18th Annual Meeting of the Special Interest Group on Discourse and Dialogue (SIGDIAL 2017)

Saarbruken, Germany
15 – 17 August 2017

ISBN: 978-1-5108-4860-3

SIGDIAL 2017

18th Annual Meeting of the
Special Interest Group on Discourse and Dialogue

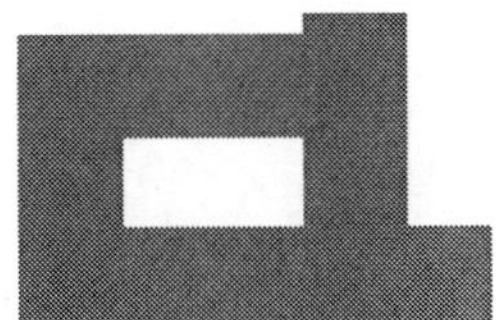  

Proceedings of the Conference

15-17 August 2017
Saarbrücken, Germany

In cooperation with:
Association for Computational Linguistics (ACL)
International Speech Communication Association (ISCA)
Association for the Advancement of Artificial Intelligence (AAAI)

We thank our sponsors:

Interactions	Microsoft	Maluuba: A Microsoft Company
Adobe Research	Amazon	DFKI
Facebook	Honda Research Institute	PARC
ETS	Charamel GmbH	SemVox
Universität des Saarlandes		
Spoken Languages Systems Group, Universität des Saarlandes		

Platinum

Gold

Silver

Bronze

In cooperation with

Association for Computational Linguistics (ACL)
209 N. Eighth Street
Stroudsburg, PA 18360
USA
Tel: +1-570-476-8006
Fax: +1-570-476-0860
acl@aclweb.org

ISBN 978-1-945626-82-1

Introduction

We are excited to welcome you to this year's SIGdial Conference, the 18th Annual Meeting of the Special Interest Group on Discourse and Dialogue. We are pleased to hold the conference in Saarbrücken on August 15-17th, co-located with SemDial 2017, and in close proximity to both INTERSPEECH 2017 and YRRSDS 2017, the Young Researchers' Roundtable on Spoken Dialog Systems.

The SIGdial conference remains a premier publication venue for research in discourse and dialogue. This year, the program includes oral presentations, poster sessions, and one demo session. SIGdial 2017 also hosts three special sessions, two joint with SemDial 2017.

We received 113 submissions this year. In only one previous year has there been a greater number of submissions to SIGdial. All long and short papers received at least 3 reviews. We carefully considered both the numeric ratings and the tenor of the comments in making our selections for the program. Overall, the members of the Program Committee did an excellent job in reviewing the submitted papers. We thank them for their important role in selecting the accepted papers and for helping to come up with a high quality program for the conference. We also thank Pierre Lison, Mentoring Chair for SIGdial 2017, for his dedicated work on the mentoring process. The goal of mentoring is to assist authors of papers that contain important ideas but lack clarity. In line with the SIGdial tradition, our aim has been to create a balanced program that accommodates as many favorably rated papers as possible. We accepted 29 long papers, 11 short papers and 7 demo presentations. These numbers give an overall acceptance rate of 41.6%. The rates separately for types of papers are 42% for long papers, 30% for short and 87% for demo submissions. Of the long papers, 18 were presented as oral presentations. The remaining 11 long papers and all the short papers were presented as posters, split into two poster sessions.

This year SIGdial has three special sessions on topics of growing interest. The chosen sessions were (i) the Special Session on Negotiation Dialog organized by Amanda Stent, Aasish Pappu, Diane Litman and Marilyn Walker; (ii) the Second WOCHAT Special Session on Chatbots and Conversational Agents organized by Ryuichiro Higashinaka, Ron Artstein, Rafael E. Banchs, and Wolfgang Minker; and (iii) Special Session on Natural Language Generation for Dialog Systems organized by Marilyn Walker, Verena Rieser, Vera Demberg, Dietrich Klakow, Dilek Hakkani-Tur, David M. Howcroft and Shereen Oraby. These specialized topics brought diverse paper submissions to our technical program. At the conference, the special sessions also featured panel discussions and position talks, allowing for active engagement of the conference participants. This year, two of these special sessions, the one on negotiation and on conversational agents, are part of the joint SIGdial/SemDial program at the conference bringing both communities to participate in them.

This year's SIGdial conference runs 3 full days compared to previous years where it was 2.5 days. We have designed our program to be balanced and inviting to SIGdial and SemDial participants alike. One keynote and one special session is held each day with remaining time given to oral and poster presentations. Two of the special sessions were run as joint sessions with SemDial and the poster/demo sessions contained presentations from both venues. We hope that we achieved a tighter bond between the two communities this year, and we hope the two communities will continue to foster their common interests and research ideas.

A conference of this scale requires advice, help and enthusiastic participation of many parties and we have a big 'thank you' to say to all of them.

We thank our three keynote speakers, Elisabeth André (Augsburg University, Germany), Andrew Kehler (UC San Diego, USA) and Oliver Lemon (Heriot-Watt University, Edinburgh, UK) for their inspiring talks and views on the many modern aspects of research in discourse and dialog.

We are incredibly grateful to the Program co-Chairs of SemDial 2017, Volha Petukhova and Ye Tian who tirelessly worked with us throughout all stages of planning for SIGdial, from deadlines to submissions and acceptance decisions, conference scheduling, special session organization, and local arrangements. We also thank the organizers of the three special sessions who handled reviewers for their papers, designed the schedule for their accepted papers, and organized the session at the venue. We are grateful for their smooth and efficient coordination with the main conference. We also extend special thanks to our Local co-Chairs, Volha Petukhova and Ivana Kruijff-Korbayova, and their local organizing team and student volunteers. SIGdial 2017 would not have been possible without their effort in arranging the conference venue and accommodations, handling registration, making banquet arrangements, and numerous preparations for the conference. The student volunteers for on-site assistance also deserve our sincere appreciation.

Ethan Selfridge, our Sponsorships Chair, has conducted the massive task of recruiting and liaising with our conference sponsors, many of whom continue to contribute year after year. Sponsorships support valuable aspects of the program, such as the invited speakers and conference banquet. We thank him for his dedicated work and coordination in conference planning. We gratefully acknowledge the support of our sponsors: (Platinum level) Interactions, Microsoft, and Maluuba: A Microsoft Company, (Gold level) Adobe Research, Amazon, DFKI, Facebook, Honda Research Institute and PARC, (Silver level) ETS, (Bronze level) Charamel GmbH and SemVox. We also thank Universität des Saarlandes and the Spoken Languages Systems Group at the Universität des Saarlandes for their generous sponsorship.

We also thank the SIGdial board, especially officers Amanda Stent, Jason Williams and Kristiina Jokinen for their advice and support from beginning to end. We also thank Priscilla Rasmussen at the ACL for tirelessly handling the financial aspects of sponsorship for SIGdial 2017, and for securing our ISBN.

We once again thank our program committee members for committing their time to help us select a superb technical program. Finally, we thank all the authors who submitted to the conference and all the conference participants for making SIGdial 2017 a grand success and for growing the research areas of discourse and dialogue with their fine work.

Kristiina Jokinen and Manfred Stede
General Co-Chairs

David DeVault and Annie Louis
Program Co-Chairs

SIGDIAL 2017

General Co-Chairs:

Kristiina Jokinen, University of Helsinki, Finland and University of Tartu, Estonia
Manfred Stede, Potsdam University, Germany

Technical Program Co-Chairs:

Annie Louis, University of Edinburgh, UK
David DeVault, University of Southern California, USA

Mentoring Chair:

Pierre Lison, Norwegian Computing Center, Norway

Local Chairs:

Ivana Kruijff-Korbayova, Saarland University and German Research Center for Artificial Intelligence
Volha Petukhova, Saarland University, Germany

Sponsorship Chair:

Ethan Selfridge, Interactions, USA

SIGdial Officers:

President: Amanda Stent, Bloomberg, USA
Vice President: Jason D. Williams, Microsoft Research, USA
Secretary-Treasurer: Kristiina Jokinen, University of Helsinki, Finland and University of Tartu, Estonia

Program Committee:

Stergos Afantenos, University of Toulouse, France
Jan Alexandersson, DFKI GmbH, Germany
Masahiro Araki, Kyoto Institute of Technology, Japan
Ron Artstein, University of Southern California, USA
Rafael E. Banchs, Institute for Infocomm Research, Singapore
Timo Baumann, Carnegie Mellon University, USA
Frederic Bechet, Aix Marseille Universite - LIF/CNRS, France
Steve Beet, Aculab plc, UK
Jose Miguel Benedi, Universitat Politecnica de Valencia, Spain
Timothy Bickmore, Massachusetts Institute of Technology, USA
Nate Blaylock, Nuance Communications, Canada
Dan Bohus, Microsoft Research, USA
Johan Boye, KTH, Sweden
Kristy Boyer, University of Florida, USA
Hendrik Buschmeier, Bielefeld University, Germany
Christophe Cerisara, CNRS, France
Joyce Chai, Michigan State University, USA
Mark Core, University of Southern California, USA

Paul Crook, Microsoft, USA
Heriberto Cuayáhuitl, Heriot-Watt University, Edinburgh, UK
Xiaodong Cui, IBM T. J. Watson Research Center, USA
Nina Dethlefs, University of Hull, UK
Vera Demberg, Saarland University, Germany
Barbara Di Eugenio, University of Illinois at Chicago, USA
Giuseppe Di Fabbrizio, Rakuten, USA
Jacob Eisenstein, Georgia Institute of Technology, USA
Maxine Eskenazi, Carnegie Mellon University, USA
Keelan Evanini, Educational Testing Service, USA
Mauro Falcone, Fondazione Ugo Bordoni, Italy
Raquel Fernandez, ILLC, University of Amsterdam, Netherlands
Kotaro Funakoshi, Honda Research Institute Japan
Milica Gasic, Cambridge University, UK
Kallirroi Georgila, University of Southern California, USA
Jonathan Ginzburg, Université Paris-Diderot, France
Curry Guinn, University of North Carolina at Wilmington, USA
Thomas Hain, University of Sheffield, UK
Mark Hasegawa-Johnson, University of Illinois at Urbana-Champaign, USA
Helen Hastie, Heriot-Watt University, Edinburgh, UK
Larry Heck, Google, USA
Peter Heeman, Oregon Health and Sciences University, USA
Ryuichiro Higashinaka, Nippon Telegraph and Telephone Corporation, Japan
Keikichi Hirose, University of Tokyo, Japan
David Janiszek, Universite Paris Descartes, France
Yangfeng Ji, Georgia Tech, USA
Pamela Jordan, University of Pittsburgh, USA
Shafiq Joty, Qatar Computing Research Institute, Qatar
Tatsuya Kawahara, Kyoto University, Japan
Simon Keizer, Heriot-Watt University, Edinburgh, UK
Casey Kennington, Boise State University, Idaho
Dongho Kim, Yonsei University, Korea
Norihide Kitaoka, Nagoya University, Japan
Kazunori Komatani, Nagoya University, Japan
Stefan Kopp, Bielefeld University, Germany
Romain Laroche, Orange Labs, France
Staffan Larsson, University of Gothenburg, Sweden
Kornel Laskowski, Carnegie Mellon University, USA
Sungjin Lee, Microsoft Research, USA
Fabrice Lefevre, University of Avignon, France
Oliver Lemon, Heriot-Watt University, Edinburgh, UK
James Lester, North Carolina State University, USA
Diane Litman, University of Pittsburgh, USA
Eduardo Lleida Solano, University of Zaragoza, Spain
Ramon Lopez-Cozar, University of Granada, Spain
Matthew Marge, U.S. Army Research Laboratory, USA
Michael McTear, University of Ulster, Northern Ireland
Raveesh Meena, KTH, Sweden

Yashar Mehdad, Yahoo! Labs, USA
Teruhisa Misu, Honda Research Institute USA, USA
Helena Moniz, INESC-ID and FLUL, Universidade de Lisboa, Portugal
Satoshi Nakamura, Nara Institutes of Science and Technology, Japan
Mikio Nakano, Honda Research Institute Japan, Japan
Vincent Ng, University of Texas at Dallas, USA
Douglas O'Shaughnessy, INRS-EMT (University of Quebec), Canada
Alexandros Papangelis, Toshiba Research Europe Limited, UK
Aasish Pappu, Yahoo! Inc, USA
Paul Piwek, The Open University, UK
Andrei Popescu-Belis, Idiap Research Institute, Switzerland
Massimo Poesio, University of Essex, UK
Matthew Purver, Queen Mary, University of London, UK
Norbert Reithinger, DFKI GmbH, Germany
Giuseppe Riccardi, University of Trento, Italy
Sophie Rosset, LIMSI, France
Michael Roth, UIUC/Saarland
Alexander Rudnicky, Carnegie Mellon University, USA
Sakriani Sakti, Nara Institutes of Science and Technology, Japan
Niko Schenk, Goethe-Universität Frankfurt am Main
David Schlangen, Bielefeld University, Germany
Ethan Selfridge, Interactions Corporation, USA
Gabriel Skantze, KTH Speech Music and Hearing, Sweden
Georg Stemmer, Intel Corp., Germany
Amanda Stent, Bloomberg LP, USA
Matthew Stone, Rutgers, The State University of New Jersey, USA
Svetlana Stoyanchev, Interactions Corporation, USA
Kristina Striegnitz, Union College, USA
Reid Swanson, University of Southern California, USA
Björn Schuller, Imperial College London, UK and University of Passau, Germany
Marc Swerts, Tilburg University, Netherlands
Antonio Teixeira, University of Aveiro, Portugal
Joel Tetreault, Yahoo! Labs, USA
Takenobu Tokunaga, Tokyo Institute of Technology, Japan
Gokhan Tur, Microsoft Research, USA
Stefan Ultes, Cambridge University, UK
David Vandyke, Cambridge University, UK
Marilyn Walker, UCSC, USA
Hsin-Min Wang, Academia Sinica, Taiwan
Nigel Ward, University of Texas at El Paso, USA
Bonnie Webber, University of Edinburgh, UK
Jason Williams, Microsoft Research, USA
Kai Yu, Shanghai Jiao Tong University, China
Jian Zhang, Dongguan University of Technology and the Hong Kong University of Science and
Technology, China

Invited Speakers:

Elisabeth André, Augsburg University, Germany
Andrew Kehler, UC San Diego, USA
Oliver Lemon, Heriot-Watt University, Edinburgh, UK

Student Volunteers:

Christophe Biwer
Margarita Chikobava
Xiaoyu Shen
Anna Welker

Table of Contents

Conference Program

Tuesday 15th August 2017

10:30-11:45   **Oral Session 1: Task-Oriented Dialogue Systems**

10:30-10:55   *Key-Value Retrieval Networks for Task-Oriented Dialogue*
Mihail Eric, Lakshmi Krishnan, Francois Charette and Christopher D. Manning

10:55-11:20   *Generative Encoder-Decoder Models for Task-Oriented Spoken Dialog Systems with Chatting Capability*
Tiancheng Zhao, Allen Lu, Kyusong Lee and Maxine Eskenazi

11:20-11:45   *Sample-efficient Actor-Critic Reinforcement Learning with Supervised Data for Dialogue Management*
Pei-Hao Su, Paweł Budzianowski, Stefan Ultes, Milica Gasic and Steve Young

13:00-15:00   **Joint Special Session on Negotiation Dialog**

13:30-13:55   *Automatic Measures to Characterise Verbal Alignment in Human-Agent Interaction*
Guillaume Dubuisson Duplessis, Chloé Clavel and Frédéric Landragin

15:30-17:00   **Poster Session 1**
Beyond On-hold Messages: Conversational Time-buying in Task-oriented Dialogue
Soledad López Gambino, Sina Zarrieß and David Schlangen

Enabling robust and fluid spoken dialogue with cognitively impaired users
Ramin Yaghoubzadeh and Stefan Kopp

Exploring Joint Neural Model for Sentence Level Discourse Parsing and Sentiment Analysis
Bita Nejat, Giuseppe Carenini and Raymond Ng

Finding Structure in Figurative Language: Metaphor Detection with Topic-based Frames
Hyeju Jang, Keith Maki, Eduard Hovy and Carolyn Rose

Inferring Narrative Causality between Event Pairs in Films
Zhichao Hu and Marilyn Walker

Interaction Quality Estimation Using Long Short-Term Memories
Niklas Rach, Wolfgang Minker and Stefan Ultes

Neural-based Context Representation Learning for Dialog Act Classification
Daniel Ortega and Ngoc Thang Vu

Predicting Success in Goal-Driven Human-Human Dialogues
Michael Noseworthy, Jackie Chi Kit Cheung and Joelle Pineau

Wednesday 16th August 2017

10:30-11:45   Oral Session 2: Turn-Taking and Real-Time Interaction

10:30-10:55   *Towards a General, Continuous Model of Turn-taking in Spoken Dialogue using LSTM Recurrent Neural Networks*
Gabriel Skantze

10:55-11:20   *Attentive listening system with backchanneling, response generation and flexible turn-taking*
Divesh Lala, Pierrick Milhorat, Koji Inoue, Masanari Ishida, Katsuya Takanashi and Tatsuya Kawahara

11:20-11:45   *Using Reinforcement Learning to Model Incrementality in a Fast-Paced Dialogue Game*
Ramesh Manuvinakurike, David DeVault and Kallirroi Georgila

13:00-15:00   Special Session: Natural Language Generation for Dialogue Systems

13:10-13:35   *Redundancy Localization for the Conversationalization of Unstructured Responses*
Sebastian Krause, Mikhail Kozhevnikov, Eric Malmi and Daniele Pighin

13:35-14:00   *Neural-based Natural Language Generation in Dialogue using RNN Encoder-Decoder with Semantic Aggregation*
Van-Khanh Tran and Le-Minh Nguyen

15:30-17:30   Poster Session 2

A surprisingly effective out-of-the-box char2char model on the E2E NLG Challenge dataset
Shubham Agarwal and Marc Dymetman

Adversarial evaluation for open-domain dialogue generation
Elia Bruni and Raquel Fernandez

Are you serious?: Rhetorical Questions and Sarcasm in Social Media Dialog
Shereen Oraby, Vrindavan Harrison, Amita Misra, Ellen Riloff and Marilyn Walker

Automatic Mapping of French Discourse Connectives to PDTB Discourse Relations
Majid Laali and Leila Kosseim

Generating and Evaluating Summaries for Partial Email Threads: Conversational Bayesian Surprise and Silver Standards
Jordon Johnson, Vaden Masrani, Giuseppe Carenini and Raymond Ng

How Would You Say It? Eliciting Lexically Diverse Dialogue for Supervised Semantic Parsing
Abhilasha Ravichander, Thomas Manzini, Matthias Grabmair, Graham Neubig, Jonathan Francis and Eric Nyberg

Thursday 17th August 2017

10:30-11:45   Oral Session 3: Modeling Semantics and Pragmatics

10:30-10:55   *Frames: a corpus for adding memory to goal-oriented dialogue systems*
Layla El Asri, Hannes Schulz, Shikhar Sharma, Jeremie Zumer, Justin Harris,
Emery Fine, Rahul Mehrotra and Kaheer Suleman

10:55-11:20   *Modelling Protagonist Goals and Desires in First-Person Narrative*
Elahe Rahimtoroghi, Jiaqi Wu, Ruimin Wang, Pranav Anand and Marilyn Walker

11:20-11:45   *The Role of Conversation Context for Sarcasm Detection in Online Interactions*
Debanjan Ghosh, Alexander Richard Fabbri and Smaranda Muresan

13:00-15:00   Special Session: Second WOCHAT Special Session on Chatbots and Conversational Agents

13:10-13:35   *Lexical Acquisition through Implicit Confirmations over Multiple Dialogues*
Kohei Ono, Ryu Takeda, Eric Nichols, Mikio Nakano and Kazunori Komatani

13:35-14:00   *Evaluating Natural Language Understanding Services for Conversational Question Answering Systems*
Daniel Braun, Adrian Hernandez-Mendez, Florian Matthes and Manfred Langen

14:00-14:25   *A data-driven model of explanations for a chatbot that helps to practice conversation in a foreign language*
Sviatlana Höhn

15:30-16:50   Oral Session 4: Context in Discourse and Dialogue

15:30-15:55   *Towards Full Text Shallow Discourse Relation Annotation: Experiments with Cross-Paragraph Implicit Relations in the PDTB*
Rashmi Prasad, Katherine Forbes-Riley and Alan Lee

15:55-16:20   *Sequential Dialogue Context Modeling for Spoken Language Understanding*
Ankur Bapna, Gokhan Tur, Dilek Hakkani-Tur and Larry Heck

16:20:16:50   *Not All Dialogues are Created Equal: Instance Weighting for Neural Conversational Models*
Pierre Lison and Serge Bibauw

Automatic Mapping of French Discourse Connectives
to PDTB Discourse Relations

Majid Laali   **Leila Kosseim**

Department of Computer Science and Software Engineering

Concordia University, Montreal, Quebec, Canada

`{m_laali, kosseim}@encs.concordia.ca`

Abstract

In this paper, we present an approach to exploit phrase tables generated by statistical machine translation in order to map French discourse connectives to discourse relations. Using this approach, we created ConcoLeDisCo, a lexicon of French discourse connectives and their PDTB relations. When evaluated against LEX-CONN, ConcoLeDisCo achieves a recall of 0.81 and an Average Precision of 0.68 for the CONCESSION and CONDITION relations.

1 Introduction

Discourse connectives (DCs) (e.g. *because, although*) are terms that explicitly signal discourse relations within a text. Building a lexicon of DCs, where each connective is mapped to the discourse relations it can signal, is not an easy task. To build such lexicons, it is necessary to have linguists manually analyse the usage of individual DCs through a corpus study, which is an expensive endeavour both in terms of time and expertise. For example, LEXCONN (Roze et al., 2012), a manually built lexicon of French DCs, was initiated in 2010 and released its first edition in 2012. The latest version, LEXCONN V2.1 (Danlos et al., 2015), contains 343 DCs mapped to an average of 1.3 discourse relations. This project is still ongoing as 37 DCs still have not been assigned to any discourse relation. Because of this, only a limited number of languages currently possess such lexicons (e.g. French (Roze et al., 2012), Spanish (Alonso Alemany et al., 2002), German (Stede and Umbach, 1998)).

In this paper, we propose an approach to automatically map French DCs to their associated PDTB discourse relations using parallel texts. Our approach can also automatically identify the usage of a DC where the DC signals a specific discourse relation. This can help linguists to study a DC in parallel texts and/or to find evidence for an association between discourse relations and DCs. Our approach is based on phrase tables generated by statistical machine translation and makes no assumption about the target language except the availability of a parallel corpus with another language for which a discourse parser exists; hence the approach is easy to expand to other languages.

We applied our approach to the Europarl corpus (Koehn, 2005) and generated ConcoLeDisCo[1], a lexicon mapping French DCs to their associated Penn Discourse Treebank (PDTB) discourse relations (Prasad et al., 2008a). To our knowledge, ConcoLeDisCo is the first lexicon of French discourse connectives mapped to the PDTB relation set. When compared to LEX-CONN, ConcoLeDisCo achieves a recall of 0.81 and an Average Precision of 0.68 for the CONCESSION and CONDITION discourse relations.

2 Related Work

Lexicons of DCs have been developed for several languages: English (Knott, 1996), Spanish (Alonso Alemany et al., 2002), German (Stede and Umbach, 1998), Czech (Poláková et al., 2013), and French (Roze et al., 2012). However, constructing such lexicons requires linguistic expertise and is a time-consuming task.

Discourse connectives and their translations have been studied within parallel texts by many (Meyer, 2011; Meyer et al., 2011; Taboada and de los Ángeles Gómez-González, 2012; Cartoni et al., 2013; Zufferey and Degand, 2014; Zufferey and Cartoni, 2014; Zufferey and Gygax, 2015;

---

[1]ConcoLeDisCo is publicly available at `https://github.com/mjlaali/ConcoLeDisCo`.

1

Proceedings of the SIGDIAL 2017 Conference, pages 1–6,
Saarbrücken, Germany, 15-17 August 2017. ©2017 Association for Computational Linguistics

Hoek and Zufferey, 2015). These works have either focused on the effect of the translation of discourse connectives on machine translation systems (Meyer, 2011; Meyer et al., 2011; Cartoni et al., 2013) or on a small number of discourse connectives due to the cost of manual annotations (Taboada and de los Ángeles Gómez-González, 2012; Zufferey and Degand, 2014; Zufferey and Cartoni, 2014; Zufferey and Gygax, 2015; Hoek and Zufferey, 2015).

To our knowledge, very little research has addressed the automatic construction of lexicons of DCs. Hidey and McKeown (2016) proposed an automatic approach to identify English expressions that signal the CAUSAL discourse relation. On the other hand, Laali and Kosseim (2014) automatically extracted French DCs from parallel texts; however, they did not associate discourse relations to the extracted DCs. The proposed approach goes beyond this work by mapping DCs to their associated discourse relations.

3 Methodology

3.1 Corpus Preparation

For our experiments, we used the English-French part of Europarl (Koehn, 2005) which contains 2 million[2] parallel sentences. To prepare the dataset, we parsed the English sentences with the CLaC discourse parser (Laali et al., 2016) to identify English DCs and the discourse relation that they signal. The CLaC parser has been learned on Section 02-20 of the PDTB and can disambiguate the usage of the 100 English DCs listed in the PDTB with an F1-score of 0.90 and label them with their PDTB discourse relation with an F1-score of 0.76 when tested on the blind test set of the CoNLL 2016 shared task (Xue et al., 2016). This parser was used because its performance is very close to that of the state of the art (Oepen et al., 2016) (i.e. 0.91 and 0.77 respectively), but is more efficient at running time than Oepen et al. (2016).

Note that since the CoNLL 2016 blind test set was extracted from Wikipedia and its domain and genre differ significantly from the PDTB, the 0.90 and 0.76 F1-scores of the CLaC parser can be considered as an estimation of its performance on texts with a different domain/genre such as Europarl.

<hr>

[2]2,007,723 to be exact.

3.2 Mapping Discourse Relations

To label French DCs with a PDTB discourse relation, we assumed that if a French DC is aligned to an English DC tagged with a discourse relation *Rel*, then it should signal the same discourse relation *Rel*. For our experiment, we used the inventory of 100 English DCs from the PDTB (Prasad et al., 2008a) and the 371 French DCs from LEXCONN V2.1 (Danlos et al., 2015). For the mapping, we used the subset of 14 PDTB discourse relations that was used in the CoNLL shared task (Xue et al., 2015). This list is based on the second-level types and a selected number of third-level subtypes of the PDTB discourse relations.

To have statistically reliable results, we ignored French DCs that appeared less than 50 times in Europarl. Out of the 371 French DCs listed in LEXCONN, seven do not appear in Europarl and 55 have a frequency lower than 50. This means that 89% (309/371) of the French DCs have a frequency higher than 50 and were thus used in the analysis. A manual inspection of the infrequent DCs shows that they are either informal (e.g. *des fois que*) or rare expression (e.g. *en dépit que*). Table 1 shows the distribution of the LEXCONN French DCs in Europarl.

Freq.	= 0	≤ 50	> 50	Total
# FR-DC	7	55	309	371

Table 1: Distribution of LEXCONN French DCs in the Europarl corpus.

We used the Moses statistical machine translation system (Koehn et al., 2007) to extract the number of alignments between French DCs and English DCs. As part of its translation model, Moses generates a phrase table (see Table 2) which aligns phrases between the language pairs. The phrase table is constructed based on statistical word alignment models and contains the frequency of the alignments between phrase pairs. We used the Och and Ney (2003) heuristic and combined IBM Model 4 word alignments (Brown et al., 1993) to construct the phrase table.

Because an English DC can signal different discourse relations, to ensure that Moses's phrase table distinguishes the different usages of the same English DC, we modified its English tokenizer so that each English DC and its discourse relation make up a single token. For example, the token '*although*-CONCESSION' will be created for the DC *although* when it signals the discourse relation CONCESSION. Table 2 shows a few entries of the phrase table for the French DC *même si*. As the table shows, *même si* was aligned to three English DCs: *although*, labeled by the CLaC parser as a CONTRAST or as a CONCESSION and to *even if* and *even though* which were not tagged .

FR-DC	EN-DC	Relation	Freq
même si	*even if*	-	2538
même si	*even though*	-	1895
même si	*although*	CONTRAST	1446
même si	*although*	CONCESSION	858

Table 2: A few entries of the phrase table for the connective *même si*.

In total, 1,970 entries of the phrase table contained a French DC, an English DC and a discourse relation[3]. From these, we computed the number of times a French DC was aligned to each discourse relation, then, created ConcoLeDisCo: tuples of *<FR-DC, Rel, Prob>*, where *FR-DC* and *Rel* indicate a French DC and a discourse relation and *Prob* indicates the probability that *FR-DC* signals *Rel*. To calculate *Prob*, we divided the number of times *FR-DC* is associated to *Rel* by the frequency of *FR-DC* in Europarl. In total, the approach generated a lexicon of 900 such tuples, a few of which are shown in Table 3.

FR-DC	Relation	Prob
si	CONDITION	0.27
même si	CONCESSION	0.08
lorsque	CONDITION	0.05
néanmoins	CONCESSION	0.07

Table 3: A few entries of ConcoLeDisCo.

4   Evaluation

To evaluate ConcoLeDisCo, because LEXCONN uses a different inventory of discourse relations than the PDTB, we only considered the discourse relations that are common across these inventories: CONCESSION and CONDITION. According to LEXCONN, 61 French DCs can signal a CONCESSION or a CONDITION discourse relation. Out

---

[3]We only considered entries whose texts are an exact match of an English DC listed in the PDTB and a French DC listed in LEXCONN.

of these, 44 have a frequency higher than 50 in Europarl.

4.1   Automatic Evaluation

To measure the quality of ConcoLeDisCo, we ranked the *<FR-DC, Rel, Prob>* tuples based on their probability and measured the quality of the ranked list using 11-point interpolated average precision (Manning et al., 2008). This curve shows the highest precision at the 11 recall levels of 0.0, 0.1, 0.2, ..., 1.0. This method allows us to evaluate the ranked list without considering any arbitrary cut-off point. As Figure 1 shows, the approach retrieved 50% of the French DCs in LEXCONN with a precision of 0.81.

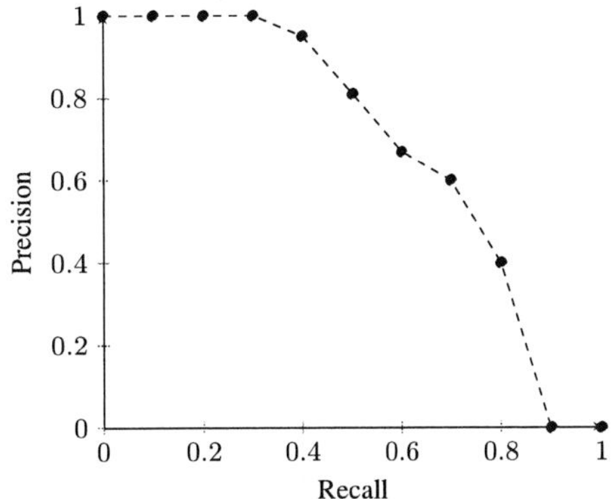

Figure 1: 11-Point Interpolated Average Precision Curve.

In addition, we also computed Average Precision (AveP) (Manning et al., 2008); the average of the precision obtained after seeing a correct LEXCONN entry in ConcoLeDisCo. More specifically, given a list of ranked tuples:

$$AveP = \frac{1}{N} \sum_{i=1}^{N} Precision(DC_i) \qquad (1)$$

where N is the number of LEXCONN French DCs that signals the CONCESSION or CONDITION discourse relations (i.e. 44), DC_i is the rank of the ith LEXCONN DC in ConcoLeDisCo, and $Precision(DC_i)$ is the precision at the rank DC_i of the ranked tuples. It can be shown that $AveP$ approximates the area under the interpolated precision-recall curve (Manning et al., 2008). The proposed approach identified 36 (81%) of these 44 French DCs with an $AveP$ of 0.68.

FR-DC	Relation	Jdg	FR-DC	Relation	Jdg
à défaut de/if	CONDITION	✓	*tout de même/nonetheless*	CONCESSION	✓
cependant/nonetheless	CONCESSION	✓	*toutefois/nonetheless*	CONCESSION	✓
faute de/if	CONDITION	✓	*pour autant/if*	CONDITION	✗
malgré tout/nonetheless	CONCESSION	✓	*sinon/if*	CONDITION	✗
néanmoins/nonetheless	CONCESSION	✓	*certes/although*	CONCESSION	✗
nonobstant/although	CONCESSION	✓	*lorsque/if*	CONDITION	✗
quand même/nonetheless	CONCESSION	✓	*pour que/if*	CONDITION	✗

Table 4: Error analysis of the potential false positive entries. ✓ indicates newly discoursed mappings which are not included in LEXCONN.

4.2 Manual Evaluation

In addition to the quantitative evaluation, we also performed a manual analysis of the false-positive errors to see if they really constituted errors. To do so, we looked at the tuples with a probability higher than 0.01 but which did not appear in LEX-CONN. 14 such cases, shown in Table 4, were found.

For example, while the French connective *à défaut de* (#1 in Table 4) signals a CONDITION discourse relation in Sentence (1) below, only the EXPLANATION and the CONCESSION discourse relations were associated with this connective in LEXCONN.

(1) **FR:** À défaut de se montrer très ambitieux, notre industrie, nos chercheurs et nos experts ne disposeront purement et simplement pas du brevet moderne dont ils ont besoin.
EN: If we are anything less than ambitious in this field, we shall simply not provide our industry, our research and development experts with the modern patent which they need.

To evaluate if these 14 cases were true mistakes, we randomly selected five English-French parallel sentences from Europarl that contained the French DC and one of its English DC translations signalling the discourse relation. Then, we showed the French DCs within their sentence to two native French speakers and asked them to confirm if the discourse relation identified was indeed signaled by the French DCs or not. The Kappa agreement between the two annotators was 0.72. For 9 French connectives, both annotators agreed that indicated that in at least one of the five sentences, the discourse relation was signalled by the connective. This indicates that 64% (9/14) are in fact true-positives, i.e. correct mappings that are not listed in LEXCONN. Table 4 shows the 14 pairs of

<FR-DC/English translation, Discourse relation> used in the manual evaluation and indicates the newly discovered mappings by ✓.

We also observed that if multiple explicit connectives occur in the same clause (e.g. *certes* and *mais*), one of them can affect the discourse relation signaled by the other. This is an interesting phenomenon as it seems to indicate that the connectives are not independent. For example, in Sentence (2), the combination of *certes* and *mais* signals a CONCESSION discourse relation.

(2) **FR:** Cela coûte <u>certes</u> un peu plus cher, <u>mais</u> est sans conséquence pour l'environnement.
EN: <u>Although</u> it is a little more expensive, it does not harm the environment.

Note that according to LEXCONN, neither *certes* nor *mais* can signal a CONCESSION discourse relation. The same phenomenon was also reported in the PDTB corpus (Prasad et al., 2008b, p. 5).

5 Conclusion and Future Work

In this paper, we proposed a novel approach to automatically map PDTB discourse relations to French DCs. Using this approach, we generated ConcoLeDisCo: a lexicon of French DCs and their PDTB discourse relations. When compared with LEXCONN, our approach achieved a recall of 0.81 and an Average Precision of 0.68 for the CONCESSION and CONDITION discourse relations. A manual error analysis of the false-positives showed that the approach identified new discourse relations for 9 French DCs which are not included in LEXCONN. As future work, we plan to evaluate all the discourse relations in ConcoLeDisCo and apply the approach to other languages.

Acknowledgement

The authors would like to thank the anonymous referees for their insightful comments on an earlier version of the paper. Many thanks also to Andre Cianflone for his help on the evaluation of this work. This work was financially supported by an NSERC grant.

References

Laura Alonso Alemany, Irene Castellón Masalles, and Lluís Padró Cirera. 2002. Lexicón computacional de marcadores del discurso. *Procesamiento del Lenguaje Natural* 29:239–246.

Peter F. Brown, Vincent J. Della Pietra, Stephen A. Della Pietra, and Robert L. Mercer. 1993. The mathematics of statistical machine translation: Parameter estimation. *Computational linguistics* 19(2):263–311.

Bruno Cartoni, Sandrine Zufferey, and Thomas Meyer. 2013. Annotating the meaning of discourse connectives by looking at their translation: The translation-spotting technique. *Dialogue & Discourse* 4(2):65–86.

L. Danlos, M. Colinet, and J. Steinlin. 2015. FDTB1: Repérage des connecteurs de discours en corpus. In *Actes de la 22e conférence sur le Traitement Automatique des Langues Naturelles (TALN 2015)*. Caen, France, pages 350–356.

Christopher Hidey and Kathleen McKeown. 2016. Identifying Causal Relations Using Parallel Wikipedia Articles. In *Proceedings of the 54th Annual Meeting of the Association for Computational Linguistics (ACL 2016)*. Berlin, Germany, pages 1424–1433.

Jet Hoek and Sandrine Zufferey. 2015. Factors influencing the implicitation of discourse relations across languages. In *Proceedings 11th Joint ACL-ISO Workshop on Interoperable Semantic Annotation (isa-11)*. TiCC, Tilburg center for Cognition and Communication, page 39–45.

Alistair Knott. 1996. *A data-driven methodology for motivating a set of coherence relations*. PhD dissertation, University of Edinburgh, Computer Science Department.

Philipp Koehn. 2005. Europarl: A parallel corpus for statistical machine translation. In *Proceedings of the 10th Machine Translation Summit*. Phuket, Thailand, volume 5, pages 79–86.

Philipp Koehn, Hieu Hoang, Alexandra Birch, Chris Callison-Burch, Marcello Federico, Nicola Bertoldi, Brooke Cowan, Wade Shen, Christine Moran, Richard Zens, Chris Dyer, Ondrej Bojar, Alexandra Constantin, and Evan Herbst. 2007. Moses: Open source toolkit for statistical machine translation. In *Proceedings of the 45th Annual Meeting of the ACL on Interactive Poster and Demonstration Sessions*. Prague, pages 177–180.

Majid Laali, Andre Cianflone, and Leila Kosseim. 2016. The CLaC Discourse Parser at CoNLL-2016. In *Proceedings of the 20th Conference on Computational Natural Language Learning (CoNLL 2016)*. Berlin, Germany, pages 92–99.

Majid Laali and Leila Kosseim. 2014. Inducing discourse connectives from parallel texts. In *Proceedings of the 25th International Conference on Computational Linguistics: Technical Papers (COLING 2014)*. Dublin, Ireland, pages 610–619.

C.D. Manning, P. Raghavan, and H. Schutze. 2008. *Introduction to information retrieval*, volume 1. Cambridge University Press Cambridge.

Thomas Meyer. 2011. Disambiguating Temporal–Contrastive Discourse Connectives for Machine Translation. In *Proceedings of the 49th Annual Meeting of the Association for Computational Linguistics: Human Language Technologies (ACL-HLT 2011)*. Portland, OR, USA, pages 46–51.

Thomas Meyer, Charlotte Roze, Bruno Cartoni, L. Danlos, and A. Popescu-Belis. 2011. Disambiguating discourse connectives using parallel corpora: senses vs. translations. In *Proceedings of Corpus Linguistics*. Birmingham.

F.J. Och and H. Ney. 2003. A systematic comparison of various statistical alignment models. *Computational Linguistics* 29(1):19–51.

Stephan Oepen, Jonathon Read, Tatjana Scheffler, Uladzimir Sidarenka, Manfed Stede, Erik Velldal, and Lilja Ovrelid. 2016. OPT: Oslo—Potsdam—Teesside Pipelining Rules, Rankers, and Classifier Ensembles for Shallow Discourse Parsing. In *Proceedings of the 20th Conference on Computational Natural Language Learning (CoNLL 2016)*. Berlin, Germany, pages 20–26.

Lucie Poláková, Jiří Mírovský, Anna Nedoluzhko, Pavlína Jínová, Šárka Zikánová, and Eva Hajičová. 2013. Introducing the Prague Discourse Treebank 1.0. In *Proceedings of the 6th International Joint Conference on Natural Language Processing (IJNLP 2013)*. Nagoya, Japan, pages 91–99.

Rashmi Prasad, Nikhil Dinesh, Alan Lee, Eleni Miltsakaki, Livio Robaldo, Aravind K. Joshi, and Bonnie L. Webber. 2008a. The Penn Discourse Tree-Bank 2.0. In *Proceedings of the Sixth International Conference on Language Resources and Evaluation (LREC 2008)*. Marrakech, Morocco, pages 28–30.

Rashmi Prasad, Eleni Miltsakaki, Nikhil Dinesh, Alan Lee, Aravind Joshi, Livio Robaldo, and Bonnie L. Webber. 2008b. The Penn Discourse Treebank 2.0 annotation manual. Technical Report IRCS-08-01, Institute for Research in Cognitive Science, University of Pennsylvania, Philadelphia, USA.

Charlotte Roze, Laurence Danlos, and Philippe Muller. 2012. LEXCONN: A French lexicon of discourse connectives. *Discours [En ligne]* 10. https://doi.org/10.4000/discours.8645.

Manfred Stede and Carla Umbach. 1998. DiMLex: A lexicon of discourse markers for text generation and understanding. In *Proceedings of the 17th International Conference on Computational Linguistics (COLING 1998)*. Montreal, Canada, pages 1238–1242.

Maite Taboada and María de los Ángeles Gómez-González. 2012. Discourse markers and coherence relations: Comparison across markers, languages and modalities. *Linguistics and the Human Sciences* 6(1-3):17–41.

Nianwen Xue, Hwee Tou Ng, Sameer Pradhan, Rashmi PrasadO Christopher Bryant, and Attapol T. Rutherford. 2015. The CoNLL-2015 shared task on shallow discourse parsing. In *Proceedings of the Nineteenth Conference on Computational Natural Language Learning - Shared Task (CoNLL 2015)*. Beijing, China, pages 1–16.

Nianwen Xue, Hwee Tou Ng, Attapol Rutherford, Bonnie Webber, Chuan Wang, and Hongmin Wang. 2016. CoNLL 2016 Shared Task on Multilingual Shallow Discourse Parsing. In *Proceedings of the 20th Conference on Computational Natural Language Learning (CoNLL 2016)*. Berlin, Germany, pages 1–19.

Sandrine Zufferey and Bruno Cartoni. 2014. A multifactorial analysis of explicitation in translation. *Target. International Journal of Translation Studies* 26(3):361–384.

Sandrine Zufferey and Liesbeth Degand. 2014. Representing the meaning of discourse connectives for multilingual purposes. *Corpus Linguistics and Linguistic Theory* 10. https://doi.org/10.1515/cllt-2013-0022.

Sandrine Zufferey and Pascal M. Gygax. 2015. The role of perspective shifts for processing and translating discourse relations. *Discourse Processes* 53(7):532–555. https://doi.org/10.1080/0163853X.2015.1062839.

Towards Full Text Shallow Discourse Relation Annotation: Experiments with Cross-Paragraph Implicit Relations in the PDTB

Rashmi Prasad
University of Wisconsin-Milwaukee
prasadr@uwm.edu

Katherine Forbes Riley
University of Pittsburgh
katherineforbesriley@gmail.com

Alan Lee
University of Pennsylvania
aleewk@seas.upenn.edu

Abstract

Full text discourse parsing relies on texts comprehensively annotated with discourse relations. To this end, we address a significant gap in the inter-sentential discourse relations annotated in the Penn Discourse Treebank (PDTB), namely the class of cross-paragraph implicit relations, which account for 30% of inter-sentential relations in the corpus. We present our annotation study to explore the incidence rate of adjacent vs. non-adjacent implicit relations in cross-paragraph contexts, and the relative degree of difficulty in annotating them. Our experiments show a high incidence of non-adjacent relations that are difficult to annotate reliably, suggesting the practicality of backing off from their annotation to reduce noise for corpus-based studies. Our resulting guidelines follow the PDTB adjacency constraint for implicits while employing an underspecified representation of non-adjacent implicits, and yield 62% inter-annotator agreement on this task.

1 Introduction

Empirical approaches for modeling discourse relations rely on corpora annotated with such relations, such as the PDTB (Prasad et al., 2008), the RST-DT (Carlson et al., 2003), and the ANN-ODIS corpus (Afantenos et al., 2012). The PDTB is currently the largest of these annotated corpora and widely used for theoretical and empirical research on discourse relations. However, it does not provide exhaustive annotation of its source texts (Prasad et al., 2014). A critical kind of gap is found within the class of inter-sentential relations, i.e., relations with arguments in different sentences. In particular, while the PDTB pro-

vides annotations of explicit inter-sentential relations within and across paragraphs, and of implicit relations between adjacent sentences within paragraphs, it ignores cross-paragraph implicit relations. Ex. (1) illustrates the problem in a PDTB-annotated text, showing 6 sentences (S1-S6) in the first four paragraphs of a longer article. (Empty lines indicate paragraph boundaries.) While all annotation elements are not shown here, the key issue to note is that the relations of sentences S2 and S3 with the prior text are left *unannotated* because they are paragraph-initial sentences lacking any inter-sentential explicit connectives.

(1) **S1:** As competition heats up in Spain's crowded bank market, Banco Exterior de Espana is seeking to shed its image of a state-owned bank and move into new activities.

(unannotated)
S2: Under the direction of its new chairman, Francisco Luzon, Spain's seventh largest bank is undergoing a tough restructuring that analysts say may be the first step toward the bank's privatization.

(unannotated)
S3: The state-owned industrial holding company Instituto Nacional de Industria and the Bank of Spain jointly hold a 13.94% stake in Banco Exterior.
(Conjunction)
S4: The government directly owns 51.4% and Factorex, a financial services company, holds 8.42%.
(Conjunction)
S5: The rest is listed on Spanish stock exchanges.

(Contrast)
S6: Some analysts are concerned, however, that Banco Exterior may have waited too long to diversify from its traditional export-related activities.

There are more than 12K such unannotated tokens in the current version of PDTB (PDTB-2), constituting 30% of all inter-sentential discourse contexts and 87% of all cross-paragraph inter-sentential contexts. Furthermore, research on discourse parsing shows that there is value in filling these gaps. For example, Pitler et al. (2009) report improvements in implicit relation sense classification with a sequence model. And more re-

Proceedings of the SIGDIAL 2017 Conference, pages 7–16,
Saarbrücken, Germany, 15-17 August 2017. ©2017 Association for Computational Linguistics

cent systems, including the best systems (Wang and Lan, 2015; Oepen et al., 2016) at the recent CONLL shared tasks on PDTB-style shallow discourse parsing (Xue et al., 2015, 2016), while not using a sequence model, still incorporate features about neighboring relations. Such systems have many applications, including summarization (Louis et al., 2010), information extraction (Huang and Riloff, 2012), question answering (Blair-Goldensohn, 2007), opinion analysis (Somasundaran et al., 2008), and argumentation (Zhang et al., 2016).

This paper describes our experiments in annotating cross-paragraph implicit relations in the PDTB (Section 2), with the goal of producing a set of guidelines (Section 3) to annotate such relations reliably (Section 4) and produce a representative dataset annotated with complete sequences of inter-sentential relations.

Our main findings from the experiments are as follows:

- The ratio of cross-paragraph implicit relations between non-adjacent sentences and between adjacent sentences is almost 1 to 1 (47% vs 51% in our experiment). This is similar to the distribution of cross-paragraph explicit relations (Prasad et al., 2010). Hence, non-adjacency is a non-trivial factor to consider when annotating cross-paragraph implicit relations.

- Inter-annotator agreement for the non-adjacent cross-paragraph implicits is substantially lower compared to their adjacent counterparts (47% versus 68%). Furthermore, the disagreements, while possible to resolve through discussion, are time-consuming and therefore prohibitive to large-scale annotation.

On the basis of these findings, we established the following guidelines for our annotation of cross-paragraph implicit relations:

- We fall back to the PDTB strategy of fully annotating only adjacent implicit relations, while also employing an underspecified marking of non-adjacent ones.

- We introduce new guidelines to (a) better represent the inter-dependency of relations in a

text, (b) represent new senses we have encountered, and (c) better represent the relation of entity-based coherence. These new guidelines are discussed at various points in Section 3.

We achieve a final overall agreement of 62% with our guidelines.

We discuss related work in Section 5 and conclude in Section 6, outlining our goals for this task and future work beyond.

2   A Brief Review of PDTB

Our study is carried out within the annotation framework of the PDTB, and incorporates the most recent PDTB (PDTB-3) sense hierarchy (Webber et al., 2016), shown in Fig. 1 (with two modifications – see Section 3.2). Annotated over the ˜1 million word WSJ corpus (Marcus et al., 1993), the PDTB follows a lexically-grounded approach to the representation of discourse relations (Webber et al., 2003) while remaining theory-neutral in its annotation approach. Discourse relations are taken to hold between two abstract object arguments, named Arg1 and Arg2 using syntactic conventions, and are triggered either by *explicit* connectives (Ex. 2) or, otherwise, by adjacency between clauses and sentences. (Throughout the paper, the expression of a relation is <u>underlined</u>, its Arg2 is **bolded**, its Arg1 is *italicized*, and its type and sense are in parentheses.)

(2) *The Manhattan U.S. attorney's office stressed criminal cases from 1980 to 1987, averaging 43 for every 100,000 adults.*
(Explicit, Contrast)
<u>But</u> **the New Jersey U.S. attorney averaged 16**.

(3) *So far, the mega-issues are a hit with investors.*
(Implicit, Arg2-as-instance, <u>For example</u>)
Earlier this year, Tata Iron & Steel Co.'s offer of $355 million of convertible debentures was oversubscribed.

(4) *When the plant was destroyed, "I think everyone got concerned that the same thing would happen at our plant," a KerrMcGee spokeswoman said.*
(AltLex, Reason)
That prompted Kerr-McGee to consider moving the potentially volatile storage facilities and cross-blending operations away from town.

(5) *The proposed petrochemical plant would use naphtha to manufacture the petrochemicals propylene and ethylene and their resin derivatives, polypropylene and polyethylene.*
(EntRel)
These are the raw materials used in making plastic

Temporal	Synchronous	--
	Asynchronous	Precedence
		Succession

Comparison	Contrast	--
	Similarity	--
	Concession +/-β, +/-ζ	Arg1-as-denier
		Arg2-as-denier

Contingency	Cause +/-β, +/-ζ	Reason
		Result
	Condition +/-ζ	Arg1-as-cond
		Arg2-as-cond
	Negative condition +/-ζ	Arg1-as-negcond
		Arg2-as-negcond
	Purpose	Arg1-as-goal
		Arg2-as-goal

Expansion	Conjunction	--
	Disjunction	--
	Equivalence	--
	Hypophora	--
	Instantiation	Arg1-as-instance
		Arg2-as-instance
	Level-of-detail	Arg1-as-detail
		Arg2-as-detail
	Substitution	Arg1-as-subst
		Arg2-as-subst
	Exception	Arg1-as-excpt
		Arg2-as-excpt
	Manner	Arg1-as-manner
		Arg2-as-manner

Figure 1: PDTB-3 Sense Hierarchy (Webber et al., 2016) Modified to Include Arg1/Arg2-as-instance and Hypophora. Only asymmetric relations are specified further at Level-3, to differentiate directionality of the arguments. Superscript symbols on Level-2 senses indicate features for implicit beliefs ($+/-\beta$) and speech-acts ($+/-\zeta$) that may or may not be associated with one of the defined arguments of the relation.

(6) The executive producer of "Saturday Night With Connie Chung," Andrew Lack, declines to discuss recreations as a practice or his show, in particular. *"I don't talk about my work," he says.*
(NoRel)
The president of CBS News, David W. Burke, didn't return numerous telephone calls.

In adjacent contexts not related by a connective, an inferred relation is annotated as either an *implicit* relation (Ex. 3) when it can be expressed by inserting a connective, or an *AltLex* (alternatively lexicalized) relation (Ex. 4) if insertion of a connective leads to a perception of relation redundancy, indicating the presence of some alternative lexico-syntactic marking of the relation. When a discourse relation is not inferred, the context is annotated as *EntRel* (Ex. 5) if an entity-based relation is perceived, and as *NoRel* (Ex. 6) otherwise. Section 3.2 discusses in further detail how the EntRel and NoRel relations are used in PDTB.

Where a relation's arguments can be annotated depends on the type of relation. The Arg2 of explicit relations is always some part of the sentence or clause containing the connective, but the Arg1 can be anywhere in the prior text. For all other relation types, Arg1 and Arg2 are only annotated when adjacent. Arguments can be extended to include additional clauses/sentences in all cases except NoRel, but a minimality constraint requires inclusion of only the minimally necessary text needed to interpret the relation.

3 The Experiment

To identify challenges and explore the feasibility of annotating cross-paragraph implicit relations on a large scale, texts from the PDTB corpus were selected to cover a range of sub-genres (Webber, 2009) and lengths. These texts contained 440 current paragraph first sentence (CPFS) tokens (excluding the first sentence in each text) not already related to the prior text by an inter-sentential explicit connective. These tokens were annotated in the PDTB Annotation Tool (Lee et al., 2016) over the three phases described below.

3.1 Phase One

Phase One involved guidelines training and developing a preliminary understanding of the task. Two expert annotators worked together to discuss and annotate 10 texts (130 tokens) with the PDTB guidelines, except we did not enforce the PDTB adjacency constraint in order to explore the full complexity of the task. Each token was annotated for its type (Implicit, EntRel or Altlex), sense (Fig. 1), and minimal argument spans. From this exercise, two observations emerged. First, while 52% of the CPFS tokens took their prior (Arg1) argument from a unit involving the prior paragraph's last sentence (PPLS), the remaining 48% of the CPFSs took their Arg1 from somewhere else in the prior discourse, i.e. formed a non-adjacent relation. This suggested that the argument distribution of cross-paragraph implicits was similar to that of cross-paragraph explicits, which are also non-adjacent roughly half (51%) the time (Prasad et al., 2010). Thus, whether this would be shown more generally became a hypothesis to explore in Phase Two.

Second, it was found that working together, the two annotators could isolate and agree upon the arguments not only of the adjacent implicit relations, but also the non-adjacent ones. Therefore, and also because of the observed high incidence of non-adjacent relations, a second hypothesis to explore in Phase Two became whether both adjacent and non-adjacent Arg1s could be reliably identified and annotated. Ex. (7) shows a CPFS (Arg2) and its Arg1 in a non-adjacent Contrast relation. In this case, the intervening material is excluded because of the minimality constraint: it only provides further detail about the Arg1 eventuality and can thus be excluded without loss of interpretation.

(7) Kidder, Peabody & Co. is trying to struggle back.

> *Only a few months ago, the 124-year-old securities firm seemed to be on the verge of a meltdown, racked by internal squabbles and defections.* Its relationship with parent General Electric Co. had been frayed since a big Kidder insider-trading scandal two years ago. Chief executives and presidents had come and gone.

(Contrast, <u>But</u>)
Now, the firm says it's at a turning point. By the end of this year, 63-year-old Chairman Silas Cathcart – the former chairman of Illinois Tool Works who was derided as a "tool-and-die man" when GE brought him in to clean up Kidder in 1987 – retires to his Lake Forest, Ill., home, possibly to build a shopping mall on some land he owns.

3.2 Phase Two

Based on Phase One observations, we decided in Phase Two to fully explore the feasibility of reliably annotating adjacent *and* non-adjacent cross-paragraph implicits. To this end, a further 103 tokens (10 texts) were separately annotated by each annotator for type, sense and minimal argument spans, regardless of whether arguments were adjacent or non-adjacent.

Table 1 presents the results of the Phase Two study. As shown, the adjacency distribution of arguments in the 76% (45%+31%) tokens agreed to be adjacent (46/103) or non-adjacent (32/103) supports our hypothesis that non-adjacent cross-paragraph implicit relations occur with high frequency (32/78, 41%), approaching half of all agreed tokens. For each of these agreed tokens, we computed sense and argument agreement to obtain

Arg1-Arg2 Tokens	Count	Pct	RelPct
Agree Adjacent:	**46**	**45%**	**100%**
Exact Match	11	11%	24%
Sent-level Match	3	3%	7%
Agree Sense, Args Overlap	14	14%	30%
Disagree Sense	18	17%	39%
Agree Non-Adjacent:	**32**	**31%**	**100%**
Exact Match	7	7%	22%
Sent-level Match	5	5%	16%
Agree Sense, Args Overlap	3	3%	9%
Agree Sense, Args Disagree	3	3%	9%
Disagree Sense	14	14%	44%
Disagree Adjacent/Non	**25**	**24%**	**100%**

Table 1: Cross-Paragraph Implicit Relations, Phase Two Agreement Counts, Percentages over all Tokens (Pct) and Relative Percentages over Subgroups (RelPct). 103 Tokens, 10 Texts.

(a) 'Exact Match', i.e., fully agreed for type, sense, and argument spans, (b) 'Sent-level match', i.e., slightly relaxing the minimality constraint subsententially to include tokens agreed for type and sense whose argument boundaries only disagreed inside a sentence boundary (e.g. because one annotator included an adjunct clause the other excluded), (c) 'Agree Sense, Args Overlap', i.e., relaxing the minimality constraint supra-sententially to include tokens agreed for type and sense whose Arg1 and Arg2 boundaries overlapped but did not exactly match (e.g. because one annotator included additional sentence(s) the other considered non-minimal), (d) 'Agree Sense, Args Disagree', i.e., agreed for type and sense but unmatched in all of the aforementioned ways, which can only occur for non-adjacent relations and not adjacent relations, and (e) 'Disagree Sense', i.e., disagreed as to type or sense, although arguments may or may not have matched in some way.

As the table shows, Exact Match agreement was low at 18% (11%+7%) for both adjacent (11/103) and non-adjacent (7/103) relations, illustrating the difficulty of the task. Agreement is boosted to 26% (26/103) when including Sentence-Level matches on argument spans (3 adjacent and 5 non-adjacent) and to 43% (43/103) when including tokens that matched for type and sense and had overlapping spans (14 adjacent and 3 non-adjacent), which we also take as the overall agreement on the task, with the most relaxed metric for argument span agreement. The table also shows that with this metric, agreement was worse for non-adjacent relations ((7+5+3)/32, 47%) than adjacent relations ((11+3+14)/46, 61%).

Discussion of the disagreements showed that while it was almost always possible to reach consensus, the time and effort required was often much greater for non-adjacent relations – twice the amount of time required for adjacent relations – and therefore prohibitive to large-scale annotation. Therefore a decision was made to maintain the PDTB adjacency constraint and focus on full annotation of only adjacent relations. Tokens perceived as forming a non-adjacent implicit relation would be annotated as **NoSemRel**, as described below, providing an underspecified marking to indicate its presence.

Also based on the Phase Two findings, two further enhancements were made to the PDTB-2 guidelines. First, two new senses were introduced (Fig. 1), as illustrated in Exs. (8-9). Our texts provide evidence of both directionalities for the asymmetric Instantiation sense, and so its Level-3 labels, **Arg1-as-instance** and **Arg2-as-instance**, were introduced. Arg2-as-instance is the more common case. In addition, a **Hypophora** label was introduced as a placeholder for question-answer pairs, until further study can shed light on the appropriate senses to capture their semantics.

(8) NBC's re-creations are produced by Cosgrove-Meurer Productions, which also makes the successful prime-time NBC Entertainment series Unsolved Mysteries.

(Arg1-as-instance, More generally)
The marriage of news and theater, if not exactly inevitable, has been consummated nonetheless.

(9) *How can we turn this situation around?*

(Hypophora)
Reform starts in the Pentagon.

The second enhancement involves a refinement of the EntRel and NoRel labels. In the absence of a semantic discourse relation between adjacent sentences, the PDTB-2 labels the relation between them as follows: **(a)** as EntRel if an entity-based coherence relation holds between Arg1 and Arg2 and the discourse is expanded around that entity in Arg2, either by continuing the narrative around it or supplying background about it; **(b)** as EntRel if (a) doesn't hold but some entity co-reference exists between Arg1 and Arg2 (even if an implicit relation also holds between Arg2 and a non-adjacent sentence); **(c)** as NoRel if neither (a) nor (b) holds (even if an implicit relation also holds between Arg2 and a non-adjacent sentence); and **(d)** as NoRel if none of (a)-(c) hold, which occurs when

Arg2 is not part of the discourse (e.g., bylines or the start of a new article in a single WSJ file).

However, given our goal to encode the presence of non-adjacent implicit relations, the manner in which these labels are currently assigned is a problem because this information is spread across both labels, by way of scenarios (b) and (c) above. Further, (a) and (b) confound the presence of a semantic coherence relation with the presence of coreference. Both of these considerations therefore led us to create two new labels for our task: **SemEntRel** (Semantic EntRel) for scenario (a), to unambiguously identify cases of entity-based coherence relations, and **NoSemRel** for scenarios (b) and (c), to unambiguously identify cases of non-adjacent implicit relations. To maintain consistency with the PDTB-2 corpus, the EntRel label for (b) was noted as a comment feature where relevant. Scenario (d) continued to be labeled as NoRel.

A SemEntRel relation is shown in Ex. (10), where Arg2 provides background about the "humanitarian assistance" conceptual entity in Arg1. Though not yet applied to the rest of PDTB-2, we find Semantic Entrels occur quite frequently in cross-paragraph contexts (see Section 4). An example of a NoSemRel relation is the underspecified annotation of the non-adjacent relation of Ex. (7), shown below as Ex. (11).

(10) *And important U.S. lawmakers must decide at the end of November if the Contras are to receive the rest of the $49 million in so-called humanitarian assistance under a bipartisan agreement reached with the Bush administration in March.*

(SemEntRel)
The humanitarian assistance, which pays for supplies such as food and clothing for the rebels amassed along the Nicaraguan border with Honduras, replaced the military aid cut off by Congress in February 1988.

(11) Only a few months ago, the 124-year-old securities firm seemed to be on the verge of a meltdown, racked by internal squabbles and defections. Its relationship with parent General Electric Co. had been frayed since a big Kidder insider-trading scandal two years ago. *Chief executives and presidents had come and gone.*

(NoSemRel)
Now, the firm says it's at a turning point. By the end of this year, 63-year-old Chairman Silas Cathcart – the former chairman of Illinois Tool Works who was derided as a "tool-and-die man" when GE brought him in to clean up Kidder in 1987 – retires to his Lake Forest, Ill., home, possibly to build a shopping mall on some land he owns.

3.3 Phase Three

Employing the enhancements to the PDTB-2 guidelines developed during Phase Two, 207

CPFS-PPLS implicit relation tokens from 34 texts were separately annotated by the two annotators in Phase Three for type, sense and minimal argument spans. However, prior to initiating the Phase Three annotation, all Phase One and Phase Two texts were reannotated by the two annotators according to the enhanced guidelines, and a close analysis of the disagreements was performed. This yielded three recurring patterns of disagreements as well as procedures for resolving them via careful application of the guidelines, detailed below.

a) Multi-sentential or discontinuous arguments may exclude supporting relations. Minimality requires that all and only the semantic material minimally needed to interpret a relation be specified by its arguments. Therefore, relations that support Arg1 and Arg2 but aren't necessary for their interpretation should be excluded from those arguments' boundaries. Common supporting relations typically excluded include Arg2-as-Instance, Arg2-as-Detail, and Reason, as well as Semantic Entrel or Temporal relations that supply background information. Ex. (12) shows supporting sentences after the CPFS that are excluded from Arg2 for minimality.

(12) *Although bullish dollar sentiment has fizzled,* many currency analysts say *a massive sell-off probably won't occur in the near future.*

> (Implicit, Reason, <u>because</u>)
> **While Wall Street's tough times and lower U.S. interest rates continue to undermine the dollar, weakness in the pound and the yen is expected to offset those factors.** "By default," the dollar probably will be able to hold up pretty well in coming days, says Francoise Soares-Kemp, a foreign-exchange adviser at Credit Suisse. "We're close to the bottom" of the near-term ranges, she contends.

b) A CPFS may appear to relate to both an adjacent and a non-adjacent unit. Often, however, the adjacent unit will be providing supporting content to the non-adjacent unit, rather than continuing the more global narrative flow. The stronger relation in this case will be the non-adjacent one. E.g., in Ex. (13), Arg2 creates an Instantiation relation regarding the names of specific judges to be included. Some annotators may perceive this relation as capable of being formed with the prior adjacent sentence or the non-adjacent italicized one. However, the prior adjacent sentence itself provides supporting detail on the italicized one, concerning the number of judges to be included. Thus, the adjacent sentence and the bolded sentence are neither directly related themselves, nor advancing the more global narrative flow. Therefore, this token is labeled NoSemRel.

(13) Several organizations, including the Industrial Biotechnical Association and the Pharmaceutical Manufacturers Association, have asked the White House and Justice Department to name candidates with both patent and scientific backgrounds. *The associations would like the court to include between three and six judges with specialized training.*

> (NoSemRel)
> **Some of the associations have recommended Dr. Alan D. Lourie, 54, a former patent agent with a doctorate in organic chemistry who now is associate general counsel with SmithKline Beckman Corp. in Philadelphia.**

c) Multiple tokens can relate differently to the same sentence. Often in the PDTB, texts begin with a single complex sentence followed by other sentences or paragraphs each discussing some aspect of it. By minimality, tokens should only be grouped into a single Arg2 if they share the same relation to the same Arg1 unit. The text in Ex. 7 provides an illustration of this. The italicized and bolded CPFSs together form the Arg2 of an Arg2-as-detail relation with the first sentence, providing detail on the eventuality of the company trying to struggle back. In contrast, in Ex. (14), the bolded Arg2 in the first CPFS provides detail on the trade deficit worsening in the first sentence. The bolded Arg2 in the second CPFS, on the other hand, displays entity coreference with the first bolded unit, but more generally and strongly, continues the global narrative flow about the Treasury Department's statement, that is, it is in a SemEntRel relation with the non-adjacent Arg1 (in italics). Given the new guidelines for Phase Three, the relation is thus labeled NoSemRel.

(14) The Treasury Department said *the U.S. trade deficit may worsen next year, after two years of significant improvement.*

> (Implicit=Arg2-as-detail)
> In its report to Congress on international economic policies, the Treasury said **that any improvement in the broadest measure of trade, known as the current account, "is likely at best to be very modest," and "the possibility of deterioration in the current account next year cannot be excluded."**

> (NoSemRel)
> **The statement was the U.S. government's first acknowledgement of what other groups, such as the International Monetary Fund, have been predicting for months.**

Arg1-Arg2 Pairs	Count	Pct	RelPct
Agree Adjacent:	**95**	**46%**	**100%**
Exact Match	40	19%	42%
Sent-level Match	13	7%	14%
Agree Sense, Args Overlap	12	6%	13%
Disagree Sense	30	14%	31%
Agreed Non-Adjacent:	**63**	**30%**	**100%**
Disagreed Adjacent/Non	**49**	**24%**	**100%**

Table 2: Cross-Paragraph Implicit Relations, Phase Three Agreement, 207 Tokens, 34 Texts.

	Implct	AltLex	SemEnt	NoSmRel	NoRel
Ct	152	8	62	207	11
Pct	35%	2%	14%	47%	3%

Table 3: Gold Cross-Paragraph Implicit Relation Counts and Percentages Across All Phases, 440 Tokens, 54 Texts.

4   Results and Discussion

Table 2 presents the Phase Three inter-annotator agreement results. As shown, agreement on whether a relation was adjacent (95) or non-adjacent (63) was approximately the same as in Phase Two, at 76% (46%+30%), Furthermore, over these 158 (95+63) tokens, the proportion of non-adjacent tokens (63/158, 40%) was similar to Phase Two, again supporting our hypothesis about their high frequency. Because of the backoff to annotating only adjacent cross-paragraph implicit relations, overall agreement with the most relaxed metric on argument spans[1] is higher in Phase Three (62%) than in Phase Two (43%). However, there is also substantial improvement in the sense annotation of the adjacent discourse relations, from 61% in Phase Two to 69% (42%+14%+13%) in this phase,[2] which we attribute partly to our enhanced guidelines for annotating SemEntRel. The increase in tokens agreed on sense also more accurately represents the agreement on arguments. Exactly matched arguments show an increase to 42% from 24% in Phase Two and there are fewer disagreements due to supra-sentential overlapping spans, which have reduced to 13% from 30% in Phase Two. The number of sentence-level disagreements increased to 14% from 7% in Phase Two, but most of these reflect minor syntactic differences (e.g., inclusion/exclusion of adjuncts or attributions) rather than semantic ones.

Following Phase Three, gold standard annotations were produced through consensus labeling over all phases. Table 3 shows the counts and percentages for each token type. Of the 440 tokens, 207 (47%) conveyed a non-adjacent relation and thus the adjacent relation was labeled NoSem-Rel, confirming our initial hypothesis of an almost equal distribution of cross-paragraph adjacent and non-adjacent implicit relations. Among the remaining 233 (53%) tokens, 153 (35%) were of the Implicit type in that a connective could be inserted to express the relation, while 8 (2%) conveyed the relation through an AltLex. 62 (14%) tokens were annotated as SemEntRels, and 11 (3%) were annotated as NoRels. Table 4 presents the counts and percentages for the Implicit and AltLex gold-labeled senses. As shown, Arg2-as-Detail occurs most frequently but still accounts for only 40% of the relations. Six other senses occurring with 5% or greater frequency account for 45% of the tokens, and include Conjunction (12%), Arg2-as-instance (9%), Reason (7%), Result (6%), Arg2-as-denier (6%) and Contrast (5%). The remaining 15% of the tokens occurring with less than 5% frequency are spread across nine different senses.

5   Related Work

Given that the end goal of this research is to produce full-text annotation of discourse relations, in this section we compare our work with two related approaches to full text discourse relation annotation, focusing on how they handle non-adjacent discourse relations, or in other words, long-distance discourse relation dependencies.

In the RST-based (Mann and Thompson, 1988) RST-DT corpus (Carlson et al., 2003), texts are first segmented into elementary discourse units (EDUs) and relations are then built recursively (i.e., as trees) between increasingly complex adjacent structures. Long-distance dependencies come about when the "nuclear" elements within a pair of complex adjacent structures are not adjacent in the text. In this approach, then, long-distance dependencies fall out as a function of the theory and its implementation in the annotation procedure. A disadvantage of such an approach, however, is that it tends to undervalue the evaluation and intuition of annotators with regards to such dependencies (Stede, 2012). As illustration, in the RST-DT tree (Fig. 2) for Ex. (15), the Antithesis relation clearly

---

[1] Exact Match + Sent-Level Match + Agree Sense, Args Overlap + Agreed Non-Adjacent

[2] The sense agreement for this task is on par with the agreement for intra-paragraph implicit relations reported in Miltsakaki et al. (2004).

Types	Senses (Count/Relative Percent of 160)							
	Detail2	Conjunction	Instance2	Reason	Result	Denier2	Contrast	Precedence
Implicit	62/39%	18/11%	13/8%	11/7%	10/6%	9/6%	8/5%	7/4%
AltLex	2/1%	1/<1%	2/1%	0	0	0	0	0
	Equivalence	Reason+β	Detail1	Instance1	Synchronous	Hypophora	Result+β	Succession
Implicit	3/2%	3/2%	2/1%	2/1%	1/<1%	1/<1%	1/<1%	1/<1%
AltLex	0	1/<1%	0	0	1/<1%	0	0	1/<1%

Table 4: Gold Cross-Paragraph Adjacent Implicit and AltLex Sense Counts and Relative Percentages Across All Phases, 160 Tokens. Detail(1/2) = Arg(1/2)-as-detail; Instance(1/2) = Arg(1/2)-as-instance; Denier2 = Arg2-as-denier.

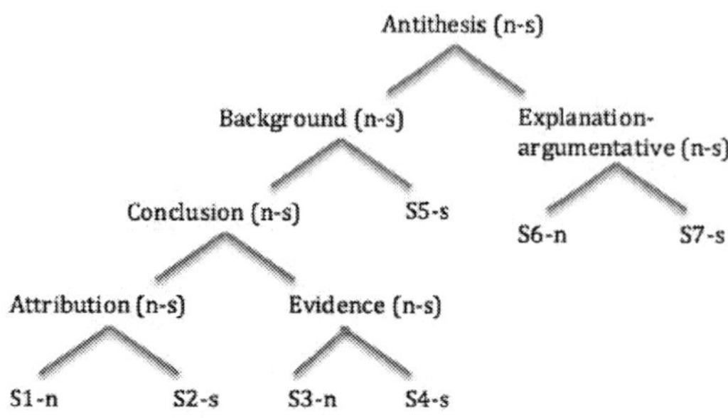

Figure 2: RST Structure for Ex. (15). Intrasentential relations are not shown. Nodes are labeled with RST mononuclear (n-s) or multinuclear (n-n) relations and leaves are anchored by sentences IDs marked with their nuclearity status.

seems to hold between S3 and S6, but this does not fall out from the RST-DT annotation, where S1 is promoted as the nucleus of the S1-S5 complex, not S3.

(15) **S1:** FEDERAL PROSECUTORS are concluding fewer criminal cases with trials.

S2: That's a finding of a new study of the Justice Department by researchers at Syracuse University.
S3: David Burnham, one of the authors, says fewer trials probably means a growing number of plea bargains.
S4: In 1980, 18% of federal prosecutions concluded at trial; in 1987, only 9% did.

S5: The study covered 11 major U.S. attorneys' offices – including those in Manhattan and Brooklyn, N.Y., and New Jersey – from 1980 to 1987.

S6: The Justice Department rejected the implication that its prosecutors are currently more willing to plea bargain.
S7: "Our felony caseloads have been consistent for 20 years," with about 15% of all prosecutions going to trial, a department spokeswoman said.

Like the RST-DT corpus, The SDRT-based (Asher and Lascarides, 2003) ANNODIS corpus (Afantenos et al., 2012) also constructs hierarchical structures - termed complex discourse units

(CDUs) - out of EDUs. A structure like Fig. 2 is thus possible in that corpus. However, CDUs are explicitly distinguished from EDUs in ANNODIS and there is at present no analogous concept of nuclearity within the theory that would promote some EDU(s) to become the prominent nucleus of the complex. The problem of identifying minimal arguments in long-distance dependencies is therefore sidestepped in the corpus; instead, the whole CDU serves as the argument. Nevertheless, identifying minimal arguments based on some principle, whether through annotation guidelines such as PDTB's "minimality constraint" or through theoretical mechanisms such as RST-DT's "nuclearity principle", is important in eliminating noise from the arguments. For example, a learning algorithm extracting features from non-minimal argument spans for sense labeling would wind up with a lot of extraneous or conflicting data. It is also an open question as to whether the speaker/hearer retains or requires such hierarchically-structured non-minimal complex units when establishing/interpreting discourse relations in speech/text. In many other respects, however, the ANNODIS approach is on par with the one addressed in this paper. Relations are defined in semantic terms, and long-distance relations are annotated regardless of whether or not they may lead to crossing dependencies in the *emergent* composite discourse structures.

6 Conclusion and Future Work

In sum, our study shows that adjacent implicit discourse relations across paragraphs can be annotated reliably. Furthermore, the gold-standard sense distributions found in our study, together with the frequency of Semantic EntRels, suggest that cross-paragraph implicit relations carry varied semantic content in substantial proportions and are therefore worth annotating. Given this, one goal of our future work is to annotate ~200 texts of the PDTB corpus with adjacent cross-paragraph implicit relations, following the enhanced guidelines developed here, and publicly distribute the annotations via github.[3] The subset of texts to be annotated contain approximately 700 tokens of cross-paragraph implicit relations, which we have estimated (from our Phase1 to Phase3 annotations) to require 3 minutes per token on average, i.e., approximately 35 hours of annotation time per annotator. Once this corpus is completed, we can then study the distribution of senses and patterns of senses in the texts, along the lines of Pitler et al. (2008), but now over full text relation sequences. In addition, the high incidence of the underspecified implicit non-adjacent relations found in this study suggests the value of developing guidelines for their more difficult annotation to ensure it can be done reliably, and thus, this is a goal of our future work as well.

More generally, our study is the first to quantitatively assess the difficulty of annotating long-distance discourse relation dependencies. We find that annotating non-adjacent cross-paragraph implicit relations is difficult and time-consuming. Another future goal is, therefore, to develop more effective tools and methodologies to increase annotation ease, speed and reliability. These include enhancements to the PDTB annotation tool to better allow simultaneous visualization of intersentential relations and their arguments in a text. In addition, a two-pass annotation methodology would allow the more difficult cross-paragraph non-adjacent implicit relations to be annotated in a second pass. Sequences of inter-sentential relations from the first pass could then reveal systematic structures to inform the second pass.

Acknowledgments

This work was partially supported by NSF grant IIS-1421067.

References

Stergos Afantenos, Nicholas Asher, Farah Benamara, Myriam Bras, Ccile Fabre, Lydia-Mai Ho-Dac, Anne Le Draoulec, Philippe Muller, Marie-Paule Pry-Woodley, Laurent Prevot, Josette Rebeyrolle, Ludovic Tanguy, Marianne Vergez-Couret, and Laure Vieu. 2012. An empirical resource for discovering cognitive principles of discourse organisation: the ANNODIS corpus. In *Proceedings of the 8th International Conference on Language Resources and Evaluation*. Istanbul, Turkey, pages 2727–2734.

Nicholas Asher and Alex Lascarides. 2003. *Logics of conversation*. Cambridge University Press.

Sasha J. Blair-Goldensohn. 2007. *Long-Answer Question Answering and Rhetorical-Semantic Relations*. Ph.D. thesis, Columbia University.

Lynn Carlson, Daniel Marcu, and Mary Ellen Okurowski. 2003. Building a discourse-tagged corpus in the framework of Rhetorical Structure Theory. In Jan van Kuppevelt and Ronnie Smith, editors, *Current Directions in Discourse and Dialogue*, Kluwer Academic Publishers, pages 85–112.

Ruihong Huang and Ellen Riloff. 2012. Modeling textual cohesion for event extraction. In *Proceedings of the 26th Conference on Artificial Intelligence*. Toronto, Canada, pages 1664–1670.

Alan Lee, Rashmi Prasad, Bonnie Webber, and Aravind Joshi. 2016. Annotating discourse relations with the PDTB annotator. In *Proceedings of the 26th International Conference on Computational Linguistics: System Demonstrations*. Osaka, Japan, pages 121–125.

Annie Louis, Aravind Joshi, and Ani Nenkova. 2010. Discourse indicators for content selection in summarization. In *Proceedings of the 11th Annual Meeting of the Special Interest Group on Discourse and Dialogue*. Tokyo, Japan, pages 147–156.

William C. Mann and Sandra A. Thompson. 1988. Rhetorical structure theory. Toward a functional theory of text organization. *Text* 8(3):243–281.

Mitchell Marcus, Beatrice Santorini, and Mary Ann Marcinkiewicz. 1993. Building a large annotated corpus of English: The Penn TreeBank. *Computational Linguistics* 19(2):313–330.

Eleni Miltsakaki, Rashmi Prasad, Aravind Joshi, and Bonnie Webber. 2004. Annotating discourse connectives and their arguments. In *Proceedings of the HLT/NAACL Workshop on Frontiers in Corpus Annotation*. Boston, MA, pages 9–16.

Stephan Oepen, Jonathon Read, Tatjana Scheffler, Uladzimir Sidarenka, Manfred Stede, Erik Velldal, and Lilja Øvrelid. 2016. OPT: Oslo-Potsdam-Teesside pipelining rules, rankers, and classifier ensembles for shallow discourse parsing. In *Proceedings of the CoNLL-16 shared task on Multilingual Shallow Discourse Parsing*. Berlin, Germany, pages 20–26.

Emily Pitler, Annie Louis, and Ani Nenkova. 2009. Automatic sense prediction for implicit discourse relations in text. In *Proceedings of the Joint Conference of the 47th Annual Meeting of the ACL and the 4th International Joint Conference on Natural Language Processing of the AFNLP: Volume 2*. Suntec, Singapore, pages 683–691.

---

[3]http://www.github.com

Emily Pitler, Mridhula Raghupathy, Hena Mehta, Ani Nenkova, Alan Lee, and Aravind Joshi. 2008. Easily identifiable discourse relations. In *Proceedings of the 22nd International Conference on Computational Linguistics*. Manchester, UK, pages 87–90.

Rashmi Prasad, Nikhil Dinesh, Alan Lee, Eleni Miltsakaki, Livio Robaldo, Aravind Joshi, and Bonnie Webber. 2008. The Penn Discourse TreeBank 2.0. In *Proceedings of the 6th International Conference on Language Resources and Evaluation*. Marrakech, Morocco, pages 2961–2968.

Rashmi Prasad, Aravind Joshi, and Bonnie Webber. 2010. Exploiting scope for shallow discourse parsing. In *Proceedings of the 7th International Conference on Language Resources and their Evaluation*. Valletta, Malta, pages 2076–2083.

Rashmi Prasad, Bonnie Webber, and Aravind Joshi. 2014. Reflections on the Penn Discourse TreeBank, comparable corpora and complementary annotation. *Computational Linguistics* 40(4):921–950.

Swapna Somasundaran, Janyce Wiebe, and Josef Ruppenhofer. 2008. Discourse level opinion interpretation. In *Proceedings of the 22nd International Conference on Computational Linguistics, Volume 1*. Manchester, U.K., pages 801–808.

Manfred Stede. 2012. *Discourse processing*. Synthesis Lectures on Human Language Technologies (series editor, Graeme Hirst). Morgan & Claypool Publishers.

Jianxiang Wang and Man Lan. 2015. A refined end-to-end discourse parser. In *Proceedings of the CoNLL-2015 Shared Task*. Beijing, China, pages 17–24.

Bonnie Webber. 2009. Genre distinctions for discourse in the Penn TreeBank. In *Proceedings of the Joint Conference of the 47th Annual Meeting of the ACL and the 4th International Joint Conference on Natural Language Processing of the AFNLP*. Suntec, Singapore, page 674–682.

Bonnie Webber, Aravind Joshi, Matthew Stone, and Alistair Knott. 2003. Anaphora and discourse structure. *Computational Linguistics* 29(4):545–587.

Bonnie Webber, Rashmi Prasad, Alan Lee, and Aravind Joshi. 2016. A discourse-annotated corpus of conjoined VPs. In *Proceedings of the 10th Linguistic Annotation Workshop*. ACL, Berlin, Germany, pages 22–31.

Nianwen Xue, Hwee Tou Ng, Sameer Pradhan, Rashmi Prasad, Christopher Bryant, and Attapol Rutherford. 2015. The CoNLL-2015 shared task on shallow discourse parsing. In *Proceedings of the CoNLL-15 shared task*. Beijing, China, pages 1–16.

Nianwen Xue, Hwee Tou Ng, Attapol Rutherford, Bonnie Webber, Chuan Wang, and Hongmin Wang. 2016. The CoNLL-2016 shared task on multilingual shallow discourse parsing. In *Proceedings of the CoNLL-16 shared task*. Berlin, Germany, pages 1–19.

Fan Zhang, Diane Litman, and Katherine Forbes Riley. 2016. Inferring discourse relations from PDTB-style discourse labels for argumentative revision classification. In *Proceedings of the 26th International Conference on Computational Linguistics: Technical Papers*. Osaka, Japan, pages 2615–2624.

User-initiated Sub-dialogues
in State-of-the-art Dialogue Systems

Staffan Larsson

Centre for Linguistic Theory and Studies in Probability (CLASP)

Department of Philosophy, Linguistics and Theory of Science

University of Gothenburg

`sl@ling.gu.se`

Abstract

We test state of the art dialogue systems for their behaviour in response to user-initiated sub-dialogues, i.e. interactions where a system question is responded to with a question or request from the user, who thus initiates a sub-dialogue. We look at sub-dialogues both within a single app (where the sub-dialogue concerns another topic in the original domain) and across apps (where the sub-dialogue concerns a different domain). The overall conclusion of the tests is that none of the systems can be said to deal appropriately with user-initiated sub-dialogues.

Index Terms: dialogue, dialogue systems, dialogue management, human-machine interaction, dialogue structure

1 Introduction

This paper follows Larsson (2015) in taking a look at how dialogue systems from some of the major players on the market actually deal with some conversational behaviours frequently encountered in human-human dialogue. It should be noted that the tests necessarily reflect the behaviour of the systems tested at the time of the test. As any other app in your mobile, conversational agents are frequently updated and new behaviours are added. The tests described here were carried out in March 2017.

The work presented here builds on the "Trindi Tick-list" (Bos et al., 1999) which was constructed in the TRINDI project[1] to examine whether certain dialogue behaviours can be reliably manifested by a dialogue system. The original tick-list is still being used (Hofmann et al., 2014), and there have

been later revisions and amendments (although these remain to be published). With the advent of widely available spoken dialogue systems in smartphones, the kind of evaluation exemplified by the Trindi Tick-list has again become relevant.

In this paper, we will choose a small subset of the questions in the current tick-list, and investigate how systems deal with dialogue behaviours related to *user-initiated sub-dialogues*, i.e. cases where a system question is responded to with a user question (or request). According to Łupkowski and Ginzburg (2013), responding to a query with a query is a common occurrence, representing on a rough estimate more than 20% of all responses to queries found in the British National Corpus. Also, many of us are used to being able to multi-task using our computers and smartphones, jumping back and forth at will between several apps or programs, and there seems to be no particular reason why we should not be able to do so just because we are interacting using spoken dialogue.

2 The systems in the test

We tested five systems: Siri[2], API.AI[3], Houndify[4], Cortana[5] and Alexa[6]. The choice of these systems was based on (1) availability, (2) being reasonably well-known, and (3) allowing testing the dialogue phenomena in question[7]. While previous tests (Larsson, 2015) used complete off-the-shelf

---

[1] `http://www.ling.gu.se/projekt/trindi/`

[2] `http://www.apple.com/ios/siri/`

[3] `https://api.ai/`

[4] `https://www.houndify.com/`

[5] `https://www.microsoft.com/en-us/mobile/experiences/cortana/`

[6] `https://developer.amazon.com/alexa`

[7] For example, the Google Assistant and Google Home systems rarely if ever ask questions to the user; instead, they generally try to take whatever information they have and do something with it. This means that there no natural place to initiate a sub-dialogue when interacting with these systems. For these reasons, they have not been included in this test.

Proceedings of the SIGDIAL 2017 Conference, pages 17–22,
Saarbrücken, Germany, 15-17 August 2017. ©2017 Association for Computational Linguistics

end-to-end dialogue applications (e.g. for calling people up), the market has shifted towards offering developers various degrees of freedom and support in implementing dialogue applications on top of a dialogue system (or dialogue system platform). In this respect, the systems in the test differ to a large extent – not only with respect to the extent to which they support various dialogue behaviours, but also as to whether they offer any dialogue management capabilities at all. Roughly speaking, the systems fall into three broad classes:

- **Closed systems**: A fixed set of non-configurable dialogue applications (e.g. Siri).

- **Configurable service platforms** provide dialogue management and domain implementations[8]; developers select domains and connect services to these ready-made domain implementations (e.g. SiriKit, Houndify[9]).

- **Domain development platforms** provide generic dialogue management; developers implement their own domains or select from a set of predefined domains (e.g. API.AI, (Houndify[10]))

- **Dialogue shells** offer ASR, NLU and TTS; developers implement dialogue managers (including domain implementations) (e.g. Cortana, Alexa).

In Section 3, we discuss some complications arising from applying a single test to systems of all four classes. First, however, we provide a brief description of each of the tested systems.

2.1 Siri

Siri runs on the iPhone and on a variety of Apple devices. SiriKit[11] offers some minimal opportunities for developers to connect their own external services to Siri, but only for a limited range of service types (currently VoIP calling, messaging, payments, photo and workouts) for which ready-made language understanding and dialogue management knowledge is provided by Siri (and unavailable for developers). For each service type, a fixed set of "intents" (tasks) are defined, that the developer use to connect their service. In the current tests, we used ready-made Siri applications on an iPhone,

2.2 API.AI

API.AI (which can be used in Google Assistant and Google Home apps) offers an interactive GUI tool for building a dialogue application by giving sample user sentences and mapping these onto interpretations in terms of intents and entities. The user-defined app can be combined with a number of pre-defined apps (not editable). For the current test, we used a combination of one "home-made" application and a selection of predefined domains, since this gave us the opportunity to define a domain with several intents as well as intents with multiple parameters (necessary for performing all our tests). Specifically, a simple phone domain was implemented by the author using the API.AI developer GUI. The tests were conducted using the text interface on the API.AI developer website.

2.3 Houndify

Houndify is very similar to API.AI but we have so far not been able to get access to the developer tools. For this reason, we used only predefined applications in the tests. The tests were conducted using the text interface on the Houndify developer website.

2.4 Cortana

Cortana runs on a variety of Windows devices, and essentially allows developers to build apps that use Cortana's built-in ASR and TTS (as well as the phone touch-screen for graphical output and haptic input) with a Cortana look-and-feel. This means that NLU, dialogue management and NLG need to be implemented more or less from scratch by the developer. In this test, we used existing ready-made Cortana domains on a Nokia Lumia phone.

2.5 Alexa

Amazon's Alexa runs on the Amazon Echo, and is similar to Cortana, except it also offers generic and configurable NLU capabilities. For our tests, we used ready-made Alexa domains. While broadly classified as a "dialogue shell", Alexa does offer a general mechanism for switching between domains ("skills") that is relevant for our current

---

[8]Roughly, we use *(dialogue) app* to refer to the entity with which a user communicates about a certain domain, given some *domain implementation* encoding the knowledge required to talk about that domain.

[9]The openly available Houndify only allows accessing existing domains.

[10]Building custom domains for Houndify is currently by invitation only. We have not been able to test this feature.

[11]https://developer.apple.com/sirikit/

concerns. The tests were conducted on an Amazon Echo.

3   Complications

Our main interest is to evaluate *general* (domain independent) dialogue management features, which may be problematic in some cases where it is not clear if a certain behaviour is implemented in a general dialogue manager, or if it is produced by a domain-specific dialogue management script. In many cases, the source of an observed behaviour can be inferred from documentation, but in other cases more indirect evidence has to be used. For example, if a system displays identical behaviours across several domains, this may be evidence that it is produced by a general dialogue manager.

Note that we are not mainly interested in what is *possible* in a given system, but rather in what is *supported* by the system. That is, the developer should not have to implement all or most of the code required to deal with the dialogue feature in question. Ideally, the developer should not have to do anything to enable it (other than possibly selecting or deselecting the feature). In the case of "dialogue shells", very few dialogue features are supported. Pretty much any behaviour can *in principle* be implemented, but this is not necessarily very helpful for the developer.

Another problem concerns the notion of a domain (or "app"). Whereas in some cases it is clear whether two tasks (or "skills") are implemented as separate domains. We have assumed e.g. that asking about missed calls and calling people up both belong to the "phone" domain, while asking for the time or setting an alarm probably instead belong to the "clock" domain.

Despite these complications, we believe the tests in this paper can be of interest, and we have tried to make clear the specific characteristics of the systems to enable the reader to assess the reliability of the tests.

4   Results

The overall results of the tests are shown in Table 1. In this section, we present the details of these results and provide concrete interactions as evidence.

4.1   User anytime jump to task within app

The first three tests consider the capabilities of the systems to deal with user utterances that respond to a system question related to a task T with a request or question related to another task T' (where T and T' are both in the same domain). We refer to such a request or question as "jump to task". The "anytime" refers to the fact the the jump to T' can occur at any point during the dialogue related to task T (not only e.g. after T' is done). The tests are the following (indexed Fn for "feature n"):

- (F1) User anytime jump to task within app. Does the system respond adequately to jumps, i.e. does it shift the topic of conversation to T'?

- (F2) System resume after within-app subdialogue. After finishing T', does the system return the dialogue to the previous (unfinished) topic T?

- (F3) Signal task resumption. If the system resumes T, does it also indicate this somehow?

Note that F2 and F3 are not applicable if F1 is answered negatively, and that F3 is not applicable if F2 is answered negatively. Here is an example of a dialogue with a system that would yield "yes"-answers to all three questions:

U:	Make a call
S:	Who do you want to call?
U:	Do I have any missed calls?
S:	No. Returning to making a call. Who do you want to call?

Here, the system's last utterance (starting with "No") first shows that it can deal with the embedded question by answering it (F1). It also shows that it returns to the unfinished topic of making a call, by repeating the question "who do you want to call." (F2) Finally, it signals task resumption explicitly ("Returning to making a call") (F3).

Siri accepts the embedded question T' and responds to it, but does not manage to return to the previous unfinished topic T.

U:	Make a call
S:	Who do you want to call?
U:	Do I have any missed calls?
S:	No
U:	Okay
S:	-

	Siri	API.AI	Houndify	Cortana	Alexa
F1. User anytime jump to task within app	+	+	?	-	+
F2. System resume after within-app sub-dialogue	-	-	?	-	-
F3. Signal task resumption	N/A	N/A	?	-	N/A
F4. User anytime jump across apps	+	-	-	-	(+)
F5. System resume after other-app subdialog	-	N/A	N/A	N/A	-
F6. Signal app (and task) resumption	N/A	N/A	N/A	N/A	N/A

Table 1: Dialogue behaviours related to user-initiated sub-dialogues in five dialogue systems

API.AI produces the same behaviour as Siri, failing to return to the unfinished topic.

Unfortunately, **Houndify** could not be tested for this feature, since none of the available domains featured (1) more than one task, whereof (2) at least one task involved asking a question to the user.

Since **Alexa** does not implement calling people up, we instead used the clock domain for testing F1-F3. The results were the same as for Siri and API.AI.

```
U:   Set the alarm
S:   Alarm for what time?
U:   What time is it?
S:   10.15
U:   OK
S:   -
```

Cortana did slightly worse than the other systems, failing to understand the embedded question (again we used the clock domain)[12].

```
U:   Set the alarm
S:   Set you alarm for what time?
U:   What time is it?
S:   What time did you want the alarm?
```

4.2 User anytime jump across apps

The next three tests (F4-F6) consider the capabilities of the systems to deal with user utterances that respond to a system question related to a task T in a domain D with a request or question related to a task T' in another domain $D' \neq D$. We refer to such a request or question as "jump across apps". Again, "anytime" refers to the fact the the jump to T' can occur at any point during the dialogue related to task T (not only e.g. after T' is done). The tests are the following:

- (F4) User anytime implicit jump across apps. After having asked a question related to a task T in a domain D, does the system respond adequately to a request or question related to a task T' belonging to a domain D' (but not mentioning D'), i.e. does it shift the topic of conversation to T' and D'?

- (F5) System resume after other-app sub-dialogue. After finishing T', does the system return the dialogue to the previous (unfinished) topic T?

- (F6) Signal app (and task) resumption. If the system resumes T, does it also indicate this somehow?

Note that F5 and F6 are not applicable if F4 is answered negatively, and that F6 is not applicable if F5 is answered negatively. Here is an example of a dialogue with a system that would yield "yes"-answers to F4, F5 and F6:

```
U:   Make a call
S:   Who do you want to call?
U:   What time is it?
S:   8 pm. Returning to making a call. Who
     do you want to call?
```

Siri offers user anytime jump across apps[13]. The behaviour concerning F5 and F6 parallels that of F2 and F3.

```
U:   Call John
S:   Which number for John?
U:   What time is it?
S:   8 pm.
U:   OK
S:   -
```

API.AI does not provide F4:

---

[12]Cortana had no problem understanding "What time is it" when the question was not embedded.

[13]This assumes that calling people up and asking the time belong to different domains

U: Make a call
S: Who do you want to call?
U: What time is it?
S: Who do you want to call?

For **Houndify**, we used a different combination of domains to test for F4-F6, with tip calculation taking the place of calling someone up. The result is similar to that for API.AI, but instead of simply ignoring the embedded request, the system indicates that it does not understand it.

U: Calculate tip
S: What is the amount of the bill?
U: What time is it
S: Sorry, I did not understand that. The bill amount is indicated on the check. What is the amount of the bill?

The results for **Cortana** were similar to those for API.AI.

In many cases, **Alexa** requires the user to explicitly address the app, thus requiring what we may call "gated commands" as opposed to "gateless commands" (wich can be issued without explicitly addressing the relevant app).

U: Alexa, play Abba *on Spotify*

Regardless of whether gated or gateless commands were used, Alexa would switch topic as requested, but did not manage to return to the original topic.

U: Alexa, set the alarm
S: Alarm for what time?
U: Alexa, play Abba on Spotify
S: (plays music)

5 Discussion and future work

An obvious extension of the work presented here is to include more systems, i.e. Luis (from Microsoft) and Watson (from IBM). This also points to the need for regularly testing both new and established systems for a wide range of dialogue phenomena, preferably in a standardised manner.

Another obvious extension of the work presented here would be to relate the various dialogue behaviours to measurements of the quality, usefulness and attractiveness of dialogue systems that have or lack the respective features. Here, the PARADISE framework (Walker et al., 1997) could potentially be very useful. Such investigations, however, must take into account variability in the usefulness of various dialogue features with respect to the overall activity and other situational factors. A feature which is very useful in one context may be of little interest in another.

It seems likely that at least in some cases, the user may not expect or want a conversational partner to return to a previous topic. For example, the user may switch to another topic as a way of steering the conversation away from the current topic. How to distinguish cases where a user initiative is intended an interruption of the ongoing topic, vs. when it is intended as an embedded subdialogue, is an interesting area for future research.

It is also possible that real-time factors may play a role. If embedded sub-dialogues can be dealt with in an efficient and highly interactive manner, with minimal delay between turns, this reduces the user's perceived cost (in terms of time and effort) of entering into a sub-dialogue, and may boost the usefulness of such sub-dialogues.

It should be noted that although none of the tested systems dealt adequately with user-initiated sub-dialogues, there are systems that do handle these phenomena. We know of at least two such systems, Indigo[14] from Artificial Solutions, and the Talkamatic Dialogue Manager (TDM) from Talkamatic[15,16]. These systems deal appropriately with most of the phenomena listed in Table 1[17].

6 Conclusion

We have tested five different well-publicised dialogue systems for their behaviour in response to user-initiated sub-dialogues within and across apps. The overall conclusion of the tests is that none of the systems tested deal appropriately with user-initiated sub-dialogues. In light of how frequent this behaviour is in human-human dialogue, we regard this as a serious shortcoming.

We hope that the kind of evaluation presented here can improve our understanding of the state of the art in commercial dialogue systems, and suggest ways in which to improve such systems with respect to dialogue management.

---

[14] http://www.hello-indigo.com/

[15] talkamatic.se

[16] For transparency, it should be noted that the author is co-founder and co-owner of Talkamatic AB.

[17] TDM handles all of F1-F7. Indigo handles F1-F4 and F6-F7. However, Indigo has trouble with the over- and other-answering tests described in Larsson (2015).

References

Johan Bos, Staffan Larsson, I Lewin, C Matheson, and D Milward. 1999. Survey of existing interactive systems. Technical Report D1.3, TRINDI (Task Oriented Instructional Dialogue) project.

Hansjörg Hofmann, Anna Silberstein, Ute Ehrlich, André Berton, Christian Müller, and Angela Mahr. 2014. Development of speech-based in-car hmi concepts for information exchange internet apps. In *Natural Interaction with Robots, Knowbots and Smartphones*, Springer, pages 15–28.

Staffan Larsson. 2015. The state of the art in dealing with user answers. In Christine Howes and Staffan Larsson, editors, *Proceedings of the 19th Workshop on the Semantics and Pragmatics of Dialogue (go-DIAL)*.

Paweł Łupkowski and Jonathan Ginzburg. 2013. A corpus-based taxonomy of question responses. In *IWCS 2013 (International Workshop on Computational Semantics)*.

M. A. Walker, D. J. Litman, C. A. Kamm, and A. Abella. 1997. PARADISE: A framework for evaluating spoken dialogue agents. In *Proc. of the ACL*. Madrid, pages 271–280.

A Multimodal Dialogue System for Medical Decision Support in Virtual Reality

Alexander Prange, Margarita Chikobava, Peter Poller, Michael Barz, Daniel Sonntag

German Research Center for Artificial Intelligence (DFKI)

66123 Saarbrücken, Germany

{Firstname}.{Lastname}@dfki.de

Abstract

We present a multimodal dialogue system that allows doctors to interact with a medical decision support system in virtual reality (VR). We integrate an interactive visualization of patient records and radiology image data, as well as therapy predictions. Therapy predictions are computed in real-time using a deep learning model.

1 Introduction

Modern hospitals and clinics rely on digital patient data. Simply storing and retrieving patient records is not enough; in order for computer systems to provide interactive decision support, one must represent the semantics in a machine readable form using medical ontologies (Sonntag et al., 2009b). In this paper, we present a novel real-time decision support dialogue for the medical domain, where the physician can visualize and interact with patient data in an virtual reality environment by using natural speech and hand gestures.

Our multimodal dialogue system is an extension of previous work by Luxenburger et al. (Luxenburger et al., 2016) where we used an Oculus Rift with an integrated eye-tracker in a medical remote collaboration setting. First, the radiologist fills out a findings form using a mobile tablet with a stylus. The data is then transcribed in real-time using automated handwriting recognition, parsed, and represented based on medical ontologies. Then, the doctor, or any other health professional, enters virtual reality and interacts with patient records using the multimodal dialogue system. Through the temporal synchronization of visual and auditory events in VR, we support multisensory integration (Morein-Zamir et al., 2003). This way we profit from superadditivity (Oviatt, 2013) to further enhance multisensory perception.

2 Architecture

Modern hospitals and clinics are highly digitalized; in order to integrate our system seamlessly into everyday processes, we designed a highly flexible architecture, which can be connected to existing hospital systems (e.g., PACS, a picture archiving and communication system) and connects novel interaction devices such as VR glasses and head-mounted displays (HMDs). As depicted in Figure 1, all devices in this scenario are either connected directly or through adapters to the *Proxy Server* using XML-RPC, a remote procedure call protocol which uses XML to encode information that is sent via HTTP between clients and server. The Proxy Server manages and relays the cross-platform communication between the different devices. The mobile device for instance retrieves patient data and medical images through the Proxy Server from the hospital's *PACS* and *RIS* (radiology information system). The doctor then fills out the report, and the results are send back. Some components, like the PACS and RIS, are not connected directly through XML-RPC to the rest of the system, but through the *Patient Data Provider*, which provides an abstraction layer to the other devices. This way we can ensure a flexible integration of different proprietary software solutions that are already being used in hospitals.

2.1 Mobile Device

Even though modern hospitals and clinics are highly digitalized, there are many everyday processes that are still performed using pen and paper. Our approach in this scenario is based on the work of Sonntag et al. (Sonntag et al., 2014) where they use digital pens to improve reporting practices in the radiology domain. Instead of using a digital pen on normal paper, we create a fully digital version of the radiology findings form (in

Proceedings of the SIGDIAL 2017 Conference, pages 23–26,
Saarbrücken, Germany, 15-17 August 2017. ©2017 Association for Computational Linguistics

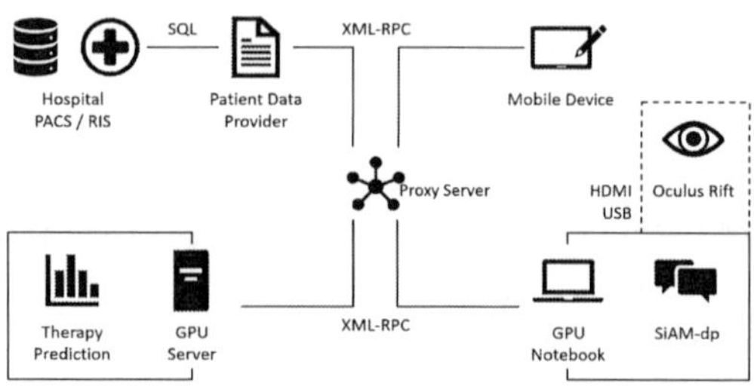

Figure 1: Architecture diagram

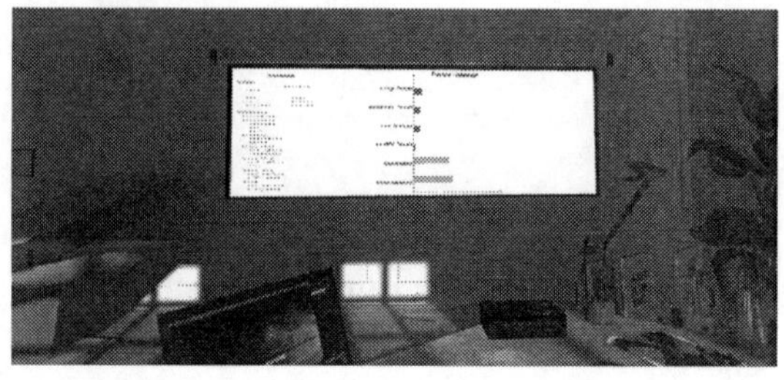

Figure 2: Screenshot of therapy prediction results inside virtual reality

this case mammography), to be used on a mobile device with integrated stylus. The radiologist writes the report directly onto the tablet using the stylus and through real-time handwriting, gesture, and sketch recognition, the entire content is transcribed, exported and written into the hospital's database. Our approach has several advantages over the traditional form filling process: (1) the contents are instantly transcribed and parsed into concepts of medical ontologies, (2) real-time feedback about the handwriting recognition process allows for a direct validation of input data, and (3) medical images are taken directly from the hospital's PACS, are then displayed on the screen and can be annotated by the radiologist. We use the Samsung Note series as mobile devices, because they feature a special Wacom digitiser technology for the stylus input; we built our software on top of the MyScript[1] handwriting recognition engine.

2.2 Virtual Reality

We created a Unity3D application[2] that resembles a real world doctor's office. The user can move freely inside the room using positional tracking and may also look around using head tracking. To enable immersive and remote interaction with medical multimedia data, we use a projection on the wall, where the patient files, the previously annotated digital form, and the therapy predictions are shown (see Figure 2). Navigation inside the documents, like zooming or scrolling through pages, can be achieved either through natural speech interaction or by using the Oculus Touch controllers, which we render as hands inside VR.

---

[1]http://myscript.com/
[2]http://unity3d.com/

2.3 Decision Support

Our medical dialogue system facilitates support for deciding which therapy is most suitable for a given patient. We integrated a prediction model for clinical decision support based on deep learning (Esteban et al., 2016) as backend service running on a dedicated GPU server. They presented a recurrent neural network (RNN) to include dynamic sequences of examinations which was modified to take dynamic patient data as additional input. This model was trained on a set of structured data from 475 patients, containing a total of 19438 diagnoses, 15352 procedures, 59202 laboratory results and 13190 medications. All personal data, such as names, date of birth, patient-IDs were anonymized accordingly and all date and time references were shifted. For our dialogue system, fast response times are of particular interest. We use TensorFlow (Abadi et al., 2016) to enable GPU-accelerated predictions on a scalable platform. Our service runs on a dedicated high-performance computer and is accessible to the dialogue system through our Proxy Server.

3 Dialogue

In order to facilitate coordinated interactions on the patient data within the virtual reality environment, we developed a multimodal dialogue interface that allows us to operate and interact by speech and gestures. The multimodal dialogue system supports three different types of interactions: (1) interactions with the patient data shown on the virtual display (e.g., *"Open the patient file for Gerda Meier.", "Show the next page."*); (2) interactive question answering (QA) about the contents of a patient record (e.g., *"When was the last examination?"*); and (3) control of the therapy prediction component (e.g., *"Which therapy is recommended?"*). Within the dialogue the following speech interactions and phenomena are realized:

- Navigation inside patient records (e.g., open/close file, scroll, zoom, turn page)
- Anaphoric reference resolution (e.g., *"What is her current medication?"*)
- Elliptic speech input (e.g., *"... and the age?"*)
- Multimodal (deictic) dialog interactions (e.g., *"Zoom in here"* + [user points on a region on the display])
- Cross-modal reference resolution (e.g., *"What is the second best therapy recommendation?"*)

3.1 Dialogue Implementation

The implementation of the dialogue follows the rapid engineering principles (Sonntag et al., 2009a) and is implemented with SiAM-dp (Neßelrath, 2015), an open development platform for multimodal dialogue systems. All knowledge representations and dialogue structures follow a declarative specification with ontology structures. First, the already existing patient data model of the patient database was mapped onto the corresponding domain ontology for SiAM-dp's knowledge manager, which is initialized with the specific patient instances at the beginning of each dialogue session. The speech recognition grammar is loaded into Nuance's speech recognizer[3].

The dialogue model is based on finite-state machines; the mapping of user intentions to matching multimodal system reactions is defined declaratively. The determination of the user intention in SiAM-dp follows a fusion process: SiAM-dp's modality specific user input analysis components (speech recognition, gesture analysis) and their fusion in conjunction with reference resolution within the discourse manager. The realization of multimodal output (speech output, virtual display content modifications, therapy prediction invocation) is coordinated by SiAM-dp's presentation planning component. The software itself runs on the same machine that has the Oculus Rift and the Touch controllers attached. Technically speaking, SiAM-dp is operated with standard speech recognition and synthesis (Nuance, SVOX), connected to Oculus Rift's microphone and speakers as audio

---

³`http://www.nuance.com`

input and output devices. An example dialogue is as follows:

U.1 *"Show the patient file for Gerda Meier."*
S.1 *"Here is the patient file for Gerda Meier."* [patient data is displayed on the display inside the VR room]
U.2 *"What was the last examination?"*
S.2 *"Mrs. Meier recently received a mammography."*
U.3 *"When was it?"*
S.3 *"The mammography was made on the 10th of March."*
U.4 *"Now show me the patient file for Paula Fischer."*
S.4 *"Here is the patient file for Paula Fischer."* [new patient data is displayed]
U.5 *"Zoom in here."* [user points on a region on the display using the Oculus Touch controller]
S.5 [virtual display is zoomed accordingly]
U.6 *"Which therapy is recommended?"*
S.6 *"For Paula Fischer chemotherapy is recommended."* [bar chart with therapy prediction is displayed]

In (U.1) the user requests a patient file to be presented on the display inside the VR room. The corresponding system output (S.1) is multimodal: speech output is synchronized with the presentation of the patient file. The user then requests information about the patient data currently shown on the display (U.2), e.g. anamneses and previous therapies. This user input contains an ellipsis: the name of the patient is not mentioned. SiAM-dp's discourse manager resolves it from the dialogue context that was filled in (U.1). Further questions about specifics may be asked (U.3). The context infers that "it" refers to the mammography just mentioned (rule-based anaphora resolution).

The next utterance (U.4) shows that users may shift the topic at any point, for instance by requesting other patient data. (U.5) is an example of a multimodal input consisting of a speech input and a corresponding pointing gesture. Processing this user input is only possible if both modalities are in a certain time frame and correctly fused.

The main dialogue move is (U.6), as it triggers the real-time therapy prediction process on the GPU Server. The system's response in (S.6) is again multimodal as the requested therapy is presented on the virtual display, together with synthesized speech output.

Anaphora resolution is also handled in our system. Since the patient file represented on the display is always synchronized with the current discourse model and within SiAM-dp depending on the context modelled as discourse memory (Sonntag, 2010) the system can resolve utterances like *"when was her last examination?"*

4 Conclusions and Future Work

In this paper, we presented our multimodal dialogue system implementation in virtual reality. It provides a first example of an automated decision support system that computes therapy predictions in real-time using deep learning techniques. Our multimodal dialogue system, in combination with interactive data visualization in virtual reality, is meant to provide an intuitive dialogue component for helping the doctor in his or her therapy decision. Preliminary evaluations in the clinical data intelligence project (Sonntag et al., 2016) are encouraging and we believe that such multimodal-multisensor interfaces in VR can already be designed and implemented to effectively advance human performance in medical decision support.

Currently we are investigating how displaying complex 3D medical images (e.g., DICOM) in VR can improve the diagnostic process. We are also looking into possibilities to include additional input modalities such as gaze information from eye-tracking to further improve the multimodal interaction.

As an extension to the dialogue it is planned to include ambiguity resolution by asking clarification questions. If a patient name is ambiguous, the system could ask for clarification (U: "Open the patient file of Mrs. Meier." S: "Gerda Mayer or Anna Maier?"). In addition users should be able to change or add patient data through natural speech.

Acknowledgments

This research is part of the project "clinical data intelligence" (KDI) which is founded by the Federal Ministry for Economic Affairs and Energy (BMWi).

References

Martín Abadi, Paul Barham, Jianmin Chen, Zhifeng Chen, Andy Davis, Jeffrey Dean, Matthieu Devin, Sanjay Ghemawat, Geoffrey Irving, Michael Isard, Manjunath Kudlur, Josh Levenberg, Rajat Monga, Sherry Moore, Derek G. Murray, Benoit Steiner, Paul Tucker, Vijay Vasudevan, Pete Warden, Martin Wicke, Yuan Yu, and Xiaoqiang Zheng. 2016. Tensorflow: A system for large-scale machine learning. In *12th USENIX Symposium on Operating Systems Design and Implementation (OSDI 16)*. USENIX Association, GA, pages 265–283.

C. Esteban, O. Staeck, S. Baier, Y. Yang, and V. Tresp. 2016. Predicting clinical events by combining static and dynamic information using recurrent neural networks. In *2016 IEEE International Conference on Healthcare Informatics (ICHI)*. pages 93–101.

Andreas Luxenburger, Alexander Prange, Mohammad Mehdi Moniri, and Daniel Sonntag. 2016. Medicalvr: Towards medical remote collaboration using virtual reality. In *Proceedings of the 2016 ACM International Joint Conference on Pervasive and Ubiquitous Computing: Adjunct*. ACM, New York, NY, USA, UbiComp '16, pages 321–324.

S. Morein-Zamir, S. Soto-Faraco, and A. Kingstone. 2003. Auditory capture of vision: examining temporal ventriloquism. *Brain Res Cogn Brain Res* 17(1):154–163.

Robert Neßelrath. 2015. *SiAM-dp : An open development platform for massively multimodal dialogue systems in cyber-physical environments*. Ph.D. thesis, Universität des Saarlandes, Postfach 151141, 66041 Saarbrücken.

S. Oviatt. 2013. *The Design of Future Educational Interfaces*. Taylor & Francis.

Daniel Sonntag. 2010. *Ontologies and Adaptivity in Dialogue for Question Answering*, volume 4 of *Studies on the Semantic Web*. IOS Press.

Daniel Sonntag, Gerhard Sonnenberg, Robert Nesselrath, and Gerd Herzog. 2009a. Supporting a rapid dialogue engineering process. In *Proceedings of the First International Workshop On Spoken Dialogue Systems Technology. International Workshop On Spoken Dialogue Systems Technology (IWSDS-2009), December 9-11, Kloster Irsee, Germany*. o.A.

Daniel Sonntag, Volker Tresp, Sonja Zillner, Alexander Cavallaro, Matthias Hammon, André Reis, Peter A. Fasching, Martin Sedlmayr, Thomas Ganslandt, Hans-Ulrich Prokosch, Klemens Budde, Danilo Schmidt, Carl Hinrichs, Thomas Wittenberg, Philipp Daumke, and Patricia G. Oppelt. 2016. The clinical data intelligence project. *Informatik-Spektrum* 39(4):290–300.

Daniel Sonntag, Markus Weber, Alexander Cavallaro, and Matthias Hammon. 2014. Integrating digital pens in breast imaging for instant knowledge acquisition. *AI Magazine* 35(1):26–37.

Daniel Sonntag, Pinar Wennerberg, Paul Buitelaar, and Sonja Zillner. 2009b. Pillars of ontology treatment in the medical domain. *J. Cases on Inf. Techn.* 11(4):47–73.

Generative Encoder-Decoder Models for Task-Oriented Spoken Dialog Systems with Chatting Capability

Tiancheng Zhao, Allen Lu, Kyusong Lee and Maxine Eskenazi
Language Technologies Institute
Carnegie Mellon University
Pittsburgh, Pennsylvania, USA
{tianchez,arlu,kyusongl,max+}@cs.cmu.edu

Abstract

Generative encoder-decoder models offer great promise in developing domain-general dialog systems. However, they have mainly been applied to open-domain conversations. This paper presents a practical and novel framework for building task-oriented dialog systems based on encoder-decoder models. This framework enables encoder-decoder models to accomplish slot-value independent decision-making and interact with external databases. Moreover, this paper shows the flexibility of the proposed method by interleaving chatting capability with a slot-filling system for better out-of-domain recovery. The models were trained on both real-user data from a bus information system and human-human chat data. Results show that the proposed framework achieves good performance in both offline evaluation metrics and in task success rate with human users.

1   Introduction

Task-oriented spoken dialog systems have transformed human-computer interaction by enabling people interact with computers via spoken language (Raux et al., 2005; Young, 2006; Bohus and Rudnicky, 2003). The task-oriented SDS is usually domain-specific. The system creators first map the user utterances into semantic frames that contain domain-specific slots and intents using spoken language understanding (SLU) (De Mori et al., 2008). Then a set of domain-specific dialog state variables is tracked to retain the context information over turns (Williams et al., 2013). Lastly, the dialog policy decides the next move from a list of dialog acts that covers the expected communicative functions from the system.

Although the above approach has been successfully applied to many practical systems, it has limited ability to generalize to out-of-domain (OOD) requests and to scale up to new domains. For example, even within in a simple domain, real users often make requests that are not included in the semantic specifications. Due to this, proper error handling strategies that guide users back to the in-domain conversation are crucial to dialog success (Bohus and Rudnicky, 2005). Past error handling strategies were limited to a set of predefined dialog acts, e.g. request repeat, clarification etc., which constrained the system's capability in keeping users engaged. Moreover, there has been an increased interest in extending task-oriented systems to multiple topics (Lee et al., 2009; Gašić et al., 2015b) and multiple skills, e.g. grouping heterogeneous types of dialogs into a single system (Zhao et al., 2016). Both cases require the system to be flexible enough to extend to new slots and actions.

Our goal is to move towards a domain-general task-oriented SDS framework that is flexible enough to expand to new domains and skills by removing domain-specific assumptions on the dialog state and dialog acts (Bordes and Weston, 2016). To achieve this goal, the neural encoder-decoder model(Cho et al., 2014; Sutskever et al., 2014) is a suitable choice, since it has achieved promising results in modeling open-domain conversations (Vinyals and Le, 2015; Sordoni et al., 2015). It encodes the dialog history using deep neural networks and then generates the next system utterance word-by-word via recurrent neural networks (RNNs). Therefore, unlike the traditional SDS pipeline, the encoder-decoder model is theoretically only limited by its input/output vocabulary.

Proceedings of the SIGDIAL 2017 Conference, pages 27–36,
Saarbrücken, Germany, 15-17 August 2017. ©2017 Association for Computational Linguistics

A naïve implementation of an encoder-decoder-based task-oriented system would use RNNs to encode the raw dialog history and generate the next system utterance using a separate RNN decoder. However, while this implementation might achieve good performance in an offline evaluation of a closed dataset, it would certainly fail when used by humans. There are several reasons for this: 1) real users can mention new entities that do not appear in the training data, such as a new restaurant name. These entities are, however, essential in delivering the information that matches users' needs in a task-oriented system. 2) a task-oriented SDS obtains information from a knowledge base (KB) that is constantly updated ("today's" weather will be different every day), so simply memorizing KB results that occurred in the training data would produce false information. Instead, an effective model should learn to query the KB constantly to get the most up-to-date information. 3) users may give OOD requests (e.g. say, "how is your day", to a slot-filling system), which must be handled gracefully in order to keep the conversation moving in the intended direction.

This paper proposes an effective encoder-decoder framework for building task-oriented SDSs. We propose *entity indexing* to tackle the challenges of out-of-vocabulary (OOV) entities and to query the KB. Moreover, we show the extensibility of the proposed model by adding chatting capability to a task-oriented encoder-decoder SDS for better OOD recovery. This approach was assessed on the Let's Go Bus Information data from the 1st Dialog State Tracking Challenge (Williams et al., 2013), and we report performance on both offline metrics and real human users. Results show that this model attains good performance for both of these metrics.

2 Related Work

Past research in developing domain-general dialog systems can be broadly divided into three branches. The first one focuses on learning domain-independent dialog state representation while still using hand-crafted dialog act system actions. Researchers proposed the idea of extracting slot-value independent statistics as the dialog state (Wang et al., 2015; Gašić et al., 2015a), so that the dialog state representation can be shared across systems serving different knowledge sources. Another approach uses RNNs to auto-

matically learn a distributed vector representation of the dialog state by accumulating the observations at each turn (Williams and Zweig, 2016; Zhao and Eskenazi, 2016; Dhingra et al., 2016; Williams et al., 2017). The learned dialog state is then used by the dialog policy to select the next action. The second branch of research develops a domain-general action space for dialog policy. Prior work replaced the domain-specific dialog acts with domain-independent natural language semantic schema as the action space of dialog managers (Eshghi and Lemon, 2014), e.g. Dynamic Syntax (Kempson et al., 2000). More recently, Wen, et al. (2016) have shown the feasibility of using an RNN as the decoder to generate the system utterances word by word, and the dialog policy of the proposed model can be fine tuned using reinforcement learning (Su et al., 2016). Furthermore, to deal with the challenge of developing end-to-end task-oriented dialog models that are able to interface with external KB, prior work has unified the special KB query actions via deep reinforcement learning (Zhao and Eskenazi, 2016) and soft attention over the database (Dhingra et al., 2016). The third branch strives to solve both problems at the same time by building an end-to-end model that maps an observable dialog history directly to the word sequences of the system's response. By using an encoder-decoder model, it has been successfully applied to open-domain conversational models (Serban et al., 2015; Li et al., 2015, 2016; Zhao et al., 2017), as well as to task oriented systems (Bordes and Weston, 2016; Yang et al., 2016; Eric and Manning, 2017). In order to better predict the next correct system action, this branch has focused on investigating various neural network architectures to improve the machine's ability to reason over user input and model long-term dialog context.

This paper is closely related to the third branch, but differs in the following ways: 1) these models are slot-value independent by leveraging domain-general entity recognizer, which is more extensible to OOV entities, 2) these models emphasize the interactive nature of dialog and address out-of-domain handling by interleaving chatting in task-oriented conversations, 3) instead of testing on a synthetic dataset, this approach focuses on real world use by testing the system on human users via spoken interface.

3 Proposed Method

Our proposed framework consists of three steps as shown in Figure 2: a) entity indexing (EI), b) slot-value independent encoder-decoder (SiED), c) system utterance lexicalization (UL). The intuition is to leverage domain-general named entity recognition (NER) (Tjong Kim Sang and De Meulder, 2003) techniques to extract salient entities in the raw dialog history and convert the lexical values of the entities into entity indexes. The encoder-decoder model is then trained to focus solely on reasoning over the entity indexes in a dialog history and to make decisions about the next utterance to produce (including KB query). In this way, the model can be unaffected by the inclusion of new entities and new KB, while maintaining its domain-general input/output interface for easy extension to new types of conversation skills. Lastly, the output from the decoder networks are lexicalized by replacing the entity indexes and special KB tokens with natural language. The following sections explain each step in detail.

3.1 Entity Indexing and Utterance Lexicalization

Entity Indexing EI has two parts. First, the EI utilizes an existing domain-general NER to extract entities from both the user and system utterances. Note that the entity here is assumed to be a super-set of the slots in the domain. For example, for a flight-booking system, the system may contain two slots: [from-LOCATION] and [to-LOCATION] for the departure and arrival city, respectively. However, EI only extracts every mention of [LOCATION] in the utterances and leaves the task of distinguishing between departure and arrival to the encoder-decoder model. Furthermore, this step replaces each KB search result with its search query (e.g. the weather is cloudy → [kb-search]-[DATETIME-0]). The second step of EI involves constructing a *indexed entity table*. Each entity is indexed by its order of occurrence in the conversation. Figure 1 shows an example in which there are two [LOCATION] mentions.

Properties of Entity Indexing In this section, several properties of EI and their assumptions are addressed. First, each entity is indexed uniquely by its entity type and index. Note that the index is not associated with the entity value, but rather solely by the order of appearance in the dialog. Despite the actual words being hidden,

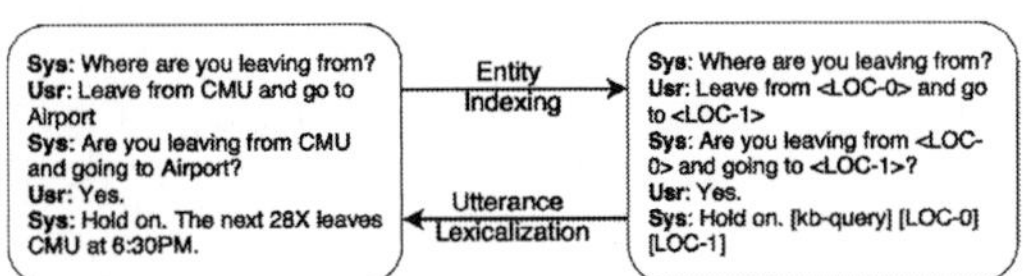

Figure 1: An example of entity indexing and utterance lexicalization.

a human can still easily predict which entity the system should confirm or search for in the KB based on logical reasoning. Therefore, that the EI not only alleviates the OOV problem of deploying the encoder-decoder model in the real world, but also forces the encoder-decoder model's focus on learning the reasoning process of task-oriented dialogs instead of leveraging too much information from the language modeling.

Moreover, most slot-filling SDSs, apart from informing the concepts from KBs, usually do not introduce novel entities to users. Instead, systems mostly corroborate the entities introduced by the users. With this assumption, every entity mention in the system utterances can always be found in the users' utterances in the dialog history, and therefore can also be found in the indexed entity table. This property reduces the grounding behavior of the conventional task-oriented dialog manager into selecting an entity from the indexed entity table and confirming it with the user.

Utterance Lexicalization is the reverse of EI. Since EI is a deterministic process, its effect can always be reversed by finding the corresponding entity in the indexed entity table and replacing the index with its word. For KB search, a simple string matching algorithm can search for the special [kb-search] token and take the following generated entities as the argument to the KB. Then the actual KB results can replace the original KB query. Figure 1 shows an example of utterance lexicalization.

3.2 Encoder-Decoder Models

The encoder-decoder model can then read in the EI-processed dialog history and predict the system's next utterance in EI format. Specifically, a dialog history of k turns is represented by $[(a_0, u_0, c_0), ...(a_{k-1}, u_{k-1}, c_{k-1})]$, in which a_i, u_i and c_i are, respectively, the system, user utterance and ASR confidence score at turn i. Each utterance in the dialog history is encoded into fixed-size vectors using Convolutional Neural Networks

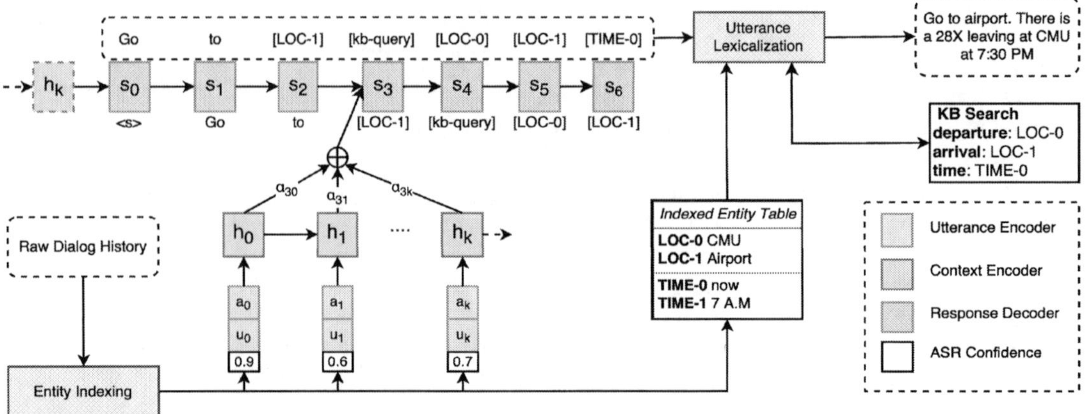

Figure 2: The proposed pipeline for task-oriented dialog systems.

(CNNs) proposed in (Kim, 2014). Specifically, each word in an utterance x is mapped to its word embedding, so that an utterance is represented as a matrix $R \in R^{|x| \times D}$, in which D is the size of the word embedding. Then L filters of size 1,2,3 conduct convolutions on R to obtain a feature map, c, of n-gram features in window size 1,2,3. Then c is passed through a nonlinear ReLu (Glorot et al., 2011) layer, followed by a max-pooling layer to obtain a compact summary of salient n-gram features, i.e. $e^t(x) = \text{maxpool}(\text{ReLu}(c + b))$. Using CNNs to capture word-order information is crucial, because the encoder-decoder has to be able to distinguish between fine-grained differences between entities. For example, a simple bag-of-word embedding approach will fail to distinguish between the two location entities in "leave from [LOCATION-0] and go to [LOCATION-1]", while a CNN encoder can capture the context information of these two entities.

After obtaining utterance embedding, a turn-level dialog history encoder network similar to the one proposed in (Zhao and Eskenazi, 2016) is used. Turn embedding is a simple concatenation of system, user utterance embedding and the confidence score $t = [e^u(a_i); e^u(u_i); c_i]$. Then an Long Short-Term Memory (LSTM) (Hochreiter and Schmidhuber, 1997) network reads the sequence turn embeddings in the dialog history via recursive state update $s_{i+1} = \text{LSTM}(t_{i+1}, h_i)$, in which h_i is the output of the LSTM hidden state.

Decoding with/without Attention A vanilla decoder takes in the last hidden state of the encoder as its initial state and decodes the next system utterance word by word as shown

in (Sutskever et al., 2014). This assumes that the fixed-size hidden state is expressive enough to encode all important information about the history of a dialog. However, this assumption may often be violated for a task that has long-dependency or complex reasoning of the entire source sequence. An attention mechanism proposed (Bahdanau et al., 2014) in the machine translation community has helped encoder-decoder models improve state-of-art performance in various tasks (Bahdanau et al., 2014; Xu et al., 2015). Attention allows the decoder to look over every hidden state in the encoder and dynamically decide the importance of each hidden state at each decoding step, which significantly improves the model's ability to handle long-term dependency. We experiment decoders both with and without attention. Attention is computed similarly multiplicative attention described in (Luong et al., 2015). We denote the hidden state of the decoder at time step j by s_j, and the hidden state outputs of the encoder at turn i by h_i. We then predict the next word by

$$a_{ji} = \text{softmax}(h_i^T W_a s_j + b_a) \quad (1)$$

$$c_j = \sum_i a_{ji} h_i \quad (2)$$

$$\widetilde{s_j} = tanh(W_s \begin{bmatrix} s_j \\ c_j \end{bmatrix}) \quad (3)$$

$$p(w_j | s_j, c_j) = \text{softmax}(W_o \widetilde{s_j}) \quad (4)$$

The decoder next state is updated by $s_{j+1} = \text{LSTM}(s_j, e(w_{j+1}), \widetilde{s_j})$.

3.3 Leveraging Chat Data to Improve OOD Recovery

Past work has shown that simple supervised learning is usually inadequate for learning robust sequential decision-making policy (Williams and Young, 2003; Ross et al., 2011). This is because the model is only exposed to the expert demonstration, but not to examples of how to recover from its own mistakes or users' OOD requests. We present a simple yet effective technique that leverages the extensibility of the encoder-decoder model in order to obtain a more robust policy in the setting of supervised learning. Specifically, we artificially augment a task-oriented dialog dataset with chat data from an open-domain conversation corpus. This has been shown to be effective in improving the performance of task-oriented systems (Yu et al., 2017). Let the original dialog dataset with N dialogs be $\mathcal{D} = [d_0..., d_n, ...d_N]$, where d_n is a multi-turn task-oriented dialog of $|d_n|$ turns. Furthermore, we assume we have access to a chat dataset $\mathcal{D}_c = [(q_0, r_0), ...(q_m, r_m), ...(q_M, r_M)]$, where q_m, r_m are common adjacency pairs that appear in chats, (e.g. q = hello, r = hi, how are you). Then we can create a new dataset $\mathcal{D}^*$ by repeating the following process a certain number of times:

1. Randomly sample dialog d_n from $\mathcal{D}$

2. Randomly sample turn $t_i = [a_i, u_i]$ from d_n

3. Randomly sample an adjacency pair (q_m, r_m) from $\mathcal{D}_c$

4. Replace the user utterance of t_i by q_m so that $t_i = [a_i, q_m]$

5. Insert a new turn after t_i, i.e. $t_{i+1} = [r_m + e_{i+1}, u_i]$

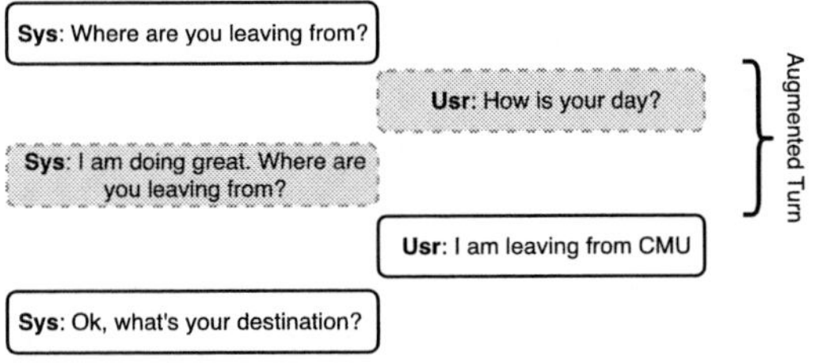

Figure 3: Illustration of data augmentation. The turn in the dashed line is inserted in the original dialog.

In Step 5, e_i is an error handling system utterance after the system answers the user's OOD request, q_m. In this study, we experimented with a simple case where $e_{i+1} = a_i$ so that the system should repeat its previous prompt after responding to q_m via r_m. Figure 3 shows an example of an augmented turn. Eventually, we train the model on the union of the two datasets $\mathcal{D}^+ = \mathcal{D} \cup \mathcal{D}^*$

Discussion: There are several reasons that the above data augmentation process is appealing. First, the model effectively learns an OOD recovery strategy from $\mathcal{D}^*$, i.e. it first gives chatting answers to users' OOD requests and then tries to pull users back to the main-task conversation. Second, chat data usually has a larger vocabulary and more diverse natural language expressions, which can reduce the chance of OOVs and enable the model to learn more robust word embeddings and language models.

4 Experiment Setup

4.1 Dataset and Domain

The CMU Let's Go Bus Information System (Raux et al., 2005) is a task-oriented spoken dialog system that contains bus information. We combined the train1a and train1b datasets from DSTC 1 (Williams et al., 2013), which contain 2608 total dialogs. The average dialog length is 9.07 turns. The dialogs were randomly splitted into 85/5/10 proportions for train/dev/test data. The data was noisy since the dialogs were collected from real users via telephone lines. Furthermore, this version of Let's Go used an in-house database containing the Port Authority bus schedule. In the current version, that database was replaced with the Google Directions API, which both reduces the human burden of maintaining a database and opens the possibility of extending Let's Go to cities other than Pittsburgh. Connecting to Google Directions API involves a POST call to their URL, with our given access key as well as the parameters needed: departure place, arrival place and departure time, and the travel mode, which we always set as TRANSIT to obtain relevant bus routes. There are 14 distinct dialog acts available to the system, and each system utterance contains one or more dialog acts. Lastly, the system vocabulary size is 1311 and the user vocabulary size is 1232. After the EI process, the sizes become 214 and 936, respectively.

For chat data, we use a publicly available chat

corpus used in (Yu et al., 2015)[1]. In total, there are 3793 chatting adjacency pairs. We control the number of data injections to 30% of the number of turns in the original DTSC dataset, which leads to a user vocabulary size of 3537 and system vocabulary size of 4047.

4.2 Training Details

For all experiments, the word embedding size was 100. The sizes of the LSTM hidden states for both the encoder and decoder were 500 with 1 layer. The attention context size was also 500. We tied the CNN weights for the encoding system and user utterances. Each CNN has 3 filter windows, 1, 2, and 3, with 100 feature maps each. We trained the model end-to-end using Adam (Kingma and Ba, 2014), with a learning rate of 1e-3 and a batch size of 40. To combat overfitting, we apply dropout (Zaremba et al., 2014) to the LSTM layer outputs and the CNN outputs after the maxpooling layer, with a dropout rate of 40%.

5 Experiments Results

This approach was assessed both offline and online evaluations. The offline evaluation contains standard metrics to test open-domain encoder-decoder dialog models (Li et al., 2015; Serban et al., 2015). System performance was assessed from three perspectives that are essential for task-oriented systems: dialog acts, slot-values, and KB query. The online evaluation is composed of objective task success rate, the number of turns, and subjective satisfaction with human users.

5.1 Offline Evaluation

Dialog Acts (DA): Each system utterance is made up of one or more dialog acts, e.g. "leaving at [TIME-0], where do you want to go?" → [implicit-confirm, request(arrival place)]. To evaluate whether a generated utterance has the same dialog acts as the ground truth, we trained a multi-label dialog tagger using one-vs-rest Support Vector Machines (SVM) (Tsoumakas and Katakis, 2006), with bag-of-bigram features for each dialog act label. Since the natural language generation module in Let's Go is handcrafted, the dialog act tagger achieved 99.4% average label accuracy on a held-out dataset. We used this dialog act tagger to tag both the ground truth and the generated

---

[1] github.com/echoyuzhou/ticktock_text_api

responses. Then we computed the micro-average precision, recall, and the F-score.

Slots: This metric measures the model's performance in generating the correct slot-values. The slot-values mostly occur in grounding utterances (e.g. explicit/implicit confirm) and KB queries. We compute precision, recall, and F-score.

KB Queries: Although the slots metric already covers the KB queries, here the precision/recall/F-score of system utterances that contain KB queries are also explicitly measured, due to their importance. Specifically, this action measures whether the system is able to generate the special [kb-query] symbol to initiate a KB query, as well as how accurate the corresponding KB query arguments are.

BLEU (Papineni et al., 2002): compares the n-gram precision with length penalty, and has been a popular score used to evaluate the performance of natural language generation (Wen et al., 2015) and open-domain dialog models (Li et al., 2016). Corpus-level BLEU-4 is reported.

Metrics	Vanilla	EI	EI +Attn	EI+Attn +Chat
DA	83.5	79.7	80.0	81.8
(p/r/f1)	77.9	80.1	83.1	83.5
	80.5	80.0	81.5	82.7
Slot	42.0	60.6	63.7	64.6
(p/r/f1)	30.3	63.6	64.7	69.1
	35.2	62.1	64.2	66.8
KB	N/A	48.9	55.4	58.2
(p/r/f1)		55.3	70.8	71.9
		51.9	62.2	64.4
BLEU	36.9	54.6	59.3	60.5

Table 1: Performance of each model on automatic measures.

Four systems were compared: the basic encoder-decoder models without EI (vanilla), the basic model with EI pre-processing (EI), the model with attentional decoder (EI+Attn) and the model trained on the dataset augmented with chatting data (EI+Attn+Chat). The comparison was carried out on exactly the same held-out test dataset that contains 261 dialogs. Table 1 shows the results. It can be seen that all four models achieve similar performance on the dialog act metrics, even the vanilla model. This confirms the capacity of encoder-decoders models to learn the "shape" of a conversation, since they have achieved impressive results in more challenging settings, e.g. modeling open-domain conversations. Furthermore, since the DSTC1 data was collected over several months, there were minor updates made to the dialog manager. Therefore, there are inherent ambiguities in the data (the dialog manager may take different actions in the same situation). We conjecture that $\sim$80% is near the upper limit of our data in modeling the system's next dialog act given the dialog history.

On the other hand, these proposed methods significantly improved the metrics related to slots and KB queries. The inclusion of EI alone was able to improve the F-score of slots by a relative 76%, which confirms that EI is crucial in developing slot-value independent encoder-decoder models for modeling task-oriented dialogs. Likewise, the inclusion of attention further improved the prediction of slots in system utterances. Adding attention also improved the performance of predicting KB queries, more so than the overall slot accuracy. This is expected, since KB queries are usually issued near the end of a conversation, which requires global reasoning over the entire dialog history. The use of attention allows the decoder to look over the history and make better decisions rather than simply depending on the context summary in the last hidden layer of the encoder. Because of the good performance achieved by the models with the attentional decoder, the attention weights in Equation 1 at every step of the decoding process in two example dialogs from test data are visualized. For both figures, the vertical axes show the dialog history flowing from the top to the bottom. Each row is a turn in the format of (system utterance # user utterance). The top horizontal axis shows the predicted next system utterance. The darkness of a bar indicates the value of the attention calculated in Equation 1.

The first example shows attention for grounding the new entity [LOCATION-1] in the previous turn. The attention weights become focus on the previous turn when predicting [LOCATION-1] in the implicit confirm action. The second dialog example shows a more challenging situation, in which the model is predicting a KB query. We can see that the attention weights when generating each input argument of the KB query clearly focus on the specific mention in the dialog history. The visualization confirms the effectiveness of the attention mechanism in dealing with long-term de-

pendency at discourse level.

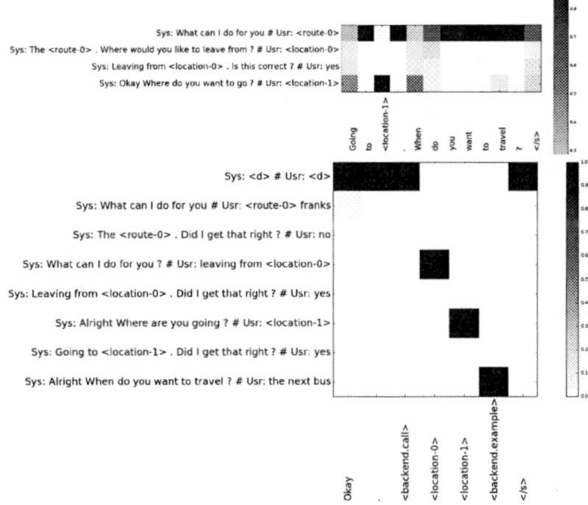

Figure 4: Visualization of attention weights when generating implicit confirm (top) and KB query (bottom).

Surprisingly, the model trained on the data augmented with chat achieved slightly better slot accuracy performance, even though the augmented data is not directly related to task-oriented dialogs. Furthermore, the model trained on chat-augmented data achieved better scores for the KB query metrics. Several reasons may explain this improvement: 1) since chat data exposes the model to a significantly larger vocabulary, the resulting model is more robust to words that it had not seen in the original task-oriented-only training data, and 2) the augmented dialog turn can be seen as noise in the dialog history, which adds extra regularization to the model and enables the model to learn more robust long-term reasoning mechanisms.

5.2 Human Evaluation

Although the model achieves good performance in offline evaluation, this may not carray over to real user dialogs, where the system must simultaneously deal with several challenges, such as automatic speech recognition (ASR) errors, OOD requests, etc. Therefore, a real user study was conducted to evaluate the performance of the proposed systems in the real world. Due to the limited number of real users, only two best performing system were compared, EI+Attn and EI+Attn+Chat. Users were able to talk to a web interface to the dialog systems via speech. Google

Chrome Speech API [2] served as the ASR and text-to-speech (TTS) modules. Turn-taking was done via the built-in Chrome voice activity detection (VAD) plus a finite state machine-based end-of-turn detector (Zhao et al., 2015). Lastly, a hybrid named entity recognizer (NER) was trained using Conditional Random Field (CRF) (McCallum and Li, 2003) and rules to extract 4 types of entities (location, hour, minute, pm/am) for the EI process.

The experiment setup is as follows: when a user logs into the website, the system prompts the user with a goal, which is a randomly chosen combination of departure place, arrival place and time (*e.g. leave from CMU and go to the airport at 10:30 AM*). The system also instructs the user to say goodbye if the he/she thinks the goal is achieved or wants to give up. The user begins a conversation with one of the two evaluated systems, with a 50/50 chance of choosing either system (not visible to the user). After the user's session is finished, the system asks the him/her to give two scores between 1 and 5 for correctness and naturalness of the system respectively. The subjects in this study consist of undergraduate and graduate students. However, many subjects did not follow the prompted goal, but rather asked about bus routes of their own. Therefore, the dialog was manually labeled for dialog success. A dialog is successful if and only if the systems give at least one bus schedule that matches with all three slots expressed by the users. Table 2 shows the

Metrics	EI+Attn	EI+Attn +Chat
# of Dialog	75	74
Slot Precision	73.3%	71.8%
KB Precision	88.6%	93.7%
Success Rate	73.3%	77.0%
Avg Turns	4.88	4.91
Avg Correctness	3.45 (1.32)	3.22 (1.40)
Avg Naturalness	3.46 (1.41)	3.53 (1.34)

Table 2: Performance of each model on automatic measures. The standard deviations of subjective scores are in parentheses.

results. Overall, our systems achieved reasonable performance in terms of dialog success rate. The EI+Attn+Chat model achieves slightly higher success and subjective naturalness metrics (although the difference between EI+Attn+Chat and EI+Attn

was not statistically significant due to the limited number of subjects). The precision of grounding the correct slots and predicting the correct KB query was also manually labelled. EI+Attn model performs slightly better than the EI+Attn+Chat model in slot precision, while the latter model performs significantly better in KB query precision. In addition, EI+Attn+Chat leads to slightly longer dialogs because sometimes it generates chatting utterances with users when it cannot understand users' utterances.

At last, we investigated the log files and identified the following major types of sources of dialog failure: **RNN Decoder Invalid Output:** Occasionally, the RNN decoder outputs system utterances as "Okay going to [LOCATION-2]. Did I get that right?", in which [LOCATION-2] cannot be found in the indexed entity table. Such invalid output confuses users. This occurred in 149 of the dialogs, where 4.1% of system utterances contain invalid symbols. **Imitation of Suboptimal Dialog Policy:** Since our models are only trained to imitate the suboptimal hand-crafted dialog policy, their limitations show when the original dialog manager cannot handle the situation, such as failing to understand slots that appeared in compound utterances. Future plans involves improving the models to perform better than the suboptimal teacher policy.

6   Conclusions

In conclusion, this paper discusses constructing task-oriented dialog systems using generative encoder decoder models. EI is effective in solving both the OOV entity and KB query challenges for encoder-decoder-based task-oriented SDSs. Additionally, the novel data augmentation technique of interleaving task-oriented dialog corpus with chat data led to better model performance in both online and offline evaluation. Future work includes developing more advanced encoder-decoder models that to better deal with long-term dialog history and complex reasoning challenges than current models do. Furthermore, inspired by the success of mixing chatting with slot-filling dialogs, we will take full advantage of the extensibility of encoder-decoder models by investigating how to make systems that are able to interleave various conversational tasks, e.g. different domains, chatting or task-oriented, which in turn can create a more versatile conversational agent.

---

[2]www.google.com/intl/en/chrome/demos/speech.html

References

Dzmitry Bahdanau, Kyunghyun Cho, and Yoshua Bengio. 2014. Neural machine translation by jointly learning to align and translate. *arXiv preprint arXiv:1409.0473* .

Dan Bohus and Alexander I Rudnicky. 2003. Ravenclaw: Dialog management using hierarchical task decomposition and an expectation agenda .

Dan Bohus and Alexander I Rudnicky. 2005. Error handling in the ravenclaw dialog management framework. In *Proceedings of the conference on Human Language Technology and Empirical Methods in Natural Language Processing*. Association for Computational Linguistics, pages 225–232.

Antoine Bordes and Jason Weston. 2016. Learning end-to-end goal-oriented dialog. *arXiv preprint arXiv:1605.07683* .

Kyunghyun Cho, Bart Van Merriënboer, Caglar Gulcehre, Dzmitry Bahdanau, Fethi Bougares, Holger Schwenk, and Yoshua Bengio. 2014. Learning phrase representations using rnn encoder-decoder for statistical machine translation. *arXiv preprint arXiv:1406.1078* .

Renato De Mori, Frédéric Bechet, Dilek Hakkani-Tur, Michael McTear, Giuseppe Riccardi, and Gokhan Tur. 2008. Spoken language understanding. *IEEE Signal Processing Magazine* 25(3).

Bhuwan Dhingra, Lihong Li, Xiujun Li, Jianfeng Gao, Yun-Nung Chen, Faisal Ahmed, and Li Deng. 2016. End-to-end reinforcement learning of dialogue agents for information access. *arXiv preprint arXiv:1609.00777* .

Mihail Eric and Christopher D Manning. 2017. A copy-augmented sequence-to-sequence architecture gives good performance on task-oriented dialogue. *arXiv preprint arXiv:1701.04024* .

Arash Eshghi and Oliver Lemon. 2014. How domain-general can we be? learning incremental dialogue systems without dialogue acts. *DialWattSemdial 2014* page 53.

M Gašić, N Mrkšić, Pei-hao Su, David Vandyke, Tsung-Hsien Wen, and Steve Young. 2015a. Policy committee for adaptation in multi-domain spoken dialogue systems. In *Automatic Speech Recognition and Understanding (ASRU), 2015 IEEE Workshop on*. IEEE, pages 806–812.

Milica Gašić, Dongho Kim, Pirros Tsiakoulis, and Steve Young. 2015b. Distributed dialogue policies for multi-domain statistical dialogue management. In *Acoustics, Speech and Signal Processing (ICASSP), 2015 IEEE International Conference on*. IEEE, pages 5371–5375.

Xavier Glorot, Antoine Bordes, and Yoshua Bengio. 2011. Deep sparse rectifier neural networks. In *Aistats*. volume 15, page 275.

Sepp Hochreiter and Jürgen Schmidhuber. 1997. Long short-term memory. *Neural computation* 9(8):1735–1780.

Ruth Kempson, Wilfried Meyer-Viol, and Dov M Gabbay. 2000. *Dynamic syntax: The flow of language understanding*. Wiley-Blackwell.

Yoon Kim. 2014. Convolutional neural networks for sentence classification. *arXiv preprint arXiv:1408.5882* .

Diederik Kingma and Jimmy Ba. 2014. Adam: A method for stochastic optimization. *arXiv preprint arXiv:1412.6980* .

Cheongjae Lee, Sangkeun Jung, Seokhwan Kim, and Gary Geunbae Lee. 2009. Example-based dialog modeling for practical multi-domain dialog system. *Speech Communication* 51(5):466–484.

Jiwei Li, Michel Galley, Chris Brockett, Jianfeng Gao, and Bill Dolan. 2015. A diversity-promoting objective function for neural conversation models. *arXiv preprint arXiv:1510.03055* .

Jiwei Li, Will Monroe, Alan Ritter, Michel Galley, Jianfeng Gao, and Dan Jurafsky. 2016. Deep reinforcement learning for dialogue generation. *arXiv preprint arXiv:1606.01541* .

Minh-Thang Luong, Hieu Pham, and Christopher D Manning. 2015. Effective approaches to attention-based neural machine translation. *arXiv preprint arXiv:1508.04025* .

Andrew McCallum and Wei Li. 2003. Early results for named entity recognition with conditional random fields, feature induction and web-enhanced lexicons. In *Proceedings of the seventh conference on Natural language learning at HLT-NAACL 2003-Volume 4*. Association for Computational Linguistics, pages 188–191.

Kishore Papineni, Salim Roukos, Todd Ward, and Wei-Jing Zhu. 2002. Bleu: a method for automatic evaluation of machine translation. In *Proceedings of the 40th annual meeting on association for computational linguistics*. Association for Computational Linguistics, pages 311–318.

Antoine Raux, Brian Langner, Dan Bohus, Alan W Black, and Maxine Eskenazi. 2005. Lets go public! taking a spoken dialog system to the real world. In *in Proc. of Interspeech 2005*. Citeseer.

Stéphane Ross, Geoffrey J Gordon, and Drew Bagnell. 2011. A reduction of imitation learning and structured prediction to no-regret online learning. In *AISTATS*. volume 1, page 6.

Iulian V Serban, Alessandro Sordoni, Yoshua Bengio, Aaron Courville, and Joelle Pineau. 2015. Building end-to-end dialogue systems using generative hierarchical neural network models. *arXiv preprint arXiv:1507.04808* .

Alessandro Sordoni, Michel Galley, Michael Auli, Chris Brockett, Yangfeng Ji, Margaret Mitchell, Jian-Yun Nie, Jianfeng Gao, and Bill Dolan. 2015. A neural network approach to context-sensitive generation of conversational responses. *arXiv preprint arXiv:1506.06714* .

Pei-Hao Su, Milica Gasic, Nikola Mrksic, Lina Rojas-Barahona, Stefan Ultes, David Vandyke, Tsung-Hsien Wen, and Steve Young. 2016. Continuously learning neural dialogue management. *arXiv preprint arXiv:1606.02689* .

Ilya Sutskever, Oriol Vinyals, and Quoc V Le. 2014. Sequence to sequence learning with neural networks. In *Advances in neural information processing systems*. pages 3104–3112.

Erik F Tjong Kim Sang and Fien De Meulder. 2003. Introduction to the conll-2003 shared task: Language-independent named entity recognition. In *Proceedings of the seventh conference on Natural language learning at HLT-NAACL 2003-Volume 4*. Association for Computational Linguistics, pages 142–147.

Grigorios Tsoumakas and Ioannis Katakis. 2006. Multi-label classification: An overview. *International Journal of Data Warehousing and Mining* 3(3).

Oriol Vinyals and Quoc Le. 2015. A neural conversational model. *arXiv preprint arXiv:1506.05869* .

Zhuoran Wang, Tsung-Hsien Wen, Pei-Hao Su, and Yannis Stylianou. 2015. Learning domain-independent dialogue policies via ontology parameterisation. In *16th Annual Meeting of the Special Interest Group on Discourse and Dialogue*. page 412.

Tsung-Hsien Wen, Milica Gasic, Nikola Mrksic, Pei-Hao Su, David Vandyke, and Steve Young. 2015. Semantically conditioned lstm-based natural language generation for spoken dialogue systems. *arXiv preprint arXiv:1508.01745* .

Tsung-Hsien Wen, David Vandyke, Nikola Mrksic, Milica Gasic, Lina M Rojas-Barahona, Pei-Hao Su, Stefan Ultes, and Steve Young. 2016. A network-based end-to-end trainable task-oriented dialogue system. *arXiv preprint arXiv:1604.04562* .

Jason Williams, Antoine Raux, Deepak Ramachandran, and Alan Black. 2013. The dialog state tracking challenge. In *Proceedings of the SIGDIAL 2013 Conference*. pages 404–413.

Jason Williams and Steve Young. 2003. Using wizard-of-oz simulations to bootstrap reinforcement-learning-based dialog management systems. In *Proceedings of the 4th SIGDIAL Workshop on Discourse and Dialogue*.

Jason D Williams, Kavosh Asadi, and Geoffrey Zweig. 2017. Hybrid code networks: practical and efficient end-to-end dialog control with supervised and reinforcement learning. *arXiv preprint arXiv:1702.03274* .

Jason D Williams and Geoffrey Zweig. 2016. End-to-end lstm-based dialog control optimized with supervised and reinforcement learning. *arXiv preprint arXiv:1606.01269* .

Kelvin Xu, Jimmy Ba, Ryan Kiros, Kyunghyun Cho, Aaron C Courville, Ruslan Salakhutdinov, Richard S Zemel, and Yoshua Bengio. 2015. Show, attend and tell: Neural image caption generation with visual attention. In *ICML*. volume 14, pages 77–81.

Zichao Yang, Phil Blunsom, Chris Dyer, and Wang Ling. 2016. Reference-aware language models. *arXiv preprint arXiv:1611.01628* .

Steve J Young. 2006. Using pomdps for dialog management. In *SLT*. pages 8–13.

Zhou Yu, Alan W Black, and Alexander I Rudnicky. 2017. Learning conversational systems that interleave task and non-task content. *arXiv preprint arXiv:1703.00099* .

Zhou Yu, Alexandros Papangelis, and Alexander Rudnicky. 2015. Ticktock: A non-goal-oriented multimodal dialog system with engagement awareness. In *Proceedings of the AAAI Spring Symposium*.

Wojciech Zaremba, Ilya Sutskever, and Oriol Vinyals. 2014. Recurrent neural network regularization. *arXiv preprint arXiv:1409.2329* .

Tiancheng Zhao, Alan W Black, and Maxine Eskenazi. 2015. An incremental turn-taking model with active system barge-in for spoken dialog systems. In *16th Annual Meeting of the Special Interest Group on Discourse and Dialogue*. page 42.

Tiancheng Zhao and Maxine Eskenazi. 2016. Towards end-to-end learning for dialog state tracking and management using deep reinforcement learning. In *17th Annual Meeting of the Special Interest Group on Discourse and Dialogue*.

Tiancheng Zhao, Maxine Eskenazi, and Kyusong Lee. 2016. Dialport: A general framework for aggregating dialog systems. *EMNLP 2016* page 32.

Tiancheng Zhao, Ran Zhao, and Maxine Eskenazi. 2017. Learning discourse-level diversity for neural dialog models using conditional variational autoencoders. *arXiv preprint arXiv:1703.10960* .

Key-Value Retrieval Networks for Task-Oriented Dialogue

Mihail Eric[1], **Lakshmi Krishnan**[2],
Francois Charette[2], and **Christopher D. Manning**[1]
`meric@cs.stanford.edu`, `lkrishn7@ford.com`
`fcharett@ford.com`, `manning@stanford.edu`
Stanford NLP Group[1] Ford Research and Innovation Center[2]

Abstract

Neural task-oriented dialogue systems often struggle to smoothly interface with a knowledge base. In this work, we seek to address this problem by proposing a new neural dialogue agent that is able to effectively sustain grounded, multi-domain discourse through a novel key-value retrieval mechanism. The model is end-to-end differentiable and does not need to explicitly model dialogue state or belief trackers. We also release a new dataset of 3,031 dialogues that are grounded through underlying knowledge bases and span three distinct tasks in the in-car personal assistant space: calendar scheduling, weather information retrieval, and point-of-interest navigation. Our architecture is simultaneously trained on data from all domains and significantly outperforms a competitive rule-based system and other existing neural dialogue architectures on the provided domains according to both automatic and human evaluation metrics.

1   Introduction

With the success of new speech-based human-computer interfaces, there is a great need for effective task-oriented dialogue agents that can handle everyday tasks such as scheduling events and booking hotels. Current commercial dialogue agents are often brittle pattern-matching systems which are unable to maintain the kind of flexible conversations that people desire. Neural dialogue agents present one of the most promising avenues for leveraging dialogue corpora to build statistical models directly from data by using powerful distributed representations (Bordes and Weston, 2016; Wen et al., 2016b; Dhingra et al., 2016).

Event	Time	Date	Party	Agenda
opt. appt.	10am	Thursday	sister	-
dinner	8pm	the 13th	Ana	-
opt. appt.	7pm	the 20th	Jeff	-
opt. appt.	4pm	the 13th	Alex	-
...	...	...	...	...

DRIVER:	I need to find out the time and parties attending my optometrist appointment.
CAR:	I have 3 appointments scheduled, with Alex, your sister, and Jeff. Which are you referring to?
DRIVER:	I want to know about the one that Alex is joining me at
CAR:	That optometrist appointment is at 4 pm.
DRIVER:	Thanks
CAR:	no problem

Figure 1: Sample dialogue from our dataset. Note some columns and rows from the knowledge base are not included due to space constraints. A dash indicates a missing value.

While this work has been somewhat successful, these task-oriented neural dialogue models suffer from a number of problems: 1) They struggle to effectively reason over and incorporate knowledge base information while still preserving their end-to-end trainability and 2) They often require explicitly modelling user dialogues with belief trackers and dialogue state information, which necessitates additional data annotation and also breaks differentiability.

To address some of the modelling issues in previous neural dialogue agents, we introduce a new architecture called the Key-Value Retrieval Network. This model augments existing recurrent network architectures with an attention-based key-value retrieval mechanism over the entries of a knowledge base, which is inspired by recent work on key-value memory networks (Miller et al., 2016). By doing so, it is able to learn how to extract useful information from a knowledge base directly from data in an end-to-end fashion, with-

Proceedings of the SIGDIAL 2017 Conference, pages 37–49,
Saarbrücken, Germany, 15-17 August 2017. ©2017 Association for Computational Linguistics

out the need for explicit training of belief or intent trackers as is done in traditional task-oriented dialogue systems. The architecture has no dependence on the specifics of the data domain, learning how to appropriately incorporate world knowledge into its dialogue utterances via attention over the key-value entries of the underlying knowledge base.

In addition, we introduce and make publicly available a new corpus of 3,031 dialogues spanning three different domain types in the in-car personal assistant space: calendar scheduling, weather information retrieval, and point-of-interest navigation. The dialogues are grounded through knowledge bases. This makes them ideal for building dialogue architectures that seamlessly reason over world knowledge. The multi-domain nature of the dialogues in the corpus also makes this dataset an apt test bed for generalizability of modelling architectures.[1]

The main contributions of our work are therefore two-fold: 1) We introduce the Key-Value Retrieval Network, a highly performant neural task-oriented dialogue agent that is able to smoothly incorporate information from underlying knowledge bases through a novel key-value retrieval mechanism. Unlike other dialogue agents which only rely on prior dialogue history for generation (Kannan et al., 2016; Eric and Manning, 2017), our architecture is able to access and use database-style information, while still retaining the text generation advantages of recent neural models. By doing so, our model outperforms a competitive rule-based system and other baseline neural models on a number of automatic metrics as well as human evaluation. 2) We release a new publicly-available dialogue corpus across three distinct domains in the in-car personal assistant space that we hope will help further work on task-oriented dialogue agents.

2 Key-Value Retrieval Networks

While recent neural dialogue models have explicitly modelled dialogue state through belief and user intent trackers (Wen et al., 2016b; Dhingra et al., 2016; Henderson et al., 2014b), we choose instead to rely on learned neural representations for implicit modelling of dialogue state, forming a truly end-to-end trainable system. Our model starts with an encoder-decoder sequence architecture and is further augmented with an attention-based retrieval mechanism that effectively reasons over a key-value representation of the underlying knowledge base. We describe each component of our model in the subsequent sections.

2.1 Encoder

Given a dialogue between a user (u) and a system (s), we represent the dialogue utterances as $\{(u_1, s_1), (u_2, s_2), \dots, (u_k, s_k)\}$ where k denotes the number of turns in the dialogue. At the ith turn of the dialogue, we encode the aggregated dialogue context composed of the tokens of $(u_1, s_1, \dots, s_{i-1}, u_i)$. Letting $x_1, \dots, x_m$ denote these tokens, we first embed these tokens using a trained embedding function ϕ^{emb} that maps each token to a fixed-dimensional vector. These mappings are fed into the encoder to produce context-sensitive hidden representations $h_1, \dots, h_m$, by repeatedly applying the recurrence:

$$h_i = \text{LSTM}(\phi^{emb}(x_i), h_{i-1}) \qquad (1)$$

where the recurrence uses a long-short-term memory unit, as described by (Hochreiter and Schmidhuber, 1997).

2.2 Decoder

The vanilla sequence-to-sequence decoder predicts the tokens of the ith system response s_i by first computing decoder hidden states via the recurrent unit. We denote $\tilde{h}_1, \dots, \tilde{h}_n$ as the hidden states of the decoder and $y_1, \dots, y_n$ as the output tokens. We extend this decoder with an attention-based model (Bahdanau et al., 2015; Luong et al., 2015a), where, at every time step t of the decoding, an attention score a_i^t is computed for each hidden state h_i of the encoder, using the attention mechanism of (Vinyals et al., 2015). Formally this attention can be described by the following equations:

$$u_i^t = w^T \tanh(W_2 \tanh(W_1[h_i, \tilde{h}_t])) \qquad (2)$$
$$a_i^t = \text{Softmax}(u_i^t) \qquad (3)$$
$$\tilde{h}_t' = \sum_{i=1}^{m} a_i^t h_i \qquad (4)$$
$$o_t = U[\tilde{h}_t, \tilde{h}_t'] \qquad (5)$$
$$y_t = \text{Softmax}(o_t) \qquad (6)$$

---

[1] The data is available for download at https://nlp.stanford.edu/blog/a-new-multi-turn-multi-domain-task-oriented-dialogue-dataset/

where U, W_1, W_2, and w are trainable parameters of the model and o_t represents the logits over the tokens of the output vocabulary V. In (2) above, the attention logit on h_i is computed via a two-layer MLP function with a $\tanh$ nonlinearity at the intermediate layers. During training, the next token y_t is predicted so as to maximize the log-likelihood of the correct output sequence given the input sequence.

2.3 Key-Value Knowledge Base Retrieval

Recently, some neural task-oriented dialogue agents that query underlying knowledge bases (KBs) and extract relevant entities either do the following: 1) create and execute well-formatted API calls to the KB, operations which require intermediate supervision in the form of training slot trackers and which break differentiability (Wen et al., 2016b), or 2) softly attend to the KB and combine this probability distribution with belief trackers as state input for a reinforcement learning policy (Dhingra et al., 2016). We choose to build off the latter approach as it fits nicely into the end-to-end trainable framework of sequence-to-sequence modelling, though we are in a supervised learning setting and we do away with explicit representations of belief trackers or dialogue state.

For storing the KB of a given dialogue, we take inspiration from the work of (Miller et al., 2016) which found that a key-value structured memory allowed for efficient machine reading of documents. We store every entry of our KB using a *(subject, relation, object)* representation. In our representation a KB entry from the dialogue in Figure 1 such as (**event**=*dinner*, **time**=*8pm*, **date**=*the 13th*, **party**=*Ana*, **agenda**=*"-"*) would be normalized into four separate triples of the form (*dinner*, *time*, *8pm*). Every KB has at most 230 normalized triples. This formalism is similar to a neo-Davidsonian or RDF-style representation of events.

Recent literature has shown that incorporating a copying mechanism into neural architectures improves performance on various sequence-to-sequence tasks (Jia and Liang, 2016; Gu et al., 2016; Ling et al., 2016; Gulcehre et al., 2016; Eric and Manning, 2017). We build off this intuition in the following way: at every timestep of decoding, we take the decoder hidden state and compute an attention score with the key of each normalized KB entry. For our purposes, the key of an entry corresponds to the sum of the word embeddings of the subject (*meeting*) and relation (*time*). The attention logits then become the logits of the value for that KB entry. For our KB attentions, we replace the embedding of the value with a canonicalized token representation. For example, the value *5pm* is replaced with the canonicalized representation *meeting_time*. At runtime, if we decode this canonicalized representation token, we convert it into the actual value of the KB entry (*5pm* in our running example) through a KB lookup. Note that this means we are expanding our original output vocabulary to $|V| + n$ where n is the number of separate canonical key representation KB entries.

In particular, let k_j denote the word embedding of the key of our j^{th} normalized KB entry. We can now formalize the decoding for our KB attention-based retrieval. Assume that we have m distinct triples in our KB and that we are in the tth timestep of decoding:

$$u_j^t = r^T \tanh(W_2' \tanh(W_1'[k_j, \tilde{h}_t]))) \quad (7)$$
$$o_t = U[\tilde{h}_t, \tilde{h}_t'] + \bar{v}^t \quad (8)$$
$$y_t = \text{Softmax}(o_t) \quad (9)$$

where r, W_1', and W_2' are trainable parameters. In (8) above, $\bar{v}^t$ is a sparse vector with length $|V| + n$. Within $\bar{v}^t$, the entry for the value embedding v_j corresponding to the key k_j is equal to the logit score u_j^t on k_j. Hence, the m entries of $\bar{v}^t$ corresponding to the values in the KB are non-zero, whereas the remaining entries corresponding to the original vocabulary tokens are 0. This sparse vector contains our aggregated KB logit scores which we combine with the original logits to get a modified o_t. We then select the argmax token as input to the next timestep. This description seeks to capture the intuition that in response to the query *What time is my meeting*, we want the model to put a high attention weight on the key representation for the (*meeting*, *time*, *5pm*) KB triple, which should then lead the model to favor outputting the value token at the given timestep. We provide a visualization of the Key-Value Retrieval Network in Figure 2.

3 A Multi-Turn, Multi-Domain Dialogue Dataset

In an effort to further work in multi-domain dialogue agents, we built a corpus of multi-turn

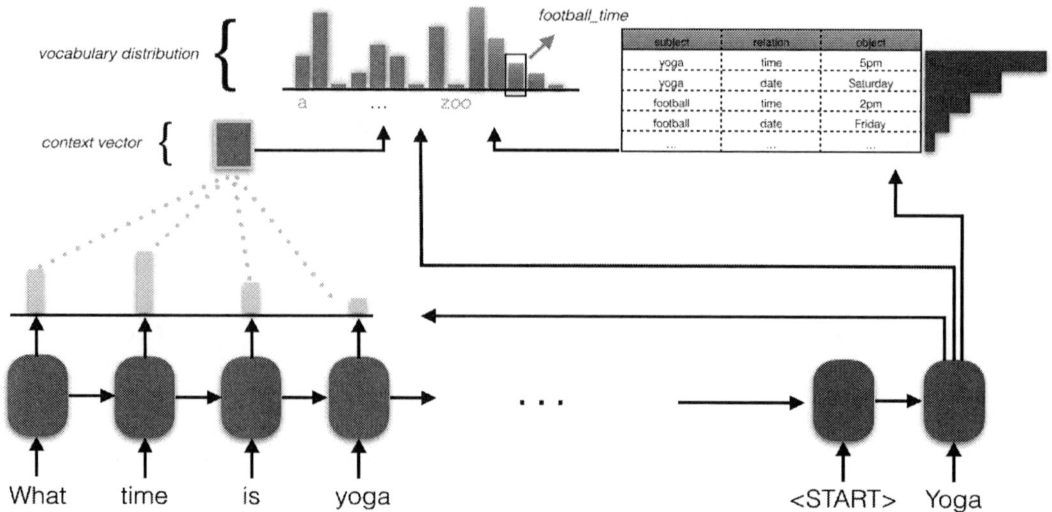

Figure 2: Key-value retrieval network. For each time-step of decoding, the cell state is used to compute an attention over the encoder states and a separate attention over the key of each entry in the KB. The attentions over the encoder are used to generate a context vector which is combined with the cell state to get a distribution over the normal vocabulary. The attentions over the keys of the KB become the logits for their associated values and are separate entries in a now augmented vocabulary that we argmax over.

dialogues in three distinct domains: calendar scheduling, weather information retrieval, and point-of-interest navigation. While these domains are different, they are all relevant to the overarching theme of tasks that users would expect of a sophisticated in-car personal assistant.

3.1 Data Collection

The data for the multi-turn dialogues was collected using a Wizard-of-Oz scheme inspired by that of (Wen et al., 2016b). In our scheme, users had two potential modes they could play: *Driver* and *Car Assistant*. In the *Driver* mode, users were presented with a task that listed certain information they were trying to extract from the *Car Assistant* as well as the dialogue history exchanged between *Driver* and *Car Assistant* up to that point. An example task presented could be: *You want to find what the temperature is like in San Mateo over the next two days*. The *Driver* was then only responsible for contributing a single line of dialogue that appropriately continued the discourse given the prior dialogue history and the task definition.

Tasks were randomly specified by selecting values (*5pm*, *Saturday*, *San Francisco*, etc.) for three to five slots (time, date, location, etc.), de-pending on the domain type. Values specified for the slots were chosen according to a uniform distribution from a per-domain candidate set.

In the *Car Assistant* mode, users were presented with the dialogue history exchanged up to that point in the running dialogue and a private knowledge base known only to the *Car Assistant* with information that could be useful for satisfying the *Driver* query. Examples of knowledge bases could include a calendar of event information, a collection of weekly forecasts for nearby cities, or a collection of nearby points-of-interest with relevant information. The *Car Assistant* was then responsible for using this private information to provide a single utterance that progressed the user-directed dialogues. The *Car Assistant* was also asked to fill in dialogue state information for mentioned slots and values in the dialogue history up to that point.

Each private knowledge base had six to seven distinct rows and five to seven attribute types. The private knowledge bases used were generated by uniformly selecting a value for a given attribute type, where each attribute type had a variable number of candidate values. Some knowledge bases intentionally lacked attributes to encourage diversity in discourse.

During data collection, some of the dialogues

	Calendar Scheduling	**Weather Information Retrieval**	**POI Navigation**
Slot Types	event, time, date, party, room, agenda	location, weekly time, temperature, weather attribute	POI name, traffic info, POI category, address, distance
# Distinct Slot Values	79	65	140

Table 1: Slots types and number distinct slot values for different domains. POI denotes point-of-interest.

Training Dialogues	2,425
Validation Dialogues	302
Test Dialogues	304
Calendar Scheduling Dialogues	1034
Navigation Dialogues	1000
Weather Dialogues	997
Avg. # of Utterances Per Dialogue	5.25
Avg. # of Tokens Per Utterance	9
Vocabulary Size	1,601
# of Distinct Entities	284
# of Entity (or Slot) Types	15

Table 2: Statistics of Dataset.

in the calendar scheduling domain did not explicitly require the use of a KB. For example, in a task such as *Set a meeting reminder at 3pm*, we hoped to encourage dialogues that required the *Car Assistant* to execute a task while asking for *Driver* clarification on underspecified information. Roughly half of the scheduling dialogues fell into this category.

While specifying the attribute types and values in each task presented to the *Driver* allowed us to ground the subject of each dialogue with our desired entities, it would occasionally result in more mechanical discourse exchanges. To encourage more naturalistic, unbiased utterances, we had users record themselves saying commands in response to underspecified visual depictions of an action a car assistant could perform. These commands were transcribed and then inserted as the first exchange in a given dialogue on behalf of the *Driver*. Roughly ∼1,500 of the dialogues employed this transcribed audio command first-utterance technique.

241 unique workers from Amazon Mechanical Turk were anonymously recruited to use the interface we built over a period of about six days. Data statistics are provided in Table 1 and slot types and values are provided in Table 2. A screenshot of the user-facing interfaces for the data collection, as well as a visual used to prompt user recorded commands, are provided in the supplementary material.

4 Related Work

Task-oriented agents for spoken dialogue systems have been the subject of extensive research effort. One line of work by (Young et al., 2013) has tackled the problem using partially observable Markov decision processes and reinforcement learning with carefully designed action spaces, though the number of distinct action states makes this approach often brittle and computationally intractable.

The recent successes of neural architectures on a number of traditional natural language processing subtasks (Bahdanau et al., 2015; Sutskever et al., 2014; Vinyals et al., 2015) have motivated investigation into dialogue agents that can effectively make use of distributed neural representations for dialogue state management, belief tracking, and response generation. Recent work by (Wen et al., 2016b) has built systems with modularly-connected representation, belief state, and generation components. These models learn to explicitly represent user intent through intermediate supervision, which breaks end-to-end trainability. Other work by (Bordes and Weston, 2016; Liu and Perez, 2016) stores dialogue context in a memory module and repeatedly queries and reasons about this context to select an adequate system response from a set of all candidate responses.

Another line of recent work has developed task-oriented models which are amenable to both supervised learning and reinforcement learning and are able to incorporate domain-specific knowledge via explicitly-provided features and model-output restrictions (Williams et al., 2017). Our model contrasts with these works in that training is done in a strictly supervised fashion via a per utterance token generative process, and the model does not need dialogue state trackers, relying instead on latent neural embeddings for accurate system response generation.

Research in task-oriented dialogue often struggles with a lack of standard, publicly available datasets. Several classical corpora have consisted of moderately-sized collections of dialogues related to travel-booking (Hemphill et al., 1990;

Bennett and Rudnicky, 2002). Another well-known corpus is derived from a series of competitions on the task of dialogue-state tracking (Williams et al., 2013). While the competitions were designed to test systems for state tracking, recent work has chosen to repurpose this data by only using the transcripts of dialogues without state annotation for developing systems (Bordes and Weston, 2016; Williams et al., 2017). More recently, Maluuba has released a dataset of hotel and travel-booking dialogues collected in a Wizard-of-Oz Scheme with elaborate semantic frames annotated (Asri et al., 2017). This dataset aims to encourage research in non-linear decision-making processes that are present in task-oriented dialogues.

5   Experiments

In this section we first introduce the details of the experiments and then present results from both automatic and human evaluation.

5.1   Details

For our experiments, we divided the dialogues into train/validation/test sets using a 0.8/0.1/0.1 data split and ensured that each domain type was equally represented in each of the splits.

To reduce lexical variability, in a pre-processing step, we map the variant surface expression of entities to a canonical form using named entity recognition and linking. For example, the surface form *20 Main Street* is mapped to *Pizza My Heart address*. During inference, our model outputs the canonical forms of the entities, and so we realize their surface forms by running the system output through an inverse lexicon. The inverse lexicon converts the entities back to their surface forms by sampling from a multinomial distribution with parameters of the distribution equal to the frequency count of a given surface form for an entity as observed in the training and validation data. Note that for the purposes of computing our evaluation metrics, we operate on the canonicalized forms, so that any non-deterministic variability in surface form realization does not affect the computed metrics.

5.2   Hyperparameters

We trained using a cross-entropy loss and the Adam optimizer (Kingma and Ba, 2015) with learning rates sampled from the interval $[10^{-4}, 10^{-3}]$. We applied dropout (Hinton et al., 2012) as a regularizer to the input and output of the LSTM. We also added an l_2 regularization penalty on the weights of the model. We identified hyperparameters by random search, evaluating on the held-out validation subset of the data. Dropout keep rates were sampled from $[0.8, 0.9]$ and the l_2 coefficient was sampled from $[3 \cdot 10^{-6}, 10^{-5}]$. We used word embeddings, hidden layer, and cell sizes with size 200. We applied gradient clipping with a clip-value of 10 to avoid gradient explosions during training. The attention, output parameters, word embeddings, and LSTM weights were randomly initialized from a uniform unit-scaled distribution in the style of (Sussillo and Abbott, 2015). We also added a bias of 1 to the LSTM cell forget gate in the style of (Pham et al., 2014).

5.3   Baseline Models

We provide several baseline models for comparing performance of the Key-Value Retrieval Network:

- **Rule-Based Model**: This model is a traditional rule-based system with modular dialogue state trackers, KB query, and natural language generation components. It first does an extensive domain-dependent keyword search in the user utterances to detect intent. The user utterances are also provided to a lexicon to extract any entities mentioned. Collectively, this information forms the dialogue state up to a given point in the dialogue. This dialogue state is used to query the KB as appropriate, and the returned KB values are used to fill in predefined template system responses.

- **Copy-Augmented Sequence-to-Sequence Network**: This model is derived from the work of (Eric and Manning, 2017). It augments a sequence-to-sequence architecture with encoder attention, with an additional attention-based hard-copy mechanism over the KB entities mentioned in the encoder context. This model does not explicitly incorporate information from the underlying KB and instead relies solely on dialogue history for system response generation. Unlike the best performing model of (Eric and Manning, 2017), we do not enhance the inputs to the encoder with additional entity type features, as we found that the

Model	BLEU	Ent. F_1	Scheduling Ent. F_1	Weather Ent. F_1	Navigation Ent. F_1
Rule-Based	6.6	43.8	61.3	39.5	40.4
Copy Net	11.0	37.0	28.1	**50.1**	28.4
Attn. Seq2Seq	10.2	30.0	30.0	42.4	17.9
KV Retrieval Net (no enc. attn.)	10.8	40.9	59.5	35.6	36.6
KV Retrieval Net	**13.2**	**48.0**	**62.9**	47.0	**41.3**
Human Performance	13.5	60.7	64.3	61.6	55.2

Table 3: Evaluation on our test data. Bold values indicate best model performance. We provide both an aggregated F_1 score as well as domain-specific F_1 scores. Attn. Seq2Seq refers to a sequence-to-sequence model with encoder attention. KV Retrieval Net (no enc. attn.) refers to our new model with no encoder attention context vector computed during decoding.

model performed worse on our data with this added mechanism. We choose this model for comparison as it is also end-to-end trainable and implicitly models dialogue state through learned neural representations, putting it in the same class of dialogue models as our key-value retrieval net. This model has also been shown to be a competitive task-oriented dialogue baseline that can accurately interpret user input and act on this input through latent distributed representation. We refer to this model as Copy Net in the results tables.

5.4 Automatic Evaluation

5.4.1 Metrics

Though prior work has shown that automatic evaluation metrics often correlate poorly with human assessments of dialogue agents (Liu et al., 2016), we report a number of automatic metrics in Table 3. These metrics are provided for coarse-grained evaluation of dialogue response quality:

- **BLEU**: We use the BLEU metric, commonly employed in evaluating machine translation systems (Papineni et al., 2002), which has also been used in past literature for evaluating dialogue systems both of the chatbot and task-oriented variety (Ritter et al., 2011; Li et al., 2016; Wen et al., 2016b). While work by (Liu et al., 2016) has demonstrated that n-gram based evaluation metrics such as BLEU and METEOR do not correlate well with human performance on non-task-oriented dialogue datasets, recently (Sharma et al., 2017) have shown that these metrics can show comparatively stronger correlation with human assessment on task-oriented datasets. We, therefore, calculate average BLEU score over all responses generated by the system, and primarily report these scores to gauge our

model's ability to accurately generate the language patterns seen in our data.

- **Entity F_1**: Each human Turker's *Car Assistant* response in the test data defines a gold set of entities. To compute an entity F_1, we micro-average over the entire set of system dialogue responses and use the entities in their canonicalized forms. This metric evaluates the model's ability to generate relevant entities from the underlying knowledge base and to capture the semantics of the user-initiated dialogue flow. Given that our test set contains dialogues from all three domains, we compute a per-domain entity F_1 as well as an aggregated dataset entity F_1. We note that other work on task-oriented dialogue by (Wen et al., 2016b; Henderson et al., 2014a) have reported the slot-tracking accuracy of their systems, which is a similar but perhaps more informative and fine-grained notion of a system's ability to capture user semantics. Because our model does not have provisions for slot-tracking by design, we are unable to report such a metric and hence report our entity F_1.

5.4.2 Results

We see that of our baseline models, Copy Net has the lowest aggregate entity F_1 performance. Though it has the highest model entity F_1 for the weather domain dialogues, it performs very poorly in the other domains, indicating its inability to generalize well to multiple dialogue domains and to accurately integrate relevant entities into its responses. Copy Net does, however, have the second highest BLEU score, which is not surprising given that the model is a powerful extension to the sequence-to-sequence modelling class, which is known to have very robust language modelling capabilities.

Our rule-based model has the lowest BLEU score, which is a consequence of the fact that the naturalness of the system output is very limited by the number of diverse and distinct response templates we manually provided. This is a common issue with heuristic dialogue agents and one that could be partially alleviated through a larger collection of lexically rich response templates. However, the rule-based system has a very competitive aggregate entity F_1. This is because it was designed to accurately parse the semantics of user utterances and query the underlying KB of the dialogue, through manually-provided heuristics.

As precursors to our key-value retrieval net, we first report results of a model that does not compute an attention over the KB (referred to as Attn. Seq2Seq) and show that without computing attention over the KB, the model performs poorly in entity F_1 as its output is agnostic to the world state represented in the KB. Note that this model is effectively a sequence-to-sequence model with encoder attention. If we include an attention over the KB but do not compute an encoder attention (referred to as KV Retrieval Net no enc. attn.), the entity F_1 increases drastically, showing that the model is able to incorporate relevant entities from the KB. Finally, we combine these two attention mechanisms to get our final key-value retrieval net. Our proposed key-value retrieval net has the highest modelling performance in BLEU, aggregate entity F_1, and entity F_1 for the scheduling and navigation domains. It outperforms the rule-based aggregate entity F_1 by 4.2% and outperforms the Copy Net BLEU score by 2.2 points as well as its entity F_1 by 11%. These salient gains are noteworthy because our model is able to achieve them by learning its latent representationts directly from data, without the need for heuristics or manual labelling.

We also report human performance on the provided metrics. These scores were computed by taking the dialogues of the test set and having a second distinct batch of Amazon Mechanical Turk workers provide system responses given prior dialogue context. This, in effect, functions as an interannotator agreement score and sets a human upper bound on model performance. We see that there is a sizable gap between human performance on entity F_1 and that of our key-value retrieval net ($\sim$ 12.7%), though our model is on par with human performance in BLEU score.

5.5 Human Evaluation

We randomly generated 120 distinct scenarios across the three dialogue domains, where a scenario is defined by an underlying KB as well as a user goal for the dialogue (e.g. *find the nearest gas station, avoiding heavy traffic*). We then paired Amazon Mechanical Turkers with one of our systems in a real-time chat environment, where each Turker played the role of the *Driver*. We evaluated the rule-based model, Copy Net, and key-value retrieval network on each of the 120 scenarios. We also paired a Turker with another Turker for each of the scenarios, in order to get evaluations of human performance. At the end of the chat, the Turker was asked to judge the quality of their partner according to fluency, cooperativeness, and humanlikeness on a scale from 1 to 5. The average scores per pairing are reported in Table 4. In a separate experiment, we also had Turkers evaluate the outputs of the systems on 80 randomly selected dialogues from the test split of our dataset. Those outputs were evaluated according to correctness, appropriateness, and humanlikeness of the responses, and the scores are reported in Table 5.

We see that on real-time dialogues the key-value retrieval network outperforms the baseline models on all of the metrics, with especially sizeable performance gains over the Copy Net which is the only other recurrent neural model evaluated. We also see that human performance on this assessment sets the upper bound on scores, as expected. The results on human evaluation of test outputs show that the rule-based model provides the most correct system responses, the KV network provides the most appropriate responses, and the Copy Net gives the most humanlike responses by small margins. We should note, however, that the second regime for human evaluation is more unrealistic because it involves providing a dialogue context that is directly sampled from our dataset, whereas the first regime of real-time dialogues measures the models' abilities to adapt to new and noisier user input. This suggests that the first set of results are more meaningful and representative for assessing overall model efficacy.

Examples of dialogues conducted between our model and Turkers are included in Figure 3. Particularly noteworthy is our model's ability to seamlessly integrate world information from the underlying KBs in the respective dialogues, while

Model	Fluency	Cooperative	Humanlike
Rule-based	3.20	3.39	2.87
Copy Net	2.33	2.42	2.02
KV Ret. Net	**3.36**	**3.43**	**3.09**
Human	3.98	3.95	4.04

Table 4: Human evaluation results on realtime dialogues.

still producing very naturalistic utterances. The model is able to do this effectively across multiple domains.

POI	Category	Traffic Info	...
Civic Center	parking garage	car collision	...
Valero	gas station	road block	...
Webster Garage	parking garage	car collision	...
Trader Joes	grocery store	heavy	...
Mandarin Rts.	chinese rest.	moderate	...
...	...	...	...

DRIVER: I am looking for a gas station near me with the shortest route from me.
CAR: *the closest gas station is valero but, but there is a road block nearby.*
DRIVER: What is the next nearest gas station?
CAR: *valero is the only gas station that i can find*
DRIVER: Thanks
CAR: *here to serve.*

Event	Time	Date	Party	Agenda
swimming act.	3pm	the 11th	sister	-
dinner	7pm	the 3rd	mother	-
football	2pm	the 20th	mother	-
lab appt.	10am	the 17th	Jeff	-
...	...	...	...	...

DRIVER: car when is gonna be my next swimming activity?
CAR: *your next swimming activity is on the 11th at 3pm.*
DRIVER: who is gonna attend with me?
CAR: *your swimming activity is on the 11th, one at 3pm with sister*
DRIVER: thank you!
CAR: *you are welcome*

Figure 3: Sample dialogues from our human evaluation, conducted between a Turker and the KV Retrieval Net. In the dialogue, our model responses are italicized. Additional dialogues are included in the supplementary material.

6 Conclusion and Future Work

In this work, we have presented a novel neural task-oriented dialogue model that is able to sustain grounded discourse across a variety of domains by retrieving world knowledge represented in knowledge bases. It smoothly incorporates

Model	Correct	Appropriate	Humanlike
Rule-based	**3.96**	3.57	3.28
Copy Net	3.52	3.63	**3.56**
KV Ret. Net	3.70	**3.64**	3.50

Table 5: Human evaluation of system outputs on test set.

this world knowledge into natural-sounding system responses in an end-to-end trainable fashion, without the need to explicitly model dialogue state. Our model outperforms competitive heuristic and neural baselines on both automatic and human evaluation metrics. In addition, we have introduced a publicly available dialogue dataset across three domains in the in-car personal assistant space that we hope will help the data scarcity issue present in task-oriented dialogue research.

Future work will address closing the margin between the Key-Value Retrieval Network and human performance on the various metrics. This will include developing new methods for robust handling of joint KB attributes as well as usage of the KB that requires more pragmatic understanding of the world via notions such as temporal reasoning.

Acknowledgments

The authors wish to thank He He, Peng Qi, Urvashi Khandelwal, and Reid Pryzant for their valuable feedback and insights. We gratefully acknowledge the funding of the Ford Research and Innovation Center, under Grant No. 124344.

References

L. El Asri, H. Schulz, S. Sharma, J. Zumer, J. Harris, E. Fine, R. Mehrotra, and K. Suleman. 2017. Frames: A corpus for adding memory to goal-oriented dialogue systems. *http://www.maluuba.com/publications/* .

Dzimitry Bahdanau, Kyunghyun Cho, and Yoshua Bengio. 2015. Neural machine translation by jointly learning to align and translate. In *International Conference on Learning Representations (ICLR2015)*.

Christina Bennett and Alexander I. Rudnicky. 2002. The carnegie mellon communicator corpus. In *ICSLP*.

Antoine Bordes and Jason Weston. 2016. Learning end-to-end goal-oriented dialog. *arXiv preprint arXiv:1605.07683* .

Bhuwan Dhingra, Lihong Li, Xiujun Li, Jianfeng Gao, Yun-Nung Chen, Faisal Ahmed, and Li Deng.

2016. End-to-end reinforcement learning of dialogue agents for information access. *arXiv preprint arXiv:1609.00777* .

Mihail Eric and Christopher Manning. 2017. A copy-augmented sequence-to-sequence architecture gives good performance on task-oriented dialogue. In *Proceedings of the 15th Conference of the European Chapter of the Association for Computational Linguistics: Volume 2, Short Papers*. Association for Computational Linguistics, pages 468–473. http://aclweb.org/anthology/E17-2075.

Jiatao Gu, Zhengdong Lu, Hang Li, and Victor O.K. Li. 2016. Incorporating copying mechanism in sequence-to-sequence learning. In *Proceedings of the 54th Annual Meeting of the Association for Computational Linguistics (Volume 1: Long Papers)*. Association for Computational Linguistics, Berlin, Germany, pages 1631–1640. http://www.aclweb.org/anthology/P16-1154.

Caglar Gulcehre, Sungjin Ahn, Ramesh Nallapati, Bowen Zhou, and Yoshua Bengio. 2016. Pointing the unknown words. In *Proceedings of the 54th Annual Meeting of the Association for Computational Linguistics (Volume 1: Long Papers)*. Association for Computational Linguistics, Berlin, Germany, pages 140–149. http://www.aclweb.org/anthology/P16-1014.

C.T. Hemphill, J. J. Godfrey, and G. R. Doddington. 1990. The atis spoken language systems pilot corpus. In *Proceedings of the DARPA speech and natural language workshop*.

Matthew Henderson, Blaise Thomson, and Jason Williams. 2014a. The second dialog state tracking challenge. *15th Annual Meeting of the Special Interest Group on Discourse and Dialogue* page 263.

Matthew Henderson, Blaise Thomson, and Steve Young. 2014b. Word-based dialog state tracking with recurrent neural networks. In *Proceedings of the SIGDIAL 2014 Conference*.

Geoffrey E. Hinton, Nitish Srivastava, Alex Krizhevsky, Ilya Sutskever, and Ruslan R. Salakhutdinov. 2012. Improving neural networks by preventing co-adaptation of feature detectors. *arXiv preprint arXiv:1207.0580* .

Sepp Hochreiter and Jurgen Schmidhuber. 1997. Long short-term memory. *Neural Computation* pages 1735–1780.

Robin Jia and Percy Liang. 2016. Data recombination for neural semantic parsing. In *Proceedings of the 54th Annual Meeting of the Association for Computational Linguistics (Volume 1: Long Papers)*. Association for Computational Linguistics, Berlin, Germany, pages 12–22. http://www.aclweb.org/anthology/P16-1002.

Anjuli Kannan, Karol Kurach, Sujith Ravi, Tobias Kaufman, Balint Miklos, Greg Corrado, Andrew Tomkins, Laszlo Lukacs, Marina Ganea, Peter Young, and Vivek Ramavajjala. 2016. Smart reply: Automated response suggestion for email. In *Proceedings of the ACM SIGKDD Conference on Knowledge Discovery and Data Mining (KDD) (2016)..* https://arxiv.org/pdf/1606.04870v1.pdf.

Diederik Kingma and Jimmy Ba. 2015. Adam: a method for stochastic optimization. In *International Conference on Learning Representations (ICLR2015)*.

Jiwei Li, Michel Galley, Chris Brockett, Jianfeng Gao, and Bill Dolan. 2016. A diversity-promoting objective function for neural conversation models. In *Proceedings of the 2016 Conference of the North American Chapter of the Association for Computational Linguistics: Human Language Technologies*. Association for Computational Linguistics, San Diego, California, pages 110–119. http://www.aclweb.org/anthology/N16-1014.

Wang Ling, Phil Blunsom, Edward Grefenstette, Karl Moritz Hermann, Tomáš Kočiský, Fumin Wang, and Andrew Senior. 2016. Latent predictor networks for code generation. In *Proceedings of the 54th Annual Meeting of the Association for Computational Linguistics (Volume 1: Long Papers)*. Association for Computational Linguistics, Berlin, Germany, pages 599–609. http://www.aclweb.org/anthology/P16-1057.

Chia-Wei Liu, Ryan Lowe, Iulian Serban, Mike Noseworthy, Laurent Charlin, and Joelle Pineau. 2016. How not to evaluate your dialogue system: An empirical study of unsupervised evaluation metrics for dialogue response generation. In *Proceedings of the 2016 Conference on Empirical Methods in Natural Language Processing*. Association for Computational Linguistics, Austin, Texas, pages 2122–2132. https://aclweb.org/anthology/D16-1230.

Fei Liu and Julien Perez. 2016. Gated end-to-end memory networks. *arXiv preprint arXiv:1610.04211* .

Minh-Thang Luong, Hieu Pham, and Christopher D. Manning. 2015a. Effective approaches to attention-based neural machine translation. *Empirical Methods in Natural Language Processing* pages 1412–1421.

Alexander Miller, Adam Fisch, Jesse Dodge, Amir-Hossein Karimi, Antoine Bordes, and Jason Weston. 2016. Key-value memory networks for directly reading documents. In *Proceedings of the 2016 Conference on Empirical Methods in Natural Language Processing*. Association for Computational Linguistics, Austin, Texas, pages 1400–1409. https://aclweb.org/anthology/D16-1147.

Kishore Papineni, Salim Roukos, Todd Ward, and Wei-Jing Zhu. 2002. Bleu: a method for automatic evaluation of machine translation. In *Proceedings of 40th Annual Meeting of the Association for Computational Linguistics*. Association for Computational Linguistics, Philadelphia, Pennsylvania, USA, pages 311–318. https://doi.org/10.3115/1073083.1073135.

Vu Pham, Theodore Bluche, Christopher Kermorvant, and Jerome Louradour. 2014. Dropout improves recurrent neural networks for handwriting recognition. *arXiv preprint arXiv:1312.4569v2* .

Alan Ritter, Colin Cherry, and William B. Dolan. 2011. Data-driven response generation in social media. *Empirical Methods in Natural Language Processing* pages 583–593.

Sikhar Sharma, Layla El Asri, Hannes Schulz, and Jeremie Zumer. 2017. Relevance of unsupervised metrics in task-oriented dialogue for evaluating natural language generation. *arXiv preprint arXiv:1706.09799* .

David Sussillo and L.F. Abbott. 2015. Random walk initialization for training very deep feed forward networks. *arXiv preprint arXiv:1412.6558* .

Ilya Sutskever, Oriol Vinyals, and Quoc V Le. 2014. Sequence to sequence learning with neural networks. In Z. Ghahramani, M. Welling, C. Cortes, N. D. Lawrence, and K. Q. Weinberger, editors, *Advances in Neural Information Processing Systems 27*, Curran Associates, Inc., pages 3104–3112. http://papers.nips.cc/paper/5346-sequence-to-sequence-learning-with-neural-networks.pdf.

Oriol Vinyals, Ł ukasz Kaiser, Terry Koo, Slav Petrov, Ilya Sutskever, and Geoffrey Hinton. 2015. Grammar as a foreign language. In C. Cortes, N. D. Lawrence, D. D. Lee, M. Sugiyama, and R. Garnett, editors, *Advances in Neural Information Processing Systems 28*, Curran Associates, Inc., pages 2773–2781. http://papers.nips.cc/paper/5635-grammar-as-a-foreign-language.pdf.

Tsung-Hsien Wen, David Vandyke, Milica Gasic, Nikola Mrksic, Lina. M. Rojas-Barahona, Pei-Hao Su, Stefan Ultes, and Steve Young. 2016b. A network-based end-to-end trainable task-oriented dialogue system. *arXiv preprint arXiv:1604.04562* .

Jason D. Williams, Kavosh Asadi, and Geoffrey Zweig. 2017. Hybrid code networks: practical and efficient end-to-end dialog control with supervised and reinforcement learning. *arXiv preprint arXiv:1702.03274* .

Jason D. Williams, Antoine Raux, Deepak Ramachadran, and Alan Black. 2013. The dialog state tracking challenge. In *Proceedings of the SIGDIAL*. Metz, France.

Steve Young, Milica Gasic, Blaise Thomson, and Jason D. Williams. 2013. POMDP-based statistical spoken dialog systems: a review. *Proceedings of the IEEE* 28(1):114–133.

POI	Category	Address	Traffic Info	Distance
Dish Parking	parking garage	550 Alester Ave	no traffic	3 miles
Cafe Venetia	coffee or tea place	329 El Camino Real	road block nearby	4 miles
Mandarin Roots	chinese restaurant	271 Springer St	car collision nearby	3 miles
Dominos	pizza restaurant	776 Arastradero Rd	moderate traffic	6 miles
Travelers Lodge	rest stop	333 Arbol Dr	moderate traffic	4 miles

> **DRIVER:** What is the nearest parking garage within 4 miles that has no traffic.
> **CAR:** *the nearest is dish parking at 550 alester ave, 3 miles away*
> **DRIVER:** Does it have any traffic?
> **CAR:** *there is no traffic on the route to dish parking*
> **DRIVER:** Thanks
> **CAR:** *you're welcome!*

Event	Time	Date	Party	Agenda	Location
dinner	5pm	the 4th	brother	-	-
meeting	1pm	the 18th	vice president	discuss company picnic	room 100
conference	11am	the 1st	HR	go over budget	room 50
meeting	4pm	the 9th	HR	onboard new members	room 100
lab appt.	6pm	the 14th	Jon	-	-
dinner	6pm	the 1st	Jon	-	-

> **DRIVER:** When is my dinner going to be and who will be attending
> **CAR:** *your next dinner is on the 1st at 6 pm with your jon*
> **DRIVER:** Great, thanks.
> **CAR:** *you're welcome!*

POI	Category	Address	Traffic Info	Distance
Dominos	pizza restaurant	776 Arastradero Rd	moderate traffic	7 miles
Stanford Express Care	hospital	214 El Camino Real	car collision nearby	1 miles
Travelers Lodge	rest stop	333 Arbol Dr	no traffic	4 miles
Coupa	coffee or tea place	394 Van Ness Ave	moderate traffic	7 miles
The Clement Hotel	rest stop	657 Ames Ave	road block nearby	6 miles
5672 barringer st.	certain address	5672 barringer st.	car collision nearby	4 miles

> **DRIVER:** Hi, I'd like to find a coffee place near me
> **CAR:** *we're 7 miles away from coupa but there is a moderate traffic*
> **DRIVER:** What's the address?
> **CAR:** *the address is 394 van ness ave, i sent it on your screen*
> **DRIVER:** Great. Can you find me the fastest route there?
> **CAR:** *the fastest route is for coupa.*
> **DRIVER:** Ok, so coupa is the closest place and you have the fastest route there
> **CAR:** *the fastest route has moderate traffic and there is a moderate traffic on the route do you want to go there?*
> **DRIVER:** yes
> **CAR:** *i sent the info on your screen, drive carefully!*
> **DRIVER:** Thanks
> **CAR:** *you're welcome, have a great day.*

	monday	tuesday	wednesday	thursday	friday	...
los angeles	hail, 60-70f	foggy, 30-40f	cloudy, 20-30f	stormy 30-40f	drizzle, 30-50f	...
durham	rain, 80-90f	cloudy, 50-70f	misty, 40-60f	dry, 80-100f	rain, 50-70f	...
boston	overcast, 30-50f	misty, 40-60f	foggy, 40-50f	foggy, 40-50f	clear skies 20-30f	...
seattle	warm, 60-70f	foggy, 30-40f	cloudy, 20-30f	stormy, 30-40f	drizzle, 30-50f	...
fresno	clear skies, 40-60f	drizzle, 70-80f	humid, 70-90f	stormy, 60-70f	cloudy, 90-100f	...
san francisco	foggy, 40-60f	hot, 90-100f	humid, 50-70f	rain, 80-100f	misty, 20-40f	...
alhambra	dew, 30-40f	dry, 30-50f	dry, 50-60f	humid, 80-90f	snow, 60-80f	...

> **DRIVER:** how is the weather
> **CAR:** *what city would you like the weather for?*
> **DRIVER:** is it foggy in seattle?
> **CAR:** *it will not be foggy in seattle today*
> **DRIVER:** thanks
> **CAR:** *you're welcome!*

Figure 4: Sample dialogues from our model. Note in the weather dialogue, the current day is italicized.

Figure 5: An image provided to users to elicit unbiased audio commands for prompting more naturalistic dialogues

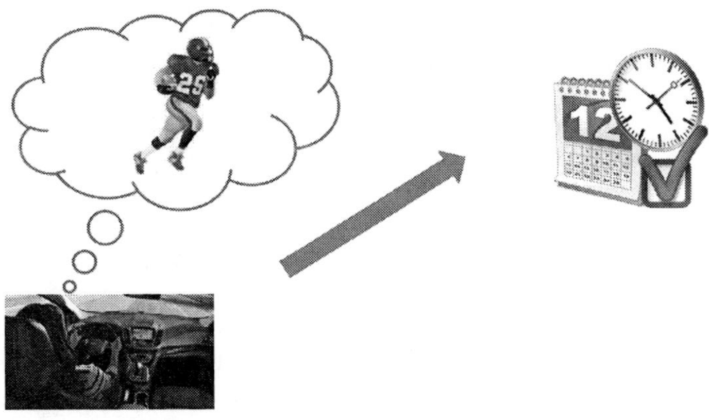

Figure 6: *Driver* mode in the wizard-of-oz collection scheme

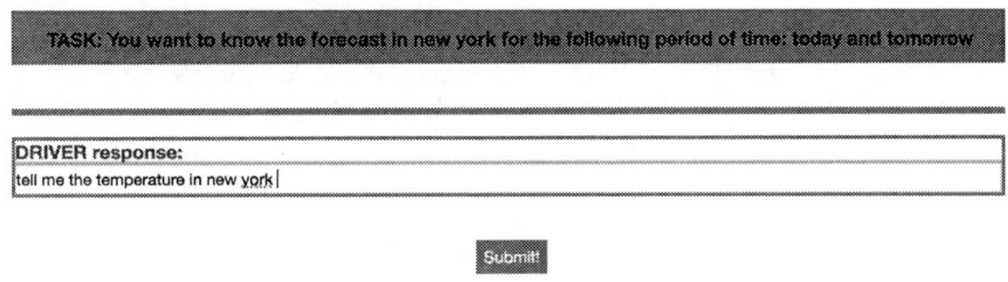

Figure 7: *Car Assistant* mode in the wizard-of-oz collection scheme

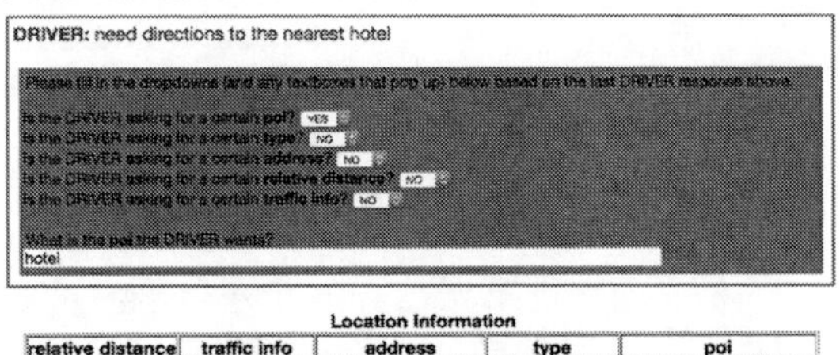

Location Information

relative distance	traffic info	address	type	poi
5 miles	no traffic	465 Arcadia Pl	rest stop	Four Seasons
3 miles	no traffic	550 Alester Ave	parking garage	Dish Parking
6 miles	moderate traffic	347 Alta Mesa Ave	friends house	jills house
5 miles	no traffic	5677 springer street	certain address	5677 springer street
5 miles	no traffic	638 Amherst St	grocery store	Sigona Farmers Market

Now, fill in what you as the CAR ASSISTANT would say to the DRIVER below

CAR ASSISTANT response:

End of dialogue? ONLY click this if the last DRIVER statement above suggests the task is done ->

Submit!

Lexical Acquisition through
Implicit Confirmations over Multiple Dialogues

Kohei Ono[†], Ryu Takeda[†], Eric Nichols[‡], Mikio Nakano[‡] and Kazunori Komatani[†]
† The Institute of Scientific and Industrial Research (ISIR), Osaka University
Ibaraki, Osaka 567-0047, Japan
‡ Honda Research Institute Japan Co., Ltd.
Wako, Saitama 351-0188, Japan

Abstract

We address the problem of acquiring the ontological categories of unknown terms through implicit confirmation in dialogues. We develop an approach that makes implicit confirmation requests with an unknown term's predicted category. Our approach does not degrade user experience with repetitive explicit confirmations, but the system has difficulty determining if information in the confirmation request can be correctly acquired. To overcome this challenge, we propose a method for determining whether or not the predicted category is correct, which is included in an implicit confirmation request. Our method exploits multiple user responses to implicit confirmation requests containing the same ontological category. Experimental results revealed that the proposed method exhibited a higher precision rate for determining the correctly predicted categories than when only single user responses were considered.

1 Introduction

Much attention has recently been paid to *non-task-oriented* dialogue systems —or *chat-oriented* dialogue systems— both in research (Higashinaka et al., 2014; Yu et al., 2016) and in industry. In addition to pure chat-oriented systems, some task-oriented dialogue systems can engage in chat-oriented dialogues (Lee et al., 2009; Dingli and Scerri, 2013; Kobori et al., 2016; Papaioannou and Lemon, 2017) because such dialogues are expected to build *rapport* (Bickmore and Picard, 2005) between users and systems. For simplicity, we will call any system that can engage in chat-oriented dialogue a *chat-*

bot. Since an open-domain chatbot that always generates appropriate utterances is still difficult to build (Higashinaka et al., 2015), we think it is worth building a closed-domain chatbot, which tries to continue dialogues in a specific domain.

One problem in building closed-domain chatbots is that, although they should preferably have comprehensive lexical knowledge in their domains, all the knowledge cannot realistically be prepared in advance. Therefore, we must consider the case where a user uses terms outside of the system's vocabulary[1], i.e. terms that have ontological categories the system does not know. If the system can acquire the term's category during dialogues, it will be able to interact with users more naturally and the cost of expanding its knowledge base will be reduced.

We call the problem of acquiring the category of an unknown term *lexical acquisition*. If the system can predict the category of an unknown term, it can ask the user if it is correct (Otsuka et al., 2013; Komatani et al., 2016). However, repeating such explicit confirmation requests can degrade the user experience in chat-oriented dialogues[2]. We therefore need to find a way to enable chatbots to: (1) interact with the user naturally and (2) acquire lexical information. To solve this dilemma, we proposed an approach using *implicit confirmation* (Ono et al., 2016), where the system makes a confirmation request about the predicted category and uses the user's response to decide if the category is correct or not. However, whether such an approach is really possible or not has not been well studied.

This paper proposes a method that utilizes im-

---

[1]Here, we use *term* to mean an expression denoting an entity that can be in the knowledge base. A term may consist of multiple words.

[2]Some typical examples will be shown in Section 2. We will verify this intuition by conducting a user study.

Proceedings of the SIGDIAL 2017 Conference, pages 50–59,
Saarbrücken, Germany, 15-17 August 2017. ©2017 Association for Computational Linguistics

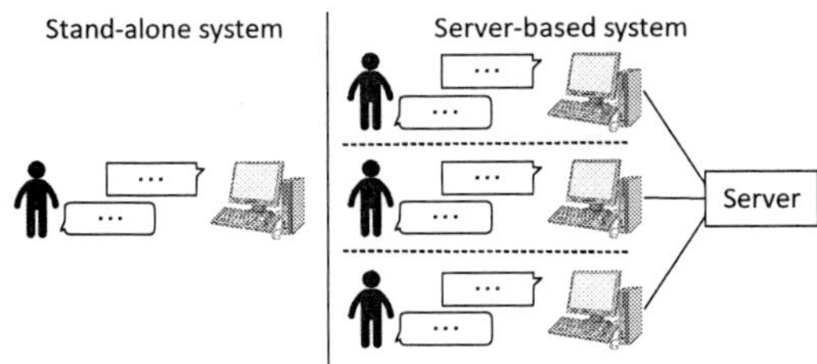

Figure 1: Server-based system can confirm the same prediction with different users

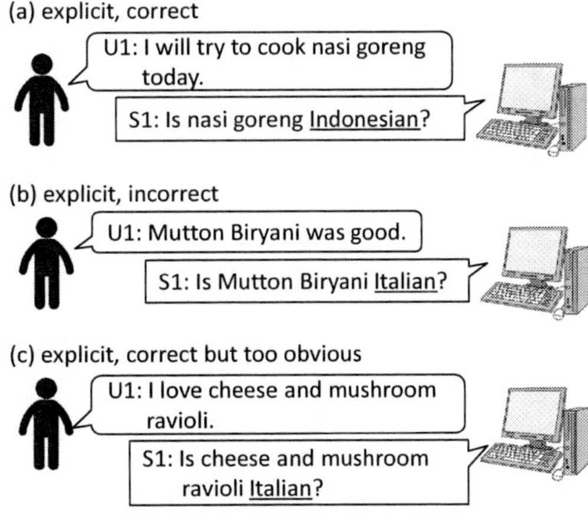

Figure 2: Examples of explicit confirmation requests

plicit confirmation dialogues from multiple users to increase the accuracy for determining if the predicted category is correct or not[3]. The system estimates the confidence score that the category prediction is correct from the responses of multiple users to the same implicit confirmation requests (Figure 1: right). Our proposed method has the goal of improving the confidence score estimation by using implicit confirmation sub-dialogues with multiple users. Then the system can determine if it should add the lexical information to the system's knowledge. For a sub-task, we consider the problem of estimating how likely the predicted category is to be correct from implicit confirmation sub-dialogues with one user (Figure 1: left).

It is reasonable to assume that the system can make confirmation requests about the same unknown term with different users because chatbots typically run on servers so they can share interaction logs for different users. Furthermore, it is difficult to ask a single user to respond to confirmation requests with the same predicted category many times, so collecting responses from multiple users is desirable.

This paper is organized as follows. The problem settings and related work are discussed in the next two sections. Section 4 describes the proposed method to determine correct categories in implicit confirmation requests on the basis of multiple implicit confirmation sub-dialogues with different users. Sections 5 and 6 show the data collection by crowdsourcing and several results as preparation for the main experimental evaluation of the proposed method, which is detailed in Section 7. Section 8 concludes this paper and discusses future work.

2   Problem Setting

This section describes the problem we address in this paper in detail. We are building a closed-domain Japanese language chatbot targeting the food and restaurant domain, so we use examples in this domain throughout this paper. In this domain, the problem is to acquire the categories of foods that the system does not know. We assume that the system can identify a food name in the user's input even if it is not in the system's vocabulary by using methods such as named entity recognition (Mesnil et al., 2015). Note that in this paper we also assume the category of an unknown term is predicted with an existing method (Otsuka et al., 2013; Ono et al., 2016). We do not assume any ontological structure of foods.

This paper focuses on deciding if the predicted category of unknown terms is correct or not in dialogues. To this end, methods for generating explicit confirmation have been proposed. Otsuka et al. (2013) proposed lexical acquisition methods that explicitly ask the user questions on the basis of category prediction results. For example, if the system does not know *nasi goreng* in the user input (denote as U1) in Figure 2 (a), the system predicts its category as *Indonesian food* and asks the user "Is nasi goreng Indonesian?"[4] Komatani et al. (2016) also proposed a utility-based method for selecting appropriate questions

---

[3]We do not deal with multi-party dialogues but utilize the interaction logs of two-party dialogues with different users.

[4]Note that Figures 2 through 4 show artificial examples, rather than those excerpted from the experimental data described in Section 5 because the experimental data are in Japanese and their direct translations are not natural.

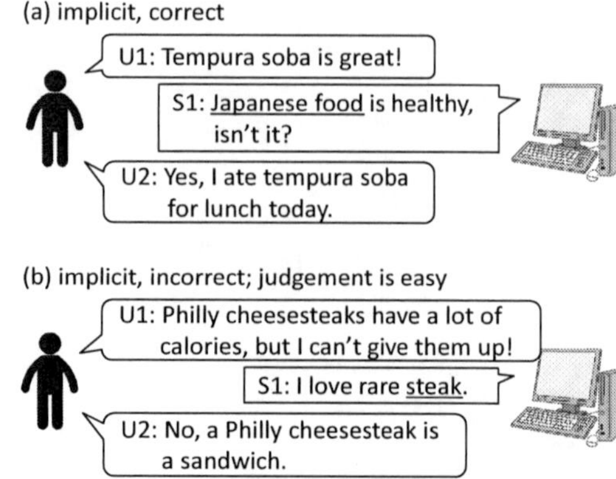

Figure 3: Examples of implicit confirmation requests

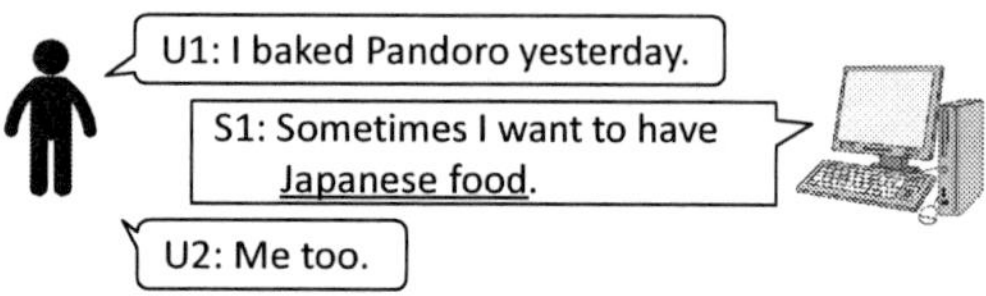

Figure 4: Example of implicit confirmation request for which judgement is difficult

on the basis of the results of category prediction. However, such explicit confirmation requests can degrade the user experience in chat-oriented dialogues, especially when the predicted category is incorrect as in Figure 2 (b), or the category of the unknown term is obvious as in Figure 2 (c).

We have proposed using implicit confirmation (Ono et al., 2016). For example, S1 in Figure 3 (a) does not explicitly ask the user if the category of *tempura soba* is Japanese, but from U2, it is possible to determine the category is correct. As another example, in Figure 3 (b), the system can determine the predicted category is incorrect from U2.

Determining if the predicted category is correct or not in implicit confirmation, however, is not always easy. Since user responses to implicit confirmation requests can come in various forms, looking at just the linguistic expressions of the user responses is not enough. For example, in Figure 4, the system incorrectly predicts the category *Japanese food* for *Pandoro* mentioned in U1 although it is Italian and generates an implicit confirmation request, S1. The user then talks about Japanese food to continue the dialogue (U2). In

such cases, it is not simple to determine if the category is incorrect. If the system's determination is wrong, it might add incorrect information to its database. Thus, we need to find a way to accurately determine the correctness of the predicted categories through implicit confirmation.

3 Related Work

So far, several studies have addressed lexical acquisition in dialogues. Meng et al. (2004) and Takahashi et al. (2002) proposed methods for predicting the categories of unknown terms. They acquire coarse categories for unknown terms, which roughly correspond to named entity categories. Those categories can be acquired more easily than the more specific categories that we are trying to acquire. Holzapfel et al. (2008) proposed a method for a robot to acquire fine-grained categories for unknown terms by iteratively asking questions. We do not think this method is suitable for chatbots as it repeats explicit questions. Whereas a previous study tried to acquire relationships among domain-dependent entities in dialogues (Pappu and Rudnicky, 2014), here we focus on acquiring lexical information, which is required before such relations are obtained.

We address the problem of deciding if the content of an implicit confirmation request is correct or not. Some studies related to this problem have tried to classify affirmative and negative sentences by using rules or statistical methods. For example, de Marneffe et al. (2009) built rules for judging if a response to a yes/no question is affirmative or negative when it is not a simple "yes" or "no." Gokcen and de Marneffe (2015) investigated features for detecting disagreement in the corpus of arguments on the Web. In contrast, in this paper, we do not try to classify user responses into affirmative and negative ones but try to determine whether a category in an implicit confirmation request is correct or not. Furthermore, we utilize multiple sub-dialogues with different users.

Our method can be considered as an instance of implicitly supervised learning (Banerjee and Rudnicky, 2007; Komatani and Rudnicky, 2009) in that user responses to implicit confirmation requests are used as indicators for acquisition, though the target knowledge is different from those works.

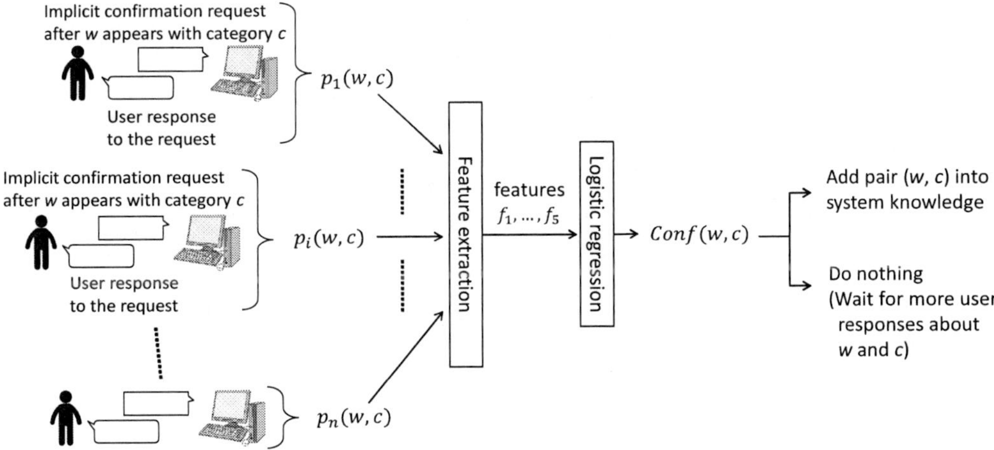

Figure 5: Overview of calculating confidence score $Conf(w, c)$

4 Determining Correct Categories Using Responses from Multiple Users

The purpose of our method is to prevent the system from learning incorrect categories for an unknown term by using multiple implicit confirmation sub-dialogues with different users. This is possible because our system is designed as a server-based dialogue system and can give implicit confirmation requests with the same predicted category to different users. The proposed method determines more accurately whether or not the predicted category in the implicit confirmation request is correct by exploiting multiple responses to them.

Let $p_i(w, c)$ be the probability that a predicted category c of an unknown term w is correct after a single implicit confirmation request. The category can be predicted using surface information of the unknown term such as character n-gram and character types in Japanese (Otsuka et al., 2013). The index i denotes the i-th response to implicit confirmation requests. Our goal here is to obtain a confidence score $Conf(w, c)$ representing how likely category c of the unknown term w is to be correct on the basis of replies to implicit confirmation requests from n different users. We can then determine whether or not the system can add the pair of the unknown term w and category c into the system knowledge by setting a threshold for $Conf(w, c)$.

4.1 Procedure

Figure 5 gives an overview of the proposed method. The steps below initially start with $i = 1$.

1. Generate an implicit confirmation request containing a predicted category c for user i after an unknown term w appears.

2. Obtain the probability $p_i(w, c)$ from the implicit confirmation sub-dialogue with user i. The probability can be obtained by machine learning that has features based on expressions from the user response and its context.

3. Extract features from $p_1(w, c), ..., p_i(w, c)$ and calculate the confidence score $Conf(w, c)$ that represents how likely the category c of the unknown term w is to be correct.

4. If $Conf(w, c)$ exceeds a predetermined threshold, c is regarded as correct and is acquired as knowledge. Otherwise, increment i, go to Step 1, and generate one more implicit confirmation with c to another user after the unknown term w appears.

4.2 Obtaining Confidence Scores for Correct Categories

The problem of obtaining the confidence score $Conf(w, c)$ can be formulated as a regression using probabilities of n user responses $\{p_1(w, c), ..., p_n(w, c)\}$ as its input. Intuitively, the category c can be regarded as more likely to be correct when $p_i(w, c)$ with higher values are obtained more times.

Table 1 lists the features used in this regression for when probabilities $p_i(w, c)$ are obtained n times. To use the same regression function when

Table 1: Features from n responses ($1 \leq i \leq n$)

f1	Average of $p_i(w, c)$
f2	n
f3	$\max_i p_i(w, c)$
f4	$\min_i p_i(w, c)$
f5	$|\{i|p_i(w, c) \geq 0.5\}|/n$

Table 2: Features for $p_i()$ with single user responses

g1	U2 includes an expression affirmative to S1
g2	U2 includes an expression negative to S1
g3	U2 includes an expression correcting S1
g4	U1 and U2 contain the same word
g5	U2 includes the category name used in S1
g6	U2 includes a category name not used in S1, excluding cases that fall under g3
g7	U2 includes a word preventing change of topic in S1
g8	U1 includes the category name used in S1
g9	U1 includes a category name not used in S1
g10	U1 includes any interrogative
g11	U1 includes an expression corresponding to the category mentioned in S1

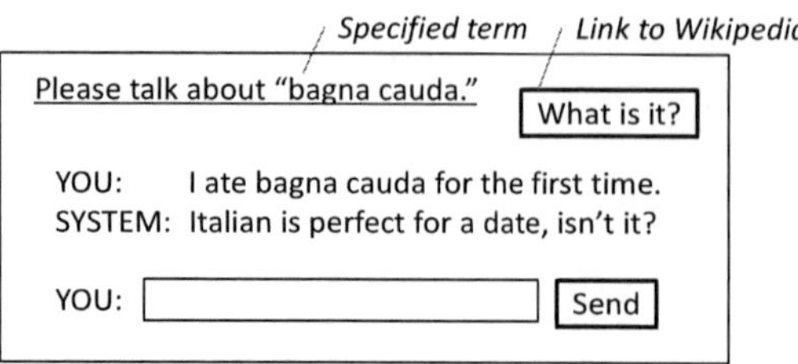

Figure 6: Schematic diagram of GUI used in crowdsourcing

n increases, we design features that consist of a constant number even when n varies and that are derived from n responses to implicit confirmation requests with category c.

5 Data Collection via Crowdsourcing

We conducted experiments to verify if our method is effective. Although it would have been desirable to collect experimental data by incorporating our method into the chatbot we are developing and having it used by many people without giving any instructions, this would have required a huge amount of interactions to collect enough data to verify our method. We therefore collected user responses to implicit confirmation requests from 100 workers via crowdsourcing[5]. The data collection procedure consists of three steps: (1) a worker inputs an utterance containing a term specified on the interface at the crowdsourcing site, (2) the system generates an implicit confirmation request about the term, and (3) the worker fills in the response to the confirmation request. This procedure was repeated for 20 specified terms per worker.

Figure 6 shows a schematic diagram of the graphical user interface (GUI) used in the crowdsourcing. Note that it was actually in Japanese. The lines starting with "YOU" and "SYSTEM" denote the worker's and the system's utterances, respectively. At Step (1), the worker was asked to input an utterance that contains a term specified in the uppermost part in Figure 6. The worker was able to check the Wikipedia page for the specified term by following a link on the GUI. This was to prevent them from talking without understanding the term.

We prepared 20 terms and their corresponding implicit confirmation requests used at Step (2): 10 had correct categories and the other 10 had incorrect categories. For example, for "shurasuko" (the Japanese rendering of churrasco), an implicit confirmation request with its correct category "meat dish[6]" is "Eating meat is fun, isn't it?" On the other hand, for "sangria," an implicit confirmation request with an incorrect category "yogashi[7]" is "Yogashi have a rich taste, don't they?" Furthermore, expressions of the implicit confirmation request were altered to make the confirmation request more natural when a worker's input was interrogative or negative.

We obtained 1,956 responses from 98 workers, half of which were responses to implicit confirmation requests with correct categories, and the other half were responses to those with incorrect ones. We removed data from two workers who just input only specified words or repeated the same sentences. We also removed four invalid inputs consisting of only spaces.

6 Preliminary Experiment with Single User Responses

6.1 Features for Obtaining Probabilities with Single User Responses

Table 2 lists the features for estimating how likely the categories in system confirmations are to be

---

[5] We used a crowdsourcing platform provided by Crowdworks, Inc. https://crowdworks.co.jp/

[6]Food category hierarchies usually used in Japan are different from those used in other countries.

[7]Yogashi means western sweets in Japanese.

correct. Here, U1, S1, and U2 respectively denote a user input, the implicit confirmation request by the system after U1, and the user response to the request. All feature values are binary; if the sentence for a feature is true, its value is 1, otherwise it is 0. These features were designed to represent differences in expressions of user responses to implicit confirmation requests with either a correct or incorrect category.

We briefly explain some important features by using the examples below. A user often uses affirmative expressions when responding to an implicit confirmation request with a correct category. This is represented by Feature g1, for which 15 affirmative expressions in Japanese were used such as "Yes" and "That's right."

When a category in an implicit confirmation request is correct, a user tends to continue with the same topic in U2 as in U1. In the example in Figure 3 (a), the user continues with the same topic and uses the same term *tempura soba* in U1 and U2. This is represented by Feature g4.

When the system makes an implicit confirmation request on the basis of an incorrect category, users tend to feel the system has suddenly changed the topic. In this case, the user tries to return the topic in U2 to the original one in U1. An example is as follows.

> U1: I like sangria with its fruity taste.
> S1: Yogashi have a rich taste, don't they?
> U2: I am talking about the alcoholic beverage.

In this example, the system generates an implicit confirmation with the incorrect category "yogashi" in S1 although the correct category of sangria is "alcoholic beverage." Then the user says that the topic is an alcoholic beverage and tries to return to the original topic. Here, another category name not used in S1 is included in U2. This is represented as Feature g6.

For Feature g2, 17 negative expressions were used such as "is not [category name used in S1]" and "No." For Feature g3, six expressions such as "It is [category name not used in S1]" that tries to correct the system's previous confirmation request were used. Our system has 20 categories, and five more names such as "cheese" and "pasta" were used as category names for Features g6 and g9. Eighteen expressions including interrogatives were used for Feature g10.

Table 3: Confusion matrices with single responses

| Features | Output | Reference | |
		Correct	Incorrect
all	Correct	742	313
	Incorrect	236	665
g1, g2 only	Correct	320	220
	Incorrect	658	758

Table 4: Classification results with single responses

Features		P	R	F
all	Correct	0.703	0.759	0.730
	Incorrect	0.738	0.680	0.708
g1, g2 only	Correct	0.593	0.327	0.422
	Incorrect	0.535	0.775	0.633

P: precision, R: recall, F: F-measure

6.2 Classification Performance with Single User Responses

We conducted a preliminary experiment to classify responses to implicit confirmation requests with correct and incorrect categories. The data consists of the 1,956 responses and their contexts obtained by crowdsourcing as described in Section 5. We applied logistic regression to them with the features listed in Table 2. We used the module in Weka (version 3.8.1) (Hall et al., 2009) as its implementation. The parameters were the default values. The classification was performed by setting a threshold to the obtained probability $p_i(w, c)$. The threshold was 0.5, which is also the default value of Weka. Evaluation was conducted with a 10-fold cross validation.

We compared two feature sets: one consists of all 11 features listed in Table 2 and the other consists of Features g1 and g2 only. The latter corresponds to a baseline condition that only considers affirmative and negative expressions of U2 and does not consider any relationship with S1 and U1.

The results are shown in Tables 3 and 4. Table 3 shows confusion matrices of the raw outputs for the two feature sets. Table 4 summarizes the results as precision and recall rates and F-measures of the two categories (correct and incorrect) also for the two feature sets. The average-F scores, i.e. the arithmetic means of F-measures for the two categories, were 0.719 and 0.528 when all features and only g1 and g2 were used, respectively.

Table 5: Top-10 feature sets after removing arbitrary features for classification with single responses

Removed features	Correct			Incorrect			avg-F
	P	R	F	P	R	F	
g10	.704	.759	.730	.738	.681	.709	.719
None	.703	.759	.730	.738	.680	.708	.719
g7,g10	.701	.760	.729	.738	.676	.705	.717
g1,g4,g10	.699	.764	.730	.740	.672	.704	.717
g1,g4	.699	.765	.730	.740	.671	.704	.717
g7	.701	.759	.729	.737	.676	.705	.717
g4,g10	.691	.784	.735	.751	.649	.696	.715
g4	.690	.784	.734	.750	.648	.696	.715
g1,g4,g7,g10	.696	.765	.729	.739	.666	.700	.715
g1,g4,g7	.695	.766	.729	.739	.665	.700	.715

P: precision, R: recall, F: F-measure

This indicates that using the features representing context improves the classification more than using only the features obtained from U2.

We also performed feature selection to analyze which features were effective for the classification. More specifically, we performed the same experiments with all combinations of the 11 features, i.e., $2047(= 2^{11} - 1)$ feature sets, and calculated their average-F scores. Table 5 lists top-10 feature sets sorted by the scores. "None" denotes the case when all the 11 features were used. First, the "None" condition was ranked second in the table, which shows that almost all features were effective for the classification. Next, when Feature g10 was removed, the F-value for the Incorrect category slightly improved and thus the average-F score also improved, as shown in the table. Because Feature g10 also appears in the table several times, Feature g10 was implied to be less helpful in this classification. On the other hand, the weight value for Feature g8 of the logistic regression function had the largest and positive value when Feature g10 was removed. This shows Feature g8 gave strong evidence and resulting $p_i(w, c)$ tended to be higher when Feature g8 was 1. This means that, when the common category name is included both in U1 and S1, the category included in S1 tended to be correct because the topic is not changed abruptly.

The results shown above indicate the classification performance was about 70% precision and recall rates on the basis of the user response and its context. However, we need higher precision because pairs of an unknown term and its predicted category will be added to the system knowledge, which must not contain errors. Thus, we have proposed a method using multiple user responses as described in Section 4, the effectiveness of which is verified in the following section.

7 Experimental Evaluation in Dialogues with Multiple Users

7.1 Data Preparation

In this section, we explain how to prepare data for training and evaluating the regression function to obtain $Conf(w, c)$. We performed the experiment in a perfectly open manner: no data were shared in training and test phases from the viewpoint of either workers or questions. More specifically, we had 98 (or 97) responses to implicit confirmation requests with 10 correct and 10 incorrect categories for making implicit confirmation requests, as explained in Section 5. Thus, we divided them into four disjointed groups, i.e., one group consists of 49 (or 48) workers with five correct and five incorrect categories.

The data were generated using responses collected from multiple users. The responses are mutually independent because they are obtained by a server-based dialogue system, so they can be combined in an arbitrary order. Thus, when we have N responses to single implicit confirmation requests, we can generate $\binom{N}{n}$ patterns. In our experiment, N was 49 (or 48) in each group. Since the values of $\binom{N}{n}$ become very large, we set a cut-off value when generating the combination randomly. The value was set to $1,000$ when $\binom{N}{n}$ exceeds $1,000$.

From this data combination, we obtained feature values listed in Table 1 with the reference values for every case. The reference value was set to either 1 or 0 depending on whether the category used in the implicit confirmation request was correct or not, respectively.

We then trained the regression function with each set of divided data of the four groups. We selected test data sets to be completely disjointed

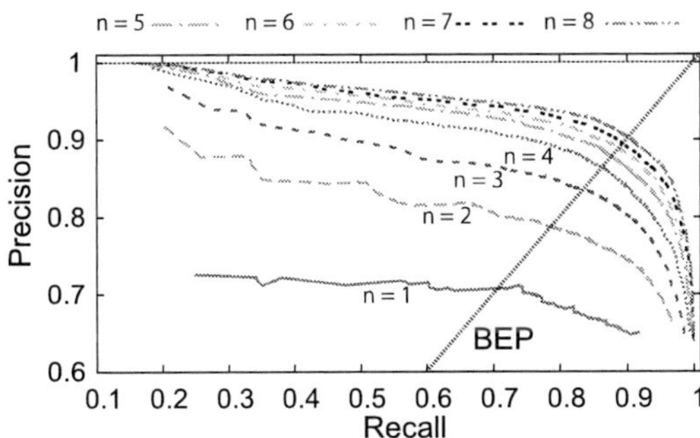

Figure 7: Precision and recall curves with BEP

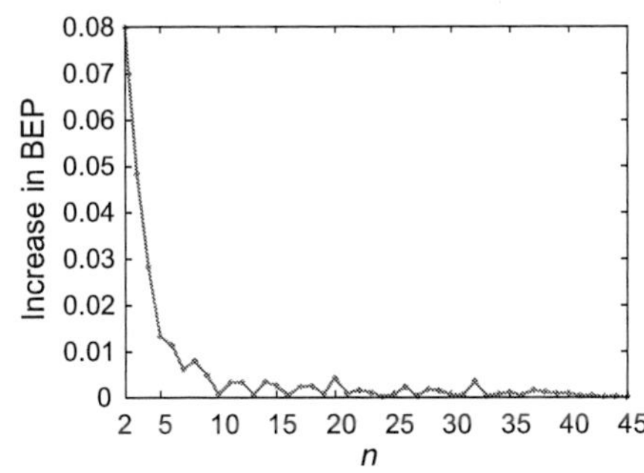

Figure 8: Increase in BEP values when n was incremented by 1

7.2 Performance of Regression with Multiple Responses

We first investigated if the performance was better when the system used multiple responses from users. The precision and recall rates were calculated by setting various thresholds to $Conf(w, c)$ representing how likely a category c is to be correct for an unknown term w.

Figure 7 depicts the precision and recall curves for n up to 8. It also shows a line indicating the breakeven points (BEPs), meaning the value where the two rates are equal. The BEP is used as a single point representing a precision and recall curve and to show how good the estimated confidence score is when n changes. Note that $n = 1$ corresponds to the case when only single responses were used for the regression.

The performance represented by the BEP values became better as n became larger. In particular, the BEP values of $n \geq 2$ were larger than that of $n = 1$. This proves that the proposed method using multiple user responses more accurately determines whether the predicted category is correct or not.

We also performed feature selection by removing arbitrary features listed in Table 1. The performance of the regression function was measured by the summation of BEP values for each n ($1 \leq$ $n \leq 48$). The result revealed the best performance in the case was obtained when we used only Features f3 and f4. One reason for this result was that the correlations among the features might be high. We still need to further investigate feature sets to obtain better $Conf(w, c)$, which is future work.

7.3 Discussion on Reasonable Number of Responses

We discuss the relationship between the values of n and the performance of the regression function in more detail. Figure 7 shows that the performance represented by the BEP improved when n increased. On the other hand, cost will need to be incurred for increasing n, i.e., collecting responses from more human users. Thus, we investigate how much the performance of the regression function changed when n increased.

We first investigated how the BEP values increased in accordance with n values. Figure 8 depicts the increases in the BEP values when n was incremented by 1. It shows the increases were large while $n \leq 5$. This result indicates that it is worthwhile to ask more users implicit confirmation requests with predicted category c especially while n is small, to more accurately determine whether or not the category is correct. The figure also shows that the improvement mostly diminished, especially when $n \geq 10$. This indicates that the effect by asking implicit confirmation requests to more human users shows diminishing returns as n increases from the viewpoint of the performance represented by the BEP.

We furthermore investigated recall rates when thresholds were set to $Conf(w, c)$ so as to keep precision rates high. In our problem setting, high precision rates rather than high recall rates are re-

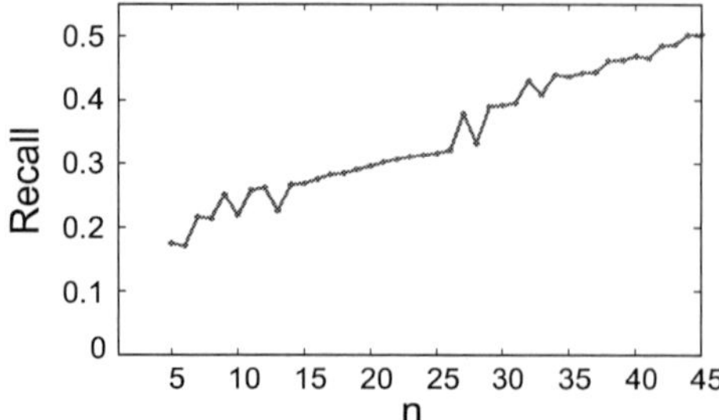

Figure 9: Recall rates with precision at 0.995

quired to avoid incorrect information being mistakenly added to the system knowledge. Figure 7 also shows the precision rate approached 1 for $n \geq 5$ by setting very large thresholds to $Conf(w, c)$. These cases indicate that the system can be almost perfectly confident that the predicted category c is correct. The recall rates were low for such cases because the precision and recall rates are in a trade-off relationship. We investigated the recall rates for such cases when n increased.

Figure 9 depicts the recall rates when we set very high threshold values for $Conf(w, c)$ so that the precision rates become almost one, i.e., $1 - \epsilon$. Here, we set $\epsilon = 0.005$[8]. First, the graph shows that the precision rate existed when n was 5 or more. For example, the recall rate for $n = 5$ was 0.175. This recall rate was rather low, but we think high precision rates should be prioritized over recall rates, even if some correct information is discarded at the current n. Second, the graph also shows that the recall rates increased with n. This means that, if the system asks more implicit confirmation requests with category c, more unknown terms the categories of which are c will be acquired with a sufficiently high precision rate.

8   Concluding Remarks

We have proposed a method to determine if the ontological category of an unknown term included in an implicit confirmation request is correct or not. Although responses to implicit confirmation requests seem to be insufficient for determining this, our method makes it effective by using the information on the context of the responses and exploiting responses from multiple users. Exper-

imental results revealed that the proposed method exhibited higher performance than when only single user responses were used. We hope the performance will be improved with further feature engineering.

The proposed method is expected to enable a chatbot to acquire knowledge through dialogues without annoying users with repetitive simple explicit confirmation requests, while it can avoid acquiring wrong knowledge by achieving a high precision rate for determining the correctness of the knowledge.

We are planning to address several issues before deploying this method in a chatbot. Although we intuitively think implicit confirmation requests do not degrade users' impressions compared with repetitive explicit confirmation requests, we need to experimentally verify this by a user study. On the basis of its results, we will define a strategy of when to make implicit confirmation requests and when to make explicit confirmation requests. Despite these remaining issues, we believe that the experimental results presented in this paper are valuable in that they show the possibility of lexical acquisition through implicit confirmation.

Acknowledgments

This work was partly supported by JSPS KAKENHI Grant Number JP16H02869.

References

Satanjeev Banerjee and Alexander I. Rudnicky. 2007. Segmenting meetings into agenda items by extracting implicit supervision from human note-taking. In *Proc. International Conference on Intelligent User Interfaces (IUI)*. pages 151–159.

Timothy W. Bickmore and Rosalind W. Picard. 2005. Establishing and maintaining long-term human-computer relationships. *ACM Transactions on Computer-Human Interaction (TOCHI)* 12(2):293–327.

Marie-Catherine de Marneffe, Scott Grimm, and Christopher Potts. 2009. Not a simple yes or no: Uncertainty in indirect answers. In *Proc. Annual Meeting of the Special Interest Group on Discourse and Dialogue (SIGDIAL)*. pages 136–143.

Alexiei Dingli and Darren Scerri. 2013. Building a hybrid: Chatterbot – dialog system. In *Proc. International Conference on Text, Speech, and Dialogue (TSD)*. pages 145–152.

Ajda Gokcen and Marie-Catherine de Marneffe. 2015. I do not disagree: leveraging monolingual alignment

---

[8] The margin ϵ is required because the confidence score obtained by the logistic regression function cannot be 1 theoretically (the score can only converge to 1). Therefore, we selected the smallest ϵ with which we can calculate reasonable recall values.

to detect disagreement in dialogue. In *Proc. Annual Meeting of the Association for Computational Linguistics (ACL)*. pages 94–99.

Mark Hall, Eibe Frank, Geoffrey Holmes, Bernhard Pfahringer, Peter Reutemann, and Ian H. Witten. 2009. The WEKA data mining software: an update. *SIGKDD Explor. Newsl.* 11:10–18.

Ryuichiro Higashinaka, Kotaro Funakoshi, Masahiro Araki, Hiroshi Tsukahara, Yuka Kobayashi, and Masahiro Mizukami. 2015. Towards taxonomy of errors in chat-oriented dialogue systems. In *Proc. Annual Meeting of the Special Interest Group on Discourse and Dialogue (SIGDIAL)*. pages 87–95.

Ryuichiro Higashinaka, Kenji Imamura, Toyomi Meguro, Chiaki Miyazaki, Nozomi Kobayashi, Hiroaki Sugiyama, Toru Hirano, Toshiro Makino, and Yoshihiro Matsuo. 2014. Towards an open-domain conversational system fully based on natural language processing. In *Proc. International Conference on Computational Linguistics (COLING)*. pages 928–939.

Hartwig Holzapfel, Daniel Neubig, and Alex Waibel. 2008. A dialogue approach to learning object descriptions and semantic categories. *Robotics and Autonomous Systems* 56(11):1004–1013.

Takahiro Kobori, Mikio Nakano, and Tomoaki Nakamura. 2016. Small talk improves user impressions of interview dialogue systems. In *Proc. Annual Meeting of the Special Interest Group on Discourse and Dialogue (SIGDIAL)*. pages 370–380.

Kazunori Komatani, Tsugumi Otsuka, Satoshi Sato, and Mikio Nakano. 2016. Question selection based on expected utility to acquire information through dialogue. In *Proc. International Workshop on Spoken Dialogue Systems (IWSDS)*. pages 27–38.

Kazunori Komatani and Alexander I. Rudnicky. 2009. Predicting barge-in utterance errors by using implicitly-supervised asr accuracy and barge-in rate per user. In *Proc. Annual Meeting of the Association for Computational Linguistics and International Joint Conference on Natural Language Processing (ACL-IJCNLP)*. pages 89–92.

Cheongjae Lee, Sangkeun Jung, Seokhwan Kim, and Gary Geunbae Lee. 2009. Example-based dialog modeling for practical multi-domain dialog system. *Speech Communication* 51(5):466 – 484.

Helen Meng, P. C. Ching, Shuk Fong Chan, Yee Fong Wong, and Cheong Chat Chan. 2004. ISIS: An adaptive, trilingual conversational system with interleaving interaction and delegation dialogs. *ACM Transactions on Computer-Human Interaction (TOCHI)* 11(3):268–299.

Gregoire Mesnil, Yann Dauphin, Kaisheng Yao, Yoshua Bengio, Li Deng, Dilek Hakkani-Tur, Xiaodong He, Larry Heck, Gokhan Tur, Dong Yu, and Geoffrey Zweig. 2015. Using recurrent neural networks for slot filling in spoken language understanding. *IEEE/ACM Transactions on Audio, Speech, and Language Processing* 23(3):530–539.

Kohei Ono, Ryu Takeda, Eric Nichols, Mikio Nakano, and Kazunori Komatani. 2016. Toward lexical acquisition during dialogues through implicit confirmation for closed-domain chatbots. In *Proc. of Second Workshop on Chatbots and Conversational Agent Technologies (WOCHAT)*.

Tsugumi Otsuka, Kazunori Komatani, Satoshi Sato, and Mikio Nakano. 2013. Generating more specific questions for acquiring attributes of unknown concepts from users. In *Proc. Annual Meeting of the Special Interest Group on Discourse and Dialogue (SIGDIAL)*. pages 70–77.

Ioannis Papaioannou and Oliver Lemon. 2017. Combining chat and task-based multimodal dialogue for more engaging HRI: A scalable method using reinforcement learning. In *Proc. ACM/IEEE International Conference on Human-Robot Interaction (HRI)*. pages 365–366.

Aasish Pappu and Alexander I. Rudnicky. 2014. Learning situated knowledge bases through dialog. In *Proc. Annual Conference of the International Speech Communication Association (INTERSPEECH)*. pages 120–124.

Yasuhiro Takahashi, Kohji Dohsaka, and Kiyoaki Aikawa. 2002. An efficient dialogue control method using decision tree-based estimation of out-of-vocabulary word attributes. In *Proc. International Conference on Spoken Language Processing (ICSLP)*. pages 813–816.

Zhou Yu, Ziyu Xu, Alan W Black, and Alexander Rudnicky. 2016. Strategy and policy learning for non-task-oriented conversational systems. In *Proc. Annual Meeting of the Special Interest Group on Discourse and Dialogue (SIGDIAL)*. pages 404–412.

Utterance Intent Classification of a Spoken Dialogue System with Efficiently Untied Recursive Autoencoders

Tsuneo Kato
Doshisha University

Atsushi Nagai
Doshisha University

Naoki Noda
Doshisha University

Ryosuke Sumitomo
KDDI Research, Inc.

Jianming Wu
KDDI Research, Inc.

Seiichi Yamamoto
Doshisha University

Abstract

Recursive autoencoders (RAEs) for compositionality of a vector space model were applied to utterance intent classification of a smartphone-based Japanese-language spoken dialogue system. Though the RAEs express a nonlinear operation on the vectors of child nodes, the operation is considered to be different intrinsically depending on types of child nodes. To relax the difference, a data-driven untying of autoencoders (AEs) is proposed. The experimental result of the utterance intent classification showed an improved accuracy with the proposed method compared with the basic tied RAE and untied RAE based on a manual rule.

1 Introduction

A spoken dialogue system needs to estimate the utterance intent correctly despite of various oral expressions. It has been a basic approach to classify the result of automatic speech recognition (ASR) of an utterance into one of multiple predefined intent classes, followed with slot filling specific to the estimated intent class.

There have been active studies on word embedding techniques (Mikolov et al., 2013), (Pennington et al., 2014), where a continuous real vector of a relatively low dimension is estimated for every word from a distribution of word co-occurence in a large-scale corpus, and on compositionality techniques (Mitchell and Lapata, 2010), (Guevara, 2010), which estimate real vectors of phrases and clauses through arithmetic operations on the word embeddings. Among them, a series of compositionality models by Socher, such as recursive autoencoders (Socher et al., 2011), matrix-vector model which models the dependencies explicitly (Socher et al., 2012), compositional vector grammar which combines a probabilistic context free grammar (PCFG) parser with compositional vectors (Socher et al., 2013a) and the neural tensor network (Socher et al., 2013b) are gaining attention. The methods which showed effectiveness in polarity estimation, sentiment distribution and paraphrase detection are effective in utterance intent classification task (Guo et al., 2014), (Ravuri and Stolcke, 2015). The accuracy of intent classification should improve if the compositional vector gives richer relations between words and phrases compared to thesaurus combined with a conventional bag-of-words model.

Japanese, an agglutative language, has a relatively flexible word order though it does have an underlying subject-object-verb (SOV) order. In colloquial expressions, the word order becomes more flexible. In this paper, we applied the recursive autoencoder (RAE) to the utterance intent classification of a smartphone-based Japanese-language spoken dialogue system. The original RAE uses a single tied autoencoder (AE) for all nodes in a tree. We applied multiple AEs that were untied depending on node types, because the operations must intrinsically differ depending on the node types of word and phrases. In terms of syntactic untying, the convolutional vector grammar (Socher et al., 2013a) introduced syntactic untying. However, a syntactic parser is not easy to apply to colloquial Japanese expressions.

Hence, to obtain an efficient untying of AEs, we propose a data-driven untying of AEs based on a regression tree. The regression tree is formed to reduce the total error of reconstructing child nodes with AEs. We compare the accuracies of utterance intent classification among the RAEs of a single tied AE, AEs untied with a manually defined rule, and AEs untied with a data-driven split method.

Proceedings of the SIGDIAL 2017 Conference, pages 60–64,
Saarbrücken, Germany, 15-17 August 2017. ©2017 Association for Computational Linguistics

Table 1: Relative frequency distribution of utterance intent classes

intent class tag	freq	sample utterance (translation)
CheckWeather	20.4	How's the weather in Tokyo now?
Greetings	16.5	Good morning.
AskTime	11.3	What time is it now?
CheckSchedule	7.2	Check today's schedule.
SetAlarm	5.7	Wake me up at 6AM tomorrow.
Thanks	3.6	Thank you.
Yes	3.1	Yes.
Goodbye	2.4	Good night.
WebSearch	2.2	Search (keyword)
Praise	2.2	You are so cute.
Time	1.9	Tomorrow.
MakeFun	1.6	Stupid.
GoodFeeling	0.9	I'm fine.
BadFeeling	0.8	I am tired
CheckTemp	0.8	What is the temperature today?
BackChannel	0.7	Sure.
AddSchedule	0.7	Schedule a party at 7 on Friday.
FortuneTeller	0.7	Tell my fortune today.
Call	0.6	Ho.
No	0.6	No way.

freq. : relative frequency distribution in percent.

2 Spoken Dialog System on Smartphone

The target system is a smartphone-based Japanese-language spoken dialog application designed to encourage users to constantly use its speech interface. The application adopts gamification to promote the use of interface. Variations of responses from an animated character are largely limited in the beginning, but variations and functionality are gradually released along with the use of the application. Major functions include weather forecast, schedule management, alarm setting, web search and chatting.

Most of user utterances are short phrases and words, with a few sentences of complex contents and nuances. The authors reviewed ASR log data of 139,000 utterances, redifined utterance intent classes, and assigned a class tag to every utterance of a part of the data. Specifically, three of the authors annotated the most frequent 3,000 variations of the ASR log, which correspond to 97,000 utterances i.e. 70.0 % of the total, redefined 169 utterance intent classes including an *others* class, and assigned a class tag to each 3,000 variations.

Frequent utterance intent classes and their relative frequency distribution are listed in Table 1. A small number of major classes occupy more than half of the total number of utterances, while there are a large number of minor classes having small portions.

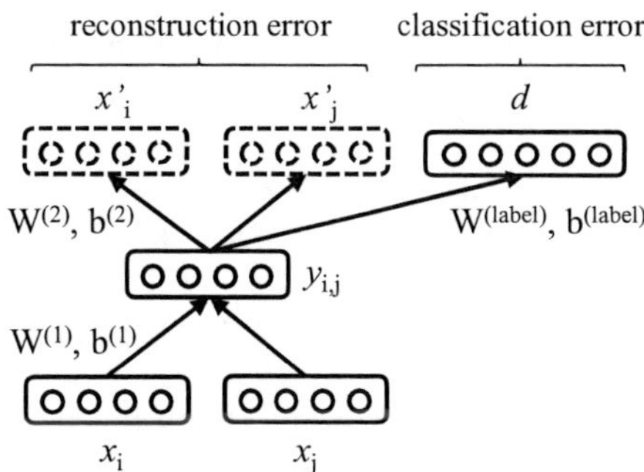

Figure 1: Model parameters and error functions of the recursive autoencoder

3 Intent Class Estimation based on Untied RAE

3.1 Training of Basic RAE

Classification based on RAE takes word embeddings as leaves of a tree and applies an AE to neighboring node pairs in a bottom-up manner repeatedly to form a tree. The RAE obtains vectors of phrases and clauses at intermediate nodes, and that of a whole utterance at the top node of the tree. The classification is performed by another softmax layer which takes the vectors of the words, phrases, clauses and whole utterance as inputs and then outputs an estimation of classes.

An AE applies a neural network of model parameters: weighting matrix $W^{(1)}$, bias $b^{(1)}$ and activation function f to a vector pair of neighboring nodes x_i and x_j as child nodes, and obtains a composition vector $y_{(i,j)}$ of the same dimension as a parent node.

$$y_{(i,j)} = f(W^{(1)}[x_i; x_j] + b^{(1)}) \qquad (1)$$

The AE applies another neural network of an inversion which reproduces x_i and x_j as x'_i and x'_j from $y_{(i,j)}$ as accurately as possible. The inversion is expressed as equation (2).

$$[x'_i; x'_j] = f(W^{(2)}y_{(i,j)} + b^{(2)}) \qquad (2)$$

The error function is reconstruction error E_{rec} in (3).

$$E_{rec} = \frac{1}{2}|[x'_i; x'_j] - [x_i; x_j]|^2 \qquad (3)$$

The tree is formed in accordance with a syntactic parse tree conceptually, but it is formed by greedy search minimizing the reconstruction error in reality. Among all pairs of neighboring nodes at a time, a pair that produces the minimal reconstruction error E_{rec} is selected to form a parent node.

Here, the AE applied to every node is a single common one, specifically, a set of model parameters $W^{(1)}$, $b^{(1)}$, $W^{(2)}$ and $b^{(2)}$. The set of model parameters of the tied RAE is trained to minimize the total of E_{rec} for all the training data.

The softmax layer for intent classification takes the vectors of nodes as inputs, and outputs posterior probabilities of K units. It outputs d_k expressed in equation (4).

$$d_k = f(W^{(label)}y + b^{(label)}) \qquad (4)$$

The correct signal is one hot vector.

$$t = [0, \ldots, 0, 1, 0, \ldots, 0]^t \qquad (5)$$

The error function is cross-entropy error E_{ce} expressed in (6).

$$E_{ce}(y, t) = -\sum_{k=1}^{K} t_k \log d_k(y) \qquad (6)$$

Figure 1 lists the model parameters and error functions of RAE. While AE aims to obtain a condensed vector representation best reproducing two child nodes of neighboring words or phrases, the whole RAE aims to classify the utterance intent accurately. Accordingly, the total error function is set as a weighted sum of two error functions in equation (7).

$$E = \alpha E_{rec} + (1 - \alpha)E_{ce} \qquad (7)$$

The training of RAE optimizes the model parameters in accordance with a criterion of minimizing the total error function for all training data.

3.2 Rule-based Syntactic Untying of RAE

To relax the difference of the nonlinear operation depending on types of nodes, we designed a rule to switch two AEs depending on types of two child nodes manually. At the leaf level of a tree, most of words are nouns, while a sentence or a phrase is composed of a predicate with a subject or an object or a complement. The operation of vectors between words and noun phrases, and that between phrases and clauses are assumed to differ considerably. Hence, the manual rule switches two AEs, one for words and noun phrases, and the other for phrases and clauses. Along a tree, the

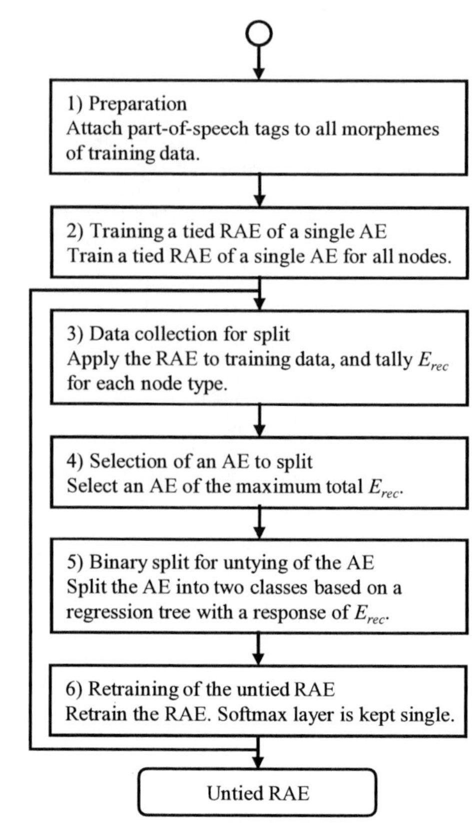

Figure 2: Procedure for training RAE of multiple AEs with data-driven untying

AE for words and noun phrases is applied at lower nodes around leaves, and the AE for phrases and clauses is applied at upper nodes close to the root node.

The node type is determined as follows. At leaf nodes, every word of a sentence is given a part-of-speech tag as a node type by Japanese morpheme analyzer (Kudo et al., 2004). The number of tags is set at 10. At upper nodes, the node type is determined by the combination of node types of two child nodes. A look-up table of the node type is defined on the basis of Japanese grammar. Another look-up table determining which AE to apply on the basis of the node type is defined as well.

3.3 Data-driven Untying of RAE

To obtain a more effective untied RAE, we designed a training method including data-driven untying of RAE. The method is based on sequentially splitting an AE with regression trees to reduce the total reconstruction error E_{rec}. Specifically, the method splits an AE into two on the basis of a re-

Table 2: Precision, recall, and accuracy of utterance intent classification of 65 classes

method	training set			test set		
	prec.	recall	acc.	prec.	recall	acc.
(1) Cosine similarity of bag-of-words (BoW)	-	-	-	76.0%	74.2%	**85.1%**
(2) Tied RAE based on random word vectors	37.2%	33.2%	**70.6%**	32.0%	65.6%	**66.4%**
(3) Tied RAE based on word2vec vectors	81.2%	78.8%	**88.7%**	74.7%	70.5%	**82.7%**
(4) RAE of two AEs untied by manual rule	65.9%	68.3%	**88.1%**	63.0%	62.5%	**84.0%**
(5) RAE of two AEs untied by data-driven split	80.3%	79.8%	**91.3%**	72.4%	72.3%	**85.6%**
(6) RAE of three AEs untied by data-driven split	73.9%	75.2%	**90.3%**	70.8%	67.9%	**84.8%**

gression tree with the response of the reconstruction error E_{rec}, and optimizes the model parameters of split AEs alternatively.

Figure 2 shows the procedure. The procedure starts with giving a part-of-speech tag to every word of a sentence. While forming a tree, a unique node type is given according to the node types of child nodes. To be precise, a new node type is given to an unseen combination of node types of two child nodes, whereas the same node type is given when the combination of node types has been seen before.

Initially, a single tied AE for all node types is trained. Applying the AE to all training data, reconstruction error E_{rec} is tallied for each node type. Then, a class of all node types is split into two classes based on a regression tree of CART (Breiman et al., 1984) with the response of E_{rec}. The predictor variables are the node types of the left and right child nodes. Then, the AEs are retrained with L2 regularization after every binary split. Note that the softmax layer is kept single in order not to make the generated vector space completely different.

4   Experiments

4.1   Experimental Setup

An experiment of utterance intent classification was conducted with the annotated data described in Section 2. The number of classes was reduced to 65 by merging classes with few pieces of data with a similar class or into the *others* class. Considering the balance of frequent utterances and less-frequent ones, the frequencies of utterances were smoothed by applying a square root function. The numbers of utterances in the training and test sets were 7,833 and 870, respectively. The ratio of unknown utterances in the test set was 15 percent.

4.2   Conditions of Experiments

Two types of word vectors, ramdom word vectors and word2vec vectors, were compared as the minimal elements of a tree. A total of 1.08 million word2vec vectors were trained with Japanese wikipedia texts of 1.1 billion words. The dimension of the vectors was fixed at 100. The word2vec vectors were trained by using skip-gram mode on the basis of results of preliminary experiments.

Three types of RAE, that is, a single tied AE, two AEs untied by the manual rule, and multiple AEs untied by the data-driven split, and a baseline method of cosine similarity of bag-of-words were evaluated.

4.3   Experimental Results

Table 2 shows the precision, recall, and accuracy of the classification for the training and test sets. The baseline method (1) showed relatively high performance, because the test set randomly chosen in consideration of the smoothed frequencies contained many known utterances and words seen in the training set. The tied RAE based on word2vec vectors (3) showed significantly better performance than the tied RAE based on random word vectors (2). While the RAE of two AEs untied by a manual rule (4) made a slight improvement, the RAE of two AEs untied by data-driven split (5) made more improvement. The resulting split was not simple, but one of the two AEs was to add a modifier, roughly speaking. However, the RAE of three AEs untied by data-driven split (6) showed a fall. We believe that the RAE was probably overlearned with thousands pieces of training data.

5   Conclusions

RAE was applied to utterance intent classification of a smartphone-based Japanese-language spoken dialogue system. To improve the classification accuracy, we examined the RAE of multiple AEs untied by a manual rule and RAEs of multiple AEs untied by data-driven split.

Comparing the untied RAEs of two AEs between the manual rule and data-driven split, the AEs untied by the data-driven split showed better accuracy. This means that splitting AEs based on a regression tree with the response of the reconstuction error is effective to some extent.

Reducing the model parameters effectively to circumvent overlearning, and utterance intent classification with more variations of utterances are future work.

References

L. Breiman, J. H. Friedman, R. A. Olshen, and C. J. Stone. 1984. *Classification And Regression Trees*. Chapman & Hall CRC.

E. Guevara. 2010. A regression model of adjective-noun compositionality in distributional semantics. *Proc. of the 2010 Workshop on Geometrical Models of Natural Language Semantics 2010* pages 33–37.

D. Guo, G. Tur, W. Yih, and G. Zweig. 2014. Joint semantic utterance classification and slot filling with recursive neural networks. *Proc. Spoken Language Technology Workshop 2014* pages 266–267.

T. Kudo, K. Yamamoto, and Y. Matsumoto. 2004. Applying conditional random fields to japanese morphological analysis. *Proc. EMNLP 2004* pages 230–237.

T. Mikolov, I. Sutskever, K. Chen, G. Corrado, and J. Dean. 2013. Efficient estimation of word representation in vector space. *arXiv: 1301.3781* .

J. Mitchell and M. Lapata. 2010. Composition in distributional models of semantics. *Cognitive Science* 34(8):1388–1429.

J. Pennington, R. Socher, and C. D. Manning. 2014. Glove: Global vectors for word representation. *Proc. EMNLP 2014* pages 1532–1543.

S. Ravuri and A. Stolcke. 2015. Recurrent neural network and lstm models for lexical utterance cllasification. *Proc. Interspeech 2015* pages 135–139.

R. Socher, J. Bauer, C. D. Manning, and A. Y. Ng. 2013a. Parsing with compositional vector grammars. *Proc. ACL 2013* pages 455–465.

R. Socher, J. Pennington, E. H. Huang, A. Y. Ng, and C. D. Manning. 2011. Semi-supervised recursive autoencoders for predicting sentiment distributions. *Proc. EMNLP 2011* pages 151–161.

R. Socher, A. Perelygin, J. Y. Wu, J. Chuang, C. D. Manning, A. Y. Ng, and C. Potts. 2013b. Recursive deep models for semantic compositionality over a sentiment treebank. *Proc. EMNLP 2013* pages 1631–1642.

R. Socher et al. 2012. Semantic compositionality through recursive matrix-vector spaces. *Proc. EMNLP 2012* pages 1201–1211.

Reward-Balancing for Statistical Spoken Dialogue Systems using Multi-objective Reinforcement Learning

Stefan Ultes, Paweł Budzianowski, Iñigo Casanueva, Nikola Mrkšić,
Lina Rojas-Barahona, Pei-Hao Su, Tsung-Hsien Wen, Milica Gašić and Steve Young
Engineering Department, University of Cambridge, Cambridge, United Kingdom
`{su259,pfb30,ic340,nm480,lmr46,phs26,thw28,mg436,sjy11}@cam.ac.uk`

Abstract

Reinforcement learning is widely used for dialogue policy optimization where the reward function often consists of more than one component, e.g., the dialogue success and the dialogue length. In this work, we propose a structured method for finding a good balance between these components by searching for the optimal reward component weighting. To render this search feasible, we use multi-objective reinforcement learning to significantly reduce the number of training dialogues required. We apply our proposed method to find optimized component weights for six domains and compare them to a default baseline.

1 Introduction

In a Spoken Dialogue System (SDS), one of the main problems is to find appropriate system behaviour for any given situation. This problem is often modelled using reinforcement learning (RL) where the task is to find an optimal policy $\pi(b) = a$ which maps the current belief state b—an estimate of the user goal— to the next system action a. To do this, RL algorithms seek to optimize an objective function, the reward r, using sample dialogues. In contrast to other RL tasks (like AlphaGo (Silver et al., 2016)), the reward used in goal-oriented dialogue systems usually consists of more than one objective (e.g., task success and dialogue length (Levin et al., 1998; Lemon et al., 2006; Young et al., 2013)).

However, balancing these rewards is rarely considered and the goal of this paper is to propose a structured method for finding the optimal weights for a multiple objective reward function. Finding a good balance between multiple objectives is usually domain-specific and not straight-forward. For example, in the case of task success and dialogue length, if the reward for success is too high, the learning algorithm is insensitive to potentially irritating actions such as `repeat` provided that the dialogue is ultimately successful. Conversely, if the reward for success is too small, the resulting policy may irritate users by offering inappropriate solutions before fully illiciting the user's requirements.

In this paper, we propose to find a suitable reward balance by searching through the space of reward component weights. Doing this with conventional RL techniques is infeasible as a policy must be trained for each candidate balance and this requires an enormous number of training dialogues. To alleviate this, we propose to use multi-objective RL (MORL) which is specifically designed for this task (among others (Roijers et al., 2013)). Then, only one policy needs to be trained which may be evaluated with several candidate balances. To the best of our knowledge, this is the first time MORL has been applied to dialogue policy optimization.

In contrast to previous work which explicitly selects component weights to maximize user satisfaction (Walker, 2000) explicitly, the proposed method enables optimisation of an implicit goal by allowing the interplay each reward component to be explored at low computational cost.

Several different algorithms have previously been used for MORL (Castelletti et al., 2013; Van Moffaert et al., 2015; Pirotta et al., 2015; Mossalam et al., 2016). In this work, we propose a novel MORL algorithm based on Gaussian processes. This is described in Section 2 along with a brief introduction to MORL. In Section 3, the proposed method for finding a good reward balance with MORL is presented. Section 4 describes the application and evaluation of the balancing method on six different domains. Finally conclusions are drawn in Section 5.

Proceedings of the SIGDIAL 2017 Conference, pages 65–70,
Saarbrücken, Germany, 15-17 August 2017. ©2017 Association for Computational Linguistics

2 Multi-objective Reinforcement Learning with Gaussian Processes

In this Section we present our proposed extension of the GPSARSA algorithm for MORL after giving a brief introduction to single- and multi-objective RL and the GPSARSA algorithm itself.

Reinforcement Learning Reinforcement learning (RL) is used in a sequential decision-making process where a decision-model (the policy π) is trained based on sample data and a potentially delayed objective signal (the reward r) (Sutton and Barto, 1998). Implementing the Markov assumption, the policy selects the next action $a \in A$ based on the current system belief state b to optimise the accumulated future reward R_t at time t:

$$R_t = \sum_{k=0}^{\infty} \gamma^k r_{t+k+1} \ . \tag{1}$$

Here, k denotes the number of future steps, γ a discount factor and r_τ the reward at time τ.

The Q-function models the expected accumulated future reward R_t when taking action a in belief state b and then following policy π:

$$Q^\pi(b,a) = E_\pi[R_t | b_t = b, a_t = a] \ . \tag{2}$$

GPSARSA For most real-world problems, finding the exact optimal Q-values is not feasible. Instead, Engel et al. (2005) have proposed the GP-SARSA algorithm which uses Gaussian processes (GP) to approximate the Q-function. Gašić and Young (2014) have shown that this works well when applied to the problem of spoken dialogue policy optimisation. GPSARSA is a Bayesian on-line learning algorithm which models the Q-function as a zero-mean GP which is fully defined by a mean and a kernel function k:

$$Q^\pi(b,a) \sim \mathcal{GP}(0, k(b,a),(b,a))) \ , \tag{3}$$

where the kernel models the correlation between data points. Based on sample data, the GP is trained to approximate Q such that the variance derived from the kernel represents the uncertainty of the approximation.

In dialogue management, the following kernel has been successfully used:

$$k((b,a),(b',a')) = \delta(a,a') \cdot k_{lin}(b,b') \ . \tag{4}$$

It consists of a linear kernel for the continuous belief representation b and the δ-kernel for the discrete system action a.

Multi-objective Reinforcement Learning In multi-objective reinforcement learning (MORL), the objective function does not consist of only one but of many dimensions. Thus, the reward r_t becomes a vector $\mathbf{r}_t = (r_t^1, r_t^2, \ldots, r_t^m)$, where m is the number of objectives.

To define the contribution of each objective, a scalarization function f is introduced which uses weights $\mathbf{w}$ for the different objectives to map the vector representation to a scalar value. The solution to a MORL problem is a set of optimal policies containing an optimal policy for any given weight configuration.

In MORL, the Q-function may either be modelled as a vector of Q-functions or directly as the expectation of the scalarized vector of $(R_t^1 \ldots R_t^m)$:

$$Q_{\mathbf{w}}^\pi(b) = E[f(\mathbf{R}_t, \mathbf{w}) | \pi, b, a] \ . \tag{5}$$

In practice, the scalarization function is often modelled as a linear function (the weighted sum):

$$f(\mathbf{r}_t, \mathbf{w}) = \sum_m w_m r_t^m \ . \tag{6}$$

Multi-objective GPSARSA The proposed multi-objective (MO) GPSARSA is based on Equation 5. By approximating the scalarized Q-function directly using a GP, the GPSARSA algorithm may be applied for MORL. The GP (and thus the Q-function) is extended by one parameter—the weight vector $\mathbf{w}$: $Q(b, a, \mathbf{w})$.

Approximating the Q-function with a GP relies on the fact that the accumulated future reward R_t (Eq. 1) may be decomposed as

$$R_t = r_{t+1} + \gamma R_{t+1} \ . \tag{7}$$

Accordingly, for using a GP to directly estimate the scalarized reward in MO-GPSARSA, the equation

$$\begin{aligned} f(\mathbf{R}_t, \mathbf{w}) &= f(\mathbf{r}_{t+1} + \gamma \mathbf{R}_{t+1}, \mathbf{w}) \\ &\overset{!}{=} f(\mathbf{r}_{t+1}, \mathbf{w}) + \gamma f(\mathbf{R}_{t+1}, \mathbf{w}) \end{aligned} \tag{8}$$

must hold. This is true in case of using a linear scalarization function f (Eq. 6).

To alter the kernel accordingly, a linear kernel for $\mathbf{w}$ is added to the state kernel[1] resulting in

$$\begin{aligned} &k((b, a, \mathbf{w}), (b', a', \mathbf{w}')) \\ &= \delta(a, a') \cdot \big(k_{lin}(b, b') + k_{lin}(\mathbf{w}, \mathbf{w}')\big) \ . \end{aligned} \tag{9}$$

---

[1] A similar type of kernel extension has been proposed previously in a different context, e.g., (Casanueva et al., 2015).

Algorithm 1: Training of the MO-GPSARSA.

Input: dialogue success reward r_s, dialogue length penalty r_l

1 **foreach** *training dialogue* **do**
2   select w_s, w_l randomly
3   execute dialogue and record $(b_t, a_t, \mathbf{w})$ in D for each turn t
       `// dialogue length penalty`
4      $r \leftarrow w_l \cdot |D| \cdot r_l$
       `// dialogue success reward`
5   **if** *dialogue successful* **then**
6        $r \leftarrow r + w_r \cdot r_s$
7   update GP using D and r
8   reset D

Since a linear scalarization function is applied, the correlations with other data points are also assumed to be linear.

To train a policy using multi-objective GP-SARSA, a new weight configuration is sampled randomly for each training dialogue. An example of the training process being applied to dialogue policy optimization with the two objectives task success and dialogue length is depicted in Algorithm 1.

3 Reward Balancing using MORL

The main contribution of this paper is to provide a structured method for finding a good balance between multiple rewards for learning dialogue policies. For the two-objective problem of having a task success reward r_s and a dialogue length reward r_l, $\mathbf{r} = (r_s, r_l)$, the scalarized reward is

$$r = f(\mathbf{r}, \mathbf{w}) = \mathbb{1}_{TS} \cdot w_s r_s + T \cdot w_s r_l$$
$$= \mathbb{1}_{TS} \cdot r_s^w + T \cdot r_l^w , \quad (10)$$

where T is the number of turns and $\mathbb{1}_{TS} = 1$ iff the dialogue is successful, zero otherwise.

To find a good reward balance, we adopt the following procedure:

1. Set initial reward values r_s^w and r_l^w along with the initial weight configuration.

2. Apply MORL to train a policy for a given number of training dialogues and evaluate with different weight configurations.

3. Select an appropriate balance based on success-weight and length-weight curves to optimise the individual implicit goal.

The method may be refined by applying it recursively with different grid sizes. After selecting a suitable weight configuration, a single-objective policy may be trained.

4 Experiments and Results

The reward balancing method described in the previous section is applied to six domains: finding TVs, laptops, restaurants or hotels (the latter two in Cambridge and San Francisco). The following table depicts the domain statistics with the number of search constraints, the number of informational items the user can request, and the number of database entities:

Domain	# constr.	# requests	# entities
CamRestaurants	3	9	110
CamHotels	5	11	33
SFRestaurants	6	11	271
SFHotels	6	10	182
TV	6	14	94
Laptops	11	21	126

For consistency with previous work (Gašić and Young, 2014; Young et al., 2013; Su et al., 2016) the rewards $r_s^w = 20$ and $r_l^w = -1$ are used representing the weight configuration $\mathbf{w} = (0.5, 0.5)$. This results in $r_s = 40$ and $r_l = -2$.

For the evaluation, simulated dialogues were created using the statistical spoken dialogue toolkit PyDial (Ultes et al., 2017). It contains an agenda-based user simulator (Schatzmann and Young, 2009) with an error model to simulate the semantic error rate (SER) encountered in real systems due to the noisy speech channel.

A policy has been trained for each domain using multi-objective GPSARSA with 3,000 dialogues and an SER of 15%. Each policy was evaluated with 300 dialogues for each weight configuration in $\{(0.1, 0.9), (0.2, 0.8), \ldots, (0.9, 0.1)\}$. The results in Figure 1 are the averages of five trained policies with different random seeds. All curves follow a similar pattern: at some point, the success curve reaches a plateau where the performance does not increase any further with higher w_s.

The following weights were selected: CamRestaurants $w_s = 0.4$; CamHotels $w_s = 0.6$; SFRestaurants $w_s = 0.6$; SFHotels $w_s = 0.7$; TV $w_s = 0.6$; Laptops $w_s = 0.7$. These weights were selected by hand according to the success rate[2] as well as the average dialogue length.

The selected weights were scaled to keep the

---

[2]Taking into account the overall performance and the proximity to the edge of the plateau. To compensate for possible inaccuracies of the MO-GPSARSA, the configuration right at the edge has not been chosen.

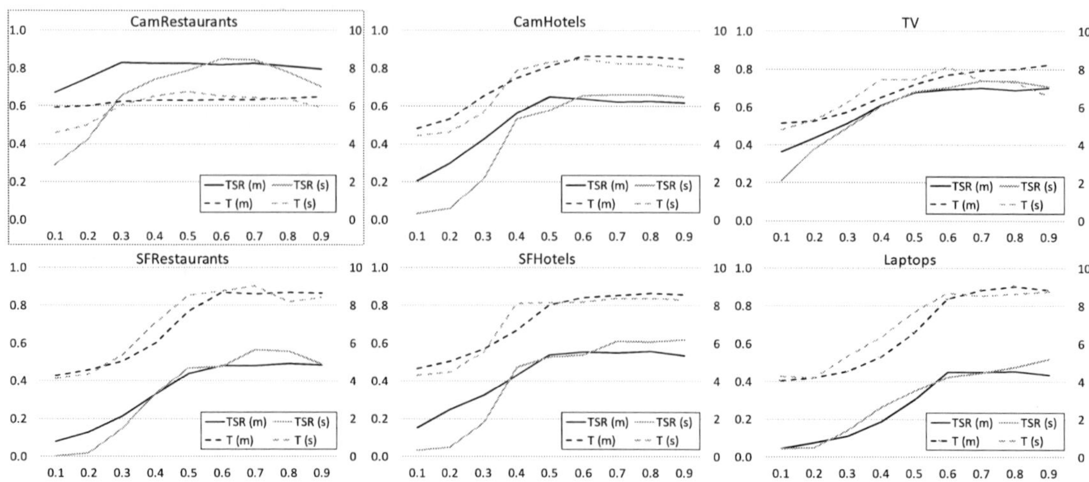

Figure 1: The MORL success-weight and length-weight curves (m, task success rate (TSR) on left, number of turns T on right vertical axes; success weights w_s on horizontal axes) after 3,000 training dialogues. Each data point is the average over five policies with different seeds where each policy/weight configuration is evaluated with 300 dialogues. As a comparison, the same curves using single-objective RL (s, separate policies trained for each balance) have been created *after* selecting the weights.

	r_s^w	TSR		# Turns	
		base.	*opt.*	*base.*	*opt.*
CamRestaurants	14	88.8%	86.2%	6.4	6.3
CamHotels	30	75.1%	79.8%	8.1	8.2
SFRestaurants	47	62.4%	65.7%	8.5	9.1
SFHotels	30	66.7%	69.4%	8.0	8.0
TV	30	75.7%	80.5%	7.4	7.4
Laptops	47	44.6%	54.6%	7.5	8.7

Table 1: Task success rates (TSRs) and number of turns after 4,000 training dialogues using a success reward of 20 (baseline) compared to the optimised success reward r_s^w. All TSR differences are statistically significant (t-test, $p < 0.05$).

turn penalty w_l^w constant at -1. Using these reward settings, each domain was evaluated with 4,000 dialogues in 10 batches. After each batch, the policies were evaluated with 300 dialogues. The final results shown in Table 1 (selection of learning curves in Figure 2) are compared to the baseline of $\mathbf{w} = (0.5, 0.5)$ (i.e. standard unoptimised reward component weight balance). Evidently, optimising the balance has a significant impact on the performance of the trained polices.

To analyse the performance of multi-objective GPSARSA, policies were trained and evaluated for each reward balance with single-objective (SO) GPSARSA (see Figure 1) *after* the weights had been selected. Each SO policy was trained with 1,000 dialogues and evaluated with 300 dialogues, all averaged over five runs. The success-weight curves for SORL clearly resemble the MORL curves for almost all domains except for CamRestaurants where it leads to an incorrect selection of weights. This may be attributed to the kernel used for multi-objective GPSARSA.

It is worth noting that for the presented full MORL analysis, 3,000 training dialogues were necessary for each domain to find a good balance. This is significantly less than the 9,000 dialogues needed for the SORL analysis and this difference would increase further for a finer grain search grid.

5 Conclusion

In this work, we have addressed the problem of finding a good balance between multiple rewards for learning dialogue policies. We have shown the relevance of the problem and demonstrated the usefulness of multi-objective reinforcement learning to facilitate the search for a suitable balance. Using the proposed procedure, only one policy needs to be trained which can then be evaluated for an arbitrary number of reward balances thus drastically reducing the total amount of training dialogues needed.

We have proposed and employed an extension of the GPSARSA algorithm for multiple objectives and applied it to six domains. The ex-

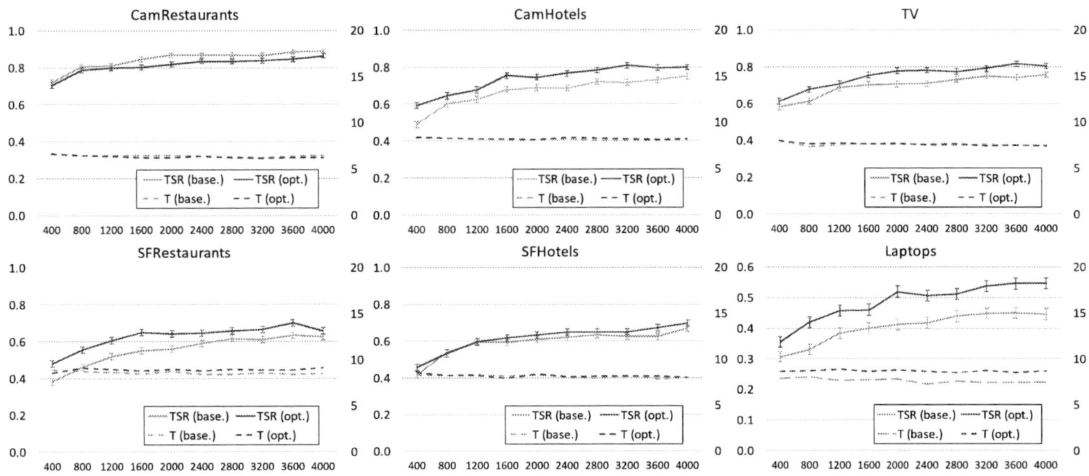

Figure 2: The task success rates (TSR, left axes) and dialogue length in number of turns (T, right axes) for all six domains comparing the baseline ($r_s^w = 20$, $w = (0.5, 0.5)$) with the optimised balance. The horizontal axes show the number of training dialogues. Each data point is the average over five policies with different seeds where each policy is evaluated with 300 dialogues.

periments show the successful application of our method: the optimal balance improved task success without unduly impacting on dialogue length in all domains except CamRestaurants, where it is clear that the weight selection criteria failed. In practice, this could have been easily trapped by applying a minimum weight to the success criteria. Furthermore, the domain-dependence of the reward balance has been confirmed.

For future work, the accuracy of the proposed multi-objective GPSARSA will be further improved with the ultimate goal of using the proposed method to directly learn a multi-objective policy through interaction with real users. To achieve this, alternative weight kernels will be explored. The resulting multi-objective policy may then directly be applied (without the need of re-training a single-objective policy) and the weights may even be adjusted according to a specific situation or user preferences.

Future work will also include an automatic method to find the optimal balance as well as investigating the relationship between the optimal success reward value and the domain characteristics (similar to Papangelis et al. (2017)).

Acknowledgments

Tsung-Hsien Wen, Paweł Budzianowski and Stefan Ultes are supported by Toshiba Research Europe Ltd, Cambridge Research Laboratory. This research was partly funded by the EPSRC grant EP/M018946/1 *Open Domain Statistical Spoken Dialogue Systems*.

Data

All experiments were run in simulation. The corresponding source code is included in the PyDial toolkit which can be found on www.pydial.org.

References

Inigo Casanueva, Thomas Hain, Heidi Christensen, Ricard Marxer, and Phil Green. 2015. Knowledge transfer between speakers for personalised dialogue management. In *16th Annual Meeting of the Special Interest Group on Discourse and Dialogue*. page 12.

A Castelletti, F Pianesi, and M Restelli. 2013. A multiobjective reinforcement learning approach to water resources systems operation: Pareto frontier approximation in a single run. *Water Resources Research* 49(6):3476–3486.

Yaakov Engel, Shie Mannor, and Ron Meir. 2005. Reinforcement learning with gaussian processes. In *Proceedings of the 22nd international conference on Machine learning*. ACM, pages 201–208.

Milica Gašić and Steve J. Young. 2014. Gaussian processes for POMDP-based dialogue manager optimization. *IEEE/ACM Transactions on Audio, Speech, and Language Processing* 22(1):28–40.

Oliver Lemon, Kalliroi Georgila, James Henderson, and Matthew Stuttle. 2006. An isu dialogue system exhibiting reinforcement learning of dialogue policies: generic slot-filling in the talk in-car system. In *Proceedings of the Eleventh Conference of the European Chapter of the Association for Computational Linguistics: Posters & Demonstrations*. Association for Computational Linguistics, pages 119–122.

Esther Levin, Roberto Pieraccini, and Wieland Eckert. 1998. Using markov decision process for learning dialogue strategies. In *Acoustics, Speech and Signal Processing, 1998. Proceedings of the 1998 IEEE International Conference on*. IEEE, volume 1, pages 201–204.

Hossam Mossalam, Yannis M. Assael, Diederik M Roijers, and Shimon Whiteson. 2016. Multi-objective deep reinforcement learning. *CoRR* abs/1610.02707. http://arxiv.org/abs/1610.02707.

Alexandros Papangelis, Stefan Ultes, and Yannis Stylianou. 2017. Domain complexity and policy learning in task-oriented dialogue systems. In *Proceedings of the 8th International Workshop On Spoken Dialogue Systems (IWSDS)*.

Matteo Pirotta, Simone Parisi, and Marcello Restelli. 2015. Multi-objective reinforcement learning with continuous pareto frontier approximation. In *Proceedings of the Twenty-Ninth AAAI Conference on Artificial Intelligence*. pages 2928–2934.

Diederik M Roijers, Peter Vamplew, Shimon Whiteson, and Richard Dazeley. 2013. A survey of multi-objective sequential decision-making. *Journal of Artificial Intelligence Research (JAIR)* 48:67–113.

Jost Schatzmann and Steve J. Young. 2009. The hidden agenda user simulation model. *Audio, Speech, and Language Processing, IEEE Transactions on* 17(4):733–747.

David Silver, Aja Huang, Chris J Maddison, Arthur Guez, Laurent Sifre, George Van Den Driessche, Julian Schrittwieser, Ioannis Antonoglou, Veda Panneershelvam, Marc Lanctot, et al. 2016. Mastering the game of go with deep neural networks and tree search. *Nature* 529(7587):484–489.

Pei-Hao Su, M. Gašić, N. Mrkšić, L. Rojas-Barahona, Stefan Ultes, D. Vandyke, T. H. Wen, and S. Young. 2016. On-line active reward learning for policy optimisation in spoken dialogue systems. In *Proceedings of the 54th Annual Meeting of the Association for Computational Linguistics*. Association for Computational Linguistics, pages 2431–2441.

Richard S. Sutton and Andrew G. Barto. 1998. *Reinforcement Learning: An Introduction*. MIT Press, Cambridge, MA, USA, 1st edition. http://portal.acm.org/citation.cfm?id=551283.

Stefan Ultes, Lina M. Rojas-Barahona, Pei-Hao Su, David Vandyke, Dongho Kim, Iñigo Casanueva, Paweł Budzianowski, Nikola Mrkšić, Tsung-Hsien Wen, Milica Gašić, and Steve J. Young. 2017. Pydial: A multi-domain statistical dialogue system toolkit. In *ACL Demo*. Association of Computational Linguistics.

Kristof Van Moffaert, Tim Brys, and Ann Nowé. 2015. Risk-sensitivity through multi-objective reinforcement learning. In *Evolutionary Computation (CEC), 2015 IEEE Congress on*. IEEE, pages 1746–1753.

Marilyn Walker. 2000. An application of reinforcement learning to dialogue strategy selection in a spoken dialogue system for email. *Journal of Artificial Intelligence Research* 12:387–416.

Steve J. Young, Milica Gašić, Blaise Thomson, and Jason D. Williams. 2013. POMDP-based statistical spoken dialog systems: A review. *Proceedings of the IEEE* 101(5):1160–1179.

Automatic Measures to Characterise Verbal Alignment in Human-Agent Interaction

Guillaume Dubuisson Duplessis
Sorbonne Universités,
UPMC Univ Paris 06,
CNRS, ISIR,
75005 Paris, France
`gdubuisson@isir.upmc.fr`

Chloé Clavel
LTCI, Télécom ParisTech,
Université Paris-Saclay
75013 Paris, France
`clavel@enst.fr`

Frédéric Landragin
Lattice Laboratory, CNRS, ENS,
Université de Paris 3,
Université Sorbonne Paris Cité,
PSL Research University
Paris/Montrouge, France
`frederic.landragin@ens.fr`

Abstract

This work aims at characterising verbal alignment processes for improving virtual agent communicative capabilities. We propose computationally inexpensive measures of verbal alignment based on expression repetition in dyadic textual dialogues. Using these measures, we present a contrastive study between Human-Human and Human-Agent dialogues on a negotiation task. We exhibit quantitative differences in the strength and orientation of verbal alignment showing the ability of our approach to characterise important aspects of verbal alignment.

1 Introduction

Convergence of behaviour is an important feature of Human-Human (H-H) interaction that occurs both at low-level (e.g., body postures, accent and speech rate, word choice, repetitions) and at high-level (e.g., mental, emotional, cognitive) (Gallois et al., 2005). In particular, dialogue participants (DPs) automatically align their communicative behaviour at different linguistic levels including the lexical, syntactic and semantic ones (Pickering and Garrod, 2004). A key ability in dialogue is to be able to align (or not) to show a convergent, engaged behaviour or at the opposite a divergent one. Such convergent behaviour may facilitate successful task-oriented dialogues (Nenkova et al., 2008; Friedberg et al., 2012). Our goal is to provide a virtual agent with the ability to detect the alignment behaviour of its human interlocutor, as well as the ability to align with the user to enhance its believability, to increase interaction naturalness and to maintain user's engagement (Yu et al., 2016). In this paper, we aim at providing measures characterising verbal alignment processes based on repetitions between DPs. We propose a framework based on repetition at the lexical level which deals with textual dialogues (e.g., transcripts), along with automatic and generic measures indicating verbal alignment between interlocutors. We offer a study that contrasts H-H and Human-Agent (H-A) dialogues on a negotiation task and show how our proposed measures can be used to quantify verbal alignment. We confirm quantitatively some predictions from previous literature regarding the strength and orientation of verbal alignment in Human-Machine Interaction (Branigan et al., 2010).

Section 2 presents and discusses the related work. Section 3 describes the proposed model and outlines its main features. Next, Section 4 presents the corpus-based experimentation protocol and states the main investigated hypotheses. Then, Section 5 presents the quantitative analysis and discusses the main results. Finally, Section 6 concludes this paper.

2 Related Work

When people are engaged in a dialogue there is evidence that their behaviours tend to converge (Gallois et al., 2005) and automatically align at several levels (Pickering and Garrod, 2004). This includes non-linguistic levels such as facial expressions and body postures as well as linguistic levels such as lexical, syntactic and semantic ones. In particular, alignment theory predicts the existence of patterns of repetition via a priming mechanism stating that "encountering an utterance that activates a particular representation makes it more likely that the person will subsequently produce an utterance that uses that representation" (Pickering and Garrod, 2004). Thus, DPs tend to reuse lexical as well as syntactic structure (Reitter et al., 2006; Ward and Litman, 2007). One consequence

Proceedings of the SIGDIAL 2017 Conference, pages 71–81,
Saarbrücken, Germany, 15-17 August 2017. ©2017 Association for Computational Linguistics

of successful alignment at several levels between DPs is a certain repetitiveness in dialogue and the development of a lexicon of fixed expressions established during dialogue (Pickering and Garrod, 2004). DPs tend to automatically establish and use fixed expressions that become dialogue routines via a process called "routinization". Recent work argues that these patterns of repetition may be specific to task-oriented dialogues and do not generalise to ordinary conversation in H-H interactions (Healey et al., 2014). Here, we are specifically interested in verbal alignment in H-H and H-A task-oriented interactions. We use the term alignment to say that DPs converge at the lexical level by using the same words and expressions (e.g., by employing the expression "that's not gonna work for me" to reject a proposition).

Studies point out evidence that lexical items and syntactic structures used by a system are subsequently adopted by users (Brennan, 1996; Stoyanchev and Stent, 2009; Parent and Eskenazi, 2010; Branigan et al., 2010). (Branigan et al., 2010) argue that linguistic alignment should occur in Human-Machine interaction. In particular, they outline the fact that the strength of alignment may be dependent on the human's belief about the communicative capability of the machine. As such, alignment might be stronger from a human participant who believes that it might improve communication and understanding. In this work, we bring quantitative evidence supporting the fact that human align more with a virtual agent than with another human based on a study contrasting H-H and H-A interactions at the level of repetition of expressions. While previous studies have mainly focused on H-H dialogues, we offer in this work an analysis of verbal alignment in H-A dialogues based on a corpus.

Several studies aim at providing virtual agents with the ability to verbally align with the user in order to improve credibility, naturalness, and also to foster user engagement (Clavel et al., 2016). It involves high-level alignment such as politeness (De Jong et al., 2008) or aligning on appreciations (Campano et al., 2015). Work on convergence in the spoken dialogue system community has mainly focused on lexical entrainment, i.e. the tendency to use the same terms when DPs refer repeatedly to the same objects (Brennan and Clark, 1996). Several entrainment models have been proposed to let the system entrains to user utterances

(e.g., (Brockmann et al., 2005; Buschmeier et al., 2010; Hu et al., 2014; Lopes et al., 2015)). These models are completely or partially rule-based and focus on specific aspects of entrainment. Recent work aims at introducing entrainment in a fully trainable natural language system by exploiting the preceding user utterance (Dušek and Jurcıcek, 2016).

Several metrics have been employed to automatically measure linguistic alignment in written corpora. At the word or token levels, (Nenkova et al., 2008) quantify verbal alignment based on high-frequency words while (Campano et al., 2014) quantify verbal alignment based on vocabulary overlap between DPs. (Healey et al., 2014) compute similarity at the syntax and lexical levels on windows of a fixed number of turns. (Fusaroli and Tyln, 2016) employ (cross-)recurrence quantification analysis to quantify interactive alignment and interpersonal synergy at the lexical, prosodic and speech/pause levels. (Reitter et al., 2006; Ward and Litman, 2007) focus on regression models to study priming effects within a small window of time in single dialogues. (Stenchikova and Stent, 2007) use a frequency-based approach (Church, 2000) to measure adaptation *between* dialogues. In this paper, we propose global and speaker-specific measures based on the automatic construction of the expression lexicon built by the DPs. An originality of our approach is to consider lexical patterns predicted by the routinization process of the interactive alignment theory. These measures rely on efficient algorithms making an online usage in a dialogue system realistic. They indicate both verbal alignment at the level of repetitions and the orientation of verbal alignment between DPs in single dialogues.

3 Model: Expression-based Measures of Verbal Alignment

To address the problem of detecting (possibly overlapping) repetitions between DPs, we propose a framework defining key features of repeated expressions, along with an efficient computational mean of building an expression lexicon.

In this work, we define an *expression* as a surface text pattern at the utterance level that has been produced by both speakers in a dialogue. In other words, it is a contiguous sequence of tokens that appears in at least two utterances produced by two different speakers. An expression may be a single token (e.g., "you", "I"). However, an expression should contain at least one non-punctuation token. Thus, sequences like "?", "!", "," are not expressions. An *instance of an expression* can either be free or constrained in a given utterance[1]. A *free* instance is an instance of an expression that appears in an utterance without being a subexpression of a larger expression. A *constrained* instance is an expression that appears in a turn as a subexpression of a larger expression. The *initiator* of the expression is the interlocutor that first produced an instance of the expression either in a free or constrained form. Lastly, an expression is established as soon as the two following criteria are met: (i) the expression has been produced by both interlocutors (either in a free or constrained form), and (ii) the expression has been produced at least once in a free form. The first turn in which these criteria are all met is the *establishment turn* of the expression. Eventually, the *expression lexicon* of a dialogue is the set of established expressions that appear in this dialogue. Importantly, the expression lexicon contains all expressions that appear in a dialogue at least once in a free form. Expressions that are always constrained (i.e. which instances are always a subpart of a larger expression) are discarded.

Table 1 presents an excerpt of dialogue extracted from the corpus used in this work. In this example, "that's not gonna work for me" is an expression initiated by A in turn 1 and established in turn 4. This expression is free in this excerpt, and it belongs to the expression lexicon. Similarly, "work for" is an expression initiated by A in turn 1 and established in turn 2. It appears in a constrained form in the expression "that's not gonna work for me" in turns 1 and 4, and in a free form in turn 2. It belongs to the expression lexicon. The expression "that's not gonna" occurs in a constrained form in turns 1 and 4, and never occurs in a free form. This expression is never established (contrary to its parent expression "that's not gonna work for me") and thus is not included in the expression lexicon.

The automatic extraction of expressions from a dialogue is an instance of sequential pattern mining (Mooney and Roddick, 2013) applied to textual dialogues. In this work, we follow a similar approach than (Dubuisson Duplessis et al., 2017)

Loc.	Utterance
A_1	well, that's an interesting idea. but no, that's not gonna work for me.
B_2	what will *work for* you?
A_3	*what* do *you* think about me getting two chairs and one plate and *you* getting one chair, one plate, and *the clock*?
B_4	*that's not gonna work for me*
A_5	well which of these items would be your first choice?
B_6	*well* i don't want *the clock*
A_7	oh really?

Table 1: Excerpt of dialogue extracted from the H-A corpus (described in Section 4.1). Expressions are coloured. Established expressions are in italic.

by employing a generalised suffix tree in order to solve the multiple common subsequence problem (MCSP) (Gusfield, 1997) to extract frequent surface text patterns between utterances, and then filtering patterns used by both DPs. Notably, the MCSP is solved in linear time with respect to the number of tokens in a dialogue (Gusfield, 1997).

3.1 Properties of Expressions

An expression has a *frequency* which corresponds to the number of utterances in which the expression appears. For example, the expression "work for" has a frequency of 3 because it appears in utterance 1, 2 and 4. Next, the *size* of an expression is its number of tokens (e.g., expression "the clock" has size 2). Then, the *span* of an expression is the number of utterances between the first production and the last production of this expression in the dialogue (including the first and last utterances). The minimum span is 2, meaning the expression has been established in two adjacent utterances. For instance, the expression "the clock" has a span of 4 because it appears first in utterance 3 and last in utterance 6. We derive the *density* of an expression which is given by the ratio between its frequency and its span. For instance, the density of the expression "well" is 0.5. Eventually, the *priming* of an expression is the number of repetitions of the expression by the initiator before being used by the other interlocutor (either in a free or constrained form). For example, the expression "well" has a priming of 2 because it is repeated by speaker A in utterance 1 and 5 before being established in utterance 6.

---

[1]This terminology is borrowed and adapted from the textual data analysis field and the notion of "repeated segment" (Lebart et al., 1997)

3.2 Measures

Globally, we derive the following measures from the model:

Expression lexicon size (ELS) the number of items in the expression lexicon, i.e. the number of established expressions in the dialogue

Expression variety (EV) the expression lexicon size normalised by the total number of tokens in the dialogue. It is given by: $EV = \frac{ELS}{\#\,Tokens}$. This ratio indicates the variety of the expression lexicon relatively to the length of the dialogue. The higher it is, the more there are different expressions established between DPs.

Expression repetition (ER) the ratio of produced tokens belonging to an instance of an established expression, i.e. the ratio of tokens belonging to a repetition of an expression. It is given by: $ER = \frac{\#\,Tokens\ in\ an\ established\ expr.}{\#\,Tokens}$, $ER \in [0,1]$. The higher the ER is, the more DPs dedicate tokens to the repetition of established expressions.

We also derive the following measures for each speaker S:

Initiated expressions (IE_S) number of expressions initiated by S (and further established) normalised by the expression lexicon size. It is given by: $IE_S = \frac{\#\,Expr.\ initiated\ by\ S}{ELS}$, $\forall\,S, IE_S \in [0,1]$. Note that in a dyadic dialogue involving speaker S_1 and S_2, $IE_{S_1} + IE_{S_1} = 1$.

Expression repetition (ER_S) ratio of produced tokens belonging to an instance of an established expression, i.e. ratio of tokens belonging to a repetition of an expression. It is given by: $ER_S = \frac{\#\,Tokens\ from\ S\ in\ an\ established\ expr.}{\#\,Tokens\ from\ S}$, $\forall\,S, ER_S \in [0,1]$

Eventually, we also consider a measure independent of the model: the *Token Overlap* (TO) which is the ratio of shared tokens between locutor S_1 and locutor S_2 in a dialogue. It is given by: $TO = \frac{\#(Tokens_{S_1} \cap Tokens_{S_2})}{\#(Tokens_{S_1} \cup Tokens_{S_2})}$. The higher is TO, the more vocabulary is shared between S_1 and S_2.

4 Experimentation

Our methodology aims at comparing quantitatively both H-H and H-A task-oriented corpora at the level of the repetition of expressions.

4.1 Negotiation Corpora

The corpus of this study focuses on a negotiation task between two DPs and is detailed in (Gratch et al., 2016). It focuses on a common abstraction of negotiation known as the multi-issue bargaining task (Kelley and Schenitzki, 1972). Here, it requires two interlocutors to find an agreement over the amount of a product each player wishes to buy. Each player receives some payoff for each possible agreement, usually unknown to the other party. Negotiation can take two structures in this scenario. The integrative structure represents a negotiation that can turn out to be a win-win for both players (if they realise through conversation that this is a cooperative negotiation). On the other hand, the distributive negotiation represents a competitive (zero-sum) negotiation where players share the same interests in objects. However, players do not know in advance and often assume a distributive negotiation (i.e. their opponent wants the same thing as them) rather than an integrative negotiation. This corpus can be broken down into two parts: a H-H corpus and a H-A corpus. In both parts, people were given similar instructions, i.e. humans are told that they must negotiate with another player how to divide the contents of a storage locker filled with three classes of valuable items (such as records, lamps or painting).

In the H-H corpus, pairs of people performed one negotiation which was either distributive or integrative in structure. Independently, they were given information in the instructions that suggested the negotiation was integrative or distributive. Note that this condition does not affect the results presented below.

In the H-A corpus, the human participant engaged in two negotiations with two different virtual agents (a male called Brad and a female called Ellie). The first negotiation was a cooperative/integrative negotiation while the second was a competitive/distributive negotiation. The order of interaction with the agents (Brad-Ellie or Ellie-Brad) was randomly chosen. The interaction was framed. Half of the human participants was told they were interacting with an autonomous agent while the other half was told they were interacting with a human wizard (though the agent was always controlled by a wizard). The Woz system controlling virtual agents has been designed to be

Table 2: Figures about the H-H corpus and the H-A corpus. U = Unique, T/Utt.=Tokens per Utterance, med. = median

	H-H	H-A
Dialogue	84	154
Utterance (U)	10319 (7840)	17125 (6109)
...avg (std)	122.8 (84.1)	111.2 (57.5)
Token (U)	79396 (2516)	90479 (1335)
T/Utt.		
avg/med. (std)	7.7/6.0 (7.4)	5.3/4.0 (5.7)
avg (std)	7.7 (7.4)	5.3 (5.7)
min/max	1/66	1/154

as natural as possible (DeVault et al., 2015). It involves low-level functions carried out automatically (such as the selection of gestures and expressions related to speech) and high-level decisions about verbal and non-verbal behaviour carried out by two wizards. Notably, it includes a large number of possible utterances (more than 11,000) along with a specific interface enabling the human operator to rapidly select among those (DeVault et al., 2015). For both virtual human agents, wizards were rather free but followed some guidelines. First, the goal in both negotiations is for the agent to win. Next, in the distributive condition, wizards were requested to be soft, polite and vague trying hard to get the human participant to make the first offer and avoiding revealing what they wanted (unless the human directly asks). In the integrative condition, wizards could share preferences and were not requested to be vague. However, they were requested to try getting the human share first and make the first offer. Table 1 presents an excerpt from a competitive negotiation from the H-A corpus.

Figures about both corpora can be found in Table 2. Globally, dialogues in both corpora contains more than 100 utterances. It shows that H-A dialogues are a bit shorter than H-H dialogues but still comparable. Besides, utterances are shorter in terms of tokens in the H-A dialogues than in the H-H dialogues.

4.2 Randomised Corpora

To investigate hypotheses stated in Section 4.3, we constituted two randomised corpora HH_R and HA_R respectively for the randomised version of the H-H corpus and the H-A corpus. This randomisation process is similar to the ones adopted by various work investigating verbal alignment (e.g., (Ward and Litman, 2007), (Healey et al., 2014), (Fusaroli and Tyln, 2016)). To constitute the HH_R corpus, the following process is performed for each dialogue of the initial corpus: each interlocutor's real turns in sequence are interleaved with turns randomly chosen from the H-H corpus. A similar process is followed for the HA_R corpus with the exception that each human turn is substituted by a random human turns from the H-A corpus when keeping the sequence of wizard turns; while each wizard turn is substituted by a random wizard turns from the H-A corpus when keeping the sequence of human turns. In all, two dialogues are generated by these processes for each original H-H/A dialogue (one for each locutor). These surrogate corpora lack the coherence of dialogues in the H-H and H-A corpora. Indeed, utterances are no longer in their original relationship with their response utterances. We thus expect to find reduced verbal alignment at the level of expressions in these corpora.

4.3 Hypotheses

4.3.1 "Above Chance" Hypotheses

Our first hypothesis is that DPs should verbally align at the level of expressions in both the H-H corpus and the H-A corpus more than would be expected by chance. This hypothesis can be expressed in the following way:

routinization DPs should constitute a richer expression lexicon than they would by chance (this should be indicated by the EV measure)

repetition DPs should repeat expressions more often than chance (this should be indicated by the ER and the TO measures)

4.3.2 H-H VS H-A Hypotheses

Following Branigan et al's hypothesis (Branigan et al., 2010), we should expect more verbal alignment at the level of expressions in the H-A corpus than in the H-H corpus. Besides, we should expect more verbal alignment from the human participant than from the agent. Indeed, the human participant both has the ability to verbally align (contrary to the agent) and may be influenced by beliefs about the communicative limitations of the agent. This hypothesis can be expressed in the following way:

routinization DPs should constitute a richer expression lexicon in the H-A corpus than in the H-H corpus (this should be indicated by the EV measure)

repetition DPs should dedicate more tokens to the repetition of established expressions in the H-A corpus than in the H-H corpus (this should be indicated by the ER and the TO measures)

orientation the human participant should repeat more expressions initiated by the agent than the other way around (this should be indicated by the IE_S and the ER_S measures)

4.3.3 H-A-specific Hypotheses

In this study, we also consider conditions that affects only the H-A corpus. First, interactions with the virtual agent were randomly "framed" meaning that, prior interactions, the human participant was either told that the agent was controlled by a human operator (72 dialogues) or that it was autonomous (82 dialogues). This condition affects the mediated component of verbal alignment i.e. the beliefs of the human participant about the communicative capabilities of the agent (e.g., in terms of understanding). This leads us to the following hypothesis:

framing framing should impact verbal alignment in the routinization, repetition and orientation aspects.

More specifically, "human" framing should lead to a more "human-like verbal alignment" while "agent" framing should lead to a "HMI-like verbal alignment" (Branigan et al., 2010).

Moreover, the human participants interacted with two versions of the virtual agent. One was Ellie, a female agent, while the other was Brad, a male agent. Interaction order was random (Brad-Ellie or Ellie-Brad). This condition leads us to the following hypothesis:

gender gender matching (Male-Male or Female-Female) or unmatching (Male-Female, Female-Male) should not impact verbal alignment

Lastly, interactions involved two types of negotiations (integrative and distributive). We study the impact of the negotiation type on the verbal alignment at the level of expressions.

5 Quantitative Analysis and Results

5.1 Comparisons to the Surrogate Corpora

We compare the H-H and H-A corpora of real interactions to the surrogate HH_R and HA_R corpora to ensure that established expressions in the dialogues are actually due to the coherent sequence of utterances and are not incidental.

We investigated whether DPs in the H-H corpus verbally align at the level of expressions more than would be expected by chance by comparing it to the HH_R corpus (following hypotheses stated in Section 4.3.1). First, the expression variety is significantly higher for the H-H corpus (mean=0.118, std=0.023) than for the HH_R corpus (mean=0.110, std=0.015). Statistical difference is checked by a Wilcoxon rank sum test ($U = 8951$, $p = 0.00051 < 0.001$, $r = 0.22$)[2]. This indicates that H-H interactions lead to a richer expression lexicon. However, the expression repetition is not significantly different ($p = 0.3446$) between the H-H corpus (mean=0.436, std=0.107) and the HH_R corpus (mean=0.420, std=0.108). This means that the amount of tokens dedicated to the repetition of expressions is similar between the H-H corpus and the HH_R corpus. An explanation of this may be that the dialogues happen in a closed domain on a specific task (negotiations of a set of objects) and thus in a constrained vocabulary. This inevitably leads random dialogues to include repetitions though in a lesser variety. This is confirmed by the token overlap that is significantly higher for the H-H corpus (mean=0.316, std=0.073) than for the HH_R corpus (mean=0.276, std=0.058) ($U = 9468.5$, $p = 9.781 \times 10^{-6} < 0.001$, $r = 0.28$). DPs share a richer vocabulary than what would happen by chance.

We performed a similar analysis by comparing the H-A corpus and the HA_R corpus. It turns out that both the expression lexicon variety and the expression repetition are significantly higher in the H-A corpus than in the HA_R corpus. Indeed, the expression variety is significantly higher ($U = 30126$, $p = 2.155 \times 10^{-6} < 0.001$, $r = 0.22$) for the H-A corpus (mean=0.134, std=0.022) than for the HA_R corpus (mean=0.124, std=0.020). Besides, the expression repetition is significantly higher ($U = 28124$, $p = 0.0011 < 0.01$, $r = 0.15$) for the H-A corpus (mean=0.416, std=0.086) than for the HA_R corpus (mean=0.386, std=0.088). This is comforted by the fact that the token overlap is significantly higher ($U = 30164$, $p = 1.875 \times 10^{-6} < 0.001$, $r = 0.22$) for the H-A corpus (mean=0.322, std=0.06) than for the HA_R corpus (mean=0.293, std=0.06).

All in all, it turns out that both H-H and H-A di-

---

[2]For each test, we report the test statistics (U/W), the p-value (p) and the effect size (r).

alogues constitute a richer expression lexicon than they would by chance (routinization hypothesis). As for the repetition hypothesis, DPs clearly repeat expressions more often than chance in the H-A corpus. However, repetition in the H-H corpus is comparable to what would happen by chance in closed domain task-oriented dialogues. All things considered, our indicators show that both corpora tends to verbally align at the level of shared expressions more than they would by chance.

5.2 Differences between H-H/A Interactions

We compare verbal alignment at the expression level between the H-H corpus and the H-A corpus globally, per speaker and at the lexicon level.

5.2.1 Global Interaction Analysis

It turns out that the expression variety is significantly lower for the H-H corpus (mean=0.118, std=0.023) than for the H-A corpus (mean=0.134, std=0.022). This is checked via a Wilcoxon rank sum test ($U = 4056.5, p = 2.035 \times 10^{-6} < 0.001$, $r = 0.31$). This indicates that DPs constitute a richer expression lexicon in the H-A corpus than in the H-H corpus. However, we noticed that there is no significant difference between the H-H corpus and the H-A corpus in terms of expression repetition and token overlap. Indeed, the expression repetition is not significantly different between the H-H corpus (mean=0.436, std=0.107) and the H-A corpus (mean=0.416, std=0.086) by a Wilcoxon rank sum test ($p = 0.1261$). Besides, the token overlap is not significantly different between the H-H corpus (mean=0.316, std=0.073) and the H-A corpus (mean=0.322, std=0.06) by a similar test ($p = 0.6618$).

H-A interactions lead to a richer expression lexicon than the H-H interactions (routinization hypothesis). This indicates more verbal alignment at the level of shared expressions in H-A dialogues. However, DPs do not dedicate more tokens to the repetition of established expressions in the H-A corpus than in the H-H corpus (repetition hyp.).

5.2.2 Speaker Perspective Analysis

We investigated verbal alignment at the level of expressions by having a closer look at each speaker in a dialogue in terms of initiated expressions (IE) and expression repetition (ER). In the H-H corpus, both speakers play a symmetrical role at the level of expressions. First, they initiate a similar amount of expressions. Indeed, IE_{S_1} and

the IE_{S_2} are not significantly different (Wilcoxon signed rank test, $p = 0.5978$). Next, they dedicate the same amount of tokens to the repetition of expressions (see Figure 1). In fact, ER_{S_1} and the ER_{S_2} are not significantly different ($p = 0.9875$).

On the contrary, the H-A corpus shows an asymmetrical role at the level of expressions between the Woz and the human participant. First, the Woz initiates more expressions than the human participant. Indeed, $\mathrm{IE}_{\mathrm{Woz}}$ (mean=0.596, std=0.116) is significantly higher than IE_{H} (mean=0.404, std=0.116) (Wilcoxon signed rank test, $W = 10161, p < 2.2 \times 10^{-16} < 0.001, r = 0.87$). Then, the human participant dedicates more tokens to the repetition of an established expression than the Woz (see Figure 1). As a matter of fact, $\mathrm{ER}_{\mathrm{Woz}}$ (mean=0.347, std=0.104) is significantly lower than ER_{H} (mean=0.492, std=0.086) (Wilcoxon signed rank test, $W = 545, p < 2.2 \times 10^{-16} < 0.001, r = 0.87$). Notably, this asymmetry does not appear when considering the number of tokens produced by each speaker, i.e. the Woz and the human tend to produce the same amount of tokens. Indeed, there is not a significant difference in the proportion of tokens produced by the Woz (mean=0.483, std=0.134) and by the human participant (mean=0.517, std=0.134) (Wilcoxon signed rank test, $p = 0.08067$). Besides, a closer look at the shared vocabulary shows that there is not a significant difference in the proportion of vocabulary shared by the Woz (mean=0.4853, std=0.116) and by the human participant (mean=0.515, std=0.093)[3] (Wilcoxon signed rank test, $p = 0.08029$). That is, globally, the Woz does not share more of its vocabulary than the human participants, and conversely.

It turns out that verbal alignment at the level of shared expressions is symmetrical in the H-H corpus. On the contrary, it is asymmetrical in the H-A corpus (orientation hypothesis) where it indicates that the human participant verbally align more by (i) adopting more Woz-initiated expressions (than the Woz adopting Human-initiated expressions), and (ii) dedicating more tokens to the repetition of established expressions.

5.2.3 Expression Lexicon Analysis

Eventually, we took a closer look at the expression lexicon produced in the H-H corpus and the

---

[3]Relative shared vocabulary for S_1 is computed as follow:
$$\mathrm{SV}_{S_1} = \frac{\#(\mathrm{Tokens}_{S_1} \cap \mathrm{Tokens}_{S_2})}{\#(\mathrm{Tokens}_{S_1})}$$

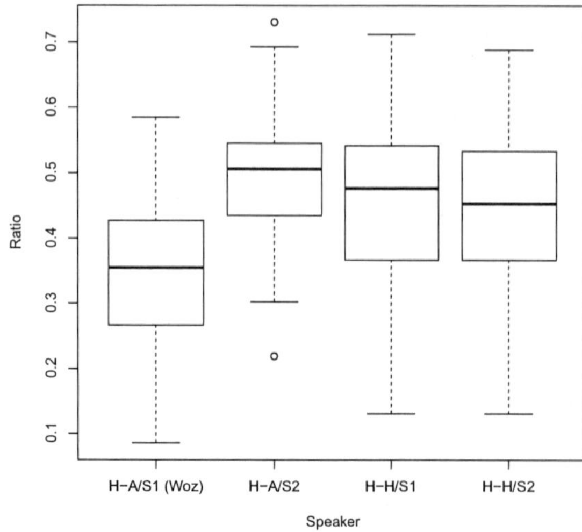

Figure 1: Comparison of the H-H/A corpora for ER$_S$. Difference is significant for H-A ($p <$ 0.001), not for H-H (cf. Section 5.2.2).

H-A corpus. Regarding the size in tokens of the expressions, there is no significant difference between the two corpora (Wilcoxon rank sum test, $p = 0.9897$). The majority of expressions contains less than 3 tokens. Around 70% of expressions are 1-token expressions, 20% are 2-token expressions, 5% are 3-token expressions, and the other 5% are 4-token and more expressions.

Considering the priming of an expression (i.e. the number of repetitions of the expression by the initiator before being used by the other interlocutor), most expressions have a priming of less than 3 repetitions in both corpora. However, there is a significant difference between the two corpora (Wilcoxon rank sum test, $U = 57185000$, $p < 2.2 \times 10^{-16} < 0.001$). The most striking one is about the proportion of 1-repetition priming expressions. 63% of expressions have a 1-repetition priming in the H-H corpus while it is higher in the H-A corpus at 72%. 20% of expressions have a 2-repetition priming in the H-H corpus while it is 17% in the H-A corpus. Lastly, 8% of the H-H expressions have a 3-repetition priming while it reaches 6% for the H-A corpus. The main reason of the difference at the priming level may be found in the functions that serve expression repetition in the corpora. This is supported by the study of the density of expressions (i.e. their ratio frequency/span) in both corpora. Expressions in the H-A corpus are denser (mean=0.174, std=0.238) than expressions in the H-H corpus

(mean=0.146, std=0.206). This difference is significant (Wilcoxon rank sum test, $U = 45419000$, $p < 2.2 \times 10^{-16} < 0.001$). Expressions in the H-A corpus tend to occur more frequently between their first and last appearance in the dialogue than in the H-H corpus.

5.3 Other Conditions in Human-Agent Interactions

We studied the impact of the "human operator" framing against the "AI" framing on the verbal alignment at the level of expressions. It turns out there is no difference in the variety of the expression lexicon between the two framing modes. Indeed, the expression variety is not significantly different between "human operator" framing (mean=0.131, std=0.023) and the "AI" framing (mean=0.136, std=0.021) (Wilcoxon rank sum test, $p = 0.1338$). Study about repetition does not reveal any effect from the framing condition. As a matter of fact, the expression repetition is not significantly different between "human operator" framing (mean=0.423, std=0.087) and "AI" framing (mean=0.409, std=0.085) ($p = 0.2915$). Similarly, no effect is found at the token overlap. Besides, analyses on the expression initiation (EI) and the expression repetition at the speaker level (ER$_S$) yield the same results than the entire H-A corpus i.e. the verbal alignment is asymmetrical between the agent and the human. Contrary to our hypothesis, framing does not quantitatively impact verbal alignment at the level of expressions.

A similar analysis at the gender mismatch or match between the human participant and the agent (Brad or Ellie) does not reveal any difference at the expression variety, expression repetition (globally or by speaker), token overlap, and expression initiation. These analyses confirm our hypothesis that gender does not quantitatively impact verbal alignment at the level of expressions in our H-A corpus.

It turns out that some significant differences exist between the two types of negotiation (integrative and distributive) in the H-A corpus. First, distributive negotiation leads to longer dialogues in number of utterances (mean=144.3, std=58.757) than integrative negotiation (mean=82.5, std=41.09). Despite this difference in dialogue length, the expression variety is similar between the integrative negotiations (mean=0.133, std=0.022) and the distributive ones (mean=0.133, std=0.020) (Wilcoxon signed rank test, $p = 0.9847$). However, a major difference can be observed at the expression repetition which is significantly higher for the distributive negotiations (mean=0.456, std=0.073) than for the integrative negotiations (mean=0.375, std=0.084) ($W = 142$, $p = 7.665 \times 10^{-10} < 0.001$, $r = 0.87$). All in all, this indicates that participants align more at the level of expressions in competitive negotiations than in cooperative ones. This may be due to the fact that they need to verbally align more on (counter-)propositions in competitive negotiations.

5.4 Discussion

We have presented automatic and generic measures of verbal alignment based on an expression framework focusing on repetition between DPs at the level of surface of text utterances. This framework mainly takes into account lexical cues by building a lexicon of shared expressions emerging during dialogue, but also syntactic cues to the extent of expressions (other work on conversations report a strong correlation between lexical and syntactic cues regarding alignment (Healey et al., 2014)). The proposed measures make it possible to quantify the routinization process (via EV), the degree of repetition between DPs (via ER), and the orientation of the verbal alignment (via IE_S and ER_S) at the level of expressions. Besides, these measures are based on efficient algorithms (Gusfield, 1997) that make it realistic to envision an on-line usage in a dialogue system. They have made it possible to check quantitatively that verbal alignment was real in both H-H and H-A task-oriented interactions (i.e. it is not likely to happen randomly). Next, they have helped contrasting quantitatively H-H interactions from H-A interactions, showing that verbal alignment was symmetrical in H-H interactions while being asymmetrical in H-A (comforting previous hypotheses (Branigan et al., 2010)). Finally, we have observed that H-A verbal alignment was independent of the gender of the agent (male or female) and of the framing of the experiment (human operator VS AI). However, the proposed measures indicate more verbal alignment in competitive negotiations than in cooperative ones that may be due to the need to reach more agreements during competitive negotiations.

Nevertheless, this work is limited to automatically quantifying repetitions at the lexical level. Hence, it does not take into account other aspects of alignment such as linguistic style (Niederhoffer and Pennebaker, 2002) or higher level such as concepts (Brennan and Clark, 1996). However, the alignment theory proposes that alignment "percolates" between levels. As such, alignment at the level of repetition of expressions indicate alignment at other levels to some extent. Besides, this work does not consider the functions behind repetition such as conveying the reception of a message, appraising a proposal, introducing a disagreement, complaining (Tannen, 2007; Schenkein, 1980). A functional analysis could explain more in depth the differences between the H-H and the H-A corpora. Lastly, an interesting perspective would be to confirm these results on another corpora involving comparable H-H and H-A dialogues.

6 Conclusion and Future Work

This paper has presented a framework based on expression repetition at the surface text of dialogue utterances involving automatic and computationally inexpensive measures. These measures make it possible to quantitatively characterise the strength and orientation of verbal alignment between DPs in a task-oriented dialogue. A promising perspective of this work lies in the exploitation of these measures to adapt and align the verbal communicative behaviour of a virtual agent.

Acknowledgments

This work was supported by the European project H2020 ARIA-VALUSPA and the French ANR project IMPRESSIONS (ANR-15-CE23-0023). We warmly thank Jonathan Gratch and David DeVault for sharing the negotiation corpora, and Catherine Pelachaud for valuable and enriching discussions. We would like to thank the anonymous reviewers for their valuable comments and suggestions.

References

Holly P Branigan, Martin J Pickering, Jamie Pearson, and Janet F McLean. 2010. Linguistic alignment between people and computers. *Journal of Pragmatics* 42(9):2355–2368.

Susan E Brennan. 1996. Lexical entrainment in spontaneous dialog. *Proceedings of International Symposium on Spoken Dialogue (ISSD)* 96:41–44.

Susan E Brennan and Herbert H Clark. 1996. Conceptual pacts and lexical choice in conversation. *Journal of Experimental Psychology: Learning, Memory, and Cognition* 22(6):1482.

Carsten Brockmann, Amy Isard, Jon Oberlander, and Michael White. 2005. Modelling alignment for affective dialogue. In *Workshop on adapting the interaction style to affective factors at the 10th international conference on user modeling (UM-05)*.

Hendrik Buschmeier, Kirsten Bergmann, and Stefan Kopp. 2010. Modelling and evaluation of lexical and syntactic alignment with a priming-based microplanner. In *Empirical Methods in Natural Language Generation*, Springer, pages 85–104.

Sabrina Campano, Jessica Durand, and Chloé Clavel. 2014. Comparative analysis of verbal alignment in human-human and human-agent interactions. In *International Conference on Language Resources and Evaluation (LREC)*. pages 4415–4422.

Sabrina Campano, Caroline Langlet, Nadine Glas, Chloé Clavel, and Catherine Pelachaud. 2015. An eca expressing appreciations. In *International Conference on Affective Computing and Intelligent Interaction (ACII)*. IEEE, pages 962–967.

Kenneth W Church. 2000. Empirical estimates of adaptation: the chance of two noriegas is closer to p/2 than p 2. In *Proceedings of the 18th conference on Computational Linguistics*. Association for Computational Linguistics, volume 1, pages 180–186.

Chloé Clavel, Angelo Cafaro, Sabrina Campano, and Catherine Pelachaud. 2016. Fostering user engagement in face-to-face human-agent interactions: a survey. In *Toward Robotic Socially Believable Behaving Systems-Volume II*, Springer, pages 93–120.

Markus De Jong, Mariët Theune, and Dennis Hofs. 2008. Politeness and alignment in dialogues with a virtual guide. In *Proceedings of the 7th international joint conference on Autonomous agents and multiagent systems (AAMAS)*. International Foundation for Autonomous Agents and Multiagent Systems, pages 207–214.

David DeVault, Johnathan Mell, and Jonathan Gratch. 2015. Toward natural turn-taking in a virtual human negotiation agent. In *AAAI Spring Symposium on Turn-taking and Coordination in Human-Machine Interaction. AAAI Press, Stanford, CA*.

Guillaume Dubuisson Duplessis, Franck Charras, Vincent Letard, Anne-Laure Ligozat, and Sophie Rosset. 2017. Utterance Retrieval based on Recurrent Surface Text Patterns. In *39th European Conference on Information Retrieval (ECIR)*. Aberdeen, United Kingdom, pages 199–211.

Ondrej Dušek and Filip Jurcıcek. 2016. A context-aware natural language generator for dialogue systems. In *17th Annual Meeting of the Special Interest Group on Discourse and Dialogue (SIGDIAL)*. pages 185–190.

Heather Friedberg, Diane Litman, and Susannah BF Paletz. 2012. Lexical entrainment and success in student engineering groups. In *Spoken Language Technology Workshop (SLT)*. IEEE, pages 404–409.

Riccardo Fusaroli and Kristian Tyln. 2016. Investigating conversational dynamics: Interactive alignment, interpersonal synergy, and collective task performance. *Cognitive Science* 40(1):145–171.

Cindy Gallois, Tania Ogay, and Howard H. Giles. 2005. Communication accommodation theory: A look back and a look ahead. *W. Gudykunst (red.): Theorizing about intercultural communication. Thousand Oaks, CA: Sage* pages 121–148.

Jonathan Gratch, David DeVault, and Gale Lucas. 2016. The benefits of virtual humans for teaching negotiation. In *International Conference on Intelligent Virtual Agents (IVA)*. Springer, pages 283–294.

Dan Gusfield. 1997. *Algorithms on Strings, Trees and Sequences*. Cambridge University Press, Cambridge, UK.

Patrick GT Healey, Matthew Purver, and Christine Howes. 2014. Divergence in dialogue. *PloS one* 9(6):e98598.

Zhichao Hu, Gabrielle Halberg, Carolynn R Jimenez, and Marilyn A Walker. 2014. Entrainment in pedestrian direction giving: How many kinds of entrainment? In *In Proceedings of 5th International Workshop on Spoken Dialog System (IWSDS)*. Citeseer.

Harold H Kelley and Donald P Schenitzki. 1972. Bargaining. *Experimental Social Psychology. New York: Holt, Rinehart, and Winston* pages 298–337.

Ludovic Lebart, André Salem, and Lisette Berry. 1997. *Exploring textual data*, volume 4. Springer Science & Business Media.

José Lopes, Maxine Eskenazi, and Isabel Trancoso. 2015. From rule-based to data-driven lexical entrainment models in spoken dialog systems. *Computer Speech & Language* 31(1):87–112.

Carl H. Mooney and John F. Roddick. 2013. Sequential pattern mining – approaches and algorithms. *ACM Computing Surveys* 45(2):19:1–19:39.

Ani Nenkova, Agustin Gravano, and Julia Hirschberg. 2008. High frequency word entrainment in spoken dialogue. In *Proceedings of the 46th annual meeting of the association for computational linguistics on human language technologies (ACL-HLT): Short papers*. Association for Computational Linguistics, pages 169–172.

Kate G Niederhoffer and James W Pennebaker. 2002. Linguistic style matching in social interaction. *Journal of Language and Social Psychology* 21(4):337–360.

Gabriel Parent and Maxine Eskenazi. 2010. Lexical entrainment of real users in the let's go spoken dialog system. In *INTERSPEECH*. pages 3018–3021.

Martin J. Pickering and Simon Garrod. 2004. Toward a mechanistic psychology of dialogue. *Behavioral and brain sciences* 27(02):169–190.

David Reitter, Frank Keller, and Johanna D Moore. 2006. Computational modelling of structural priming in dialogue. In *Proceedings of the Human Language Technology Conference of the North American Chapter of the ACL (NAACL-HLT): Short Papers*. Association for Computational Linguistics, pages 121–124.

James Schenkein. 1980. A taxonomy for repeating action sequences in natural conversation. *Language production* 1:21–47.

Svetlana Stenchikova and Amanda Stent. 2007. Measuring adaptation between dialogs. In *8th Annual Meeting of the Special Interest Group on Discourse and Dialogue (SIGDIAL)*.

Svetlana Stoyanchev and Amanda Stent. 2009. Lexical and syntactic priming and their impact in deployed spoken dialog systems. In *Proceedings of the Human Language Technology Conference of the North American Chapter of the ACL (NAACL-HLT): Short Papers*. Association for Computational Linguistics, pages 189–192.

Deborah Tannen. 2007. *Talking voices: Repetition, dialogue, and imagery in conversational discourse*, volume 26. Cambridge University Press.

Arthur Ward and Diane J Litman. 2007. Automatically measuring lexical and acoustic/prosodic convergence in tutorial dialog corpora. In *Speech and Language Technology in Education (SLaTE2007)*. pages 57–60.

Zhou Yu, Leah Nicolich-Henkin, Alan W Black, and Alex I Rudnicky. 2016. A wizard-of-oz study on a non-task-oriented dialog systems that reacts to user engagement. In *17th Annual Meeting of the Special Interest Group on Discourse and Dialogue (SIGDIAL)*. pages 55–63.

Demonstration of interactive teaching for end-to-end dialog control with hybrid code networks

Jason D. Williams
Microsoft Research
jason.williams@microsoft.com

Lars Liden
Microsoft
lars.liden@microsoft.edu

Abstract

This is a demonstration of interactive teaching for practical end-to-end dialog systems driven by a recurrent neural network. In this approach, a developer teaches the network by interacting with the system and providing on-the-spot corrections. Once a system is deployed, a developer can also correct mistakes in logged dialogs. This demonstration shows both of these teaching methods applied to dialog systems in three domains: pizza ordering, restaurant information, and weather forecasts.

1 Introduction

Whereas traditional dialog systems consist of a pipeline of components such as intent detection, state tracking, and action selection, an end-to-end dialog system is driven by a machine learning model which takes observable dialog history as input, and directly outputs a distribution over dialog actions. The benefit of this approach is that intermediate quantities such as intent or dialog state do not need to be labeled – rather, learning can be done directly on example dialogs.

In practice, purely end-to-end methods can require large amounts of data to learn seemingly simple behaviors, such as sorting database results. This is problematic because when building a new dialog system, typically no in-domain dialog data exists, so data efficiency is crucial. Moreover, machine-learned models alone cannot guarantee practical constraints are followed – for example a bank would require that a user must be logged in before they are allowed to transfer funds. For these reasons, in past work we introduced *Hybrid Code Networks* (HCN) (Williams et al., 2017). HCNs make end-to-end learning of task-oriented dialog systems practical by combining a recurrent neural network (RNN) with domain-specific software provided by the developer; domain-specific action templates; and a conventional entity extraction module for identifying entity mentions in text. Experiments on a public corpus show that HCNs can substantially reduce the number of training dialogs required compared to purely end-to-end learning methods, and also outperform purely rule-based systems.

This demonstration shows a practical implementation of HCNs, as a web service for building task-oriented dialog systems. Once the developer has provided their domain-specific software, they can add training dialogs in several ways. First, the developer can simply upload dialogs to the training set. Second, the developer can *interactively teach* the HCN, and make on-the-spot corrections. Finally, as the HCN interacts with end-users, the developer can inspect logged dialogs, make corrections if needed, and add the dialogs to the training set.

2 Dialog learning platform

The practical operation of the HCN is shown in Figure 1, where the left-hand block in white shows an end-user messaging client, the center block in blue shows a web service implemented by the system developer that hosts domain-specific logic, and the right-hand block in green is the HCN web service. A software development kit (SDK) facilitates using the HCN web service.

When interacting with end users, the process begins when the end user provides input text, such as "What's the 5 day forecast for Seattle?", shown as item 1 in Figure 1. This text can be typed or output by a standard speech recognizer. This text is passed to the developer's web service, which in turn calls the HCN service to perform entity ex-

Proceedings of the SIGDIAL 2017 Conference, pages 82–85,
Saarbrücken, Germany, 15-17 August 2017. ©2017 Association for Computational Linguistics

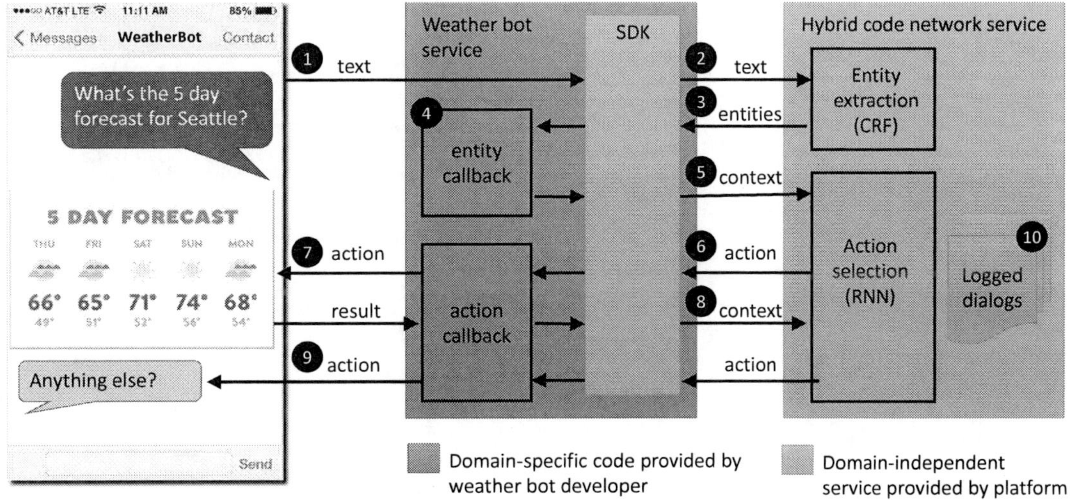

Figure 1: Development platform for interactive dialog learning. Entity extraction is done with Conditional Random Fields (CRFs). See text for full details.

traction (item 2). The HCN service then returns entity mentions detected in text, such as "location=Seattle" (3). Domain-specific code on the developer's service then resolves entity mentions to a canonical form, such as a latitude/longitude pair, and to store entities for use in later turns in the dialog (4). The developer's code then calls the HCN service again, optionally passing in *context* which can include which entities have been recognized so far in the dialog, as well as an action mask that limits which action templates are available at the current step (5).

The HCN service returns a distribution over all un-masked action templates, and the developer code executes the highest-ranked action (6). If this action template is an API call – such as displaying rich content to the user, executing a transaction in a database, or raising a robot's arm – that API is invoked (7), and the HCN service is called again to choose the next action. If the API call returns context features, those can be passed to the HCN service (8). If the action template is text, the developer's code can substitute in entity values such as a weather forecast, and the text is rendered to the end user (9). The cycle then repeats.

Dialogs conducted with users are logged by the HCN service, and can later be reviewed and corrected by the system developer through a web user interface (10). Also, the cycle can be augmented to support interactive teaching. These aspects are described in the next section.

3   Illustrative interactions

When creating a new dialog system, typically no in-domain data exists. To address this, the dialog learning platform supports *interactive teaching*. In interactive teaching, the developer alternates between the role of the end user, and the role of the teacher. The operational loop shown in Figure 1 is modified so that results of entity extraction and action selection can be corrected before continuing.

Figure 4 shows an example of interactive teaching for pizza ordering. The developer – playing the part of the user – enters "medium pizza with olives". The current entity extraction model finds entity mentions for the $pizza and $size entities, but not the "olive" $topping. So, the developer corrects this by adding a corrected entity label, and this corrected label is used going forward. The interface then displays the contents of the developer-defined state, and provides a list of actions, each with their score under the current RNN model. In this example, all but one of the actions are shown as "disqualified", meaning that the action mask prohibits them. For example, the action "Would you like a Small, Medium, or Large $crust pizza ..." is masked because the pizza size is already known. The developer enters the index of the action to take ("1") and the dialog continues. At this point, the developer could have alternatively entered a new action – for example, by typing "So you want $toppings, is that right?". As each correction is made, the CRF and RNN models are re-

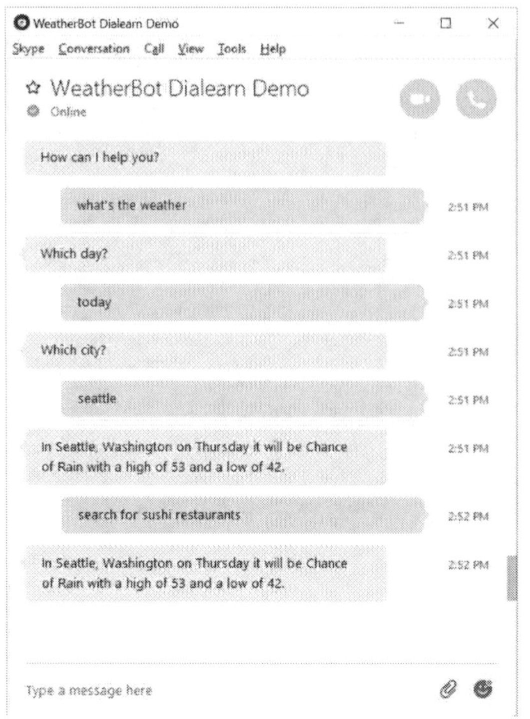

Figure 2: Example interaction with an end user. Note the system mistake after the user enters "search for sushi restaurants".

trained.

Once a rudimentary model is in place, end-users can start using the system. An example dialog with an end-user is shown in Figure 2, which shows an error at the last system turn. Figure 3 shows how this dialog appears to the developer, and how a correction can be made. Each system utterance is shown in a drop-down box. If the developer identifies a turn where the system output the wrong action, the developer can select the correct action from the drop-down. When an action which differs from the action in the log is selected, the remainder of the dialog is discarded, since it is no longer known how the user would have responded. If none of the actions is appropriate, the developer can choose "new action...", and enter a new action into a provided text box. When the dialog has been corrected, the developer clicks on "submit", which saves the labeled dialog to the training set, re-trains the model, and re-deploys the new model. In the example in Figure 3, the user's fourth input was "search for sushi

Figure 3: Example of off-line dialog correction, showing the dialog collected in Figure 2. After the user says "search for sushi restaurants", the developer changed the action "$forecast" to "new action..." and typed in "Sorry, I can't help with that".

restaurants", and the system had answered with a weather forecast. The developer changed this response to "new action..." and typed in the new action "Sorry, I can't help with that".

In the demonstration, we have three working dialog systems available, for pizza ordering, restaurant information, and weather forecasts. The demonstration shows applying the two interactive methods described above to each of these three domains.

References

Jason D Williams, Kavosh Asadi, and Geoffrey Zweig. 2017. Hybrid code networks: practical and efficient end-to-end dialog control with supervised and reinforcement learning. In *Proc ACL, Vancouver*.

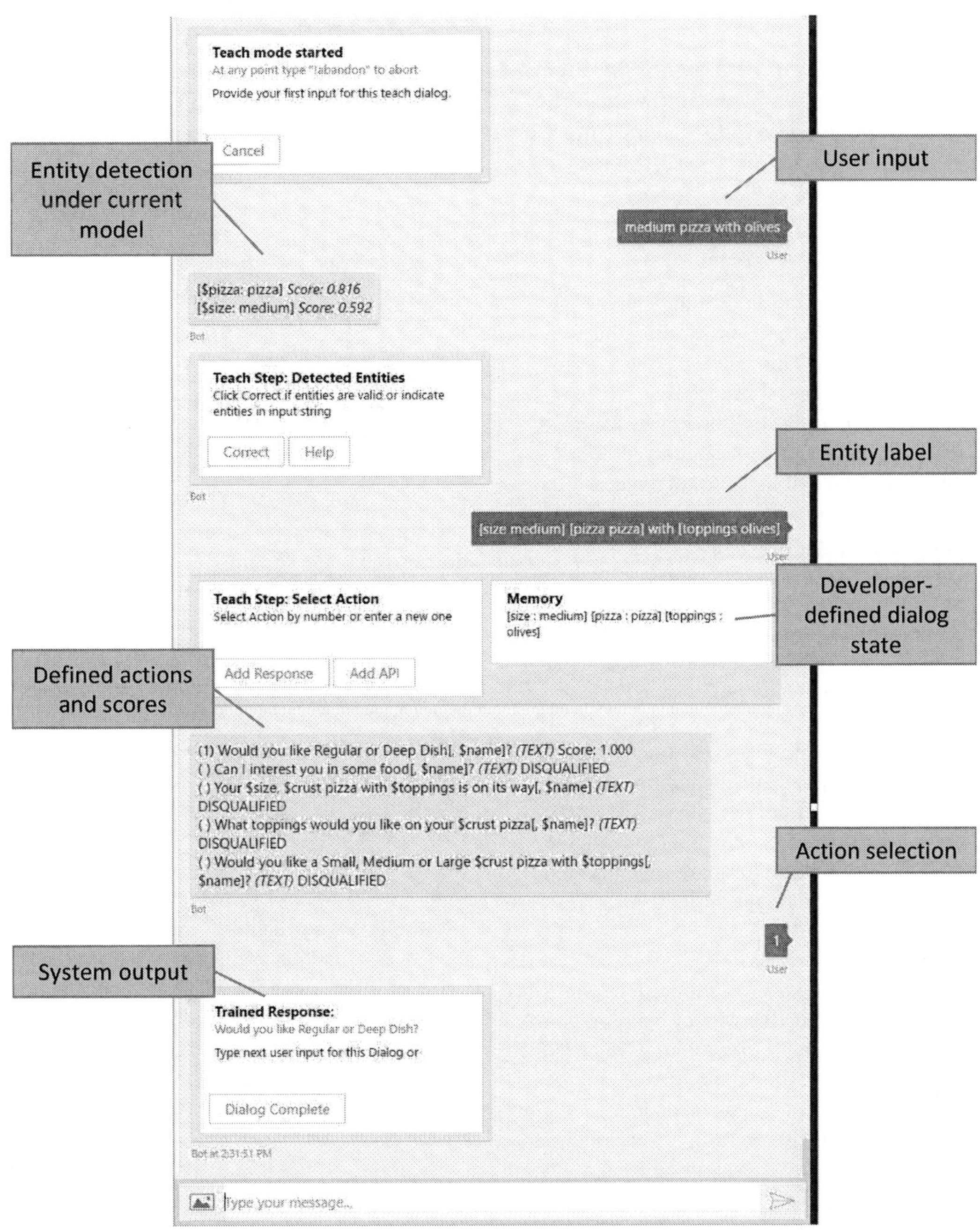

Figure 4: Example of interactive dialog teaching. The developer's input is in blue boxes on the right side, and the system's responses are in grey and white boxes on the left side. The developer alternates between playing the role of an end user, and providing corrective input.

Sub-domain Modelling for Dialogue Management
with Hierarchical Reinforcement Learning

Paweł Budzianowski, Stefan Ultes, Pei-Hao Su, Nikola Mrkšić,
Tsung-Hsien Wen, Iñigo Casanueva, Lina Rojas-Barahona and Milica Gašić
Cambridge University, Engineering Department, Trumpington Street, Cambridge, UK
`{pfb30,mg436}@cam.ac.uk`

Abstract

Human conversation is inherently complex, often spanning many different topics/domains. This makes policy learning for dialogue systems very challenging. Standard flat reinforcement learning methods do not provide an efficient framework for modelling such dialogues. In this paper, we focus on the under-explored problem of multi-domain dialogue management. First, we propose a new method for hierarchical reinforcement learning using the *option* framework. Next, we show that the proposed architecture learns faster and arrives at a better policy than the existing flat ones do. Moreover, we show how pretrained policies can be adapted to more complex systems with an additional set of new actions. In doing that, we show that our approach has the potential to facilitate policy optimisation for more sophisticated multi-domain dialogue systems.

1 Introduction

The statistical approach to dialogue modelling has proven to be an effective way of building conversational agents capable of providing required information to the user (Williams and Young, 2007; Young et al., 2013). Spoken dialogue systems (SDS) usually consist of various statistical components, dialogue management being the central one. Optimising dialogue management can be seen as a planning problem and is normally tackled using reinforcement learning (RL). Many approaches to policy management over single domains have been proposed over the last years with ability to learn from scratch (Fatemi et al., 2016; Gašić and Young, 2014; Su et al., 2016; Williams and Zweig, 2016).

The goal of this work is to propose a coherent framework for a system capable of managing conversations over multiple dialogue domains. Recently, a number of frameworks were proposed for handling multi-domain dialogue as multiple independent single-domain sub-dialogues (Lison, 2011; Wang et al., 2014; Mrkšić et al., 2015; Gašić et al., 2015). Cuayáhuitl et al. (2016) proposed a network of deep Q-networks with an SVM classifier for *domain selection*. However, such frameworks do not scale to modelling complex conversations over large state/action spaces, as they do not facilitate conditional training over multiple domains. This inhibits their performance, as domains often share sub-tasks where decisions in one domain influence learning in the other ones.

In this paper, we apply *hierarchical reinforcement learning* (HRL) (Barto and Mahadevan, 2003) to dialogue management over complex dialogue domains. Our system learns how to handle complex dialogues by learning a multi-domain policy over different domains that operate on independent time-scales with temporally-extended actions.

HRL gives a principled way for learning policies over complex problems. It overcomes the curse of dimensionality which plagues the majority of complex tasks by reducing them to a sequence of sub-tasks. It also provides a learning framework for managing those sub-tasks at the same time (Dietterich, 2000; Sutton et al., 1999b; Bacon et al., 2017).

Even though the first work on HRL dates back to the 1970s, its usefulness for dialogue management is relatively under-explored. A notable exception is the work of Cuayáhuitl (2009; 2010), whose method is based on the MAXQ algorithm (Dietterich, 2000) making use of hierarchical abstract machines (Parr and Russell, 1998). The main limitation of this work comes from the tabular approach which prevents the efficient approximation of the state space and the objective function. This is crucial for scalability of spoken dia-

Proceedings of the SIGDIAL 2017 Conference, pages 86–92,
Saarbrücken, Germany, 15-17 August 2017. ©2017 Association for Computational Linguistics

logue systems to more complex scenarios. Parallel to our work, Peng et al. (2017) proposed another HRL approach, using deep Q-networks as an approximator. In separate work, we found deep Q-networks to be unstable (Su et al., 2017); in this work, we focus on more robust estimators.

The contributions of this paper are threefold. First, we adapt and validate the option framework (Sutton et al., 1999b) for a multi-domain dialogue system. Second, we demonstrate that hierarchical learning for dialogue systems works well with function approximation using the GPSARSA algorithm. We chose the Gaussian process as the function approximator as it provides uncertainty estimates which can be used to speed up learning and achieve more robust performance. Third, we show that independently pre-trained domains can be easily integrated into the system and adapted to handle more complex conversations.

2 Hierarchical Reinforcement Learning

Dialogue management can be seen as a control problem: it estimates a distribution over possible user requests – *belief states*, and chooses what to say back to the user, i.e. which *actions* to take to maximise positive user feedback – the *reward*.

Reinforcement Learning The framework described above can be analyzed from the perspective of the *Markov Decision Process* (MDP). We can apply RL to our problem where we parametrize an optimal policy $\pi : \mathcal{B} \times \mathcal{A} \to [0, 1]$. The learning procedure can either directly look for the optimal policy (Sutton et al., 1999a) or model the Q-value function (Sutton and Barto, 1999):

$$Q^\pi(\mathbf{b}, a) = \mathrm{E}_\pi \{ \sum_{k=0}^{T-t} \gamma^k r_{t+k} | \mathbf{b}_t = \mathbf{b}, a_t = a \},$$

where r_t is the reward at time t and $0 < \gamma \leq 1$ is the discount factor. Both approaches proved to be an effective and robust way of training dialogue systems online in interaction with real users (Gašić et al., 2011; Williams and Zweig, 2016).

Gaussian Processes in RL Gaussian Process RL (GPRL) is one of the state-of-the-art RL algorithms for dialogue modelling (Gašić and Young, 2014) where the Q-value function is approximated using Gaussian processes with a zero mean and chosen kernel function $k(\cdot, \cdot)$, i.e.

$$Q(\mathbf{b}, a) \sim \mathcal{GP}\left(0, k((\mathbf{b}, a), (\mathbf{b}, a))\right).$$

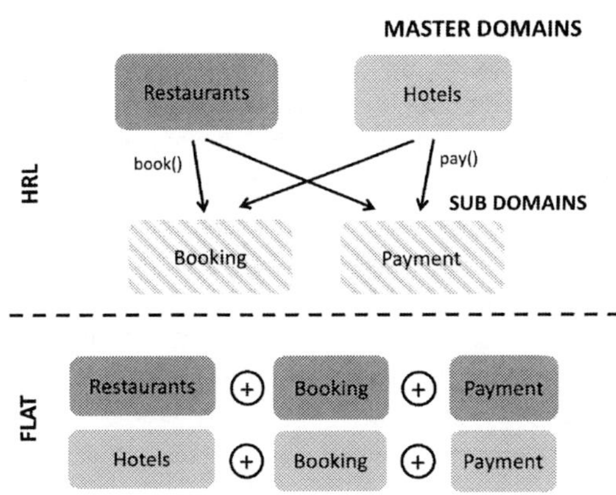

Figure 1: Comparison of two analysed architectures.

Gaussian processes follow a pure Bayesian framework, which allows one to obtain the posterior given a new collected pair $(\mathbf{b}, a)$. The trade-off between exploration and exploitation is handled naturally as given belief state $\mathbf{b}$ at the time t we can sample from posterior $Q(\mathbf{b}, a)$ over set of available actions $\mathcal{A}$ to choose the action with the highest sampled Q-value.

Hierarchical Policy Standard *flat* models where a single Markov Decision Process is responsible for solving multi-task problems have proven to be inefficient. These models have trouble overcoming the cold start problem and/or suffer from the curse of dimensionality (Barto and Mahadevan, 2003). This pattern was also observed with state-of-the-art models proposed recently (Mnih et al., 2013; Duan et al., 2016).

To overcome this issue, many frameworks have been proposed in the literature (Fikes et al., 1972; Laird et al., 1986; Parr and Russell, 1998). They make use of hierarchical control architectures and learning algorithms whereby specifying a hierarchy of tasks and reusing parts of the state space across many sub-tasks can greatly improve both learning speed and agent performance.

The key idea is the notion of *temporal abstraction* (Sutton et al., 1999b) where decisions at the given level are not required at each step but can call temporally-extended sub-tasks with their own policies.

The Option Framework One of the most natural generalisations of flat RL methods to complex tasks and easily interchangeable with primitive actions is the *option* model (Sutton et al., 1999b). The option is a generalisation of a single-step action that might span across more than one time-step and can be used as a standard action.From mathematical perspective option is a tuple $\langle \pi, \beta, \mathcal{I} \rangle$ that consists of policy $\pi : \mathcal{S} \times \mathcal{A} \rightarrow [0, 1]$ which conducts the option, stochastic termination condition $\beta : \mathcal{S} \rightarrow [0, 1]$ and an input set $\mathcal{I} \subseteq \mathcal{S}$ which specifies when the option is available.

As we consider hierarchical architectures with temporally extended activities, we have to generalise the MDP to the semi-Markov Decision Process (SMDP) (Parr and Russell, 1998) where actions can take a variable amount of time to complete. This creates a division between *primitive* actions that span over only one action (and can be seen as a classic reinforcement learning approach) and *composite* actions (options) that involve an execution of a sequence of primitive actions. This introduces a policy μ over options that selects option o in state s with probability $\mu(s, o)$, o's policy might in turn select other options until o terminates and so on. The value function for option policies can be defined in terms of the value functions of the semi-Markov flat policies (Sutton et al., 1999b). Define the value function under a semi-Markov flat policy as:

$$V^{\pi}(s) = \mathbb{E}\{r_{t+1} + \gamma r_{t+2} + ...|E(\pi, s, t)\},$$

where $E(\pi, s, t)$ is the event of π being initiated at time t in s. The value function for the policy over options μ can be defined as the value function for corresponding flat policy. This means we can apply off-the-shelf RL methods in HRL using different time-scales.

3   Hierarchical Policy Management

We propose a multi-domain dialogue system with a pre-imposed hierarchy that uses the option framework for learning an optimal policy. The user starts a conversation in one of the *master* domains and switches to the other domains (having satisfied his/her goal) that are seen by the model as *sub-domains*. To model individual policies, we can use any RL algorithm. In separate work, we found deep RL models performing worse in noisy environment (Su et al., 2017). Thus, we employ the GPSARSA model from section 2 which proves to handle efficiently noise in the environment. The

Algorithm 1 Hierarchical GPRL

1: Initialize dictionary sets $\mathcal{D}_{\mathcal{M}}, \mathcal{D}_{\mathcal{S}}$ and policies $\pi_{\mathcal{M}}, \pi_{\mathcal{S}}$ for master and sub-domains accordingly
2: **for** episode=1:N **do**
3:     Start dialogue and obtain initial state **b**
4:     **while b** is not terminal **do**
5:         Choose action a according to π_m
6:         **if** a is primitive **then**
7:             Execute a and obtain next state **b**$'$
8:             Obtain extrinsic reward r_e
9:         **else**
10:             Switch to chosen sub-domain
11:             **while b** is not terminal **or** a terminates **do**
12:                 Choose action a according to π_s
13:                 Obtain next state **b**$'$
14:                 Obtain intrinsic reward r_i
15:                 Store transition in $\mathcal{D}_s$
16:                 **b** $\leftarrow$ **b**$'$
17:             Store transition in $\mathcal{D}_m$
18:             **b** $\leftarrow$ **b**$'$
19:     Update parameters with $\mathcal{D}_m, \mathcal{D}_s$

system is trained from scratch where the system has to learn appropriate policy using both primitive and temporally extended actions.

We consider two task-oriented master domains providing restaurant and hotel information for the Cambridge (UK) area. Having found the desired entity, the user can then book it for a specified amount of time or pay for it. The two domains have a set of primitive actions (such as *request, confirm* or *inform* (Ultes et al., 2017)) and a set of composite actions (e.g., *book, pay*) which call sub-domains shared between them.

The `Booking` and `Payment` domains were created in a similar fashion: the user wants to reserve a table in a restaurant or a room in a hotel for a specific amount of money or duration of time. The system's role is to determine whether it is possible to make the requested booking. The sub-domains operates only on primitive actions and it's learnt following standard RL framework.

Figure 1 shows the analysed architecture: the `Booking` and `Payment` tasks/sub-domains are shared between two master domains. This means we can train general policies for those sub-tasks that adapt to the current dialogue given the information passed to them by the master domains.

Learning proceeds on two different time-scales. Following (Dieterich, 2000; Kulkarni et al., 2016), we use pseudo-rewards to train sub-domains using an internal critic which assesses whether the sub-goal has been reached.

The master domains are trained using the reward signal from the environment. If a one-step option (i.e., a primitive action) is chosen, we ob-

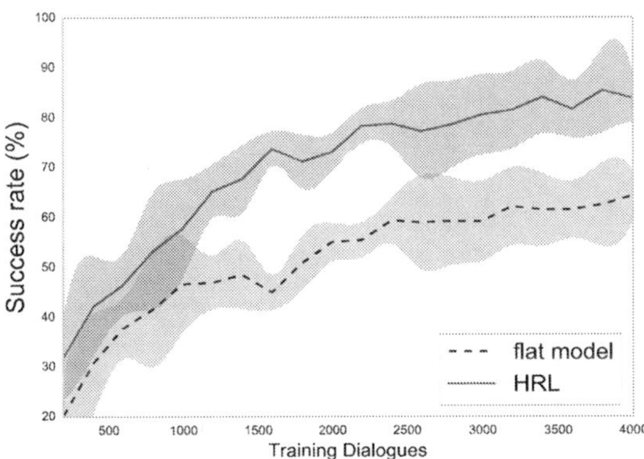

Figure 2: Learning curves for flat and the hierarchical reinforcement learning models.

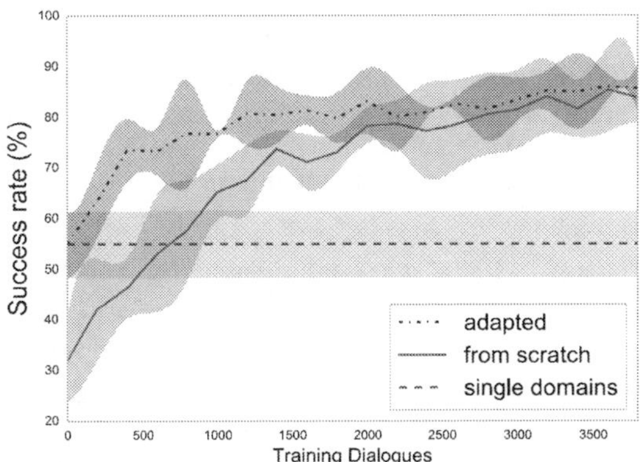

Figure 3: Comparison of policies learnt from scratch and those pre-trained on master domains.

tain immediate extrinsic reward while for the composite actions the master domain waits until the sub-domain terminates and the cumulative reward information is passed back to the master domain. The pseudo-code for the learning algorithm is given in Algorithm 1.

4 Experiments

The PyDial dialogue modelling tool-kit (Ultes et al., 2017) was used to evaluate the proposed architecture. The restaurant domain consists of approximately 100 venues with 3 search constraint slots while the hotel domain has 33 entities with 5 properties. There are 5 slots in the booking domain that the system can ask for while the payment domain has 3 search constraints slots.

In the case of the flat approach, each master domain was combined with the sub-domains, resulting in 11 and 13 requestable slots for the restaurants and hotel domains, respectively.

The input for all models was the full belief state **b**, which expresses the distribution over the user intents and the requestable slots. The belief state has size 311, 156, 431 and 174 for the restaurants, hotels, booking and payment domains in the hierarchical approach. The flat models have input spaces of sizes 490 and 333 for the restaurant and hotel domains accordingly.

The proposed models were evaluated with an agenda-based simulated user (Schatzmann et al., 2006) where the user intent was perfectly captured in the dialogue belief state. For both intrinsic and extrinsic evaluation, the total return of each dialogue was set to $\mathbb{1}(\mathcal{D}) * 20 - T$, where T is the dialogue length and $\mathbb{1}(\mathcal{D})$ is the success indicator for dialogue $\mathcal{D}$. Maximum dialogue length was set

to 30 in both hierarchical and flat model scenarios with $\gamma = 0.99$.

At the beginning of each dialogue, the master domain is chosen randomly and the user is given a goal which consists of finding an entity and either booking it (for a specific date) or paying for it. The user was allowed to change the goal with a small probability and could not proceed with the sub-domains before achieving the master domain goal.

4.1 Hierarchical versus the Flat Approach

Following (Dietterich, 2000; Kulkarni et al., 2016), we apply a more exploratory policy in the case of master domains, allowing greater flexibility in managing primitive and composite actions during the initial learning stages. Figure 2 presents the results with 4000 training dialogues, where the policy was evaluated after each 200 dialogues.

The results validate the option framework: it learns faster and leads to a better final policy than the flat approach. The flat model did overcome the cold start problem but it could not match the performance of the hierarchical model. The policies learnt for sub-tasks with the flat approach perform only 10% worse (on average) than in the hierarchical case. However, providing the entity in both master domains has around 20% lower success rate compared to HRL.

Moreover, the flat model was not able to match the performance of the HRL approach even with more training dialogues. We let it run for another 6000 dialogues and did not observe any improvements in success rate (not reported here). This confirms the findings from other RL tasks - the flat approach is not able to remember successful strategies across different tasks (Peng et al., 2017;

Duan et al., 2016). An example of two successful dialogues for both models is presented in the Figure 4.

4.2 Adaptation of Pretrained Policies

Following the idea of curriculum learning (Bengio et al., 2009), we test the adaptation capabilities of pre-trained policies to more complex situations. Adaptation has proven to be an effective way of reusing existing dialogue policies in new domains (Gašić et al., 2014). Since the kernel function is factored into the kernel for the belief state space and the action space, we can consider them separately. Following (Gašić et al., 2014) the action kernel function is defined only on actions that appear both in original and extended sets and defined 0 otherwise. The kernel for the belief state space is not changed as we operate on the same belief space.

We first train both master domains (without subgoals) until robust policies are learned. Subsequently, both master domains are re-trained in a hierarchical manner for 4000 dialogues (testing after each 200). Figure 3 shows the results compared to the policy learnt from scratch. Both policies trained on independent domains were able to adapt to more complicated tasks very quickly using the hierarchical framework with new options. This confirms that our approach can substantially speed up learning time by training a policy in a supervised way with the available data and then adapting it to more complex multi-task conversations.

5   Conclusion and Future Work

This paper introduced a hierarchical policy management model for learning dialogue policies which operate over composite tasks. The proposed model uses hierarchical reinforcement learning with the Gaussian Process as the function approximator. Our evaluation showed that our model learns substantially faster and achieves better performance than standard (flat) RL models. The natural next step towards the generalisation of this approach is to deepen the hierarchy and apply to more complex tasks.

Acknowledgments

Paweł Budzianowski is supported by EPSRC Council and Toshiba Research Europe Ltd, Cambridge Research Laboratory.

constraint	slot
pricerange	moderate
kind	guesthouse
stars	don't care
hasparking	no
hour	4 pm
peopleNo	4
durationDays	4
day	don't care

requestable slots
name of hotel
price of hotel

S:	Hello, welcome to the Cambridge Multi-Domain dialogue system. How may I help you? **[master domain]**
U:	Hello.
S:	Do you want a hotel or a guesthouse?
U:	I'm looking for a guesthouse in a moderate pricerange. I don't care about stars and don't need a parking access.
S:	A and B guest house is in a moderate pricerange and has 4 stars.
U:	How much does it cost?
S:	Cheapest single room is 50 pounds and a cheapest double room is 70 pounds .
U:	Ok. Can you book it for 4 people?
S:	book() **[option action]**
S:	What time are you planning to check in? **[sub-domain]**
U:	4 pm.
S:	How long do you want to stay?
U:	4 days anytime soon.
S:	You want to book it for 4 people, is that right?
U:	Yes.
S:	I confirm a reservation for 4 days on Saturday for 4 people. Reservation number is 8.
U:	Bye.
S:	Goodbye. **[master domain]**

S:	Hello, welcome to the Cambridge Multi-Domain dialogue system. How may I help you?
U:	I am looking for a guesthouse.
S:	How many stars should the place have? From 0 to 4.
U:	I don't need a parking access.
S:	How many stars should the place have? From 0 to 4.
U:	I don't care but the price should be moderate.
S:	A and B guest house is in a moderate pricerange and has 4 stars.
U:	How much does it cost?
S:	Cheapest single room is 50 pounds and a cheapest double room is 70 pounds.
U:	Ok. Can you book it for 4 people anytime soon?
S:	It doesn't have to have a parking, right? **[wrong domain]**
U:	Yes.
S:	For what day should I make a reservation?
U:	I don't care.
S:	You are looking for a 4 stars hotel right? **[wrong domain]**
U:	Yes.
S:	Would you like the place to have a parking? **[wrong domain]**
U:	No.
S:	How many days do you want to stay there?
U:	4.
S:	I confirm a reservation for 4 days on Saturday. Reservation number is 10.
U:	Bye.
S:	Goodbye.

Figure 4: An example dialogue with the same user goal (top) handled by HRL (middle) and flat (bottom) models.

References

P.-L. Bacon, J. Harb, and D. Precup. 2017. The Option-Critic Architecture. *31AAAI Conference On Artificial Intelligence* .

Andrew G Barto and Sridhar Mahadevan. 2003. Recent advances in hierarchical reinforcement learning. *Discrete Event Dynamic Systems* 13(4):341–379.

Yoshua Bengio, Jérôme Louradour, Ronan Collobert, and Jason Weston. 2009. Curriculum learning. In *Proceedings of the 26th annual international conference on machine learning*. ACM, pages 41–48.

Heriberto Cuayáhuitl. 2009. Hierarchical reinforcement learning for spoken dialogue systems. *PhD Thesis, University of Edinburgh* .

Heriberto Cuayáhuitl, Steve Renals, Oliver Lemon, and Hiroshi Shimodaira. 2010. Evaluation of a hierarchical reinforcement learning spoken dialogue system. *Computer Speech & Language* 24(2):395–429.

Heriberto Cuayáhuitl, Seunghak Yu, Ashley Williamson, and Jacob Carse. 2016. Deep reinforcement learning for multi-domain dialogue systems. *NIPS Workkshop* .

Thomas G Dietterich. 2000. Hierarchical reinforcement learning with the maxq value function decomposition. *J. Artif. Intell. Res.(JAIR)* 13:227–303.

Yan Duan, Xi Chen, Rein Houthooft, John Schulman, and Pieter Abbeel. 2016. Benchmarking deep reinforcement learning for continuous control. In *Proceedings of The 33rd International Conference on Machine Learning*. pages 1329–1338.

Mehdi Fatemi, Layla El Asri, Hannes Schulz, Jing He, and Kaheer Suleman. 2016. Policy networks with two-stage training for dialogue systems. *Proc of SigDial* .

Richard E Fikes, Peter E Hart, and Nils J Nilsson. 1972. Learning and executing generalized robot plans. *Artificial intelligence* 3:251–288.

Milica Gašić, Filip Jurcicek, Blaise. Thomson, Kai Yu, and Steve Young. 2011. On-line policy optimisation of spoken dialogue systems via live interaction with human subjects. In *IEEE ASRU*.

Milica Gašić, Dongho Kim, Pirros Tsiakoulis, Catherine Breslin, Matthew Henderson, Martin Szummer, Blaise Thomson, and Steve Young. 2014. Incremental on-line adaptation of pomdp-based dialogue managers to extended domains .

Milica Gašić, Nikola Mrkšić, Pei-hao Su, David Vandyke, Tsung-Hsien Wen, and Steve Young. 2015. Policy committee for adaptation in multi-domain spoken dialogue systems. In *Automatic Speech Recognition and Understanding (ASRU), 2015 IEEE Workshop on*. IEEE, pages 806–812.

Milica Gašić and Steve Young. 2014. Gaussian processes for pomdp-based dialogue manager optimization. *TASLP* 22(1):28–40.

Tejas D Kulkarni, Karthik Narasimhan, Ardavan Saeedi, and Josh Tenenbaum. 2016. Hierarchical deep reinforcement learning: Integrating temporal abstraction and intrinsic motivation. In *Advances in Neural Information Processing Systems*. pages 3675–3683.

John E Laird, Paul S Rosenbloom, and Allen Newell. 1986. Chunking in soar: The anatomy of a general learning mechanism. *Machine learning* 1(1):11–46.

Pierre Lison. 2011. Multi-policy dialogue management. In *Proceedings of the SIGDIAL 2011 Conference*. Association for Computational Linguistics, pages 294–300.

Volodymyr Mnih, Koray Kavukcuoglu, David Silver, Alex Graves, Ioannis Antonoglou, Daan Wierstra, and Martin Riedmiller. 2013. Playing atari with deep reinforcement learning. *arXiv preprint arXiv:1312.5602* .

Nikola Mrkšić, Diarmuid Ó Séaghdha, Blaise Thomson, Milica Gašić, Pei-Hao Su, David Vandyke, Tsung-Hsien Wen, and Steve Young. 2015. Multi-domain Dialog State Tracking using Recurrent Neural Networks. In *Proceedings of ACL*.

Ronald Parr and Stuart J Russell. 1998. Reinforcement learning with hierarchies of machines. In *Advances in Neural Information Processing Systems*. pages 1043–1049.

B. Peng, X. Li, L. Li, J. Gao, A. Celikyilmaz, S. Lee, and K.-F. Wong. 2017. Composite Task-Completion Dialogue System via Hierarchical Deep Reinforcement Learning. *ArXiv e-prints* .

Jost Schatzmann, Karl Weilhammer, Matt Stuttle, and Steve Young. 2006. A survey of statistical user simulation techniques for reinforcement-learning of dialogue management strategies. *The knowledge engineering review* 21(02):97–126.

Pei-Hao Su, Paweł Budzianowski, Stefan Ultes, Milica Gašić, and Steve J. Young. 2017. Sample-efficient actor-critic reinforcement learning with supervised data for dialogue management. In *Proceedings of the SIGDIAL 2017 Conference*.

Pei-Hao Su, Milica Gasic, Nikola Mrksic, Lina Rojas-Barahona, Stefan Ultes, David Vandyke, Tsung-Hsien Wen, and Steve Young. 2016. Continuously learning neural dialogue management. *arXiv preprint arXiv:1606.02689* .

Richard S. Sutton and Andrew G. Barto. 1999. *Reinforcement Learning: An Introduction*. MIT Press.

Richard S Sutton, David A McAllester, Satinder P Singh, Yishay Mansour, et al. 1999a. Policy gradient methods for reinforcement learning with function approximation. In *Proceedings of NIPS*. volume 99.

Richard S Sutton, Doina Precup, and Satinder Singh. 1999b. Between mdps and semi-mdps: A framework for temporal abstraction in reinforcement learning. *Artificial intelligence* 112(1-2):181–211.

Stefan Ultes, Lina M. Rojas-Barahona, Pei-Hao Su, David Vandyke, Dongho Kim, Iñigo Casanueva, Paweł Budzianowski, Nikola Mrkšić, Tsung-Hsien Wen, Milica Gašić, and Steve J. Young. 2017. Pydial: A multi-domain statistical dialogue system toolkit. In *ACL Demo*. Association of Computational Linguistics.

Zhuoran Wang, Hongliang Chen, Guanchun Wang, Hao Tian, Hua Wu, and Haifeng Wang. 2014. Policy learning for domain selection in an extensible multi-domain spoken dialogue system. pages 57–67.

Jason D. Williams and Steve Young. 2007. Partially observable Markov decision processes for spoken dialog systems. *Computer Speech and Language* 21(2):393–422.

Jason D Williams and Geoffrey Zweig. 2016. End-to-end lstm-based dialog control optimized with supervised and reinforcement learning. *arXiv preprint arXiv:1606.01269* .

Steve Young, Milica Gašić, Blaise Thomson, and Jason D Williams. 2013. Pomdp-based statistical spoken dialog systems: A review. *Proceedings of the IEEE* 101(5):1160–1179.

MACA: A Modular Architecture for Conversational Agents

Hoai Phuoc Truong,* Prasanna Parthasarathi,† and Joelle Pineau‡
School of Computer Science
McGill University

Abstract

We propose a software architecture designed to ease the implementation of dialogue systems. The Modular Architecture for Conversational Agents (MACA) uses a plug-n-play style that allows quick prototyping, thereby facilitating the development of new techniques and the reproduction of previous work. The architecture separates the domain of the conversation from the agent's dialogue strategy, and as such can be easily extended to multiple domains. MACA provides tools to host dialogue agents on Amazon Mechanical Turk (mTurk) for data collection and allows processing of other sources of training data. The current version of the framework already incorporates several domains and existing dialogue strategies from the recent literature.

1 Introduction

Recent research in building sophisticated AI-based dialogue management systems has led to many new models supporting goal oriented or chit-chat style dialogue agents. These models have been applied to a variety of consumer domains, such as restaurant booking (Kim and Banchs, 2014), flight booking (Young, 2006), etc. However, the lack of tools for easy prototyping of newer models remains an impediment to developing new models and properly benchmarking against previous models. Furthermore, the different types of conversational agents– e.g., generative (Hochreiter and Schmidhuber, 1997; Serban et al., 2015, 2016), retrieval-based (Schatzmann et al.,

2005a; Lowe et al., 2015a), slot-based (Young, 2006) or POMDP agents (Png and Pineau, 2011)– have different working mechanisms, which pose challenges to the development of a unified platform for conversational agents with multi-domain support.

To address this gap, we propose a new, ready-to-use, cross-platform framework for text-based conversational agents – MACA[1] (**M**odularized **A**rchitecture for **C**onversational **A**gents)– that supports *plug-n-play* use of several existing dialogue agents, as well as facilitates easy prototyping of new dialogue agents. The architecture simplifies the specification of different types of dialogue agents and plugs in an already-built dialogue agent. The framework also maintains a clear separation between domain knowledge and the dialogue agent, which improves agent and domain knowledge reusability. MACA separates task definition from task selection and thereby supports multi-task agents that can extend to multiple turns.

The key characteristics of the MACA framework include:

- strong separation between domain knowledge and a dialogue agent
- a unified architecture to support goal-oriented, POMDP, generative, and retrieval-based dialogue agents
- easy plug-n-play of custom-built agents
- multi-task support for domain specification
- reusability of slots across different tasks
- tool to collect data from mTurk with ease
- template to construct dialogue agents within the framework
- independence from dialogue agents' implementation libraries
- open source code ready for public sharing

---

*phuoc.truong2@mail.mcgill.ca
†prasanna.p@cs.mcgill.ca
‡jpineau@cs.mcgill.ca

[1]https://github.com/ppartha03/MACA

93

Proceedings of the SIGDIAL 2017 Conference, pages 93–102,
Saarbrücken, Germany, 15-17 August 2017. ©2017 Association for Computational Linguistics

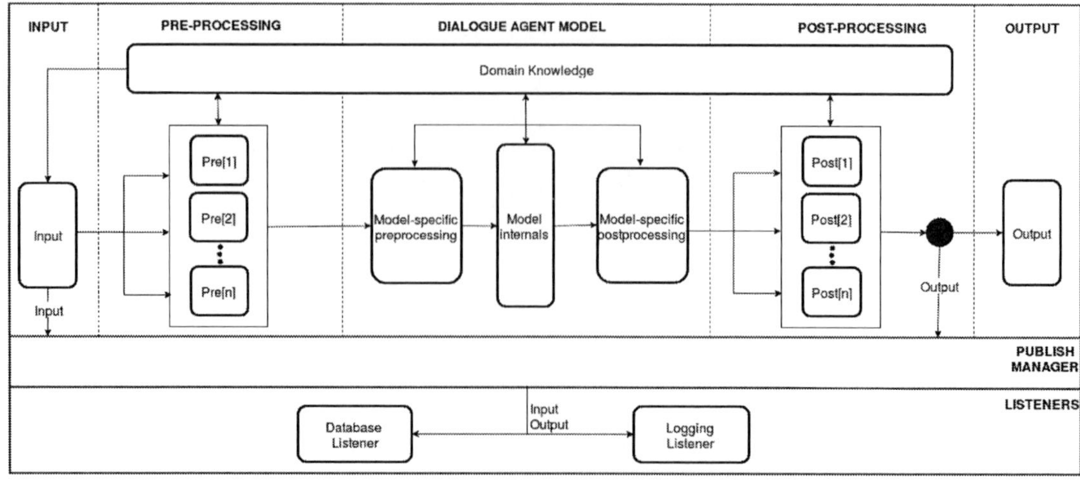

Figure 1: Overview of MACA: A Modular Architecture for Conversational Agents.

2   Related Work

There are a few proposed frameworks in recent years that provide easy prototyping of dialogue agents.

Ravenclaw (Bohus and Rudnicky, 2003), proposed as a successor to Agenda (Allen et al., 2001), is a two-tiered dialogue architecture supporting rapid development of dialogue agents. This flexible architecture provides a clear separation between the domain knowledge and dialogue agent, and maintains a hierarchical task structure. Systems can be built on the architecture with the hierarchical task layout but adding a new task requires the hierarchy to be rebuilt, which impedes application to new domains.

A hierarchical architecture similar to Ravenclaw, called Task Completion Platform (TCP) (Crook et al., 2016), addresses domain knowledge extensibility with minimal changes to a configuration file. In addition, it allows the goal oriented tasks to be defined easily using a TaskForm language to maintain slot information. Although TCP facilitates extension of slot-based agents to multiple domains, it cannot be extended for other dialogue agent types *viz.*, generative models and retrieval models.

Another notable architecture is ClippyScript (Seide and McDirmid, 2012), but its task definition is tied to a task condition by rule. Rules are therefore constrained to be explicitly defined on a per task basis. This is significantly more restrictive than our proposed architecture.

As much research focuses on proposing different architectures for dialogue models, there have also been some progress made in proposing efficient protocols for agent-agent interaction such as DialPort (Zhao et al., 2016), which provides tools for enabling multi-modal interaction between agents. Our proposed work is different from this line of research, focusing on a unifying architecture for dialogue agents and little on the inter-agent communication.

3   Architecture Description

An overview of the Modular Architecture for Conversational Agents (MACA) is presented in Figure 1. The system is setup as a pipeline with six major components: *Input, Pre-processing, Dialogue Model, Post-processing, Output, and Listeners*. Each component contains independent subcomponents that interact across it. All components within the architecture abstract away their underlying implementations and therefore allow their extensions to be straightforward. This helps in block-wise designing of newer systems by preserving the original functionality, yet also providing a free hand in customizing of each component.

3.1   Component Details

3.1.1   Domain Knowledge

Domain knowledge contains static background information about the conversation topic. This can take the form of training data (e.g. transcribed conversations), constants, dictionaries, or restrictions on produced responses (e.g. sentence length, banned phrases). Data stored in domain knowledge must be independent of the model implementation, and can be shared between different models and components.

3.1.2 Input

The *Input* module provides or generates input utterances (i.e. statements, sentences) to the conversation pipeline. This component represents an abstract input device whose source of context varies depending on the use case. This could include a database of previous collected conversations, a terminal interface (i.e. stdin) to acquire data in real-time, or a web interface to a data source (e.g. mTurk).

3.1.3 Preprocessing

The *Pre-processing* module serves as a bridge between raw data acquired via the *Input* component and the input format required of components of the *Dialogue model* module. The system architect may choose to include one or several pre-processing operations within this module. These pre-processing operations by default are performed in parallel and their results are fed into the next component as an array. This allows the dialogue model to have multiple input representations. Alternatively, the framework also allows these operations to be sequentially processed in a specified order (e.g. spelling correction, followed by stemming).

Pre-processing operations currently implemented in MACA include: getting POS tags, removing stop-words, sentence tokenizing (Loper and Bird, 2002), Byte-Pair encoding (BPE) (Gage, 1994) and can be extended to accommodate trained sentence2vec model (Le and Mikolov, 2014), trained word2vec model (Mikolov et al., 2013), etc. These nodes can also interact with the *Domain Knowledge* component to acquire domain specific information required for the operations.

3.1.4 Dialogue Model

This module is the core of the architecture, and contains implementations of agents capable of producing dialogue acts in response to the pre-processed Input information. This module can have up to three sub-components: *Model Specific Pre-processing*, *Model Internals* and *Model Specific Post-processing*, to accommodate dialogue agent models with various interface requirements.

The *Model internals* sub-module contains the central dialogue model, which may be an existing model, such as a POMDP (Png and Pineau, 2011), Dual Encoder (Lowe et al., 2015a), HRED agent (Serban et al., 2015), or a newly designed model. This sub-module receives inputs from the *Model Specific Pre-processing* sub-module. The space of possible responses, vocabulary or dialogue acts are stored in the *Domain Knowledge* module. The *Model internals* and *Model specific Pre/Post-processing* sub-modules share the model information. Similar to the *Pre-processing* component, they can access any information required for their operations by querying the *Domain Knowledge* component. A specific illustration of this interaction is in goal-oriented dialogue agents, where the slot information – *askQueries* and other attributes of the slot and these slot objects – are maintained in the domain knowledge, which enables the framework to support multiple agents. In such settings, the Dialogue Model is initialized with a generic agent that tries to gauge the user intent, and then queries the domain knowledge for the appropriate slots.

Model specific Pre-processing and Post-processing sub-components are provided to give the luxury of designing fine-tuned pre-processing for a model. *Model Specific Pre-processing* sub-component transforms pre-processed input(s) into appropriate representations compatible with the model internals (e.g. array of word indices into vector, matrix or lookup table, etc). On the other hand, *Model Specific Post-processing* sub-component transforms model outputs into more comprehensible forms for the next independent component in the system (e.g. matrix/vector representation to array of words/sentences).

Although certain interpretations suggest analogies between the above sub-modules and conventional units of a goal-oriented dialogue system such as Dialogue Manager (DM) as *Model internals*, Natural Language Understanding (NLU) as *Model specific Pre-processing*, and Natural Language Generation (NLG) as *Model specific Post-processing*, MACA does not impose any restriction on how the framework's sub-modules should correspond with these conventional parts of a dialogue system. For example, the architect may choose to have the *Model internals* sub-module act as a NLU unit, while *Model specific Post-processing* act as both NLG Unit and DM unit.

In addition, as the model may also be an ensemble of dialogue models, the model specific pre-

and post-processing sub-components can also be used to keep processing units specific to each of the model in the architecture. For clarification, in a typical implementation of an ensemble of models, the *Model specific Pre-processing* sub-component can be used to provide separate inputs parsed from the *Pre-processing* component to the corresponding models, while *Model specific Post-processing* sub-component can be used to perform a majority voting or other ensemble techniques to select the response *pool*.

3.1.5 Postprocessing

The Posprocessing component connects the *Dialogue Model* and the *Output* components. It allows the architect to choose the response in the case of multi-response retrieval, to alter responses based on linguistic characteristics, or to modify a response in accordance with the conversation domain. It may also serve as a translation of text to system calls, which is useful in the case where a dialogue agent placed as the front-end interface to another software system. Similar to the *Pre-processing* module, this component includes one or multiple post-processing operations, which process the output in parallel or in sequence, depending on the specification of the designer. In addition, these post-processing operations within the *Post-processing* component can also query the *Domain Knowledge* component for relevant data required for the generation of text response.

3.1.6 Output

Through the output component, the architecture provides a generic way to output the response to appropriate audience(s) depending on the use case. Currently, implemented options are *command line, file based, web based*, and *database*. Similar to the *Input* component, the output component provides flexibility for the architect to change the destination of produced outputs and to separate the output programming logic from that of other components.

3.1.7 Pubsub system/Listeners

In addition to the main pipeline presented above, the proposed system also includes a passive pubsub layer to facilitate monitoring, conversation recording, and independent evaluation of the model. This pubsub system allows the architect to choose or plug in a wide range of peripheral components (called *Listeners*) to passively monitor the main system for execution behaviors and performance. On top of several default channels (see Operation modes section below) that the system writes to and reads from, users can freely add their own channels to communicate between the main system and the pubsub layer hosting the peripherals.

Listeners, as previously mentioned, are optional modules that can be plugged in to passively monitor the system over different channels. These modules are useful when the architect is interested in observing the system inputs and/or outputs, or visualizing internal parameters or states of the dialogue model at execution time. Passive monitoring logic can be independently introduced into the system without modifying the other components' implementations.

3.2 Operation modes

MACA can be operated in three different modes: *Data Collection, Training* and *Execution*. This section describes the data flow in the architecture along with abstract setups of the framework's components in these different operation modes for several dialogue models from the recent literature.

3.2.1 Data Collection Mode

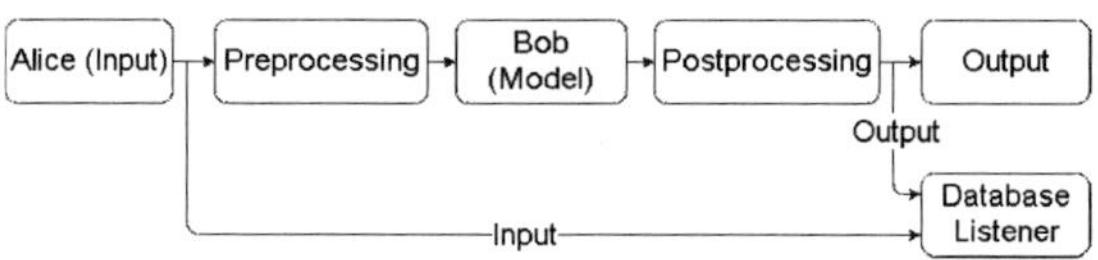

Figure 2: Data flow in data collection mode.

The goal of the data collection mode is to collect conversations as training datasets for dialogue models. In this mode, the two agents *Alice* and *Bob* involved in the conversation are considered the *Input* component and the *Dialogue Model* component respectively. Figure 2 describes a typical setup for the data collection process with said configuration. The conversation is recorded using a database listener that receives both input (context) and output (response) for each speaking turn, similar to the scheme presented in section 3.2.3 above.

This setup realizes the infrastructure required for two common dialogue data collection scenarios. The first scenario is collection of both contexts and responses. In this case, both agents are humans. In the second scenario, the goal is to collect human responses for a given set of contexts. In this case, agent Alice can be an implementation of the *Input* component fetching contexts from a database, while Bob is a human agent responding to the fetched contexts.

3.2.2 Training Mode

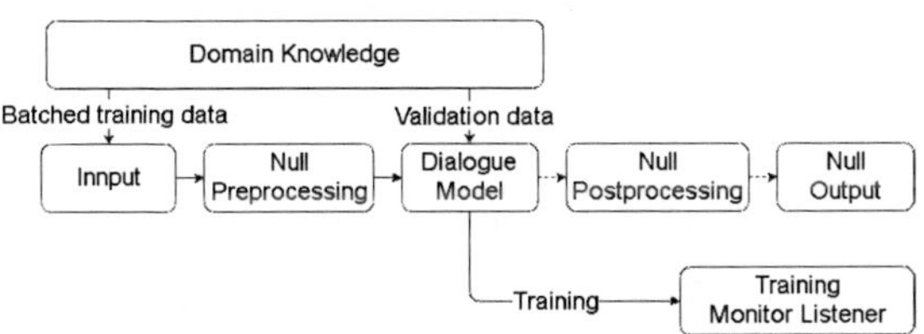

Figure 3: Data flow in training mode.

The goal of the training and validation mode is to use the data obtained in the data collection stage to train one or multiple dialogue models, as illustrated in figure 3. Assuming a dataset is available from the *Domain Knowledge* component, training data can be fetched as batches by the *Input* component and fed into the *VoidPreprocessing* component. This component simply forwards the data as is to the *Dialogue Model* component, which performs model training, and occasionally queries the domain knowledge for validation data to verify its training progress. Since system output is irrelevant within the training scenario, *Post-processing* and *Output* components are implemented with null operations, which simply discard their received contents. Once certain validation accuracy is achieved, the model can save its internals on to the disk and terminate the system. In addition to the core training process, the architect may opt to emit training information to a listener through the *training* channel to monitor the training progress.

3.2.3 Execution Mode

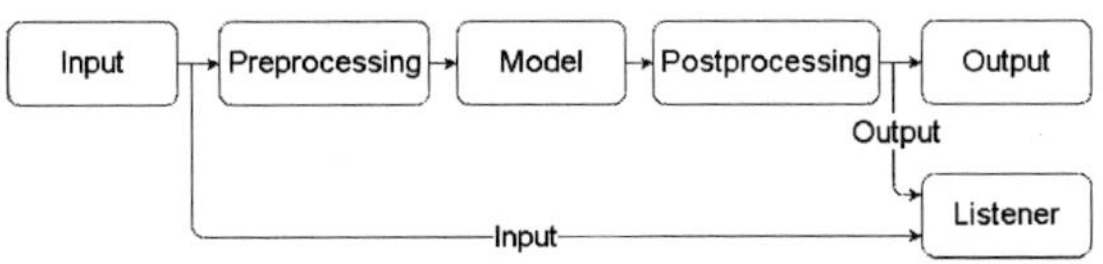

Figure 4: Data flow in execution mode.

Data flow in execution mode is illustrated in figure 4. In this mode, all core components in the system are enabled and active. Given that the dialogue model has been successfully trained and fine-tuned, its internal states (e.g. weights, hyperparameters) are loaded into the *Dialogue Model* component at system initialization time. Input data is retrieved in real time (through local user interface (e.g. terminal, GUI) or via an interface with the Internet (e.g. web page, chat client)). This input then enters the pipeline and goes through *Preprocessing, Dialogue model, Postprocessing* and finally *Output* component. At the end of the pipeline, the output component is responsible for sending the generated responses to relevant audiences (e.g. print to stdout, HTTP response, ...).

From the peripheral components perspective, conversation logging and system monitoring can be done through two default channels: *input* and *output*. Specifically, as shown in figure 4, the passive *listener* receives a notification for every input received from the *Input* component on the *input* channel, and a notification for every output received by the *Output* component on the *output* channel.

4   Feature Highlights

As discussed in the previous sections, MACA can be used to plug in different types of existing dialogue agents. The architecture abstracts the implementation details, similar to popular machine learning libraries such as Theano (Theano Development Team, 2016), Tensorflow (Abadi et al., 2016), or PyTorch. The modular design enables rapid prototyping and should facilitate reproducing previous results. The support for experimentation, extension, and development of slot-based dialogue agents for goal-oriented tasks has also been provided. In addition, the current implementation has rule-based approach for slot disambiguation and has provisions for the easy extension of slot disambiguation to *machine learning* (ML) based modules. The clear separation of domain knowledge from the agent aids in multi-agent systems with little dependence on the domain – the intent identification is provided at a higher level to identify and trigger the task, defined as a set of slots and *ask queries*. Intent identification supports hosting of multiple tasks.

The framework provides tools for easy hosting of dialogue tasks as HIT (Human Intelligence Task) on Amazon mTurk to collect human responses; the framework also supports modelling dialogue tasks as an agent-agent interaction that can be used to test a dialogue agent against simulated users (Schatzmann et al., 2005b). A summary of MACA's features is provided in Table 1.

	MACA	TCP	Ravenclaw
Multi Domain Support	✓	✓	✓
Plug-and-Play	✓	✓	✗
Adaptation for FCA	✓	✗	✗
Agent Abstraction	✓	✗	✗
Integration with mTurk	✓	✗	✗

Table 1: Feature Comparison of MACA with existing similar frameworks. Note: FCA: Frequently used Conversational Agents.

5 Implementation Highlights[2]

MACA's current implementation is in Python and includes standard libraries to ensure the framework's portability, as well as to facilitate rapid prototyping of different dialogue model strategies. Each component of the framework (e.g. *Input* component) is described with an abstract Python class, whose concrete implementation instances (i.e. Python objects) are manifestations of that component (e.g. Command line input, Database input). This corresponds to the abstraction layer of the architecture's module to foster independence of the pipeline implementation from that of the underlying dialogue model(s). The assembly of these components are then specified in a central configuration file representing an instantiation of the architecture. With this design, changes in the instantiation specifications can be done within the central configuration file by modifying the names of invoked modules. On the other hand, this setup allows system specifications to be completely contained within the central configuration file, which reduces maintenance effort and simplifies configuration modification during development. In addition, the open source nature of the framework encourages sharing and reusing of components, which allows researchers to easily develop from existing models and save time by reusing common components written by others.

6 Case Studies

MACA was deployed for several studies within our research group. All conducted studies have the same template for the central configuration file, whose content is then modified corresponding to the purpose of each study. Listing 1 shows the configuration template representing a system with a simple dialogue agent, which repeats its input

(echo agent). The configuration file requires several attributes to be mentioned and provides a general outlook of the experiment being run. The template contains the following attributes: *input, output, preprocessing, postprocessing, agent, domain knowledge* and *listeners*. The *class* sub-attribute of the attributes refers to the Python class implementation of the component being invoked.

6.1 Building a simple agent

The Echo agent is designed to simply listen and store the input to file; this is a good first test case for new users of MACA. In this setup, the *input* attribute is instantiated with *StdinInputDevice*, which is the commandline inputs, and the *output* attribute is instantiated with *FileOutputDevice*, which writes the results to a file. Likewise, the instantiations of the other attributes, like *postprocessing, preprocessing* and *domain knowledge*, point to *VoidPostprocessor, VoidPreprocessor*, and *EmptyDomainKnowledge* respectively, since Echo agent does not require them. The *agent* attribute is instantiated with the appropriate dialogue agent, which in this case is Echo agent. Along with these components, *LoggingListener*, which logs the input and output of the system on to an output file, is included as a *listener* component.

```
1   'input' : { 'class' : StdinInputDevice },
2   'output' : {
3       'class' : FileOutputDevice,
4       'args' : ['out.gods']
5   },
6   'preprocessing' : {
7       'modules' : [{ 'class' : VoidPreprocessor, }],
8       'parallel' : False, # Optional
9   },
10  'postprocessing' : {
11      'output_index' : 0, # Index of the pipe to output
12      'parallel' : False, # Optional
13      'modules' : [ { 'class' : VoidPostprocessor, } ]
14  },
15  'agent' : { 'class' : EchoAgent },
16  'domain_knowledge' : { 'class' : EmptyDomainKnowledge },
17  'listeners' : { 'unnamed': [{ 'class' : LoggingListener }] }
```

Listing 1: Configuration Template.

6.2 Building a goal oriented system

Next, we consider using MACA to build goal oriented agents for the restaurant, flight booking, and other toy domains. These slot-based agents were developed using the tools provided in the framework that aids in hierarchical task decomposition and slot sharing across tasks (as in the example reusing the same Python variables). With regard to hosting a multi-task agent, the invocation of Goal

---

[2]Some of the configuration file samples provided in the listings in this section are slightly modified to fit the page limit constraint.

oriented policies/sub-agents for each task happens with the description of slots – askQuery, disambiguation strategy etc. As with providing multi-agent support, the architecture can handle multiple intents with intent triggers defined for each of them. For example, "I would like to book a flight" will trigger the flight booking policy which will fill in slots specific to this task based on the information provided in the domain knowledge, whereas "What's a good restaurant nearby?" will trigger the restaurant booking policy. The configuration file modification in the agent and domain knowledge attributes is provided in Listing 2.

```
1   first_name_slot = Slot('first_name')
2   last_name_slot = Slot('last_name')
3   'agent' : {
4     'class' : PersonalInformationAskingModel,
5     'kwargs' : {
6       'intents' : [
7         AddressAskingAgent('address'),
8         NameAskingAgent('name')
9       ]
10    }
11  },
12  'domain_knowledge' : {
13    'class' : GoalOrientedDomainKnowledge,
14    'args' : [{
15      'address' : [
16        first_name_slot, last_name_slot,
17        Slot('street', ['apt', 'street_name']),
18        Slot('city'),
19        Slot('country'),
20        Slot('zip_code', enabling_condition = \
21        lambda slots: slots['country'].value() == "US")
22      ],
23      'flight_booking' : [
24        first_name_slot, last_name_slot,
25        Slot('origin'),
26        Slot('destination'),
27        Slot('return_date')
28      ]
29    }]
30  },
```

Listing 2: Sample Agent attribute in Goal Oriented Dialogue models' Configuration.

An overview of the architecture components in the goal oriented setting is provided in Table 2.

6.3 Building a neural response generation agent

We also used MACA to prototype neural response generation agents based on the Hierarchical Encoder-Decoder framework (Serban et al., 2015).

6.3.1 HRED in training mode

MACA's *training* mode was tested with the training process of an HRED agent. The modifications for the central configuration files for this

Component		Description	Note
Domain Knowledge		GoalOriented Do-mainKnowledge	Specifying slots information for known domains.
Input		StdInputDevice	Inputs from stdin.
Preprocessing		VoidPreprocessor	None.
Model	Preprocessing	VoidProcessing	None.
	Postprocessing	Model specific	None.
	Internal	PersonalInformation AskingModel	Intent disambiguation and execution policies.
Postprocessing		VoidProcessing	None.
Output		FileOutputDevice	Output to a file.
Listeners		LoggingListener	Log all pubsub notifications to file.

Table 2: Setup for goal oriented system in execution mode.

setup are presented in Listing 3. *HREDTraining-InputDevice* simply invokes the training process by sending an *initiate* message to the model while the dialogue model *HREDAgent*, configured to be in *training* mode, starts its regular training process and writes the trained weights to disk. The training dataset is specified using the *prototype* sub-attribute (in compliance with the HRED code base) within the *train_args* attribute of *agent*. All other components of the pipeline are unchanged as it is unnecessary to postprocess or to output data. The HRED agent was trained using both the Twitter Corpus (Ritter et al., 2011) and Ubuntu Dialogue Corpus (Lowe et al., 2015b).

```
1   'input' : {
2     'class' : HREDTrainingInputDevice
3   }, ...
4   'agent' : {
5     'class' : HREDAgent,
6     'kwargs' : {
7       'train_args' : { 'prototype' : 'ubuntu_HRED' },
8       'mode' : system_modes.TRAINING,
9     }
10  },
```

Listing 3: Modified attributes for HRED training.

6.3.2 HRED in execution mode

We also tested using a trained HRED agent in *execution* and *data collection* modes. In the execution mode, MACA used the command-line as the input and the output units to fetch user responses and show model responses from HRED. In the data collection mode, MACA was hosted on a local psiTurk (Gureckis et al., 2016) server emulating mTurk. A layout that lets the users chat and score the model responses was provided, and user inputs were logged by a database listener through the pubsub architecture. In this scenario, the pre-trained HRED model can be seen as a case of custom built dialogue agent adapted to MACA.

```
1   'agent' : {
2     'class' : HREDAgent,
3     'kwargs' : {
4       'ignore_unknown_words' : True,
5       'normalize' : False,
6       'prototype' : 'prototype_twitter_HRED',
7       'train_dialogues' : 'Training.dialogues.pkl',
8       'test_dialogues' : 'Test.dialogues.pkl',
9       'valid_dialogues' : 'Validation.dialogues.pkl',
10      'dictionary_path' : 'Dataset.dict.pkl',
11      'model_prefix' : './334.74_Model'
12    }
13  },
```

Listing 4: Agent attribute in HRED Configuration.

The central configuration file from Listing 1 is updated for HRED in *execution* mode, as shown in Listing 4. The model specific arguments, provided between lines 3 and 14, in Listing 4 demonstrate MACA's support for plugging in customized or pre-trained dialogue agents. Furthermore, an overview of the architecture, with the instantiated components, and their roles is provided in Table 3.

Component		Description	Role
Domain Knowledge		EmptyDomainKnowledge	An empty domain.
Input		StdInputDevice	Inputs from stdin.
Preprocessing		HredPreprocessing	Tokenize input sentence.
Model	Preprocessing	Model specific	Add model specific tokens.
	Postprocessing	Model specific	Remove speaker tokens.
	Internal	HredAgent	HRED internals.
Postprocessing		VoidProcessing	None.
Output		FileOutputDevice	Output to a file.
Listeners		LoggingListener	Log all pubsub notifications to file.

Table 3: Setup of HRED system: Execution mode.

6.4 Building a neural response retrieval agent

Finally, we built an architecture that incorporates a neural response retrieval agent operating using the Dual Encoder method (Lowe et al., 2015a).

6.4.1 Dual Encoder in training mode

Listing 5 presents changes to the template configuration to incorporate a Dual Encoder dialogue agent in training mode. Similar to the HRED model training case, we replace the *Input* and *Model* modules in the template configuration. In the case of Dual Encoder, the specified data set will be loaded into *DomainKnowledge* and will become accessible after initialization. During the training process, *RetrievalModelTrainingInputDevice* retrieves the data from the specified train-

ing data set via *DomainKnowledge* and feeds it to the *Dialogue Model* while the *RetrievalModelAgent* contains the relevant training parameters. Once training finishes, *RetrievalModelTrainingInputDevice* issues a message to the agent to write out trained weights to disk.

```
1   'input' : {
2     'class' : RetrievalModelTrainingInputDevice,
3     'kwargs' : { 'n_epochs' : 500, 'shuffle_batch' : False }
4   }, ...
5   'agent' : {
6     'class' : RetrievalModelAgent,
7     'args' : [ 'twitter_dataset/W_twitter_bpe.pkl' ],
8     'kwargs' : {
9       'model_fname' : 'model.pkl',
10      'mode' : system_modes.TRAINING,
11      'model_params' : {
12        'encoder' : 'lstm',
13        'batch_size' : 512, 'hidden_size' : 200,
14        'optimizer' : 'adam', 'lr' : 0.001,
15      }
16    }
17  }, ...
18  'dataset' : {
19    'class' : RetrievalTwitterDataset,
20    'args' : [ 'twitter_dataset', 'dataset_twitter_bpe.pkl' ]
21  },
```

Listing 5: Modified attributes for Dual Encoder training.

6.4.2 Dual Encoder in execution mode

We also tested the Dual Encoder agent in *execution* mode, which is an instance of adapting a retrieval based model to the proposed framework. The execution mode in this case obtained inputs from a database of previously collected context-response pairs. The configuration file for the Dual Encoder model looks mostly similar to the generic template, with modification on the *agent* attribute, described in Listing 6.

```
1   'preprocessing' : {
2     'modules': [{
3       'class' : RetrievalModelPreprocessor,
4       'args' : ['./retrieval/BPE/Twitter_Codes_5000.txt']
5     }],
6   }, ...
7   'agent' : {
8     'class' : RetrievalModelAgent,
9     'args' : [ '../../twitter_dataset/W_twitter_bpe.pkl' ],
10    'kwargs' : {
11      'model_params' : {
12        'encoder' : 'lstm',
13        'batch_size' : 512, 'hidden_size' : 100,
14        'input_dir' : '../../twitter_dataset',
15        'W_fname' : 'W_twitter_bpe.pkl'
16      }
17    }
18  },
```

Listing 6: Agent attribute in Dual Encoder (Retrieval Model) Configuration.

The configuration file's flexibility allows customized agents to be plugged in with ease, while providing the parameters for the model to run in the *model_params* sub-attribute. Further, an overview of MACA with its instantiated components and their roles is provided in Table 4; specification of these attributes within MACA is achieved through the configuration file.

Component		Description	Role
Domain Knowledge		EmptyDomainKnowledge	An empty domain.
Input		StdInputDevice	Inputs from stdin.
Preprocessing		RetrievalModelPreprocessing	Compute BPE on all utterances.
Model	Preprocessing	Model specific	None.
	Postprocessing	Model specific	None.
	Internal	RetrievalModelAgent	Dual Encoder internals.
Postprocessing		VoidProcessing	None.
Output		FileOutputDevice	Output to a file.
Listeners		LoggingListener	Log all pubsub notifications to file.

Table 4: Setup for Dual Encoder system in execution mode.

7 Discussion

MACA offers a unified architecture for dialogue agents that supports the plug-n-play of different types of dialogue agents and different domains. We hope that this will facilitate the fast development of new models, but also foster reproducibility in dialogue system research.

A few possible limitations in the current implementation of MACA include simplicity of the pubsub system, lack of support for distributed hosting of different components of the architecture, and lack of support for parallel conversations. As future work, the pubsub system could be improved by capturing a wider range of system information with more monitoring pubsub channels. In addition, we plan to incorporate new domains and agents as they become available, along with comprehensive ML based slot-disambiguation modules.

Acknowledgments

Acknowledgements The authors gratefully acknowledge financial support for this work by the Samsung Advanced Institute of Technology (SAIT) and the Natural Sciences and Engineering Research Council of Canada (NSERC).

References

M. Abadi, A. Agarwal, P. Barham, E. Brevdo, Z. Chen, C. Citro, G. S Corrado, A. Davis, J. Dean, and M. et. al Devin. 2016. Tensorflow: Large-scale machine learning on heterogeneous distributed systems. *arXiv:1603.04467* .

J. F Allen, D. K Byron, M. Dzikovska, G. Ferguson, L. Galescu, and A. Stent. 2001. Toward conversational human-computer interaction. *AI magazine* .

D. Bohus and A. I Rudnicky. 2003. Ravenclaw: Dialog management using hierarchical task decomposition and an expectation agenda .

PA Crook, A Marin, V Agarwal, K Aggarwal, T Anastasakos, R Bikkula, D Boies, A Celikyilmaz, S Chandramohan, and Z et. al Feizollahi. 2016. Task completion platform: A self-serve multi-domain goal oriented dialogue platform. *NAACL HLT* .

P. Gage. 1994. A new algorithm for data compression. *The C Users Journal* .

T. M. Gureckis, J. Martin, J. McDonnell, A. S. Rich, D. Markant, A. Coenen, D. Halpern, J. B. Hamrick, and P. Chan. 2016. psiturk: An open-source framework for conducting replicable behavioral experiments online. *Behavior research methods* .

S. Hochreiter and J. Schmidhuber. 1997. Long short-term memory. *Neural computation* .

S. Kim and R. E. Banchs. 2014. R-cube: a dialogue agent for restaurant recommendation and reservation. In *Asia-Pacific Signal and Information Processing Association, 2014 Annual Summit and Conference (APSIPA)*. IEEE.

Q. V. Le and T. Mikolov. 2014. Distributed representations of sentences and documents. In *ICML*.

E. Loper and S. Bird. 2002. Nltk: The natural language toolkit. In *Proceedings of the ACL-02 Workshop on Effective tools and methodologies for teaching natural language processing and computational linguistics-Volume 1*.

R. Lowe, N. Pow, I. Serban, and J. Pineau. 2015a. The ubuntu dialogue corpus: A large dataset for research in unstructured multi-turn dialogue systems. *arXiv:1506.08909* .

R. Lowe, N. Pow, I. Serban, and J. Pineau. 2015b. The ubuntu dialogue corpus: A large dataset for research in unstructured multi-turn dialogue systems. In *16th Annual Meeting of the Special Interest Group on Discourse and Dialogue*.

T. Mikolov, K. Chen, G. Corrado, and J. Dean. 2013. Efficient estimation of word representations in vector space. *arXiv:1301.3781* .

S. Png and J. Pineau. 2011. Bayesian reinforcement learning for pomdp-based dialogue systems. In *Acoustics, Speech and Signal Processing (ICASSP), IEEE International Conference on*. IEEE.

A. Ritter, C. Cherry, and W. B. Dolan. 2011. Data-driven response generation in social media. In *EMNLP*.

J. Schatzmann, K. Georgila, and S. Young. 2005a. Quantitative evaluation of user simulation techniques for spoken dialogue systems. In *6th SIGdial Workshop on DISCOURSE and DIALOGUE*.

J. Schatzmann, K. Georgila, and S. Young. 2005b. Quantitative evaluation of user simulation techniques for spoken dialogue systems. In *6th SIGdial Workshop on DISCOURSE and DIALOGUE*.

F. Seide and S. McDirmid. 2012. Clippyscript: A programming language for multi-domain dialogue systems. In *Thirteenth Annual Conference of the International Speech Communication Association*.

I. Serban, A. Sordoni, Y. Bengio, A. Courville, and J. Pineau. 2015. Building end-to-end dialogue systems using generative hierarchical neural network models. *arXiv:1507.04808* .

I. Serban, A. Sordoni, R. Lowe, L. Charlin, J. Pineau, A. Courville, and Y. Bengio. 2016. A hierarchical latent variable encoder-decoder model for generating dialogues. *arXiv:1605.06069* .

Theano Development Team. 2016. Theano: A Python framework for fast computation of mathematical expressions. *arXiv:1605.02688* .

S. Young. 2006. Using pomdps for dialog management. In *Spoken Language Technology Workshop*. IEEE.

T. Zhao, K. Lee, and M. Eskenazi. 2016. Dialport: Connecting the spoken dialog research community to real user data. *arXiv:1606.02562* .

Sequential Dialogue Context Modeling for Spoken Language Understanding

Ankur Bapna   **Gokhan Tür**   **Dilek Hakkani-Tür**   **Larry Heck**

Google Research, Mountain View

ankurbpn@google.com {gokhan.tur, dilek, larry.heck}@ieee.org

Abstract

Spoken Language Understanding (SLU) is a key component of goal oriented dialogue systems that would parse user utterances into semantic frame representations. Traditionally SLU does not utilize the dialogue history beyond the previous system turn and contextual ambiguities are resolved by the downstream components. In this paper, we explore novel approaches for modeling dialogue context in a recurrent neural network (RNN) based language understanding system. We propose the Sequential Dialogue Encoder Network, that allows encoding context from the dialogue history in chronological order. We compare the performance of our proposed architecture with two context models, one that uses just the previous turn context and another that encodes dialogue context in a memory network, but loses the order of utterances in the dialogue history. Experiments with a multi-domain dialogue dataset demonstrate that the proposed architecture results in reduced semantic frame error rates.

1 Introduction

Goal oriented dialogue systems help users with accomplishing tasks, like making restaurant reservations or booking flights, by interacting with them in natural language. The capability to understand user utterances and break them down into task specific semantics is a key requirement for these systems. This is accomplished in the spoken language understanding module, which typically parses user utterances into semantic frames, composed of domains, intents and slots (Tur and De Mori, 2011), that can then be processed by downstream dia-

$u1$	Can you get me a restaurant reservation ?					
s	Sure, where do you want to go ?					
$u2$	table	for	2	at	Pho	Nam
	↓	↓	↓	↓	↓	↓
S	O	O	B-#	O	B-Rest	I-Rest
D	restaurants					
I	reserve_restaurant					

Figure 1: An example semantic parse of an utterance ($u2$) with slot (S), domain (D), intent (I) annotations, following the IOB (in-out-begin) representation for slot values.

logue system components. An example semantic frame is shown for a restaurant reservation related query in Figure 1.

As the complexity of the task supported by a dialogue system increases, there is a need for an increased back and forth interaction between the user and the agent. For example, a restaurant reservation task might require the user to specify a restaurant name, date, time and number of people required for the reservation. Additionally, based on reservation availability, the user might need to negotiate on date, time, or any other attribute with the agent. This puts the burden of parsing in-dialogue contextual user utterances on the language understanding module. The complexity increases further when the system supports more than one task and the user is allowed to have goals spanning multiple domains within the same dialogue. Natural language utterances are often ambiguous, and the context from previous user and system turns could help resolve the errors arising from these ambiguities.

In this paper, we explore approaches to improve dialogue context modeling within a Recurrent Neural Network (RNN) based spoken language understanding system. We propose a novel model architecture to improve dialogue context modeling for spoken language understanding on a

103

Proceedings of the SIGDIAL 2017 Conference, pages 103–114,
Saarbrücken, Germany, 15-17 August 2017. ©2017 Association for Computational Linguistics

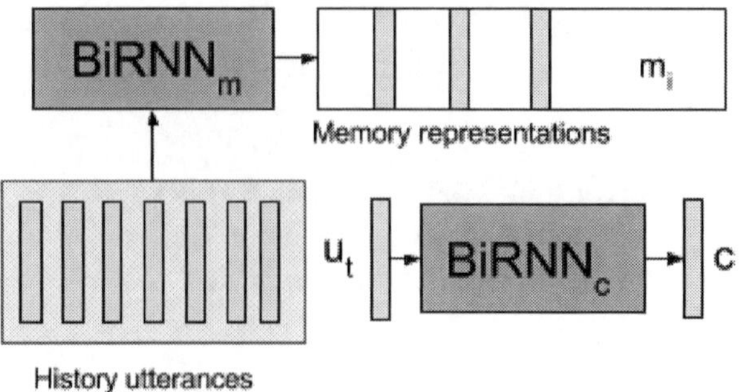

Figure 2: Architecture of the Memory and current utterance context encoder.

multi-domain dialogue dataset. The proposed architecture is an extension of Hierarchical Recurrent Encoder Decoders (HRED) (Sordoni et al., 2015), where we combine the query level encodings with a representation of the current utterance, before feeding it into the session level encoder. We compare the performance of this model to a RNN tagger injected with just the previous turn context and a single hop memory network that uses an attention weighted combination of the dialogue context (Chen et al., 2016; Weston et al., 2014).

Furthermore, we describe a dialogue recombination technique to enhance the complexity of the training dataset by injecting synthetic domain switches, to create a better match with the mixed domain dialogues in the test dataset. This is, in principle, a multi-turn extension of (Jia and Liang, 2016). Instead of inducing and composing grammars to synthetically enhance single turn text, we combine single domain dialogue sessions into multi-domain dialogues to provide richer context during training.

2   Related Work

The task of understanding a user utterance is typically broken down into 3 tasks: domain classification, intent classification and slot-filling (Tur and De Mori, 2011). Most modern approaches to Spoken language understanding involve training machine learning models on labeled training data (Young, 2002; Hahn et al., 2011; Wang et al., 2005, among others). More recently, recurrent neural network (RNN) based approaches have been shown to perform exceedingly well on spoken language understanding tasks (Mesnil et al., 2015; Hakkani-Tür et al., 2016; Kurata et al., 2016, among others). RNN based approaches have also been applied successfully to other tasks for di-

alogue systems, like dialogue state tracking (Henderson, 2015; Henderson et al., 2014; Perez and Liu, 2016, among others), policy learning (Su et al., 2015) and system response generation (Wen et al., 2015, 2016, among others).

In parallel, joint modeling of tasks and addition of contextual signals has been shown to result in performance gains for several applications. Modeling domain, intent and slots in a joint RNN model was shown to result in reduction of overall frame error rates (Hakkani-Tür et al., 2016). Joint modeling of intent classification and language modeling showed promising improvements in intent recognition, especially in the presence of noisy speech recognition (Liu and Lane, 2016).

Similarly, models incorporating more context from dialogue history (Chen et al., 2016) or semantic context from the frame (Dauphin et al., 2014; Bapna et al., 2017) tend to outperform models without context and have shown potential for greater generalization on spoken language understanding and related tasks. (Dhingra et al., 2016) show improved performance on an informational dialogue agent by incorporating knowledge base context into their dialogue system. Using dialogue context was shown to boost performance for end to end dialogue (Bordes and Weston, 2016) and next utterance prediction (Serban et al., 2015).

In the next few sections, we describe the proposed model architecture, the dataset and our dialogue recombination approach. This is followed by experimental results and analysis.

3   Model Architecture

We compare the performance of 3 model architectures for encoding dialogue context on a multi-domain dialogue dataset. Let the dialogue be a sequence of system and user utterances $D_t =$

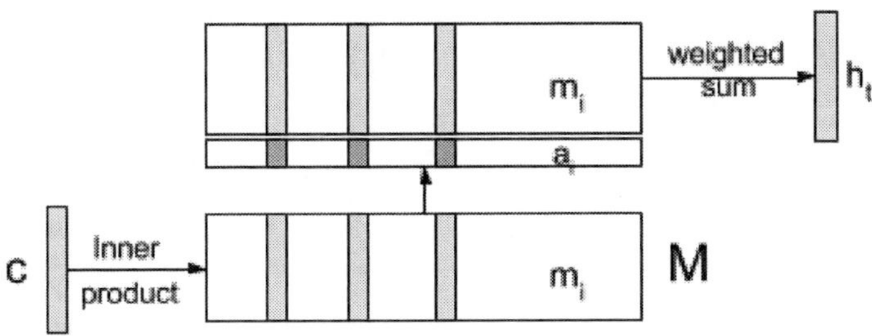

Figure 3: Architecture of the dialogue context encoder for the cosine similarity based memory network.

$\{u_1, u_2...u_t\}$ and at time step t we are trying to output the parse of a user utterance u_t, given D_t. Let any utterance u_k be a sequence of tokens given by $\{x_1^k, x_2^k...x_{n_k}^k\}$.

We divide the model into 2 components, the context encoder that acts on D_t to produce a vector representation of the dialogue context denoted by $h_t = H(D_t)$, and the tagger, which takes the dialogue context encoding h_t, and the current utterance u_t as input and produces the domain, intent and slot annotations as output.

3.1 Context Encoder Architectures

In this section we describe the architectures of the context encoders used for our experiments. We compare the performance of 3 different architectures that encode varying levels of dialogue context.

3.1.1 Previous Utterance Encoder

This is the baseline context encoder architecture. We feed the embeddings corresponding to tokens in the previous system utterance, $u_{t-1} = \{x_1^{t-1}, x_2^{t-1}...x_{n_{t-1}}^{t-1}\}$, into a single Bidirectional RNN (BiRNN) layer with Gated Recurrent Unit (GRU) (Chung et al., 2014) cells and 128 dimensions (64 in each direction). The embeddings are shared with the tagger. The final state of the context encoder GRU is used as the dialogue context.

$$h_t = BiGRU_c(u_{t-1}) \qquad (1)$$

3.1.2 Memory Network

This architecture is identical to the approach described in (Chen et al., 2016). We encode all dialogue context utterances, $\{u_1, u_2...u_{t-1}\}$, into memory vectors denoted by $\{m_1, m_2, ...m_{t-1}\}$ using a Bidirectional GRU (BiGRU) encoder with 128 dimensions (64 in each direction). To add temporal context to the dialogue history utter-

ances, we append special positional tokens to each utterance.

$$m_k = BiGRU_m(u_k) \quad for \quad 0 \leq k \leq t-1 \quad (2)$$

We also encode the current utterance with another BiGRU encoder with 128 dimensions (64 in each direction), into a context vector denoted by c, as in equation 3. This is conceptually depicted in Figure 2

$$c = BiGRU_c(u_t) \qquad (3)$$

Let M be a matrix with the ith row given by m_i. We obtain the cosine similarity between each memory vector, m_i, and the context vector c. The softmax of this similarity is used as an attention distribution over the memory M, and an attention weighted sum of M is used to produce the dialogue context vector h_t (Equation 4). This is conceptually depicted in Figure 3.

$$a = softmax(Mc)$$
$$h_t = a^T M \qquad (4)$$

3.1.3 Sequential Dialogue Encoder Network

We enhance the memory network architecture described above by adding a session encoder (Sordoni et al., 2015) that temporally combines a joint representation of the current utterance encoding, c, (Eq. 3) and the memory vectors, $\{m_1, m_2...m_{t-1}\}$, (Eq. 2).

We combine the context vector c with each memory vector m_k, for $1 \leq k \leq n_k$, by concatenating and passing them through a feed forward layer (FF) to produce 128 dimensional context encodings, denoted by $\{g_1, g_2...g_{t-1}\}$ (Eq. 5).

$$g_k = sigmoid(FF(m_k, c)) \quad for \quad 0 \leq k \leq t-1 \qquad (5)$$

These context encodings are fed as token level inputs into the session encoder, which is a 128 di-

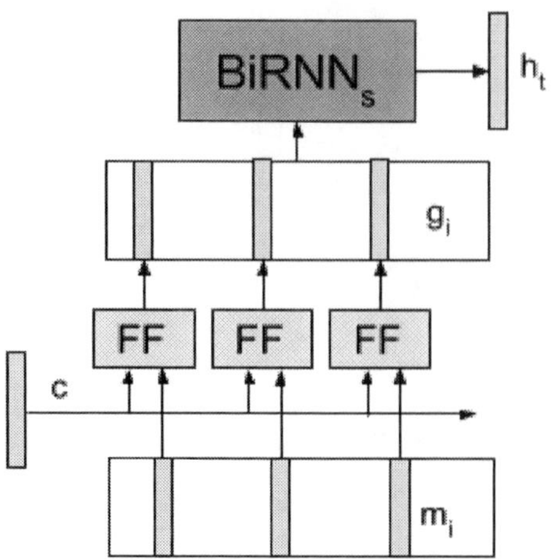

Figure 4: Architecture of the Sequential Dialogue Encoder Network. The feed-forward networks share weights across all memories.

mensional BiGRU layer. The final state of the session encoder represents the dialogue context encoding h_t (Eq. 6).

$$h_t = BiGRU_s(\{g_1, g_2, ...g_{t-1}\}) \qquad (6)$$

The architecture is depicted in Figure 4.

3.2 Tagger Architecture

For all our experiments we use a stacked BiRNN tagger to jointly model domain classification, intent classification and slot-filling, similar to the approach described in (Hakkani-Tür et al., 2016). We feed learned 256 dimensional embeddings corresponding to the current utterance tokens into the tagger.

The first RNN layer uses GRU cells with 256 dimensions (128 in each direction) as in equation 7. The token embeddings are fed into the token level inputs of the first RNN layer to produce the token level outputs $o^1 = \{o^1_1, o^1_2...o^1_{n_t}\}$.

$$o^1 = BiGRU_1(u_t) \qquad (7)$$

The second layer uses Long Short Term Memory (LSTM) (Hochreiter and Schmidhuber, 1997) cells with 256 dimensions (128 in both dimensions). We use a LSTM based second layer since that improved slot-filling performance on the validation set for all architectures. We apply dropout to the outputs of both layers. The initial states of both forward and backward LSTMs of the second tagger layer are initialized with the dialogue encoding h_t as in equation 8. The token level outputs of the first RNN layer, o^1, are fed as input

into the second RNN layer to produce token level outputs $o^2 = \{o^2_1, o^2_2...o^2_{n_t}\}$ and the final state s^2.

$$o^2, s^2 = BiLSTM_2(o^1, h_t) \qquad (8)$$

The final state of the second layer, s^2, is used as input to classification layers for domain and intent classification.

$$\begin{aligned} p^{domain} &= softmax(Us^2) \\ p^{intent} &= sigmoid(Vs^2) \end{aligned} \qquad (9)$$

The token level outputs of the second layer, o^2, are used as input to a softmax layer that outputs the IOB slot labels. This results in a softmax layer with $2N+1$ dimensions for a domain with N slots.

$$p^{slot}_i = softmax(So^2_i) \quad for \quad 0 \leq i \leq n^t \qquad (10)$$

The architecture is depicted in Figure 5.

4   Dataset

We crowd sourced multi-turn dialogue sessions for 3 tasks: buying movie tickets, searching for a restaurant and reserving tables at a restaurant. Our data collection process comprises of two steps: (i) Generating user-agent interactions comprising of dialog acts and slots based on the interplay of a simulated user and a rule based dialogue policy. (ii) Using a crowd sourcing platform to elicit natural language utterances that align with the semantics of the generated interactions.

The goal of the spoken language understanding module of our dialogue system is to map each user utterance into frame based semantics that can be processed by the downstream components. Tables describing the intents and slots present in the dataset can be found in the appendix.

We use a stochastic agenda-based user simulator (Schatzmann et al., 2007; Shah et al., 2016) for interplay with our rule based system policy. The user goal is specified in terms of a tuple of slots, which denote the user constraints. Some constraints might be unspecified, in which case the user is indifferent to the value of those slots. At any given turn, the simulator samples a user dialogue act from a set of acceptable actions based on (i) the user goal and agenda that includes slots that still need to be specified, (ii) a randomly chosen user profile (co-operative/aggressive, verbose/succinct etc.) and (iii) the previous user and

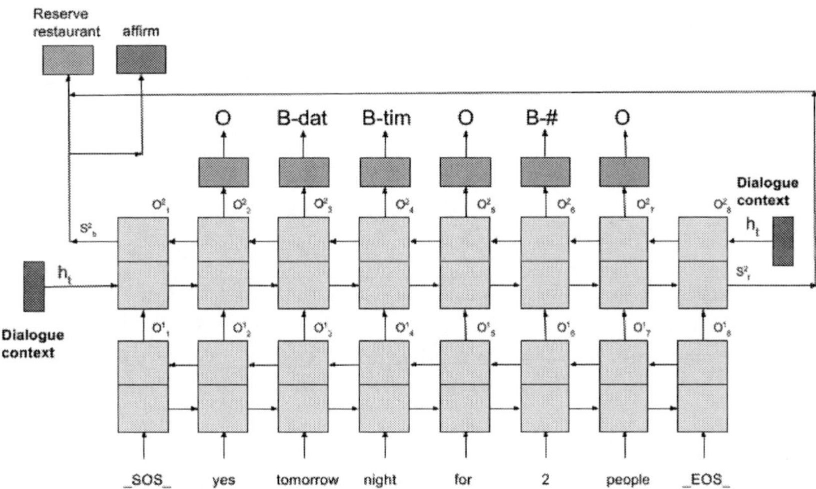

Figure 5: Architecture of the stacked BiRNN tagger. The dialogue context obtained from the context encoder is fed into the initial states of the second RNN layer.

Domain	Attributes
movies	date, movie, num_tickets, theatre_name, time
find-restaurants	category, location, meal, price_range, rating, restaurant_name
reserve-restaurant	date, num_people, restaurant_name, time

Table 1: List of attributes supported for each domain.

system actions. Based on the chosen user dialogue act, the rule based policy might make a backend call to inquire for restaurant or movie availability. Based on the user act and the backend response the system responds back with a dialogue act or a combination of dialogue acts, based on a hand designed rule based policy. These generated interactions were then translated to their natural language counterparts and sent out to crowd-workers for paraphrasing into natural language human-machine dialogues.

The simulator and policy were also extended to handle multiple goals spanning different domains. In this set-up, the user goal for the simulator would include multiple tasks and slot values could be conditioned on the previous task, for example, the simulator would ask for booking a table "after the movie", or search for a restaurant "near the the-ater". The set of slots supported by the simulator is enumerated in Table 1. We collected 1319 dialogues for restaurant reservation, 976 dialogues for finding restaurants and 1048 dialogues for buy-ing movie tickets. All single domain datasets were used for training. The multi-domain simulator was used to collect 467 dialogues for training, 50 for validation and 273 for the test set. Since the natural language dialogues were paraphrased versions of known dialogue- act and slot combinations, they were automatically labeled. These labels were verified by an expert annotator, and turns with missing annotations were manually annotated by the expert.

5 Dialogue Recombination

As described in the previous section, we train our models on a large set of single domain dialogue datasets and a small set of multi-domain dialogues. These models are then evaluated on a test set composed of multi-domain dialogues, where the user attempts to fulfill multiple goals spanning several domains. This results in a distribution drift that might result in performance degradation. To counter this drift in the training-test data distributions we device a dialogue recombination scheme to generate multi-domain dialogues from single domain training datasets.

Dialogue x	Dialogue y	Dialogue d_r
U: Get me 5 tickets to see Inferno.		U: Get me 5 tickets to see Inferno.
S: Sure, when is this booking for ?		S: Sure, when is this booking for ?
U: Around 5 pm tomorrow night.		U: Around 5 pm tomorrow night.
S: Do you have a theatre in mind?		S: Do you have a theatre in mind?
U: AMC newpark 12.	U: Find italian restaurants in Mountain View	U: Find italian restaurants in Mountain View
S: Does 4:45 pm work for you ?	S: What price range are you looking for ?	S: What price range are you looking for ?
U: Yes.	U: cheap	U: cheap
S: Your booking is complete.	S: Ristorante Giovanni is a nice Italian restaurant in Mountain View.	S: Ristorante Giovanni is a nice Italian restaurant in Mountain View.
	U: That works. thanks.	U: That works. thanks.

Table 2: A sample dialogue obtained from recombining a dialogue from the movies and find-restaurant datasets.

The key idea behind the recombination approach is the conditional independence of sub-dialogues aimed at performing distinct tasks (Grosz and Sidner, 1986). We exploit the presence of task intents, or intents that denote a switch in the primary task the user is trying to perform, since they are a strong indicator of a switch in the focus of the dialogue. We exploit the independence of the sub-dialogue following these intents from the previous dialogue context, to generate synthetic dialogues with multi-domain context. The recombination process is described as follows:

Let a dialogue d be defined as a sequence of turns and corresponding semantic labels (domain, intent and slot annotations) $\{(t_{d1}, f_{d1}), (t_{d2}, f_{d2}), ...(t_{dn_d}, f_{dn_d}\}$. To obtain a re-combined dataset composed of dialogues from dataset $dataset_1$ and $dataset_2$, we repeat the following steps 10000 times, for each combination of $(dataset_1, dataset_2)$ from the three single domain datasets.

- Sample dialogues x and y from $dataset_1$ and $dataset_2$ respectively.

- Find the first user utterance labeled with a task intent in y. Let this be turn l.

- Randomly sample an insertion point in dialogue x. Let this be turn k.

- The new recombined dialogue is $\{(t_{x1}, f_{x1}), ...(t_{xk}, f_{xk}), (t_{yl}, f_{yl}), ...(t_{yn_y}, f_{yn_y})\}$.

A sample dialogue generated using the above procedure is described in table 2. We drop the utterances from dialogue x following the insertion point (turn k) in the recombined dialogue since these turns become ambiguous or confusing in the absence of preceding context. In a sense our approach is one of partial dialogue recombination.

6 Experiments

We compare the domain classification, intent classification and slot-filling performances, and the overall frame error rates of the encoder-decoder, memory network and sequential dialogue encoder network on the dataset described above. The frame error rate of a SLU system is the percentage of utterances where it makes a wrong prediction i.e. any of domain, intent or slot is predicted incorrectly.

We trained all 3 models with RMSProp for 100000 training steps with a batch size of 100. We started with a learning rate of 0.0003 which was decayed by a factor of 0.95 every 3000 steps. Gradient norms were clipped if they exceed a magnitude of 2.5. All model and optimization hyper-parameters were chosen based on a grid search, to minimize validation set frame error rates.

Model	Domain F1	Intent F1	Slot Token F1	Frame Error Rate
ED	0.937	0.865	0.891	31.87%
MN	0.964	0.890	0.896	26.72%
SDEN	0.960	0.870	0.896	31.31%
ED + DR	0.936	0.885	0.911	30.72%
MN + DR	0.968	**0.902**	0.904	27.48%
SDEN + DR	**0.975**	0.898	**0.926**	**25.85%**

Table 3: Test set performances for the encoder decoder (ED) model, Memory Network (MN) and the Sequential Dialogue Encoder Network (SDEN) with and without recombined data (DR).

utterance				MN+DR	SDEN+DR
hi!				0.00	0.13
hello ! i want to buy movie tickets for *8* pm at cinclux plaza				0.05	**0.34**
which movie , how many , and what day ?				0.13	**0.24**
Trolls , *6* tickets for today					

	True	ED+DR	MN+DR	SDEN+DR
Domain	buy-movie-tickets	movies	movies	movies
Intent	contextual	contextual	contextual	contextual
date	today	today	today	today
num_tickets	*6*	*6*	*6*	*6*
movie	*Trolls*	*Trolls*	-	*Trolls*

Table 4: Dialogue from the test set with predictions from Encoder Decoder with recombined data (ED+DR), Memory Network with recombined data (MN+DR) and Sequential Dialogue Encoder Network with dialogue recombination (SDEN+DR).Tokens that have been italicized in the dialogue were out of vocabulary or replaced with special tokens. The columns to the right of the dialogue history detail the attention distributions. For SDEN+DR, we use the magnitude of the change in the session GRU state as a proxy for the attention distribution. Attention weights might not sum up to 1 if there is non-zero attention on history padding.

We restrict the model vocabularies to contain only tokens occurring more than 10 times in the training set, to prevent over-fitting to training set entities. Digits were replaced with a special "#" token to allow better generalization to unseen numbers. The dialogue history was padded to 40 utterances for batch processing. We report results with and without the recombined dataset in Table 3.

7 Results

The encoder decoder model trained on just the previous turn context performs worst on almost all metrics, irrespective of the presence of recombined data. This can be explained by worse performance on in-dialogue utterances, where just the previous turn context isn't sufficient to accurately identify the domain, and in several cases, the intents and slots of the utterance.

The memory network is the best performing model in the absence of recombined data, indicating that the model is able to encode additional context effectively to improve performance on all tasks, even when only a small amount of multi-domain data is available.

The Sequential dialogue encoder network performs slightly worse than the memory network in the absence of recombined data. This could be explained by the model over-fitting to the single domain context seen during training and failure to utilize context effectively in a multi-domain setting. In the presence of recombined dialogues it outperforms all other implementations.

Apart from increasing the noise in the dialogue context, adding recombined dialogues to the training set increases the average turn length of the training data, bringing it closer to that of the test dialogues. Our augmentation approach is, in spirit, an extension of the data recombination described in (Jia and Liang, 2016) to conversations. We hypothesize that the presence of synthetic con-

utterance	MN+DR	SDEN+DR
hello	0.01	0.10
hello . i need to buy tickets at cinemark redwood downtown *20* for xd at *6 : 00* pm	0.00	0.06
which movie do you want to see at what time and date .	0.00	0.04
I didn't understand that.	0.00	0.03
please tell which movie , the time and date of the movie	0.01	0.02
the movie is queen of katwe today and the number of tickets is *4*	0.00	0.00
So 4 tickets for the *6 : 00* pm showing	0.02	0.01
yes	0.01	0.01
I bought you *4* tickets for the *6 : 00* pm showing of queen of katwe at cinemark redwood downtown *20*	0.06	0.04
thank you	0.03	0.03
i want a *Brazilian* restaurant	**0.61**	**0.29**
which one of *Fogo de Cho Brazilian* steakhouse , *Espetus Churrascaria* san mateo or *Fogo de Cho* would you prefer	0.02	**0.26**
Fogo de Cho Brazilian steakhouse		

	True	ED+DR	MN+DR	SDEN+DR
Domain	find-restaurants	movies	find-restaurants	find-restaurants
Intent	affirm(restaurant)	-	-	-
restaurant name	*Fogo de Cho Brazilian* steakhouse	-	-	*Fogo de Cho Brazilian* steakhouse

Table 5: Dialogue from the test set with predictions from Encoder Decoder with recombined data (ED+DR), Memory Network with recombined data (MN+DR) and Sequential Dialogue Encoder Network with dialogue recombination (SDEN+DR). Tokens that have been italicized in the dialogue were out of vocabulary or replaced with special tokens. The columns to the right of the dialogue history detail the attention distributions. For SDEN+DR, we use the magnitude of the change in the session GRU state as a proxy for the attention distribution. Attention weights might not sum up to 1 if there is non-zero attention on history padding.

text has a regularization-like effect on the models. Similar effects were observed by (Jia and Liang, 2016), where training with longer, synthetically-augmented utterances resulted in improved semantic parsing performance on a simpler test set. This is also supported by the observation that performance improvements obtained by addition of recombined data increase as the complexity of the model increases.

8 Discussion and Conclusions

Table 4 demonstrates an example dialogue from the test set, along with the gold and model annotations from all 3 models. We observe that Encoder Decoder (ED) and Sequential Dialogue Encoder Network (SDEN) are able to successfully identify the domain, intent and slots, while the Memory Network (MN) fails to identify the movie name.

Looking at the attention distributions, we notice that the MN attention is very diffused, whereas SDEN is focusing on the most recent last 2 utterances, which directly identify the domain and the presence of the *movie* slot in the final user utterance. ED is also able to identify the presence of a *movie* in the final user utterance from the previous utterance context.

Table 5 displays another example where the SDEN model outperforms both MN and ED. Constrained to just the previous utterance ED is unable to correctly identify the domain of the user utterance. The MN model correctly identifies the domain, using its strong focus on the task-intent bearing utterance, but it is unable to identify presence of a restaurant in the user utterance. This highlights its failure to combine context from multiple history utterances. On the other hand, as indicated by its attention distribution on the final two utterances, SDEN is able to successfully combine context from the dialogue to correctly identify the domain and the restaurant name from the user utterance, despite the presence of several out-of-vocabulary tokens.

The above two examples hint that SDEN performs better in scenarios where multiple history utterances encode complementary information that could be useful to interpret user utterances. This is usually the case in more natural goal oriented dialogues, where several tasks and sub tasks go in and out of the focus of the conversation (Grosz, 1979).

On the other hand, we also observed that SDEN performs significantly worse in the absence of recombined data. Due to its complex architecture and a much larger set of parameters SDEN is prone to over-fitting in low data scenarios.

In this paper, we collect a multi-domain dataset of goal oriented human-machine conversations and analyze and compare the SLU performance of multiple neural network based model architectures that can encode varying amounts of context. Our experiments suggest that encoding more context from the dialogue, and enabling the model to combine contextual information in a sequential order results in a reduction in overall frame error rate. We also introduce a data augmentation scheme to generate longer dialogues with richer context, and empirically demonstrate that it results in performance improvement for multiple model architectures.

9 Acknowledgements

We would like to thank Pararth Shah, Abhinav Rastogi, Anna Khasin and Georgi Nikolov for their help with the user-machine conversation data collection and labeling. We would also like to thank the anonymous reviewers for their insightful comments.

References

Ankur Bapna, Gokhan Tür, Dilek Hakkani-Tür, and Larry Heck. 2017. Towards zero-shot frame semantic parsing for domain scaling. In *In Proceedings of the Interspeech*. Stockholm, Sweden.

Antoine Bordes and Jason Weston. 2016. Learning end-to-end goal-oriented dialog. *arXiv preprint arXiv:1605.07683* .

Y.-N. Chen, D. Hakkani-Tür, G. Tur, J. Gao, and L. Deng. 2016. End-to-end memory networks with knowledge carryover for multi-turn spoken language understanding. In *Proceedings of the Interspeech*. San Francisco, CA.

Junyoung Chung, Caglar Gulcehre, KyungHyun Cho, and Yoshua Bengio. 2014. Empirical evaluation of gated recurrent neural networks on sequence modeling. *arXiv preprint arXiv:1412.3555* .

Y. Dauphin, G. Tur, D. Hakkani-Tür, and L. Heck. 2014. Zero-shot learning and clustering for semantic utterance classification. In *Proceedings of the ICLR*.

Bhuwan Dhingra, Lihong Li, Xiujun Li, Jianfeng Gao, Yun-Nung Chen, Faisal Ahmed, and Li Deng. 2016. End-to-end reinforcement learning of dialogue agents for information access. *arXiv preprint arXiv:1609.00777* .

Barbara J Grosz. 1979. Focusing and description in natural language dialogues. Technical report, DTIC Document.

Barbara J Grosz and Candace L Sidner. 1986. Attention, intentions, and the structure of discourse. *Computational linguistics* 12(3):175–204.

S. Hahn, M. Dinarelli, C. Raymond, F. Lefevre, P. Lehnen, R. De Mori, A. Moschitti, H. Ney, and G. Riccardi. 2011. Comparing stochastic approaches to spoken language understanding in multiple languages. *IEEE Transactions on Audio, Speech, and Language Processing* 19(6):1569–1583.

D. Hakkani-Tür, G. Tur, A. Celikyilmaz, Y.-N. Chen, J. Gao, L. Deng, and Y.-Y. Wang. 2016. Multi-domain joint semantic frame parsing using bi-directional RNN-LSTM. In *Proceedings of the Interspeech*. San Francisco, CA.

Matthew Henderson. 2015. Machine learning for dialog state tracking: A review. In *Proceedings of The First International Workshop on Machine Learning in Spoken Language Processing*.

Matthew Henderson, Blaise Thomson, and Jason D Williams. 2014. The second dialog state tracking challenge.

Sepp Hochreiter and Jürgen Schmidhuber. 1997. Long short-term memory. *Neural computation* 9(8):1735–1780.

Robin Jia and Percy Liang. 2016. Data recombination for neural semantic parsing. *arXiv preprint arXiv:1606.03622* .

G. Kurata, B. Xiang, B. Zhou, and M. Yu. 2016. Leveraging sentence-level information with encoder LSTM for semantic slot filling. In *Proceedings of the EMNLP*. Austin, TX.

Bing Liu and Ian Lane. 2016. Joint online spoken language understanding and language modeling with recurrent neural networks. *CoRR* abs/1609.01462. http://arxiv.org/abs/1609.01462.

G. Mesnil, Y. Dauphin, K. Yao, Y. Bengio, L. Deng, D. Hakkani-Tür, X. He, L. Heck, G. Tur, and D. Yu. 2015. Using recurrent neural networks for slot filling in spoken language understanding. *IEEE Transactions on Audio, Speech, and Language Processing* 23(3):530–539.

Julien Perez and Fei Liu. 2016. Dialog state tracking, a machine reading approach using memory network. *arXiv preprint arXiv:1606.04052* .

Jost Schatzmann, Blaise Thomson, Karl Weilhammer, Hui Ye, and Steve Young. 2007. Agenda-based user simulation for bootstrapping a pomdp dialogue system. In *Human Language Technologies 2007: The Conference of the North American Chapter of the Association for Computational Linguistics; Companion Volume, Short Papers*. Association for Computational Linguistics, pages 149–152.

Iulian Vlad Serban, Alessandro Sordoni, Yoshua Bengio, Aaron C. Courville, and Joelle Pineau. 2015. Hierarchical neural network generative models for movie dialogues. *CoRR* abs/1507.04808. http://arxiv.org/abs/1507.04808.

Pararth Shah, Dilek Hakkani-Tür, and Larry Heck. 2016. Interactive reinforcement learning for task-oriented dialogue management.

Alessandro Sordoni, Yoshua Bengio, Hossein Vahabi, Christina Lioma, Jakob Grue Simonsen, and Jian-Yun Nie. 2015. A hierarchical recurrent encoder-decoder for generative context-aware query suggestion. In *Proceedings of the 24th ACM International on Conference on Information and Knowledge Management*. ACM, New York, NY, USA, CIKM '15, pages 553–562. https://doi.org/10.1145/2806416.2806493.

Pei-Hao Su, David Vandyke, Milica Gasic, Nikola Mrksic, Tsung-Hsien Wen, and Steve Young. 2015. Reward shaping with recurrent neural networks for speeding up on-line policy learning in spoken dialogue systems. *arXiv preprint arXiv:1508.03391* .

Gokhan Tur and Renato De Mori. 2011. *Spoken language understanding: Systems for extracting semantic information from speech*. John Wiley & Sons.

Y.-Y. Wang, L. Deng, and A. Acero. 2005. Spoken language understanding - an introduction to the statistical framework. *IEEE Signal Processing Magazine* 22(5):16–31.

Tsung-Hsien Wen, Milica Gasic, Nikola Mrksic, Lina M Rojas-Barahona, Pei-Hao Su, David Vandyke, and Steve Young. 2016. Multi-domain neural network language generation for spoken dialogue systems. *arXiv preprint arXiv:1603.01232* .

Tsung-Hsien Wen, Milica Gasic, Nikola Mrksic, Pei-Hao Su, David Vandyke, and Steve Young. 2015. Semantically conditioned lstm-based natural language generation for spoken dialogue systems. *arXiv preprint arXiv:1508.01745* .

Jason Weston, Sumit Chopra, and Antoine Bordes. 2014. Memory networks. *arXiv preprint arXiv:1410.3916* .

S. Young. 2002. Talking to machines (statistically speaking). In *Proceedings of the ICSLP*. Denver, CO.

Table 6: **Supported Intents:** List of intents and dialogue acts supported by the user simulator, with descriptions and representative examples. Acts parametrized with **slot** can be instantiated for any attribute supported within the domain.

Intent	Intent descriptions	Sample utterance
affirm	generic affirmation	U: sounds good.
cant_understand	expressing failure to understand system utterance	U: What do you mean ?
deny	generic negation	U: That doesn't work.
good_bye	expressing end of dialogue	U: bye
thank_you	expressing gratitude	U: thanks a lot!
greeting	greeting	U: Hi
request_alts	request alternatives to a system offer	S: Doppio Zero is a nice italian restaurant near you. U: Are there any other options available ?
affirm(**slot**)	affirming values corresponding to a particular attribute	U: 5 pm sounds good to me.
deny(**slot**)	negating a particular attribute.	U: None of those times would work for me.
dont_care(**slot**)	expressing that any value is acceptable for a given attribute	U: Any time should be ok.
movies	explicit intent to buy movie tickets	U: Get me 3 tickets to Inferno
reserve-restaurants	explicit intent to reserve a table at a restaurant	U: make a reservation at Max Brenner's
find-restaurants	explicit intent to search for restaurants	U: find cheap italian restaurants near me
contextual	implicit intent continuing from context, also used in place of inform	S: What time works for you ? U: 5 pm tomorrow.
unknown_intent	intents not supported by the dialogue system	U: What's the weather like in San Francisco ?

Table 7: **Sample dialogue:** Sample dialogue generated using a crowd working platform. The LHS consists of the instructions shown to the crowd workers based on the dialog act interactions between the user simulator and the rule based policy. The RHS describes the natural language dialog generated by the crowd workers.

Instructions	Natural language paraphrase
S: greetings	hi
U:buy movie tickets AND date is DontCare	buy some movie tickets for any date
S: provide preference for: theatre name	Which theatre would you like to make the reservation at ?
U: theatre name is GB	the GB theatre
S: provide preference for: time	When is the reservation for?
U: number of tickets is 6 and time is DontCare	get 6 tickets for any time
S: provide preference for: movie	Which movie would you like to go for ?
U: movie is Power Rangers	The power rangers movie
S: found the following: date is March 25 and time is 8:00 am	I found 6 tickets available for 8 am on March 25.
U: disagree	That doesn't work for me
S: found the following: date is March 25 and time is 6:00 pm	Does 6 pm on March 25 work for you ?
U: accept	Sounds good, make the booking
S: purchase confirmed with given details theatre name is GB and date is March 25 and time is 6:00 pm and number of tickets is 6 and movie is Power Rangers	Ok, I've reserved 6 tickets for the 6 pm showing of Power Rangers at the GB theatre on March 25.
U: thank you	Thanks.

Redundancy Localization for the Conversationalization of Unstructured Responses

Sebastian Krause[1,*], **Mikhail Kozhevnikov**[2], **Eric Malmi**[3,*], **Daniele Pighin**[2]

[1]DFKI Language Technology Lab, Berlin, Germany
`sebastian.krause@dfki.de`
[2]Google, Zürich, Switzerland
`{qnan,biondo}@google.com`
[3]Aalto University, Espoo, Finland
`eric.malmi@aalto.fi`

Abstract

Conversational agents offer users a natural-language interface to accomplish tasks, entertain themselves, or access information. Informational dialogue is particularly challenging in that the agent has to hold a conversation on an open topic, and to achieve a reasonable coverage it generally needs to digest and present unstructured information from textual sources. Making responses based on such sources sound natural and fit appropriately into the conversation context is a topic of ongoing research, one of the key issues of which is preventing the agent's responses from sounding repetitive. Targeting this issue, we propose a new task, known as redundancy localization, which aims to pinpoint semantic overlap between text passages. To help address it systematically, we formalize the task, prepare a public dataset with fine-grained redundancy labels, and propose a model utilizing a weak training signal defined over the results of a passage-retrieval system on web texts. The proposed model demonstrates superior performance compared to a state-of-the-art entailment model and yields encouraging results when applied to a real-world dialogue.

1   Introduction

Recent years have seen a growing interest in research on conversational agents. Several strands of dialogue systems have emerged which differ in underlying goals and methods. Some systems focus on data-driven learning of models which can autonomously hold conversations with humans or one another, potentially even on open domains (Vinyals and Le, 2015; Sordoni et al., 2015; Li

---

User: *What is Malaria?*

Agent: *A disease caused by a plasmodium parasite, transmitted by the bite of infected mosquitoes.*

User: *Is it a virus?*

Agent: <u>*Malaria is a parasitic infection spread by Anopheles mosquitoes. The Plasmodium parasite that causes Malaria*</u> *is neither a virus nor a bacterium – it is a single-celled parasite that multiplies in red blood cells of humans as well as in the mosquito intestine.*

Figure 1: Informational-dialogue example between a human and a conversational agent. The second agent utterance is partially redundant (the underlined text).

et al., 2016). Other works deal with task-oriented dialogues, which offer natural-language interfaces to real-world services like restaurant booking (Bordes and Weston, 2016; Dhingra et al., 2016; Crook et al., 2016). We focus in this paper on a third dialogue setting where the goal is to have a natural conversation with a user, during which the user's information needs are satisfied in an iterative manner. Such a setting is common in question-answering experiences implemented in personal digital assistants (Sarikaya et al., 2016).

We call this setting *informational dialogues.* They start with the user posing a fact-seeking question, e.g., to learn about current events or to explore unknown terms and concepts. Consider the example dialogue in Fig. 1, which is initiated by the user requesting a definition of a specific disease and which also features a subsequent question on the same topic. Many approaches have been proposed which can produce suitable replies to such questions. Examples include techniques which find pertinent passages or short text chunks in collections of documents (Hermann et al., 2015; Miller et al., 2016; Trischler et al., 2016) or find rele-

---

*Work performed during an internship at Google.

115

Proceedings of the SIGDIAL 2017 Conference, pages 115–126,
Saarbrücken, Germany, 15-17 August 2017. ©2017 Association for Computational Linguistics

vant entries in structured knowledge bases (Bordes et al., 2014, 2015; Yin et al., 2016a,b). Generation techniques can then be employed to generate well-formed natural-language utterances from the candidate replies (Wen et al., 2015, 2016a,b; Zhou et al., 2016; Dušek and Jurcicek, 2016). In the dialogue in Fig. 1, both agent replies are coherent wrt. the questions. However, they sound strange when occurring together in a single dialogue context because information is partially reiterated (see the underlined part in the second agent reply). It is this very problem that we focus on in this work, i.e., the *localization of redundancy* in conversation. Information on the location of non-novel portions of a passage could either be fed back to the retrieval model, so that only text passages with new information would be selected, or alternatively this localized redundancy might be used as input to a summarization model (Rush et al., 2015).

The specific contributions of this work are as follows:

- We propose a new task, motivated by practical issues that dialogue applications face (Sec. 3).

- We release a new dataset with manual annotations for this task, which allows to evaluate and compare competing approaches (Sec. 4).

- Due to the insufficient amount of annotated data for training purposes, we report on a weak supervision signal over a large collection of passages with partially redundant content (Sec. 5).

- We augment a recently introduced entailment model (Parikh et al., 2016) with means for representing local similarities in passages in a unidirectional way (Sec. 6) and find that this extension outperforms the original model (Sec. 8).

- Furthermore, we briefly discuss an experiment on real-world dialogue data (Sec. 9), which gives insights on the application-relevance of the proposed task and model.

2   Related Work

A lot of work has been presented on reasoning with short texts for tasks on similarity and entailment. Knowledge-rich approaches define lexical and syntactic inference rules over phrase pairs and employ decision algorithms that rely on matches of these rules in input texts (Magnini et al., 2014). Other approaches generate structured representations of

the input to enable sophisticated alignment of the texts with now available rich lexical, syntactic, and semantic information (Liang et al., 2016). The use of kernel methods for similarity tasks has also been reported (Filice et al., 2015). In contrast to these approaches, neither do we use external knowledge nor do we build explicit syntactic representations of input texts.

Sentence fusion (Barzilay and McKeown, 2005; Filippova and Strube, 2008) is a technique that is related to the overall problem setting of this paper. This technique is used in the context of abstractive multi-document summarization, where a particular challenge is to identify shared content in a cluster of sentences and to subsequently produce a single sentence that covers all information fragments. In our work, we focus on a similar but different problem formulation, in which we fix one text fragment and want to find reiterations of its content in other texts. Furthermore, we focus on identifying and localizing redundancy and leave the generation of low-redundancy text mostly as future work.

Neural approaches are common for bi-sequence classification problems (Laha and Raykar, 2016). Yin and Schütze (2015), He et al. (2015), and He and Lin (2016) use convolutional networks to represent input texts on multiple granularity levels and model the interactions of these. We also aim to find fine-granular interactions in texts, but in addition to their models, we aim to make these interactions explicit rather than latent intermediate results. Another line of research has proposed recurrent networks for modeling phrases/sentences, including various forms of neural attention (Bowman et al., 2015; Rocktäschel et al., 2015; Zhao et al., 2016). These approaches come with high computational cost during training and inference, in contrast we rely on cheaper feed-forward connections.

3   Problem Definition

We focus in this work on the problem of *redundancy localization* in a passage with respect to another text, i.e., we aim to understand when a sub-passage is redundant with what is mentioned in the context.[1] Consider the following example with a context passage **c** and a follow-up passage **p** with sub-sequences s_0–s_3, which need to be ranked according to the extent to which their semantics are covered by **c**. In this case, one may expect the

---

[1]Note that the problem definition is not limited to the dialogue scenario used as motivation in the introduction.

order to be $(\mathbf{s}_1, \mathbf{s}_2, \mathbf{s}_3, \mathbf{s}_0)$:

$\mathbf{c}$: *The Allianz Arena is a football stadium in Munich, Bavaria, Germany, with a seating capacity of more than 70,000.*

— — — — — — — — — — — —

$\mathbf{s}_0$: *Bayern to increase stadium capacity.*

$\mathbf{s}_1$: *Bayern Munich have revealed plans to increase the capacity of Allianz Arena to 75,000,*

$\mathbf{s}_2$: *which would make it the second largest stadium in Germany.*

$\mathbf{s}_3$: *The Allianz Arena is currently the third largest stadium in Germany.*

More formally, let $\mathbf{p}$ be a sequence of n tokens. Let $\mathbf{S} = \{\mathbf{s}_k\}_{k=0}^{m-1}$ be a set of m sub-sequences of $\mathbf{p}$ such that for integers $s_0, s_1, \ldots, s_m$ with $s_0 = 0 < s_1 < \ldots < s_{m-1} < s_m = n$, each sub-sequence $\mathbf{s}_k \in \mathbf{S}$ is ranging from tokens s_k to $(s_{k+1} - 1)$, inclusive. Given a context sequence $\mathbf{c}$, the task of redundancy localization is to produce a ranking function $rank(\mathbf{s}_k) \in \{1, \ldots, m\}$ that induces an ordering of the subsequences $\mathbf{s}_k \in \mathbf{S}$ of $\mathbf{p}$ which corresponds to the degree of information in $\mathbf{s}_k$ that is semantically covered by $\mathbf{c}$. Here, a low rank corresponds to a high semantic overlap of a subsequence with $\mathbf{c}$, where segments are allowed to have equal ranks.

We formulate this task as a ranking problem instead of a more expressive yet also more complex regression setting in order to pose less restrictions on the collection of data for training and evaluation. The design decision to rank sub-sequences rather than individual tokens is intended to keep manual annotation feasible and cost-effective.

Relation to Other Tasks The problem we pose here is related to bi-sequence problems like *semantic textual similarity* (STS) (Agirre et al., 2016a) and *recognizing textual entailment* (RTE) (Bowman et al., 2015). In contrast to these tasks, we are not interested in determining the overall relation between sequences, but aim to generate more fine-grained sub-passage-level information. The task of *interpretable semantic textual similarity* (Agirre et al., 2016b) requires systems to provide human-understandable explanations for STS ratings of *sentence* pairs. Chunks from both sentences need to be paired and for each such pairing, similarity and relation type need to be assessed. While this type of annotation is richer than what we propose, it is also harder to produce, likely requiring specially-trained raters, and would likely be impossible to

predict accurately using a surrogate supervision signal like we rely on. Besides, it does not scale well beyond single sentences, since the number of ratings per sequence pair grows proportionally to the multiple of their lengths, while the model we present can handle longer, multi-sentence passages. The setting proposed in the next section is more restricted, but easier to learn and directly applicable in downstream applications.

4 A Testbed for Redundancy Localization

The evaluation dataset (EVAL) is constructed from pairs of *potentially* redundant passages from Wikipedia, which were segmented into sub-passages and presented to human raters for manual redundancy assessment. The collection of passages was guided by a need for text pairs with various degrees of semantic overlap; we employed a *passage-retrieval* system for the purpose of text selection. Passage retrieval (Khalid and Verberne, 2008; Aktolga et al., 2011; Xu et al., 2011) is a common intermediate step in information-retrieval and question-answering settings, the goal of which is to return a passage containing the answer to a given query. Most systems generate a list of candidate passages, rank them by relevance and return the top one.

We picked a random set of 1200 fact-seeking questions and retrieved corresponding passages from Wikipedia. The questions were then discarded, as they are not relevant to our task. We selected the top-scoring passage as the context $\mathbf{c}$ and paired it with a low-scoring one from further down the result list ($\mathbf{p}$). $\mathbf{p}$ was then heuristically split into chunks s_k, corresponding to verb-governed phrases. The example shown in the last section is an instance of such a pair ($\mathbf{c}$, $\mathbf{p}$).

We asked three raters per item to select for each segment $\mathbf{s}_k$ of $\mathbf{p}$ one out of three labels: NOTREDUNDANT, PARTIALLYREDUNDANT, and FULLYREDUNDANT, depending on the degree of which the content of a sub-passage is covered by the context $\mathbf{c}$. The annotators fully/partially agreed[2] on 64%/96% of examples, their annotation has an intra-class correlation of .55. We aggregated the rating by mapping the categorical labels to a numeric scale (0, 1, 2) and averaging the scores. We used 200 examples as a development

---

[2] Full: 3/3 annotators agreed on a label. Partial: At least 2/3 annotators agreed on a label.

c:	*Brewer's yeast is made from a one-celled fungus called Saccharomyces cerevisiae.*
p$^+$:	*Brewer's yeast is named so because it comes from the same fungus that's used to ferment and make beer - Saccharomyces cerevisiae.*
p$^-$:	*Because brewer's yeast is a rich source of chromium, scientists think it may help treat high blood sugar.*
c:	*The height of the net in men's volleyball is 7 feet 11 5/8 inches, and in women's volleyball, it is 7 feet 4 1/8 inches.*
p$^+$:	*Outdoor volleyball, played on grass, will use the standard net heights of 7 feet, 4 1/8 inches for women, with men and co-ed teams using the height of 7 feet, 11 5/8 inches.*
p$^-$:	*The first volleyball net was borrowed from a tennis court and was set at 6 feet 6 inches high.*
c:	*The world's tallest artificial structure is the 829.8 m tall Burj Khalifa in Dubai, United Arab Emirates.*
p$^+$:	*The 828-metre tall Burj Khalifa in Dubai has been the tallest building in the world since 2008.*
p$^-$:	*Burj Khalifa broke the height record in all four categories for completed buildings.*

Table 1: Three weakly-labeled examples (Sec. 5). Underlining used to indicate overlapping/distinct information between items.

Label	DEV #	DEV %	TEST #	TEST %
REDUNDANT	95	15.83	495	16.50
PARTIALLYREDUNDANT	81	13.50	541	18.03
NOTREDUNDANT	424	70.67	1964	65.47

Table 2: Distribution of sub-passage labels in EVAL.

dataset for the experiments in this paper (DEV), and the remaining 1000 items as a test dataset (TEST). Tab. 2 reports the label distribution in both parts of the dataset. We make the dataset publicly available at `https://github.com/kraseb/redundancy-localization`.

5 Training with a Proxy Signal

While the annotation required for our task is comparatively simple and can be performed by raters without special training, a workable fully-supervised model would require a very considerable amount of data and is likely to prove costly.[3] Suppose, however, we were supplied with a large number of short texts with varying degrees of similarity and relatedness to one another and we had a means of assessing at the coarse level of text pairs whether or not they were similar. Our hypothesis is that given appropriate model capacity and structure, a model trained to predict the passage-level similarity would learn to compare smaller units of text to make an appropriate high-level decision.

We derive a proxy signal from passage-level retrieval scores which allows to bootstrap the redundancy-localization model described in Sec. 6.

The model is presented with passage triples, where two passages are very closely related and the third one is on the same general topic, but less similar to the other two and hence likely contains less redundancy. The model is then trained to rank the more closely related passage pairs above the less closely related ones.

We retrieve lists of relevant passages from the web using the same passage-retrieval system that we utilized to collect data for manual annotation. Through manual inspection of a small subset of candidate passage lists, we identified a range of passage scores, where candidate passages are topically close to the top-scoring one, but sufficiently different in factual content. To ensure that the top-scoring passage and the lower-scoring one are on the same topic, we further require that they be extracted from the same webpage.

From each of the queries' passage lists we extract three passages, the top-scoring passage **c**, the second-highest ranking passage **p$^+$**, and a lower-scoring passage **p$^-$** from the score corridor described above. The stream of passage triples $(\mathbf{c}, \mathbf{p}^+, \mathbf{p}^-)$ generated in this way allows to train a model with a margin-based ranking objective. This objective enforces that the similarity score of the two high-scoring passages **c**, **p$^+$** is greater than the similarity of the low-scoring passage **p$^-$** and the top-scoring one, plus a margin; see Sec. 6.3. This pushes a model to find what differentiates two given text sequences, so that it can assign a higher similarity to the near-paraphrases.

Tab. 1 shows three example passage triples constructed with this signal. Here, underlining is a means of visualizing the overlapping/disjoint content between triple elements. Note that we do not

---

[3] Among other things, to accurately identify redundancy the model needs to have at least some notion of paraphrasing.

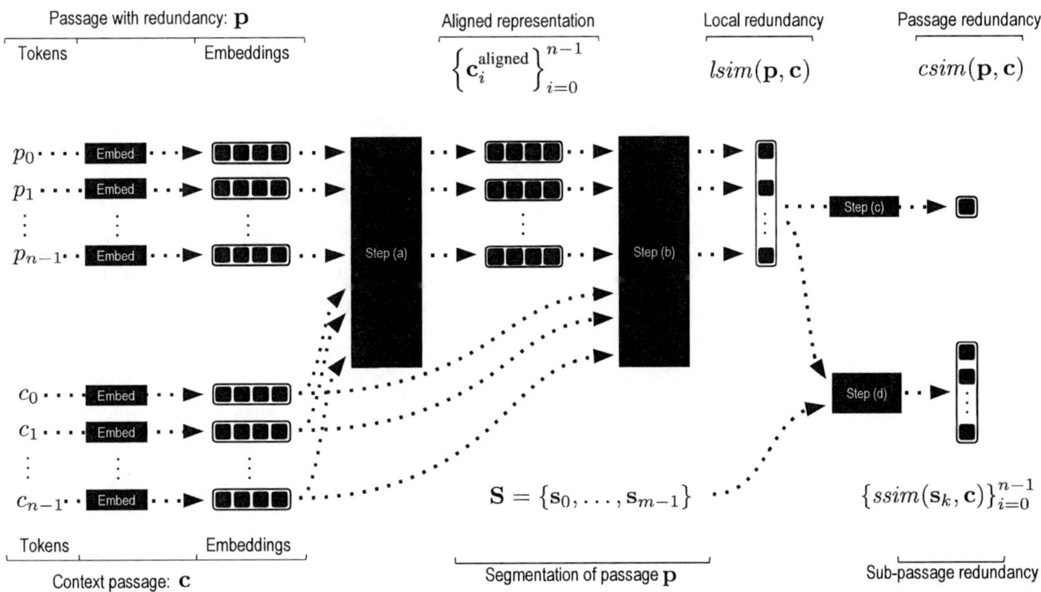

Figure 2: Overview of the model architecture.

make this information available to a model during training. In the interest of brevity, we selected short, single-sentence passages for this example.

6 Model Design

This section first gives a brief overview of the proposed model, before going into details of its architecture and use during training and inference time.

Architecture Overview Existing models for bi-sequence tasks (Bahdanau et al., 2014; Rush et al., 2015; He and Lin, 2016) often learn to align texts as an intermediate step, i.e., reasoning is done with pairs of short text units, which allows to build a task-specific output for whole sequences on top of local decisions. A particular example for RTE is the three-layer model of Parikh et al. (2016). The first layer produces a bi-directional alignment between input sentences, which is utilized in the second component to perform local comparisons, which in turn are fed to the top layer to make the final entailment decision. We follow the same pattern in the design of our model.

We implement a multi-component neural-network that takes two passages as input. It first (a) learns a *uni*-directional alignment between the passages, which is utilized to produce a customized representation of the context passage, specific to each token of the potentially redundant passage.

Next, (b) token-level redundancy scores are produced via local comparison operations. During training, (c) an additional layer aggregates the local scores and produces a passage-level similarity score on top of which a ranking objective is applied. At inference time, (d) the local scores from (b) serve as the basis for the ranking of the sub-passage elements as described in Sec. 3. Fig. 2 outlines steps (a) – (d).

6.1 Step (a): Alignment

Input to the model are two sequences of n tokens each, $\mathbf{p} = (p_0, \ldots, p_{n-1})$ and $\mathbf{c} = (c_0, \ldots, c_{n-1})$, with shorter sequences being padded to this length. The goal of this step is to generate for each $p_i \in \mathbf{p}$ a fixed-length representation $\mathbf{c}_i^{\text{aligned}}$ of $\mathbf{c}$, which captures the meaning aspects of $\mathbf{c}$ specifically relevant for p_i.

The tokens p_i, c_j are represented via word embeddings of size d_w, which are updated during model training and are stored in a matrix $W_w \in \mathbb{R}^{d_w \times |V|}$, with V being the vocabulary. For ease of notation, we use $\mathbf{p}, p_i, \mathbf{c}, c_i$ to refer to both the original tokens and their embedding representation.

We create a soft alignment of $\mathbf{c}$ to the tokens of $\mathbf{p}$ via the decomposed attention mechanism described by Parikh et al. (2016). At its core is the application of the attention function f1 to each token of the input sequences, which is implemented as a feed-forward neural network with h_{f1} layers of

d_{f1} rectified linear units (Glorot et al., 2011, ReLu) each. Using this function, unnormalized attention weights are produced:

$$\alpha_{ij} = \mathrm{f1}(p_i) \cdot \mathrm{f1}(c_j), \qquad (1)$$

then normalized per token in $\mathbf{p}$ via

$$\alpha'_{ij} = \exp\left(\alpha_{ij}\right) / \sum_k \exp\left(\alpha_{ik}\right). \qquad (2)$$

The customized (*aligned*) representation of $\mathbf{c}$ is then calculated as

$$\mathbf{c}_i^{\mathrm{aligned}} = \sum_{j=0}^{n-1} \alpha'_{ij} c_j. \qquad (3)$$

6.2 Step (b): Learning Local Redundancy

Each token p_i from $\mathbf{p}$ is compared to the corresponding representation $\mathbf{c}_i^{\mathrm{aligned}}$ of the context sequence via a single-layer feed-forward network f2 with a ReLu:

$$lsim\left(p_i, \mathbf{c}\right) := \mathrm{f2}\left(\left[p_i, \mathbf{c}_i^{\mathrm{aligned}}\right]\right) \qquad (4)$$

$$lsim\left(\mathbf{p}, \mathbf{c}\right) := \left[lsim\left(p_i, \mathbf{c}\right)\right]_{i=0}^{n-1} \qquad (5)$$

with $[]$ being the concatenation operator and $lsim(\mathbf{p}, \mathbf{c}) \in \mathbb{R}^n$. This local similarity score measures for each token the degree with which its meaning is covered by $\mathbf{c}$.

6.3 Step (c): Learning to Aggregate Local Redundancy Scores

As described in Sec. 5, supervised training with local redundancy labels is costly, which is why we add another layer on top which learns to calculate a coarse passage-level similarity score $csim(\mathbf{p}, \mathbf{c})$ from the local redundancy information. Given a passage triple $(\mathbf{c}, \mathbf{p}^+, \mathbf{p}^-)$ (Sec. 5), two such coarse scores are calculated and used to determine a loss which allows to train steps (a–c) of the network in Fig. 2 in a weakly supervised way.

The passage-level score is computed by another feed-forward network f3 with h_{f3} layers of d_{f3} ReLus, followed by another hidden layer with a logistic activation function that projects to a scalar value in $(0, 1)$:

$$csim\left(\mathbf{p}, \mathbf{c}\right) := \mathrm{f3}\left(lsim\left(\mathbf{p}, \mathbf{c}\right)\right). \qquad (6)$$

Then, for a given passage triple $(\mathbf{c}, \mathbf{p}^+, \mathbf{p}^-)$, the loss is defined as:

$$\mathcal{L} = max\{0, 0.5 - csim(\mathbf{p}^+, \mathbf{c}) + csim(\mathbf{p}^-, \mathbf{c})\} \qquad (7)$$

This ranking criterion is similar to what has been used by Collobert et al. (2011) and Bordes et al. (2013). It is intended to push the model to assign a higher coarse similarity score to the more similar sequences from the triple, and in doing so, ideally forces the model to learn to detect local redundancies.

6.4 Step (d): Generation of Sub-sequence Redundancy Scores

During inference time, the goal of this model is to rank a set of given sub-sequences $\mathbf{S}$ of $\mathbf{p}$ with respect to their redundancy with $\mathbf{c}$; note that during inference time the model is presented with pairs of passages in contrast to the triples it sees in the training phase.

We calculate a redundancy score for a subsequence $\mathbf{s}_k \in \mathbf{S}$ as follows:

$$ssim(\mathbf{s}_k, \mathbf{c}) := \frac{1}{s_{k+1} - s_k} \sum_{l=s_k}^{s_{k+1}-1} \left(lsim(p_l, \mathbf{c})\right), \qquad (8)$$

where $\mathbf{s}_k$ is the subsequence running from positions s_k to $s_{k+1} - 1$ (see Sec. 3). A ranking of the subsequences is then given by:

$$rank(\mathbf{s}_k) := |\{\mathbf{s}_l \mid ssim(\mathbf{s}_l, \mathbf{c}) \geq ssim(\mathbf{s}_k, \mathbf{c})\}| \qquad (9)$$

In other words, sub-passages are ranked by comparing the mean of their local redundancy scores. In the evaluation of Sec. 8, we refer to the model that uses this way of ranking sub-passages as UA (short for uni-directional alignment). We compare this against a number of other variants of processing internal activations of the model to extract information about local redundancy, see Sec. 8.

6.5 Baseline Ranking Method

The bi-directional alignment model (BA) of Parikh et al. (2016) can be trained in a similar fashion as our proposed model, i.e., with triples of passages and the loss from Eq. (7). Although it has not been developed with the localization of redundancy in mind, its native problem formulation (RTE) is structurally related to the problem at hand by requiring models to assess to what degree the semantic content of one passage is embedded in a second one. We believe BA constitutes a strong baseline because it has been shown to achieve state-of-the-art performance on RTE and because it has the means to decompose coarse inference decisions on two text sequences into local comparison operations,

d_w	100	η	0.01
d_{f1}	200	$\|V\|$	$10k$
d_{f3}	100	p_{f1}	0.21
h_{f1}	1	p_{f2}	0.46
h_{f3}	1	p_{f3}	0.05
batch size	256	epochs	≈ 200

Table 3: Hyperparameter settings for UA.

Dataset	Model	ρ	Model	ρ
DEV	UA	.5298	BA$'$	.1384
	UA$_\Sigma$	.4169	BA$'_\Sigma$	.2232
	UA$'$	.3862	BA$''$	.2817
	UA$'_\Sigma$	.4071	BA$''_\Sigma$	.2923
TEST	UA	.5544	BA$''_\Sigma$	.2688

Table 4: Comparison of alternative strategies for step (d) (Sec. 6.4) on DEV and results of optimal strategies on TEST.

a key requisite to successfully utilize the training signal from Sec. 5.

However, in contrast to our model, the results of comparing the aligned sequences $\mathbf{c}_i^{\text{aligned}}$ with individual tokens from $\mathbf{p}$ are not directly interpretable as redundancy scores, also the architecture is designed for a bi-directional alignment of the input sequences. In order to produce *lsim* values for the tokens of $\mathbf{p}$, we use the alignment matrices as a basis for a max-based aggregation, i.e., we take the row-wise maximum value and use this as the localized redundancy value for the corresponding token. Sub-sequence similarity is then determined either via Eq. (8) or alternatively via summation.

7 Experimental Setting, Model Training

We implemented both UA and BA in the Tensor-Flow framework (Abadi et al., 2015) and trained them with the signal from Sec. 5. As input to the passage-retrieval system we used a set of 1.5 million queries, resulting in the same amount of passage triples; 80% were used for training, 10% were used as a separate validation set for hyperparameter optimization, and the final 10% were held out and served as the basis for the smaller dataset with manually annotated labels (EVAL, Sec. 4)[4].

The hyperparameters of UA ($h_{f1}, d_{f1}, h_{f3}, d_{f3}$) and BA (like our model, plus a few additional ones) were optimized separately. We also experimented with Dropout (Srivastava et al., 2014) for the feed-forward networks in step (a–c) (p_{f1}, p_{f2}, p_{f3}), with different initial learning rates (η) for Adagrad (Duchi et al., 2011), with different batch sizes, and with different vocabulary sizes ($|V|$). The final settings for UA used in the reported experiments are shown in Tab. 3. Word embeddings were initialized with pre-trained embeddings (Mikolov et al., 2013), the other model parameters were randomly initialized; out-of-vocabulary words were hashed

---

[4]We only annotated a subset of the passages in this part of the data.

into 100 buckets. The models were trained for 1 million steps.

8 Evaluation on EVAL

We first compare the performance of different variants of generating the redundancy scores for sub-passage ranking, for both UA and BA, on DEV. We then pick the respective best-performing model variant and compare the systems on TEST. The model variants we test are the following:

- **UA**: The uni-directional alignment model described in Sec. 6.

- **UA$_\Sigma$**: Summation instead of averaging in Eq. (8), which gives higher weight to long sub-sequences with redundancy.

- **UA$'$**: Calculation of *lsim* in analogous fashion as BA (see below).

- **UA$'_\Sigma$**: Combination of two variants above.

- **BA$'$/BA$''$**: Models with bi-directional alignment of input texts. *lsim* values for tokens of $\mathbf{p}$ are produced by using the first/second one of the two alignment matrices as a basis for the max-based aggregation of the normalized attention weights described in Sec. 6.5.

- **BA$'_\Sigma$ / BA$''_\Sigma$**: Like above, but sub-sequence similarity is determined via summation rather than calculating the mean in Eq. (8).

We measure performance by calculating the Spearman correlation of the raw passage scores with the gold redundancy for all segments in the respective partition of the dataset. The top of Tab. 4 reports results of the different model variants. For UA, making direct use of the local redundancy scores calculated in step (b) of the model yields slightly better results than post-processing the alignments

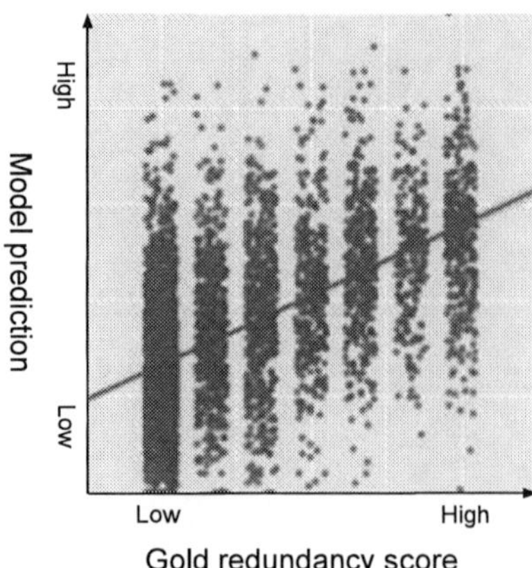

Figure 3: Plot of predictions of UA on TEST against annotated redundancy.

from step (a) of the model. The best overall results for UA are achieved when this is combined with the strategy that represents sub-sequence redundancy as the arithmetic mean of the contained tokens' local scores, meaning sub-sequence length needs to be taken into account.

For the baseline BA, exploiting the reverse alignment matrix and summing over the alignment scores without correction for sub-sequence length gives the best results. The bottom of the table reports the results of applying both models with the respective best strategy on the test partition of the dataset. The proposed uni-directional model clearly outperforms the bi-directional baseline. This indicates that the direct modeling of uni-directional redundancy during both training and inference time allows a model to better learn to compare a sub-sequence to another full passage, in comparison to the case where both passages are analyzed in a fine-granular way.

Fig. 3 depicts a scatter plot of the segments in TEST, with the x-axis corresponding to the gold redundancy scores (Sec. 4) and the y-axis showing the redundancy assessment by UA. While actually redundant segments tend to be handled correctly by the model, a certain amount of non-redundant segments get assigned a relatively high absolute redundancy value, which is not problematic as long as the actually redundant segments of the same passage are rated even higher. The next section elaborates on an experiment that looks into the quality of this internal ranking of segments for given passages, and how this ranking could potentially be utilized in an application.

9 Redundancy Localization for Passage Compression

This section briefly discusses an experiment in a dialogue setting, in which redundancy information is used for the compression of passages. Consider again the example from Fig. 1, where a conversational agent engages a human user in an informational dialogue whose quality suffers from repetition of information on the agent side. In this experiment, we asked human raters to assess whether the removal of redundancy improves the dialogue flow. Note, however, that given the small scale of the experiment, results are only indicative and not conclusive.

We selected 50 passage pairs from the held-out portion of the training data where the second passage consisted of at least three sentences. We then fed the passages to UA and removed the sentence from the second passage which had the largest semantic overlap with the context (the first passage). We asked three human raters, (a) whether the two original passages are coherent at all (as the following questions assume this), (b) whether the compressed passage sounds more or less natural (due to the dropped redundant sentence), and (c) whether the modified passage is equally informative as the original passage.

For comparison, we implemented a baseline which always dropped the first sentence of a passage, as well as one that removed the sentence with the highest term overlap. For the following example, dropping the underlined sentence from the passage would result in a more natural and equally informative text:

c : *The 1966 FIFA World Cup was won by the England national football team.*

p : *The day England won the World Cup. Long-suffering fans of the England football team can always look back with nostalgia on one year: 1966. This was the year Bobby Moore's team defeated West Germany 4-2 in the World Cup final on 30 July, after a nail-biting and controversial match.*

Among the 50 uncompressed passage pairs, only one third was rated as being coherent (question a; independent of the model). For these pairs, UA tended to produce more natural compressions (question b) compared to the baselines. This might be explained by the term-overlap baseline's restriction to only look at the level of individual words, which results in erroneously removing sentences that are essential for discourse coherence but do not repeat facts. Similarly, always dropping the first sentence can leave a passage with dangling backward references, e.g., in the case of anaphors. In terms of the informativeness dimension (question c), all approaches resulted in slightly less informative compressed passages, which is expected. However, UA's score on this metric is slightly worse than the one of the baselines.

10 Contributions and Outlook

In this paper, we described the problem of localizing redundancy in pairs of passages. We proposed a model based on a uni-directional alignment from one passage to the context passage, which can be efficiently trained using a novel weak supervision signal defined over the output of common passage-retrieval systems. We applied this signal in a one-off process to train our model and a reasonable baseline; from a held-out part of the retrieved passages we created a publicly available dataset which allows to compare and evaluate models on this task and enables other researchers to reproduce the evaluation setting of this work. The conducted evaluation showed that the proposed uni-directional alignment model is indeed capable of finding the redundant sub-segments in texts.

In future work, we would like to represent and model more facets of the naturalness and coherence of dialogues. For instance in dialogue settings, a certain amount of redundancy between the utterances of participants may actually tie the dialogue turns together, i.e., may be beneficial in terms of discourse coherence and naturalness. Incorporating this consideration into the structure of a model can potentially improve the results of passage compression techniques in settings similar to Sec. 9.

Acknowledgments

The first author was partially supported by the German Federal Ministry of Education and Research, project ALL SIDES (contract 01IW14002).

References

Martín Abadi, Ashish Agarwal, Paul Barham, Eugene Brevdo, Zhifeng Chen, Craig Citro, Greg S. Corrado, Andy Davis, Jeffrey Dean, Matthieu Devin, Sanjay Ghemawat, Ian Goodfellow, Andrew Harp, Geoffrey Irving, Michael Isard, Yangqing Jia, Rafal Jozefowicz, Lukasz Kaiser, Manjunath Kudlur, Josh Levenberg, Dan Mané, Rajat Monga, Sherry Moore, Derek Murray, Chris Olah, Mike Schuster, Jonathon Shlens, Benoit Steiner, Ilya Sutskever, Kunal Talwar, Paul Tucker, Vincent Vanhoucke, Vijay Vasudevan, Fernanda Viégas, Oriol Vinyals, Pete Warden, Martin Wattenberg, Martin Wicke, Yuan Yu, and Xiaoqiang Zheng. 2015. TensorFlow: Large-scale machine learning on heterogeneous systems. Software available from tensorflow.org.

Eneko Agirre, Carmen Banea, Daniel Cer, Mona Diab, Aitor Gonzalez-Agirre, Rada Mihalcea, German Rigau, and Janyce Wiebe. 2016a. SemEval-2016 task 1: Semantic textual similarity, monolingual and cross-lingual evaluation. In *Proceedings of the 10th International Workshop on Semantic Evaluation (SemEval-2016)*. Association for Computational Linguistics, San Diego, California, pages 497–511. https://doi.org/10.18653/v1/S16-1081.

Eneko Agirre, Aitor Gonzalez-Agirre, Inigo Lopez-Gazpio, Montse Maritxalar, German Rigau, and Larraitz Uria. 2016b. SemEval-2016 task 2: Interpretable semantic textual similarity. In *Proceedings of the 10th International Workshop on Semantic Evaluation (SemEval-2016)*. Association for Computational Linguistics, San Diego, California, pages 512–524. https://doi.org/10.18653/v1/S16-1082.

Elif Aktolga, James Allan, and David A. Smith. 2011. Passage reranking for question answering using syntactic structures and answer types. In *Advances in Information Retrieval - Proceedings of the 33rd European Conference on IR Research (ECIR)*. Springer, Dublin, Ireland, volume 6611 of *Lecture Notes in Computer Science*, pages 617–628. https://doi.org/10.1007/978-3-642-20161-5_62.

Dzmitry Bahdanau, Kyunghyun Cho, and Yoshua Bengio. 2014. Neural machine translation by jointly learning to align and translate. *CoRR* abs/1409.0473. http://arxiv.org/abs/1409.0473.

Regina Barzilay and Kathleen McKeown. 2005. Sentence fusion for multidocument news summarization. *Computational Linguistics* 31(3):297–328. https://doi.org/10.1162/089120105774321091.

Antoine Bordes, Sumit Chopra, and Jason Weston. 2014. Question answering with subgraph embeddings. In *Proceedings of the 2014 Conference on Empirical Methods in Natural Language Processing (EMNLP)*. Association for Computational Linguistics, Doha, Qatar, pages 615–620. https://doi.org/10.3115/v1/D14-1067.

Antoine Bordes, Nicolas Usunier, Sumit Chopra, and Jason Weston. 2015. Large-scale simple question answering with memory networks. *CoRR* abs/1506.02075. http://arxiv.org/abs/1506.02075.

Antoine Bordes, Nicolas Usunier, Alberto García-Durán, Jason Weston, and Oksana Yakhnenko. 2013. Translating embeddings for modeling multi-relational data. In *Advances in Neural Information Processing Systems 26 (NIPS)*. pages 2787–2795. http://papers.nips.cc/paper/5071-translating-embeddings-for-modeling-multi-relational-data.

Antoine Bordes and Jason Weston. 2016. Learning end-to-end goal-oriented dialog. *CoRR* abs/1605.07683. http://arxiv.org/abs/1605.07683.

Samuel R. Bowman, Gabor Angeli, Christopher Potts, and Christopher D. Manning. 2015. A large annotated corpus for learning natural language inference. In *Proceedings of the 2015 Conference on Empirical Methods in Natural Language Processing*. Association for Computational Linguistics, Lisbon, Portugal, pages 632–642. https://doi.org/10.18653/v1/D15-1075.

Ronan Collobert, Jason Weston, Léon Bottou, Michael Karlen, Koray Kavukcuoglu, and Pavel P. Kuksa. 2011. Natural language processing (almost) from scratch. *Journal of Machine Learning Research* 12:2493–2537. http://dl.acm.org/citation.cfm?id=2078186.

Paul Crook, Alex Marin, Vipul Agarwal, Khushboo Aggarwal, Tasos Anastasakos, Ravi Bikkula, Daniel Boies, Asli Celikyilmaz, Senthilkumar Chandramohan, Zhaleh Feizollahi, Roman Holenstein, Minwoo Jeong, Omar Khan, Young-Bum Kim, Elizabeth Krawczyk, Xiaohu Liu, Danko Panic, Vasiliy Radostev, Nikhil Ramesh, Jean-Phillipe Robichaud, Alexandre Rochette, Logan Stromberg, and Ruhi Sarikaya. 2016. Task completion platform: A self-serve multi-domain goal oriented dialogue platform. In *Proceedings of the 2016 Conference of the North American Chapter of the Association for Computational Linguistics: Demonstrations*. Association for Computational Linguistics, San Diego, California, pages 47–51. https://doi.org/10.18653/v1/N16-3010.

Bhuwan Dhingra, Lihong Li, Xiujun Li, Jianfeng Gao, Yun-Nung Chen, Faisal Ahmed, and Li Deng. 2016. End-to-end reinforcement learning of dialogue agents for information access. *CoRR* abs/1609.00777. http://arxiv.org/abs/1609.00777.

John C. Duchi, Elad Hazan, and Yoram Singer. 2011. Adaptive subgradient methods for online learning and stochastic optimization. *Journal of Machine Learning Research* 12:2121–2159. http://dl.acm.org/citation.cfm?id=2021068.

Ondřej Dušek and Filip Jurcicek. 2016. Sequence-to-sequence generation for spoken dialogue via deep syntax trees and strings. In *Proceedings of the 54th Annual Meeting of the Association for Computational Linguistics (Volume 2: Short Papers)*. Association for Computational Linguistics, Berlin, Germany, pages 45–51. https://doi.org/10.18653/v1/P16-2008.

Simone Filice, Giovanni Da San Martino, and Alessandro Moschitti. 2015. Structural representations for learning relations between pairs of texts. In *Proceedings of the 53rd Annual Meeting of the Association for Computational Linguistics and the 7th International Joint Conference on Natural Language Processing (Volume 1: Long Papers)*. Association for Computational Linguistics, Beijing, China, pages 1003–1013. https://doi.org/10.3115/v1/P15-1097.

Katja Filippova and Michael Strube. 2008. Sentence fusion via dependency graph compression. In *Proceedings of the 2008 Conference on Empirical Methods in Natural Language Processing*. Association for Computational Linguistics, pages 177–185. http://aclweb.org/anthology/D08-1019.

Xavier Glorot, Antoine Bordes, and Yoshua Bengio. 2011. Deep sparse rectifier neural networks. In *Proceedings of the Fourteenth International Conference on Artificial Intelligence and Statistics (AISTATS)*. JMLR.org, volume 15 of *JMLR Proceedings*, pages 315–323.

Hua He, Kevin Gimpel, and Jimmy Lin. 2015. Multi-perspective sentence similarity modeling with convolutional neural networks. In *Proceedings of the 2015 Conference on Empirical Methods in Natural Language Processing*. Association for Computational Linguistics, pages 1576–1586. https://doi.org/10.18653/v1/D15-1181.

Hua He and Jimmy Lin. 2016. Pairwise word interaction modeling with deep neural networks for semantic similarity measurement. In *Proceedings of the 2016 Conference of the North American Chapter of the Association for Computational Linguistics: Human Language Technologies*. Association for Computational Linguistics, pages 937–948. https://doi.org/10.18653/v1/N16-1108.

Karl Moritz Hermann, Tomás Kociský, Edward Grefenstette, Lasse Espeholt, Will Kay, Mustafa Suleyman, and Phil Blunsom. 2015. Teaching machines to read and comprehend. In *Advances in Neural Information Processing Systems 28 (NIPS)*. pages 1693–1701. http://papers.nips.cc/paper/5945-teaching-machines-to-read-and-comprehend.

Mahboob Khalid and Suzan Verberne. 2008. Passage retrieval for question answering using sliding windows. In *Coling 2008: Proceedings of the 2nd Workshop on Information Retrieval for Question Answering*. Coling 2008 Organizing Committee, pages 26–33. http://aclweb.org/anthology/W08-1804.

Anirban Laha and Vikas Raykar. 2016. An empirical evaluation of various deep learning architectures for bi-sequence classification tasks. In *Proceedings of COLING 2016, the 26th International Conference on Computational Linguistics: Technical Papers*. The COLING 2016 Organizing Committee, Osaka, Japan, pages 2762–2773. http://aclweb.org/anthology/C16-1260.

Jiwei Li, Will Monroe, Alan Ritter, Dan Jurafsky, Michel Galley, and Jianfeng Gao. 2016. Deep reinforcement learning for dialogue generation. In *Proceedings of the 2016 Conference on Empirical Methods in Natural Language Processing*. Association for Computational Linguistics, Austin, Texas, pages 1192–1202. https://doi.org/10.18653/v1/D16-1127.

Chen Liang, Praveen K. Paritosh, Vinodh Rajendran, and Kenneth D. Forbus. 2016. Learning paraphrase identification with structural alignment. In *Proceedings of the Twenty-Fifth International Joint Conference on Artificial Intelligence (IJCAI)*. IJCAI/AAAI Press, pages 2859–2865. http://www.ijcai.org/Abstract/16/406.

Bernardo Magnini, Roberto Zanoli, Ido Dagan, Kathrin Eichler, Guenter Neumann, Tae-Gil Noh, Sebastian Padó, Asher Stern, and Omer Levy. 2014. The excitement open platform for textual inferences. In *Proceedings of 52nd Annual Meeting of the Association for Computational Linguistics: System Demonstrations*. Association for Computational Linguistics, pages 43–48. https://doi.org/10.3115/v1/P14-5008.

Tomas Mikolov, Ilya Sutskever, Kai Chen, Gregory S. Corrado, and Jeffrey Dean. 2013. Distributed representations of words and phrases and their compositionality. In *Advances in Neural Information Processing Systems 26 (NIPS)*. pages 3111–3119. http://papers.nips.cc/paper/5021-distributed-representations-of-words-and-phrases-and-their-compositionality.

Alexander Miller, Adam Fisch, Jesse Dodge, Amir-Hossein Karimi, Antoine Bordes, and Jason Weston. 2016. Key-value memory networks for directly reading documents. In *Proceedings of the 2016 Conference on Empirical Methods in Natural Language Processing*. Association for Computational Linguistics, Austin, Texas, pages 1400–1409. https://doi.org/10.18653/v1/D16-1147.

Ankur Parikh, Oscar Täckström, Dipanjan Das, and Jakob Uszkoreit. 2016. A decomposable attention model for natural language inference. In *Proceedings of the 2016 Conference on Empirical Methods in Natural Language Processing*. Association for Computational Linguistics, Austin, Texas, pages 2249–2255. https://doi.org/10.18653/v1/D16-1244.

Tim Rocktäschel, Edward Grefenstette, Karl Moritz Hermann, Tomás Kocisky, and Phil Blunsom. 2015. Reasoning about entailment with neural attention. *CoRR* abs/1509.06664. http://arxiv.org/abs/1509.06664.

Alexander M. Rush, Sumit Chopra, and Jason Weston. 2015. A neural attention model for abstractive sentence summarization. In *Proceedings of the 2015 Conference on Empirical Methods in Natural Language Processing*. Association for Computational Linguistics, Lisbon, Portugal, pages 379–389. https://doi.org/10.18653/v1/D15-1044.

Ruhi Sarikaya, Paul A. Crook, Alex Marin, Minwoo Jeong, Jean-Philippe Robichaud, Asli Çelikyilmaz, Young-Bum Kim, Alexandre Rochette, Omar Zia Khan, Xiaohu Liu, Daniel Boies, Tasos Anastasakos, Zhaleh Feizollahi, Nikhil Ramesh, H. Suzuki, Roman Holenstein, Elizabeth Krawczyk, and Vasiliy Radostev. 2016.

An overview of end-to-end language understanding and dialog management for personal digital assistants. In *2016 IEEE Spoken Language Technology Workshop (SLT 2016)*. pages 391–397. https://doi.org/10.1109/SLT.2016.7846294.

Alessandro Sordoni, Michel Galley, Michael Auli, Chris Brockett, Yangfeng Ji, Margaret Mitchell, Jian-Yun Nie, Jianfeng Gao, and Bill Dolan. 2015. A neural network approach to context-sensitive generation of conversational responses. In *Proceedings of the 2015 Conference of the North American Chapter of the Association for Computational Linguistics: Human Language Technologies*. Association for Computational Linguistics, Denver, Colorado, pages 196–205. https://doi.org/10.3115/v1/N15-1020.

Nitish Srivastava, Geoffrey E. Hinton, Alex Krizhevsky, Ilya Sutskever, and Ruslan Salakhutdinov. 2014. Dropout: A simple way to prevent neural networks from overfitting. *Journal of Machine Learning Research* 15(1):1929–1958. http://dl.acm.org/citation.cfm?id=2670313.

Adam Trischler, Zheng Ye, Xingdi Yuan, Philip Bachman, Alessandro Sordoni, and Kaheer Suleman. 2016. Natural language comprehension with the EpiReader. In *Proceedings of the 2016 Conference on Empirical Methods in Natural Language Processing*. Association for Computational Linguistics, Austin, Texas, pages 128–137. https://doi.org/10.18653/v1/D16-1013.

Oriol Vinyals and Quoc V. Le. 2015. A neural conversational model. *CoRR* abs/1506.05869. http://arxiv.org/abs/1506.05869.

Tsung-Hsien Wen, Milica Gasic, Nikola Mrkšić, Lina M. Rojas Barahona, Pei-Hao Su, Stefan Ultes, David Vandyke, and Steve Young. 2016a. Conditional generation and snapshot learning in neural dialogue systems. In *Proceedings of the 2016 Conference on Empirical Methods in Natural Language Processing*. Association for Computational Linguistics, Austin, Texas, pages 2153–2162. https://doi.org/10.18653/v1/D16-1233.

Tsung-Hsien Wen, Milica Gasic, Nikola Mrkšić, Pei-Hao Su, David Vandyke, and Steve Young. 2015. Semantically conditioned LSTM-based natural language generation for spoken dialogue systems. In *Proceedings of the 2015 Conference on Empirical Methods in Natural Language Processing*. Association for Computational Linguistics, Lisbon, Portugal, pages 1711–1721. https://doi.org/10.18653/v1/D15-1199.

Tsung-Hsien Wen, Milica Gašić, Nikola Mrkšić, Lina M. Rojas-Barahona, Pei-Hao Su, David Vandyke, and Steve Young. 2016b. Multi-domain neural network language generation for spoken dialogue systems. In *Proceedings of the 2016 Conference of the North American Chapter of the Association for Computational Linguistics: Human Language Technologies*. Association for Computational

Linguistics, San Diego, California, pages 120–129. https://doi.org/10.18653/v1/N16-1015.

Wei Xu, Ralph Grishman, and Le Zhao. 2011. Passage retrieval for information extraction using distant supervision. In *Proceedings of 5th International Joint Conference on Natural Language Processing*. Asian Federation of Natural Language Processing, pages 1046–1054. http://aclweb.org/anthology/I11-1117.

Jun Yin, Xin Jiang, Zhengdong Lu, Lifeng Shang, Hang Li, and Xiaoming Li. 2016a. Neural generative question answering. In *Proceedings of the Twenty-Fifth International Joint Conference on Artificial Intelligence (IJCAI)*. IJCAI/AAAI Press, pages 2972–2978. http://www.ijcai.org/Abstract/16/422.

Pengcheng Yin, Zhengdong Lu, Hang Li, and Ben Kao. 2016b. Neural enquirer: Learning to query tables in natural language. In *Proceedings of the Twenty-Fifth International Joint Conference on Artificial Intelligence (IJCAI)*. IJCAI/AAAI Press, pages 2308–2314. http://www.ijcai.org/Abstract/16/329.

Wenpeng Yin and Hinrich Schütze. 2015. Convolutional neural network for paraphrase identification. In *Proceedings of the 2015 Conference of the North American Chapter of the Association for Computational Linguistics: Human Language Technologies*. Association for Computational Linguistics, pages 901–911. https://doi.org/10.3115/v1/N15-1091.

Kai Zhao, Liang Huang, and Mingbo Ma. 2016. Textual entailment with structured attentions and composition. In *Proceedings of COLING 2016, the 26th International Conference on Computational Linguistics: Technical Papers*. The COLING 2016 Organizing Committee, pages 2248–2258. http://aclweb.org/anthology/C16-1212.

Hao Zhou, Minlie Huang, and Xiaoyan Zhu. 2016. Context-aware natural language generation for spoken dialogue systems. In *Proceedings of COLING 2016, the 26th International Conference on Computational Linguistics: Technical Papers*. The COLING 2016 Organizing Committee, Osaka, Japan, pages 2032–2041. http://aclweb.org/anthology/C16-1191.

Attentive listening system with backchanneling, response generation and flexible turn-taking

Divesh Lala, Pierrick Milhorat, Koji Inoue
Masanari Ishida, Katsuya Takanashi and Tatsuya Kawahara
Graduate School of Informatics
Kyoto University
`[lastname]@sap.ist.i.kyoto-u.ac.jp`

Abstract

Attentive listening systems are designed to let people, especially senior people, keep talking to maintain communication ability and mental health. This paper addresses key components of an attentive listening system which encourages users to talk smoothly. First, we introduce continuous prediction of end-of-utterances and generation of backchannels, rather than generating backchannels after end-point detection of utterances. This improves subjective evaluations of backchannels. Second, we propose an effective statement response mechanism which detects focus words and responds in the form of a question or partial repeat. This can be applied to any statement. Moreover, a flexible turn-taking mechanism is designed which uses backchannels or fillers when the turn-switch is ambiguous. These techniques are integrated into a humanoid robot to conduct attentive listening. We test the feasibility of the system in a pilot experiment and show that it can produce coherent dialogues during conversation.

1 Introduction

One major application of embodied spoken dialogue systems is to improve life for elderly people by providing companionship and social interaction. Several conversational robots have been designed for this specific purpose (Heerink et al., 2008; Sabelli et al., 2011; Iwamura et al., 2011). A necessary feature of such a system is that it be an attentive listener. This means providing feedback to the user as they are talking so that they feel some sort of rapport and engagement with the system. Humans can interact with attentive listeners at any time, making them a useful tool for people such as the elderly.

Our motivation is to create a robot which can function as an attentive listener. Towards this goal, we use the autonomous android named Erica. Our long-term goal is for Erica to be able to participate in a conversation with a human user while displaying human-like speech and gesture. In this work we focus on integrating an attentive listener function into Erica and describe a new approach for this application.

The approaches to these kind of dialogue systems have focused mainly on backchanneling behavior and have been implemented in large-scale projects such as SimSensei (DeVault et al., 2014), Sensitive Artificial Listeners (Bevacqua et al., 2012) and active listening robots (Johansson et al., 2016). These systems are multimodal in nature, using human-like non-verbal behaviors to give feedback to the user. However, the backchannels are usually generated after the end of utterance and they do not necessarily create synchrony in the conversation (Kawahara et al., 2015). Moreover, the dialogue systems are still based on hand-crafted keyword matching. This means that new lines of dialogue or extensions to new topics must be handcrafted, which becomes impractical.

In this paper we present an approach to attentive listening which integrates continuous backchannels with responsive dialogue to user statements to maintain the flow of conversation. We create a continuous prediction model which is perceived as being better than a model which predicts only after an IPU (inter-pausal unit) has been received from the automatic speech recognition (ASR) system. Meanwhile, the statement response system detects focus words of the user's utterance and uses them to generate responses as a wh-question or by repeating it back to the user. We also introduce a novel approach to turn-taking which uses

Proceedings of the SIGDIAL 2017 Conference, pages 127–136,
Saarbrücken, Germany, 15-17 August 2017. ©2017 Association for Computational Linguistics

backchannels and fillers to indicate confidence in taking the speaking turn.

Our approach is not limited by the topic of conversation and no prior parameters about the conversation are required so it can be applied to open domain conversation. We also do not require perfect speech recognition accuracy, which has been identified as a limitation in other attentive listening systems (Bevacqua et al., 2012). Our system runs efficiently in real-time and can be flexibly integrated into a larger architecture, which we will also demonstrate through a conversational robot.

The next section outlines the architecture of our attentive listener. In Section 3 we describe in detail the major components of the attentive listener including results of evaluation experiments. We then implement this system into Erica as a proof-of-concept in Section 4, before the conclusion of the paper. Our system is in Japanese, but English translations are used in the paper for clarity.

2 System architecture

Figure 1 summarizes the components of attentive listening and the general system architecture. Inputs to the system are prosodic features, which is calculated continuously, and ASR results from the Japanese speech recognition system Julius (Lee et al., 2001).

We implement a dialogue act tagger which classifies an utterance into questions, statements or others such as greetings. This is currently based on a support vector machine and is moving to a recurrent neural network. Questions and others are handled by a separate module which will not be explained in this paper. Statements are handled by a statement response component. The other two components in the attentive listener are a backchannel generator and a turn-taking model.

Backchannels are generated by one component, while the statement response component can generate different types of dialogue depending on the utterance of the user. As part of our NLP functionalities we have a focus word extractor trained by a conditional random field (Yoshino and Kawahara, 2015) which identifies the focus of an utterance. For example, the statement "Yesterday I ate curry." would produce a focus word of "curry". We then send this information to the statement response component which generates a question response "What kind of curry?". Further details of the technical implementation are described in the next section.

The process flow of the system is as follows. The system performs continuous backchanneling behavior while listening to the speaker. At the same time, ASR results of the user are received. When the utterance unit is detected and its dialogue act is tagged as a statement, then a response is generated and then stored. However, a response is only actually output when the system predicts an appropriate time to take the turn. This is because the user may wish to keep talking and the system should not interrupt. Thus, we can manage turn-taking more flexibly.

In summary, the three major components required for attentive listening are backchanneling, statement response and turn-taking.

3 Attentive listening components

In this section we describe the three major components of attentive listening. We evaluate each of these components individually.

3.1 Continuous backchannel generation

Our goal is to increase rapport (Huang et al., 2011) with the user by showing that the system is interested in the content of the user's speech. There have been many works on automatic backchannel generation, with most using prosodic features for either rule-based models (Ward and Tsukahara, 2000; Truong et al., 2010) or machine learning methods (Morency et al., 2008; Ozkan et al., 2010; Kawahara et al., 2015).

In this work we use a model in which backchanneling behavior occurs continuously during the speaker's turn, not only at the end of an utterance. We take a machine learning approach by implementing a logistic regression model to predict if a backchannel would occur 500ms into the future. We predict into the future rather than at the current time point, because in the real-time system Erica requires processing time to generate nodding and mouth movements that synchronize with her utterance. We trained the model using a counseling corpus. This corpus consisted of eight one-to-one counseling sessions between a counselor and a student and were transcribed according to the guidelines of the Corpus of Spontaneous Japanese (CSJ) (Maekawa, 2003).

The model makes a prediction every 100ms by using windows of prosodic features of sizes 100, 200, 500, 1000 and 2000 milliseconds. For a win-

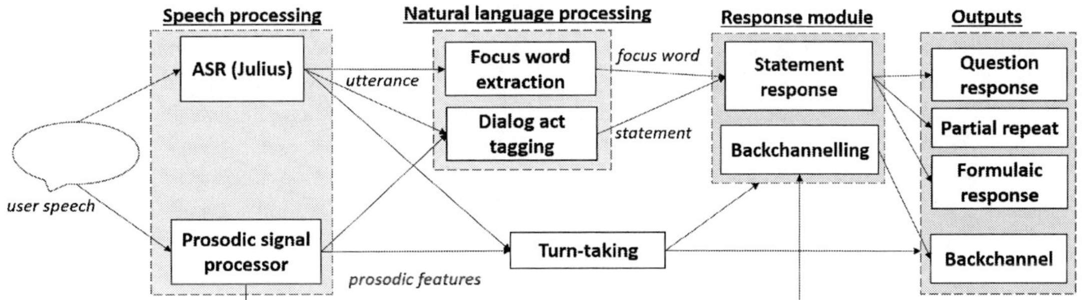

Figure 1: System architecture of attentive listener.

dow size s, feature extraction is conducted within windows every s milliseconds before the current time point, up to a maximum of $4s$ milliseconds. For example, for a time window of 100ms, prosodic features are calculated inside windows starting at 400, 300, 200 and 100 milliseconds before the current time point. The prosodic features are the mean, maximum, minimum, range and slope of the pitch and intensity. Finally, we add the durations of silence, voice activity, and overlap of the speaker and listener.

We conducted two evaluations of the backchannel timing model. The first is an objective evaluation of the precision and recall. We used 8-fold cross validation and tested on individual sessions. We compared against a baseline model which generated a backchannel after every IPU (**Fixed**) and an IPU-based model based on logistic regression which also predicted after every IPU using additional linguistic features (**IPU-based**). Our model showed that the most influential prosodic feature was the range and maximum intensity of the speech, with larger windows located just before the prediction point generally being more influential than other windows. Although we have no quantitative evidence, we propose that a reduction in the intensity of the speech provides an opportunity for the listener to produce a backchannel. The results are displayed in Table 1.

Model	AUC	Prec.	Rec.	F1
Time-based	0.851	0.344	0.889	0.496
IPU-based	0.809	0.659	0.512	0.576
Fixed	0.500	0.146	1.000	0.255

Table 1: Prediction results for backchannel timing.

We see that the time-based model performs better than the baseline and the IPU-based model with a high AUC and recall. The precision is fairly low, due to predicting a large number backchannels even though none in the corpus are found.

We also conducted a subjective evaluation of this model by comparing against the same models as the objective evaluation. We also included an additional counselor condition, in which backchannels in the real corpus were substituted with the same recorded pattern.

Participants in the experiment listened to recorded segments from the counseling corpus, lasting around 30-40 seconds each. We chose segments where the counselor acted as an attentive listener by only responding through the backchannels used in our model. The counselor's voice for backchannels was generated using a recorded pattern by a female voice actress. We created the different conditions for each recording by applying our model directly to the audio signal of the speaker. The audio channel of the counselor's voice was separated and so could be removed. When the model determined that a backchannel should be generated at a timepoint, we manually inserted the backchannel pattern into the speaker's channel using audio editing software, effectively replacing the counselor's voice.

Each condition was listened to twice by each participant through different recordings selected at random. Subjects rated each recording over five measures - naturalness and tempo of backchannels (Q1 and Q2), empathy and understanding (Q3 and Q4) and if the participant would like to talk with the counselor in the recording (Q5). Each measure was rated using a 7-point Likert scale.

For analysis we conducted a repeated measures ANOVA with Bonferroni corrections. Results are shown in Table 2. Our proposed model outperformed the baseline models and was comparable to the counselor condition.

	Fixed	IPU	Couns.	Time-based
Q1	2.74*	3.92*	4.55	4.48
Q2	3.06*	4.05	4.86	4.61
Q3	2.44*	3.75*	4.25	4.58
Q4	2.55*	3.95	4.38	4.39
Q5	2.35*	3.64*	4.23	4.21

Table 2: Average ratings of backchannel models. Asterisks indicate the difference is statistically significant from the proposed model.

The results of both evaluations show the need for backchannel timing to be done continuously and not just at the end of utterances.

3.2 Statement response

The statement response component is triggered for statements and outputs when the system takes a turn. The purpose is to encourage the user to expand on what they have just said and extend the thread of the conversation. The statement response tries to use a question phrase which repeats a word that the user has previously said. For example, if the user says "I will go to the beach.", the statement response should generate a question such as "Which beach?". It may also repeat the focus of the utterance back to the user to encourage elaboration, such as "The beach?".

Our approach uses wh-questions as a means to continue the conversation. From a linguistic perspective, they are described in question taxonomies by Graesser et al. (1994) and Nielsen et al. (2008) as concept completions (who, what, when, where) or feature specifications (what properties does X have?). We observe that listeners in everyday conversations use such phrases to get the speaker to provide more information.

From a technical perspective, there are two processes for the system. The first process is to detect the focus word of the utterance. The second is to correctly pair this with an appropriate wh-question word to form a meaningful question. The basic wh-question words are similar for both English and Japanese.

To detect the focus word we use a conditional random field classifier in previous work which uses part-of-speech tags and a phrase-level dependency tree (Yoshino and Kawahara, 2015). The model was trained with utterances from users interacting with two different dialogue systems. This corpus was then annotated to identify the focus phrases of sentences.

We use a decision tree in Figure 2 to decide from one of four response types. If a focus phrase can be detected, we take each noun in the phrase, match them to a wh-question and select the pair with the maximum likelihood. We used an n-gram language model to compute the joint probability of the focus noun being associated with each question word. The corpus used is the Balanced Corpus of Contemporary Written Japanese, which contains 100 million words from written documents. We then consider the maximum joint probability of this noun and a question word. If this is over a threshold Tf, then a question on the focus word is generated. If no question is generated, the focus noun is repeated with a rising tone.

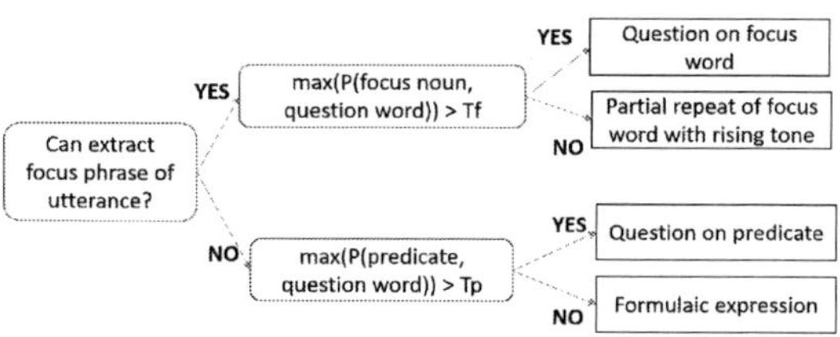

Figure 2: Decision tree of statement response system showing the four different response types.

If no focus phrase is found we match the predicate of the utterance to a question word using the same method as above. If this is above a threshold Tp, then the response is a question on the predicate, otherwise a formulaic expression is generated as a fallback response. We provide examples of each of the response types in Table 3.

We evaluated this component in two different ways. Firstly, we extracted dialogue from an existing chatting corpus created for Project Next's NLP task[1]. We selected 200 user statements from this corpus as a test set and applied the statement response system to them. Two annotators then checked if the generated responses were appropriate. The results are shown in Table 4.

The results showed that the algorithm could classify the statements reasonably well. However, in the case of a focus word being unable to be

---

[1] https://sites.google.com/site/dialoguebreakdowndetection/chat-dialogue-corpus

Response type	Example
Question on focus	U: Yesterday I ate **curry**.
	S: <u>What kind of</u> **curry**?
Partial repeat	U: I'll go and run a **marathon**.
	S: A **marathon**?
Question on predicate	U: Then I **went** out.
	S: <u>Where</u> did you **go**?
Formulaic expression	U: That's beautiful.
	S: Yeah.

Table 3: Examples of response types for user statements. Bold words indicate the detected focus noun or predicate of the utterance, while underlined words indicate matched question words.

Response type	Precision	Recall
Question on focus	0.63	0.46
Partial repeat	0.72	0.86
Question on predicate	0.14	0.30
Formulaic expression	0.94	0.78

Table 4: Classification accuracy of statement response system for chatting corpus.

found correctly identifying a question word for a predicate is a challenge.

Next, we evaluated our statement response system by testing if it could reduce the number of fallback responses used by the system. We conducted this experiment with 22 participants, and gathered data on their utterances during a first-time meeting with Erica. In most cases the participants asked questions that could be answered by the system, but sometimes the users said statements for which the question-answering system could not formulate a response. In these cases a generic fallback response was generated.

From the data we found that 39 out of 226 (17.2%) user utterances produced fallback responses. We processed all these utterances offline through the statement response component. From these 39 statements, 19 (47.7%) result in a statement which could be categorized into either a question on focus, partial repeat, or a question on predicate. Furthermore, the generated responses were deemed to be coherent with the correct focus and question words being applied. This would have continued the flow of conversation.

3.3 Flexible turn-taking

The goal of turn-taking is to manage the floor of the conversation. The system decides when it should take the turn using a decision model. One simple approach is to wait for a fixed duration of silence from the user before starting the speaking turn. However, we have found this is highly user-dependent and very challenging when the user continues talking. The major problem is that if the user has not finished their turn and the system begins speaking, they must then wait for the system's utterance to finish. This disrupts the flow of the conversation and makes the user frustrated. Solving this problem is not trivial so several works have attempted to develop a robust model for turn-taking (Raux and Eskenazi, 2009; Selfridge and Heeman, 2010; Ward et al., 2010).

Figure 3 displays our approach towards turn-taking behavior, rather than having to make a binary decision about whether or not to take the turn. When the user has the floor and the system receives an ASR result, our model outputs a likelihood score between 0 and 1 that the system should take the turn. The actual likelihood score determines the system's response. The system has four possible responses - silence, generate a backchannel, generate a filler or take the turn by speaking.

The novelty of our approach is that we do not have to immediately take a turn based on a hard threshold. Backchannels encourage the user to continue speaking and signal that the system will not take the turn. Fillers are known to indicate a willingness to take the turn (Clark and Tree, 2002; Ishi et al., 2006) and so are used to grab the turn from the user. However, the user may still wish to continue speaking and if they do the system won't grab the turn and so doesn't interrupt the flow of

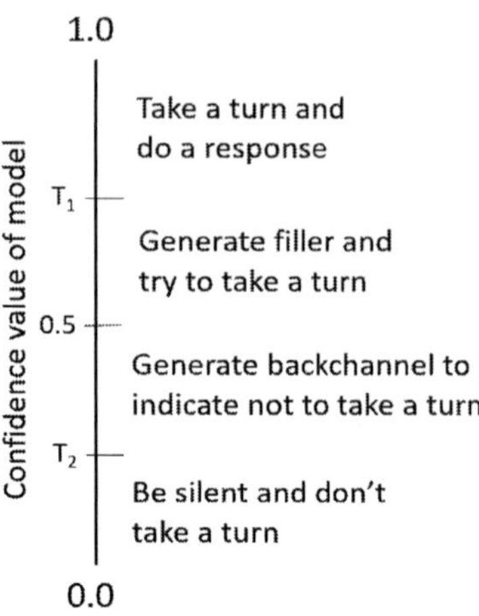

Figure 3: Conceptual diagram of Erica's turn-taking behavior. The decision of the system is dependent on the model's likelihood of the speaker has finished their turn. Decision thresholds are applied manually.

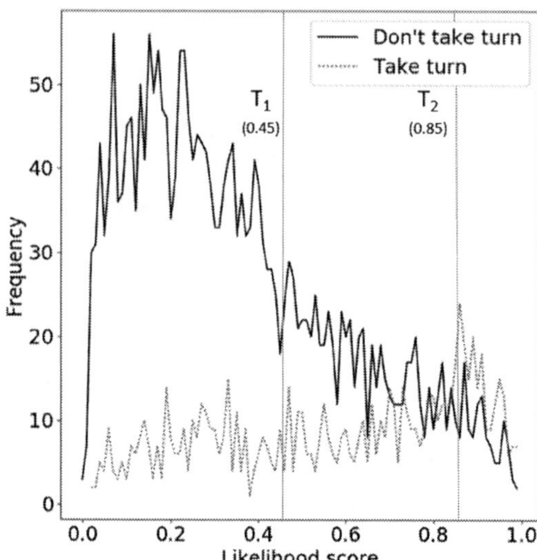

Figure 4: Distribution of likelihood scores for turn-taking.

Model	Precision	Recall	F1
	3-tier		
Don't take turn	0.856	0.683	0.760
Take turn	0.624	0.231	0.337
	Binary		
Don't take turn	0.848	0.731	0.785
Take turn	0.428	0.605	0.501

Table 5: Performance of turn-taking model compared to single-threshold logistic regression.

conversation. To guarantee that Erica will eventually take the turn, we set a threshold for the user's silence time and automatically take the turn once it elapses.

To implement this system, we used a logistic regression model with the same features as our backchanneling model. We train using the same counseling corpus and features that were used for the backchanneling model. We found 25% of the outputs within the corpus to be turn changes.

Our proposed model requires two likelihood score thresholds (T_1 and T_2) to decide whether or not to be silent ($\leq T_1$) or take the turn ($\geq T_2$). We set a threshold for deciding between backchannels and fillers to 0.5. We determined T_1 to be 0.45 and T_2 to be 0.85 based on Figure 4, which displays the distributions of likelihood score for the two classes.

The performance of this model is shown in Table 5. We compared the proposed model to a logistic regression model with a single threshold at 0.5. Results are shown in Table 5.

These two thresholds degrade the recall of turn-taking ground-truth actions because the cases in between them are discarded. However we improve the precision of taking the turn, which is critical in spoken dialogue systems, from 0.428 to 0.624. The cases discarded in this stage will be recovered by uttering fillers or backchannels.

Moreover, the ground-truth labels are based on actual turn-taking actions made by the human listener, and there should be more Transition Relevance Places (Sacks et al., 1974), where turn-taking would be allowed. This should be addressed in future work.

4 System

In this section we describe the overall system with the attentive listener being integrated into the conversational android Erica.

4.1 ERICA

Erica is an android robot that takes the appearance of a young woman. Her purpose is to use conversation to play a variety of social roles. The physical realism of Erica necessitates that her conversational behaviors are also human-like. Therefore our objective is not only to undertake natural language processing, but to also address a variety of conversational phenomena.

The environment we create for Erica reduces the need to use a physical interface such as a handheld microphone or headset to have a conversation. Instead we use a spherical microphone array placed on a table between Erica and the user. A photo of this environment is shown in Figure 5.

Figure 5: Photo of user interacting with Erica.

Based on the microphone array and the Kinect sensor, we are able to reliably determine the source of speech. Erica only considers speech from a particular user and ignores unrelated noises such as ambient sounds and her own voice.

4.2 Pilot study

We conducted an initial evaluation of our system as a pilot study to demonstrate its appropriateness for attentive listening. We have observed from previous demonstrations that users often do not speak with Erica as if she is an attentive listener. Rather, they simply ask Erica questions and wait for her answers. To overcome this issue in order to evaluate the statement response system, we first provided the subjects with dialogue prompts in the form of scripts. This allowed users familiarize themselves with Erica for free conversation. Two male graduate students were subjects in the experiment and interacted with Erica in these two different tasks.

The first task was to read from four conversational scripts of 3 to 5 turns each. These scripts were not hand-crafted, but taken from a corpus of real attentive listening conversations with a Wizard-of-Oz controlled robot. Subjects were instructed to pause after each sentence in the script to wait for a statement response. If Erica replied with a question they could answer it before con-

tinuing the scripted conversation.

The second task was to speak with Erica freely while she did attentive listening. In this scenario the subjects talked freely on the subject of their favorite travel memories. They could end the conversation whenever they wished. Statistics of the subjects' turns are shown in Table 6.

	Script	Free talk
Turns	77	13
Avg. length per turn (sec.)	3.94	2.90
Avg. characters per turn	20.9	16.4

Table 6: Statistics for the speaking turns of the subjects.

We find that the subjects reading from the script had longer turns but the speaking rate was lower than for free talk. In other words, script reading was slower and longer. We also analyzed the distribution of response types generated from the system as shown in Table 7.

	Script	Free talk	Total
Backchannel	77	13	90
Q. on focus	14	10	24
Partial repeat	10	1	11
Q. on predicate	2	1	3
Formulaic	29	6	35
Total	132	31	163

Table 7: Distribution of response types from statement response component.

Backchannels were generated most frequently, while both questions on focus and formulaic expressions were the most common response types, with questions on focus words having the highest frequency in free conversation. Partial repeats had a much higher frequency in the scripts than in free conversation. This is because the script readings were taken from conversations which used more complex sentences than the free talk, and focus nouns for which a suitable question word could not be reliably matched.

4.3 Subjective ratings

We evaluated the system by asking 8 evaluators to listen to the recording of both the scripts and free conversation. Each evaluator was assigned

Speaker	Japanese utterance	English translation	Component
User	Kono mae, tomodachi to Awajishima ni ryokou ni ikimashita.	I once took a trip with friends to Awajishima island	
Erica	*unun*	*mhm*	Backchannel
Erica	*Doko e itta no desuka?*	*Where did you go?*	Question on predicate
User	Awajishima ni itte, sono ato bokujo nado wo-	Awajishima, then-	
Erica	*un*	*mm*	Backchannel
User	mi ni ikimashita.	went to visit a farm.	
Erica	*Doko no bokujo desu ka?*	*Where was the farm?*	Question on focus
User	Etto, namae ha chotto oboetenain desukeredomo-	Um, I don't remember the name of it, but-	
Erica	*un*	*mm*	Backchannel
User	-ee, hitsuji toka wo mimashita.	-we saw sheep and other animals.	

Table 8: Example dialogue of user free talk conversation with attentive listening Erica.

one random script and both free conversations to evaluate. The evaluators rated each of Erica's backchannels and statement responses in terms of coherence (coherent, somewhat coherent, or incoherent) and timing (fast, appropriate, or slow). We used a majority vote to determine the overall rating of each speech act. The ratings on the coherence of each statement are shown in Figure 6.

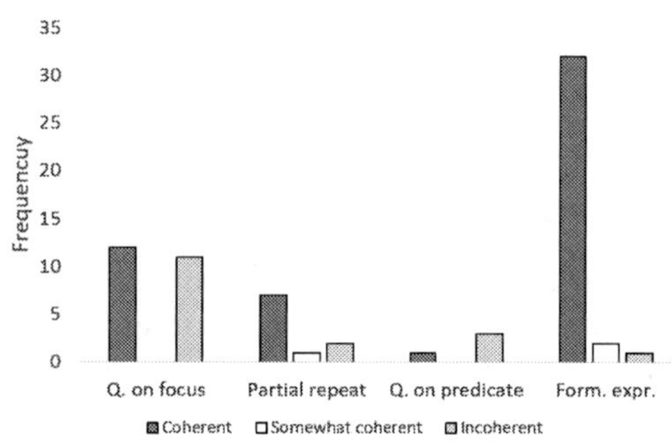

Figure 6: Rating on coherence for each response type.

We see that the results are similar to the previous evaluation of the statement response system. More than half of questions on focus words were coherent, although most of these were in response to the scripts. Formulaic expressions were mostly coherent even though they were selected at random.

Similarly, we categorized system utterances into backchannels or statements and analyzed timing. The results are shown in Figure 7.

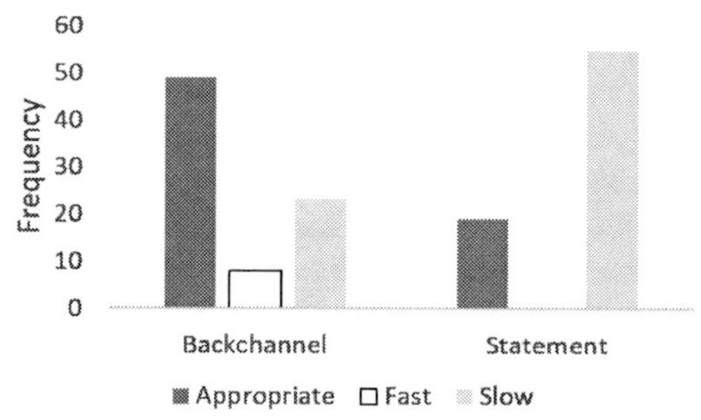

Figure 7: User rating of timing for backchannels and statements.

We can see that while most backchannels have suitable timing, statement responses are slow due to the processing of the utterance that is required.

4.4 Generated dialogue

Table 8 shows dialogue from a free talk conversation. User utterances were punctuated by backchannels and the system is able to extract a focus noun or predicate and produce a coherent response.

We also found that the system could produce a coherent response even in the case of ASR errors.

In one case the subject said "sakana tsuri wo shi-mashita (I went fishing.).". The ASR system generated "sakana wo sore wo sumashita", which is nonsensical. In this case, the word "fish" was successfully detected as the focus noun and a coherent response could be generated.

4.5 Analysis of incoherent statements

We also examined 17 utterances determined to be incoherent (excluding backchannels and formulaic expressions) and analyzed the reasons for these. Table 9 shows the sources of errors in the statement response with their associated frequencies.

Error source	Frequency
Incorrect question word match	5
Incoherent focus noun/predicate	4
Repeated statement	4
ASR errors	3
Focus word undetected	1

Table 9: Errors found in the generated statement responses.

Incorrect question word matching was found several times. For example, the user said "Tokyo ni ryokou ni ittekimashita (I went on a trip to Tokyo)", generating the reply "Donna Tokyo desu ka? (What kind of Tokyo?)" which does not make sense. Another source of error was the system detecting a focus noun or predicate which did not make sense. Repeated statements were also found. The subject had already explained something during the conversation but the system asked a question on it. This can be addressed by keeping a history of the dialogue. The ASR word error rate was approximately 10% for both script reading and free talk, so was not a major issue. In most cases, incorrect ASR results cannot be parsed and so a formulaic expression is produced.

4.6 Lessons from pilot study

Our pilot study showed that our system is feasible with no technical failures. Backchannels can be generated at appropriate times. Coherent responses could be generated by the system and errors in Erica's dialog can be addressed. We chose third-party evaluations for this experiment due to the small sample size and also because the subjects could not evaluate specific utterances while they were using the system.

However we intend to conduct a more comprehensive study where the subjects evaluate their own interaction with Erica. Subjects should engage in free talk, but we have found that motivating them to do so is not trivial. A reasonable metric for a full experiment is the subject's willingness to continue the interaction with with Erica which indicates engagement with the system. We can also use more objective metrics such as the number and length of turns taken by the user. Our strategy of using fillers and backchannels to regulate turn-taking should also be evaluated.

5 Conclusion and future work

In this paper we described our approach towards creating an attentive listening system which is integrated inside the android Erica. The major components are backchannel generation, statement response system, and a turn-taking model. We presented individual evaluations of each of these components and how they work together to form the attentive listening system. We also conducted a pilot study to demonstrate the feasibility of the attentive listener. We intend to conduct a full experiment with the system to discover if it is comparable to human conversational behavior. Our aim is for this system to be used in a practical setting, particularly with elderly people.

Acknowledgements

This work was supported by JST ERATO Ishiguro Symbiotic Human-Robot Interaction program (Grant Number JPMJER1401), Japan.

References

Elisabetta Bevacqua, Roddy Cowie, Florian Eyben, Hatice Gunes, Dirk Heylen, Mark Maat, Gary Mckeown, Sathish Pammi, Maja Pantic, Catherine Pelachaud, Etienne De Sevin, Michel Valstar, Martin Wollmer, Marc Shroder, and Bjorn Schuller. 2012. Building Autonomous Sensitive Artificial Listeners. *IEEE Transactions on Affective Computing* 3(2):165–183.

Herbert H Clark and Jean E Fox Tree. 2002. Using uh and um in spontaneous speaking. *Cognition* 84(1):73–111.

David DeVault, Ron Artstein, Grace Benn, Teresa Dey, Ed Fast, Alesia Gainer, Kallirroi Georgila, Jon Gratch, Arno Hartholt, Margaux Lhommet, Gale Lucas, Stacy Marsella, Fabrizio Morbini, Angela Nazarian, Stefan Scherer, Giota Stratou, Apar Suri, David Traum, Rachel Wood, Yuyu Xu, Albert

Rizzo, and Louis-philippe Morency. 2014. SimSensei Kiosk : A Virtual Human Interviewer for Healthcare Decision Support. In *International Conference on Autonomous Agents and Multi-Agent Systems*. 1, pages 1061–1068.

A. C. Graesser, C. L. McMahen, and B. K. Johnson. 1994. Question Asking and Answering. In Morton A. Gernsbacher, editor, *Handbook of Psycholinguistics*, Academic Press, pages 517–538.

Marcel Heerink, Ben Kröse, Bob Wielinga, and Vanessa Evers. 2008. Enjoyment intention to use and actual use of a conversational robot by elderly people. In *Proceedings of the 3rd ACM/IEEE international conference on Human robot interaction*. ACM, pages 113–120.

Lixing Huang, Louis-Philippe Morency, and Jonathan Gratch. 2011. Virtual rapport 2.0. In *International Workshop on Intelligent Virtual Agents*. Springer, pages 68–79.

Carlos Toshinori Ishi, Hiroshi Ishiguro, and Norihiro Hagita. 2006. Analysis of prosodic and linguistic cues of phrase finals for turn-taking and dialog acts. In *INTERSPEECH*.

Yamato Iwamura, Masahiro Shiomi, Takayuki Kanda, Hiroshi Ishiguro, and Norihiro Hagita. 2011. Do elderly people prefer a conversational humanoid as a shopping assistant partner in supermarkets? In *6th ACM/IEEE International Conference on Human-Robot Interaction (HRI)*. IEEE, pages 449–457.

Martin Johansson, Tatsuro Hori, Gabriel Skantze, Anja Höthker, and Joakim Gustafson. 2016. Making turn-taking decisions for an active listening robot for memory training. In Arvin Agah, John-John Cabibihan, Ayanna M. Howard, Miguel A. Salichs, and Hongsheng He, editors, *Social Robotics: 8th International Conference, ICSR 2016*. Springer International Publishing, Cham, pages 940–949.

Tatsuya Kawahara, Miki Uesato, Koichiro Yoshino, and Katsuya Takanashi. 2015. Toward adaptive generation of backchannels for attentive listening agents. In *International Workshop Series on Spoken Dialogue Systems Technology*. pages 1–10.

Akinobu Lee, Tatsuya Kawahara, and Kiyohiro Shikano. 2001. Julius – an open source real-time large vocabulary recognition engine. In *EUROSPEECH*. pages 1691–1694.

Kikuo Maekawa. 2003. Corpus of spontaneous Japanese: Its design and evaluation. In *ISCA & IEEE Workshop on Spontaneous Speech Processing and Recognition*. pages 7–12.

Louis-Philippe Morency, Iwan de Kok, and Jonathan Gratch. 2008. Predicting listener backchannels: A probabilistic multimodal approach. In *International Workshop on Intelligent Virtual Agents*. Springer, pages 176–190.

Rodney D Nielsen, Jason Buckingham, Gary Knoll, Ben Marsh, and Leysia Palen. 2008. A taxonomy of questions for question generation. In *Proceedings of the 1st Workshop on Question Generation*.

Derya Ozkan, Kenji Sagae, and Louis-Philippe Morency. 2010. Latent mixture of discriminative experts for multimodal prediction modeling. In *Proceedings of the 23rd International Conference on Computational Linguistics*. Association for Computational Linguistics, pages 860–868.

Antoine Raux and Maxine Eskenazi. 2009. A finite-state turn-taking model for spoken dialog systems. In *Proceedings of Human Language Technologies: The 2009 Annual Conference of the North American Chapter of the Association for Computational Linguistics*. Association for Computational Linguistics, pages 629–637.

Alessandra Maria Sabelli, Takayuki Kanda, and Norihiro Hagita. 2011. A conversational robot in an elderly care center: an ethnographic study. In *6th ACM/IEEE International Conference on Human-Robot Interaction (HRI)*. IEEE, pages 37–44.

Harvey Sacks, Emanuel a Schegloff, and Gail Jefferson. 1974. A simplest systematics for the organization of turn taking for conversation. *Language* 50(4):696–735.

Ethan O. Selfridge and Peter A. Heeman. 2010. Importance-driven turn-bidding for spoken dialogue systems. In *Proceedings of the 48th Annual Meeting of the Association for Computational Linguistics*. Association for Computational Linguistics, Stroudsburg, PA, USA, ACL '10, pages 177–185.

Khiet P. Truong, Ronald Poppe, and Dirk Heylen. 2010. A rule-based backchannel prediction model using pitch and pause information. In *Interspeech 2010*. International Speech Communication Association (ISCA), pages 3058–3061.

Nigel Ward and Wataru Tsukahara. 2000. Prosodic features which cue back-channel responses in English and Japanese. *Journal of Pragmatics* 32(8):1177–1207.

Nigel G Ward, Olac Fuentes, and Alejandro Vega. 2010. Dialog prediction for a general model of turn-taking. In *INTERSPEECH*. Citeseer, pages 2662–2665.

Koichiro Yoshino and Tatsuya Kawahara. 2015. Conversational system for information navigation based on pomdp with user focus tracking. *Computer Speech & Language* 34(1):275–291.

Natural Language Input for In-Car Spoken Dialog Systems: How Natural is Natural?

Patricia Braunger, Wolfgang Maier, Jan Wessling, Steffen Werner

Daimler AG

Sindelfingen

Germany

{patricia.braunger, wolfgang.mw.maier}@daimler.com
{jan.wessling, steffen.s.werner}@daimler.com

Abstract

Recent spoken dialog systems are moving away from *command and control* towards a more intuitive and natural style of interaction. In order to choose an appropriate system design which allows the system to deal with naturally spoken user input, a definition of what exactly constitutes *naturalness* in user input is important. In this paper, we examine how different user groups naturally speak to an automotive spoken dialog system (SDS). We conduct a user study in which we collect freely spoken user utterances for a wide range of use cases in German. By means of a comparative study of the utterances from the study with interpersonal utterances, we provide criteria what constitutes *naturalness* in the user input of an state-of-the-art automotive SDS.

1 Introduction

In the automotive area, speech interfaces have continuously gained importance in recent years. Current spoken dialog systems (SDS) are expected not to be restricted to a *command-and-control*-style interaction, in which functions are invoked by the user by speaking fixed key phrases. Instead, they are expected to accept *natural* input from the user, i.e., to understand the user without imposing restrictions on how he has to formulate queries.[1]

A definition of what exactly constitutes *naturalness* in user input is important, not only in order to precisely understand user expectations, but also, and especially, in order to choose an appropriate system design which allows the system to deal with flexible user input and spontaneous speech

phenomena (as described by Skantze (2007)), and to facilitate the design of meaningful system evaluation.

Since interpersonal interaction is the most natural form of interaction, it is often taken as a baseline for the development of an intuitive and natural human-machine interaction (Bonin et al., 2015). However, earlier work shows that human speech is strongly influenced by the assumptions that a speaker has about his interlocutor, e.g. (Branigan and Pearson, 2006), and also by individual properties such as age, e.g. (Möller et al., 2008; Bell, 2003). In conclusion, naturalness in user input cannot simply be equated with interpersonal speech and different user groups may have a different understanding of what is natural and intuitive. To the best of our knowledge, there are no studies investigating what exactly constitutes naturalness in user input.

In this paper, our aim is to answer the question of which kind of utterances the natural language understanding component of an SDS must be able to understand from a user perspective. Thereby, characterizing the capabilities of a dialog management, as done by Bohlin et al. (1999) (cf. TRINDI tick-list), is not enough – a thorough characterization of the characteristics of natural language user input is needed. In order to achieve this, we conduct a study in which we collect free user utterances for an in-car SDS in German. By means of a comparative analysis with interpersonal utterances, we first show to which extent utterances used for system interaction share properties with interpersonal utterances. Second, we examine to which extent different user groups speak differently in terms of naturalness.

The remainder of the paper is structured as follows. In section 2, we review previous literature which has aimed at defining naturalness of user input and describing natural language utterances respectively. The following section 3 we introduce

---

[1] Also, it is expected, that systems answer *naturally* to the user. However, a discussion of system output is beyond the scope of this paper.

Proceedings of the SIGDIAL 2017 Conference, pages 137–146,
Saarbrücken, Germany, 15-17 August 2017. ©2017 Association for Computational Linguistics

our study design. Section 4 presents the evaluation of the study, in section 5 the results are discussed and section 6 concludes the article.

2 Towards a Definition of Naturalness

In general, natural language is human language and therefore different from artificial languages which are especially created for specific purposes, e.g., computer languages. In this sense, spoken dialog systems always make use of natural language. This also applies to command-and-control systems. However, the term *natural* is often used as a qualifier of the abilities of the natural language understanding (NLU) and natural language generation (NLG) modules of an SDS.

A general definition of naturalness in this sense is given by Berg (2013), who calls SDS *natural* if their language behavior is as human-like as possible. Many authors refer to this definition of *natural language* when they demand a more natural human-machine interaction, see, e.g., (Edlund et al., 2008).

The literature that investigates the naturalness of spoken user input, which is the focus of our work, can be split into three groups.

Literature in the first group describes the users' speaking style by means of labels like *natural* and *command*. Hofmann et al. (2012), e.g., conduct a web-based study to find out how users would interact with internet services using speech. They classify the observed speaking styles into *natural*, *command* and *keyword style*. They state that *natural* reflects the way humans communicate among each other and that the *command* and *keyword style* is related to state-of-the-art human-machine interaction. Berg et al. (2010) use similar labels with a different meaning. They classify utterances collected from a human-machine interaction study into *commands*, *phrased commands* and *natural language*, whereas *commands* is used similar to *keyword style* of Hofmann et al. (2012) and *natural language* utterances consist of full sentences including phrases of civility and filler words. Similarly, in the study of Berg (2012), speaking styles are classified into *full sentences*, *medium-length commands* and *short commands*. White et al. (2014) and Pang et al. (2011) investigate written web search queries. They classify information seeking queries into *keyword queries* and *natural language questions*. *Natural language questions* are defined as utterances beginning with

a question indicator, such as *what* and *do*, and ending with a question mark.

The second group consists of literature which (linguistically) analyzes spoken user input style. Braunger et al. (2016), e.g., compare crowd-sourced natural language user input in terms of sentence constructions. They conclude that if people speak freely to an SDS, they mostly use an imperative style. Winter et al. (2010) collect naturally spoken utterances and quantify their complexity and variety. They use context information as a qualitative measurement for classification, classifying the utterance content into three categories: *information data*, *context relevant words* and *non-context relevant words*. They find that users tend to repeat similar utterance patterns composed from a limited set of different words.

Thirdly, we find work which concenctrates on the differences between human-human and human-machine communication. Guy (2016) shows that voice queries are closer to natural language than written queries. He builds two natural language models, one based on a corpus representing classic formal language and one based on a corpus representing a more colloquial web language. For measuring the similarity to a natural language model he used perplexity. He concludes that voice queries are still far from natural language questions. The authors of (Hayakawa et al., 2016) compared direct human-human dialogs to dialogs that are mediated by a speech-to-speech machine translation system. They found that in machine mediated conversation speakers use less words than in direct human-to-human communication. In (Pang and Kumar, 2011) written natural language questions posed as web search queries are compared to a natural language sample of questions posted by web users on a community-based question-answering site. Since written text tends to be structurally complete Pang et al. (2011) measure naturalness by means of the probability mass of function words.

A more intuitive and natural interaction with SDSs presupposes understanding naturally spoken user utterances. In order to choose an appropriate system design which allows the system to deal with naturally spoken utterances, a definition of what exactly constitutes naturalness in user input is necessary. Recent research in this area only focuses on the question whether users speak naturally or in a command-/keyword-based way to a speech system, whereby *naturalness* is equated with human-directed speech, e.g. (Hofmann et al., 2012; Pang and Kumar, 2011; Berg, 2012). The criteria mentioned for natural, human-directed speech are full sentences, civility, filler words and a higher number of words. Since natural is what people intuitively use, *natural language input* cannot simply be equated with interpersonal speaking style. Even though different studies found that a speaker's language behavior is influenced by beliefs about an interlocutor, cf. (Branigan and Pearson, 2006; Branigan et al., 2010; Bell, 2003) and researchers have many intuitions about the differences between human-machine and human-human communication, interpersonal speaking style is often taken as a baseline for naturalness as can be seen from the discussed literature and it has not been examined to which extent the criteria mentioned for naturalness characterize naturally spoken utterances towards state-of-the-art SDS. There exist only a few empirical studies which investigate the differences. These research works focus either on dialog issues such as turn-taking, e.g. (Doran et al., 2001), or on lexical alignment, e.g. (Branigan et al., 2011), but not on natural language input towards SDS in a car environment.

The way people address the system is not only influenced by their beliefs about the system but also by individual properties such as age or gender. Work in this area of research has been done by Bell (2003) who found that individual differences in speaker behavior are significant and by Möller (2008) who found that younger users differ from older users in the way they speak with a smart-home system. The observations show that different user groups may have a different understanding of what is natural and intuitive. Therefore, user profiles must be considered when defining natural language input.

3 Study Design

To the best of our knowledge, there are no data answering the question to which extent naturally spoken user input towards SDS differ from human-directed speech and what exactly constitutes naturalness in user input. We therefore conduct a study to examine how different user groups would naturally speak to an actual in-car SDS and how they would speak to their passenger.

In the following, we explain the experimental setup and procedure of the study.

3.1 Participants

The study is targeted at younger and elder German adults with different SDS experience and a valid driver's license. In total, 45 subjects participated in the study. 46% of them were female and 54% were male. The average age was 39.5 years (standard deviation SD: 13.5). 55.6% of the participants were aged between 20-39 years, 26.6% were 40-59 years old and 17.8% were older than 60 years. 27% were experienced in the use of spoken dialog systems; 74% had little to no experience with speech-controlled devices.

3.2 Experimental Design

The study was split into two sessions and each participant encountered both conditions (*within-subject design*). In the one session the participants had to talk to their front passenger who performed the requested action. In the other session the participants were asked to interact with an in-car spoken dialog system. According to Möller (2008; 2005) we decided to conduct a Wizard of Oz (WOZ) experiment. This method is less time consuming and less costly. In a WOZ experiment a human operator (wizard) simulates the behavior of an intelligent computer application whereby the human believes to be interacting with a fully automated prototype (Dahlbaeck et al., 1993). Within each session the participants were asked to solve twelve tasks typically performed in a car:

1. Listen to radio station SWR3
2. Play Michael Jackson Greatest Hits
3. Navigate to Stieglitzweg 23 in Berlin
4. Call Barack Obama on his mobile phone
5. Set temperature to 23 degrees
6. Send a text message to brother
7. Weather in Berlin today
8. Date of the European Football championship final game
9. Population of Berlin
10. Score VfB Stuttgart against FC Bayern
11. Cinema program in Berlin today
12. Next Shell gas station

The tasks consist of six non-information seeking tasks (1-6) and six information seeking tasks (7-12).

| Task 1 | Task 10 |

Figure 1: Task description

3.2.1 System Simulation

The system behavior was simulated with the help of the SUEDE tool (Klemmer et al., 2000). The system behavior was designed such as in an actual Mercedes-Benz E-class. The system directly provided the information requested or activated the appropriate function whereby the user input resulted in a visual and acoustic system feedback. With user input for Task 1), for example, the radio program started playing and the screen provided information on the current radio station.

3.2.2 Task Description

The tasks were presented by pictures in paper form. Different studies, e.g., (Bernsen et al., 1998; Tateishi et al., 2005), report from priming effects when using text-based task descriptions. As pictures do not bias the subjects by putting words into their mouths, the participants were shown pictures that describe the tasks. The tasks were pre-tested with friendly users to find out if the desired situation was put in the user's mind. Examples for the task descriptions are given in Fig. 1.

3.2.3 Driving Simulation Setup

Since we want to find out how users naturally interact with a spoken dialog system while driving, we put the participants in a simulated driving situation. The participants were sitting on the driver's seat in a car which was placed in front of a canvas onto which the driving simulation was projected, such as done by Hofmann et al. (2014). They were shown a driving simulation where they were driving behind a car. Their task was to brake if and only if the preceding vehicle brakes. The driving simulation setup is illustrated in Fig. 2.

3.3 Procedure

The overall procedure of the experiment was as follows. First, the participants were informed about the procedure. The participants were told that they have to orally solve tasks while driving and they were shown the graphically depicted

Figure 2: Driving simulation setup

tasks. The participants had to verbally interpret the tasks. In order to prevent wrong interpretations we gave assistance, where necessary. As for the session with the passenger, they were told that the passenger provided the information requested or activated the appropriate function. As for the system session, they were told to speak freely to the system. They had to activate the speech recognition via speaking the phrase "Hallo Auto" (eng. "Hello Car"). Afterwards, the participants got to know the driving simulation in a test drive lasting about three minutes. The instructor was sitting on the passenger seat. The instructor showed the task presentation pictures randomly while the participant was driving. The tasks were permuted to avoid order effects.

4 Evaluation and Results

In total, we collected 1.080 utterances; 540 system-directed utterances and 540 human-directed utterances. The utterances were manually transcribed and automatically analyzed. The transcription exactly matched the spoken utterances. The analysis included Part-of-Speech (POS) Tagging and Parsing with *SpaCy*.[2] The part-of-speech-tagger uses the Google Universal POS tag set of Petrov et al. (2011).

First, we analyze to which extent system-directed utterances share properties with human-directed utterances. Second, we aim at identifying salient features of intuitively spoken user input. Third, we analyze the impact of the users' age and gender on their speaking style to gain additional insights into the variability of user in-

---

[2]https://github.com/explosion/spaCy.

put. Therefore, system-directed utterances are compared with human-directed utterances broken down by the users' age and gender. The collected data are examined in terms of different linguistic criteria commonly used in the literature, e.g. (Summa et al., 2016; Johansson, 2008; Pinter et al., 2016; Pak and Paroubek, 2010), including those mentioned by the literature for naturalness:

- Lexical diversity
- Lexical density
- Big words
- POS tag frequencies
- Politeness
- Filler words
- Syntactic complexity
- Sentence types
- Utterance length

Only those features which occur significantly often in system-directed speech are considered as characteristic features of intuitively spoken user input. In order to determine the linguistic features that are associated with the respective criterion, e.g., what is polite, we rely on the findings from literature (see below).

One of the most common measures of lexical diversity is the type-token ratio which is defined as the ratio of the total number of individual word types (lemmas) to the total number of occuring word tokens, cf. (Johansson, 2008). We use the standardized type-token tatio (STTR), firstly mentioned by Johnson (1944), to normalize the impact of the size of the different corpora. Fig. 3 displays the STTR broken down by different age, gender and interlocutor.

The type-token ratio significantly differs between human-directed speech and system-directed speech (p<0.01). In addition, Fig. 3 shows that the older the users the higher the lexical diversity. That is, older participants tend to use more individual words than younger both in system-directed speech and in human-directed speech. The differences between the age groups are significant at p<0.01. The users' gender does not seem to have an impact on the lexical diversity.

One of the measures of lexical density is the content-function word ratio which is calculated by dividing the number of content words (open class words) by the number of function words

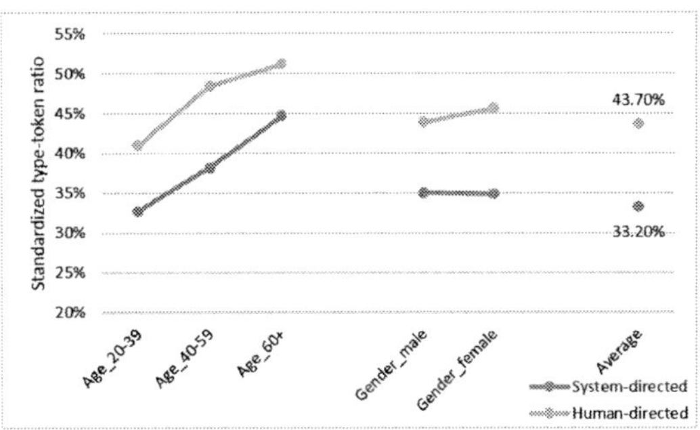

Figure 3: Type-token ratio broken down by user profiles and interlocutor

(closed class words), cf. (Johansson, 2008). This means, the higher the proportion of content words the more information is given. In human-directed speech people tend to use more content words (44.68%) than in system-directed speech (41.68%). The user profiles do not seem to have an impact.

The big word ratio is calculated by dividing the number of words longer than six characters (big words) by the total number of words. We found that people do not tend to adapt the use of big words significantly to their interlocutor. 17.11% of the system-directed words are big words and 16.50% of the human-directed. The user profiles do not seem to have an impact on the use of big words.

Next, we are interested in a difference of tag distributions between the speech sets. Table 1 shows the seven most frequent POS tags of both speech sets. Nouns (NOUN) and proper nouns (PROPN) occur much more frequently in the system-directed speech set, whereas adverbs (ADV) and verbs (VERB) occur much more frequently in the human-directed speech set. Pronouns (PRON) are less frequently used in system-directed speech (5.50%) than in human-directed speech (10.42%). The proportion of prepositions (ADP) is ranked at position seven in human-directed speech but at position four in system-directed speech. The proportions of determiners (DET) are more or less balanced. As for the user groups in both sets, we found differences in the occurrence of verbs between men and women. Women tend to use more verbs than men (in system-directed speech significant at the 0.05 level). Additionally, we found that older users tend to use more verbs and pronouns and fewer

Table 1: POS tag frequencies

System-directed		Human-directed	
NOUN	18.93%	ADV	16.73%
PROPN	17.40%	NOUN	14.16%
DET	13.28%	VERB	13.05%
ADP	12.65%	PROPN	12.47%
ADV	12.38%	DET	11.02%
VERB	9.50%	PRON	10.42%
PRON	5.50%	ADP	10.06%

proper nouns than younger people. These tendencies hold for both system-directed speech and human-directed speech.

Our evaluation of how polite users speak to an SDS is based on the empirical findings of (Danescu-Niculescu-Mizil et al., 2013). They characterized politeness marking in requests. Out of the 14 strategies which are perceived as being polite the following strategies appear in our data:

- Sentence-medial please: Could you **please**

- Counterfactual modal: **Could/Would** you...

- Indicative modal: **Can/Will** you...

- 1st person start: **I** search...

- 1st person pl.: Could **we** find...

The distribution of utterances with politeness indicators are shown in Fig. 4.[3] The results in Fig. 4 confirm that politeness strategies are salient features of human-directed utterances but not of system-directed utterances. Overall, only 19.63% of the system-directed utterances contain politeness markers, whereas 53.33% of the human-directed utterances are polite (p<0.01). Fig. 4 shows that politeness strategies have been used more often by women in both corpora (p<0.01). Furthermore, younger people (20-39 years) are far more likely to avoid politeness strategies when speaking to the system than older people (p<0.01).

As for the categorie *filler words*, we investigate the number of utterances that contain disfluencies such as *äh* and *ähm* (eng. "uh") and modal particles. We use the definition of modal

---

[3]Direct questions such as *What is your native language?*, direct variants such as imperatives and sentence-initial *please* are perceived as being impolite, cf. (Danescu-Niculescu-Mizil et al., 2013). In our data, 8% of all utterances contain an imperative with sentence-medial *please*. Since imperatives with *please* are perceived as not being polite we did not count *please* in this morphosyntactic context.

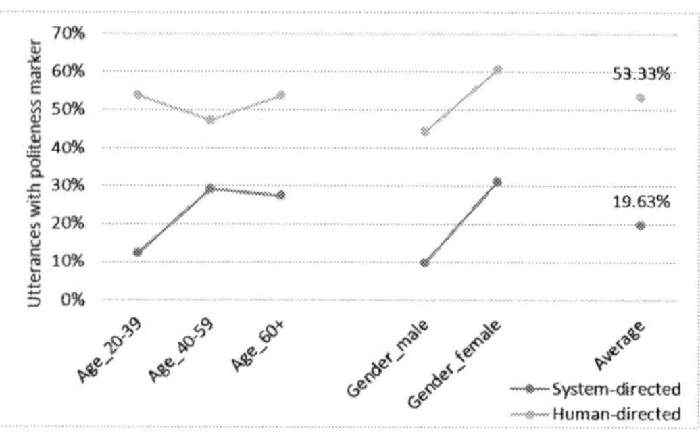

Figure 4: Distribution of polite utterances broken down by user profiles and interlocutor

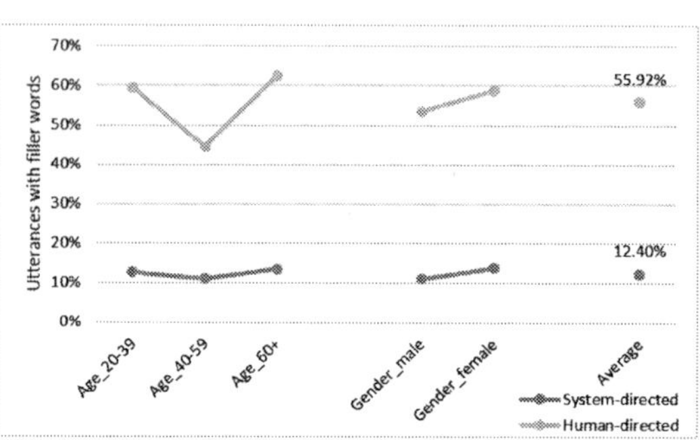

Figure 5: Distribution of utterances containing filler words broken down by user profiles and interlocutor

particles according to Bross (2012), namely that modal particles do not contribute to the sentence meaning. The following modal particles occur in our data: *doch, einmal, nochmal, mal, denn, eigentlich, vielleicht*. Fig. 5 shows the percentage of utterances with disfluencies and modal particles. The results show that all user groups avoid filler words when speaking to the system. Only 12.40% of the system-directed utterances contain filler words. In contrast, 55.92% of the human-directed utterances contain filler words. Significant differences (p<0.01) also appear in the use of filler words between the different age groups. 40-59 years old people tend to use less filler words than the younger (20-39) and older (60+) when speaking to their passenger.

Besides lexical and pragmatic aspects we analyze our data in terms of syntactic features. One of the measures of syntactic complexity is tree depth. Tree depth is defined as the number of edges in the longest path from the root node to a leaf, cf. (Pinter et al., 2016). We have calculated the median and mean depth of the dependency

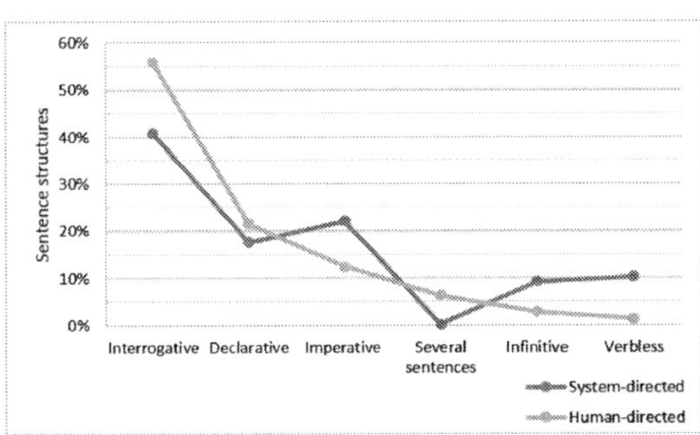

Figure 6: Distribution of sentence structures broken down by interlocutor

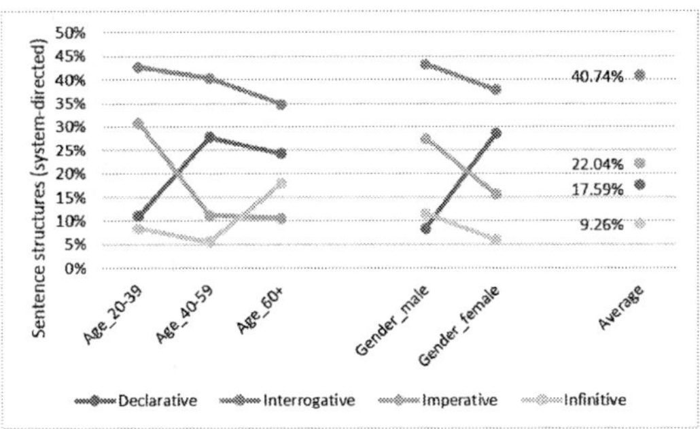

Figure 7: Distribution of sentence structures broken down by user profiles (system-directed)

trees. However, the differences are not significant at p<0.05. Overall, the median tree depth of the system-directed utterances is 3 with an interquartile range of 2. The same holds for the human-directed utterances.

Another syntactic criterion mentioned by the literature for naturalness is the use of full sentences. The criterion *full sentence* comprises sentences containing a finite verb form. We further subdivided the category *full sentence* into four categories based on sentence types. In addition, we identified patterns without verb or just with an infinitive. We also found utterances composed of two or three sentences that are categorized as *several sentences*. An overview and examples of the sentence structures we identified are given in Table 2. The frequency of the occurrence of the sentence structures is shown in Fig. 6. Across all tasks, an interrogative structure predominates. This is due to the fact that the twelve tasks consist of six information seeking tasks. As Fig. 6 implies, 95,93% of the human-directed utterances are full sentences but only 80,56% of the system-directed. The frequency of an imperative, infinitive and verbless construction increases significantly (p<0.05) in system-directed speech. In human-directed speech people tend to use more interrogative constructions and several sentences to verbalize their request.

Fig. 7 displays the distribution of sentence structures broken down by user profiles for the system-directed utterances. Only those sentence structures are displayed which show significantly different distributions at the 0.05 level. Younger people (20-39 years) and males tend to use a lot more imperative constructions than older people and females but less declarative constructions.

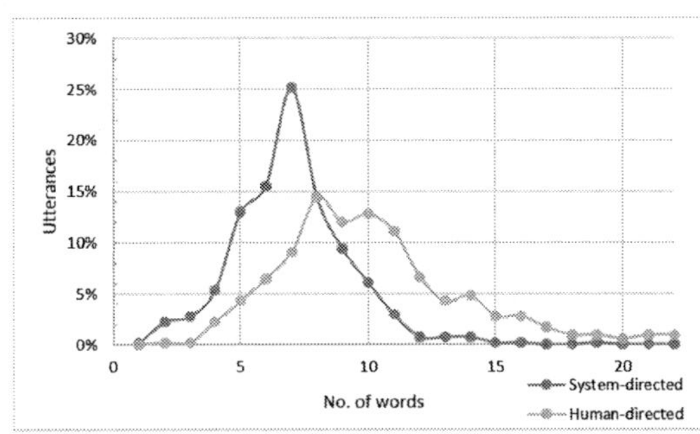

Figure 8: Utterance length broken down by interlocutor

The group of people older than 60 years used more often an infinitive construction than the younger but fewer interrogative constructions. The older participants used fewer interrogative constructions also when speaking to the passenger. As for the distribution of the other sentence structures occured in the human-directed set, the user groups are more or less balanced.

In order to conclude the syntactic analysis we compare the utterance length. Fig. 8 shows the distribution of the number of words per utterance. The utterances towards the system were shorter, Ø 7.01 words per utterance (SD 1.95), than the utterances towards the passenger, Ø 10.22 (SD 3.64).

5 Discussion

Our comparative study shows that certain features, e.g., full sentences or filler words, are characteristic features of interpersonal speaking but not of system-directed speech. We found that although people are told to utter freely they still use syntactic incomplete sentences and they are likely to avoid politeness strategies and filler words, cf. examples given in a) and b).

Table 2: Sentence structures

Sentence Structure	Example
Interrogative	Wo ist die nächste Shell-Tankstelle?
	"Where is the nearest Shell gas station?"
Imperative	Spiele SWR3!
	"Play SWR3!"
Declarative	Ich möchte SWR3 hören.
	"I would like to listen to SWR3."
Infinitive	SWR3 spielen.
	No corresponding syntax existing in English
Verbless	Radio SWR3
	"Radio SWR3"
Several sentences	Wir könnten ja heute Abend ins Kino. Was kommt denn heute in Berlin?
	"We could go to the cinema this evening. What's the program in Berlin?"

a) Bitte Radiosender SWR3 einstellen.
   "Please radio station SWR3 *infinite verb*"

b) Temperatur auf 23 Grad.
   "Temperature to 23 degrees."

Our analysis results confirm that people adapt their speaking style depending on whom they are talking to. According to the findings of (Levin et al., 2013; Pearson et al., 2006; Branigan et al., 2011) we assume that speakers are strongly influenced by the assumptions that a speaker has about his interlocutor, not only in human-machine communication but also in human-human communication. Thus, people always utter in a way they believe the system is able to understand, also if the system behaves more human-like. We therefore argue that freely spoken user input should not be considered synonymous with human-directed speech, namely with full sentences, civility, with the occurrence of filler words etc. The use of short and concise phrases (such as a verbless construction) just seems to be an effect of the user adapting to the system as conversational partner in the sense of (Pearson et al., 2006; Branigan et al., 2011) and is as natural (in the sense of intuitive) as using full sentences including politeness markers or filler words. If system developers follow the assumption that the linguistics of freely spoken user input is equated with interpersonal speaking style they hardly meet the user expectations of an intuitive and natural speaking. Instead, we suggest to add incomplete syntactic structures such as verbless and infinite sentences to the criteria for naturally spoken user input. Since 71% of the system-directed utterances do not contain filler words or

politeness markers we also suggest not to equate natural language input with the occurrence of filler words and politeness indicators.

6   Conclusion

In this paper, we have contributed to the question of how we can define *naturalness* in user input towards a state-of-the-art SDS.

We have presented a user study in which we have collected freely spoken user utterances for a wide range of automotive use cases in German. By means of a comparative study of human-directed and system-directed utterances, we have shown that *naturalness* cannot simply be equated with *human-human* communication: users will use shorter and concise phrases in order to interact with the machine. We have argued that this is an effect of the user adapting to the machine as conversational partner in the sense of (Pearson et al., 2006; Branigan et al., 2011). In addition, we found that the users' age and gender have an impact on the way they speak to an SDS. We have shown that women did more often make use of politeness strategies and of a declarative construction and that older users tended to use more individual words.

Our further goal is to define evaluation criteria which consider freely spoken user input to compare different SDS. This will be subject of future work.

References

Linda Bell. 2003. *Linguistic Adaptions in Spoken Human-Computer Dialogues: Empirical Studies of User Behavior*. Ph.D. thesis, KTH Royal Institute of Technology.

Markus Berg. 2012. Survey on spoken dialogue systems: User expectations regarding style and usability. In *14th International PhD Workshop OWD*.

Markus Berg. 2013. Natürlichsprachlichkeit in dialogsystemen. *Informatik-Spektrum* 36(4):371–381.

Markus Berg, Petra Gröber, and Martina Weicht. 2010. User study: Talking to computers. In *Proceedings of the 3rd Workshop on Inclusive eLearning*.

Niels O. Bernsen, Hans Dybkjaer, and Laila Dybkjaer. 1998. *Designing Interactive Speech Systems: From First Ideas to User Testing*. Springer.

Peter Bohlin, Johan Bos, Staffan Larsson, Ian Lewin, Collin Matheson, and David Milward. 1999. Survey of existing interactive systems. trindi project deliverable d1.3. Technical report, University of Gothenburg.

Francesca Bonin, Ronald Böck, Nick Campbell, and Ronald Poppe, editors. 2015. *Multimodal Analyses enabling Artificial Agents in Human-Machine Interaction*. Springer.

Holly P. Branigan and Jamie Pearson. 2006. Alignment in human-computer interaction. In *Proceedings of the Workshop on How People Talk to Computers, Robots, and Other Artificial Communication Partners*.

Holly P. Branigan, Martin J. Pickering, Jamie Pearson, and Janet F. McLean. 2010. Linguistic alignment between people and computers. *Journal of Pragmatics* 42:2355–2368.

Holly P. Branigan, Martin J. Pickering, Jamie Pearson, Janet F. McLean, and Ash Brown. 2011. The role of beliefs in lexical alignment: Evidence from dialogs with humans and computers. *Cognition* 121(1):41–57.

Patricia Braunger, Hansjörg Hofmann, Steffen Werner, and Maria Schmidt. 2016. A comparative analysis of crowdsourced natural language corpora for spoken dialog systems. In *Proceedings of the 10th International Conference on Language Resources and Evaluation (LREC)*.

Fabian Bross. 2012. German modal particles and the common ground. *Helikon. A Multidisciplinary Online Journal* 2:182–209.

Nils Dahlbaeck, Arne Joensson, and Lars Ahrenberg. 1993. Wizard of oz-studies – why and how. In *Proceedings of the Workshop on Intelligent User Interfaces*.

Cristian Danescu-Niculescu-Mizil, Moritz Sudhof, Dan Jurafsky, Jure Leskovec, and Christopher Potts. 2013. A computational approach to politeness with application to social factors. In *Proceedings of the 51st Annual Meeting of the Association for Computational Linguistics (ACL)*.

Christine Doran, John Aberdeen, Laurie Damianos, and Lynette Hirschman. 2001. Comparing several aspects of human-computer and human-human dialogues. In *Proceedings of the 2nd SigDial Workshop on Discourse and Dialogue*.

Jens Edlund, Joakim Gustafson, Matthias Heldner, and Anna Hjalmarsson. 2008. Towards human-like spoken dialog systems. *Speech Communication* 50:630–645.

Ido Guy. 2016. Searching by talking: Analysis of voice queries on mobile web search. In *Proceedings of the 39th International ACM SIGIR Conference on Research and Development in Information Retrieval*.

Akira Hayakawa, Luz Saturnino, and Nick Campbell. 2016. Talking to a system and talking to a human: A study from a speech-to-speech, machine translation mediated map task. In *Proceedings of INTERSPEECH*.

Hansjörg Hofmann, Ute Ehrlich, André Berton, and Wolfgang Minker. 2012. Speech interaction with the internet - a user study. In *Proceedings of the 8th International Conference on Intelligent Environments*.

Hansjörg Hofmann, Mario Hermanutz, Vanessa Tobisch, Ute Ehrlich, André Berton, and Wolfgang Minker. 2014. Evaluation of in-car sds notification concepts for incoming proactive events. In *Proceedings of 5th International Workshop on Spoken Dialog Systems (IWSDS)*.

Victoria Johansson. 2008. *The Department of Linguistics and Phonetics: Working Papers 53*, Lund University, chapter Lexical diversity and lexical density in speech and writing: a developmental perspective, pages 61–79.

Wendell Johnson. 1944. Studies in language behavior: I.a program of research. *Psychological Monographs* 56:1–15.

Scott R. Klemmer, Anoop K. Sinha, Jack Chen, James A. Landay, Nadeem Aboobaker, and Annie Wang. 2000. Suede: A wizard of oz prototyping tool of speech user interfaces. In *Proceedings of the 13th Annual ACM Symposium on User interface Software and Technology*.

Daniel T. Levin, Stephen S. Killingsworth, Megan M. Saylor, Stephen M. Gordon, and Kazuhiko Kawamura. 2013. Tests of concepts about different kinds of minds: Predictions about the behavior of computers, robots, and people. *Human-Computer Interaction* 28(2):161–191.

145

Sebastian Möller, Florian Gödde, and Maria Wolters. 2008. Corpus aanalysis of spoken smart-home interactions with older users. In *Proceeding of the 6th International Conference on Language Resources and Evaluation (LREC)*.

Alexander Pak and Patrick Paroubek. 2010. Twitter as a corpus for sentiment analysis and opinion mining. In *Proceedings of the 7th International Conference on Language Resources and Evaluation (LREC)*.

Bo Pang and Ravi Kumar. 2011. Search in the lost sense of "query": Question formulation in web search queries and its temporal changes. In *Proceedings of the 49th Annual Meeting of the Association for Computational Linguistics: Human Language Technologies: Short Papers - Volume 2*.

Jamie Pearson, Jiang Hu, Holly P. Branigan, Martin J. Pickering, and Clifford I. Nass. 2006. Adaptive language behavior in hci: How expectations and beliefs about a system affect users' word choice. In *Proceedings of the 2006 Conference on Human Factors in Computing Systems (CHI)*.

Slav Petrov, Dipanjan Das, and Ryan T. McDonald. 2011. A universal part-of-speech tagset. *CoRR* .

Yuval Pinter, Roi Reichart, and Idan Szpektor. 2016. Syntactic parsing of web queries with question intent. In *Conference of the North American Chapter of the Association for Computational Linguistics: Human Language Technologies*.

Gabriel Skantze. 2007. *Error Handling in Spoken Dialogue Systems: Managing Uncertainty, Grounding and Miscommunication*. Ph.D. thesis, KTH Stockholm.

Anja Summa, Bernd Resch, and Michael Strube. 2016. Microblog emotion classification by computing similarity in text, time, and space. In *Proceedings of the Workshop on Computational Modeling of People's Opinions, Personality, and Emotions in Social Media*.

Masahiko Tateishi, Katsushi Asami, Ichiro Akahori, Scott Judy, Yasunari Obuchi, Teruko Mitamura, Eric Nyberg, and Nobuo Hataoka. 2005. *A Spoken Dialog Corpus for Car Telematics Services*, Springer, chapter DSP for In-Vehicle and Mobile Systems, pages 47–64.

Ryen White, Matthew Richardson, and Wen tau Yih. 2014. Questions vs. queries in informational search tasks. Technical report, Microsoft.

Ute Winter, Tim J. Grost, and Omer Tsimhoni. 2010. Language pattern analysis for automotive natural language speech application. In *Proceedings of the 2nd International Conference on Automotive User Interfaces and Interactive Vehicular Applications (AutomotiveUI)*.

Sample-efficient Actor-Critic Reinforcement Learning
with Supervised Data for Dialogue Management

Pei-Hao Su, Paweł Budzianowski, Stefan Ultes, Milica Gašić, and Steve Young
Department of Engineering, University of Cambridge, Cambridge, UK
`{phs26, pfb30, su259, mg436, sjy11}@cam.ac.uk`

Abstract

Deep reinforcement learning (RL) methods have significant potential for dialogue policy optimisation. However, they suffer from a poor performance in the early stages of learning. This is especially problematic for on-line learning with real users. Two approaches are introduced to tackle this problem. Firstly, to speed up the learning process, two sample-efficient neural networks algorithms: trust region actor-critic with experience replay (TRACER) and episodic natural actor-critic with experience replay (eNACER) are presented. For TRACER, the trust region helps to control the learning step size and avoid catastrophic model changes. For eNACER, the natural gradient identifies the steepest ascent direction in policy space to speed up the convergence. Both models employ off-policy learning with experience replay to improve sample-efficiency. Secondly, to mitigate the cold start issue, a corpus of demonstration data is utilised to pre-train the models prior to on-line reinforcement learning. Combining these two approaches, we demonstrate a practical approach to learning deep RL-based dialogue policies and demonstrate their effectiveness in a task-oriented information seeking domain.

1 Introduction

Task-oriented Spoken Dialogue Systems (SDS) aim to assist users to achieve specific goals via speech, such as hotel booking, restaurant information and accessing bus-schedules. These systems are typically designed according to a structured *ontology* (or a database *schema*), which defines the domain that the system can talk about. The development of a robust SDS traditionally requires a substantial amount of hand-crafted rules combined with various statistical components. This includes a spoken language understanding module (Chen et al., 2016; Yang et al., 2017), a dialogue belief state tracker (Henderson et al., 2014; Perez and Liu, 2016; Mrkšić et al., 2017) to predict user intent and track the dialogue history, a dialogue policy (Young et al., 2013; Gašić and Young, 2014; Budzianowski et al., 2017) to determine the dialogue flow, and a natural language generator (Rieser and Lemon, 2009; Wen et al., 2015; Hu et al., 2017) to convert conceptual representations into system responses.

In a task-oriented SDS, teaching a system how to respond appropriately in all situations is non-trivial. Traditionally, this *dialogue management* component has been designed manually using flow charts. More recently, it has been formulated as a planning problem and solved using reinforcement learning (RL) to optimise a dialogue policy through interaction with users (Levin and Pieraccini, 1997; Roy et al., 2000; Williams and Young, 2007; Jurčíček et al., 2011). In this framework, the system learns by a *trial and error* process governed by a potentially delayed learning objective called the *reward*. This reward is designed to encapsulate the desired behavioural features of the dialogue. Typically it provides a positive reward for success plus a per turn penalty to encourage short dialogues (El Asri et al., 2014; Su et al., 2015a; Vandyke et al., 2015; Su et al., 2016b).

To allow the system to be trained on-line, Bayesian sample-efficient learning algorithms have been proposed (Gašić and Young, 2014; Daubigney et al., 2014) which can learn policies from a minimal number of dialogues. However, even with such methods, the initial performance is still relatively poor, and this can impact negatively

Proceedings of the SIGDIAL 2017 Conference, pages 147–157,
Saarbrücken, Germany, 15-17 August 2017. ©2017 Association for Computational Linguistics

on the user experience.

Supervised learning (SL) can also be used for dialogue action selection. In this case, the policy is trained to produce an appropriate response for any given dialogue state. Wizard-of-Oz (WoZ) methods (Kelley, 1984; Dahlbäck et al., 1993) have been widely used for collecting domain-specific training corpora. Recently an emerging line of research has focused on training neural network-based dialogue models, mostly in text-based systems (Vinyals and Le, 2015; Shang et al., 2015; Serban et al., 2015; Wen et al., 2017; Bordes et al., 2017). These systems are directly trained on past dialogues without detailed specification of the internal dialogue state. However, there are two key limitations of using SL in SDS. Firstly, the effect of selecting an action on the future course of the dialogue is not considered and this may result in sub-optimal behaviour. Secondly, there will often be a large number of dialogue states which are not covered by the training data (Henderson et al., 2008; Li et al., 2014). Moreover, there is no reason to suppose that the recorded dialogue participants are acting optimally, especially in high noise levels. These problems are exacerbated in larger domains where multi-step planning is needed.

In this paper, we propose a network-based approach to policy learning which combines the best of both SL- and RL-based dialogue management, and which capitalises on recent advances in deep RL (Mnih et al., 2015), especially off-policy algorithms (Wang et al., 2017).

The main contribution of this paper is two-fold:

1. improving the sample-efficiency of actor-critic RL: trust region actor-critic with experience replay (TRACER) and episodic natural actor-critic with experience replay (eNACER).

2. efficient utilisation of demonstration data for improved early stage policy learning.

The first part focusses primarily on increasing the RL learning speed. For TRACER, trust regions are introduced to standard actor-critic to control the step size and thereby avoid catastrophic model changes. For eNACER, the natural gradient identifies steepest ascent direction in policy space to ensure fast convergence. Both models exploit the off-policy learning with experience replay (ER) to improve sample-efficiency. These are compared with various state-of-the-art RL methods.

The second part aims to mitigate the cold start issue by using *demonstration data* to pre-train an RL model. This resembles the training procedure adopted in recent game playing applications (Silver et al., 2016; Hester et al., 2017). A key feature of this framework is that a single model is trained using both SL and RL with different training objectives but without modifying the architecture.

By combining the above, we demonstrate a practical approach to learning deep RL-based dialogue policies for new domains which can achieve competitive performance without significant detrimental impact on users.

2   Related Work

RL-based approaches to dialogue management have been actively studied for some time (Levin et al., 1998; Lemon et al., 2006; Gašić and Young, 2014). Initially, systems suffered from slow training, but recent advances in data efficient methods such as Gaussian Processes (GP) have enabled systems to be trained from scratch in on-line interaction with real users (Gašić et al., 2011). GP provides an estimate of the uncertainty in the underlying function and a built-in noise model. This helps to achieve highly sample-efficient exploration and robustness to recognition/understanding errors.

However, since the computation in GP scales with the number of points memorised, sparse approximation methods such as the *kernel span* algorithm (Engel, 2005) must be used and this limits the ability to scale to very large training sets. It is therefore questionable as to whether GP can scale to support commercial wide-domain SDS. Nevertheless, GP provides a good benchmark and hence it is included in the evaluation below.

In addition to increasing the sample-efficiency of the learning algorithms, the use of reward shaping has also been investigated in (El Asri et al., 2014; Su et al., 2015b) to enrich the reward function in order to speed up dialogue policy learning.

Combining SL with RL for dialogue modelling is not new. Henderson et al. (2008) proposed a hybrid SL/RL model that, in order to ensure tractability in policy optimisation, performed exploration only on the states in a dialogue corpus. The policy was then defined manually on parts of the space which were not found in the corpus. A method of initialising RL models using logistic regression was also described (Rieser and Lemon, 2006). For GPRL in dialogue, rather than using a linear kernel that imposes heuristic data pair correlation, a pre-optimised Gaussian kernel learned using SL from a dialogue corpus has been proposed (Chen et al., 2015). The resulting kernel was more accurate on data correlation and achieved better performance, however, the SL corpus did not help to initialise a better policy. Better initialisation of GPRL has been studied in the context of domain adaptation by specifying a GP prior or re-using an existing model which is then pre-trained for the new domain (Gašić et al., 2013).

A number of authors have proposed training a standard neural-network policy in two stages (Fatemi et al., 2016; Su et al., 2016a; Williams et al., 2017). Asadi and Williams (2016) also explored off-policy RL methods for dialogue policy learning. All these studies were conducted in simulation, using error-free text-based input. A similar approach was also used in a conversational model (Li et al., 2016). In contrast, our work introduces two new sample-efficient actor-critic methods, combines both two-stage policy learning and off-policy RL, and testing at differing noise levels.

3 Neural Dialogue Management

The proposed framework addresses the dialogue management component in a modular SDS. The input to the model is the belief state **b** that encodes a distribution over the possible user intents along with the dialogue history. The model's role is to select the system action a at every turn that will lead to the maximum possible cumulative reward and a successful dialogue outcome. The system action is mapped into a system reply at the semantic level, and this is subsequently passed to the natural language generator for output to the user.

The semantic reply consists of three parts: the *intent* of the response, (e.g. inform), which *slots* to talk about (e.g. area), and a *value* for each slot (e.g. east). To ensure tractability, the policy selects a from a restricted action set which identifies the *intent* and sometimes a *slot*, any remaining information required to complete the reply is extracted using heuristics from the tracked belief state.

3.1 Training with Reinforcement Learning

Dialogue policy optimisation can be seen as the task of learning to select the sequence of responses (actions) at each turn which maximises the long-term objective defined by the reward function. This can be solved by applying either value-based

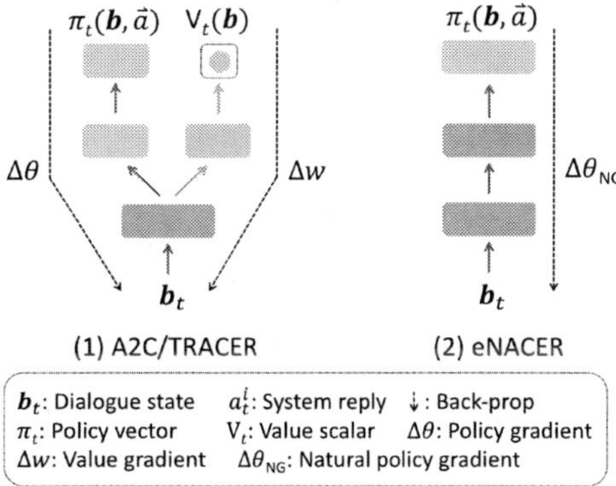

Figure 1: A2C, TRACER and eNACER architectures using feed-forward neural networks.

or policy-based methods. In both cases, the goal is to find an optimal policy π^* that maximises the discounted total return $R = \sum_{t=0}^{T-1} \gamma^t r_t(\mathbf{b}_t, a_t)$ over a dialogue with T turns where $r_t(\mathbf{b}_t, a_t)$ is the reward when taking action a_t in dialogue belief state $\mathbf{b}_t$ at turn t and γ is the discount factor.

The main difference between the two categories is that policy-based methods have stronger convergence characteristics than value-based methods. The latter often diverge when using function approximation since they optimise in value space and a slight change in value estimate can lead to a large change in policy space (Sutton et al., 2000).

Policy-based methods suffer from low sample-efficiency, high variance and often converge to local optima since they typically learn via Monte Carlo estimation (Williams, 1992; Schulman et al., 2016). However, they are preferred due to their superior convergence properties. Hence in this paper we focus on policy-based methods but also include a value-based method as a baseline.

3.1.1 Advantage Actor-Critic (A2C)

In a policy-based method, the training objective is to find a parametrised policy $\pi_\theta(a|\mathbf{b})$ that maximises the expected reward $J(\theta)$ over all possible dialogue trajectories given a starting state.

Following the *Policy Gradient Theorem* (Sutton et al., 2000), the gradient of the parameters given the objective function has the form:

$$\nabla_\theta J(\theta) = \mathbb{E}\left[\nabla_\theta \log \pi_\theta(a|\mathbf{b}) Q^{\pi_\theta}(\mathbf{b}, a)\right]. \quad (1)$$

Since this form of gradient has a potentially high variance, a baseline function is typically introduced to reduce the variance whilst not changing the estimated gradient (Williams, 1992; Sutton and Barto, 1999). A natural candidate for this baseline is the value function $V(\mathbf{b})$. Equation 2 then becomes:

$$\nabla_\theta J(\theta) = \mathbb{E}\left[\nabla_\theta \log \pi_\theta(a|\mathbf{b}) A_w(\mathbf{b}, a)\right], \quad (2)$$

where $A_w(\mathbf{b}, a) = Q(\mathbf{b}, a) - V(\mathbf{b})$ is the *advantage function*. This can be viewed as a special case of the *actor-critic*, where π_θ is the actor and $A_w(\mathbf{b}, a)$ is the critic, defined by two parameter sets θ and w. To reduce the number of required parameters, temporal difference (TD) errors $\delta_w = r_t + \gamma V_w(\mathbf{b_{t+1}}) - V_w(\mathbf{b_t})$ can be used to approximate the advantage function (Schulman et al., 2016). The left part in Figure 1 shows the architecture and parameters of the resulting A2C policy.

3.1.2 The TRACER Algorithm

To boost the performance of A2C policy learning, two methods are introduced:

I. Experience replay with off-policy learning for speed-up

On-policy RL methods update the model with the samples collected via the current policy. Sample-efficiency can be improved by utilising *experience replay* (ER) (Lin, 1992), where mini-batches of dialogue experiences are randomly sampled from a replay pool $\mathcal{P}$ to train the model. This increases learning efficiency by re-using past samples in multiple updates whilst ensuring stability by reducing the data correlation. Since these past experiences were collected from different policies compared to the current policy, the use of ER leads to *off-policy* updates.

When training models with RL, ϵ-greedy action selection is often used to trade-off between exploration and exploitation, whereby a random action is chosen with probability ϵ otherwise the top-ranking action is selected. A policy used to generate a training dialogues (episodes) is referred to as a *behaviour policy* μ, in contrast to the policy to be optimised which is called the *target policy* π.

The basic A2C training algorithm described in §3.1.1 is *on-policy* since it is assumed that actions are drawn from the same policy as the target to be optimised ($\mu = \pi$). In *off-policy* learning, since the current policy π is updated with the samples generated from old behaviour policies μ, an importance sampling (IS) ratio is used to rescale each sampled reward to correct for the sampling bias at time-step t: $\rho_t = \pi(a_t|\mathbf{b_t})/\mu(a_t|\mathbf{b_t})$ (Meuleau et al., 2000).

For A2C, the off-policy gradient for the parametrised value function V_w thus has the form:

$$\Delta w^{\text{off}} = \sum_{t=0}^{T-1} \left(\bar{R}_t - \hat{V}_w(\mathbf{b_t})\right) \nabla_w \hat{V}_w(\mathbf{b_t}) \prod_{i=0}^{t} \rho_i, \quad (3)$$

where $\bar{R}_t$ is the off-policy Monte-Carlo return (Precup et al., 2001):

$$\bar{R}_t = r_t + \gamma r_{t+1} \prod_{i=1}^{1} \rho_{t+i} + \cdots + \gamma^{T-t-1} r_{T-1} \prod_{i=1}^{T-1} \rho_{t+i}. \quad (4)$$

Likewise, the updated gradient for policy π_θ is:

$$\Delta \theta^{\text{off}} = \sum_{t=0}^{T-1} \rho_t \nabla_\theta \log \pi_\theta(a_t|\mathbf{b_t}) \hat{\delta}_w, \quad (5)$$

where $\hat{\delta}_w = r_t + \gamma \hat{V}_w(\mathbf{b_{t+1}}) - \hat{V}_w(\mathbf{b_t})$ is the TD error using the estimated value of $\hat{V}_w$.

Also, as the gradient correlates strongly with the sampled reward, reward r_t and total return R are normalised to lie in [-1,1] to stabilise training.

II. Trust region constraint for stabilisation

To ensure stability in RL, each per-step policy change is often limited by setting a small learning rate. However, setting the rate low enough to avoid occasional large destabilising updates is not conducive to fast learning.

Here, we adopt a modified Trust Region Policy Optimisation method introduced by Wang et al. (2017). In addition to maximising the cumulative reward $J(\theta)$, the optimisation is also subject to a Kullback-Leibler (KL) divergence limit between the updated policy θ and an *average policy* θ_a to ensure safety. This average policy represents a running average of past policies and constrains the updated policy to not deviate far from the average $\theta_a \leftarrow \alpha \theta_a + (1 - \alpha)\theta$ with a weight α.

Thus, given the off-policy policy gradient $\Delta \theta^{\text{off}}$ in Equation 5, the modified policy gradient with trust region g is calculated as follows:

$$\underset{g}{\text{minimize}} \quad \frac{1}{2}\|\Delta \theta^{\text{off}} - g\|_2^2,$$

$$\text{subject to} \quad \nabla_\theta D_{KL}\left[\pi_{\theta_a}(\mathbf{b_t})\|\pi_\theta(\mathbf{b_t})\right]^T g \leq \xi,$$

where π is the policy parametrised by θ or θ_a, and ξ controls the magnitude of the KL constraint. Since the constraint is linear, a closed form solution to this quadratic programming problem can be derived using the KKT conditions. Setting $k = \nabla_\theta D_{KL}\left[\pi_{\theta_a}(\mathbf{b_t})\|\pi_\theta(\mathbf{b_t})\right]$, we get:

$$g_{tr}^* = \Delta\theta^{\text{off}} - \max\left\{\frac{k^T\Delta\theta^{\text{off}} - \xi}{\|k\|_2^2}, 0\right\}k. \quad (6)$$

When this constraint is satisfied, there is no change to the gradient with respect to θ. Otherwise, the update is scaled down along the direction of k and the policy change rate is lowered. This direction is also shown to be closely related to the *natural gradient* (Amari, 1998; Schulman et al., 2015), which is presented in the next section.

The above enhancements speed up and stabilise A2C. We call it the Trust Region Actor-Critic with Experience Replay (TRACER) algorithm.

3.1.3 The eNACER Algorithm

Vanilla gradient descent algorithms are not guaranteed to update the model parameters in the steepest direction due to re-parametrisation (Amari, 1998; Martens, 2014). A widely used solution to this problem is to use a *compatible function approximation* for the advantage function in Equation 2: $\nabla_w A_w(b, a) = \nabla_\theta \log \pi_\theta(a|b)$, where the update of w is then in the same update direction as θ (Sutton et al., 2000). Equation 2 can then be rewritten as:

$$\begin{aligned}\nabla_\theta J(\theta) &= \mathbb{E}\left[\nabla_\theta \log \pi_\theta(a|\mathbf{b})\nabla_\theta \log \pi_\theta(a|\mathbf{b})^T w\right] \\ &= F(\theta) \cdot w,\end{aligned}$$

where $F(\theta)$ is the Fisher information matrix. This implies $\Delta\theta_{NG} = w = F(\theta)^{-1}\nabla_\theta J(\theta)$ and it is called the *natural gradient*. The Fisher Matrix can be viewed as a correction term which makes the natural gradient independent of the parametrisation of the policy and corresponds to steepest ascent towards the objective (Martens, 2014). Empirically, the natural gradient has been found to significantly speed up convergence.

Based on these ideas, the Natural Actor-Critic (NAC) algorithm was developed by Peters and Schaal (2006). In its episodic version (eNAC), the Fisher matrix does not need to be explicitly computed. Instead, the gradient is estimated by a least squares method given the n-th episode consisting of a set of transition tuples $\{(\mathbf{b}_t^n, a_t^n, r_t^n)\}_{t=0}^{T_n-1}$:

$$R^n = \left[\sum_{t=0}^{T_n-1} \nabla_\theta \log \pi_\theta(a_t^i|\mathbf{b}_t^i; \theta)^T\right] \cdot \Delta\theta_{NG} + C, \quad (7)$$

which can be solved analytically. C is a constant which is an estimate of the baseline $V(\mathbf{b})$.

As in TRACER, eNAC can be enhanced by using ER and off-policy learning, thus called eNACER, whereby R^n in Equation 7 is replaced by the off-policy Monte-Carlo return $\bar{R}_0^n$ at time-step $t = 0$ as in Equation 4. For very large models, the inversion of the Fisher matrix can become prohibitively expensive to compute. Instead, a truncated variant can be used to calculate the natural gradient (Schulman et al., 2015).

eNACER is structured as a feed forward network with the output π as in the right of Figure 1, updated with natural gradient $\Delta\theta_{NG}$. Note that by using the compatible function approximation, the value function does not need to be explicitly calculated. This makes eNACER in practice a policy-gradient method.

3.2 Learning from Demonstration Data

From the user's perspective, performing RL from scratch will invariably result in unacceptable performance in the early learning stages. This problem can be mitigated by an off-line corpus of *demonstration data* to bootstrap a policy. This data may come from a WoZ collection or from interactions between users and an existing policy. It can be used in three ways: A: Pre-train the model, B: Initialise a supervised replay buffer $\mathcal{P}_{sup}$, and C: a combination of the two.

(A) For model pre-training, the objective is to 'mimic' the response behaviour from the corpus. This phase is essentially standard SL. The input to the model is the dialogue belief state $\mathbf{b}$, and the training objective for each sample is to minimise a joint cross-entropy loss $\mathcal{L}(\theta) = -\sum_k y_k \log(p_k)$ between action labels y and model predictions p, where the policy is parametrised by a set θ.

A policy trained by SL on a fixed dataset may not generalise well. In spoken dialogues, the noise levels may vary across conditions and thus can significantly affect performance. Moreover, a policy trained using SL does not perform any long-term planning on the conversation. Nonetheless, supervised pre-training offers a good model starting point which can then be fine-tuned using RL.

(B) For supervised replay initialisation, the demonstration data is stored in a replay pool $\mathcal{P}_{sup}$ which is kept separate from the ER pool used for RL and is never over-written. At each RL update iteration, a small portion of the demonstration data $\mathcal{P}'_{sup}$ is sampled, and the supervised cross-entropy loss $\mathcal{L}(\theta)$ computed on this data is added to the RL objective $J(\theta)$. Also, an L2 regularisation loss $\|\cdot\|_2^2$ is applied to θ to help prevent it from over-fitting on the sampled demonstration dataset. The total loss to be minimised is thus:

$$\mathcal{L}_{all}(\theta) = -J(\theta) + \lambda_1 \mathcal{L}(\theta; \mathcal{P}'_{sup}) + \lambda_2 \|\theta\|_2^2, \quad (8)$$

where λ's are weights. In this way, the RL policy is guided by the sampled demonstration data while learning to optimise the total return.

(C) The learned parameters of the pre-trained model in method A above might distribute differently from the optimal RL policy and this may cause some performance drop in early stages while learning an RL policy from this model. This can be alleviated by using the composite loss proposed in method B. A comparison between the three options is included in the experimental evaluation.

4 Experimental Results

Our experiments utilised the software tool-kit Py-Dial (Ultes et al., 2017), which provides a platform for modular SDS. The target application is a live telephone-based SDS providing restaurant information for the Cambridge (UK) area. The task is to learn a policy which manages the dialogue flow and delivers requested information to the user. The domain consists of approximately 100 venues, each with 6 slots out of which 3 can be used by the system to constrain the search (food-type, area and price-range) and 3 are system-informable properties (phone-number, address and postcode) available once a database entity has been found.

The input for all models was the full dialogue belief state $\mathbf{b}$ of size 268 which includes the last system act and distributions over the user intention and the three requestable slots. The output includes 14 restricted dialogue actions determining the system intent at the semantic level. Combining the dialogue belief states and heuristic rules, it is then mapped into a spoken response using a natural language generator.

4.1 Model Comparison

Two value-based methods are shown for comparison with the policy-based models described. For both of these, the policy is implicitly determined by the action-value (Q) function which estimates the expected total return when choosing action a given belief state $\mathbf{b}$ at time-step t. For an optimal policy π^*, the Q-function satisfies the *Bellman*

equation (Bellman, 1954):

$$Q^*(\mathbf{b}_t, a_t) = \mathbb{E}_{\pi^*}\{r_t + \gamma \max_{a'} Q^*(\mathbf{b}_{t+1}, a')|\mathbf{b}_t, a_t\}. \quad (9)$$

4.1.1 Deep Q-Network (DQN)

DQN is a variant of the Q-learning algorithm whereby a neural network is used to non-linearly approximate the Q-function. This suggests a sequential approximation in Equation 9 by minimising the loss:

$$L(w_t) = \mathbb{E}\left[(y_t - Q(\mathbf{b}_t, a_t; w_t))^2\right], \quad (10)$$

where $y_t = r_t + \gamma \max_{a'} Q(\mathbf{b}_{t+1}, a'; w_t^-)$ is the target to update the parameters w. Note that y_t is evaluated by a target network w^- which is updated less frequently than the network w to stabilise learning, and the expectation is over the tuples $(\mathbf{b}_t, a_t, r_{t+1}, \mathbf{b}_{t+1})$ sampled from the experience replay pool described in §3.1.2.

DQN often suffers from over-estimation on Q-values as the max operator is used to select an action as well as to evaluate it. Double DQN (DDQN) (Van Hasselt et al., 2016) is thus used to de-couple the action selection and Q-value estimation to achieve better performance.

4.1.2 Gaussian Processes (GP) RL

GPRL is a state-of-the-art value-based RL algorithm for dialogue modelling. It is appealing since it can learn from a small number of observations by exploiting the correlations defined by a *kernel function* and provides an uncertainty measure of its estimates. In GPRL, the Q-function is modelled as a GP with zero mean and kernel: $Q(B, A) \sim \mathcal{GP}(0, (k(\mathbf{b}, a), k(\mathbf{b}, a))$. This Q-function is then updated by calculating the posterior given the collected belief-action pairs $(\mathbf{b}, a)$ (dictionary points) and their corresponding rewards (Gašić and Young, 2014). The implicit knowledge of the distance between data points in observation space provided by the kernel greatly speeds up learning since it enables Q-values in as yet unexplored space to be estimated. Note that GPRL was used by Fatemi et al. (2016) to compare with deep RL but no uncertainty estimate was used to guide exploration and as a result had relatively poor performance. Here GPRL with uncertainty estimate is used as the benchmark.

4.2 Reinforcement Learning from Scratch

The proposed models were first evaluated under 0% semantic error rate with an agenda-based simulator which generates user interactions at the

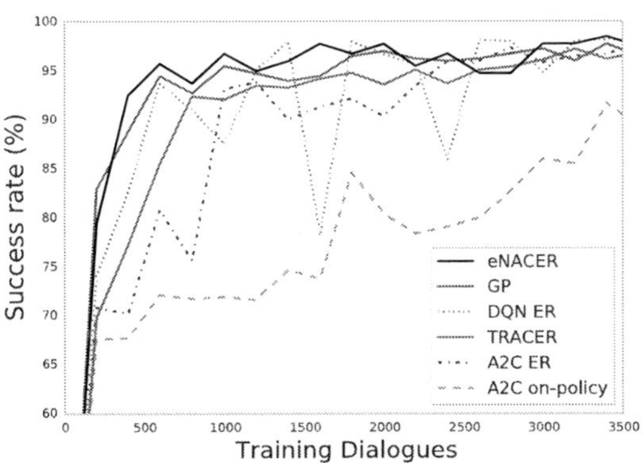

Figure 2: The success rate learning curves of on-policy A2C, A2C with ER, TRACER, DQN with ER, GP and eNACER in user simulation under noise-free condition.

semantic-level (Schatzmann et al., 2006). In this case, the user intent is perfectly captured in the dialogue belief state without noise.

The total return of each dialogue was set to $\mathbb{1}(\mathcal{D}) - 0.05 \times T$, where T is the dialogue length and $\mathbb{1}(\mathcal{D})$ is the success indicator for dialogue $\mathcal{D}$. The maximum dialogue length was set to 20 turns and γ was 0.99. All deep RL models (A2C, TRACER, eNACER and DQN) contained two hidden layers of size 130 and 50. The Adam optimiser was used (Kingma and Ba, 2014) with an initial learning rate of 0.001. During training, an ϵ-greedy policy was used, which was initially set to 0.3 and annealed to 0.0 over 3500 training dialogues. For GP, a linear kernel was used.

The ER pool $\mathcal{P}$ size was 1000, and the mini-batch size was 64. Once an initial 192 samples had been collected, the model was updated after every 2 dialogues. Note that for DQN, each sample was a state transition $(\mathbf{b}_t, a_t, r_t, \mathbf{b}_{t+1})$, whereas in A2C, TRACER and eNACER, each sample comprised the whole dialogue with all its state transitions. For eNACER, the natural gradient was computed to update the model weights of size $\sim$ 42000. For TRACER, α was set to 0.02, and ξ was 0.01. Since the IS ratio has a high variance and can occasionally be extremely large, it was clipped between [0.8,1.0] to maintain stable training.

Figure 2 shows the success rate learning curves of on-policy A2C, A2C with ER, TRACER, DQN with ER, GP and eNACER. All were tested with 600 dialogues after every 200 training dialogues. As reported in previous studies, the benchmark

GP model learns quickly and is relatively stable. eNACER provides comparable performance. DQN also showed high sample-efficiency but with high instability at some points. This is because an iterative improvement in value space does not guarantee an improvement in policy space. Although comparably slower to learn, the difference between on-policy A2C and A2C with ER clearly demonstrates the sample-efficiency of reusing past samples in mini-batches. The enhancements incorporated into the TRACER algorithm do make this form of learning competitive although it still lags behind eNACER and GPRL.

4.2.1 Learning from Demonstration Data

Regardless of the choice of model and learning algorithm, training a policy from scratch on-line will always result in a poor user experience until sufficient interactions have been experienced to allow acceptable behaviours to be learned.

As discussed in §3.2, an off-line corpus of demonstration data can potentially mitigate this problem. To test this, a corpus of 720 real user spoken dialogues in the Cambridge restaurant domain was utilised. The corpus was split in a 4:1:1 ratio for training, validation and testing. It contains interactions between real users recruited via the Amazon Mechanical Turk service and a well-behaved SDS as described in Su et al. (2016b).

For A2C with ER and TRACER, the three ways of exploiting demonstration data in §3.2 were explored. The exploration parameter ϵ was also set to 0.3 and annealed to 0.0 over 2000 training dialogues. Since TRACER has similar patterns to A2C with ER, we first explored the impact of demonstration data on the A2C with ER results since it provides more headroom for identifying performance gains.

Figure 3a shows the different combinations of demonstration data using A2C with ER in noise-free conditions. The supervised pre-trained model (SL model) provides reasonable starting performance. The A2C ER model with supervised pre-training (A2C ER+SL_model) improves on this after only 400 dialogues whilst suffering initially. We hypothesise that the optimised SL pre-trained parameters distributed very differently to the optimal A2C ER parameters. Also, the A2C ER model with SL replay (A2C ER+SL_replay) shows clearly how the use of a supervised replay buffer can accelerate learning from scratch. Moreover, when SL pre-training is combined with SL replay

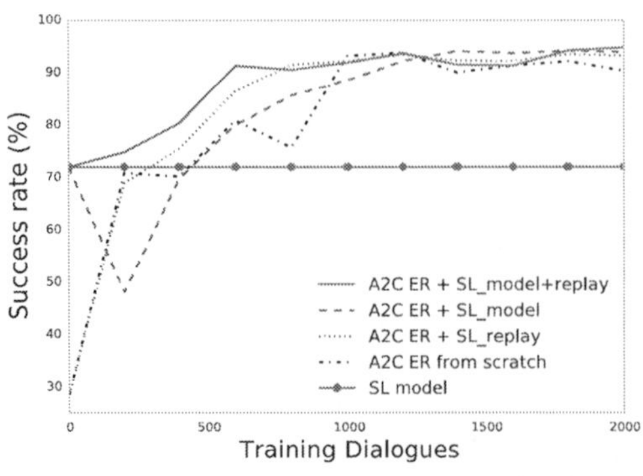

(a) Learning for A2C ER with demonstration data.

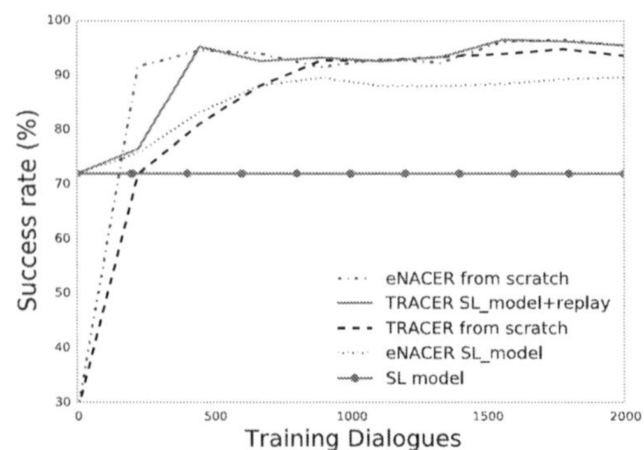

(b) Learning for TRACER and eNACER with demonstration data.

Figure 3: Utilising demonstration data for improving RL learning speed.

(A2C ER+SL_model+replay), it achieved the best result. Note that λ_1 and λ_2 in Equation 8 were 10 and 0.01 respectively. In each policy update, 64 demonstration data were randomly sampled from the supervised replay pool $\mathcal{P}_{sup}$, which is the same number of RL samples selected from ER for A2C learning. Similar patterns emerge when utilising demonstration data to improve early learning in the TRACER and eNACER algorithms as shown in Figure 3b. However, in this case, eNACER is less able to exploit demonstration data since the training method is different from standard actor-critics. Hence, the supervised loss $\mathcal{L}$ cannot be directly incorporated into the RL objective J as in Equation 8. One could optimise the model using $\mathcal{L}$ separately after every RL update. However, in our experiments, this did not yield improvement. Hence, only eNACER learning from a pre-trained SL model is reported here. Compared to eNACER learning from scratch, eNACER from SL model started with good performance but learned more slowly. Again, this may be because the optimised SL pre-trained parameters distributed very differently from the optimal eNACER parameters and led to sub-optimality. Overall, these results suggest that the proposed SL+RL framework to exploit demonstration data is effective in mitigating the cold start problem and TRACER provides the best solution in terms of avoiding poor initial performance, rapid learning and competitive fully trained performance.

In addition to the noise-free performance, we also investigated the impact of noise on the TRACER algorithm. Figure 4 shows the results after training on 2000 dialogues via interaction with

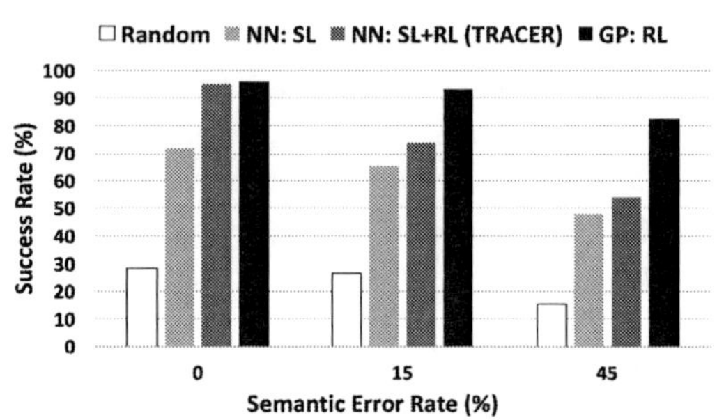

Figure 4: The success rate of TRACER for a random policy, policy trained with corpus data (NN:SL) and further improved via RL (NN:SL+RL) respectively in user simulation under various semantic error rates.

the user simulator under different semantic error rates. The random policy (white bars) uniformly sampled an action from the set of size 14. This can be regarded as the average initial performance of any learning system. We can see that SL generates a robust model which can be further fine-tuned using RL over a wide range of error rates. It should be noted, however, that the drop-off in performance at high noise levels is more rapid than might be expected, comparing to the GPRL. We believe that deep architectures are prone to over-fitting and in consequence do not handle well the uncertainty of the user behaviour. We plan to investigate this issue in future work. Overall, these outcomes validate the benefit of the proposed two-phased approach where the system can be effectively pre-trained using corpus data and further be refined via user interactions.

5   Conclusion

This paper has presented two compatible approaches to tackling the problem of slow learning and poor initial performance in deep reinforcement learning algorithms. Firstly, trust region actor-critic with experience replay (TRACER) and episodic natural actor-critic with experience replay (eNACER) were presented, these have been shown to be more sample-efficient than other deep RL models and broadly competitive with GPRL. Secondly, it has been shown that demonstration data can be utilised to mitigate poor performance in the early stages of learning. To this end, two methods for using off-line corpus data were presented: simple pre-training using SL, and using the corpus data in a replay buffer. These were particularly effective when used with TRACER which provided the best overall performance.

Experimental results were also presented for mismatched environments, again TRACER demonstrated the ability to avoid poor initial performance when trained only on the demonstration corpus, yet still improve substantially with subsequent reinforcement learning. It was noted, however, that performance still falls off rather rapidly in noise compared to GPRL as the uncertainty estimates are not handled well by neural networks architectures.

Finally, it should be emphasised that whilst this paper has focused on the early stages of learning a new domain where GPRL provides a benchmark and is hard to beat, the potential of deep RL is its readily scalability to exploit on-line learning with large user populations as the model size is not related with experience replay buffer.

Acknowledgments

Pei-Hao Su is supported by Cambridge Trust and the Ministry of Education, Taiwan. Paweł Budzianowski is supported by EPSRC Council and Toshiba Research Europe Ltd, Cambridge Research Laboratory. The authors would like to thank the other members of the Cambridge Dialogue Systems Group for their valuable comments.

References

Shun-Ichi Amari. 1998. Natural gradient works efficiently in learning. In *Neural computation*. MIT Press, volume 10, pages 251–276.

Kavosh Asadi and Jason D Williams. 2016. Sample-efficient deep reinforcement learning for dialog control. In *arXiv preprint arXiv:1612.06000*.

Richard Bellman. 1954. The theory of dynamic programming. Technical report, DTIC Document.

Antoine Bordes, Y-Lan Boureau, and Jason Weston. 2017. Learning end-to-end goal-oriented dialog. In *Proc of ICLR*.

Paweł Budzianowski, Stefan Ultes, Pei-Hao Su, Nikola Mrkšić, Tsung-Hsien Wen, Inigo Casanueva, Lina M. Rojas Barahona, and Milica Gašić. 2017. Sub-domain modelling for dialogue management with hierarchical reinforcement learning. In *Proc of SIG-DIAL*.

Lu Chen, Pei-Hao Su, and Milica Gašic. 2015. Hyper-parameter optimisation of gaussian process reinforcement learning for statistical dialogue management. In *Proc of SigDial*.

Yun-Nung Chen, Dilek Hakkani-Tür, Gokhan Tur, Jianfeng Gao, and Li Deng. 2016. End-to-end memory networks with knowledge carryover for multi-turn spoken language understanding. In *Proc of INTERSPEECH*.

Nils Dahlbäck, Arne Jönsson, and Lars Ahrenberg. 1993. Wizard of oz studies: why and how. In *Proc of Intelligent user interfaces*.

Lucie Daubigney, Matthieu Geist, Senthilkumar Chandramohan, and Olivier Pietquin. 2014. A comprehensive reinforcement learning framework for dialogue management optimisation. volume 6.

Layla El Asri, Romain Laroche, and Olivier Pietquin. 2014. Task completion transfer learning for reward inference. In *Proc of MLIS*.

Yaakov Engel. 2005. *Algorithms and representations for reinforcement learning*. PhD Thesis.

Mehdi Fatemi, Layla El Asri, Hannes Schulz, Jing He, and Kaheer Suleman. 2016. Policy networks with two-stage training for dialogue systems. In *Proc of SigDial*.

Milica Gašić, Catherine Breslin, Matt Henderson, Dongho Kim, Martin Szummer, Blaise Thomson, Pirros Tsiakoulis, and Steve Young. 2013. Pomdp-based dialogue manager adaptation to extended domains. In *Sigdial*.

Milica Gašić, Filip Jurcicek, Blaise. Thomson, Kai Yu, and Steve Young. 2011. On-line policy optimisation of spoken dialogue systems via live interaction with human subjects. In *IEEE ASRU*.

Milica Gašić and Steve Young. 2014. Gaussian processes for pomdp-based dialogue manager optimization. IEEE, volume 22, pages 28–40.

James Henderson, Oliver Lemon, and Kallirroi Georgila. 2008. Hybrid reinforcement/supervised learning of dialogue policies from fixed data sets. In *Computational Linguistics*. MIT Press, volume 34, pages 487–511.

M. Henderson, B. Thomson, and S. J. Young. 2014. Word-based Dialog State Tracking with Recurrent Neural Networks. In *Proc of SIGdial*.

Todd Hester, Matej Vecerik, Olivier Pietquin, Marc Lanctot andTom Schaul, Bilal Piot, Andrew Sendonaris, Gabriel Dulac-Arnold, Ian Osband, John Agapiou, Joel Z. Leibo, and Audrunas Gruslys. 2017. Learning from demonstrations for real world reinforcement learning. In *arXiv:1704.03732*.

Zhiting Hu, Zichao Yang, Xiaodan Liang, Ruslan Salakhutdinov, and Eric P Xing. 2017. Controllable text generation. *Proc of ICML* .

Filip Jurčíček, Blaise Thomson, and Steve Young. 2011. Natural actor and belief critic: Reinforcement algorithm for learning parameters of dialogue systems modelled as pomdps. In *ACM TSLP*. ACM, volume 7, page 6.

John F. Kelley. 1984. An iterative design methodology for user-friendly natural language office information applications.

Diederik Kingma and Jimmy Ba. 2014. Adam: A method for stochastic optimization. In *arXiv preprint arXiv:1412.6980*.

Oliver Lemon, Kallirroi Georgila, and James Henderson. 2006. Evaluating effectiveness and portability of reinforcement learned dialogue strategies with real users: the talk towninfo evaluation. In *SLT*. pages 178–181.

Esther Levin and Roberto Pieraccini. 1997. A stochastic model of computer-human interaction for learning dialogue strategies. In *Eurospeech*.

Esther Levin, Roberto Pieraccini, and Wieland Eckert. 1998. Using markov decision process for learning dialogue strategies. In *ICASSP*.

Jiwei Li, Will Monroe, Alan Ritter, and Dan Jurafsky. 2016. Deep reinforcement learning for dialogue generation. In *Proc of EMNLP*.

Lihong Li, He He, and Jason D Williams. 2014. Temporal supervised learning for inferring a dialog policy from example conversations. In *Spoken Language Technology Workshop (SLT), 2014 IEEE*. IEEE, pages 312–317.

Long-Ji Lin. 1992. Self-improving reactive agents based on reinforcement learning, planning and teaching. In *Machine learning*. volume 8, pages 293–321.

James Martens. 2014. New insights and perspectives on the natural gradient method. *arXiv preprint arXiv:1412.1193* .

Nicolas Meuleau, Leonid Peshkin, Leslie P Kaelbling, and Kee-Eung Kim. 2000. Off-policy policy search. In *Technical report, MIT AI Lab*.

Volodymyr Mnih, Koray Kavukcuoglu, David Silver, Andrei A Rusu, Joel Veness, Marc G Bellemare, Alex Graves, Martin Riedmiller, Andreas K Fidjeland, Georg Ostrovski, et al. 2015. Human-level control through deep reinforcement learning. In *Nature*. Nature Publishing Group, volume 518, pages 529–533.

Nikola Mrkšić, Diarmuid Ó Séaghdha, Blaise Thomson, Tsung-Hsien Wen, and Steve Young. 2017. Neural Belief Tracker: Data-driven dialogue state tracking. In *Proc of ACL*.

Julien Perez and Fei Liu. 2016. Dialog state tracking, a machine reading approach using memory network. *arXiv preprint arXiv:1606.04052* .

Jan Peters and Stefan Schaal. 2006. Policy gradient methods for robotics. In *IEEE RSJ*.

Doina Precup, Richard S Sutton, and Sanjoy Dasgupta. 2001. Off-policy temporal-difference learning with function approximation. In *Proc of ICML*.

Verena Rieser and Oliver Lemon. 2006. Using logistic regression to initialise reinforcement-learning-based dialogue systems. In *Spoken Language Technology Workshop, 2006. IEEE*. IEEE, pages 190–193.

Verena Rieser and Oliver Lemon. 2009. Natural language generation as planning under uncertainty for spoken dialogue systems. In *Proc of EACL*. pages 683–691.

Nicholas Roy, Joelle Pineau, and Sebastian Thrun. 2000. Spoken dialogue management using probabilistic reasoning. In *Proc of SigDial*.

Jost Schatzmann, Karl Weilhammer, Matt Stuttle, and Steve Young. 2006. A survey of statistical user simulation techniques for reinforcement-learning of dialogue management strategies. In *The knowledge engineering review*. Cambridge Univ Press, volume 21, pages 97–126.

John Schulman, Sergey Levine, Philipp Moritz, Michael I Jordan, and Pieter Abbeel. 2015. Trust region policy optimization. In *Proc of ICML*.

John Schulman, Philipp Moritz, Sergey Levine, Michael Jordan, and Pieter Abbeel. 2016. High-dimensional continuous control using generalized advantage estimation. In *Proc of ICLR*.

Iulian V Serban, Alessandro Sordoni, Yoshua Bengio, Aaron Courville, and Joelle Pineau. 2015. Hierarchical neural network generative models for movie dialogues. In *arXiv preprint arXiv:1507.04808*.

Lifeng Shang, Zhengdong Lu, and Hang Li. 2015. Neural responding machine for short-text conversation. In *arXiv preprint arXiv:1503.02364*.

David Silver, Aja Huang, Chris J Maddison, Arthur Guez, Laurent Sifre, George Van Den Driessche, Julian Schrittwieser, Ioannis Antonoglou, Veda Panneershelvam, Marc Lanctot, et al. 2016. Mastering the game of go with deep neural networks and tree search. In *Nature*. Nature Publishing Group, volume 529, pages 484–489.

Pei-Hao Su, Milica Gasic, Nikola Mrksic, Lina Rojas-Barahona, Stefan Ultes, David Vandyke, Tsung-Hsien Wen, and Steve Young. 2016a. Continuously learning neural dialogue management. In *arXiv preprint arXiv:1606.02689*.

Pei-Hao Su, Milica Gašić, Nikola Mrkšić, Lina Rojas-Barahona, Stefan Ultes, David Vandyke, Tsung-Hsien Wen, and Steve Young. 2016b. On-line active reward learning for policy optimisation in spoken dialogue systems. In *Proc of ACL*.

Pei-Hao Su, David Vandyke, Milica Gašić, Dongho Kim, Nikola Mrkšić, Tsung-Hsien Wen, and Steve Young. 2015a. Learning from real users: Rating dialogue success with neural networks for reinforcement learning in spoken dialogue systems. In *Proc of Interspeech*.

Pei-Hao Su, David Vandyke, Milica Gašić, Nikola Mrkšić, Tsung-Hsien Wen, and Steve Young. 2015b. Reward shaping with recurrent neural networks for speeding up on-line policy learning in spoken dialogue systems. In *Proc of SigDial*.

Richard S. Sutton and Andrew G. Barto. 1999. *Reinforcement Learning: An Introduction*. MIT Press.

Richard S Sutton, David A McAllester, Satinder P Singh, Yishay Mansour, et al. 2000. Policy gradient methods for reinforcement learning with function approximation. In *Proc of NIPS*.

Stefan Ultes, Lina M. Rojas Barahona, Pei-Hao Su, David Vandyke, Dongho Kim, Inigo Casanueva, Pawel Budzianowski, Nikola Mrkšić, Tsung-Hsien Wen, Milica Gašić, and Steve Young. 2017. CU-PyDial: A Multi-domain Statistical Dialogue System Toolkit. In *ACL Demo*.

Hado Van Hasselt, Arthur Guez, and David Silver. 2016. Deep reinforcement learning with double q-learning. In *Proc of AAAI*.

David Vandyke, Pei-Hao Su, Milica Gašić, Nikola Mrkšić, Tsung-Hsien Wen, and Steve Young. 2015. Multi-domain dialogue success classifiers for policy training. In *IEEE ASRU*.

Oriol Vinyals and Quoc Le. 2015. A neural conversational model. In *arXiv preprint arXiv:1506.05869*.

Ziyu Wang, Victor Bapst, Nicolas Heess, Volodymyr Mnih, Remi Munos, Koray Kavukcuoglu, and Nando de Freitas. 2017. Sample efficient actor-critic with experience replay. In *Proc of ICLR*.

Tsung-Hsien Wen, Milica Gašić, Nikola Mrkšić, Lina M. Rojas-Barahona, Pei-Hao Su, Stefan Ultes, David Vandyke, and Steve Young. 2017. A network-based end-to-end trainable task-oriented dialogue system. In *Proc of EACL*.

Tsung-Hsien Wen, Milica Gašić, Nikola Mrkšić, Pei-Hao Su, David Vandyke, and Steve Young. 2015. Semantically conditioned lstm-based natural language generation for spoken dialogue systems. In *EMNLP*.

Jason D Williams, Kavosh Asadi, and Geoffrey Zweig. 2017. Hybrid code networks: practical and efficient end-to-end dialog control with supervised and reinforcement learning. In *ACL*.

Jason D. Williams and Steve Young. 2007. Partially observable Markov decision processes for spoken dialog systems. volume 21, pages 393–422.

Ronald J Williams. 1992. Simple statistical gradient-following algorithms for connectionist reinforcement learning. In *Machine learning*. Springer, volume 8, pages 229–256.

Xuesong Yang, Yun-Nung Chen, Dilek Hakkani-Tür, Paul Crook, Xiujun Li, Jianfeng Gao, and Li Deng. 2017. End-to-end joint learning of natural language understanding and dialogue manager. In *IEEE ICASSP*. pages 5690–5694.

Steve Young, Milica Gašic, Blaise Thomson, and Jason Williams. 2013. Pomdp-based statistical spoken dialogue systems: a review. In *Proc of IEEE*. volume 99, pages 1–20.

A surprisingly effective out-of-the-box char2char model on the *E2E NLG Challenge* dataset

Shubham Agarwal   **Marc Dymetman**

NAVER Labs Europe*, Grenoble, France

shubhamagarwal92@gmail.com, marc.dymetman@naverlabs.com

Abstract

We train a char2char model on the *E2E NLG Challenge* data, by exploiting "out-of-the-box" the recently released *tf-seq2seq* framework, using some of the standard options of this tool. With minimal effort, and in particular without delexicalization, tokenization or lowercasing, the obtained raw predictions, according to a small scale human evaluation, are excellent on the linguistic side and quite reasonable on the adequacy side, the primary downside being the possible omissions of semantic material. However, in a significant number of cases (more than 70%), a perfect solution can be found in the top-20 predictions, indicating promising directions for solving the remaining issues.

1 Introduction

Very recently, researchers (Novikova et al., 2017) at Heriot-Watt University proposed the E2E NLG Challenge[1] and released a dataset consisting of 50K (MR, RF) pairs, MR being a slot-value Meaning Representation of a restaurant, RF (human ReFerence) being a natural language utterance rendering of that representation. The utterances were crowd-sourced based on pictorial representations of the MRs, with the intention of producing more natural and diverse utterances compared to the ones directly based on the original MRs (Novikova et al., 2016).

Most of the RNN-based approaches to Natural Language Generation (NLG) that we are aware of, starting with (Wen et al., 2015), generate the output word-by-word, and resort to special delexicalization or copy mechanisms (Gu et al., 2016) to handle rare or unknown words, for instance restaurant names or telephone numbers. One exception is (Goyal et al., 2016), who employed a char-based seq2seq model where the input MR is simply represented as a character sequence, and the output is also generated char-by-char; this approach avoids the rare word problem, as the character vocabulary is very small.

While (Goyal et al., 2016) used an additional finite-state mechanism to guide the production of well-formed (and input-motivated) character sequences, the performance of their basic char2char model was already quite good. We further explore how a recent out-of-the box seq2seq model would perform on E2E NLG Challenge, when used in a char-based mode. We choose attention-based *tf-seq2seq* framework provided by authors of (Britz et al., 2017) (which we detail in next section).

Using some standard options provided by this framework, and without any pre- or post-processing (not even tokenization or lowercasing), we obtained results on which we conducted a small-scale human evaluation on one hundred MRs, involving two evaluators. This evaluation, on the one hand, concentrated on the linguistic quality, and on the other hand, on the semantic adequacy of the produced utterances. On the linguistic side, vast majority of the predictions were surprisingly grammatically perfect, while still being rather diverse and natural. In particular, and contrary to the findings of (Goyal et al., 2016) (on a different dataset), our char-based model never produced non-words. On the adequacy side, we found that the only serious problem was the tendency (in about half of the evaluated cases) of the model to omit to render one (rarely two) slot(s); on the other end, it never hallucinated, and very rarely duplicated, material. To try and assess the potential value of a simple re-ranking technique (which we did not implement at this stage, but the

---

*Previously *Xerox Research Centre Europe*.

[1] http://www.macs.hw.ac.uk/InteractionLab/E2E/

Proceedings of the SIGDIAL 2017 Conference, pages 158–163,
Saarbrücken, Germany, 15-17 August 2017. ©2017 Association for Computational Linguistics

approach of (Wen et al., 2015) and more recently the "inverted generation" technique of (Chisholm et al., 2017) could be used), we generated (using the beam-search option of the framework) 20-best utterances for each MR, which the evaluators scanned towards finding an "oracle", i.e. a generated utterance considered as perfect not only from the grammatical but also from the adequacy viewpoint. An oracle was found in the first position in around 50% of the case, otherwise among the 20 positions in around 20% of the cases, and not at all inside this list in the remaining 30% cases. On the basis of these experiments and evaluations we believe that there remains only a modest gap towards a very reasonable NLG seq2seq model for the E2E NLG dataset.

2 Model

Our model is a direct use of the seq2seq open-source software framework[2], built over TensorFlow (Abadi et al., 2016), and provided along with (Britz et al., 2017), with some standard configuration options that will be detailed in section 3. While in their large-scale NMT experiments (Britz et al., 2017) use word-based sequences, in our case we use character-based ones. This simply involves changing "delimiter" option in configuration files.

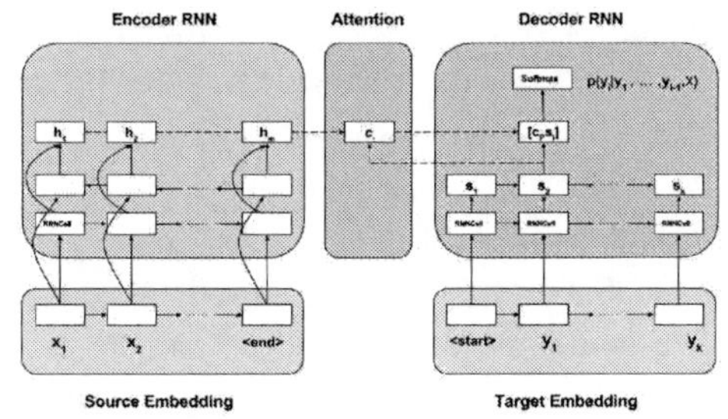

Figure 1: The seq2seq architecture of (Britz et al., 2017) (drawing borrowed from that paper). Contrary to word-based sequences, we use character-based sequences for generating grammatically correct and natural utterances.

Figure 1, borrowed from (Britz et al., 2017), provides an overview of the framework. While many options are configurable (number of layers, unidirectional *vs* bidirectional encoder, additive *vs* multiplicative attention mechanism, GRU (Cho et al., 2014) *vs* LSTM cells (Hochreiter and Schmidhuber, 1997), etc.), the core architecture is common to all models. This is by now a pretty standard attention-based encoder-decoder architecture based on (Bahdanau et al., 2015; Luong et al., 2015). The encoder RNN embeds each of the source words (in our case, characters) into vectors exploiting the hidden states computed by the RNN. The decoder RNN predicts the next word (resp. character) based on its current hidden state, previous character, and also based on the "context" vector c_i, which is an attention-based weighted average of the embeddings of the source words (resp. characters).

3 Experiments

3.1 Dataset

(Novikova et al., 2016) explain the protocol followed for crowdsourcing the *E2E NLG Challenge* dataset. Slightly different from the description in the article, there are two additional slots in the dataset: 'kidsFriendly' and 'children-friendly' which seem to be alternates for 'familyFriendly'. Thus, there are in total 10 slots (in decreasing order of frequency of being mentioned in the dataset MRs): name (100%), food (83%), customer rating (68%), priceRange (68%), area (60%), eatType (51%), near (50%), familyFriendly (25%), kidsFriendly (19%), children-friendly (19%). Also, the number of active slots in the MRs varies as: 3 (5%), 4 (17%), 5 (19%), 6 (19%), 7 (16%), 8 (4%).

3.2 Implementation

The *tf-seq2seq* toolkit (Britz et al., 2017) trains on pairs of sequences presented in parallel text format (separate source and target sequence files).[3] [4]

Taking cue from recommended configurations in Table 7 of (Britz et al., 2017) and the provided example configs in *tf-seq2seq*, we experimented with different numbers of layers in the encoder and decoder as well as different beam widths, while using the bi-directional encoder along with "additive" attention mechanism. As also observed

---

[2]https://github.com/google/seq2seq.

[3]We cleaned the E2E NLG Challenge data as there were a few erroneous newline characters (Line 603 in devset.csv as well as 30048 in trainset.csv). There were different character encodings for MR and RF, which we uniformized to utf-8. Also, there were a few wrongly encoded characters (such as on line 23191 in trainset.csv). We normalized these characters, after which there remained only two non-ascii characters: £ and é. Note: since submission, these issues have been corrected in the updated version of the Challenge data.

[4]Code for processing of the data, conversion to parallel text format as well as our configuration files for the tf-seq2seq model can be found at: https://github.com/shubhamagarwal92/sigdialSubmission/

Model Specification	Beam Width	Length Penalty	Depth (Number of layers)				
Encoder			1	1	2	4	4
Decoder			1	2	2	4	4
Cell Unit			GRU	GRU	GRU	GRU	LSTM
Greedy Search			20.94	22.59	23.5	23.84	23.98
	Beam 5	0.0	15.85	22.47	21.76	22.73	20.15
	Beam 10	0.0	14.5	21.4	19.98	21.15	18.88
Beam Search	Beam 20	0.0	13.48	20.18	18.5	19.94	17.93
	Beam 5	1.0	20.64	24.77	24.67	**24.94**	23.87
	Beam 10	1.0	21	25.05	24.88	24.69	24.27
	Beam 20	1.0	21.27	25.4	24.96	**24.6**[*]	24.05

Table 1: BLEU scores on devset with different configuration: varying the depth of both encoder and decoder RNNs, type of cell unit, different beam width and length penalty. (Results reported for only a single experiment with training and prediction.)

by Britz et al. (2017), using a non-null "length-penalty" (alias length normalization (Wu et al., 2016)), significantly improved decoding results.

3.3 Results

We report the BLEU scores[5] for different configurations of the seq2seq model in Table 1. In our initial experiments, using a beam-width 5 (with no length penalty), with 4 layers in both the encoder and decoder and GRU cells, showed the best results in terms of BLEU (score of 24.94).

We observed significant improvements using length penalty 1, and decided to use this architecture as a basis for human evaluations, with a beam-width 20 to facilitate the observation of oracles. These evaluations were thus conducted on model [encoder 4 layers, decoder 4 layers, GRU cell, beam-width 20, length penalty 1] (starred in Table 1), though we found slightly better performing models in terms of BLEU at a later stage.

4 Evaluation

The human evaluations were performed by two annotators on the top 20 predictions of the previously discussed model, for the first 100 MRs of the devset, using the following metrics:

1. Semantic Adequacy
   a) Omission [1/0]: information present in the MR that is omitted in the predicted utterance (1=No omission, 0=Omission). **b) Addition [1/0]:** information in the predicted utterance that is absent in the MR (1=No addition, 0=Addition). **c) Repetition [1/0]:** repeated information in the predicted utterance (1=No repetition, 0=Repetition).

2. Linguistic Quality
   a) Grammar [1/0]: (1=Grammatically correct, 0=incorrect). Note: one annotator punished the model even for (rare) mistakes of punctuation. **b) Naturalness [2/1/0]:** subjective score to measure the naturalness of the utterance (2 being best). **c) Comparison to reference [1/0/-1]:** subjective score comparing the prediction with the crowdsourced RF. ('vsRef' in the Table 2, 1=Prediction better than RF, 0=Prediction at par with RF, -1=RF better than prediction).

3. Oracle [1/0/-1]: 1 if the first prediction is an "oracle" (i.e. considered as perfect, see section 1), 0 when the oracle is found in the top 20, and -1 when no oracle is found there.

5 Analysis

We show a few examples of utterances (predictions in first position, i.e. most probable) produced by our model, for discussion.[6]

1. **[MR]:** name[The Punter], customer rating[high], area[riverside], kidsFriendly[yes]
   [RF]: *In riverside area, there is The Punter, which is high rated by customers and kids are friendly.*
   [Pred]: The Punter is a kid friendly restaurant in the riverside area with a high customer rating.

2. **[MR]:** name[The Golden Palace], eatType[coffeee shop], food[Japanese], priceRange[£20-25], customer rating[high], area[riverside]
   [RF]: *For highly-rated Japanese food pop along to The Golden Palace coffee shop. Its located on the riverside. Expect to pay between 20-25 pounds per person.*
   [Pred]: The Golden Palace is a coffee shop providing Japanese food in the £20-25 price range. It is located in the riverside area.

---

[5]Calculated using multi-bleu perl script bundled with *tf-seq2seq*. Note that these results were computed on the original version of Challenge devset (updated recently) which did not group the references associated with the same MR, possibly resulting in lower scores than when exploiting multi-refs.

[6]Some more examples can be found in Table 4. The full list of human annotated examples, including the 20-best predictions and oracles, can be found at `https://docs.google.com/spreadsheets/d/1wMu42g8bzyFxBUJ33QIdkqN3md3281pg6rLGrnDbEIE/edit?usp=sharing`.

Ann	O(1/0)	A(1/0)	R(1/0)	G(1/0)	N(2/1/0)	vsRef(1/0/-1)	Or(1/0/-1)
Ann 1	51/49	100/0	97/3	93/7	85/13/2	46/16/38	50/18/32
Ann 2	51/49	100/0	98/2	98/2	80/18/2	29/36/35	51/18/31
Mean	51/49	100/0	97.5/2.5	95.5/4.5	82.5/15.5/2	37.5/26/36.5	50.5/18/31.5

Table 2: Human annotations for 100 samples using different metrics defined in Sec. 4. O (Omission), A (Addition), R (Repetition) and G (Grammar) are on binary scale. Naturalness is measured as (2/1/0) and Oracle as (1/0/-1). Predictions were also judged against the reference on a scale of (1/0/-1).

Slots	DA	Or@1	Or	No Or
3	1(1%)	1(100%)	0(0%)	0(0%)
4	29(29%)	24(83%)	3(10%)	2(7%)
5	25(25%)	13(48%)	6(24%)	6(28%)
6	29(29%)	11(34%)	5(17%)	13(48%)
7	11(11%)	1(9%)	3(27%)	7(64%)
8	5(5%)	1(20%)	1(20%)	3(60%)
Total	100	51	18	31

Table 3: Human annotations for different slots using beam-width 20. 'Or@1' represents the presence of an 'oracle' at first position while 'Or' represents the presence of 'Oracle' (desirable) in the top-20 predictions. Cases where no oracle was found are marked as 'No Or'.

3. **[MR]:** name[Strada], food[Fast food], priceRange [moderate], customer rating[1 out of 5], kidsFriendly[no], near [Rainbow Vegetarian Cafe]
   [RF]: *Strada is a Fast food restaurant near the Rainbow Vegetarian caffe which has a moderate customer rating of 1 out of 5 for a non Kids friendly restaurant*
   [Pred]: Strada is a moderately priced fast food restaurant in the **moderate price range**. It is located near Rainbow Vegetarian caffe.

Among the utterances produced by the model in first position (Pred), the most prominent issue was that of omissions (underlined in example 2). There were no additions or non-words (which was one of the primary concerns for (Goyal et al., 2016)). We observed only a couple of repetitions which were actually accompanied by omission of some slot(s) in the same utterance (repetition highlighted in bold in example 3). Surprisingly enough, we observed a similar issue of omissions in human references (target for our model). We then decided to perform comparisons against the human reference ('vsRef' in Table 2). Often, the predictions were found to be semantically or grammatically better than the human reference; for example observe the underlined portion of the reference in the first example. The two annotators independently found the predictions to be mostly grammatically correct as well as natural (to a slighty lesser extent).[7]

A general feeling of the annotators was that the predictions, while showing a significant amount of linguistic diversity and naturalness, had a tendency to respect grammatical constraints *better* than the references; the crowdsourcers tended to strive for creativity, sometimes not supported by evidence in the MR, and often with little concern for linguistic quality; it may be conjectured that the seq2seq model, by "averaging" over many linguistically diverse and sometimes incorrect training examples, was still able to learn what amounts to a reasonable linguistic model for its predictions.

We also investigate whether we could find an 'oracle' (perfect solution as defined in section 1) in the top-20 predictions and observed that in around 70% of our examples the oracle could be found in the top results (see Table 3), very often (51%) at the first position. In the rest 30% of the cases, even the top-20 predictions did not contain an oracle. We found that the presence of an oracle was dependent on the number of slots in the MR. When the number of slots was 7 or 8, the presence of an oracle in the top predictions decreased significantly to approximately 40%. In contrast, with 4 slots, our model predicted an oracle right at the first place for 83% of the cases.

6 Conclusion

We employed the open source *tf-seq2seq* framework for training a char2char model on the *E2E NLG Challenge* data. This could be done with minimal effort, without requiring delexicalization, lowercasing or even tokenization, by exploiting standard options provided with the framework.

Human annotators found the predictions to have great linguistic quality, somewhat to our surprise, but also confirming the observations in (Karpathy, 2015). On the adequacy side, omissions were the major drawback; no hallucinations were observed and only very few instances of repetition. We hope our results and annotations can help understand the dataset and issues better, while also being useful for researchers working on the challenge.

---

[7]Annotator-1 was more severe in highlighting even the (rare) punctuation issues as grammatical mistakes. There was also a slight disagreement with Annotator-2 being more severe than Annotator-1 when assessing the references against the predictions.

Slots	Type	Utterance
	MR	name[Blue Spice], priceRange[£20-25], area[riverside]
3	RF	*Blue Spice has items in the £20-25 price range and is in riverside.*
	Pred	Blue Spice is located in the riverside area with a price range of £20-25.
	MR	name[The Punter], customer rating[high], area[riverside], kidsFriendly[yes]
4	RF	*In riverside area, there is The Punter, which is high rated by customers and kids are friendly.*
	Pred	The Punter is a kid friendly restaurant in the riverside area with a high customer rating.
	MR	name[Green Man], eatType[pub], food[English], area[city centre], near[Cafe Rouge]
5	RF	*Green Man is a pub that can be found in the city centre, near caffe Rouge and serves English-style food.*
	Pred	Green Man is an English pub located in the city centre near caffe Rouge.
	MR	name[The Golden Palace], eatType[coffeee shop], food[Japanese], priceRange[£20-25], **customer rating[high]**, area[riverside]
6	RF	*For highly-rated Japanese food pop along to The Golden Palace coffee shop. Its located on the riverside. Expect to pay between 20-25 pounds per person.*
	Pred	The Golden Palace is a coffee shop providing Japanese food in the £20-25 price range. It is located in the riverside area.
	MR	name[The Rice Boat], food[Chinese], priceRange[cheap], customer rating[average], area[city centre], **familyFriendly[no]**, near[Express by Holiday Inn]
7	RF	*The Rice Boat is a not family friendly,cheap, average rated Chinese food restaurant near Express by Holiday Inn.*
	Pred	The Rice Boat provides Chinese food in the cheap price range. It is located in the city centre near Express by Holiday Inn. Its customer rating is average.
	MR	name[The Eagle], eatType[coffeee shop], food[Japanese], priceRange[moderate], customer rating[1 out of 5], area[riverside], kidsFriendly[yes], near[Burger King]
8	RF	*There is a one star mid priced family friendly coffee shop The Eagle near Burger King in the City centre. It offers Chinese food.*
	Pred	The Eagle is a kid friendly Japanese coffee shop in the riverside area near Burger King. It has a moderate price range and a customer rating of 1 out of 5.

Table 4: Sample predictions. For the first MR of each arity (3 to 8) in the devset, we show the best prediction of the model (the starred one in Table 1), along with the RF. Omissions of semantic material are highlighted in bold.

Acknowledgments We thank Éric Gaussier, Chunyang Xiao, and Matthias Gallé for useful suggestions.

References

Martín Abadi, Ashish Agarwal, Paul Barham, Eugene Brevdo, Zhifeng Chen, Craig Citro, Greg S Corrado, Andy Davis, Jeffrey Dean, Matthieu Devin, Sanjay Ghemawat, Ian Goodfellow, Andrew Harp, Geoffrey Irving, Michael Isard, Yangqing Jia, Rafal Jozefowicz, Lukasz Kaiser, Manjunath Kudlur, Josh Levenberg, Dan Mane, Rajat Monga, Sherry Moore, Derek Murray, Chris Olah, Mike Schuster, Jonathon Shlens, Benoit Steiner, Ilya Sutskever, Kunal Talwar, Paul Tucker, Vincent Vanhoucke, Vijay Vasudevan, Fernanda Viegas, Oriol Vinyals, Pete Warden, Martin Wattenberg, Martin Wicke, Yuan Yu, and Xiaoqiang Zheng. 2016. Tensorflow: Large-scale machine learning on heterogeneous distributed systems. *CoRR abs/1603.04467* .

Dzmitry Bahdanau, Kyunghyun Cho, and Yoshua Bengio. 2015. Neural machine translation by jointly learning to align and translate. In *Proc. ICLR*.

Denny Britz, Anna Goldie, Thang Luong, and Quoc Le. 2017. Massive exploration of neural machine translation architectures. *CoRR abs/1703.03906* .

Andrew Chisholm, Will Radford, and Ben Hachey. 2017. Learning to generate one-sentence biographies from wikidata. *CoRR abs/1702.06235* .

Kyunghyun Cho, Bart Van Merriënboer, Caglar Gulcehre, Dzmitry Bahdanau, Fethi Bougares, Holger Schwenk, and Yoshua Bengio. 2014. Learning phrase representations using rnn encoder-decoder for statistical machine translation. In *Proc. EMNLP*.

Raghav Goyal, Marc Dymetman, and Eric Gaussier. 2016. Natural Language Generation through Character-based RNNs with Finite-State Prior Knowledge. In *Proc. COLING*. Osaka, Japan.

Jiatao Gu, Zhengdong Lu, Hang Li, and Victor OK Li. 2016. Incorporating copying mechanism in sequence-to-sequence learning. In *Proc. ACL*.

Sepp Hochreiter and Jürgen Schmidhuber. 1997. Long short-term memory. *Neural computation* 9(8):1735–1780.

Andrej Karpathy. 2015. The unreasonable effectiveness of recurrent neural networks. http://karpathy.github.io/2015/05/21/rnn-effectiveness/.

Wang Ling, Isabel Trancoso, Chris Dyer, and Alan W Black. 2016. Character-based neural machine translation. In *Proc. ICLR*. pages 1–11.

Thang Luong, Hieu Pham, and Christopher D. Manning. 2015. Effective approaches to attention-based neural machine translation. In *Proc. EMNLP*.

Jekaterina Novikova, Ondrej Dušek, and Verena Rieser. 2017. The E2E NLG Shared Task .

Jekaterina Novikova, Oliver Lemon, and Verena Rieser. 2016. Crowd-sourcing NLG Data: Pictures Elicit Better Data. *CoRR abs/1608.00339* .

Ilya Sutskever, Oriol Vinyals, and Quoc V Le. 2014. Sequence to sequence learning with neural networks. In *Proc. NIPS*. pages 3104–3112.

Tsung-Hsien Wen, Milica Gasic, Nikola Mrksic, Pei-Hao Su, David Vandyke, and Steve Young. 2015. Semantically conditioned lstm-based natural language generation for spoken dialogue systems. In *Proc. EMNLP*.

Yonghui Wu, Mike Schuster, Zhifeng Chen, Quoc V Le, Mohammad Norouzi, Wolfgang Macherey, Maxim Krikun, Yuan Cao, Qin Gao, Klaus Macherey, Jeff Klinger, Apurva Shah, Melvin Johnson, Xiaobing Liu, Lukasz Kaiser, Stephan Gouws, Yoshikiyo Kato, Taku Kudo, Hideto Kazawa, Keith Stevens, George Kurian, Nishant Patil, Wei Wang, Cliff Young, Jason Smith, Jason Riesa, Alex Rudnick, Oriol Vinyals, Greg Corrado, Macduff Hughes, and Jeffrey Dean. 2016. Google's neural machine translation system: Bridging the gap between human and machine translation. *CoRR abs/1609.08144* .

Interaction Quality Estimation Using Long Short-Term Memories

Niklas Rach[1], Wolfgang Minker[1], and Stefan Ultes[2]
[1]Institute of Communication Engineering, Ulm University
{vorname.nachname}@uni-ulm.de
[2]Department of Engineering, University of Cambridge, UK
su259@cam.ac.uk

Abstract

For estimating the Interaction Quality (IQ) in Spoken Dialogue Systems (SDS), the dialogue history is of significant importance. Previous works included this information manually in the form of precomputed temporal features into the classification process. Here, we employ a deep learning architecture based on Long Short-Term Memories (LSTM) to extract this information automatically from the data, thus estimating IQ solely by using current exchange features. We show that it is thereby possible to achieve competitive results as in a scenario where manually optimized temporal features have been included.

1 Introduction

The increasing complexity of Spoken Dialogue Systems (SDS) and the requirements that come with this progress made automatized recognition and modeling of user states crucial to ensure natural and user adaptive interaction. User Satisfaction (US) is one important part of such a state. On the dialogue level (i.e. after the interaction is complete), it provides a measure for the interaction and allows to compare different SDS (Walker et al., 1997) or to learn appropriate dialogue strategies (Walker, 2000; Ultes et al., 2017a). However, if US is available in each turn, it can also be used for user adaptation (Ultes et al., 2011, 2012, 2016, 2014a).

In the scope of this work we focus on the Interaction Quality (IQ) as a turn-wise approach to US and propose a deep learning architecture to estimate it solely using exchange parameters[1]. In doing so, we show that with the proposed approach,

---

[1]An exchange is a system turn followed by a user turn.

manually optimized, pre-computed temporal information (as employed in previous work) is no longer required.

Diverse approaches for estimating the US were already proposed, including n-gram models (Hara et al., 2010) and Hidden Markov Models (Higashinaka et al., 2010a; Engelbrech et al., 2009) in different scenarios. Although the results were above the random baseline, the respective improvement was only minor. As it was discussed by Higashinaka et al. (2010b), one difficulty of this task lies in the subjective nature of US since it depends on the appreciation of the user.

IQ is a more objective approach to US that relies on the rating of experts instead of users (Schmitt and Ultes, 2015) and thus closes the gap between subjective valuation and objective criteria. The respective rating is given on a scale between 1 (extremely unsatisfied) and five (satisfied) after listening to audio records of the dialogue in question. A detailed study on the correlation between the IQ and a measure of the real US was provided by Ultes et al. (2013) and various approaches including Hidden Markov Models (Ultes et al., 2014b; Ultes and Minker, 2014), Support Vector Machines (Schmitt et al., 2011; Ultes and Minker, 2013), Ordinal Regression (El Asri et al., 2014) and Recurrent Neural Networks (Pragst et al., 2017) have been employed to estimate the IQ from exchange parameters. Although the results show a significant improvement to alternative approaches, the classification relies in each case on precomputed features modeling the dialogue history (so called *temporal features*).

Despite the good results, using *temporal features* requires insight into the correlations between the dialogue history and the IQ score as the time-span covered by the temporal information significantly influences the outcome (Ultes et al., 2017b). The required knowledge about this correlation is

Proceedings of the SIGDIAL 2017 Conference, pages 164–169,
Saarbrücken, Germany, 15-17 August 2017. ©2017 Association for Computational Linguistics

usually not accessible and likely to be domain dependent thus rendering the respective approaches inflexible. In contrast, we employ a deep learning classifier to extract the required temporal information automatically and show that in doing so it is possible to achieve competitive results by only using exchange level parameters. In addition, we show that findings of previous works regarding the optimal amount of temporal information to be included may be retrieved in our approach by slightly varying the input sequences. Finally, the usability of our proposed architecture in real-life scenarios is discussed by looking at the percentage of usable IQ guesses.

The remainder of this paper is as follows: In Section 2 we discuss the LSTM based neural network architecture followed by a discussion of the employed data in Section 3. Section 4 presents the experiments and results and we close with a brief conclusion and outlook in Section 5.

2 LSTM-based Interaction Quality Estimation

Recurrent Neural Networks (RNN) include temporal correlations in the data into the classification process and are thus suitable for sequential tasks such as the one at hand. However, common approaches have shown to be inefficient in learning long-term dependencies (Bengio et al., 1994) due to a vanishing (or exploding) gradient. To tackle this problem, Hochreiter et al. (1997) introduced an architecture, called Long Short-Term Memory (LSTM) that allows to preserve temporal information, even if the correlated events are separated by a longer time. Since previous works showed that long time correlations are of importance for estimating the IQ, we consider LSTM a suitable approach for the reviewed scenario.

The herein employed architecture is thus built of a LSTM unit, consisting of two stacked LSTM cells, followed by a two-layer perceptron unit with sigmoid activation functions. The latter one is given as

$$F_{MLP} : y_t \rightarrow (g_2 \circ g_1)(y_t) \qquad (1)$$
$$g_i(y_t) = sigm(W_i^T y_t + b_i) \qquad (2)$$

where W_i denotes the weight matrix, b_i a bias vector and $sigm$ the element-wise sigmoid function. A LSTM cell on the other hand can be seen as function

$$f : x_t, c_{t-1}, h_{t-1} \rightarrow h_t, c_t \qquad (3)$$

with h_t the output state, c_t the internal cell state and x_t the input of the LSTM at time step t. In a multilayer scenario, the input of a layer is the output of the previous one. A deeper discussion of the LSTM architecture including the respective formulas is provided for example in (Zaremba et al., 2014). The complete LSTM unit can thus be written as a function F_{LSTM} that processes a given input through two LSTM layers and maps it to an output state y_t. Combining this description with equation 1 yields

$$z_t = (F_{MLP} \circ \sigma \circ F_{LSTM})(x_t) \qquad (4)$$

for the whole net with z_t the final IQ mapping of the input and σ the softmax normalization function. In the reviewed scenario, each LSTM layer consisted of 48 nodes whereas the perceptron unit had 48 nodes in the hidden layer and five nodes in the output layer. Therefore, the two LSTM layers are employed to extract the temporal information whereas the following perceptron layers serve as classifier that maps the output of the LSTM unit to the respective IQ scale. The whole net is depicted in Figure 1 and was implemented using Google's Tensorflow library (Abadi et al., 2016). Optimization was done by use of the Adaptive Gradient Algorithm (Duchi et al., 2011).

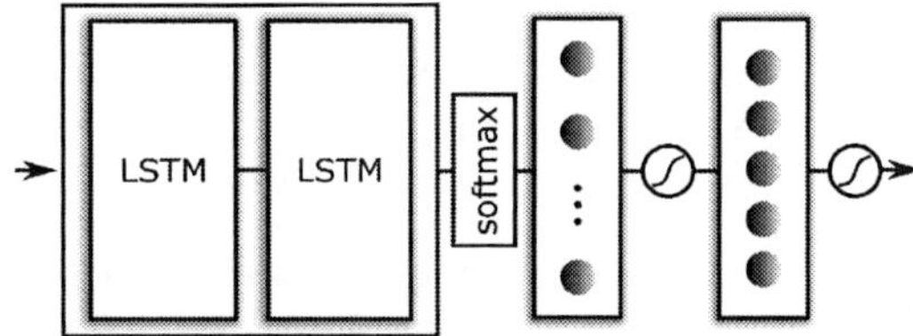

Figure 1: Sketch of the deep learning architecture in use. The left part contains the two stacked LSTM cells followed by a softmax normalization unit. The output is fed into a two layer perceptron with sigmoid activation functions.

3 The LEGO Corpus

To appropriately compare our results, we employ the LEGO coprus (Schmitt et al., 2012)—the same corpus as the authors of previous work. It is based on the "Let's Go Bus Information System" of the Carnegie Mellon university in Pittsburg (Raux et al., 2006) and consists of 200 dialogues including 4884 system-user exchanges. Each exchange was assigned with features from three instances of

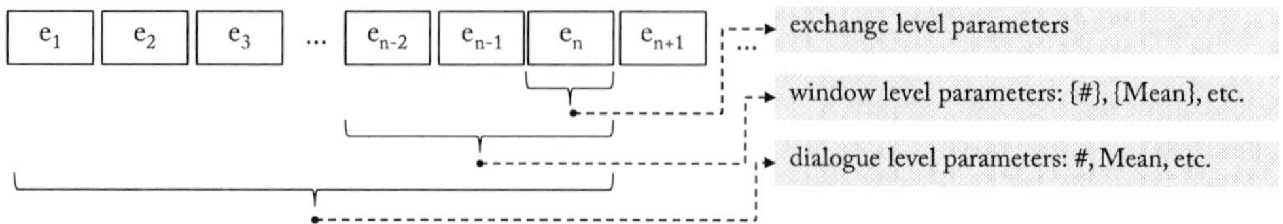

Figure 2: The three parameter levels including the temporal features of the window and the dialogue level (Schmitt et al., 2012).

the SDS, namely the Automatic Speech Recognition (ASR), Natural Language Understanding (NLU) and the Dialogue Manager (DM). Furthermore, the corpus was annotated with an IQ rating by three experts following specific guidelines to achieve an objective measure (Schmitt et al., 2011). In doing so, an inter-annotator agreement of $\kappa = 0.54$ was achieved. For the final IQ score, the median of all three ratings was taken. To include temporal features into the corpus, three different interaction levels that are depicted in Figure 2 were considered:

- The exchange level contains all features regarding the current system-user exchange.

- The window level includes counts and means of numerical exchange level features from the previous n exchanges, where n is referred to as window size.

- The dialogue level contains counts and means of numerical exchange level features from all previous exchanges.

The term temporal features thus refers to features of the window and dialogue level. The influence of these two additional levels as well as the choice of n on the automatized estimation of the IQ were studied (Ultes et al., 2017b) and serve as a baseline for this work.

4 Experiments and Results

In this section we discuss the results of the employed classifier in estimating the IQ for the annotated LEGO corpus. To distinguish the contribution of the parameters derived from different SDS instances to the IQ, three feature sets were employed that consisted of features assigned to the ASR, the DM and both:

ASR: *ASRRecognitionStatus* (string, status of the ASR), *Modality* (string, input modality of the user, either *speech* or *dtmf*), *ExMo* (string, expected modality of the user input, either *speech*, *dtmf*, *both* or *none*), *ASRConfidence* (float, confidence score of the ASR), *Barged-In?* (boolean, true if system was interrupted by the user), *UnExMo?* (boolean, true if the actual input modality did not match the expected one), *WPUT* (integer, words per user turn), *UTD* (float, utterance turn duration)

DM: *ActivityType* (string, type of activity), *RoleName* (string, function of the system turn), *RePromt?* (boolean, true if the current turn is a repromt), *WPST* (integer, words per system turn), *DD* (float, dialogue duration), *RoleIndex* (integer, tries necessary to get a desired response from the user)

Parameters that are either constant or task-related were discarded, including the two features from the NLU. To represent all parameters as a numerical input vector, non-numerical features were encoded in a one-hot vector. As in previous work, we used 10-fold cross validation to evaluate the outcomes. The results are compared in terms of Unweighted Average Recall[2] (UAR), Cohen's (linearly weighted) Kappa (Cohen, 1968) and Spearman's Rho (Spearman, 1904) to the ones achieved by Ultes et al. (2017b) with the best window size $n = 9$, the full feature set and a Support Vector Machine (SVM). Our results as well as the baseline value are shown in Table 1. For all three measures, the results with the full feature set are competitive to the baseline. Whereas the UAR is slightly below the reference value, κ and ρ show a small improvement. The results for the two subsets are visibly below the baseline for both UAR and κ whereas the DM value of ρ equals the respective reference value. Moreover, the DM features yield better results than the ASR features and thus contribute more to the overall IQ value,

---

[2]The arithmetic average of all class-wise recalls.

	features	#TF	UAR	κ	ρ
LSTM	ASR+DM	0	**0.548**	**0.684**	**0.832**
LSTM	ASR	0	0.502	0.636	0.796
LSTM	DM	0	0.516	0.654	0.812
SVM	ASR+DM	25	**0.549**	0.679	0.812

Table 1: The results of the LSTM approach in comparison to the SVM baseline (Ultes et al., 2017b), including the number of handcrafted temporal features in use (#TF) for each scenario.

which is in line with the outcomes of previous work (Ultes et al., 2015). It is stressed that none of the feature sets employed for the LSTM uses handcrafted temporal features nor needs them. Thus, we conclude that our approach is indeed capable of extracting the required temporal information automatically.

In addition, we investigate the temporal information extracted by the trained classifier by measuring the impact of one system-user exchange on following estimates. This allows a comparison of the extracted information in the herein discussed scenario with the manually set window size in previous work. To this end, we replaced the input vector of the second system-user exchange e_2 in each dialogue $D_i = (e_1^i, e_2^i, .., e_L^i)$ of the corpus $\{D_1, ..., D_M\}$ by the input associated with one out of 20 randomly picked exchanges e_r^j ($j \in \{1, ..., M\}$) with assigned IQ value of 1. The modified dialogues

$$\tilde{D}_i = (e_1^i, e_r^j, ..., e_L^i) \tag{5}$$

were then fed through a trained model of the 10-fold cross validation and the results were compared to the ones achieved with the original data by computing the sum of the absolute errors of each class. This was repeated for all 20 random picks and all 10 models (we employed different random picks for each model). The mean of this error over all dialogues, all trained models and all random picks for the replaced exchange was determined and is shown as a function of the system-user exchange number in Figure 3. This error indicates the impact one exchange has on the IQ estimate of following exchanges. We see that from exchange number 9 to exchange number 12 the error clearly decreases. A comparison with the referenced work shows that this drop is in the same range as the optimal window size $n = 9$ (that would correspond to exchange number 11).

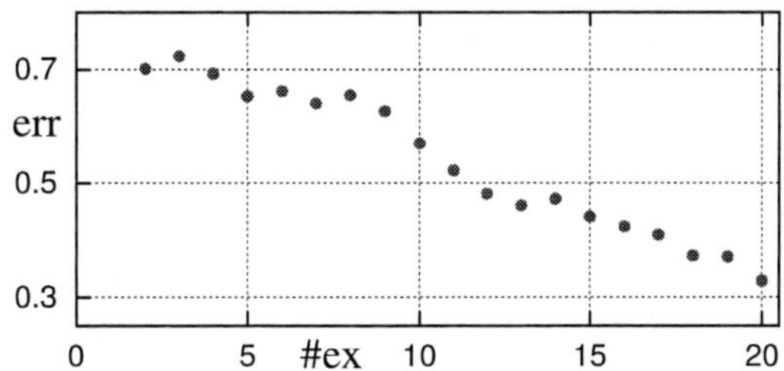

Figure 3: Mean error caused by the replacement of the second system-user exchange by a random picked exchange as a function of the exchange number.

Therefore the impact of the exchange in question is decreased in the same range as in a scenario were this impact is controlled manually. This indicates that similar temporal information that was employed therein is automatically extracted by our architecture.

In many classification scenarios, the classes are not ordered which means that in the case of a wrong guess it is irrelevant which class was chosen. However, as the IQ is an ordered scale, the distance of the wrong guess to the real class is of interest, especially in view of the application. We therefore compute the amount of guesses in which the classification was wrong only by one point (e.g. an instant of IQ 1 classified as IQ 2 or vice versa). This percentage δ can be derived directly from the confusion matrix C as

$$\delta = \frac{1}{N}(\sum_{k=1}^{K-1} C_{k,k+1} + \sum_{k=2}^{K} C_{k,k-1}) \tag{6}$$

with N the number of total entries of C and K the number of classes, i.e. the dimension of C. Adding this value to the Accuracy (ACC) gives a percentage of usable guesses of the classifier. The results for the architecture used in this work and the best feature set (ASR + DM) are ACC=0.57 and δ=0.37, resulting in a sum of 0.94. In other words, considering a real-life scenario, 94% of the classifiers guesses could be used, for example for user adaptation. Again, these results are compared to the ones achieved with a SVM and the setup of (Ultes et al., 2017b) with a sum of 0.91. Evidently, the deep learning classifier outperforms the SVM approach in this metric.

5 Conclusion and Outlook

In this work, we investigated the estimation of the IQ with a deep learning classifier by only using exchange level parameters. It was shown that by use of the presented architecture, precomputed temporal features are no longer required and the IQ can be estimated with an UAR of 0.548. The results are competitive to the ones achieved with a SVM classifier and the whole feature set in earlier work. In addition, we compared the temporal information extracted by the classifier with the optimal window size from previous work and showed that our results match previous findings. Finally, the usability of the employed classifier in applications was discussed by computing the percentage of usable guesses in such a case. The result of 94% is below the outcome of the 0.91 achieved with the SVM and a complete feature set. Moreover, since our approach does not require any domain dependent information, it is much more flexible.

It is reasonable to assume that the difficulty of estimating the interaction quality and the amount of temporal information that is required rely on the complexity of the system and the interaction. Although the herein presented slot filling dialogue is comparatively basic, the IQ is influenced not only by technical aspects (e.g., the quality of the speech recognition) but also by the ability of the system to react appropriately. This influence is even stronger in more advanced tasks, where the user satisfaction (and thus the IQ as well) may also depend on the ability of the system to appropriately react on the users state including for example emotions and culture. Although this task differs from the one addressed here, we assume the presented architecture to be a good starting point for these scenarios as well due to its above discussed flexibility.

Thus, for future work the performance of this architecture in different scenarios and systems will be of interest, especially in systems were the IQ depends on additional aspects. Moreover, applying the presented architecture to estimate other user states or features used for user adaptation is also in the focus of future work.

Acknowledgments

This work is part of a project that has received funding from the *European Unions Horizon 2020 research and innovation programme* under grant agreement No 645012.

References

Martín Abadi, Ashish Agarwal, Paul Barham, Eugene Brevdo, Zhifeng Chen, Craig Citro, Greg S Corrado, Andy Davis, Jeffrey Dean, Matthieu Devin, et al. 2016. Tensorflow: Large-scale machine learning on heterogeneous distributed systems. *arXiv preprint arXiv:1603.04467* .

Yoshua Bengio, Patrice Simard, and Paolo Frasconi. 1994. Learning long-term dependencies with gradient descent is difficult. *IEEE transactions on neural networks* 5(2):157–166.

Jacob Cohen. 1968. Weighted kappa: Nominal scale agreement provision for scaled disagreement or partial credit. *Psychological bulletin* 70(4):213.

John Duchi, Elad Hazan, and Yoram Singer. 2011. Adaptive subgradient methods for online learning and stochastic optimization. *Journal of Machine Learning Research* 12(Jul):2121–2159.

Layla El Asri, Hatim Khouzaimi, Romain Laroche, and Olivier Pietquin. 2014. Ordinal regression for interaction quality prediction. In *International Conference on Acoustics, Speech and Signal Processing (ICASSP)*. IEEE, pages 3245–3249.

Klaus-Peter Engelbrech, Florian Gödde, Felix Hartard, Hamed Ketabdar, and Sebastian Möller. 2009. Modeling user satisfaction with Hidden Markov Model. *Proceedings of the SIGDIAL 2009 Conference: The 10th Annual Meeting of the Special Interest Group on Discourse and Dialogue* (September):170–177.

Sunao Hara, Norihide Kitaoka, and Kazuya Takeda. 2010. Estimation method of user satisfaction using n-gram-based dialog history model for spoken dialog system. In *LREC*.

Ryuichiro Higashinaka, Yasuhiro Minami, Kohji Dohsaka, and Toyomi Meguro. 2010a. Modeling user satisfaction transitions in dialogues from overall ratings. In *Proceedings of the 11th Annual Meeting of the Special Interest Group on Discourse and Dialogue*. Association for Computational Linguistics, pages 18–27.

Ryuichiro Higashinaka, Yasuhiro Minami, Kohji Dohsaka, and Toyomi Meguro. 2010b. Modeling User Satisfaction Transitions in Dialogues from Overall Ratings. *Proceedings of the 11th Annual Meeting of the Special Interest Group on Discourse and Dialogue* pages 18–27.

Sepp Hochreiter and Jürgen Schmidhuber. 1997. Long short-term memory. *Neural computation* 9(8):1735–1780.

Louisa Pragst, Stefan Ultes, and Wolfgang Minker. 2017. Recurrent neural network interaction quality estimation. In Kristiina Jokinen and Graham Wilcock, editors, *Dialogues with Social Robots: Enablements, Analyses, and Evaluation*, Springer Singapore, Singapore, pages 381–393.

Antoine Raux, Dan Bohus, Brian Langner, Alan W Black, and Maxine Eskenazi. 2006. Doing research on a deployed spoken dialogue system: one year of let's go! experience. In *INTERSPEECH*.

Alexander Schmitt, Benjamin Schatz, and Wolfgang Minker. 2011. Modeling and predicting quality in spoken human-computer interaction. *Proceedings of the SIGDIAL 2011 Conference* pages 173–184.

Alexander Schmitt and Stefan Ultes. 2015. Interaction quality: assessing the quality of ongoing spoken dialog interaction by expertsand how it relates to user satisfaction. *Speech Communication* 74:12–36.

Alexander Schmitt, Stefan Ultes, and Wolfgang Minker. 2012. A parameterized and annotated spoken dialog corpus of the cmu let's go bus information system. In *International Conference on Language Resources and Evaluation (LREC)*. pages 3369–337.

Charles Spearman. 1904. The proof and measurement of association between two things. *The American journal of psychology* 15(1):72–101.

Stefan Ultes, Hüseyin Dikme, and Wolfgang Minker. 2014a. First insight into quality-adaptive dialogue. In *International Conference on Language Resources and Evaluation (LREC)*. pages 246–251.

Stefan Ultes, Hüseyin Dikme, and Wolfgang Minker. 2016. Dialogue Management for User-Centered Adaptive Dialogue. In Alexander I. Rudnicky, Antoine Raux, Ian Lane, and Teruhisa Misu, editors, *Situated Dialog in Speech-Based Human-Computer Interaction*, Springer International Publishing, Cham, pages 51–61. https://doi.org/10.1007/978-3-319-21834-2_5.

Stefan Ultes, Robert ElChab, and Wolfgang Minker. 2014b. Application and evaluation of a conditioned hidden markov model for estimating interaction quality of spoken dialogue systems. In *Natural Interaction with Robots, Knowbots and Smartphones*, Springer, pages 303–312.

Stefan Ultes, Tobias Heinroth, Alexander Schmitt, and Wolfgang Minker. 2011. A theoretical framework for a user-centered spoken dialog manager. In Ramón López-Cózar and Tetsunori Kobayashi, editors, *Proceedings of the Paralinguistic Information and its Integration in Spoken Dialogue Systems Workshop*. Springer New York, New York, NY, pages 241–246. https://doi.org/10.1007/978-1-4614-1335-6_24.

Stefan Ultes, Juliana Miehle, and Wolfgang Minker. 2017a. On the applicability of a user satisfaction-based reward for dialogue policy learning. In *Proceedings of the 8th International Workshop On Spoken Dialogue Systems (IWSDS)*.

Stefan Ultes and Wolfgang Minker. 2013. Improving Interaction Quality Recognition Using Error Correction. *Proceedings of the SIGDIAL 2013 Conference* (August):122–126.

Stefan Ultes and Wolfgang Minker. 2014. Interaction quality estimation in spoken dialogue systems using hybrid-hmms. In *Proceedings of the 15th Annual Meeting of the Special Interest Group on Discourse and Dialogue (SIGDIAL)*. Association for Computational Linguistics, pages 208–217.

Stefan Ultes, María Jesús Platero Sánchez, Alexander Schmitt, and Wolfgang Minker. 2015. Analysis of an extended interaction quality corpus. In *Natural Language Dialog Systems and Intelligent Assistants*, Springer, pages 41–52.

Stefan Ultes, Alexander Schmitt, and Wolfgang Minker. 2012. Towards quality-adaptive spoken dialogue management. In *NAACL-HLT Workshop on Future directions and needs in the Spoken Dialog Community: Tools and Data (SDCTD 2012)*. Association for Computational Linguistics, Montréal, Canada, pages 49–52. http://www.aclweb.org/anthology/W12-1819.

Stefan Ultes, Alexander Schmitt, and Wolfgang Minker. 2013. On Quality Ratings for Spoken Dialogue Systems – Experts vs. Users. *Proceedings of the 2013 Conference of the North American Chapter of the Association for Computational Linguistics: Human Language Technologies* (June):569–578.

Stefan Ultes, Alexander Schmitt, and Wolfgang Minker. 2017b. Analysis of temporal features for interaction quality estimation. In *Dialogues with Social Robots*, Springer, pages 367–379.

Marilyn Walker. 2000. An application of reinforcement learning to dialogue strategy selection in a spoken dialogue system for email. *Journal of Artificial Intelligence Research* 12:387–416.

Marilyn A. Walker, Diane J. Litman, Candace A. Kamm, Alicia Abella, Marilyn A. Walker, Diane J. Litman, Candace A. Kamm, and Alicia Abella. 1997. Paradise. *Proceedings of the eighth conference on European chapter of the Association for Computational Linguistics -* pages 271–280. https://doi.org/10.3115/979617.979652.

Wojciech Zaremba, Ilya Sutskever, and Oriol Vinyals. 2014. Recurrent neural network regularization. *arXiv preprint arXiv:1409.2329 .*

DialPort, Gone Live: An Update After A Year of Development

**Kyusong Lee, Tiancheng Zhao, Yulun Du, Edward Cai, Allen Lu, Eli Pincus[1], David Traum[1],
Stefan Ultes[2], Lina M. Rojas-Barahona[2], Milica Gasic[2], Steve Young[2] and Maxine Eskenazi**
Language Technologies Institute, Carnegie Mellon University, Pittsburgh, Pennsylvania, USA
[1]USC Institute for Creative Technologies, 12015 Waterfront Dr, Playa Vista, CA 90094, USA
[2]Department of Engineering, University of Cambridge, Cambridge, UK
{kyusongl,tianchez,yulund,edcai,arlu,max}@cs.cmu.edu
[1]{pincus, traum}@ict.usc.edu
[2]{su259,lmr46,mg436,sjyll}@eng.cam.ac.uk

Abstract

DialPort collects user data for connected
spoken dialog systems. At present six systems are linked to a central portal that directs the user to the applicable system and
suggests systems that the user may be interested in. User data has started to flow
into the system.

1 Introduction

The goal of the DialPort spoken dialog portal is
to gather large amounts of real user data for spoken dialog systems (SDS). Sophisticated statistical representations in state of the art SDS, require
large amounts of data. While industry has this,
they cannot share this treasure. Academia has difficulty getting even small amounts of similar data.
With one central portal, connected to many different systems, the task of advertising and affording
user access can be done in one centralized place
that all systems can connect to. DialPort provides
a steady stream of data, allowing system creators
to focus on developing their systems. The portal
decides what service the user wants and connects
them to the appropriate system which carries on a
dialog with the user, returning control to the portal
at the end.

DialPort (Zhao et al., 2016) began with a central
agent and the Let'sForecast weather information
system. The Cambridge restaurant system (Gasic
et al., 2015) and a general restaurant system (Let's
Eat, that handles cities that Cambridge does not
cover) joined the portal. A chatbot, Qubot, was
developed to deal with out-of-domain requests.
Later, more systems connected to the portal. A
flow of users has begun interacting with the portal. Originally envisioned as a website with a list
of the urls of systems a user could try, the portal
has become easier to use, more closely resembling

what users might expect, given their exposure to
the Amazon ECHO[1] and Google HOME[2], etc. In
order to get a flow of users started, DialPort developers expanded the number of connected systems
to make the portal offerings more attractive and
relevant. They also made the interface easier to
use. By the end of March 2017, in addition to the
above systems, the portal also included Mr. Clue, a
word game from USC (Pincus and Traum, 2016),
a restaurant opinion bot (Let's Discuss, CMU),
and a bus information system derived from Let's
Go (Raux et al., 2005). The portal offers users the
option of typing or talking and of seeing an agent
or just hearing it. With few connected systems in
previous versions it was difficult to assess the portal's switching mechanisms. The increased number of systems challenges the portal to make better decisions and have better a switching strategy.
It also demands changes in the frequency of recommendations to connected systems. And it challenged the nature of the agent: some users prefer
no visual agent; others couldn't use speech with
the system.

A short history of DialPort DialPort started
with a call for research groups to link their SDS
to the portal and a website listing SDS urls for
users to try out. It quickly evolved into one userfriendly portal where, all of the SDS are accessed
through one central agent, users being seamlessly
transferred from one system to another. System
connections go through an API that sends them
the ASR result (Chrome at present). The system
was tried out informally (Lee et al., 2017) to determine whether the portal fulfilled criteria such as:
timely response, correct transfer (to what the user
wanted), and correct recommendation of systems
(not saying for example, you can ask me about

---

[1]https://www.amazon.com
[2]https://madeby.google.com/home/

Proceedings of the SIGDIAL 2017 Conference, pages 170–173,
Saarbrücken, Germany, 15-17 August 2017. ©2017 Association for Computational Linguistics

restaurants in Cambridge just after the user has finished talking to that system).

2   External Agents (ESes)

The first assessment of the interface (Lee et al., 2017) included five External Systems (ESes, that is, systems that are joined to the portal and are thus not part of the central portal - they can be from CMU as well as from other sites): Let'sForecast, Cambridge SDS on restaurants, Lets Eat; Mr Clue word game; and Qubot chatbot handling out of domain requests. Since then, Let's Go and Let'sDiscuss, a chatbot that gives restaurant reviews, have joined. The latter systems, by the CMU portal group, offer new services hoping to attract more diverse users and encourage them to become return users.

Cambridge   The Cambridge restaurant information system helps users find a restaurant in Cambridge, UK based on the area, the price range or the food type. The current database has just over 100 restaurants and is implemented using the multi-domain statistical dialogue system toolkit PyDial (Ultes et al., 2017). To connect PyDial to Dialport, PyDial's dialogue server interface is used. It is implemented as an HTTP server expecting JSON messages from the Dialport client. The system runs a trained dialogue policy based on the GP-SARSA algorithm (Gašić et al., 2010).

Mr. Clue   Mr. Clue plays a simple word-guessing game (Pincus and Traum, 2016). Mr. Clue is the clue-giver and the user plays the role of guesser. Mr. Clue mines his clues from pre-existing web and database resources such as dictionary.com and WordNet. Clue lists used are only clues that pass an automatic filter described in (Pincus and Traum, 2016). The original Mr. Clue was updated to enable successful communication with Dialport. First, since the original Mr. Clue listens for VH messages (a variant of ActiveMQ messaging used by the Virtual Human Toolkit (Hartholt et al., 2013), we built an HTTP server that converts HTTP messages (expected in JSON format) to VH messages. Second, since DialPort has multiple users in parallel, Mr. Clue was updated to launch a new agent instance for each new HTTP session (user) that is directed to the game from the main DialPort system. Mr. Clue is always in one of 2 states (in-game or out-game). The out-game state dialogue is limited to asking if

the user wants to play another round (and offering to give instructions in the beginning of a session). The user can use goodbye keyword to exit the system at any time. This sends an exit message to DialPort and allowing it to take back control. For its 150 second rounds, timing information is kept on the back-end and sent to the front-end (DialPort) in every message. For each new session, the agent chooses 1 of 77 different pre-compiled clue lists (each with 10 unique target-words) at random. It keeps track of which lists have been used for a session so a user will never play the same round twice (for a given session).

Let'sDiscuss   LetsDiscuss responds to queries about a specific restaurant by finding relevant segments of user reviews. It searches a database of restaurant reviews obtained from Zomato and Yelp. We formed a list of general discussion points for restaurants (service, atmosphere, etc). For each discussion point, a list of relevant keywords was compiled using WordNet, thesaurus, and by categorizing the most frequently words found in reviews.

Other Systems   QuBot, a chatbot from Pohang University and CMU, is used for out-of-domain handling. Let'sForecast, from CMU, uses the NOAA website. Let's Eat from CMU is based on Yelp, finding restaurants for cities that Cambridge does not cover and for Cambridge if that system is down. Let's Go, derived from the Let's Go system (Raux et al., 2005), is based on an end-to-end recurrent neural network structure and a backend that covers cities other than Pittsburgh.

3   DialPort Platform

In informal trials, some aspects of the portal's interaction were not effective for some users. This included the use of speech (as opposed to typing), the use of a visual agent, the absence of both graphical and speech response, feedback and portal behavior. Some ES need graphics to supplement their verbal information. Since Mr Clue keeps score and timing of users' answers, its instructions and scores are shown on a blackboard. Let's Go shows a map with the bus trajectory from departure to arrival.

Feedback and communication   The portal gives users feedback for: available topics, system state, and present system state. Skylar doesn't interrupt the dialog with a list of topics. Rather it suggests one topic every few turns. This evenly steers users to all of the ES. A banner at the bottom of the screen reminds users of all the topics that can be discussed. Another box indicates the system state in order to avoid user confusion about who has the floor. It shows, for example, whether the system is processing the speech or is still waiting for them to talk. The box shows:

- idle (either from timeout or from the user clicking on the box to pause the system);
- listening (this is shown from the instant the ASR begins to process speech to when it is finished);
- speaking (from when the TTS begins output to when it is finished);
- thinking (from when the ASR output is sent to the NLU to when the DM issues its action).

Finally, the system informs the user of the present state of the dialog. *Do you still want XX (e.g. Pittsburgh)?* reveals that the user preference for Pittsburgh has not been used for a while, and Skylar's forgetting curve is ready to eliminate it. The dynamic choice of implicit or explicit confirmation covers the global dialog state.

3.1 Changes in the portal's behavior

As more ES join the portal, policies and strategies have become more flexible. There are two major changes to the portal's behavior: ES selection policy and ES recommendation policy. Starting with few ESes, each on very different topics, the agent selection policy simply tried to detect the topic in the users' request and select the corresponding ES. As more ESes connect to the portal, non-trivial relationships among ESes emerge:

1) *Dialog context sensitive agent selection:* The optimal choice of ES may depend on discourse history. For example, Let'sForecast, Cambridge restaurant and Let's Eat: after the user has weather information for city X, they say, recommend a place to have lunch. Choosing between Let's Eat and Cambridge restaurant depends on the value of city X, because Cambridge restaurant covers places to eat in Cambridge UK and Let's Eat covers other places.

2) *Discourse Obligation for Agent selection:* Users have various ways to make requests: request (tell me xxx), WH-question (what's the weather in xx) or Yes/No-question (Is it going to rain?). A natural dialog should answer a user according to the way in which they made their earlier requests (Traum and Allen, 1994). For example, the weather system should produce the natural *Yes it's going to rain* instead of a full weather report, for the third question above. We thus keep the user's initial request intent in the global dialog context and share it with the relevant ESes.

The recommendation policy has been improved in two ways: **1)** All participating system developers agreed that Skylar should give ES recommendations on a rotating basis so that all systems are recommended equally. Skylar no longer makes a recommendation at the end of each system turn. Recommendations are made about every four turns and, as mentioned above, are not for a system that the user recently interacted with. **2)** Fine grained recommendation: As more ESes joined the portal, we began to exploit the relatedness among ESs in order to generate more targeted recommendations. For instance, we tuned the policy to have a higher probability of recommending the Let'sDiscuss restaurant review function when users obtain restaurant information by prompting, *do you want to hear a review about this place?*

Finally, the NLU has been extended to support multi-intent multi-domain identification by reducing the problem to a multi-label classification task using a one-vs-all strategy. The weighted average F-1 score for multi-intent and multi-domain classification is 0.93.

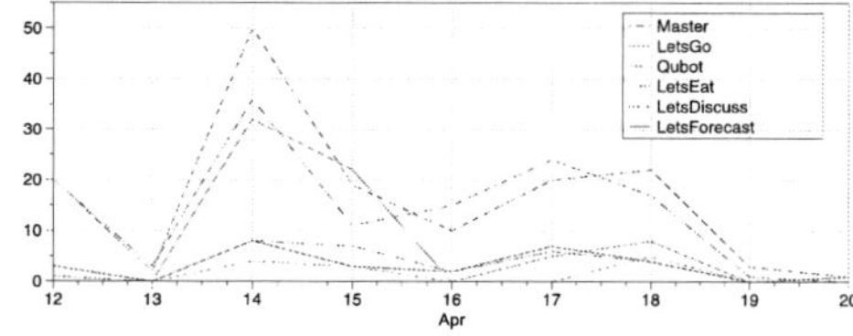

Figure 1: Number of dialog turns over time per ES

4 Go "Live"

There are several types of portal users. First, the developers themselves try out the system. Then they ask friends and family to try it. Users can be paid. Finally we have users who really need the information or gaming pleasure. We define two potential types of users (using IP addresses): explorers and real users. Explorers are trying the system for the first time. They explore several of the ESes, but they do not have any real gaming or information need. Real users have returned to use the portal, asking for something they need or enjoy. They may speak to less of the ESes during their visit, but have some real. The first advertising attempt using Google AdWords[3] attracted few explorers and no real users. The following factors may explain why users did not have a dialog with the system: presence of human study consent form; not using Chrome browser (solved by making a typing-only version); user didn't want any portal services; user didn't have a microphone; user didn't understand the purpose of the portal (we gave Skylar an opening monologue explaining what the data is for).

4.1 Can DialPort collect data?

The AdWord experience lead us to published a Facebook page on April 12, 2017. The page was to attract both explorers and real users through both organic (friends and friends of friends) and paid distribution. Despite the short time (4-12 to 4-20) that it has been published, there have been a total of 51 dialogs (excluding all dialogs from participating research teams). As of April 20, DialPort spent about $52 in advertising to reach 1776 individuals getting 147 page views, 47 likes and 346 engagements (shares or clicks). About 40% of the clicks were from mobile devices as opposed to computers. This underlines the need for mobile versions of DialPort.

The average length of a dialog is 8.7turns (7.18 stdev) and 129.51s (stdev 138.03). There were 14.9% return users, although another person could be using that computer and some places have automatic IP assignment. 52.9% of the dialogs were spoken as opposed to typed. The average ASR delay was 925.03ms. On average, users tried 4.8 systems per dialog. The distribution of dialog turns per ES and for the portal over time is shown on Figure 1. Some systems are getting less use than others. This will be countered by paid advertising campaigns that promote each specific system.

5   Conclusion

This paper has presented a novel portal that collects spoken dialog data for connected systems. It has begun to collect data for the present seven systems. In order to improve service an audio server is under construction as are smartphone and tablet versions. The portal welcomes new external systems.

---

[3]https://adwords.google.com

Acknowledgments

This work is partly funded by National Science Foundation grant CNS-1512973. The opinions expressed in this paper do not necessarily reflect those of the National Science Foundation.

References

M Gasic, Dongho Kim, Pirros Tsiakoulis, and Steve Young. 2015. Distributed dialogue policies for multi-domain statistical dialogue management. In *Acoustics, Speech and Signal Processing (ICASSP)*. pages 5371–5375.

Milica Gašić, Filip Jurčíček, Simon Keizer, François Mairesse, Blaise Thomson, Kai Yu, and Steve Young. 2010. Gaussian processes for fast policy optimisation of pomdp-based dialogue managers. In *Proceedings of the 11th Annual Meeting of the Special Interest Group on Discourse and Dialogue*. pages 201–204.

Arno Hartholt, David Traum, Stacy C Marsella, Ari Shapiro, Giota Stratou, Anton Leuski, Louis-Philippe Morency, and Jonathan Gratch. 2013. All together now. In *International Workshop on Intelligent Virtual Agents*. Springer, pages 368–381.

Kyusong Lee, Tiancheng Zhao, Stefan Ultes, Lina Rojas-Barahona, Eli Pincus, David Traum, and Maxine Eskenazi. 2017. An assessment framework for dialport. *Proceedings of the International Workshop on Spoken Dialogue Systems Technology* .

Eli Pincus and David Traum. 2016. Towards Automatic Identification of Effective Clues for Team Word-Guessing Games. In *Proceedings of the Language Resources and Evaluation Conference (LREC)*. European Language Resources Association, Portoro, Slovenia, pages 2741–2747.

Antoine Raux, Brian Langner, Dan Bohus, Alan W Black, and Maxine Eskenazi. 2005. Lets go public! taking a spoken dialog system to the real world. In *in Proc. of Interspeech 2005*. Citeseer.

David R Traum and James F Allen. 1994. Discourse obligations in dialogue processing. In *Proceedings of the 32nd annual meeting on Association for Computational Linguistics*. Association for Computational Linguistics, pages 1–8.

Stefan Ultes, Lina M. Rojas-Barahona, Pei-Hao Su, David Vandyke, Dongho Kim, Inigo Casanueva, Pawe Budzianowski, Tsung-Hsien Wen Nikola Mrksic, Milica Gasic, , and Steve J. Young. 2017. Pydial: A multi-domain statistical dialogue system toolkit. In *Proceedings of ACL Demo. Association of Computational Linguistics*.

Tiancheng Zhao, Kyusong Lee, and Maxine Eskenazi. 2016. The dialport portal: Grouping diverse types of spoken dialog systems. *Workshop on Chatbots and Conversational Agents* .

Evaluating Natural Language Understanding Services
for Conversational Question Answering Systems

Daniel Braun Adrian Hernandez Mendez Florian Matthes
Technical University of Munich
Department of Informatics
{daniel.braun,adrian.hernandez,matthes}
@tum.de

Manfred Langen
Siemens AG
Corporate Technology
manfred.langen
@siemens.com

Abstract

Conversational interfaces recently gained a lot of attention. One of the reasons for the current hype is the fact that chatbots (one particularly popular form of conversational interfaces) nowadays can be created without any programming knowledge, thanks to different toolkits and so-called Natural Language Understanding (NLU) services. While these NLU services are already widely used in both, industry and science, so far, they have not been analysed systematically. In this paper, we present a method to evaluate the classification performance of NLU services. Moreover, we present two new corpora, one consisting of annotated questions and one consisting of annotated questions with the corresponding answers. Based on these corpora, we conduct an evaluation of some of the most popular NLU services. Thereby we want to enable both, researchers and companies to make more educated decisions about which service they should use.

1   Introduction

Long before the terms *conversational interface* or *chatbot* were coined, Turing (1950) described them as the ultimate test for artificial intelligence. Despite their long history, there is a recent hype about chatbots in both, the scientific community (cf. e.g. Ferrara et al. (2016)) and industry (Gartner, 2016). While there are many related reasons for this development, we think that three key changes were particularly important:

- Rise of universal chat platforms (like Telegram, Facebook Messenger, Slack, etc.)

- Advances in machine learning (ML)

- Natural Language Understanding (NLU) as a service

In this paper, we focus on the latter. As we will show in Section 2, NLU services are already used by a number of researchers for building conversational interfaces. However, due to the lack of a systematic evaluation of theses services, the decision why one services was prefered over another, is usually not well justified. With this paper, we want to bridge this gap and enable both, researchers and companies, to make more educated decisions about which service they should use. We describe the functioning of NLU services and their role within the general architecture of chatbots. We explain, how NLU services can be evaluated and conduct an evaluation, based on two different corpora consisting of nearly 500 annotated questions, of the most popular services.

2   Related Work

Recent publications have discussed the usage of NLU services in different domains and for different purposes, e.g. question answering for localized search (McTear et al., 2016), form-driven dialogue systems (Stoyanchev et al., 2016), dialogue management (Schnelle-Walka et al., 2016), and the internet of things (Kar and Haldar, 2016).

However, none of these publications explicitly discuss, why they choose one particular NLU service over another and how this decision may have influenced the performance of their system and hence their results. Moreover, to the best of our knowledge, so far there exists no systematic evaluation of a particular NLU service, let alone a comparison of multiple services.

Dale (2015) lists five NLP cloud services and describes their capabilities, but without conducting an evaluation. In the domain of spoken dialog

Proceedings of the SIGDIAL 2017 Conference, pages 174–185,
Saarbrücken, Germany, 15-17 August 2017. ©2017 Association for Computational Linguistics

systems, similar evaluations have been conducted for automatic speech recognizer services, e.g. by Twiefel et al. (2014) and Morbini et al. (2013).

Speaking about chatbots in general, Shawar and Atwell (2007) present an approach to conduct end-to-end evaluations, however, they do not take into account the single elements of a system. Resnik and Lin (2010) provide a good overview and evaluation of Natural Language Processing (NLP) systems in general. Many of the principals they apply for their evaluation (e.g. inter-annotator agreement and partitioning of data) play an important role in our evaluation too. A comprehensive and extensive survey of question answering technologies was presented by Kolomiyets and Moens (2011). However, there has been a lot of progress since 2011, including the here presented NLU services.

One of our two corpora was labelled using Amazon Mechanical Turk (AMT, cf. Section 5.2), while there have been long discussions about whether or not AMT can replace the work of experts for labelling linguistic data, the recent consensus is that, given enough annotators, crowd-sourced labels from AMT are as reliable as expert data. (Snow et al., 2008; Munro et al., 2010; Callison-Burch, 2009)

3   Chatbot Architecture

In order to understand the role of NLU services for chatbots, one first has to look at the general architecture of chatbots. While there exist different documented chatbot architectures for concrete use cases, no universal model of how a chatbot should be designed has emerged yet. Our proposal for a universal chatbot architecture is shown in Figure 1. It consists of three main parts: Request Interpretation, Response Retrieval and Message Generation. The Message Generation follows the classical Natural Language Generation (NLG) pipeline described by Reiter and Dale (2000). In the context of Request Interpretation, a "request" is not necessarily a question, but can also be any user input like "My name is John". Equally, a "response" to this input could e.g. be "What a nice name".

4   NLU Services

The general goal of NLU services is the extraction of structured, semantic information from unstructured natural language input, e.g. chat messages. They mainly do this by attaching user-defined la-

bels to messages or parts of messages. At the time of writing, among the most popular NLU services are:

- LUIS[1]

- Watson Conversation[2]

- API.ai[3]

- wit.ai[4]

- Amazon Lex[5]

Moreover, there is a popular open source alternative which is called RASA[6]. RASA offers the same functionality, while lacking the advantages of cloud-based solutions (managed hosting, scalability, etc). On the other hand, it offers the typical advantages of self-hosted open source software (adaptability, data control, etc).

Table 1 shows a comparison of the basic functionality offered by the different services. All of them, except for Amazon Lex, share the same basic concept: Based on example data, the user can train a classifier to classify so-called intents (which represent the intent of the whole message and are not bound to a certain position within the message) and entities (which can consist of a single or multiple characters).

Service	Intents	Entities	Batch import
LUIS	+	+	+
Watson	+	+	+
API.ai	+	+	+
wit.ai	+	+	O
Lex	+	O	-
RASA	+	+	+

Table 1: Comparison basic functionality of NLU services

Figure 2 shows a labelled sentence in the LUIS web interface. The intent of this sentence was classified as FindConnection, with a confidence of 97%. The labelled entities are: (next, Criterion), (train, Vehicle), (Universität, StationStart), (Max-Weber-Platz, StationDest). Amazon Lex shares

---

[1] https://www.luis.ai
[2] https://www.ibm.com/watson/ developercloud/conversation.html
[3] https://www.api.ai
[4] https://www.wit.ai
[5] https://aws.amazon.com/lex
[6] https://www.rasa.ai

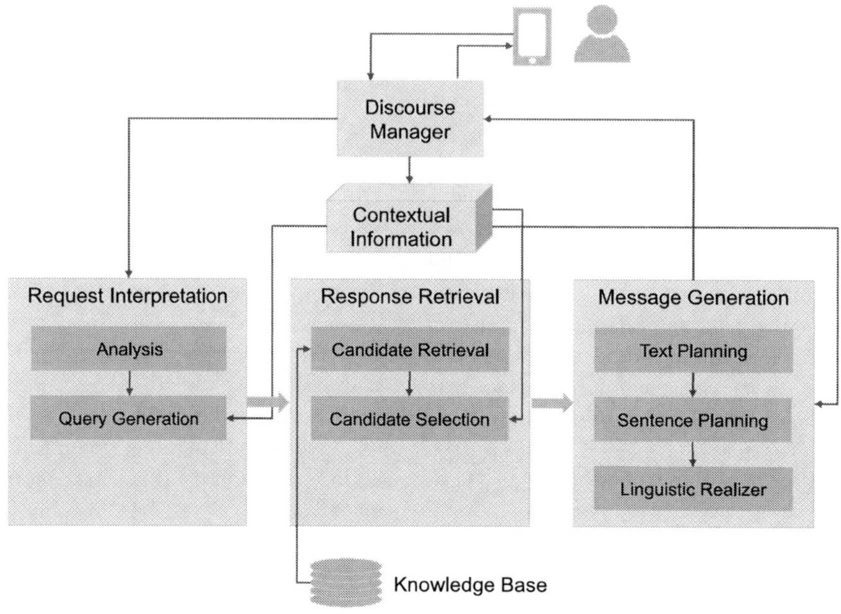

Figure 1: General Architecture for Chatbots

the concept of intents with the other services, but instead of entities, Lex is using so-called slots, which are not trained by concrete examples, but example patterns like "When is the {Criterion} {Vehicle} to {StationDest}". Moreover, all services, except for Amazon Lex, also offer an export and import functionality which uses a json-format to export and import the training data. While wit.ai offers this functionality, as of today, it only works reliably for creating backups and restoring them, but not importing new data[7].

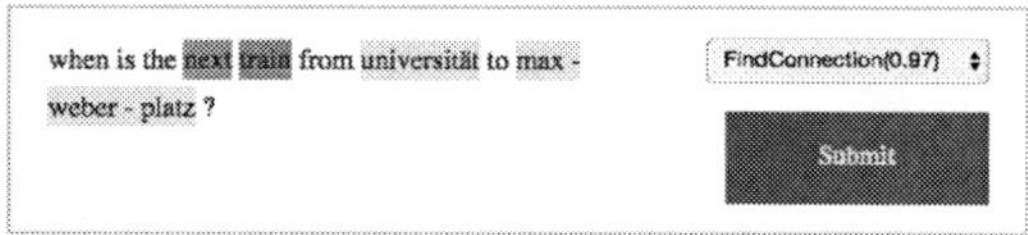

Figure 2: Labelled sentence with intent and entities in Microsoft LUIS

When it comes to the core of the services, the machine learning algorithms and the data on which they are initially trained, all services are very secretive. None of them gives specific information about the used technologies and datasets.

The exception in this case is, of course, RASA, which can either use MITIE (Geyer et al., 2016) or spaCy (Choi et al., 2015) as ML backend.

5 Data Corpus

Our evaluation is based on two very different data corpora. The Chatbot Corpus (cf. Section 5.1) is based on questions gathered by a *Telegram* chatbot in production use, answering questions about public transport connections. The StackExchange Corpus (cf. Section 5.2) is based on data from two StackExchange[8] platforms: *ask ubuntu*[9] and *Web Applications*[10]. Both corpora are available on GitHub under the Creative Commons CC BY-SA 3.0 license[11]:

```
https://github.com/sebischair/
NLU-Evaluation-Corpora.
```

5.1 Chatbot Corpus

The Chatbot Corpus consists of 206 questions, which were manually labelled by the authors. There are two different intents (Departure Time,

---

[7]cf. e.g. `https://github.com/wit-ai/wit/issues?q=is%3Aopen+is%3Aissue+label%3Aimport`

[8]`https://www.stackexchange.com`
[9]`https://www.askubuntu.com`
[10]`https://webapps.stackexchange.com`
[11]`https://creativecommons.org/licenses/by-sa/3.0/`

Find Connection) in the corpus and five different entity types (StationStart, StationDest, Criterion, Vehicle, Line). The general language of the questions was English, however, mixed with German street and station names. Example entries from the corpus can be found in Appendix A.1. For the evaluation, the corpus was split into a training dataset with 100 entries and a test dataset with 106 entries.

43% of the questions in the training dataset belong to the intent Departure Time and 57% to Find Connection. The distribution for the test dataset is 33% (Departure Time) and 67% (Find Connection). Table 2 shows how the different entity types are distributed among the two datasets. While some entity types occur very often, like Station-Start, some occur very rarely, especially Line. We do this differentiation to evaluate, if some services handle very common, or very rare, entity types better than others.

While in this corpus, there are more tagged entities in the training dataset than in the test dataset, it is the other way round in the other corpus, which will be introduced in the next section. Although one might expect that this leads to better results, the evaluation in Section 7 shows that this is not necessarily the case.

Entity Type	training	test	Σ
StationStart	91	102	193
StationDest	57	71	128
Criterion	48	34	82
Vehicle	50	35	85
Line	4	2	6
Σ	250	244	494

Table 2: Entity types within the chatbot corpus

5.2 StackExchange Corpus

For the generation of the StackExchange corpus, we used the StackExchange Data Explorer[12]. We choose the most popular questions (i.e. questions with the highest scores and most views), from the two StackExchange platforms *ask ubuntu* and *Web Applications*, because they are likely to have a better linguistic quality and a higher relevance, compared to less popular questions. Additionally, we used only questions with an accepted, i.e. correct, answer. Although we did not use the answers in

---

our evaluation, we included them in our corpus, in order to create a corpus that is not only useful for this particular evaluation, but also for research on question answering in general. In this way, we gathered 290 questions and answers in total, 100 from *Web Applications* and 190 from *ask ubuntu*.

The corpus was labelled with intents and entities using Amazon Mechanical Turk (AMT). Each question was labelled by five different workers, summing up to nearly 1,500 datapoints.

For each platform, we created a list of candidates for **intents**, which were extracted from the labels (i.e. tags) assigned to the questions by StackExchange users. For each question, the AMT workers were asked to chose one of these intents or "None", if they think no candidate is fitting.

For *ask ubuntu*, the possible intents were: "Make Update", "Setup Printer", "Shutdown Computer", and "Software Recommendation".

For *Web Applications*, the candidates were: "Change Password", "Delete Account", "Download Video", "Export Data", "Filter Spam", "Find Alternative", and "Sync Accounts".

Similarly, a set of **entity type** candidates were given. By marking parts of the questions with the mouse, workers could assign these entity types to words (or characters) within the question. For *Web Applications* the possible entity types were: "WebService", "OperatingSystem" and "Browser". For *ask ubuntu*, they were: "SoftwareName", "Printer", and "UbuntuVersion".

Moreover, workers were asked to state how confident they are in their assessment: very confident, somewhat confident, undecided, somewhat unconfident, or very unconfident.

For the generation of the annotated, final corpus, only submissions with a confidence level of "undecided" or higher were taken into account. A label, no matter if intent or entity, was only added to the corpus if the inter-annotator agreement among those confident annotators was 60% or higher. If no intent could be found for a question, satisfying these criteria, this question was not added to the corpus. The final corpus was also checked for false positives by two experts, but non were found. Therefore the final corpus consists of 251 entries, 162 from *ask ubuntu* and 89 from *Web Applications*. Example entries from the corpus are shown in Appendix A.2.

For the evaluation, we also split this corpus.

Four datasets were separated, one for training and one for testing, for each platform. The distribution of intents among these datasets is shown in Table 3, the distribution of entity types is shown in Table 4. Again, we do this differentiation to compare the classification results for frequently and rarely occurring intents and entity types.

Intent	training	test	Σ
ChangePassword	2	6	8
DeleteAccount	7	10	17
DownloadVideo	1	0	1
ExportData	2	3	5
FilterSpam	6	14	20
FindAlternative	7	16	23
SyncAccounts	3	6	9
None	2	4	6
Σ	30	54	84

(a) *Web Applications* datasets

Intent	training	test	Σ
MakeUpdate	10	37	47
SetupPrinter	10	13	23
ShutdownComputer	13	14	27
S.Recommendation	17	40	57
None	3	5	8
Σ	53	109	162

(b) *ask ubuntu* datasets

Table 3: Intents within StackExchange corpus

dataset	Entity Type	training	test	Σ
web apps	WebService	33	64	97
	OS	1	0	1
	Browser	1	0	1
	Σ	35	64	99
ubuntu	Printer	8	12	20
	Software	3	4	7
	Version	24	78	102
	Σ	35	94	129

Table 4: Entity types within the StackExchange corpus

6 Experimental Design

In order to compare the performance of the different NLU services, we used the corpora described in Section 5. We used the respective training datasets to train the NLU services LUIS, Watson Conversation, API.ai, and RASA. Amazon Lex was not included in this comparison because, as mentioned in Section 4, it does not offer a batch import functionality, which is crucial in order to effectively train all services with the exact same data. For the same reason, wit.ai was also excluded from the experiment. While it does offer an import option, currently, it only works reliable for data which was created through the wit.ai webinterface and not altered, or even created, manually.

Afterwards, the test datasets were sent to the NLU services and the labels created by the services were compared against our human created gold standard. For training, we used the batch import interfaces, offered by all compared services, in this way it was not only possible to train all different services relatively fast, despite many hundred individual labels, it also guaranteed, that all services are fed with exactly the same data. Since the data format differs from service to service, we used a Python script to automatically convert the training datasets from the format shown in the Appendix to the respective data format of the services. For retrieving the results for the test datasets from the NLU services, their respective REST-APIs were used.

In order to evaluate the results, we calculated true positives, false positives, and false negatives, based on exact matches. Based on this data, we computed precision and recall as well as F-score for single intents, entity types, and corpora, as well as overall results. We will say one service is better than another if it has a higher F-score.

6.1 Hypotheses

Before the conduction of the experiment, we had three main hypotheses:

1. **The performance varies between services**: Although it might sound obvious, it is worth mentioning that one of the reasons for this evaluation is the fact that we think, there is a difference between the compared NLU services. Despite their very similar concepts and "look and feel", we expect differences when it comes to annotation quality (i.e. F-scores), which should be taken into account when deciding for one or another service.

2. **The commercial products will (overall) perform better**:

The initial language model of RASA, which comes with MITIE, is about 300 MB of data. The commercial services, on the other hand, are fed with data by hundreds, if not thousands, of users every day. We, therefore, assume, that the commercial products will perform better in the evaluation, especially when the training data is sparse.

3. **The quality of the labels is influenced by the domain**:
   We assume that, depending on the used algorithms and models, individual services will perform differently in different domains. Therefore, we think it is not unlikely that a service which performs well on the more technical corpus from StackExchange will perform considerably worse on the chatbot corpus, which has a focus on spatial and time data, and vice versa.

6.2 Limitations

One important limitation of this evaluation is the fact that the results will not be representative for other domains. On the opposite, as already mentioned in Hypothesis 3, we do believe that there are important differences in performance between different domains. Therefore our final conclusion can not be that one service is absolutely better than the others, but rather that on the given corpus, one service performed better than the others. However, we believe that the here presented approach will help developers to conduct evaluations of NLU services for their domain and thus empower them to make better-informed decisions.

With regard to the used corpora, we made an effort to make them as naturally as possible by using only real data from real users. However, when analysing the results, one should keep in mind that the Chatbot Corpus consists of questions which were asked by users, which were aware of communicating with a chatbot. It is, therefore, conceivable that they formulated their questions in a way which they expect to be more understandable for a chatbot.

Finally, NLU services, like all other services, can change over time (and hopefully improve). While it is easy to track these changes for locally installed software, changes on cloud-based services may happen without any notice to the user. Conducting the very same experiment, described in this paper, in six months time, might, therefore,

lead to different results. This evaluation can therefore only be a snapshot of the current state of the compared services. While this might decrease the reproducibility of our experiment, it is also a good argument for a formalized, repeatable evaluation process, as we describe it in this paper.

7 Evaluation

The detailed results of the evaluation, broken down on single intents, entity types, corpora, and overall, are shown in Table 5 to 8. Each table shows the result from a different NLU service. Within the tables, each row represents one particular entity type or intent.

For each row, the corpus, type (intent/entity), and true positives, false negatives, and false positives are given. From these values, precision, recall, and F-score have been calculated. The entity types and intents are also sorted by the corpus they appear in. For each corpus, there is a summary row, which shows precision, recall, and F-score for the whole corpus. At the bottom of each table, there is also an overall summary.

From a high-level perspective, LUIS performed best with an F-score of 0.916, followed by RASA (0.821), Watson Conversation (0.752), and API.ai (0.687). LUIS also performed best on each individual dataset: chatbot, web apps, and ask ubuntu. Similarly, API.ai performed worst on every dataset, while the second place changes between RASA and Watson Conversation (cf. Figure 3).

Based on this data, the second hypothesis can be rejected. Although the best performance was indeed shown by a commercial product, RASA easily competes with the other commercial products.

The first hypothesis is supported by our findings. We can see a difference between the services, with the F-score of LUIS being nearly 0.3 higher than the F-score of API.ai. However, a conducted two-way ANOVA analysis with the F-score as dependent variable and the NLU service and the entity type/intent as fixed factors does not show a significance at the level of $p < 0.05$ ($p = 0.234, df = 3$). An even larger corpus might be necessary to get quantitatively more robust results.

With regard to the third hypothesis, the picture is less clear. Although we can see a clear influence of the domain on the F-score within each service, the ranking between different services is not

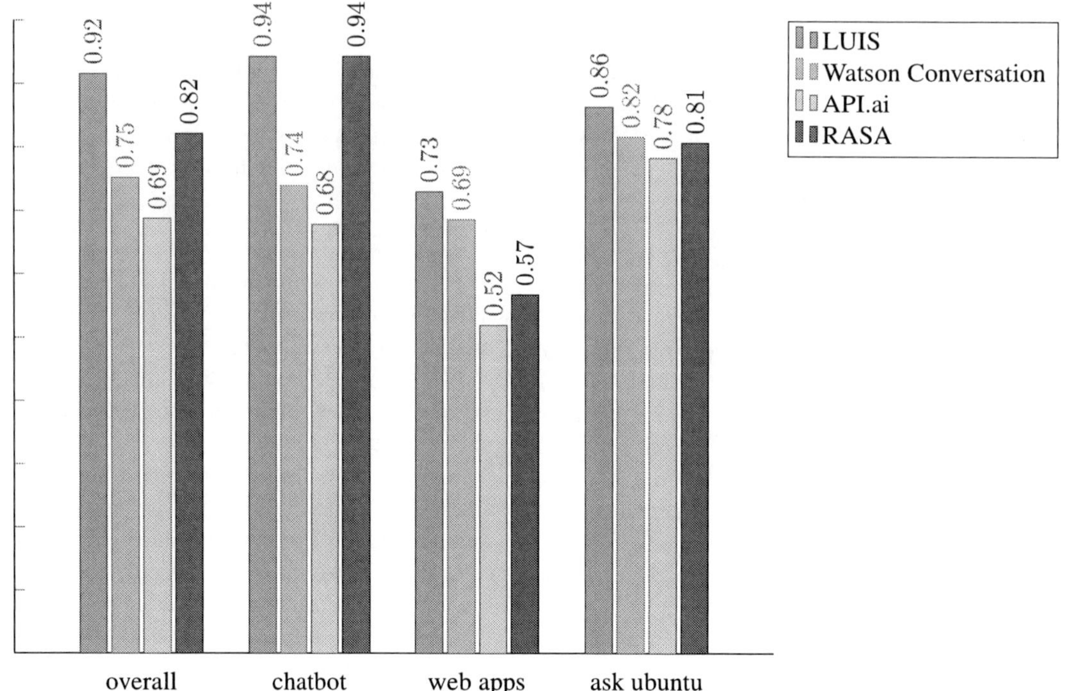

Figure 3: F-scores for the different NLU services, grouped by corpus

much influenced. LUIS always performs best, independent from the domain, API.ai always worst, also independent from the domain, merely the second and third place changes. Therefore, although the domain influences the results, it is not clear whether or not it should also influence the decision which service should be used.

On a more detailed level, we also see differences between entities and intents. Especially API.ai seems to have big troubles identifying entities. On the web apps corpus, for example, API.ai did not identify a single occurrence of the entity type WebService, which occurred 64 times in the dataset. If we calculate the F-score for this dataset only based on the intents, it would increase from 0.519 to 0.803. The overall results of API.ai were therefore heavily influenced by its shortcomings regarding entity detection.

If we look at intents and entity types with sparse training data, like Line, ChangePassword, and ExportData, other than we expected, we do not see a significantly better performance of commercial services.

8 Conclusion

The evaluation of the NLU services LUIS, Watson Conversation, API.ai, and RASA, based on the two corpora we presented in Section 5, has shown that the quality of the annotations differs between the different services. Before using an NLU service, no matter if for commercial or scientific purposes, one should therefore compare the different services with domain specific data.

For our two corpora, LUIS showed the best results, however, the open source alternative RASA could achieve similar results. Given the advantages of open source solutions (mainly adaptability), it might well be possible to achieve an even better results with RASA, after some customization.

With regard to absolute numbers, it is difficult to decide whether an F-score of 0.916 or 0.821 is satisfactory for productive use within a conversational question answering system. This decision also depends strongly on the concrete use case. We, therefore, focused on relative comparisons in our evaluation and leave this decision to future users.

corpus	entity type / intent	type	true +	false -	false +	precision	recall	F-score
chatbot	DepartureTime	Intent	34	1	1	0.971	0.971	0.971
	FindConnection	Intent	70	1	1	0.986	0.986	0.986
	Criterion	Entity	34	0	0	1	1	1
	Line	Entity	0	2	0		0	
	StationDest	Entity	65	6	3	0.956	0.915	0.935
	StationStart	Entity	90	17	5	0.947	0.841	0.891
	Vehicle	Entity	33	2	0	1	0.943	0.971
	Σ		326	29	10	0.970	0.918	0.943
web apps	ChangePassword	Intent	3	3	0	1	0.5	0.667
	DeleteAccount	Intent	8	2	0	1	0.8	0.889
	DownloadVideo	Intent	0	0	0			
	ExportData	Intent	3	0	1	0.75	1	0.857
	FilterSpam	Intent	12	2	0	1	0.857	0.923
	FindAlternative	Intent	14	2	2	0.875	0.875	0.875
	None	Intent	3	1	8	0.273	0.75	0.4
	SyncAccounts	Intent	5	1	0	1	0.833	0.909
	WebService	Entity	29	30	5	0.853	0.492	0.624
	Σ		77	41	16	0.828	0.653	0.73
ask ubuntu	MakeUpdate	Intent	36	1	4	0.900	0.973	0.935
	SetupPrinter	Intent	12	1	2	0.857	0.923	0.889
	ShutdownComputer	Intent	14	0	0	1	1	1
	SRecommendation	Intent	36	4	5	0.878	0.9	0.889
	None	Intent	0	5	0		0	
	SoftwareName	Entity	0	4	0		0	
	Printer	Entity	5	7	0	1	0.417	0.589
	UbuntuVersion	Entity	67	10	11	0.859	0.87	0.864
	Σ		170	32	22	0.885	0.842	0.863
overall			820	102	48	0.945	0.889	0.916

Table 5: Results LUIS

corpus	entity type / intent	type	true +	false -	false +	precision	recall	F-score
chatbot	DepartureTime	Intent	33	2	1	0.971	0.943	0.957
	FindConnection	Intent	70	1	2	0.972	0.986	0.979
	Criterion	Entity	34	0	0	1	1	1
	Line	Entity	1	1	0	1	0.5	0.667
	StationDest	Entity	42	29	75	0.359	0.592	0.447
	StationStart	Entity	65	37	50	0.565	0.637	0.599
	Vehicle	Entity	35	0	0	1	1	1
	Σ		280	70	128	0.686	0.8	0.739
web apps	ChangePassword	Intent	5	1	0	1	0.833	0.909
	DeleteAccount	Intent	9	1	3	0.750	0.9	0.818
	DownloadVideo	Intent	0	0	1	0		
	ExportData	Intent	2	1	2	0.500	0.667	0.572
	FilterSpam	Intent	13	1	2	0.867	0.929	0.897
	FindAlternative	Intent	15	1	1	0.938	0.938	0.938
	None	Intent	0	4	1	0	0	
	SyncAccounts	Intent	5	1	0	1	0.833	0.909
	WebService	Entity	23	41	5	0.821	0.359	0.5
	Σ		72	51	15	0.828	0.585	0.686
ask ubuntu	MakeUpdate	Intent	37	0	4	0.902	1	0.948
	SetupPrinter	Intent	13	0	1	0.929	1	0.963
	ShutdownComputer	Intent	14	0	0	1	1	1
	SRecommendation	Intent	35	5	3	0.921	0.875	0.897
	None	Intent	1	4	1	0.500	0.2	0.286
	SoftwareName	Entity	0	4	0		0	
	Printer	Entity	0	12	0		0	
	UbuntuVersion	Entity	51	7	27	0.654	0.879	0.75
	Σ		151	32	36	0.807	0.825	0.816
overall			503	153	179	0.738	0.767	0.752

Table 6: Results Watson Conversation

corpus	entity type / intent	type	true +	false -	false +	precision	recall	F-score
chatbot	DepartureTime	Intent	35	0	4	0.897	1	0.946
	FindConnection	Intent	60	11	0	1	0.845	0.916
	Criterion	Entity	31	3	0	1	0.912	0.954
	Line	Entity	1	1	0	1	0.5	0.667
	StationDest	Entity	0	71	0		0	
	StationStart	Entity	28	79	4	0.875	0.262	0.403
	Vehicle	Entity	34	1	5	0.872	0.971	0.919
	Σ		189	166	13	0.936	0.532	0.678
web apps	ChangePassword	Intent	4	2	1	0.800	0.667	0.727
	DeleteAccount	Intent	10	0	2	0.833	1	0.909
	DownloadVideo	Intent	0	0	0			
	ExportData	Intent	1	2	2	0.333	0.333	0.333
	FilterSpam	Intent	10	4	3	0.769	0.714	0.74
	FindAlternative	Intent	16	0	2	0.889	1	0.941
	None	Intent	2	2	1	0.667	0.5	0.572
	SyncAccounts	Intent	4	2	0	1	0.667	0.8
	WebService	Entity	0	64	0		0	
	Σ		47	76	11	0.810	0.382	0.519
ask ubuntu	MakeUpdate	Intent	36	1	3	0.923	0.973	0.947
	SetupPrinter	Intent	13	0	1	0.929	1	0.963
	ShutdownComputer	Intent	14	0	2	0.875	1	0.933
	SRecommendation	Intent	28	12	2	0.933	0.7	0.8
	None	Intent	2	3	8	0.200	0.4	0.267
	SoftwareName	Entity	0	4	0		0	
	Printer	Entity	0	12	0		0	
	UbuntuVersion	Entity	48	30	0	1	0.615	0.762
	Σ		141	46	32	0.815	0.754	0.783
overall			377	288	56	0.871	0.567	0.687

Table 7: Results API.ai

corpus	entity type / intent	type	true +	false -	false +	precision	recall	F-score
chatbot	DepartureTime	Intent	34	1	1	0.971	0.971	0.971
	FindConnection	Intent	70	1	1	0.986	0.986	0.986
	Criterion	Entity	34	0	0	1	1	1
	Line	Entity	0	2	0		0	
	StationDest	Entity	65	6	3	0.956	0.915	0.935
	StationStart	Entity	90	17	5	0.947	0.841	0.891
	Vehicle	Entity	33	2	0	1	0.943	0.971
	Σ		326	29	10	0.970	0.918	0.943
web apps	ChangePassword	Intent	4	2	0	1	0.667	0.8
	DeleteAccount	Intent	9	1	5	0.643	0.9	0.75
	DownloadVideo	Intent	0	0	1	0		
	ExportData	Intent	0	3	0		0	
	FilterSpam	Intent	13	1	0	1	0.929	0.963
	FindAlternative	Intent	15	1	8	0.652	0.938	0.769
	None	Intent	0	4	1	0	0	
	SyncAccounts	Intent	3	3	0	1	0.5	0.667
	WebService	Entity	45	19	87	0.341	0.703	0.459
	Σ		89	34	102	0.466	0.724	0.567
ask ubuntu	MakeUpdate	Intent	34	3	2	0.944	0.919	0.931
	SetupPrinter	Intent	13	0	2	0.867	1	0.929
	ShutdownComputer	Intent	14	0	6	0.700	1	0.824
	SRecommendation	Intent	33	7	4	0.892	0.825	0.857
	None	Intent	0	5	1	0	0	
	SoftwareName	Entity	0	4	11	0	0	
	Printer	Entity	8	4	11	0.421	0.667	0.516
	UbuntuVersion	Entity	65	13	7	0.903	0.833	0.867
	Σ		167	36	44	0.791	0.823	0.807
overall			582	99	156	0.789	0.855	0.821

Table 8: Results RASA

References

Chris Callison-Burch. 2009. Fast, cheap, and creative: evaluating translation quality using amazon's mechanical turk. In *Proceedings of the 2009 Conference on Empirical Methods in Natural Language Processing: Volume 1-Volume 1*. Association for Computational Linguistics, pages 286–295.

Jinho D. Choi, Joel R. Tetreault, and Amanda Stent. 2015. It depends: Dependency parser comparison using A web-based evaluation tool. In *Proceedings of the 53rd Annual Meeting of the Association for Computational Linguistics and the 7th International Joint Conference on Natural Language Processing of the Asian Federation of Natural Language Processing, ACL 2015, July 26-31, 2015, Beijing, China, Volume 1: Long Papers*. pages 387–396. http://aclweb.org/anthology/P/P15/P15-1038.pdf.

Robert Dale. 2015. Nlp meets the cloud. *Natural Language Engineering* 21(4):653–659. https://doi.org/10.1017/S1351324915000200.

Emilio Ferrara, Onur Varol, Clayton Davis, Filippo Menczer, and Alessandro Flammini. 2016. The rise of social bots. *Communications of the ACM* 59(7):96–104.

Gartner. 2016. Hype cycle for emerging technologies, 2016. Technical report. http://www.gartner.com/document/3383817.

Kelly Geyer, Kara Greenfield, Alyssa Mensch, and Olga Simek. 2016. Named entity recognition in 140 characters or less. In *6th Workshop on Making Sense of Microposts (#Microposts2016)*. pages 78–79.

Rohan Kar and Rishin Haldar. 2016. Applying chatbots to the internet of things: Opportunities and architectural elements. *arXiv preprint arXiv:1611.03799* .

Oleksandr Kolomiyets and Marie-Francine Moens. 2011. A survey on question answering technology from an information retrieval perspective. *Inf. Sci.* 181(24):5412–5434. https://doi.org/10.1016/j.ins.2011.07.047.

Michael McTear, Zoraida Callejas, and David Griol. 2016. *The Conversational Interface: Talking to Smart Devices*, Springer International Publishing, Cham, chapter Implementing Spoken Language Understanding, pages 187–208.

Fabrizio Morbini, Kartik Audhkhasi, Kenji Sagae, Ron Artstein, Dogan Can, Panayiotis Georgiou, Shri Narayanan, Anton Leuski, and David Traum. 2013. Which asr should i choose for my dialogue system. In *Proceedings of the 14th annual SIGdial Meeting on Discourse and Dialogue*. pages 394–403.

Robert Munro, Steven Bethard, Victor Kuperman, Vicky Tzuyin Lai, Robin Melnick, Christopher Potts, Tyler Schnoebelen, and Harry Tily. 2010. Crowdsourcing and language studies: the new generation of linguistic data. In *Proceedings of the NAACL HLT 2010 workshop on creating speech and language data with Amazon's Mechanical Turk*. Association for Computational Linguistics, pages 122–130.

Ehud Reiter and Robert Dale. 2000. *Building Natural Language Generation Systems*. Studies in Natural Language Processing. Cambridge University Press.

Philip Resnik and Jimmy Lin. 2010. Evaluation of nlp systems. *The handbook of computational linguistics and natural language processing* 57.

Dirk Schnelle-Walka, Stefan Radomski, Benjamin Milde, Chris Biemann, and Max Mühlhäuser. 2016. Nlu vs. dialog management: To whom am i speaking? In *Joint Workshop on Smart Connected and Wearable Things (SCWT'2016), co-located with IUI*. https://doi.org/10.13140/RG.2.1.1928.4247.

Bayan Abu Shawar and Eric Atwell. 2007. Different measurements metrics to evaluate a chatbot system. In *Proceedings of the Workshop on Bridging the Gap: Academic and Industrial Research in Dialog Technologies*. Association for Computational Linguistics, Stroudsburg, PA, USA, NAACL-HLT-Dialog '07, pages 89–96. http://dl.acm.org/citation.cfm?id=1556328.1556341.

Rion Snow, Brendan O'Connor, Daniel Jurafsky, and Andrew Y. Ng. 2008. Cheap and fast—but is it good?: Evaluating non-expert annotations for natural language tasks. In *Proceedings of the Conference on Empirical Methods in Natural Language Processing*. Association for Computational Linguistics, Stroudsburg, PA, USA, EMNLP '08, pages 254–263. http://dl.acm.org/citation.cfm?id=1613715.1613751.

Svetlana Stoyanchev, Pierre Lison, and Srinivas Bangalore. 2016. Rapid prototyping of form-driven dialogue systems using an open-source framework. In *Proceedings of the 17th Annual Meeting of the Special Interest Group on Discourse and Dialogue*. Association for Computational Linguistics, Los Angeles, pages 216–219. http://www.aclweb.org/anthology/W16-3626.

Alan M Turing. 1950. Computing machinery and intelligence. *Mind* 59(236):433–460.

Johannes Twiefel, Timo Baumann, Stefan Heinrich, and Stefan Wermter. 2014. Improving domain-independent cloud-based speech recognition with domain-dependent phonetic post-processing. In *AAAI*. pages 1529–1536.

A Supplemental Material

A.1 Examples Chatbot Corpus

```
{
  "text": "what is the cheapest
    ↪ connection between
    ↪ quiddestraße and
    ↪ hauptbahnhof?",
  "intent": "FindConnection",
  "entities": [
    {
      "entity": "Criterion",
      "start": 3,
      "stop": 3
    },
    {
      "entity": "StationStart",
      "start": 6,
      "stop": 6
    },
    {
      "entity": "StationDest",
      "start": 8,
      "stop": 8
    }
  ]
},
{
  "text": "when is the next u6
    ↪ leaving from garching?",
  "intent": "DepartureTime",
  "entities": [
    {
      "entity": "Line",
      "start": 4,
      "stop": 4
    },
    {
      "entity": "StationStart",
      "start": 7,
      "stop": 7
    }
  ]
}
```

A.2 Examples StackExchange Corpus

A.2.1 Web Applications Dataset

```
{
  "text": "How can I delete my
    ↪ Twitter account?",
  "url": "http://
    ↪ webapps.stackexchange.com
    ↪ /questions/57/how-can-i-
    ↪ delete-my-twitter-account
    ↪ ",
  "author": "Jared Harley",
  "answer": {
    "text": "[...]",
    "author": "Ken Pespisa"
  },
  "intent": "Delete Account",
  "entities": [
    {
      "text": "Twitter",
      "stop": 5,
      "start": 5,
      "entity": "WebService"
    }
  ]
},
{
  "text": "Is it possible to
    ↪ export my data from
    ↪ Trello to back it up?",
  "url": "http://
    ↪ webapps.stackexchange.com
    ↪ /questions/18975/is-it-
    ↪ possible-to-export-my-
    ↪ data-from-trello-to-back-
    ↪ it-up",
  "author": "Clare Macrae",
  "answer": {
    "text": "[...]",
    "author": "Daniel LeCheminant
      ↪ "
  },
  "intent": "Export Data",
  "entities": [
    {
      "text": "Trello",
      "stop": 8,
      "start": 8,
      "entity": "WebService"
    }
  ]
}
```

A.2.2 Ask Ubuntu Dataset

```
{
  "text": "How do I install the
    ↪ HP F4280 printer?",
  "url": "http://askubuntu.com/
```

```json
        ↪ questions/24073/how-do-i-
        ↪ install-the-hp-f4280-
        ↪ printer",
    "author": "ok comp",
    "answer": {
      "text": "[...]",
      "author": "nejode"
    },
    "intent": "Setup Printer",
    "entities": [
      {
        "text": "HP F4280",
        "stop": 6,
        "start": 5,
        "entity": "Printer"
      }
    ]
  },
  {
    "text": "What is a good MongoDB
        ↪ GUI client?",
    "url": "http://askubuntu.com/
        ↪ questions/196136/what-is-
        ↪ a-good-mongodb-gui-client
        ↪ ",
    "author": "Eyal",
    "answer": {
      "text": "[...]",
      "author": "Eyal"
    },
    "intent": "Software
        ↪ Recommendation",
    "entities": [
      {
        "text": "MongoDB",
        "stop": 4,
        "start": 4,
        "entity": "SoftwareName"
      }
    ]
  }
```

The Role of Conversation Context for Sarcasm Detection in Online Interactions

Debanjan Ghosh[§] Alexander Richard Fabbri[†] Smaranda Muresan[‡]
[§]School of Communication Information, Rutgers University, NJ, USA
[†]Department of Computer Science, Columbia University, NY, USA
[‡]Data Science Institute, Columbia University, NY, USA
`debanjan.ghosh@rutgers.edu, {arf2145,smara@columbia.edu}`

Abstract

Computational models for sarcasm detection have often relied on the content of utterances in isolation. However, speaker's sarcastic intent is not always obvious without additional context. Focusing on social media discussions, we investigate two issues: (1) does modeling of conversation context help in sarcasm detection and (2) can we understand what part of conversation context triggered the sarcastic reply. To address the first issue, we investigate several types of Long Short-Term Memory (LSTM) networks that can model both the conversation context and the sarcastic response.[1] We show that the conditional LSTM network (Rocktäschel et al., 2015) and LSTM networks with sentence level attention on context and response outperform the LSTM model that reads only the response. To address the second issue, we present a qualitative analysis of attention weights produced by the LSTM models with attention and discuss the results compared with human performance on the task.

1 Introduction

It has been argued that sarcasm, or verbal irony, is a type of interactional phenomenon with specific perlocutionary effects on the hearer (Haverkate, 1990), such as to break their pattern of expectation. Thus, to be able to detect speakers' sarcastic intent it is necessary (even if maybe not sufficient) to consider their utterances in the larger conversation context. Consider the Twitter conversation example in Table 1. Without the context of UserA's

Platform	Context-Reply pair
Twiter	**userA:** plane window shades are open . . . so that people can see if there is fire. **userB**: @UserA one more reason to feel really great.
Discussion Forum	**userC:** see for yourselves. The fact remains that in the caribbean, poverty and crime was near nil. Everyone was self-sufficient and contented with the standard of life. there were no huge social gaps. **userD:** Are you kidding me?! You think that Caribbean countries are "content?!" Maybe you should wander off the beach sometime and see for yourself.

Table 1: Sample Context/Reply pairs from two social media platforms

statement, the sarcastic intent of UserB's response might not be detected.

Most computational models for sarcasm detection have considered utterances in isolation (Davidov et al., 2010; González-Ibáñez et al., 2011; Liebrecht et al., 2013; Riloff et al., 2013; Maynard and Greenwood, 2014; Joshi et al., 2015; Ghosh et al., 2015; Joshi et al., 2016; Ghosh and Veale, 2016). In many instances, even humans have difficulty in recognizing sarcastic intent when considering an utterance in isolation (Wallace et al., 2014).

In this paper, we investigate the role of *conversation context* in detecting sarcasm in social media discussions (Twitter conversations and discussion forums). Table 1 shows some examples of sarcastic replies taken from two media platforms (userB

---

[1]We use response and reply interchangeably.

186

Proceedings of the SIGDIAL 2017 Conference, pages 186–196,
Saarbrücken, Germany, 15-17 August 2017. ©2017 Association for Computational Linguistics

and userD's posts, respectively) and a minimum unit of conversation context given by the prior turn (userA and userC's posts, respectively).

We address two specific issues: (1) does modeling of conversation context help in sarcasm detection and (2) can we understand what part of conversation context triggered the sarcastic reply (e.g., which sentence(s) from userC's comment triggered userD's sarcastic reply). To address the first issue, we investigate both SVM models with linguistically-motivated discrete features and several types of Long Short-Term Memory (LSTM) networks (Hochreiter and Schmidhuber, 1997) that can model both the context and the sarcastic reply (Section 3). We show that the conditional LSTM network (Rocktäschel et al., 2015) and LSTM networks with sentence level attention on context and reply outperform the LSTM model that reads only the reply (Section 4). To address the second issue, we present a qualitative analysis of attention weights produced by the LSTM models with attention, and discuss the results compared with human performance on the task (Section 4.1). We make all datasets and code available.[2]

2 Data

One goal of our investigation is to comparatively study two types of social media platforms that have been considered individually for sarcasm detection: discussion forums and Twitter. We first discuss the two datasets and then point out some differences between them that could impact results and modeling choices.

Discussion Forums. Oraby et al. (2016) have introduced the Sarcasm Corpus V2, a subset of the Internet Argument Corpus that consists of discussion forum data. This corpus consists of sarcastic responses and their context (quotes to which the posts are replies to). The annotation of sarcastic vs. non-sarcastic replies was done using crowdsourcing, where annotators were asked to label a reply as sarcastic if any part of the reply contained sarcasm (thus annotation is done at the reply/comment level and not sentence level). The final gold sarcastic label was assigned only if a majority of the annotators labeled the reply as sarcastic. Although the dataset described by Oraby et al. (2016) consists of 9,400 post, only

50% (4,692 altogether; balanced between sarcastic and non-sarcastic categories) of that corpus is currently available for research.[3]

An example from this dataset is given in Table 1, where userD's reply has been labeled as sarcastic by annotators, in the context of userC's post/comment.

Twitter: To collect sarcastic and non-sarcastic tweets, we adopt the methodology proposed in related work (González-Ibáñez et al., 2011; Riloff et al., 2013; Bamman and Smith, 2015; Muresan et al., 2016). The sarcastic tweets were collected using hashtags such as, *#sarcasm, #sarcastic, #irony*, while the non-sarcastic tweets were the ones that do not contain these hashtags, but they might contain sentiment hashtags such as *#happy, #love, #sad, #hate*. We exclude the retweets, duplicates, quotes, tweets that contain only hashtags and URLs or are shorter than three words. Also, we eliminate all tweets where the hashtags of interest were not positioned at the very end of the message. Thus, we removed utterances such as "#sarcasm is something that I love". To built the conversation context, for each sarcastic and non-sarcastic utterance we used the "reply to status" parameter in the tweet to determine whether it was in reply to a previous tweet: if so, we downloaded the last tweet (i.e., "local conversation context") to which the original tweet was replying to (Bamman and Smith, 2015). In addition, we also collected the entire threaded conversation when available (Wang et al., 2015). Although we have collected over 200K tweets in the first step, around 13% of them were a reply to another tweet and thus our final Twitter conversations set contains 25,991 instances (12,215 instances for sarcastic class and 13,776 instances for the non-sarcastic class). We observe that 30% of the tweets have more than one tweet in the conversation context.

There are two main differences between these two datasets that need to be acknowledged. First, discussion forum posts are much longer than Twitter messages. Second, the way the gold labels for the sarcastic class are obtained is different. In the discussion forum dataset the gold label is obtained via crowdsourcing, thus the gold label emphasizes whether the sarcastic intent is *perceived* by hearers (we do not know if the speaker intended to be sarcastic or not). In Twitter dataset the gold label

---

[2]https://github.com/debanjanghosh/sarcasm_context

[3]This reduction in the training size will have obvious effects in the classification performance.

is given directly by the #hashtag the speaker used, signaling clearly the speaker's sarcastic intent. A third difference should be made: the size of the forum dataset is much smaller than the size of the Twitter dataset.

3 Computational Models and Experimental Setup

To assess the effect of conversation context (c) on labeling a reply (r) as sarcastic or not sarcastic, we consider two binary classification tasks. We refer to sarcastic instances as S and non-sarcastic instances as NS. In the first task, classification is performed using the reply in isolation (S^r vs. NS^r task). In the second, the classification considers both the reply and its context (S^{c+r} vs. NS^{c+r} task). We experiment with two types of computational models: Support Vector Machines (SVM) with linguistically-motivated discrete features (used as baseline; SVM_{bl}), and approaches using distributed representations. For the latter we use the Long short-term Memory (LSTM) Networks (Hochreiter and Schmidhuber, 1997) that have been shown to be successful in various NLP tasks, such as constituency parsing (Vinyals et al., 2015), language modeling (Zaremba et al., 2014), machine translation (Sutskever et al., 2014) and textual entailment (Bowman et al., 2015; Rocktäschel et al., 2015; Parikh et al., 2016). We present these models in the next subsections.

3.1 SVM with discrete features (SVM_{bl})

For features, we used n-grams, lexicon-based features, and sarcasm indicators that are commonly used in the existing sarcasm detection approaches (Tchokni et al., 2014; González-Ibáñez et al., 2011; Riloff et al., 2013; Joshi et al., 2015; Ghosh et al., 2015; Muresan et al., 2016). Below is a short description of the features.

- **BoW:** Features are derived from unigram, bigram, and trigram representation of words.

- **Sentiment and Pragmatic features:** We use the Linguistic Inquiry and Word Count (LIWC) lexicon (Pennebaker et al., 2001) to identify the pragmatic features. Each category in this dictionary is treated as a separate feature and we define a Boolean feature that indicates if a context or a reply contains a LIWC category. Two sentiment lexicons are also used to model the utterance sentiment:

"MPQA" (Wilson et al., 2005) and "Opinion Lexicon" (Hu and Liu, 2004). To capture sentiment, we count the number of positive and negative sentiment tokens, negations, and use a boolean feature that represents whether a reply contains both positive and negative sentiment tokens. For the S^{c+r} vs. NS^{c+r} classification task, we check whether the reply r has a different sentiment than the context c (similar to Joshi et al. (2015)). Given that sarcastic utterances often contain a positive sentiment towards a negative situation, we hypothesize that this feature will capture this type of sentiment incongruity.

- **Sarcasm Indicators:** Burgers et al. (2012) introduce a set of sarcasm indicators that explicitly signal if an utterance is sarcastic. We use *morpho-syntactic* features such as interjections (e.g., "uh", "oh", "yeah"), tag questions (e.g., "is not it?", "don't they"), exclamation marks (e.g., "!", "?"); *typographic* features such as capitalization of words, quotation marks, emoticons; *tropes* such as superlative and intensifiers words (e.g., "greatest", "best", "really") that often occur in sarcastic utterances (Camp, 2012).

When building the features, we lowercased the utterances, except the words where all the characters are uppercased (i.e., we did not lowercased "GREAT", "SO", and "WONDERFUL" in "GREAT i'm SO happy; shattered phone on this WONDERFUL day!!!"). Tokenization is conducted via CMU's Tweeboparser (Gimpel et al., 2011). For the discussion forum dataset we use the NLTK tool (Bird et al., 2009) for sentence boundary detection and tokenization. We used libSVM toolkit with Linear Kernel (Chang and Lin, 2011) with weights inversely proportional to the number of instances in each class.

3.2 Long Short-Term Memory Networks

LSTMs are a type of recurrent neural networks (RNNs) able to learn long-term dependencies (Hochreiter and Schmidhuber, 1997). Recently, LSTMs have been shown to be effective in Natural Language Inference (NLI) research, where the task is to establish the *relationship* between multiple inputs (i.e., a pair of premise and hypothesis as in the case of Recognizing Textual Entailment task (Bowman et al., 2015; Rocktäschel et al., 2015;

Parikh et al., 2016)). Since our goal is to explore the role of contextual information (our *first input*) for recognizing whether the reply (our *second input*) is sarcastic or not, we argue that using LSTM networks that read the context and reply are a natural modeling choice.

Attention-based LSTM Networks: Attentive neural networks have been shown to perform well on a variety of NLP tasks (Yang et al., 2016; Yin et al., 2015; Xu et al., 2015). Using attention-based LSTM will accomplish two goals: (1) test whether they achieve higher performance than simple LSTM models and (2) use the attention weights produced by the LSTM models to perform a qualitative analysis to determine which portions of context triggers the sarcastic reply.

Although Yang et al. (2016) have included two levels of attention mechanisms – one at the word level and another at the sentence level – we primarily focus on sentence level attention for two specific reasons. First, sentence level attentions can show the exact sentence in the context that is most informative to trigger sarcasm. In the discussion forum dataset, context posts are usually three or four sentences long and it could be helpful to identify the exact text that triggers the sarcastic reply. Second, attention over both the words and sentences seek to learn a large number of model parameters and given the moderate size of the discussion forum corpus they might overfit. For tweets, we treat each individual tweet as a sentence. The majority of tweets consist of a single sentence and even if there are multiple sentences in a tweet, often one sentence contains only hashtags, URLs, and emoticons making them uninformative if treated in isolation.

Figure 1 shows the high-level structure of the model. The context (left) is read by an LSTM ($LSTM_c$) whereas the response (right) is read by another LSTM ($LSTM_r$). We represent each sentence by the average of its word embeddings.

Let the context c contain d sentences and each sentence s_{c_i} contain T_{c_i} words. Similar to the notation of Yang et al. (2016), we first feed the sentence annotation h_{c_i} through a one layer MLP to get u_{c_i} as a hidden representation of h_{c_i}, then we weight the sentence u_{c_i} by measuring similarity with a sentence level context vector u_{c_s}. This gives a normalized importance weight α_{c_i} through a softmax function. v_c is the vector that summarize all the information of sentences in the context

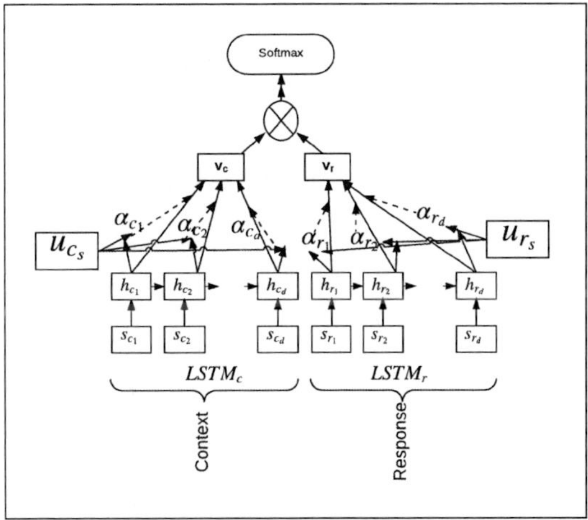

Figure 1: Sentence-level Attention Network for Context and Reply. Figure is inspired by Yang et al. (2016)

($LSTM_c$).

$$v_c = \sum_{i \in [1,d]} \alpha_{i_c} h_{i_c} \qquad (1)$$

where attention is calculated as:

$$\alpha_{i_c} = \frac{\exp(u_{c_i}^T u_{c_s})}{\sum_{i \in [1,d]} \exp(u_{c_i}^T u_{c_s})} \qquad (2)$$

Likewise we compute v_r for the response r via $LSTM_r$ (similar to eq. 1 and 2; also shown in Figure 1). Finally, we concatenate the vector v_c and v_r from the two LSTMs for the final softmax decision (i.e., predicting the S or NS class).

We also experiment with both word and sentence level attentions in a hierarchical fashion similarly to the approach proposed by Yang et al. (2016). As we show in Section 4 however, we achieve best performance for both datasets using just the sentence-level attention.

Conditional LSTM Networks: We also experiment with the *conditional encoding* model as introduced by Rocktäschel et al. (2015) for the task of recognizing textual entailment. In this architecture, two separate LSTMs are used – $LSTM_c$ and $LSTM_r$ – similar to the previous architecture without any attention, but for $LSTM_r$, its memory state is initialized with the last cell state of $LSTM_c$. In other words, $LSTM_r$ is conditioned on the representation of $LSTM_c$ that is built on the context.

Parameters and pre-trained word vectors. For both discussion forum and Twitter, we split randomly the corpus into training (80%), development (10%), and test (10%), maintaining the same distribution of sarcastic vs. non-sarcastic data in training, development and test. For Twitter we used the skip-gram word-embeddings (100-dimension) used in (Ghosh et al., 2015) that was built using over 2.5 million tweets.[4] For discussion forums, we use the standard Google n-gram $word2vec$ pre-trained model (300-dimension) (Mikolov et al., 2013). We do not optimize the word embedding during training. Out-of-vocabulary words in the training set are randomly initialized via sampling values uniformly from (-0.05,0.05). We use the development data to tune the parameters and selected dropout rate of 0.5 (from [.25,0.5, 0.75]), L_2 regularization strength and evaluate only that configuration on the test set. For both datasets mini-batch size of 16 is employed.

4 Results and Discussion

We report Precision (P), Recall (R), and F1 scores on S and NS classes. SVM_{bl}^r and SVM_{bl}^{c+r} respectively represent the performance of the SVM model using discrete features when using only the reply and the reply together with context. $LSTM^{ca}$ and $LSTM^{ra}$ are the attention-based LSTM models of context and reply, where the w, s and $w + s$ subscripts denote the word-level, sentence-level or word and sentence level attentions. $LSTM^{conditional}$ is the $conditional\ encoding$ model (no attention).

Discussion Forums: Table 2 shows the classification results on the discussion forum dataset. Although a vast majority of the context posts contain 3-4 sentences, around 100 context posts have more than ten sentences and thus we set a cutoff to a maximum of ten sentences for context modeling. For the reply r we considered the entire reply.

The SVM_{bl} models that are based on discrete features did not perform very well, and adding context actually hurt the performance. Regarding the performance of the neural network models, we observe that modeling context improves the performance using all types of LSTM architectures that read both context (c) and reply (r) (results are statistically significant when compared

[4]https://github.com/debanjanghosh/sarcasm_wsd

to $LSTM^r$). The highest performance when considering both the S and NS classes is achieved by the $LSTM^{conditional}$ model (73.32% F1 for S class and 70.56% F1 for NS, showing a 6% and 3% improvement over $LSTM^r$ for S and NS classes, respectively). The LSTM model with sentence-level attentions on both context and reply ($LSTM^{cas}$+$LSTM^{ras}$) gives the best F1 score of 73.7% for the S class. For the NS class, while we notice an improvement in precision we notice a drop in recall when compared to the LSTM model with sentence level attention only on reply ($LSTM^{ras}$). Remember that sentence-level attentions are based on average word embeddings. We also experimented with the hierarchical attention model where each sentence is represented by a *weighted average* of its word embeddings. In this case, attentions are based on words and sentences and we follow the architecture of hierarchical attention network (Yang et al., 2016). We observe the performance (69.88% F1 for S category) deteriorates, probably due to the lack of enough training data. Since attention over both the words and sentences seek to learn a lot more model parameters, adding more training data will be helpful. With the full release of the Sarcasm Corpus used by Oraby et al. (2016), we expect to achieve better accuracy for these models.

Twitter: Table 3 shows the results on the Twitter dataset. As for discussion forums, adding context using the SVM models does not show a statistically significant improvement. For the neural networks model, similar to the results on discussion forums, the LSTM models that read both context and reply outperform the LSTM model that reads only the reply ($LSTM^r$). The best performing architectures are again the $LSTM^{conditional}$ and LSTM with sentence-level attentions ($LSTM^{cas}$+$LSTM^{ras}$). $LSTM^{conditional}$ model shows an improvement of 11% F1 on the S class and 4-5%F1 on the NS class, compared to $LSTM^r$. For the attention-based models, the improvement using context is smaller ($\sim$2% F1). We kept the maximum length of context to the last five tweets in the conversation context, when available.We also conducted experiments with only word-level attentions, however, we obtain lower accuracy in comparison to sentence level attention models.

Experiment	S			NS		
	P	R	F1	P	R	F1
SVM_{bl}^{r}	65.55	66.67	66.10	66.10	64.96	65.52
SVM_{bl}^{c+r}	63.32	61.97	62.63	62.77	64.10	63.5
$LSTM^{r}$	67.90	66.23	67.1	67.08	**68.80**	67.93
$LSTM^{c}+LSTM^{r}$	66.19	79.49	72.23	74.33	59.40	66.03
$LSTM^{conditional}$	**70.03**	76.92	**73.32**	74.41	67.10	**70.56**
$LSTM^{r_{as}}$	69.45	70.94	70.19	70.30	68.80	69.45
$LSTM^{c_{as}}+LSTM^{r_{as}}$	66.90	**82.05**	**73.70**	**76.80**	59.40	66.99
$LSTM^{c_{aw+s}}+LSTM^{r_{aw+s}}$	65.90	74.35	69.88	70.59	61.53	65.75

Table 2: Experimental results for the discussion forum dataset (**bold** are best scores)

Experiment	S			NS		
	P	R	F1	P	R	F1
SVM_{bl}^{r}	64.20	64.95	64.57	69.0	68.30	68.7
SVM_{bl}^{c+r}	65.64	65.86	65.75	70.11	69.91	70.0
$LSTM^{r}$	73.25	58.72	65.19	61.47	75.44	67.74
$LSTM^{c}+LSTM^{r}$	70.89	67.95	69.39	64.94	68.03	66.45
$LSTM^{conditional}$	76.08	**76.53**	**76.30**	**72.93**	72.44	**72.68**
$LSTM^{r_{as}}$	76.00	73.18	74.56	70.52	73.52	71.9
$LSTM^{c_{as}}+LSTM^{r_{as}}$	**77.25**	75.51	**76.36**	72.65	**74.52**	**73.57**
$LSTM^{c_{aw}}+LSTM^{r_{aw}}$	76.74	69.77	73.09	68.63	75.77	72.02
$LSTM^{c_{aw+s}}+LSTM^{r_{aw+s}}$	76.42	71.37	73.81	69.50	74.77	72.04

Table 3: Experimental results for Twitter dataset (**bold** are best scores)

4.1 Qualitative Analysis

Wallace et al. (2014) showed that by providing contextual information humans are able to identify sarcastic utterances which they were unable without the context. However, it will be useful to understand whether a specific *part of the context* triggers the sarcastic reply.

To begin to address this issue, we conducted a qualitative study to understand whether (a) human annotators are able to identify parts of context that trigger the sarcastic reply and (b) attention weights are able to signal similar information. For (a) we designed a crowdsourcing experiment and for (b) we looked at the attention weights of the LSTM networks. Below is a short description of the crowdsourcing task.

4.1.1 Crowdsourcing Experiment.

We designed an Amazon Mechanical Turk task (for brevity, MTurk) framed as follow: Given a pair of context c and a sarcastic reply r from the discussion forum dataset, identify one or more sentences in c that may trigger the sarcastic reply r. Turkers could select one or more sentences

from the context c, including the entire context. From the test data, we select examples with context length between three to seven sentences since for longer posts the task will be too complicated for the Turkers.

We provided a definition of sarcasm and a few examples to the Turkers. We also explained how to carry out the task with the help of a few context/reply pairs. Each HIT contains only one task and five Turkers were allowed to attempt each HIT (a total of 85 HITS). Turkers with reasonable quality (i.e., more than 95% of acceptance rate with experience of over 8,000 HITs) were selected and paid seven cents per task.

4.1.2 Comparing Turkers' answers with attention models.

We visualize and compare the sentence-level attention weights of the LSTM models on context with Turkers' annotations (Figure 2). We first measure the overlap of Turkers choice with the attention weights. For the sentence-based attention model (i.e., $LSTM^{c_{as}}+LSTM^{r_{as}}$ model for the discussion forum), we selected the sentence with highest attention weight and matched it to the sentence selected by Turkers using majority voting. We found that 41% of times the sentence with the highest attention weight is also the one picked by Turkers. Figure 2 shows side by side the heat maps of the attention weights of LSTM models (LHS) and Turkers' choices when picking up sentences from context that they thought triggered the sarcastic reply (RHS).

Here the obvious question that we need to answer is why these sentences are selected by the models (and humans). In the next section we conduct a qualitative analysis to try answering this question.

4.1.3 Interpretation of selected context via attention weights

Semantic coherence between context and reply. Figure 2(a) depicts a case where the context contains three sentences and the attention weights given to the sentences are similar to the Turkers' choice. Looking at this example it seems the model pays attention to output vectors that are semantically coherent between c and r. The sarcastic response of this example contains a single sentence – "...hold your tongue ...in support of an anti-gay argument". The context contains the sentence S3 "...I've held my tongue on this as long as I can". The attention-based LSTM architecture is learning the attention weights simultaneously for the context c and the response r. Thus the model is showing contextual understanding by setting high weights to semantically coherent parts of the c and r. In Figure 2(b), attention weights is given to the most informative sentence –"rationally explain these creatures existence so recently in our human history if they were extinct for millions of years?". Here, the sarcastic reply mocks by claiming the author of the context is reading a lot more religious script (" you're reading waaaaay too much into your precious bible"). We also observe similar behavior in Tweets (highest attention to words –*retain* and *gerrymadering* in context: "breaking: *republicans retain majority* control of house" and reply: "hooray for *gerrymandering*" (Figure 3).

Incongruity between context and reply The meaning incongruity is an inherent characteristic of irony and sarcasm and have been extensively studied in linguistics, philosophy, communication science (Grice et al., 1975; Attardo, 2000; Burgers et al., 2012) as well as recently in NLP (Riloff

et al., 2013; Joshi et al., 2015). For instance, Riloff et al. (2013) pointed out that identifying the incongruity between *positive* sentiment towards a *negative* situation is a key characteristic of sarcasm detection in social media. We observe in discussion forums and in Tweets that the attention-based models have frequently identified sentences and words from c and r that are semantically incongruous (i.e., opposite sentiment words). For instance, in Figure 2(c), the attention model has chosen sentence S1, which contains strong negative sentiment word ("disgusting sickening ..."). Interestingly, in contrast, the attention model on the reply, has given the highest weight to sentence that contain opposite sentiment ("I love you"). Thus, the model seems to learn the context incongruity of opposite sentiment for detecting sarcasm. However, it seems the Turkers prefer the second sentence S2 ("how can you tell a man that about his mum?") as the most instructive sentence instead of the first sentence. Looking at the sarcastic reply we observe that the reply contains remarks about "mothers" and apparently that commonality assisted the Turkers to chose the second sentence.

In Twitter dataset, we observe often the attention models have selected utterance(s) from the context which have opposite sentiment (Figure 4, Figure 5, and Figure 6). Here, the word and sentence-level attention model have chosen the particular utterance from the context (i.e., the top heatmap for the context) and the words with high attention (e.g., "mediocre", "gutsy").These words again show examples of meaning incongruity which is useful for sarcasm detection. Word-models seem to also work well when words in the context/reply are semantically incongruous but connected via deeper semantics ("bums" and "welfare" in context: "someone needs to remind these *bums* they work for the people" and reply: "feels like we are paying them *welfare*" (Figure 6).

Attention weights and sarcasm markers Looking just at attention weights in reply, we notice the models are giving highest weight to sentences that contain sarcasm markers, such as emoticons (i.e., ":p", ":)") and interjections (i.e., "ah", "hmm"). Sarcasm markers are explicit indicators of sarcasm that signal that an utterance is sarcastic, such as the use of emoticons, uppercase spelling of words, or interjections. (Attardo, 2000; Burgers et al., 2012). Use of such markers in

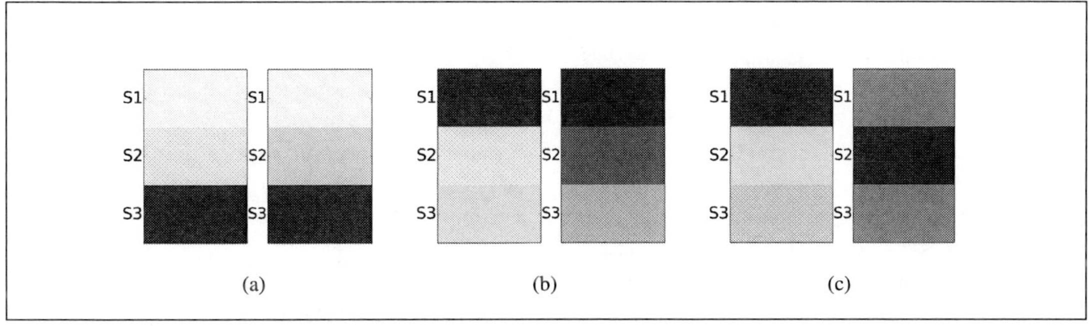

Figure 2: Context sentences that trigger sarcasm: LHS: *attention weights*; RHS: *Turkers' selections*

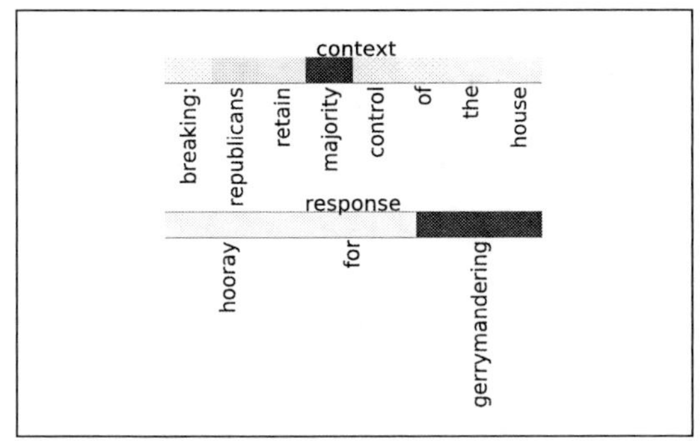

Figure 3: Attention visualization of semantic coherence between c and r

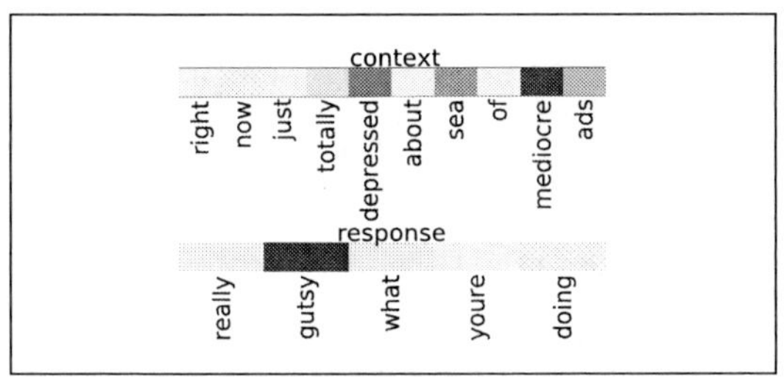

Figure 4: Attention visualization of incongruity between c and r

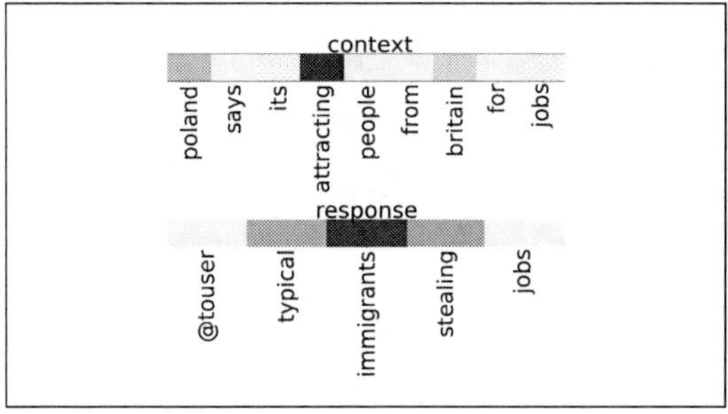

Figure 5: Attention visualization of incongruity between c and r

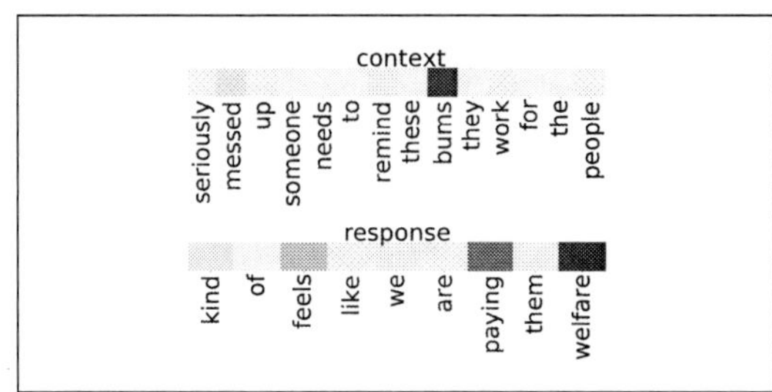

Figure 6: Attention visualization of incongruity between c and r

social media (particularly in Twitter) is extensive.

While we have started to understand the semantic of attention weights in this task, more studies need to be carry out. Rocktäschel et al. (2015) have argued that interpretations based on attentions weights have to be taken with care since the classification task is not forced to solely rely on the attentions weights. Thus in future work, we plan to analyze utterances that are more subtle and do not consist of sarcasm markers or explicit incongruence of opposite sentiment between context and response.

5   Related Work

Most computational models for sarcasm detection have considered utterances in isolation (Davidov et al., 2010; González-Ibáñez et al., 2011; Liebrecht et al., 2013; Riloff et al., 2013; Maynard and Greenwood, 2014; Ghosh et al., 2015; Joshi et al., 2016; Ghosh and Veale, 2016). However, even humans have difficulty sometimes in recognizing sarcastic intent when considering an utterance in isolation (Wallace et al., 2014). Thus, recent work on sarcasm and irony detection have started to exploit contextual information. In particular, (Khattri et al., 2015) analyzed authors' prior sentiment towards certain entities and if a new tweet deviates from the author's estimated sentiment the tweet is predicted to be sarcastic. Similar to this approach, several models have been introduced; some relied on extensive feature engineering to capture contextual information about authors, topics or conversation context whereas the rest are using deep learning techniques to embed authors' information (Rajadesingan et al., 2015). The two studies that have considered conversation context among other contextual information have shown minimal improvement when modeling conversation context using Twitter data (Bamman and Smith, 2015; Wang et al., 2015). Our work show that using better models, such as LSTM networks show a clear benefit of using context for sarcasm detection. As stated earlier in Section 3, LSTM's have been shown to be effective in NLI tasks, especially where the task is to establish the relationship between multiple inputs (i.e., in our case, between the context and the response). We observe that the $\text{LSTM}^{conditional}$ model and the sentence level attention-based models using both context and reply present the best results.

6 Conclusion

This research makes a complementary contribution to existing work of modeling context for sarcasm/irony detection by looking at a particular type of context, *conversation context*. We have addressed two issues: (1) does modeling of conversation context help in sarcasm detection and (2) can we determine what part of the conversation context triggered the sarcastic reply. To answer the first question, we show that Long Short-Term Memory (LSTM) networks that can model both the context and the sarcastic reply achieve better performance than LSTM networks that read only the reply. In particular, conditional LSTM networks (Rocktäschel et al., 2015) and LSTM networks with sentence level attention achieved significant improvement (e.g., 6-11% F1 for discussion forums and Twitter messages). To address the second issue, we presented a qualitative analysis of attention weights produced by the LSTM models with attention, and discussed the results compared with human annotators. We also showed that attention-based models are able to identify inherent characteristics of sarcasm (i.e., sarcasm markers and sarcasm factors such as context in-congruity). In future, we plan to study larger context, such as the full thread in a discussion forum that consider also the responses to the sarcastic comment, when available. We are also interested in analyzing sarcastic replies that do not contain sarcasm markers or explicit incongruence (i.e., opposing sentiment between the context and the reply).

Acknowledgements

This paper is based on work supported by the DARPA-DEFT program. The views expressed are those of the authors and do not reflect the official policy or position of the Department of Defense or the U.S. Government. The authors thank Christopher Hidey for the discussions and resources on LSTM and the anonymous reviewers for helpful comments.

References

Salvatore Attardo. 2000. Irony markers and functions: Towards a goal-oriented theory of irony and its processing. *Rask* 12(1):3–20.

David Bamman and Noah A Smith. 2015. Contextualized sarcasm detection on twitter. In *Ninth International AAAI Conference on Web and Social Media*.

Steven Bird, Ewan Klein, and Edward Loper. 2009. *Natural language processing with Python: analyzing text with the natural language toolkit.* " O'Reilly Media, Inc.".

Samuel R Bowman, Gabor Angeli, Christopher Potts, and Christopher D Manning. 2015. A large annotated corpus for learning natural language inference. *arXiv preprint arXiv:1508.05326* .

Christian Burgers, Margot Van Mulken, and Peter Jan Schellens. 2012. Verbal irony differences in usage across written genres. *Journal of Language and Social Psychology* 31(3):290–310.

Elisabeth Camp. 2012. Sarcasm, pretense, and the semantics/pragmatics distinction*. *Noûs* 46(4):587–634.

Chih-Chung Chang and Chih-Jen Lin. 2011. LIBSVM: A library for support vector machines. *ACM Transactions on Intelligent Systems and Technology* 2:27:1–27:27.

Dmitry Davidov, Oren Tsur, and Ari Rappoport. 2010. Semi-supervised recognition of sarcastic sentences in twitter and amazon. In *Proceedings of the Fourteenth Conference on Computational Natural Language Learning*. CoNLL '10.

Aniruddha Ghosh and Tony Veale. 2016. Fracking sarcasm using neural network. In *Proceedings of NAACL-HLT*. pages 161–169.

Debanjan Ghosh, Weiwei Guo, and Smaranda Muresan. 2015. Sarcastic or not: Word embeddings to predict the literal or sarcastic meaning of words. In *Proceedings of the 2015 Conference on Empirical Methods in Natural Language Processing*. Association for Computational Linguistics, Lisbon, Portugal, pages 1003–1012.

Kevin Gimpel, Nathan Schneider, Brendan O'Connor, Dipanjan Das, Daniel Mills, Jacob Eisenstein, Michael Heilman, Dani Yogatama, Jeffrey Flanigan, and Noah A Smith. 2011. Part-of-speech tagging for twitter: Annotation, features, and experiments. In *Proceedings of the 49th Annual Meeting of the ACL*. pages 42–47.

Roberto González-Ibáñez, Smaranda Muresan, and Nina Wacholder. 2011. Identifying sarcasm in twitter: A closer look. In *ACL (Short Papers)*. Association for Computational Linguistics, pages 581–586.

H Paul Grice, Peter Cole, and Jerry L Morgan. 1975. Syntax and semantics. *Logic and conversation* 3:41–58.

Henk Haverkate. 1990. A speech act analysis of irony. *Journal of Pragmatics* 14(1):77–109.

Sepp Hochreiter and Jürgen Schmidhuber. 1997. Long short-term memory. *Neural computation* 9(8):1735–1780.

Minqing Hu and Bing Liu. 2004. Mining and summarizing customer reviews. In *Proceedings of the tenth ACM SIGKDD international conference on Knowledge discovery and data mining*. ACM, pages 168–177.

Aditya Joshi, Vinita Sharma, and Pushpak Bhattacharyya. 2015. Harnessing context incongruity for sarcasm detection. In *Proceedings of the 53rd Annual Meeting of the Association for Computational Linguistics and the 7th International Joint Conference on Natural Language Processing (Volume 2: Short Papers)*. Association for Computational Linguistics, Beijing, China, pages 757–762.

Aditya Joshi, Vaibhav Tripathi, Kevin Patel, Pushpak Bhattacharyya, and Mark Carman. 2016. Are word embedding-based features useful for sarcasm detection? *arXiv preprint arXiv:1610.00883* .

Anupam Khattri, Aditya Joshi, Pushpak Bhattacharyya, and Mark James Carman. 2015. Your sentiment precedes you: Using an authors historical tweets to predict sarcasm. In *6th Workshop on Computational Approaches to Subjectivity, Sentiment and Social Media Analysis (WASSA)*. page 25.

CC Liebrecht, FA Kunneman, and APJ van den Bosch. 2013. The perfect solution for detecting sarcasm in tweets# not .

Diana Maynard and Mark A Greenwood. 2014. Who cares about sarcastic tweets? investigating the impact of sarcasm on sentiment analysis. In *Proceedings of LREC*.

Tomas Mikolov, Kai Chen, Greg Corrado, and Jeffrey Dean. 2013. Efficient estimation of word representations in vector space. *arXiv preprint arXiv:1301.3781* .

Smaranda Muresan, Roberto Gonzalez-Ibanez, Debanjan Ghosh, and Nina Wacholder. 2016. Identification of nonliteral language in social media: A case study on sarcasm. *Journal of the Association for Information Science and Technology* .

Shereen Oraby, Vrindavan Harrison, Ernesto Hernandez, Lena Reed, Ellen Riloff, and Marilyn Walker. 2016. Creating and characterizing a diverse corpus of sarcasm in dialogue .

Ankur P Parikh, Oscar Täckström, Dipanjan Das, and Jakob Uszkoreit. 2016. A decomposable attention model for natural language inference. *arXiv preprint arXiv:1606.01933* .

James W Pennebaker, Martha E Francis, and Roger J Booth. 2001. Linguistic inquiry and word count: Liwc 2001. *Mahway: Lawrence Erlbaum Associates* 71:2001.

Ashwin Rajadesingan, Reza Zafarani, and Huan Liu. 2015. Sarcasm detection on twitter: A behavioral modeling approach. In *Proceedings of the Eighth ACM International Conference on Web Search and Data Mining*. ACM, pages 97–106.

Ellen Riloff, Ashequl Qadir, Prafulla Surve, Lalindra De Silva, Nathan Gilbert, and Ruihong Huang. 2013. Sarcasm as contrast between a positive sentiment and negative situation. In *Proceedings of the Conference on Empirical Methods in Natural Language Processing*. Association for Computational Linguistics, pages 704–714.

Tim Rocktäschel, Edward Grefenstette, Karl Moritz Hermann, Tomáš Kočiský, and Phil Blunsom. 2015. Reasoning about entailment with neural attention. *arXiv preprint arXiv:1509.06664* .

Ilya Sutskever, Oriol Vinyals, and Quoc V Le. 2014. Sequence to sequence learning with neural networks. In *Advances in neural information processing systems*. pages 3104–3112.

Simo Tchokni, Diarmuid O Séaghdha, and Daniele Quercia. 2014. Emoticons and phrases: Status symbols in social media. In *Eighth International AAAI Conference on Weblogs and Social Media*.

Oriol Vinyals, Łukasz Kaiser, Terry Koo, Slav Petrov, Ilya Sutskever, and Geoffrey Hinton. 2015. Grammar as a foreign language. In *Advances in Neural Information Processing Systems*. pages 2773–2781.

Byron C Wallace, Laura Kertz Do Kook Choe, Laura
Kertz, and Eugene Charniak. 2014. Humans require
context to infer ironic intent (so computers probably
do, too). In *ACL (2)*. pages 512–516.

Zelin Wang, Zhijian Wu, Ruimin Wang, and Yafeng
Ren. 2015. Twitter sarcasm detection exploiting a
context-based model. In *International Conference
on Web Information Systems Engineering*. Springer,
pages 77–91.

Theresa Wilson, Janyce Wiebe, and Paul Hoffmann.
2005. Recognizing contextual polarity in phrase-
level sentiment analysis. In *Proceedings of the conference on human language technology and empirical methods in natural language processing*. Association for Computational Linguistics, pages 347–354.

Kelvin Xu, Jimmy Ba, Ryan Kiros, Kyunghyun Cho,
Aaron Courville, Ruslan Salakhudinov, Rich Zemel,
and Yoshua Bengio. 2015. Show, attend and tell:
Neural image caption generation with visual at-
tention. In *International Conference on Machine
Learning*. pages 2048–2057.

Zichao Yang, Diyi Yang, Chris Dyer, Xiaodong He,
Alex Smola, and Eduard Hovy. 2016. Hierarchical
attention networks for document classification. In
Proceedings of NAACL-HLT. pages 1480–1489.

Wenpeng Yin, Hinrich Schütze, Bing Xiang, and
Bowen Zhou. 2015. Abcnn: Attention-based convolutional neural network for modeling sentence pairs.
arXiv preprint arXiv:1512.05193 .

Wojciech Zaremba, Ilya Sutskever, and Oriol Vinyals.
2014. Recurrent neural network regularization.
arXiv preprint arXiv:1409.2329 .

VOILA: An Optimised Dialogue System for Interactively Learning Visually-Grounded Word Meanings (Demonstration System)

Yanchao Yu
Interaction Lab
Heriot-Watt University
`y.yu@hw.ac.uk`

Arash Eshghi
Interaction Lab
Heriot-Watt University
`a.eshghi@hw.ac.uk`

Oliver Lemon
Interaction Lab
Heriot-Watt University
`o.lemon@hw.ac.uk`

Abstract

We present VOILA: an optimised, multi-modal dialogue agent for interactive learning of visually grounded word meanings from a human user. VOILA is: (1) able to learn new visual categories interactively from users from scratch; (2) trained on real human-human dialogues in the same domain, and so is able to conduct natural spontaneous dialogue; (3) optimised to find the most effective trade-off between the accuracy of the visual categories it learns and the cost it incurs to users. VOILA is deployed on Furhat[1], a human-like, multi-modal robot head with back-projection of the face, and a graphical virtual character.

1 Introduction

As intelligent systems/robots are brought out of the laboratory and into the physical world, they must become capable of natural everyday conversation with their human users about their physical surroundings. Among other competencies, this involves the ability to learn and adapt mappings between words, phrases, and sentences in Natural Language (NL) and perceptual aspects of the external environment – this is widely known as *the grounding problem*. Our work is similar in spirit to e.g. (Roy, 2002; Skocaj et al., 2011) but advances it in several aspects (Yu et al., 2016).

In this demo paper, we present a dialogue agent that learns visually grounded word meanings interactively from a human tutor, which we call: VOILA (Visually Optimised Interactive Learning Agent). Our goal is to enable this agent to learn to identify and describe objects/attributes (colour

and shape in this case) in its immediate visual environment through interaction with human users, incrementally, over time. Unlike a lot of past work (Silberer and Lapata, 2014; Thomason et al., 2016; Matuszek et al., 2014), here we assume that the agent is in the position of a child, who does not have any prior knowledge of perceptual categories. Hence, the agent must learn from scratch: (1) the perceptual/visual categories themselves; and (2) how NL expressions map to these; and in addition, (3) as a standard conversational agent, the agent much also learn to conduct natural, spontaneous conversations with real humans.

In this demonstration, *VOILA* plays the role of an interactive, concept learning agent that takes initiative in the dialogues and actively learns novel visual knowledge from the feedback from the human tutor. What sets VOILA apart from other work in this area is:

- VOILA's dialogue strategy is *optimised* via Reinforcement Learning to achieve an optimal trade-off between the accuracy of the concepts it learns/has learnt from users, and the effort that the dialogues incur on the users: this is a form of active learning where the agent only asks about something if it doesn't already know the answer with some appropriate confidence (see (Yu et al., 2016) for more detail).

- VOILA is trained on a corpus of real Human-Human conversations (Yu et al., 2017), and is thus able to process *natural* human dialogue, which contains phenomena such as *self- corrections, repetitions and restarts, pauses, fillers, and continuations*

VOILA is deployed onto Furhat, a human-like robot head with a custom back-projected face, built-in stereo microphones, and a Microsoft

---

[1]`http://www.furhatrobotics.com/`

197

Proceedings of the SIGDIAL 2017 Conference, pages 197–200,
Saarbrücken, Germany, 15-17 August 2017. ©2017 Association for Computational Linguistics

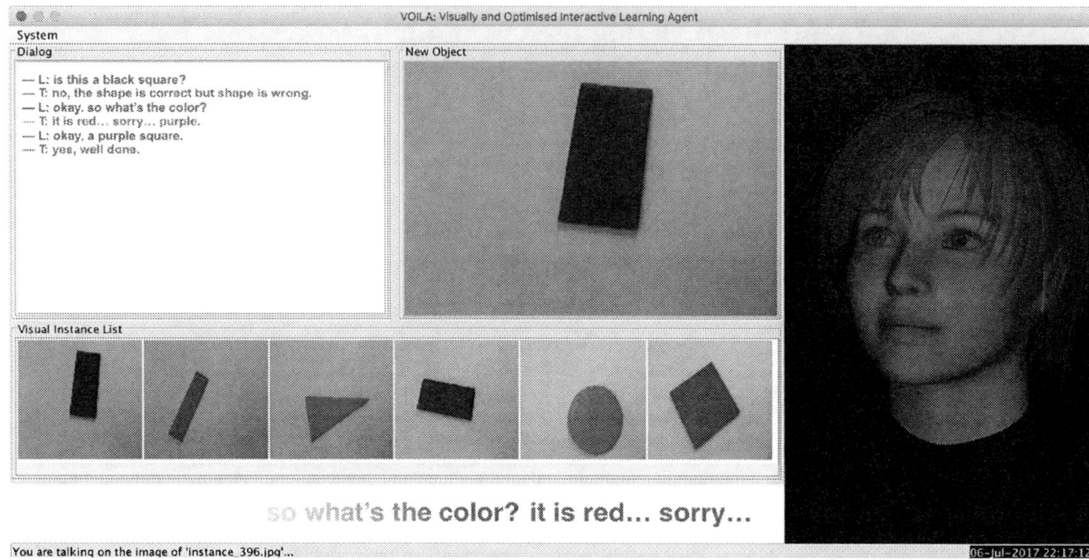

Figure 1: Interactive Visual Concept Learning in the VOILA Agent (Screenshot)

Kinect for skeletal tracking and processing non-verbal signals. A graphical version of the character can also bee used (see 1).

2 Interactive Multimodal Framework

We developed a multimodal framework in support of building an interactive learning system, which loosely follows that of Yu et al. (2016). The framework consists of two core modules:

Vision Module The vision module produces visual attribute predictions, using two base feature categories: the HSV colour space for colour attributes, and a 'bag of visual words' (i.e. PHOW descriptors) for the object shapes/class. It consists of a set of binary classifiers - Logistic Regression SVM classifiers with Stochastic Gradient Descent (SGD) (Zhang, 2004) – to incrementally learn attribute predictions. The visual classifiers ground visual attribute words such as 'red', 'circle' etc. that appear as parameters of the Dialogue Acts used in the system.

Dialogue Module This module relies on a classical architecture for dialogue systems, composed of Dialogue Management (DM) and Natural Language Understanding (NLU), as well as Generation (NLG) components. These components interact via Dialogue Act representations (Stolcke et al., 2000), e.g. *inform(color=red)*, *ask(shape)*. The Natural Language Understanding component processes user utterances by extracting a sequence of key patterns, slots and values, and then transforming them into dialogue-act representations, following a list of hand-crafted rules. The NLG component makes use of a template-based approach that chooses a suitable learner utterance for a specific dialogue act, according to the statistical distribution of utterance templates from dialogue examples. Finally, the DM component is implemented with an optimised learning policy using Reinforcement Learning (see Section 3). This optimised policy is trained to: (1) conduct interaction with human partners, and (2) achieve an optimum balance between classification performance and the cost of the dialogue to the tutor in the interactive learning process.

3 Learning How to Learn

In this section, we briefly describe our method for optimising the dialogue agent with Reinforcement Learning and in interaction with a simulated tutor, itself built from the BURCHAK human-human dialogue corpus[2] (Yu et al., 2017) within a simulated learning environment (see Fig. 2).

Given the visual attribute learning task, a smart agent must learn novel visual objects/attributes as accurately as possible through natural interactions with real humans, but meanwhile it should attempt

---

[2]BURCHAK is freely available at `https://sites.google.com/site/hwinteractionlab/babble`

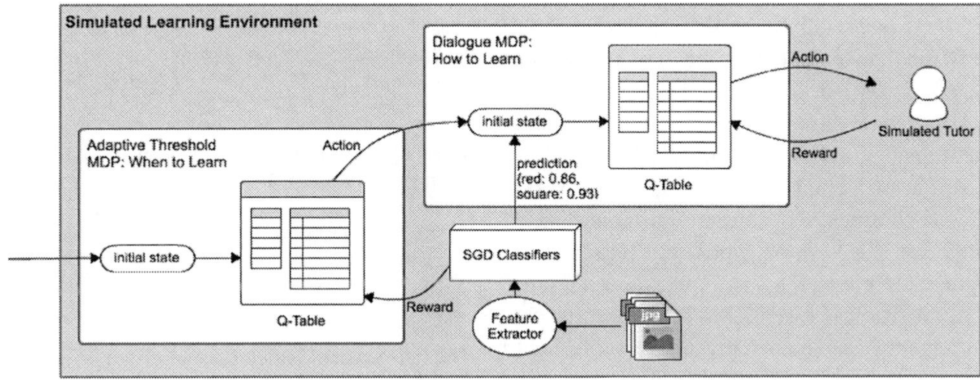

Figure 2: Architecture of Optimised Learning Policy with a Hierarchical MDP

to minimise the human involvement as much as possible in this life-long learning process. Here, we divide this interactive learning task into two sub-tasks, modeled as a hierarchical Markov Decision Process, consisting of two interdependent MDPs in charge of decisions about: *"when to learn"* and *"how to learn"*.

3.1 When to Learn: Adaptive Confidence Threshold

The first MDP performs a kind of *active learning*: the learner/agent only acquires the feedback from humans about a visual attribute if it is not confident enough already about its own predictions. Following previous work (Yu et al., 2016), here we use a positive confidence threshold, which determines when the agent believes its own predictions. For instance, the learner can ask either polar or WH-questions about an attribute if its confidence score is higher than a certain threshold; otherwise, there should be no interaction about that attribute. But as Yu et al. (2016) point out the confidence score from a classifier is not reliable enough at the early stages of learning, so in order to find an optimum dialogue policy, a threshold should be able to dynamically adjust according to the previous learning performance of the agent. We therefore assign a separate but dependent component MDP for adjusting the threshold dynamically in order to optimise the trade-off between accuracy and cost. Note now that the adjusted confidence threshold will affect the agent's dialogue behaviour, modeled in the other MDP presented in the next section (natural interaction with humans).

3.2 How to Learn: Natural Interaction with Humans

The second MDP, as a purely conversational agent, aims at managing natural, spontaneous conversation with human partners or other agents to achieve the final goal, i.e. gain useful information about visual attributes. The initial state in this MDP is determined by a combination of the adjusted threshold from the former MDP and the visual predictions from the color and shape classifiers that ground NL attributes terms ('red', 'square', etc): either the color or shape status can be assigned to: 0, if the learner has a low confidence on its predictions (i.e. the confidence score is lower than 0.5); or, 1 if the confidence score is higher than 0.5, but lower than the positive threshold; or else, 2. This together with the previous dialogue act constitutes the state space of this MDP. The agent is then trained to choose the correct dialogue action to achieve a state in which both shape and color of the current object are known with certainty (with status = 2), either through feedback from the user, or through the agent's own existing visual knowledge. Of course, the agent must also learn to produce coherent dialogues by responding to questions at the right time, giving feedback at the right time, asking for feedback at the right time, etc.

4 Demonstration

As noted, VOILA has been deployed onto Furhat: a human-like Robot Head (Moubayed et al., 2011), which provides an interaction framework for the management of multi-party, multi-modal interactions, and which employs a Microsoft Kinect for skeletal tracking. In the demonstration, the VOILA agent will randomly choose 20 visual objects, and then learn to describe them using their low-level visual attributes (e.g. color and shape) image-by-image through interaction with users. As mentioned above, we assume that VOILA is in the position of a child learning from scratch, but instead of complex real objects with noisy backgrounds, we use a set of simple toy objects (see dialogue example in Fig. 1), but without annotations or labels. It is essential to highlight that the VOILA agent would only start a conversation with a human partner when it isn't confident about its own attribute predictions.

5 Conclusion

We have presented a multi-modal learning agent – VOILA – that can learn grounded visual-concept meanings through interaction with human tutors incrementally, over time. The agent is deployed with an *adaptive* dialogue policy (optimised using Reinforcement Learning), which has learned to (1) process natural, coherent conversations with humans and (2) achieve comparable learning performance to a hand-crafted system, but with less tutoring effort needed from humans. Recently, we also extended the VOILA agent to learn real visual object classes instead of toy objects by integrating with a Load-Balancing Self-Organizing Incremental Neural Network (LB-SOINN) (Zhang et al., 2014) for object classification.

Acknowledgements

This research is supported by the EPSRC, under grant number EP/M01553X/1 (BABBLE project[3]).

References

Cynthia Matuszek, Liefeng Bo, Luke Zettlemoyer, and Dieter Fox. 2014. Learning from unscripted deictic gesture and language for human-robot interactions. In *Proceedings of the Twenty-Eighth AAAI Conference on Artificial Intelligence, July 27 -31, 2014, Québec City, Québec, Canada.*. pages 2556–2563.

Samer Al Moubayed, Jonas Beskow, Gabriel Skantze, and Björn Granström. 2011. Furhat: A back-projected human-like robot head for multiparty human-machine interaction. In *Cognitive Behavioural Systems - COST 2102 International Training School, Dresden, Germany, February 21-26, 2011, Revised Selected Papers.* pages 114–130.

Deb Roy. 2002. A trainable visually-grounded spoken language generation system. In *Proceedings of the International Conference of Spoken Language Processing.*

Carina Silberer and Mirella Lapata. 2014. Learning grounded meaning representations with autoencoders. In *Proceedings of the 52nd Annual Meeting of the Association for Computational Linguistics (Volume 1: Long Papers).* Association for Computational Linguistics, Baltimore, Maryland, volume 1, pages 721–732.

Danijel Skocaj, Matej Kristan, Alen Vrecko, Marko Mahnic, Miroslav Janíček, Geert-Jan M. Kruijff, Marc Hanheide, Nick Hawes, Thomas Keller, Michael Zillich, and Kai Zhou. 2011. A system for interactive learning in dialogue with a tutor. In *2011 IEEE/RSJ International Conference on Intelligent Robots and Systems, IROS 2011, San Francisco, CA, USA, September 25-30, 2011.* pages 3387–3394. https://doi.org/10.1109/IROS.2011.6094926.

Andreas Stolcke, Klaus Ries, Noah Coccaro, Elizabeth Shriberg, Rebecca A. Bates, Daniel Jurafsky, Paul Taylor, Rachel Martin, Carol Van Ess-Dykema, and Marie Meteer. 2000. Dialogue act modeling for automatic tagging and recognition of conversational speech. *CoRR* cs.CL/0006023.

Jesse Thomason, Jivko Sinapov, Maxwell Sevtlik, Peter Stone, and Raymond J. Mooney. 2016. Learning multi-modal grounded linguistic semantics by playing "i spy". In *To Appear: Proceedings of the Twenty-Fifth International Joint Conference on Artificial Intelligence, IJCAI-16, New York City, USA, July 9-15, 2016.*

Yanchao Yu, Arash Eshghi, and Oliver Lemon. 2016. Training an adaptive dialogue policy for interactive learning of visually grounded word meanings. In *Proceedings of SIGDIAL 2016, 17th Annual Meeting of the Special Interest Group on Discourse and Dialogue.* Los Angeles, pages 339–349.

Yanchao Yu, Arash Eshghi, Gregory Mills, and Oliver Lemon. 2017. *Proceedings of the Sixth Workshop on Vision and Language*, Association for Computational Linguistics, chapter The BURCHAK corpus: a Challenge Data Set for Interactive Learning of Visually Grounded Word Meanings, pages 1–10. http://aclweb.org/anthology/W17-2001.

Hongwei Zhang, Xiong Xiao, and Osamu Hasegawa. 2014. A Load-Balancing Self-Organizing Incremental Neural Network. *IEEE Transactions on Neural Networks and Learning Systems* 25(6):1096–1105.

Tong Zhang. 2004. Solving large scale linear prediction problems using stochastic gradient descent algorithms. In *Proceedings of the twenty-first international conference on Machine learning.* ACM, page 116.

[3]https://sites.google.com/site/hwinteractionlab/babble

The E2E Dataset: New Challenges For End-to-End Generation

Jekaterina Novikova, Ondřej Dušek and Verena Rieser
School of Mathematical and Computer Sciences
Heriot-Watt University, Edinburgh
`j.novikova, o.dusek, v.t.rieser@hw.ac.uk`

Abstract

This paper describes the E2E data, a new dataset for training end-to-end, data-driven natural language generation systems in the restaurant domain, which is ten times bigger than existing, frequently used datasets in this area. The E2E dataset poses new challenges: (1) its human reference texts show more lexical richness and syntactic variation, including discourse phenomena; (2) generating from this set requires content selection. As such, learning from this dataset promises more natural, varied and less template-like system utterances. We also establish a baseline on this dataset, which illustrates some of the difficulties associated with this data.

1 Introduction

The natural language generation (NLG) component of a spoken dialogue system typically has to be re-developed for every new application domain. Recent end-to-end, data-driven NLG systems, however, promise rapid development of NLG components in new domains: They jointly learn sentence planning and surface realisation from non-aligned data (Dušek and Jurčíček, 2015; Wen et al., 2015; Mei et al., 2016; Wen et al., 2016; Sharma et al., 2016; Dušek and Jurčíček, 2016a; Lampouras and Vlachos, 2016). These approaches do not require costly semantic alignment between meaning representations (MRs) and the corresponding natural language (NL) reference texts (also referred to as "ground truths" or "targets"), but they are trained on parallel datasets, which can be collected in sufficient quality and quantity using effective crowdsourcing techniques, e.g. (Novikova et al., 2016). So far, end-to-end approaches to NLG are limited to small, delexi-

Flat MR	NL reference
name[Loch Fyne], eatType[restaurant], food[French], priceRange[less than £20], familyFriendly[yes]	Loch Fyne is a family-friendly restaurant providing wine and cheese at a low cost.
	Loch Fyne is a French family friendly restaurant catering to a budget of below £20.
	Loch Fyne is a French restaurant with a family setting and perfect on the wallet.

Table 1: An example of a data instance.

calised datasets, e.g. BAGEL (Mairesse et al., 2010), SF Hotels/Restaurants (Wen et al., 2015), or RoboCup (Chen and Mooney, 2008). Therefore, end-to-end methods have not been able to replicate the rich dialogue and discourse phenomena targeted by previous rule-based and statistical approaches for language generation in dialogue, e.g. (Walker et al., 2004; Stent et al., 2004; Demberg and Moore, 2006; Rieser and Lemon, 2009).

In this paper, we describe a new crowdsourced dataset of 50k instances in the restaurant domain (see Section 2). We analyse it following the methodology proposed by Perez-Beltrachini and Gardent (2017) and show that the dataset brings additional challenges, such as open vocabulary, complex syntactic structures and diverse discourse phenomena, as described in Section 3. The data is openly released as part of the E2E NLG challenge.[1] We establish a baseline on the dataset in Section 4, using one of the previous end-to-end approaches.

2 The E2E Dataset

The data was collected using the Crowd-Flower platform and quality-controlled following Novikova et al. (2016). The dataset provides infor-

---

[1] `http://www.macs.hw.ac.uk/ InteractionLab/E2E/`

Proceedings of the SIGDIAL 2017 Conference, pages 201–206,
Saarbrücken, Germany, 15-17 August 2017. ©2017 Association for Computational Linguistics

Figure 1: Pictorial MR for Table 1.

Attribute	Data Type	Example value
name	verbatim string	The Eagle, ...
eatType	dictionary	restaurant, pub, ...
familyFriendly	boolean	Yes / No
priceRange	dictionary	cheap, expensive, ...
food	dictionary	French, Italian, ...
near	verbatim string	market square, ...
area	dictionary	riverside, city center, ...
customerRating	enumerable	1 of 5 (low), 4 of 5 (high), ...

Table 2: Domain ontology of the E2E dataset.

mation about restaurants and consists of more than 50k combinations of a dialogue-act-based MR and 8.1 references on average, as shown in Table 1. The dataset is split into training, validation and testing sets (in a 76.5-8.5-15 ratio), keeping a similar distribution of MR and reference text lengths and ensuring that MRs in different sets are distinct. Each MR consists of 3–8 attributes (slots), such as *name*, *food* or *area*, and their values. A detailed ontology of all attributes and values is provided in Table 2. Following Novikova et al. (2016), the E2E data was collected using pictures as stimuli (see example in Figure 1), which was shown to elicit significantly more natural, more informative, and better phrased human references than textual MRs.

3 Challenges

Following Perez-Beltrachini and Gardent (2017), we describe several different dimensions of our dataset and compare them to the BAGEL and SF Restaurants (SFRest) datasets, which use the same domain.

Size: Table 3 summarises the main descriptive statistics of all three datasets. The E2E dataset is significantly larger than the other sets in terms of instances, unique MRs, and average number of human references per MR (Refs/MR).[2] While having more data with a higher number of references per MR makes the E2E data more attractive for statistical approaches, it is also more challenging than previous sets as it uses a larger number of sentences in NL references (Sents/Ref; up to 6 in our dataset compared to typical 1–2 for other sets) and a larger number of slot-value pairs in MRs (Slots/MR). It also contains sentences of about double the word length (W/Ref) and longer sentences in references (W/Sent).

Lexical Richness: We used the Lexical Complexity Analyser (Lu, 2012) to measure various dimensions of lexical richness, as shown in Table 4. We complement the traditional measure of *lexical diversity* type-token ratio (TTR) with the more robust measure of mean segmental TTR (MSTTR) (Lu, 2012), which divides the corpus into successive segments of a given length and then calculates the average TTR of all segments. The higher the value of MSTTR, the more diverse is the measured text. Table 4 shows our dataset has the highest MSTTR value (0.75) while Bagel has the lowest one (0.41). In addition, we measure *lexical sophistication* (LS), also known as lexical rareness, which is calculated as the proportion of lexical word types not on the list of 2,000 most frequent words generated from the British National Corpus. Table 4 shows that our dataset contains about 15% more infrequent words compared to the other datasets.

We also investigate the distribution of the top 25 most frequent bigrams and trigrams in our dataset (see Figure 2). The majority of both trigrams (61%) and bigrams (50%) is only used once in the dataset, which creates a challenge to efficiently train on this data. Bigrams used more than once in the dataset have an average frequency of 54.4 (SD = 433.1), and the average frequency of trigrams used more than once is 19.9 (SD = 136.9). For comparison, neither SFRest nor Bagel dataset contains bigrams or trigrams that are only used once. The minimal frequency of bigrams is 27 for Bagel (Mean = 98.2, SD = 86.9) and 76 for SFrest (Mean = 128.4, SD = 50.5), for trigrams the minimal frequency is 24 for Bagel (Mean = 63.5, SD = 54.6) and 43 for SFRest (Mean = 67.3, SD = 18.9). Infrequent words and phrases pose a chal-

---

[2]Note that the difference is even bigger in practice as the Refs/MR ratio for the SFRest dataset is skewed: for specific MRs, e.g. *goodbye*, SFRest has up to 101 references.

	No. of instances	No. of unique MRs	Refs/MR		Slots/MR	W/Ref	W/Sent	Sents/Ref	
E2E	**50,602**	**5,751**	**8.1**	**(2–16)**	**5.43**	**20.1**	**14.3**	**1.5**	**(1–6)**
SFRest	5,192	1,950	1.82	(1–101)	2.86	8.53	8.53	1.05	(1–4)
Bagel	404	202	2	(2–2)	5.41	11.54	11.54	1.02	(1–2)

Table 3: Descriptive statistics of linguistic and computational adequacy of datasets.

No. of instances is the total number of instances in the dataset, *No. of unique MRs* is the number of distinct MRs, *Refs/MR* is the number of NL references per one MR (average and extremes shown), *Slots/MR* is the average number of slot-value pairs per MR, *W/Ref* is the average number of words per MR, *W/Sent* is the average number of words per single sentence, *Sents/Ref* is the number of NL sentences per MR (average and extremes shown).

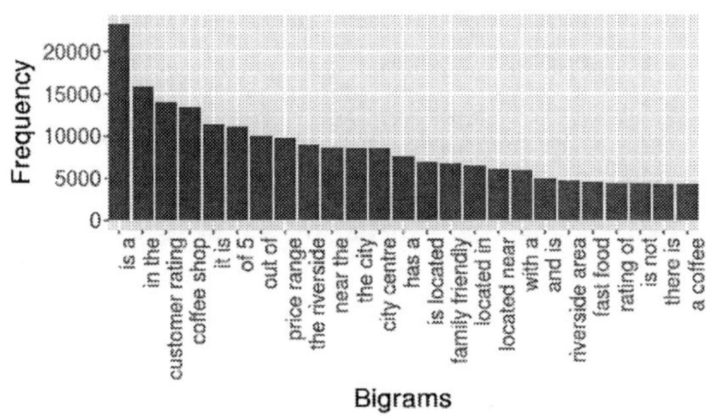
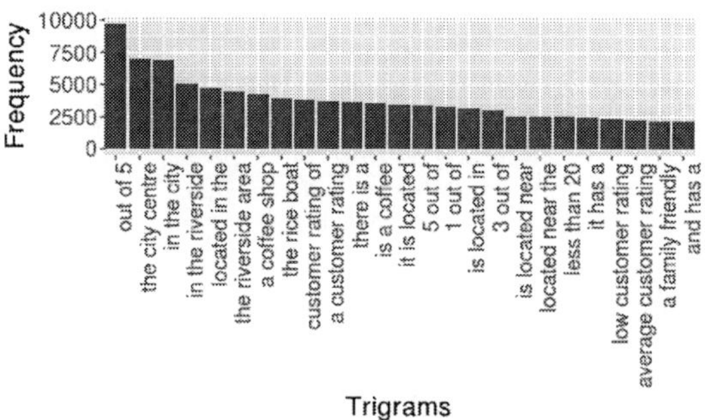

Figure 2: Distribution of the top 25 most frequent bigrams and trigrams in our dataset (left: most frequent bigrams, right: most frequent trigrams).

Dataset	Tokens	Types	LS	TTR	MSTTR
E2E	**65,710**	945	**0.57**	0.01	**0.75**
SFRest	45,791	1,187	0.43	0.03	0.62
Bagel	1,071	70	0.42	0.04	0.41

Table 4: Lexical Sophistication (LS) and Mean Segmental Type-Token Ratio (MSTTR).

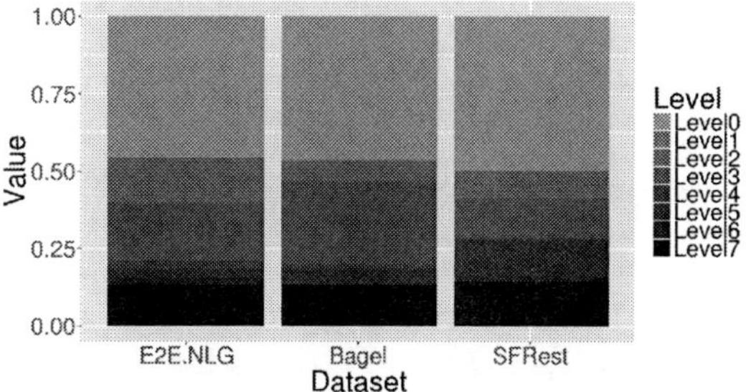

Figure 3: D-Level sentence distribution of the datasets under comparison.

lenge to current end-to-end generators since they cannot handle out-of-vocabulary words.

Syntactic Variation and Discourse Phenomena: We used the D-Level Analyser (Lu, 2009) to evaluate syntactic variation and complexity of human references using the revised D-Level Scale (Lu, 2014). Figure 3 show a similar syntactic variation in all three datasets. Most references in all the datasets are simple sentences (levels 0 and 1), although the proportion of simple texts is the lowest for the E2E NLG dataset (46%) compared to others (47-51%). Examples of simple sentences in our dataset include: "The Vaults is an Indian restaurant", or "The Loch Fyne is a moderate priced family restaurant". The majority of our data, however, contains more complex, varied syntactic structures, including phenomena explicitly modelled by early statistical approaches (Stent et al., 2004; Walker et al., 2004). For ex-

ample, clauses may be joined by a coordinating conjunction (level 2), e.g. "Cocum is a very expensive restaurant *but* the quality is great". There are 14% of level-2 sentences in our dataset, comparing to 7-9% in others. Sentences may also contain verbal gerund (*-ing*) phrases (level 4), either in addition to previously discussed structures or separately, e.g. "The coffee shop Wildwood has fairly priced food, *while being* in the same vicinity as the Ranch" or "The Vaults is a family-friendly restaurant *offering* fast food at moderate prices". Subordinate clauses are marked as level 5, e.g. "*If* you like Japanese food, try the Vaults". The highest levels of syntactic complexity involve

Dataset	O	A	C
E2E NLG	22%	18%	60%
SFRest	0%	6%	94%
Bagel	0%	0%	100%

Table 5: Match between MRs and NL references.

O: Omitted content, A: Additional content, C: Content fully covered in the reference.

Metric	Value
BLEU (Papineni et al., 2002)	0.6925
NIST (Doddington, 2002)	8.4781
METEOR (Lavie and Agarwal, 2007)	0.4703
ROUGE-L (Lin, 2004)	0.7257
CIDEr (Vedantam et al., 2015)	2.3987

Table 6: TGen results on the development set.

sentences containing referring expressions ("The Golden Curry provides Chinese food in the high price range. *It* is near the Bakers"), non-finite clauses in adjunct position ("*Serving* cheap English food, as well as *having* a coffee shop, the Golden Palace has an average customer rating and is located along the riverside") or sentences with multiple structures from previous levels. All the datasets contain 13-16% of sentences of levels 6 and 7, where Bagel has the lowest proportion (13%) and our dataset the highest (16%).

Content Selection: In contrast to the other datasets, our crowd workers were asked to verbalise all the *useful* information from the MR and were allowed to skip an attribute value considered unimportant. This feature makes generating text from our dataset more challenging as NLG systems also need to learn which content to realise. In order to measure the extent of this phenomenon, we examined a random sample of 50 MR-reference pairs. An MR-reference pair was considered a fully covered (C) match if all attribute values present in the MR are verbalised in the NL reference. It was marked as "additional" (A) if the reference contains information not present in the MR and as "omitted" (O) if the MR contains information not present in the reference, see Table 5. 40% of our data contains either additional or omitted information. This often concerns the attribute-value pair *eatType=restaurant*, which is either omitted ("Loch Fyne provides French food near The Rice Boat. It is located in riverside and has a low customer rating") or added in case *eatType* is absent from the MR ("Loch Fyne is a low-rating riverside French restaurant near The Rice Boat").

4   Baseline System Performance

To establish a baseline on the task data, we use TGen (Dušek and Jurčíček, 2016a), one of the re-

cent E2E data-driven systems.[3] TGen is based on sequence-to-sequence modelling with attention (seq2seq) (Bahdanau et al., 2015). In addition to the standard seq2seq model, TGen uses beam search for decoding and a reranker over the top k outputs, penalizing those outputs that do not verbalize all attributes from the input MR. As TGen does not handle unknown vocabulary well, the sparsely occurring string attributes (see Table 2) *name* and *near* are delexicalized – replaced with placeholders during generation time (both in input MRs and training sentences).[4]

We evaluated TGen on the development part of the E2E set using several automatic metrics. The results are shown in Table 6.[5] Despite the greater variety of our dataset as shown in Section 3, the BLEU score achieved by TGen is in the same range as scores reached by the same system for BAGEL (0.6276) and SFRest (0.7270). This indicates that the size of our dataset and the increased number of human references per MR helps statistical approaches.

Based on cursory checks, generator outputs seem mostly fluent and relevant to the input MR. For example, our setup was able to generate long, multi-sentence output, including referring expressions and ellipsis, as illustrated by the following example: "Browns Cambridge is a family-friendly coffee shop that serves French food. It has a low customer rating and is located in the riverside area near Crowne Plaza Hotel." However, TGen requires delexicalization and does not learn content selection, forcing the verbalization of all MR attributes.

---

[3]TGen is freely available at `https://github.com/UFAL-DSG/tgen`.

[4]Detailed system training parameters are given in the supplementary material.

[5]To measure the scores, we used slightly adapted versions of the official MT-Eval script (BLEU, NIST) and the COCO Caption (Chen et al., 2015) metrics (METEOR, ROUGE-L, CIDEr). All evaluation scripts used here are available at `https://github.com/tuetschek/e2e-metrics`.

5 Conclusion

We described the E2E dataset for end-to-end, statistical natural language generation systems. While this dataset is ten times bigger than similar, frequently used datasets, it also poses new challenges given its lexical richness, syntactic complexity and discourse phenomena. Moreover, generating from this set also involves content selection. In contrast to previous datasets, the E2E data is crowdsourced using pictorial stimuli, which was shown to elicit more natural, more informative and better phrased human references than textual meaning representations (Novikova et al., 2016). As such, learning from this data promises more natural and varied outputs than previous "template-like" datasets. The dataset is freely available as part of the E2E NLG Shared Task.[6]

In future work, we hope to collect data with further increased complexity, e.g. asking the user to compare, summarise, or recommend restaurants, in order to replicate previous rule-based and statistical approaches, e.g. (Walker et al., 2004; Stent et al., 2004; Demberg and Moore, 2006; Rieser et al., 2014). In addition, we will experiment with collecting NLG data within a dialogue context, following (Dušek and Jurčíček, 2016b), in order to model discourse phenomena across multiple turns.

Acknowledgements

This research received funding from the EPSRC projects DILiGENt (EP/M005429/1) and MaDrIgAL (EP/N017536/1). The Titan Xp used for this research was donated by the NVIDIA Corporation.

References

D. Bahdanau, K. Cho, and Y. Bengio. 2015. Neural machine translation by jointly learning to align and translate. In *International Conference on Learning Representations*. San Diego, CA, USA. ArXiv:1409.0473. http://arxiv.org/abs/1409.0473.

David L. Chen and Raymond J. Mooney. 2008. Learning to sportscast: A test of grounded language acquisition. In *Proceedings of the 25th international conference on Machine learning (ICML)*. Helsinki, Finland, pages 128–135. http://dl.acm.org/citation.cfm?id=1390173.

Xinlei Chen, Hao Fang, Tsung-Yi Lin, Ramakrishna Vedantam, Saurabh Gupta, Piotr Dollar, and C. Lawrence Zitnick. 2015. Microsoft COCO Captions: Data Collection and Evaluation Server. *CoRR* abs/1504.00325. http://arxiv.org/abs/1504.00325.

Vera Demberg and Johanna D Moore. 2006. Information presentation in spoken dialogue systems. In *Proceedings of the 11th Conference of the European Chapter of the ACL (EACL)*. pages 65–72. http://aclweb.org/anthology/E06-1009.

George Doddington. 2002. Automatic evaluation of machine translation quality using n-gram co-occurrence statistics. In *Proceedings of the Second International Conference on Human Language Technology Research*. San Diego, CA, USA, pages 138–145. http://dl.acm.org/citation.cfm?id=1289273.

Ondřej Dušek and Filip Jurčíček. 2015. Training a natural language generator from unaligned data. In *Proceedings of the 53rd Annual Meeting of the Association for Computational Linguistics and the 7th International Joint Conference on Natural Language Processing (Volume 1: Long Papers)*. Beijing, China, pages 451–461. http://aclweb.org/anthology/P15-1044.

Ondřej Dušek and Filip Jurčíček. 2016a. Sequence-to-sequence generation for spoken dialogue via deep syntax trees and strings. In *Proceedings of the 54th Annual Meeting of the Association for Computational Linguistics*. Berlin, Germany, pages 45–51. arXiv:1606.05491. http://aclweb.org/anthology/P16-2008.

Ondřej Dušek and Filip Jurčíček. 2016b. A context-aware natural language generator for dialogue systems. In *Proceedings of the 17th Annual Meeting of the Special Interest Group on Discourse and Dialogue*. Association for Computational Linguistics, Los Angeles, CA, USA, pages 185–190. arXiv:1608.07076. http://aclweb.org/anthology/W16-3622.

Gerasimos Lampouras and Andreas Vlachos. 2016. Imitation learning for language generation from unaligned data. In *Proceedings of COLING 2016, the 26th International Conference on Computational Linguistics: Technical Papers*. The COLING 2016 Organizing Committee, Osaka, Japan, pages 1101–1112. http://aclweb.org/anthology/C16-1105.

Alon Lavie and Abhaya Agarwal. 2007. METEOR: An automatic metric for MT evaluation with high levels of correlation with human judgments. In *Proceedings of the Second Workshop on Statistical Machine Translation*. Association for Computational Linguistics, Prague, Czech Republic, pages 228–231. http://aclweb.org/anthology/W07-0734.

Chin-Yew Lin. 2004. ROUGE: A package for automatic evaluation of summaries. In *Text summarization branches out: Proceedings of the ACL-*

---

[6]The training and development parts of our dataset can be downloaded from `http://www.macs.hw.ac.uk/InteractionLab/E2E/`.

04 workshop. Barcelona, Spain, pages 74–81. http://aclweb.org/anthology/W04-1013.

Xiaofei Lu. 2009. Automatic measurement of syntactic complexity in child language acquisition. *International Journal of Corpus Linguistics* 14(1):3–28. http://doi.org/10.1075/ijcl.14.1.02lu.

Xiaofei Lu. 2012. The relationship of lexical richness to the quality of ESL learners' oral narratives. *The Modern Language Journal* 96(2):190–208. http://doi.org/10.1111/j.1540-4781.2011.01232_1.x.

Xiaofei Lu. 2014. *Computational methods for corpus annotation and analysis*. Springer. http://doi.org/10.1007/978-94-017-8645-4.

François Mairesse, Milica Gašić, Filip Jurčíček, Simon Keizer, Blaise Thomson, Kai Yu, and Steve Young. 2010. Phrase-based statistical language generation using graphical models and active learning. In *Proceedings of the 48th Annual Meeting of the Association for Computational Linguistics*. Uppsala, Sweden, pages 1552–1561. http://aclweb.org/anthology/P10-1157.

Hongyuan Mei, Mohit Bansal, and Matthew R. Walter. 2016. What to talk about and how? Selective generation using LSTMs with coarse-to-fine alignment. In *Proceedings of the 2016 Conference of the North American Chapter of the Association for Computational Linguistics: Human Language Technologies*. San Diego, CA, USA. arXiv:1509.00838. http://aclweb.org/anthology/N16-1086.

Jekaterina Novikova, Oliver Lemon, and Verena Rieser. 2016. Crowd-sourcing NLG data: Pictures elicit better data. In *Proceedings of the 9th International Natural Language Generation Conference*. Edinburgh, UK, pages 265–273. arXiv:1608.00339. http://aclweb.org/anthology/W16-2302.

Kishore Papineni, Salim Roukos, Todd Ward, and Wei-Jing Zhu. 2002. BLEU: a method for automatic evaluation of machine translation. In *Proceedings of the 40th Annual Meeting of the Association for Computational Linguistics*. Association for Computational Linguistics, Philadelphia, PA, USA, pages 311–318. http://aclweb.org/anthology/P02-1040.

Laura Perez-Beltrachini and Claire Gardent. 2017. Analysing data-to-text generation benchmarks. In *Proceedings of the 10th International Natural Language Generation Conference*. Santiago de Compostela, Spain. http://arxiv.org/abs/1705.03802.

Verena Rieser and Oliver Lemon. 2009. Natural language generation as planning under uncertainty for spoken dialogue systems. In *Proceedings of the 12th Conference of the European Chapter of the ACL (EACL)*. Athens, Greece, pages 683–691. http://aclweb.org/anthology/E09-1078.

Verena Rieser, Oliver Lemon, and Simon Keizer. 2014. Natural language generation as incremental planning under uncertainty: Adaptive information presentation for statistical dialogue systems. *IEEE/ACM Transactions on Audio, Speech, and Language Processing* 22(5):979–993. https://doi.org/10.1109/TASL.2014.2315271.

Shikhar Sharma, Jing He, Kaheer Suleman, Hannes Schulz, and Philip Bachman. 2016. Natural language generation in dialogue using lexicalized and delexicalized data. *CoRR* abs/1606.03632. http://arxiv.org/abs/1606.03632.

Amanda Stent, Rashmi Prasad, and Marilyn Walker. 2004. Trainable sentence planning for complex information presentations in spoken dialog systems. In *Proceedings of the 42nd Meeting of the Association for Computational Linguistics*. Barcelona, Spain, pages 79–86. http://aclweb.org/anthology/P04-1011.

Ramakrishna Vedantam, C. Lawrence Zitnick, and Devi Parikh. 2015. CIDEr: Consensus-based image description evaluation. In *Proceedings of the 2015 IEEE Conference on Computer Vision and Pattern Recognition (CVPR)*. Boston, MA, USA, pages 4566–4575. https://doi.org/10.1109/CVPR.2015.7299087.

Marilyn A Walker, Stephen J Whittaker, Amanda Stent, Preetam Maloor, Johanna Moore, Michael Johnston, and Gunaranjan Vasireddy. 2004. Generation and evaluation of user tailored responses in multimodal dialogue. *Cognitive Science* 28(5):811–840. https://doi.org/10.1016/j.cogsci.2004.06.002.

Tsung-Hsien Wen, Milica Gašić, Nikola Mrkšić, Lina Maria Rojas-Barahona, Pei-hao Su, David Vandyke, and Steve J. Young. 2016. Multidomain neural network language generation for spoken dialogue systems. In *Proceedings of the 2016 Conference of the North American Chapter of the Association for Computational Linguistics: Human Language Technologies*. San Diego, CA, USA, pages 120–129. arXiv:1603.01232. http://aclweb.org/anthology/N16-1015.

Tsung-Hsien Wen, Milica Gašić, Nikola Mrkšić, Pei-Hao Su, David Vandyke, and Steve Young. 2015. Semantically conditioned LSTM-based natural language generation for spoken dialogue systems. In *Proceedings of the 2015 Conference on Empirical Methods in Natural Language Processing*. Lisbon, Portugal, pages 1711–1721. http://aclweb.org/anthology/D15-1199.

Frames: A Corpus for Adding Memory
to Goal-Oriented Dialogue Systems

Layla El Asri and **Hannes Schulz** and **Shikhar Sharma** and **Jeremie Zumer**

Justin Harris and **Emery Fine** and **Rahul Mehrotra** and **Kaheer Suleman**
Microsoft Maluuba
`first.last@microsoft.com`

Abstract

This paper proposes a new dataset, *Frames*, composed of 1369 human-human dialogues with an average of 15 turns per dialogue. This corpus contains goal-oriented dialogues between users who are given some constraints to book a trip and assistants who search a database to find appropriate trips. The users exhibit complex decision-making behaviour which involve comparing trips, exploring different options, and selecting among the trips that were discussed during the dialogue. To drive research on dialogue systems towards handling such behaviour, we have annotated and released the dataset and we propose in this paper a task called *frame tracking*. This task consists of keeping track of different semantic frames throughout each dialogue. We propose a rule-based baseline and analyse the frame tracking task through this baseline.

1 Introduction

Goal-oriented, information-retrieving dialogue systems have been designed traditionally to help users find items in a database given a set of constraints (Singh et al., 2002; Raux et al., 2003; El Asri et al., 2014; Laroche et al., 2011). For instance, the *LET'S GO* dialogue system finds a bus schedule given a bus number and a location (Raux et al., 2003).

Available resources for data-driven learning of such goal-oriented systems are often collected with an existing system (Henderson et al., 2014b; Bennett and Rudnicky, 2002) and have been proposed to study one component of dialogue. Examples are the first three Dialogue State Tracking Challenges (DSTC, Williams et al., 2016) during which a se-

ries of datasets and tasks of increasing complexity were released. These shared tasks were essential to advance the state of the art on state tracking. Other resources have allowed to study and develop different approaches to spoken language understanding and entity extraction (Mesnil et al., 2013). As for dialogue management, simulators have been proposed (Schatzmann et al., 2006) but datasets are scarce.

In most datasets collected with an existing system, the dialogues consist of sequential slot-filling: the system requests constraints until it can query the database and return several results to the user. Then, the user can ask for more information about a given result or request other possibilities. As a consequence, the tasks and methods that were based on these datasets were defined according to this sequential slot-filling process

We propose the *Frames* dataset to study more complex dialogue flows and decision-making behaviour. Our motivation comes from user studies in e-commerce which show that several information-seeking behaviours are exhibited by users who may come with a very well defined item in mind, but may also visit an e-commerce website with the intent to compare items and explore different possibilities (Moe and Fader, 2001; Saha et al., 2017). Supporting this kind of decision-making process in conversational systems implies adding *memory*. Memory is necessary to track different items or preferences set by the user during the dialogue. For instance, consider product comparisons. If a user wants to compare different items using a dialogue system, then this system should be able to separately recall properties pertaining to each item.

We collected 1369 human-human dialogues in a Wizard-of-Oz (WOz) setting – *i.e.*, users were paired up with humans, whom we refer to as *wizards*, who assumed the role of the dialogue system. Wizards were given access to a database of vaca-

207

Proceedings of the SIGDIAL 2017 Conference, pages 207–219,
Saarbrücken, Germany, 15-17 August 2017. ©2017 Association for Computational Linguistics

tion packages containing round-trip flights and a hotel. Users were tasked with finding packages based on a few constraints such as a destination and a budget. The dataset has been fully annotated by human experts and is publicly available[1].

Along with this dataset, we formalize a new task called *frame tracking*. Frame tracking is an extension of state tracking (Henderson, 2015; Williams et al., 2016). In state tracking, the information summarizing the full dialogue history is compressed into a single semantic frame which contains properties and values corresponding to the user's preferences (*e.g.*, destination city). In frame tracking, the dialogue agent must simultaneously track multiple semantic frames (*e.g.*, different destination cities; frames are defined formally in Section 4.2) throughout the conversation.

2　Data Collection

We collected the Frames data over a period of 20 days with 12 participants, who worked either for one day, one week, or 20 days. The participants alternated between the user and wizard roles on a daily basis. Due to this rotation, we can assume that we deal with returning users who know how to use the system, and focus on the decision making process, skipping the phase where the user learns about the system capabilities. The domain for all dialogues is travel: specifically, finding a vacation package that fulfils certain *a priori* requirements through a conversational search-and-compare process.

2.1　Wizard-Of-Oz Setting

Wizard-of-Oz (WOz) dialogues (Kelley, 1984; Rieser et al., 2005; Wen et al., 2016) have the considerable advantage of exhibiting realistic behaviours often beyond the capabilities of existing dialogue systems. Our setting is slightly different from the usual WOz setting because, in our case, users did not believe they were interacting with a dialogue system; they knew they were conversing with fellow humans. We chose not to give templated answers to wizards because, apart from studying decision-making, we also wanted to study information presentation and dialogue management. We work with text-based dialogues because this engenders a more controlled wizard behaviour, obviates handling time-sensitive turn taking, and speech recognition noise.

2.2　Task Templates and Instructions

User-wizard dialogues took place on Slack.[2] We deployed a Slack bot to pair up participants and record conversations. At the beginning of each dialogue, a user was paired with a wizard and given a new task. Tasks were built from templates like the following:

> "Find a vacation between [START_DATE] and [END_DATE] for [NUM_ADULTS] adults and [NUM_CHILDREN] kids. You leave from [ORIGIN_CITY]. You are travelling on a budget and you would like to spend at most $[BUDGET]."

Tasks were generated by drawing values (*e.g.*, for BUDGET) from a database. We constructed our database of flight and hotel properties by hand to simulate what one would find on a standard travel booking site. Each template was assigned a probability of success, and then constraint values were drawn in order to comply with this probability. For example, if 20 tasks were generated at probability 0.5, about 10 tasks would be generated with successful database queries and the other 10 would be generated such that the database returned no results for the constraints. This success mechanism allowed us to emulate cases when a user would find nothing meeting her constraints. If a task was unsuccessful, the user either ended the dialogue or got an alternative task such as: "If nothing matches your constraints, try increasing your budget by $200." We wrote 38 templates. 14 were generic like the one presented above and the other 24 included a background story to encourage role-playing from users and to keep them engaged. These templates were meant to add variety to the dialogues. The generic templates were also important for the users to create their own character and personality. We found that the combination of the two types of templates prevented the task from becoming too repetitive. Notably, we distributed the role-playing templates throughout the data collection process to bring some novelty and surprise. We also asked the participants to write templates (13 of them) to keep them engaged in the task.

To control data collection, we gave a set of instructions to the participants. The user instructions encouraged a variety of behaviours. As for the wizards, they were asked only to talk about the

---

[1] datasets.maluuba.com/Frames

[2] www.slack.com

database results and the task at hand. We also asked the wizards to perform untimely actions occasionally, for instance, to ask for information that the user has already provided. It is interesting from a dialogue management point of view to have examples of bad behaviour and of how it impacts user satisfaction. At the end of each dialogue, the user provided a wizard cooperativity rating on a scale of 1 to 5. The wizard, on the other hand, was shown the user's task and was asked whether she thought the user had accomplished it.

2.3 Search Interface And Suggestions

Wizards received a link to a search interface every time a user was connected to them. The search interface was a simple GUI with all the searchable fields in the database (see Appendix A). For every database search, up to 10 results were displayed, sorted by increasing price.

Another important property of human dialogue that we want to study with Frames is how to provide users with database information. When a set of user constraints leads to no results, users would benefit from knowing that relaxing a given constraint (*e.g.*, increasing the budget by a reasonable amount) leads to results. We modelled this by displaying suggestions to the wizards when a database query returned no results. Suggestions were packages obtained by randomly relaxing one or more constraints. It was up to the wizard to decide whether or not to use suggestions.

3 Statistics of the Corpus

Using the data collection process described above, we collected *1369 dialogues*. Figure 1a shows the distribution of dialogue lengths in the corpus. The average number of turns is 15, for a total of *19986 turns* in the dataset. A turn is defined as a Slack message sent by either a user or a wizard. Turns always alternate between user and wizard.

Figure 1b shows the number of acts per dialogue turn. About 25% of the dialogue turns have more than one dialogue act. The turns without dialogue acts are turns where the user asked for something that the wizard could not provide, *e.g.*, because it was not part of the database. We left such (rarely occurring) user turns unannotated, as they are usually followed up by the wizard saying she cannot provide the required information. This rarely occurs, since our users are familiar with the capabilities of the "system" after only few dialogues.

Figure 1c shows the distribution of user ratings. More than 70% of the dialogues have the maximum rating of 5. Figure 2 shows the occurrences of dialogue acts in the corpus. The dialogue acts are described in Table 9. We present the annotation scheme in the following section.

4 Annotation

We manually annotated the Frames dataset with dialogue acts, slot types and values, references to other frames, and the ID of the currently active frame for each utterance. We also computed frame descriptions based on the labels of earlier turns.

4.1 Dialogue Acts, Slot Types, Slot Values

Most of the dialogue acts used for annotation are typical of the goal-oriented setting, such as `inform` and `offer` (Henderson et al., 2014b). We also introduced dialogue acts specifically for frame tracking, such as `switch_frame` and `request_compare`. The dialogue acts are listed in Table 9.

Our annotation uses three sets of slot types. The first set, listed in Tables 7 and 8, corresponds to the fields of the database. The second set is listed in Table 10 and contains the slot types which we defined to describe specific aspects of the dialogue, such as `intent`, `action`, and `count`. The remaining slot types in Table 10 were introduced to describe frames and cross-references between them.

4.2 Frame Definition

Semantic frames form the core of our dataset. A semantic frame is defined by the following four components:

- User requests: slots whose values the user wants to know for this frame.
- User binary questions: user questions with slot types and slot values.
- Constraints: slots which have been set to a particular value by the user or the wizard.
- User comparison requests: slots whose values the user wants to know for this frame and one or more other frames.

In DSTC, a semantic frame contains the constraints set by the user, the user requests, and the user's search method (*e.g.*, by constraints or alternatives). In our case, constraints can also be set by the wizard when she suggests or offers a package. Any field in the database (see Tables 7 and 8 in Appendix A) can be constrained by the user or

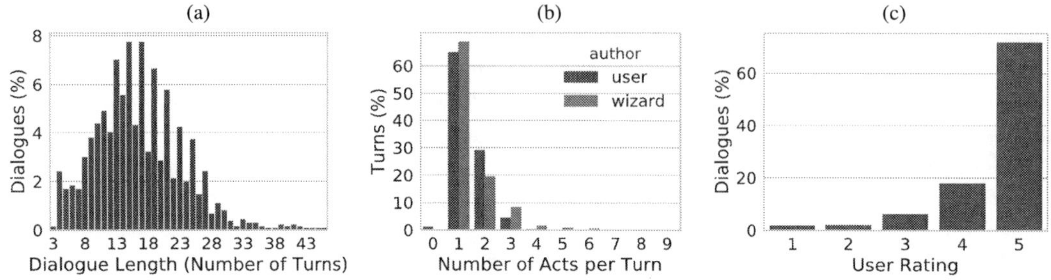

Figure 1: Overview of the Frames corpus

Table 1: Dialogue excerpt with active frame annotation

Author	Utterance	Frame
User	I'd like to book a trip to Atlantis from Caprica on Saturday, August 13, 2016 for 8 adults. I have a tight budget of 1700.	1
Wizard	Hi...I checked a few options for you, and unfortunately, we do not currently have any trips that meet this criteria. Would you like to book an alternate travel option?	1
User	Yes, how about going to Neverland from Caprica on August 13, 2016 for 5 adults. For this trip, my budget would be 1900.	2
Wizard	I checked the availability for those dates and there were no trips available. Would you like to select some alternate dates?	2

the wizard. The comparison requests and the binary questions were added after analysing the dialogues. The comparison requests correspond to the `request_compare` dialogue act. This dialogue act is used to annotate turns when a user asks to compare different results, for instance: *"Could you tell me which of these resorts offers free wifi?"*. These questions possibly relate to several frames. Binary questions are questions with slot types and slot values, *e.g.*, *"In which part of the town is the hotel located?"* (`request` act), or *"Is the trip to Marseille cheaper than to Naples?"* (`request_compare` act), as well as all `confirm` acts. Binary questions may concern one or several frames.

4.3 Frame Creation and Switching

Each dialogue starts in frame 1. New frames are introduced when the wizard offers or suggests some-

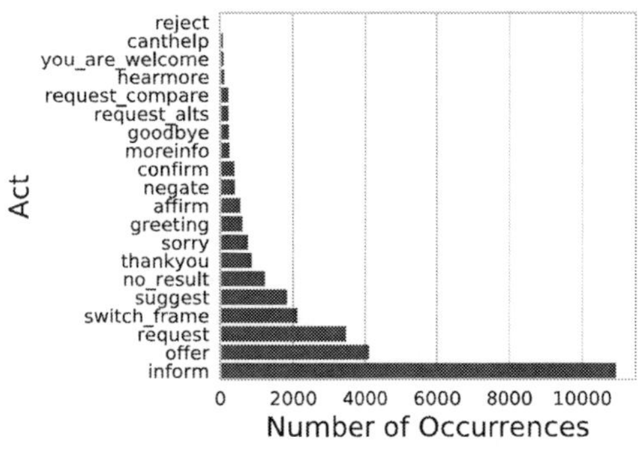

Figure 2: Dialogue act occurrences in the corpus

thing, or when the user modifies pre-established slots. Thus, all values discussed during the dialogue are recorded and the user can return to a previous set of constraints at any point. An example is given in Table 1: the frame number changes when the user modifies several slot values, namely, the destination city, the number of adults for the trip, and the budget. While modifying pre-established slots is supported by most dialogue systems, these rules allow us to clearly distinguishing creating frames from extending frames and thus define how the items in the dialogue memory, which the user can reference, are structured. Though frames are created for each offer or suggestion made by the wizard, the *active* frame can only be changed by the user so that the user has control over the dialogue. When creating frames, the annotator can explicitly mark which frame the new frame is derived from, which heuristically copies some of its content to the new frame. If not annotated, we assume it is derived from the currently active frame. If the user asks for more information about a specific offer or suggestion, the active frame is changed to the frame introduced with that offer or suggestion. This change of frame is indicated by a `switch_frame` act (see Appendix A). The rules for creating and switching frames are summarized in Table 2.

We introduced specific slot types for recording the creation and modification of frames. These slot types are `id`, `ref`, `read`, and `write` (see Table 10 in Appendix A). The frame `id` is defined when the frame is created and is used to switch to

Table 2: Frequency of frame creation and switching events

Rule Type	Author	Rule Description	Relative Frequency	Absolute Frequency
Creation	User	Changing the value of a slot	31%	2092
	Wizard	Making an offer or a suggestion	69%	4762
Switching	User	Changing the value of a slot (it causes the dialogue to switch to that frame)	50%	2092
		Considering a wizard offer or suggestion	39%	1635
		Switching to an earlier frame by mentioning its slot values	11%	458

this frame when the user decides to do so.

The other slot types are used to annotate cross-references between frames. A reference has two parts: the `id` of the frame it refers to and the slots and values that are used to refer to that frame (if any). For instance, `ref[1{name=Tropic}]` means that frame 1 is being referred to by the hotel name *Tropic*. If anaphora are used to refer to a frame, we annotated this with the slot `ref_anaphora` (*e.g.*, "This is too long" – `inform(duration=too long, ref_anaphora=this)`). Inside an `offer` dialogue act, a `ref` means that the frame corresponding to the offer is derived from another frame. This happens for instance when a wizard proposes a package with business or economy options. In this case, the business and economy offers are derived from the hotel offer.

The slot types `read` and `write` only occur inside a wizard's `inform` act and are used by wizards to provide relations between offers or suggestions: `read` is used to indicate which frame the values come from (and which slots are used to refer to this frame, if any), while `write` indicates the frame where the slot values are to be written (and which slot values are used to refer to this frame, if any). If there is a `read` without a `write`, the current frame is assumed as the storage for the slot values. A slot type without a value indicates that the value is the same as in the referenced frame, but was not mentioned explicitly *e.g.*, "for the same price".

Table 3 gives an example of how these slot types are used in practice: `inform( read=[7{dst_city=Punta Cana, category=2.5}])` means that the values *2.5* and *Punta Cana* are to be read from frame 7, and to be written in the current frame. At this turn of the dialogue, the wizard repeats information from frame 7. The annotation `inform(breakfast=False, write= [7{name=El Mar}])` means that the value

False for breakfast is written in frame 7 and that frame 7 was identified in this utterance by the name of the hotel *El Mar*.

The average number of frames created per dialogue is 6.71 and the average number of frame switches is 3.58. Figure 3 shows boxplots for the number of frame creations and the number of frame changes in the corpus.

4.4 Annotation Reproducibility

Five trained experts annotated the dataset according to the above rules. To measure inter-annotator agreement, the experts annotated the same randomly chosen 10 dialogues. On this subset, we compute the inter-annotator agreement rate as the F1-score. Note that the commonly used κ statistic cannot be directly applied here, since the annotation is not a multi-class classification problem. The provided F1 score also captures how much the annotators failed to annotate words or acts, or disagreed about the correct value. We report the mean and standard deviation over all possible pairing of annotators. On dialogue acts only, this score is 81.2 ± 3.1, on slot values, it is 95.2 ± 1.1, and on dialogue acts, slot values, and content of referenced frames, it is 62.3 ± 4.9.

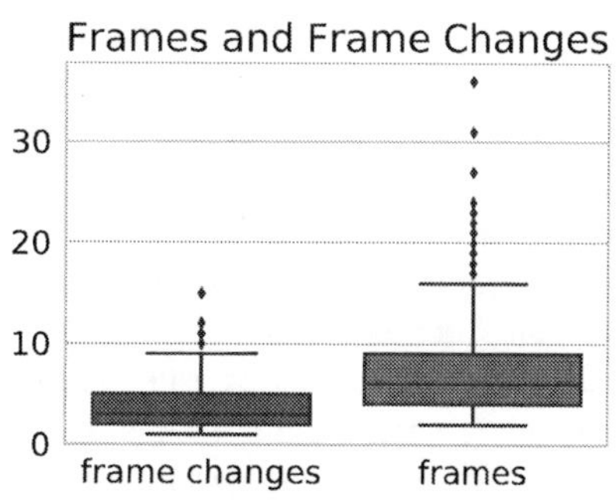

Figure 3: Number of frames and frame switches in the corpus

Table 3: Annotation example with the `write` and `read` slot types

Author	Utterance	Frame	Annotation
Wizard	I am only able to find hotels with a 2.5 star rating in Punta Cana for that time.	6	inform(*read*=[7{dst_city=Punta Cana, category=2.5}])
User	2.5 stars will do. Can you offer any additional activities?	11	inform(category=2.5)
Wizard	Unfortunately I am not able to provide this information.	11	sorry, canthelp
User	How about breakfast?	11	request(breakfast)
Wizard	El Mar does not provide breakfast.	11	inform(breakfast=False, *write*=[7{name=El Mar}])

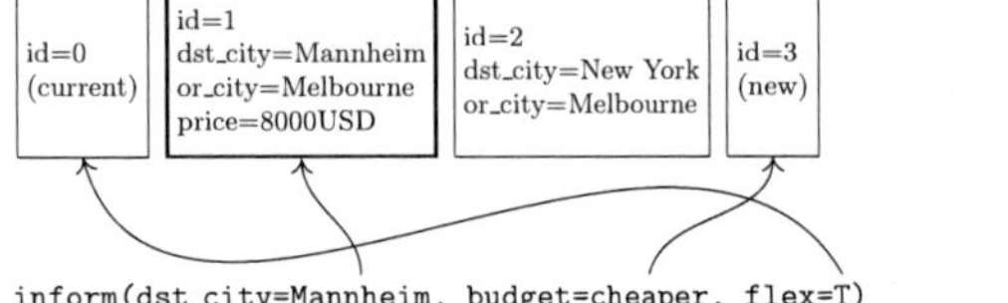

Figure 4: Illustration of the frame tracking task. The model must choose, for each slot, which frame it is referring to, given the set of available frames, the previous active frame (bold), and the potential new frame (marked "(new)").

5   Research Topics

Frames can be used to study many aspects of goal-oriented dialogue, from Natural Language Understanding (NLU) to Natural Language Generation (NLG). In this section, we propose three topics that we believe are new and representative of Frames.

5.1   Frame Tracking

5.1.1   Definition

We propose *Frame tracking* as an extension of state tracking (Henderson, 2015) to a setting where several semantic frames are tracked simultaneously. In state tracking, the dialogue history is compressed into one semantic frame. The state tracker updates a probability distribution, for each slot, over the different possible values. Every time the user sets a new value, the probability distribution is updated. This architecture prevents the user from comparing options or returning to an item discussed earlier since the values for each slot are tracked separately. In frame tracking, a new value creates a new semantic frame. The frame tracking task is significantly harder as it requires, for each user utterance, identifying the active frame as well as all the frames modified by the utterance. An example is provided in Fig. 4.

Definition 1 (Frame Tracking). At each user turn t, we assume access to the full dialogue history $H = \{f_1, ..., f_{n_{t-1}}\}$, where f_i is a frame and n_{t-1} is the number of frames created so far in the dialogue. For a user utterance u_t at time t, we provide the following NLU labels: dialogue acts, slot types, and slot values. The goal of frame tracking is to predict if a new frame is created and to predict for each dialogue act the `ref` labels (possibly none) and the `ids` of the frames referenced.

Predicting the frame that is referenced by a dialogue act requires detecting if a new frame is created and recognizing a previous frame from the values mentioned by the user (potentially synonyms, *e.g.*, NYC for New York), or by using the user utterance directly. It is necessary in many cases to use the user utterance directly because users do not always use slot values to refer to previous frames. An example in the corpus is a user asking: "Which package has the soonest departure?". In this case, the user refers to several frames (the packages) without ever explicitly describing which ones. This phenomenon is quite common for dialogue acts such as `switch_frame` (979 occurrences in the corpus) and `request_compare` (455 occurrences in the corpus). These cases can only be resolved by working on the text directly and solving anaphora.

Note that when talking with real users, a system would need to generate the frames dynamically during the dialogue. We propose the frame tracking task as a first step and we show in Section 6.2 that this simplified task entails many challenges.

5.1.2   Evaluation Metrics

We define two metrics: frame identification and frame creation. For frame identification, for each dialogue act, we compare the ground truth pair (`key-value`, `frame`) to that predicted by the frame tracker. We compute performance as the number of correct predictions over the number of pairs. The `frame` is the `id` of the referenced frame. The `key` and `value` are respectively the type and the value of the slot used to refer to the frame (these can be null).

For frame creation, we compute the number of times the frame tracker correctly predicts that a frame is created or correctly predicts that a frame has not been created over the number of dialogue turns.

5.1.3 Related Work

In previous work, some limitations of sequential slot filling dialogue systems were addressed using goal-modeling (Crook and Lemon, 2010; Crook et al., 2012; Misu et al., 2011), task tracking (Lee and Stent, 2016) and memory-augmentation of classical state tracking (Weston et al., 2015).

Crook and Lemon (2010); Crook et al. (2012) model the user goal as a subset of all possible slot value combinations and propose techniques to automatically compress this huge space into a summary space. Rewards, transitions, and observations of a POMDP system can then be projected to the reduced space, which facilitates policy learning. Misu et al. (2011) propose a method for decision support in spoken dialogue systems that aids a user who is assumed to have an (unknown) weighted preference over the possible slot values and limited knowledge about alternatives. The authors employ a user simulator that outputs dialogue acts to learn a policy that optimizes the sum of the weights of the final user selection. The Frames dataset allows learning and evaluating these techniques on a large and more realistic text-based dataset. Additionally, the memorized frames would allow a dialogue system to compare disjunct goals or return to earlier states.

Recent approaches to state tracking have been suggested to go beyond the sequential slot-filling approach. An important contribution is the Task Lineage-based Dialog State Tracking (TL-DST) proposed by Lee and Stent (2016). TL-DST is a framework that allows keeping track of tasks across different domains. Similarly to frame tracking, Lee and Stent propose building a dynamic structure of the dialogue containing different frames corresponding to different tasks. They defined different sub-tasks among which *task frame parsing* which is closely related to frame tracking except that they impose constraints on how a dialogue act can be assigned to a frame and a dialogue act can only relate to one frame. Because of the lack of data, Lee

and Stent (2016) trained their tracking model on datasets released for DSTC (DSTC2 and DSTC3, Henderson et al., 2014b,a). As a result, they could artificially mix different tasks, *e.g.*, looking for a restaurant and looking for a pub, but they could not study how human beings switch between topics. In addition, this framework can switch between different tasks but does not handle comparisons between disjunct frames, which is an important aspect of frame tracking.

Another related approach was proposed by Perez and Liu (2016) who re-interpreted the state tracking task as a question-answering task. Their state tracker is based on a memory network (Weston et al., 2015) and can answer questions about the user goal at the end of the dialogue. They also propose adding functionalities such as keeping a list of the constraints expressed by the user during the dialogue.

The Frames dataset may be used to test and validate these approaches on real data. In addition, we propose the frame tracking task as benchmark and as a first step towards modelling complex decision-making behaviour.

5.2 Dialogue Management

Most of the time, the wizard would speak about the current frame to ask or answer questions. However, sometimes, the wizard would talk about previous frames. An example is given in Table 11 in Appendix A. In the bold utterance in this dialogue, the wizard mentions a frame which is not the currently active frame. In order to reproduce this kind of behaviour, a dialogue manager would need to be able to identify potentially relevant frames for the current turn and to output actions for these frames.

Table 11 also illustrates another novelty. In the utterance in italics, the wizard actually performs two actions. The first action consists of informing the user about the price of the *regal resort* and the second action consists of proposing another option, *Hotel Globetrotter*. Performing more than one action per turn is a challenge when using reinforcement learning (Pietquin et al., 2011; Gašić et al., 2012; Fatemi et al., 2016) and, to our knowledge, has only been tackled in a simulated setting (Laroche et al., 2009).

5.3 Natural Language Generation

An interesting behaviour observed in Frames is that wizards often tend to summarize database results. An example is a wizard saying: *"The cheapest*

Table 4: F1 scores for the NLU baseline (mean and standard deviation).

Dialogue Acts	Slots
0.78 ± 0.05	0.79 ± 0.04

Table 5: Accuracy (%) of the Frame Tracking Baselines (mean and standard deviation).

	Rule-Based	Random
Frame Creation	0.49 ± 0.03	0.47 ± 0.02
Frame Identification	0.24 ± 0.02	0.18 ± 0.02

available flight is 1947.14USD." In this case, the wizard informs the user that the database has no cheaper result than the one she is proposing. To imitate this behaviour, a natural language generator (Oh and Rudnicky, 2000; Wen et al., 2015; Sharma et al., 2017) would need to reason over the database and decide how to tailor the results to the user and present them in a concise but sufficient way. Various strategies and their combinations can be employed, e.g. summarization, comparison or recommendation (Rieser and Lemon, 2009). A decision-theoretical foundation of such an approach was presented by Walker et al. (2004). A data-driven approach to attribute selection for NLG as planning under uncertainty was proposed by Rieser et al. (2014). The Frames dataset contains a larger set of dialogues as well as wizard-generated text with detailed annotations, which we believe will provide insight into when humans use which strategy and how they present the information.

6 Baselines

We developed baseline models for natural language understanding and frame tracking.

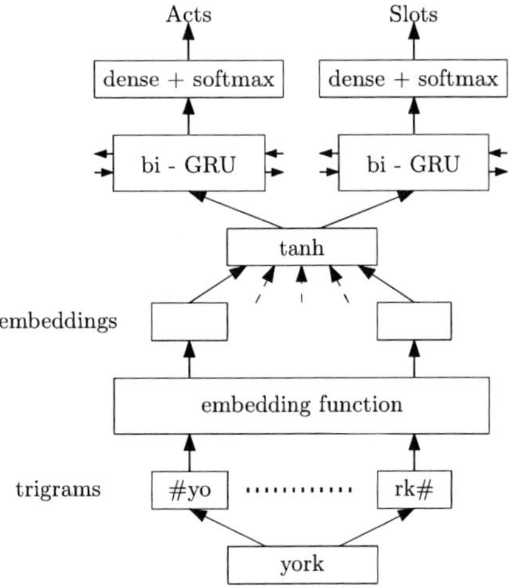

Figure 5: Illustration of the NLU model for slots and acts prediction.

6.1 Natural Language Understanding

We define the NLU task as dialogue act prediction and IOB (Inside, Outside, Beginning) tagging. The NLU model that we propose as baseline is illustrated in Fig. 5. We predict, for each word of the utterance, a pair of tags – one for the act and one for the slot. This model operates on character trigrams and is based on the robust named entity recognition model (Arnold et al., 2016) except that it has two heads instead of one: one head for the slot type (either a slot type or an *O* tag) as in the original model and one head for dialogue act prediction. These two parts share an embedding matrix for the input character trigrams.

We generated the IOB tags by matching the slot values in the manual annotations with the corresponding textual utterances. Note that the model only predicts IOB tags for slots whose values can be found in the text. Therefore, the prediction for slots such as `intent` or vicinities and amenities is not evaluated for this simple baseline. The act tags were also generated at the word level: for a given dialogue act with slot values, each word between the slot value that occurred first in the text and the one that occurred last in the text was tagged with the corresponding act. For example, for the utterance *I am only able to find hotels with a 2.5 star rating in Punta Cana for that time.*, the words *2.5 star rating in Punta Cana* are tagged with the `inform` dialogue act. The other words are tagged with *O*.

The two parts of the model are trained simultaneously, using a modified categorical crossentropy loss for both sets of outputs. We modify the loss to ignore *O* labels that are already predicted correctly by the model. We introduce this modification because *O* labels are far more frequent than other labels, and not limiting their contribution to the loss causes the model to degenerate to predicting *O* labels for every word. The losses for both parts of the model are added together and the combined objective is optimized using ADAM (Kingma and Ba, 2015).

We provide F1 scores for acts and slots for this model in Table 4. We report average and standard deviation over ten leave-one-user-out splits of the Frames dataset. We had a total of 11 participants who played the user role at least once during data collection. Two participants performed significantly fewer dialogues than the others. We merged the dialogues generated by these two participants (ids U21E41CQP and U23KPC9QV). For each of the resulting 10 users, we randomly split the combined dialogues of the nine others into training (80%) and validation (20%), and then tested on the dialogues from the held-out user.

6.2 Frame Tracking

We propose a rule-based frame tracking baseline which takes as input the dialogue acts with slot types and slot values but without the referenced frames (*i.e.*, the `ref` slots) as well as all the frames created so far during the dialogue. Based on this input, the tracker predicts the `ref` tags (for frame identification, see Section 5.1.2) for each dialogue act, and it predicts if a frame is created. We write $f[k]$ to denote the value of slot k in frame f. For an act $a(k=v)$ in frame f, the following rules are used:

- *Create and switch to a new frame* if $f[k]$ is set and a is `inform`, but v does not match $f[k]$.
- *Switch to frame g* if a is `switch_frame` and $g[k]$ matches v. If no match is found, switch to the most recently created frame.[3]
- *Assign `ref` to frame g* if a can have a `ref` tag, and $g[k]$ matches v. The most recently created frame is used in ambiguous cases. If no match is found, assign `ref` to the current frame.

We compare this baseline to random performance. For random performance, for each (dialogue act, slot type) combination, we compute priors on the corpus for each time the user would refer to the current frame *vs* a previous one. We sampled whether each slot referred to the current frame or another one based on that prior, and if it referred to another frame, the frame number for that other frame was sampled uniformly from the list of frames created so far.

Table 5 presents results for these baselines. We report results over 10 runs following the same evaluation method as for the NLU model. Table 5 shows that the rule-based model performs only slightly better than random on frame identification

Table 6: Accuracy (%) of the rule-based baseline on sub-tasks of frame tracking.

	With slots	Without slots	After an offer	Not after an offer
Frame switching	44.9	16.3	54.3	16.5

	Change of value	No frame creation
Frame creation	5.5	83.1

and performs similarly on frame creation. Table 6 presents an analysis of the performance of the rule-based model. We report the accuracy of the frame tracking baseline on the most crucial sub-tasks of frame tracking for one fold. The top table shows that the most difficult tasks consist of assigning the correct frame to a `switch_frame` act when the act is not directly preceded by an offer and when the act has no slots. As discussed previously, when the act has no slots, it is important to consider the text and solve anaphora. When the act is directly preceded by an offer, the baseline assigns the previous frame, which is the frame of the offer and which most of the time is the frame that the user switched to, *e.g.*, to ask for more information about the offer. In terms of frame creation, the baseline has very poor performance in correctly predicting that a frame is created because the user changes the value of a previously set slot. These results demonstrate that frame tracking cannot be solved with simple rules and necessitates tackling many complex sub-tasks.

7 Conclusion

We introduced the Frames dataset: a corpus of human-human dialogues in a travel domain. This dataset contains complex user behaviour such as comparing between offers. We formalized the frame tracking task, which requires tracking simultaneously several semantic frames during a dialogue. We proposed a rule-based model for this task and analysed its performance. We release Frames in the hope of driving further research on complex decision-making in the dialogue community.

References

S. Arnold, F. A. Gers, T. Kilias, and A. Löser. 2016. Robust named entity recognition in idiosyncratic domains. *arXiv:1608.06757 [cs.CL]* .

Christina L. Bennett and Alexander I. Rudnicky. 2002. The carnegie mellon communicator corpus. In *Proc. of Interspeech*.

---

[3]a reasonable assumption since this case often happens when a wizard makes an offer and the user talks about it.

Paul A Crook and Oliver Lemon. 2010. Representing uncertainty about complex user goals in statistical dialogue systems. In *Proc. of SIGDIAL*. pages 209–212.

Paul A Crook, Zhuoran Wang, Xingkun Liu, and Oliver Lemon. 2012. A statistical spoken dialogue system using complex user goals and value directed compression. In *Proc. of EACL*. Association for Computational Linguistics, pages 46–50.

Layla El Asri, Rémi Lemonnier, Romain Laroche, Olivier Pietquin, and Hatim Khouzaimi. 2014. NASTIA: Negotiating Appointment Setting Interface. In *Proc. of LREC*.

Mehdi Fatemi, Layla El Asri, Hannes Schulz, Jing He, and Kaheer Suleman. 2016. Policy networks with two-stage training for dialogue systems. In *Proc. of SIGDIAL*.

M. Gašić, M. Henderson, B. Thomson, P. Tsiakoulis, and S. Young. 2012. Policy optimisation of POMDP-based dialogue systems without state space compression. In *Proc. of SLT*.

M. Henderson, B. Thomson, and J. Williams. 2014a. The Third Dialog State Tracking Challenge. In *Proceedings of IEEE Spoken Language Technology*.

Matthew Henderson. 2015. Machine learning for dialog state tracking: A review. In *First International Workshop on Machine Learning in Spoken Language Processing*.

Matthew Henderson, Blaise Thomson, and Jason D. Williams. 2014b. The second dialog state tracking challenge. In *Proc. of SIGDIAL*.

John F. Kelley. 1984. An iterative design methodology for user-friendly natural language office information applications. *ACM Transaction on Information Systems* .

Diederik Kingma and Jimmy Ba. 2015. Adam: A method for stochastic optimization. *Proc. of ICLR* .

Romain Laroche, Ghislain Putois, Philippe Bretier, Martin Aranguren, Julia Velkovska, Helen Hastie, Simon Keizer, Kai Yu, Filip Jurčíček, Oliver Lemon, and Steve Young. 2011. Report D6.4 : Final evaluation of classic towninfo and appointment scheduling systems. Technical report, CLASSIC Project.

Romain Laroche, Ghislain Putois, Philippe Bretier, and Bernadette Bouchon-Meunier. 2009. Hybridisation of expertise and reinforcement learning in dialogue systems. In *Proc. of Interspeech*.

Sungjin Lee and Amanda Stent. 2016. Task lineages: Dialog state tracking for flexible interaction. In *Proc. of SIGDIAL*.

Grégoire Mesnil, Xiaodong He, Li Deng, and Yoshua Bengio. 2013. Investigation of recurrent-neural-network architectures and learning methods for spoken language understanding. In *Proc. of Interspeech*.

Teruhisa Misu, Komei Sugiura, Tatsuya Kawahara, Kiyonori Ohtake, Chiori Hori, Hideki Kashioka, Hisashi Kawai, and Satoshi Nakamura. 2011. Modeling spoken decision support dialogue and optimization of its dialogue strategy. *Transactions on Speech and Language Processing* 7(3):10.

Wendy W. Moe and Peter S. Fader. 2001. Uncovering patterns in cybershopping. *California Management Review* .

Alice H. Oh and Alexander I. Rudnicky. 2000. Stochastic language generation for spoken dialogue systems. In *Proc. of ANLP/NAACL workshop on Conversational Systems*.

Julien Perez and Fei Liu. 2016. Dialog state tracking, a machine reading approach using memory network. In *Proc. of EACL*.

Olivier Pietquin, Matthieu Geist, Senthilkumar Chandramohan, and Hervé Frezza-Buet. 2011. Sample-efficient batch reinforcement learning for dialogue management optimization. *ACM Transaction on Speech and Language Processing* 7(3):1–21.

Antoine Raux, Brian Langner, Allan Black, and Maxine Eskenazi. 2003. LET'S GO: Improving Spoken Dialog Systems for the Elderly and Non-natives. In *Proc. of Eurospeech*.

Verena Rieser, Ivana Kruijff-Korbayov, and Oliver Lemon. 2005. A corpus collection and annotation framework for learning multimodal clarification strategies. In *Proc. of SIGDIAL*.

Verena Rieser and Oliver Lemon. 2009. Natural language generation as planning under uncertainty for spoken dialogue systems. In *Proc. of EACL*. pages 683–691.

Verena Rieser, Oliver Lemon, and Simon Keizer. 2014. Natural language generation as incremental planning under uncertainty: adaptive information presentation for statistical dialogue systems. *Transactions on Audio, Speech and Language Processing* 22(5):979–994.

A. Saha, M. Khapra, and K. Sankaranarayanan. 2017. Multimodal Dialogs (MMD): A large-scale dataset for studying multimodal domain-aware conversations. *arXiv:1704.00200 [cs.CL]* .

Jost Schatzmann, Karl Weilhammer, Matt Stuttle, and Steve Young. 2006. A survey of statistical user simulation techniques for reinforcement-learning of dialogue management strategies. *The knowledge engineering review* 21(2):97–126.

Shikhar Sharma, Jing He, Kaheer Suleman, Hannes Schulz, and Philip Bachman. 2017. Natural language generation in dialogue using lexicalized and delexicalized data. *Proc. of ICLR Workshop* .

Satinder Singh, Michael Kearns, Diane Litman, and Marilyn Walker. 2002. Optimizing dialogue management with reinforcement learning: experiments with the njfun system. *Journal of Artificial Intelligence Research* 16:105–133.

M.a. Walker, S.j. Whittaker, A. Stent, P. Maloor, J. Moore, M. Johnston, and G. Vasireddy. 2004. Generation and evaluation of user tailored responses in multimodal dialogue. *Cognitive Science* 28(5):811–840.

Tsung-Hsien Wen, Milica Gasic, Nikola Mrksic, Lina Maria Rojas-Barahona, Pei-Hao Su, Stefan Ultes, David Vandyke, and Steve J. Young. 2016. A network-based end-to-end trainable task-oriented dialogue system. In *Proc. of EACL.*

Tsung-Hsien Wen, Milica Gasic, Nikola Mrkšić, Pei-Hao Su, David Vandyke, and Steve Young. 2015. Semantically conditioned lstm-based natural language generation for spoken dialogue systems. In *Proc. of EMNLP.*

Jason Weston, Sumit Chopra, and Antoine Bordes. 2015. Memory networks. *Proc. of ICLR* .

Jason D. Williams, Antoine Raux, and Matthew Henderson. 2016. The dialog state tracking challenge series: A review. *Dialogue and Discourse* .

A   Annotation Details and Dialogue Example

Table 7: Searchable fields in the database of packages

Field	Description
PRICE_MAX	Maximum price the user is willing to pay
PRICE_MIN	Minimum price defined by the user
DESTINATION_CITY	Destination city
MAX_DURATION	Maximum number of days for the trip
NUM_ADULTS	Number of adults
NUM_CHILDREN	Number of children
START_DATE	Start date for the trip
END_DATE	End date for the trip
ARE_DATES_FLEXIBLE	Boolean value indicating whether or not the user's dates are flexible. If True, then the search is broadened to 2 days before START_DATE and 2 days after END_DATE.
ORIGIN_CITY	Origin city

Table 8: Non-searchable fields in the database of packages

Field	Description
Global Properties	
PRICE	Price of the trip including flights and hotel
DURATION	Duration of the trip
Hotel Properties	
NAME	Name of the hotel
COUNTRY	Country where the hotel is located
CATEGORY	Rating of the hotel (in number of stars)
CITY	City where the hotel is located
GUEST_RATING	Rating of the hotel by guests (in number of stars)
BREAKFAST, PARKING, WIFI, GYM, SPA	Boolean value indicating whether or not the hotel offers this amenity.
PARK, MUSEUM, BEACH, SHOPPING, MARKET, AIRPORT, UNIVERSITY, MALL, CATHEDRAL, DOWNTOWN, PALACE, THEATRE	Boolean value indicating whether or not the hotel is in the vicinity of one of these.
Flights Properties	
SEAT	Seat type (economy or business)
DEPARTURE_DATE_DEP	Date of departure to destination
DEPARTURE_DATE_ARR	Date of return flight
DEPARTURE_TIME_DEP	Time of departure to destination
ARRIVAL_TIME_DEP	Time of arrival to destination
DEPARTURE_TIME_ARR	Time of departure from destination
ARRIVAL_TIME_ARR	Time of arrival to origin city
DURATION_DEP	Duration of flight to destination
DURATION_ARR	Duration of return flight

Table 9: List of dialogue acts in the annotation of Frames

Dialogue Act	Speaker	Description
inform	User/Wizard	Inform a slot value
offer	Wizard	Offer a package to the user
request	User/Wizard	Ask for the value of a particular slot
switch_frame	User	Switch to a frame
suggest	Wizard	Suggest a slot value or package that does not match the user's constraints
no_result	Wizard	Tell the user that the database returned no results
thankyou	User/Wizard	Thank the other speaker
sorry	Wizard	Apologize to the user
greeting	User/Wizard	Greet the other speaker
affirm	User/Wizard	Affirm something said by the other speaker
negate	User/Wizard	Negate something said by the other speaker
confirm	User/Wizard	Ask the other speaker to confirm a given slot value
moreinfo	User	Ask for more information on a given set of results
goodbye	User/Wizard	Say goodbye to the other speaker
request_alts	User	Ask for other possibilities
request_compare	User	Ask the wizard to compare packages
hearmore	Wizard	Ask the user if she'd like to hear more about a given package
you_are_welcome	Wizard	Tell the user she is welcome
canthelp	Wizard	Tell the user you cannot answer her request
reject	Wizard	Tell the user you did not understand what she meant

Table 10: List of slot types not present in the database

Slot Type	Description
count	Number of different packages
count_amenities	Number of amenities
count_name	Number of different hotels
count_dst_city	Number of destination cities
count_seat	Number of seat options (for flights)
count_category	Number of star ratings
id	Id of the frame created (for offers and suggestions)
vicinity	Vicinity of the hotel
amenities	Amenities of the hotel
ref_anaphora	Words used to refer to a frame *e.g.*, "the second package'
impl_anaphora	Used when a slot type is not specifically mentionned *e.g.*, "What is the price for Rio?"..."And for Cleveland?"
ref	Id of the frame that the speaker is referring to
read	Reads slot values specified in another frame and writes them in the current frame
write	Writes slot values in a given frame
intent	User intent (*e.g.*, book)
action	Wizard action (*e.g.*, book)

Table 11: Dialogue excerpt where the wizard talks about a frame other than the active frame

Author	Utterance
Wizard	A 5 star hotel called the Regal Resort,
Wizard	it has free wifi and a spa.
User	dates?
Wizard	Starts on august 27th until the 30th
User	ok that could work. I would like to see my options in Santos as well
Wizard	*regal resort goes for $2800 or there is the Hotel* Globetrotter in Santos it has 3 stars and comes with *breakfast and wifi. it leaves on the 25th and returns on the 30th! all for $2000*
User	ahh I can't leave until august 26 though
Wizard	**then i guess you might have to choose the Regal resort**
User	yeah. I will book it
Wizard	Thank you!

Towards a General, Continuous Model of Turn-taking
in Spoken Dialogue using LSTM Recurrent Neural Networks

Gabriel Skantze
Department of Speech Music and Hearing, KTH
Stockholm, Sweden
skantze@kth.se

Abstract

Previous models of turn-taking have mostly been trained for specific turn-taking decisions, such as discriminating between turn shifts and turn retention in pauses. In this paper, we present a predictive, continuous model of turn-taking using Long Short-Term Memory (LSTM) Recurrent Neural Networks (RNN). The model is trained on human-human dialogue data to predict upcoming speech activity in a future time window. We show how this general model can be applied to two different tasks that it was not specifically trained for. First, to predict whether a turn-shift will occur or not in pauses, where the model achieves a better performance than human observers, and better than results achieved with more traditional models. Second, to make a prediction at speech onset whether the utterance will be a short backchannel or a longer utterance. Finally, we show how the hidden layer in the network can be used as a feature vector for turn-taking decisions in a human-robot interaction scenario.

1 Introduction

One of the most fundamental aspects of dialogue is the organization of speaking between the participants. Since it is difficult to speak and listen at the same time, the interlocutors need to take turns speaking, and this turn-taking has to be co-ordinated somehow. This poses a challenge for spoken dialogue systems, where the system needs to coordinate its speaking with the user to avoid interruptions and (inappropriate) gaps and overlaps.

For a full account of turn-taking, there are many different aspects that need to be modelled. For example, the system should be able to detect whether the user is likely to continue speaking after a brief silence, or whether the system

should respond (Meena et al., 2014; Ferrer et al., 2002). Another related issue is to detect places where it is appropriate to give brief feedback (so-called backchannels) while the user is speaking (Morency et al., 2008). If the user starts speaking, it is also important to estimate whether the user is most likely initiating a longer utterance, or a shorter listener response (Neiberg and Truong, 2011; Selfridge et al., 2013). When the system is speaking, it is important to assess whether the user will interpret pauses in the system's speech as turn-yielding (an opportunity to take the turn) or not, depending on how the system's utterance is synthesized (Hjalmarsson, 2011). So far, these different problems have mostly been addressed as separate issues, using different models.

In this paper, we present a general, continuous model of turn-taking, trained on dialogue data. The model is *general*, in that we do not train it for specific turn-taking decisions, but instead train it to forecast the probability that the speakers will continue speaking over a future time window. The model is *continuous*, in that it does this at every time step, and not at certain events (such as when someone stopped speaking). We argue that this predictive model is potentially useful for a number of different types of predictions and decisions that are relevant for spoken dialogue systems.

A similar approach was taken by Ward et al. (2010). However, their experiments only yielded modest improvements over the baseline. An explanation for this might be that turn-taking is a highly context-dependent phenomenon, and that representation of dialogue context is a challenging task, typically involving a lot of heuristics and feature engineering. To address this problem, and make as few assumptions as possible, we train the model using Long Short-Term Memory (LSTM) Recurrent Neural Networks (RNN), where the context-modelling is left to the net-

Proceedings of the SIGDIAL 2017 Conference, pages 220–230,
Saarbrücken, Germany, 15-17 August 2017. ©2017 Association for Computational Linguistics

work, and we feed it with fairly basic features representing cues known to be relevant for turn-taking.

The paper is organized as follows. We start with a review of related work on the problem of turn-taking in dialogue, and give a brief overview of RNNs. We then describe the proposed model in more detail, how it was applied in this study, and how features were extracted. Using the HCRC Map Task Corpus (Anderson et al., 1991), we then present two experiments on turn-taking predictions, both at pauses and at speech onset. Finally we investigate how the model can be applied to make predictions on human-computer dialogue data.

2 Background

2.1 Turn-taking in Spoken Dialogue

Traditionally, spoken dialogue systems have rested on a very simplistic model of turn-taking, where a certain amount of silence (e.g., 700ms) is used as an indicator that the user has stopped speaking, and that the turn is yielded to the system. One obvious problem with this model is that turn-shifts often are supposed to be much more rapid than this, with very short gaps, and that pauses within a turn often might be longer. Thus, the system will sometimes appear to give sluggish responses, and sometimes interrupt the user. Several studies have shown that humans coordinate their turn-taking using much more sophisticated cues. For example, an incomplete syntactic clause or a filled pause (such as "uhm") typically indicates that the speaker is not yielding the turn (Clark and Fox Tree, 2002), and turn-taking is related to information density in the words spoken (Dethlefs et al., 2016). Prosodically, a rising or falling pitch at the end of a segment tend to be turn-yielding, whereas a flat pitch is turn-holding (Edlund and Heldner, 2005). The intensity of the voice tends be lower when yielding the turn, and the duration of the last phoneme tends to be shorter. Gaze has also been found to be an important cue – speakers tend to not look at the addressee during an utterance, but then shift the gaze towards the addressee when yielding the turn (Kendon, 1967). Studies have also shown that the more turn-yielding cues are presented together, the more likely it is that the other speaker will take the turn (Gravano and Hirschberg, 2011; Koiso et al., 1998; Duncan and Niederehe, 1974).

Several models have been presented for taking these different cues into account and to predict turn-taking events. A common approach is to segment the speech into so-called Inter-Pausal Units (IPU), which is a stretch of audio from one speaker without any silence exceeding a certain amount (such as 200ms). Given the end of an IPU, the model has to predict whether the speaker is making a pause and "holding" the turn, or whether the speaker is yielding the turn. Various feature sets and machine learning algorithms have been proposed, and tested on both human-human and human-machine dialogue data (Meena et al., 2014; Schlangen, 2006; Neiberg and Gustafson, 2011; Johansson and Skantze, 2015; Ferrer et al., 2002; Kawahara et al., 2012).

These kinds of models assume that turn-taking only occurs when a speaker has stopped speaking. However, in studies of human-human dialogue it is clear that overlaps are fairly frequent (Heldner and Edlund, 2010). A common phenomenon, that often leads to overlapping speech, is *backchannels* – short utterances (such as "mhm" or "yeah"), which the listener provides to show continued attention (Yngve, 1970). Models have been proposed to continuously detect where in the speech these are suitable (Morency et al., 2008). Given that a listener starts to speak, the current speaker must also detect whether the listener is simply providing a backchannel (so that the speaker may continue), or is intending to claim the floor to produce a longer response (Neiberg and Truong, 2011).

Another limitation of IPU-based models of turn-taking is that they are purely reactive. Several studies have shown that humans are able to predict upcoming turn-taking events (Tice and Henetz, 2011), and that this prediction facilitates rapid and accurate turn-taking (Ruiter et al., 2006). To implement this behaviour in spoken dialogue systems, it is important that they can process speech incrementally (Skantze and Schlangen, 2009), and not wait until the user is done speaking. The model proposed in this paper is based on an incremental and predictive notion of turn-taking, where the model continuously monitor the speech from the two interlocutors and makes predictions about future turn-taking events.

2.2 Modelling Context with Recurrent Neural Networks

Most attempts at creating computational models of turn-taking have only considered a brief window before the turn-taking decision is being made. Also, any dynamic events (such as a raise in pitch) in this window need to be transformed into a single feature vector using heuristics and careful feature engineering. This is an obvious drawback, since turn-taking is likely to be dependent on various contextual properties, such as previous speaking activity. To address this problem, we propose to use Recurrent Neural Networks (RNNs), which are especially designed to learn representations of context from low-level features. Whereas a typical feedforward neural network only transforms a single feature vector into an output vector (possibly through a number of hidden layers), RNNs are neural networks with loops that allow information to persist from one step in time to the next, as illustrated in Figure 1. During training and backpropagation, the updates are fed back in time, in order to adjust the weights at previous time steps, and thereby potentially learn long-term dependencies.

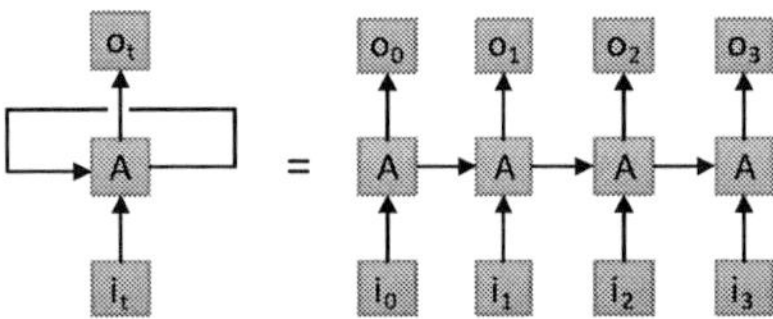

Figure 1. The principle behind RNNs with an unrolled view to the right. The neural network, *A*, looks at the input i_t at time *t* and outputs a value o_t. The loop allows the network to remember the state at time *t-1*.

A limitation of traditional RNNs is their inability to learn dependencies over longer time sequences. The reason for this is that the update gradients become too small over longer distances. This can be especially problematic for the continuous model proposed here, since important events may occur many frames before the turn-taking prediction is being made. To address this problem, it is common to use an extension called Long Short-Term Memory (LSTM), which have a cell state and a gating mechanism that allow information to pass longer paths in the network history, thereby avoiding the vanishing gradient problem (Hochreiter and Schmidhuber, 1997). LSTM has been successfully applied to a number of tasks related to speech and language processing, such as voice activity detection (Eyben et al., 2014), speech recognition (Graves et al., 2013), and spoken language understanding (Liu and Lane, 2016). To our knowledge, this is the first attempt at using LSTM RNNs for a continuous model of turn-taking.

3   Model and Data

3.1   The Model

The general principles for the model are illustrated in Figure 2. An RNN is trained to make continuous predictions about the speech activity for one of the speakers (speaker S_0) for an upcoming fixed time window, based on previous events in both speaker channels. The speech signals for the two speakers (S_0 and S_1) are segmented into equally sized frames (or time steps). For each frame, features from both speakers are extracted and fed into an RNN with one LSTM layer. For each frame, the RNN outputs an *N*-dimensional vector with predictions of the probability that S_0 will speak or not for the next *N* frames. For the experiments in this paper, we use a frame size of 50ms (20 frames per second), and a prediction window of 3 seconds (60 frames).

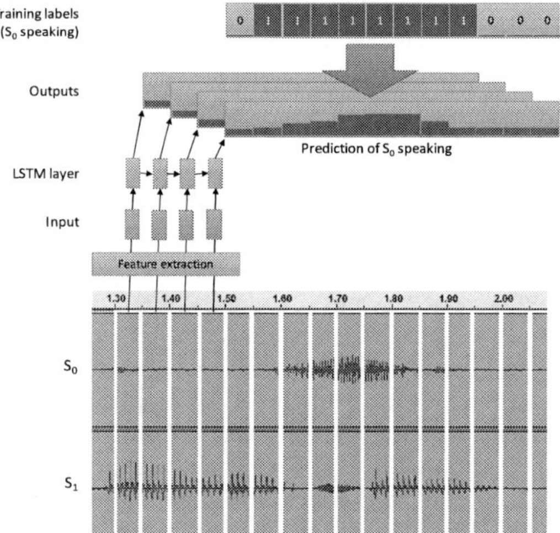

Figure 2. How the model makes predictions and is trained, with an unrolled view of the RNN. For each frame (50ms), the network predicts the probability of speaker S_0 speaking over the next *N* frames (with one output node per frame).

To train the model, we use human-human dialogue data, with the voice activity of speaker S_0 for the next *N* frames as target labels. Although these labels are binary, the output nodes will be trained to provide a probabilistic score (between 0 and 1). To allow the model to train to make predictions for both speakers, the same network is trained on each dialogue twice, with each speaker serving as both speaker S_0 and S_1.

When applying the model, two network instances are used, one in which speaker A serves as S_0 (to get predictions for speaker A), and one where speaker B serves as S_0 (to get predictions for speaker B), with the speaker features switched between the two networks. Some examples of what the predictions can look like are shown in the Appendix[1]. Note that although we will here assume two speakers, the model is not limited to dyadic interaction. In principle, it could be applied to dialogues with any number of speakers, where each speaker is modelled with its own network at application time.

The model should also be applicable for making decisions in dialogue systems. By feeding the two networks (as described above) in real time with both the user's speech and the system's own speech, the user's network will make predictions of how likely it is that the user will speak in the near future. But the system's network will also predict how likely it is that the system *should* be speaking in the future time window, given the assumption that a human-like behaviour is desired. The output of the two models could then be combined to make decisions of whether the system should speak or not. In the simplest case, the two predictions can be compared, and if the system's network has a stronger prediction than the user's network, it would constitute a good place to take the turn. Since the model is probabilistic, a more sophisticated decision theoretic approach could take the probabilities of the predictions, together with a utility, into account. For example, it could still be desirable for the system to take the turn even if it is an unlikely place to do so, given that the system has something important to say. Since the probabilities are updated continuously, even during silences, the model could naturally generate variable gap lengths in the system's response.

Another potential application of the model would be for the generation of system responses. Given different prosodic and syntactic realisations of a response, the model could predict whether the user is likely to take the turn, for example in pauses. To select a response which signals the intended turn-taking cues, the system could feed different candidate responses into the networks and predict how the user would react to them. Yet another application would be to enhance Voice Activity Detection (VAD) with the probability that the user will be speaking, given the dialogue context.

In this paper, we will mainly evaluate the model on its predictive power when observing human-human interaction. However, we will also

---

[1] A video of live predictions can be seen at https://www.youtube.com/watch?v=wE2pPZQGR6U

investigate whether it could be used for turn-taking decisions in a spoken dialogue system, according to the simple method outlined above.

3.2 Data

To train and evaluate the model, we have used the HCRC Map Task corpus (Anderson et al., 1991). This corpus consists of 128 dialogues, where one speaker (the information giver) is explaining a route on a map to another speaker (the follower), using landmarks on the map. The gender of the speakers is balanced, in some dialogue with mixed gender and in other dialogues with same gender. In half of the sessions, the speakers knew each other, in the other half they didn't. Another variable was whether they could see each other (face-to-face) or not.

For our experiments, the data set was split into one training set with 96 dialogues, and one test set with 32 dialogues. Care was taken to balance the variables described above across training set and test set. The average dialogue length was 6.7 minutes, giving 10.7 hours of training data and 3.6 hours of test data. Since the frame rate was 20 frames per second and the model was trained for both speakers, the RNN was trained on about 1 540 800 frames.

3.3 Feature extraction

Features were chosen based on the findings in related literature. For each frame (spanning 50ms), we produce a feature vector as input for the network. We only use momentary features (e.g., the current pitch level), and do not encode delta (such as a rising pitch) or context (e.g., for how long someone has been speaking), with the assumption that these derivations in the time-domain will be learned by the RNN.

Voice activity: A binary feature representing the current voice activity (speech/no speech) of the two speakers. The voice activity was extracted from the manual annotation of the corpus. These features are also used for the target labels during training (the projection of voice activity for the next 3 seconds), as can be seen in Figure 2.

Pitch: The pitch was automatically extracted using the Snack toolkit (Sjölander and Beskow, 2000), transformed into semitones, and then z-normalized for the individual speaker. Both the relative and absolute values were used as individual features. In addition, a binary feature indicating whether the current frame was voiced or not was included.

Power: The power (intensity) in dB, was automatically extracted using Snack, and then z-normalized for the individual speaker.

Spectral stability: Since final lengthening is known to be an indicator for turn-taking, a measure of spectral stability was derived. First, the Snack FFT analysis was used to get the power spectrum divided into N bands (up to 4 kHz), at each time step. Then the following equation was used to calculate the stability S_t at time t:

$$S_t = \sum_{n=0}^{N} p_{n,t} - \sum_{n=0}^{N} abs(p_{n,t} - p_{n,t-1})$$

where $p_{n,t}$ is the power in band n at time t. As is evident from the equation, S_t will be high when the total power in the spectrum is high, but when the power profile of the spectrum is stable, and should therefore be an indication of phonetic lengthening. Just like with the other prosodic features, this stability score was z-normalized for the individual speaker.

Part-of-Speech (POS): Previous studies have found the final POS tags to be indicative of turn-taking (Gravano and Hirschberg, 2011; Koiso et al., 1998). The corpus was already manually annotated with 59 different POS tags. A one-hot representation (with 59 features per speaker) was used. These features were all set to 0 as default, but 100ms after a word ended, the corresponding POS feature was set to 1 for one frame. This was done to simulate what could ideally be achieved in a real dialogue system, given that the spoken word would be available from an incremental speech recognizer immediately after it is spoken. Although this is a somewhat idealistic assumption, it serves an indication of the upper limit performance.

Since the POS features are the most challenging to extract in a live system, and the value of prosodic and syntactic features for turn-taking prediction has been debated (Ruiter et al., 2006; Edlund and Heldner, 2005), we are interested in evaluating two sets of features. The first set (**Full**) comprises all features listed above. The second set (**Prosody**), uses all features except POS, i.e., features that can be extracted directly from the speech signal without any speech recognition. In total, 12 features were used for the Prosody model (6 for each speaker), and 130 features for the Full model (65 for each speaker).

4 Experiments

4.1 Training the Model

To train and evaluate the model, we used the Deeplearning4j framework (Deeplearning4j, 2017). The training data was partitioned into mini-batches of 32 examples, with a sequence length of 60 seconds. Since these sequences are too computationally demanding to fully train, the Truncated Back-propagation Through Time (BPTT) procedure was applied, with a length of 10 seconds. The learning rate was set to 0.01. To avoid overfitting, an l2 regularization of 0.001 was used. The weights were updated using RMSProp, which is often used for LSTM. A sigmoid activation function was used for the output layer, and a *tanh* function for the hidden layer. The network was optimised using a mean-squared error loss function.

For the Full model, we used 40 hidden nodes in the LSTM layer, and for the Prosody model we used 10 hidden nodes, reflecting the different number of input nodes. Both models were trained for 100 epochs. This took about 2 days for the Full model on an Intel core i7 laptop.

Some examples of the predictions the model makes on the test set are shown in the Appendix. To evaluate the performance of the model, we measured the Mean Absolute Error across all 60 output nodes, at all time steps, when applying the model to the test set. The average performance of different sets of output nodes (covering different future windows) for the Full model, are shown in Figure 3.

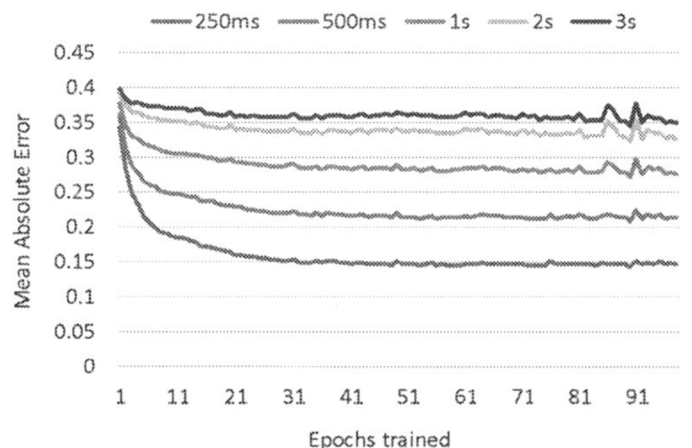

Figure 3. Prediction performance of the Full model on the test set, for different time windows (prefixes of output vectors) and depending on the number of epochs trained.

As can be seen, the performance varied a lot depending on the time window – predictions within the first second are much more accurate than predictions further into the future. It also looks like the network seems to learn and stabilize the performance fairly early on. However, it is important to stress that this is a crude overall performance over all time steps. As we will see in the next section, it might hide improvements for more specific predictions.

4.2 Predictions at Pauses

One of the most common turn-taking decisions that has been modelled in related work is to predict whether a speaker will continue speaking when a brief pause is detected (HOLD), or whether the turn will shift to the other speaker (SHIFT). This is important to model in spoken dialogue systems, in order to know when the system should take the turn, but it could also be applied to predict whether the user is likely to take the turn or not after the system has made a pause.

To investigate whether the trained model could be used for such predictions in the test set (without being specifically trained for this decision), we identified all places where 10 frames (500ms) of silence had just passed since the last speaker was speaking (we will investigate different pause lengths further down). This amounted to 2876 instances in the test set. Of these, we selected instances where one (and only one) of the speakers continued within 1 second (2079 in total). We then averaged the predictions of the first second for the two networks associated with each speaker. The network with the highest average score was selected as the predicted next speaker. This binary classification task (SHIFT vs. HOLD) gives us an F-score with which we can compare the performance of different network configurations. Since the two classes are fairly well balanced (881 vs. 1198), a majority-class baseline (always HOLD) only yields an F-score of 0.421.

Figure 4 shows the performance for the Prosody and the Full models, depending on the total number of epochs trained. As can be seen, the performance of this specific decision is fairly unstable across epochs – probably because the model is not specifically trained towards this decision – and thus it might be hard to know which epoch model to choose. However, we found that the performance on the test set and the training set were highly correlated across epochs (r = 0.98). Thus, if the model that performs best on the training set is chosen, it will most likely be optimal for the test set. As the figure shows, the performance of the Prosody model quickly stabilizes and reaches an F-score of 0.724 at epoch 30

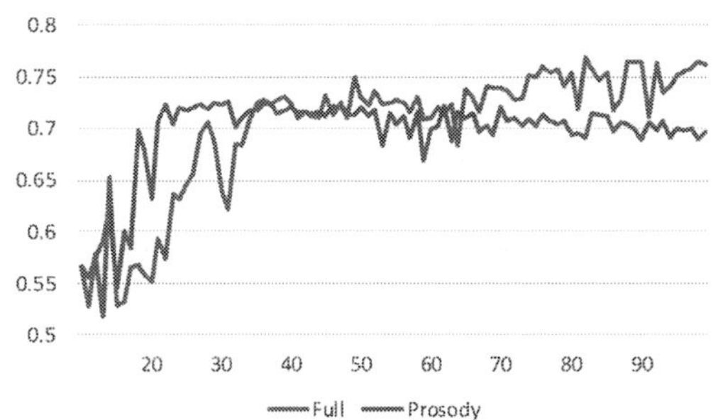

Figure 4. Prediction performance (F-score) of turn-shifts at pauses for the two models when applied to the test set, depending on the number of epochs trained.

(and then degrades somewhat), whereas the Full model continues to learn, reaching an F-score of 0.762 at epoch 100.

In the experiments above, we have studied the prediction performance after a pause of 500ms. However, turn-shifts might of course be much more rapid than this, and a dialogue system should be able to assess whether it should take the turn immediately when a pause is detected, or possibly wait a longer time if it is uncertain. Previous approaches have done this by training specific models at different pause lengths, which are then applied after each other as the pause progresses (Ferrer et al., 2002). Since our model is continuous, it can be directly applied at each time step during a pause. To assess the performance of the model after very brief pauses, we also evaluated the model after just 50ms (1 frame) or 250ms (5 frames) of silence. The results are shown in Table 1.

Table 1: Prediction performance of turn-shifts at pauses for the Full model, depending on pause length.

	50ms	**250ms**	**500ms**
Instances	4933	3405	2079
% HOLD	62.3%	59.8%	57.6%
Precision SHIFT	0.752	0.726	0.711
Recall SHIFT	0.583	0.703	0.738
Precision HOLD	0.778	0.805	0.802
Recall HOLD	0.884	0.822	0.780
F-score	**0.763**	**0.774**	**0.762**
Baseline F-score (always HOLD)	0.479	0.448	0.421

Interestingly, as the precision/recall numbers show, the model seems to be biased towards making HOLD predictions early on in the pause. This is arguably a good trade-off, since it means that the model would be inclined to wait a little bit longer to make another decision, instead of interrupting the user. In any case, the F-score is very similar regardless of pause length, which shows that a relatively good prediction performance can be achieved already after very brief pauses, potentially allowing dialog systems to give responses with barely any gap.

It is not obvious what to compare the performance with. Since a lot of turn-taking behaviour is optional, and we are evaluating the model based on what the humans actually did, we could never expect these predictions to be 100% correct. One comparison is Neiberg and Gustafson (2011), who also used the HCRC Map Task data to predict turn SHIFT vs. HOLD, with a model specifically trained for this. Using Gaussian Mixture Modelling with prosodic features derived right before the pause, their best performance was an average recall of 0.578–0.614, depending on which part of the corpus they were targeting. However, since their data preparations and definitions were not exactly the same as ours, we also trained a set of more traditional models on our data set, using Naive Bayes, Support Vector Machines and Logistic Regression, to classify each 500ms pause as either HOLD or SHIFT. Since these are not sequential models, we cannot use the features directly in the same way as was used for the RNN. Instead, we used feature engineering similar to Meena et al. (2014), including syntactic features (last POS unigram and bigram), prosodic features (pitch slope, mean pitch, mean intensity, and mean spectral stability in the final 300ms voiced region), and context (length of last IPU and last turn). The models were trained on the training set and evaluated on the test set. The best result on the full feature set was obtained using Naive Bayes, which yielded an F-score of 0.677. When using only prosodic features, Logistic Regression yielded the best F-score of 0.590, which similar to Neiberg and Gustafson (2011). These performances are clearly below the performance of our model, even though we did not train it specifically for this decision.

Another possible comparison is how well a human would perform the task. To test this, we used the Crowdflower platform, where human subjects were paid to judge which speaker would continue after a brief silence, given 10 seconds of interaction ending just after a pause of 500ms (i.e., the same task ask the RNN was given). To simplify the task, we selected a random subset of the corpus where there was a man and a woman talking (207 instances), and asked the annotator "do you think the man or the woman will speak

next?" As a quality control question, we also asked whether it was the man or the woman that was the last speaker, and excluded annotators who gave an incorrect answer. Three different annotators judged each instance. Using the majority vote, the humans reached an F-score of 0.709, which is below the performance of our best models. A summary of the different comparisons made here with our model is shown in Table 2.

Table 2: Summary of F-score comparisons for predicting turn-shifts at 500ms pauses.

Majority-class baseline	0.421
Human performance	0.709
Logistic Regression, Prosody only	0.590
RNN, Prosody only	0.724
Naive Bayes, All features	0.677
RNN, All features	0.762

4.3 Predictions at Speech Onset

Next, we wanted to see if the same model can be applied to a different task: to predict utterance length at the onset of speech. As discussed in 2.1, this prediction would be useful for a dialogue system, in order to determine whether it should stop speaking or not, given that the user has just started to speak. If the user is just giving a brief response (i.e., a backchannel), the system typically does not have to stop speaking. However, if the user is initiating a longer response, the system might decide to stop speaking and allow the user to "barge-in" (cf. Selfridge et al., 2013) .

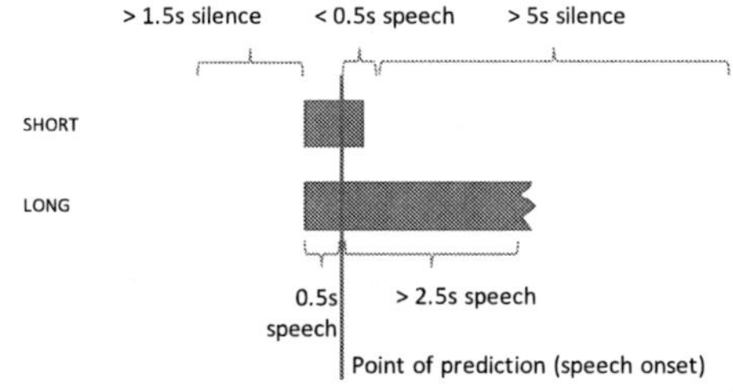

Figure 5. Definitions of SHORT and LONG utterances.

We therefore wanted to test if our model can, already at the speech onset, predict whether the utterance will be very brief or longer. To test this, we identified instances in the data where a speaker had just initiated a LONG or a SHORT utterance (i.e., something like a backchannel). The definitions of these categories are illustrated in Figure 5. To fall in any of these categories, at least 1.5s of silence by one participant has to be followed by an onset of 500ms of speech. If this onset was followed by a maximum of 500ms of more speech, and then no speech (by the same speaker) for 5s, it was categorized as a SHORT utterance. If it was followed by at least 2.5s of speech, it was categorized as a LONG utterance. With these definitions, the test set contained 196 SHORT utterances and 179 LONG utterances. At each onset, the prediction score over the 60 output nodes in the model were averaged. Figure 6 shows the number of instances in the test set that received different prediction scores (rounded to deciles) by the Full model, depending on whether it was in fact a SHORT or LONG utterance. As is evident, the model manages to make a fairly good separation between short and long utterances. Using the best prediction score separation threshold derived from the training set (0.404), the F-score for classifying SHORT vs. LONG utterances in the test set was 0.786.

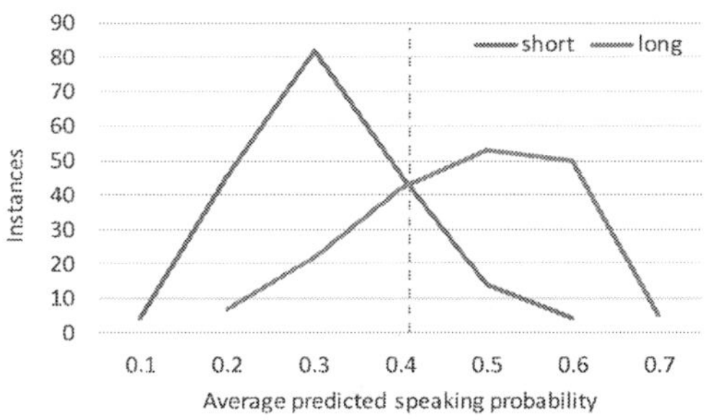

Figure 6. Number of instances with different prediction scores in the test set, using the Full model, at the onset of short and long utterances.

As a minimum comparison, a majority class baseline yields an F-score of 0.359. Another comparison is (Neiberg and Truong, 2011), who trained a model specifically for this decision and achieved a somewhat lower performance. However, they used a different dataset and it is therefore not directly comparable. Just like for the previous task above (4.2), we therefore also trained more traditional models for comparison. We used features that were deemed to be relevant for the task, including the preceding POS unigrams and bigrams for the two speakers, the mean power of the speech onset, whether it was voiced, whether it was overlapping with the other speaker, and time since last speech for both speakers. The best F-score of 0.684 was achieved using a Naive Bayes classifier. Again, our generic model achieves a better performance than traditional non-sequential models that were trained specifically for the task.

4.4 Application to Spoken Dialogue Systems

One important question is whether the models trained on human-human data could also be used to predict turn-taking in human-computer dialogue. Or, rather, could they be used to predict a *desired* behaviour for the system, given the dialogue history between the human and the computer up to some point in time, as discussed in 3.1 above? This is of course challenging, partly because human-human interaction and human-computer interaction typically look very different, but also because human-human turn-taking behaviour might not necessarily be a role model for how we want systems to behave. To test this, we used data from a previous study on human-robot interaction (Johansson et al., 2016). In that setting, the user was asked to tell the robot about a past visit to a foreign country, while the robot listened actively by giving backchannels and asking various follow-up questions to elicit more elaborate descriptions. The corpus consists of 30 dialogues with 15 different subjects. Each end of an IPU was manually annotated as either HOLD, OPTIONAL or TAKE. To make the task clearer, we excluded the OPTIONAL instances, and tested whether the model could distinguish between HOLD (213 instances) and TAKE (303 instances).

For this data, we used the Prosody model (at epoch 30), since we did not have any POS features. We first applied the model directly according to the simple approach outlined in 3.1 above, i.e., we fed the user's and the system's speech into two networks and then compared the predictions for the user and the system at the end of each IPU. If the system's prediction was stronger than the user's, a TAKE was selected, otherwise a HOLD. However, this only yielded an F-score of 0.582, which is a very modest improvement over the majority class baseline of 0.434.

As discussed above, there are a number of reasons why it is hard for the model to make direct predictions towards the labels in this dataset. A training set more similar to the testing set is most likely needed. However, it is still possible that the network might model phenomena relevant to turn-taking in the dialogue, and be useful for feature extraction. To test this, we partitioned the human-robot interaction data into a training and testing set, and applied a Logistic Regression model trained on the manual annotations (TAKE/HOLD). As input features, we used the hidden nodes in the RNN network, at the time of the prediction. In a 10-fold cross validation, this yielded an F-score 0.751. Thus, it seems like the network had learned to transform the feature space, and the logistic regression only has to make a final linear separation in this new feature space. This would also mean that it should be possible to train with relatively few training examples. Indeed, when training on only 20% of the data (and evaluating on the other 80%), this approach still yields a relatively high average F-score of 0.72. This is promising, since it means that the model could at least be used for feature extraction to make turn-taking decisions in spoken dialogue systems, with only a small amount of manually labelled training data.

5   Conclusions and Discussion

In this paper, we have presented a first step towards a general model of turn-taking in spoken dialogue. Unlike most previous models, the proposed model is not trained towards specific turn-taking decisions, but instead makes continuous predictions of future speech activity. To evaluate the model, we have applied it to two different turn-taking decisions for which it was not specifically trained. First, to detect the next speaker at pauses, where the model achieves a better performance than more traditional attempts on the same dataset, and better than human performance. Second, to project the length of an utterance at speech onset, where the model also yields a better performance than traditional models. Finally, we have tested the model on human-robot dialogue data. Most likely due to the large differences in training and testing conditions, the model was not directly applicable for making turn-taking decisions in this setting. However, it could at least be used for feature extraction to train a separate model on a small set of manually labelled data.

So far, we have relied on manually labelled POS features (for the Full model). For future studies, we would like to see how well the model would cope with automatic online POS tagging of ASR results. Although we have worked with manually annotated speech segments, these could also be extracted with a VAD. All other features were automatically extracted.

As noted earlier, the model should be applicable to multi-party interaction. Another obvious extension is to use multi-modal features, such as gaze and gestures, which have shown to be important for turn-taking (Kawahara et al., 2012; Johansson and Skantze, 2015).

So far, we have only tested the model on binary decisions, in order to make the results as clear and comparable as possible. However, this clearly only hints at some of the potential applications of the model (which can be grasped by looking at the examples in the Appendix). For example, since the model is continuous and predictive, it should be possible to use it for preparing a dialogue system to make responses before the user's utterance is completed. Since the model is probabilistic, it should be possible to use it in a decision-theoretic framework, as discussed in 3.1 above. However, to make the model directly applicable to spoken dialogue systems, it should probably be trained on a more diverse set of interactions, more similar to the actual dialogue system application.

Acknowledgements

This work is supported by the SSF (Swedish Foundation for Strategic Research) project COIN, and the Swedish research council (VR) project *Online learning of turn-taking behaviour in spoken human-robot interaction*.

References

A Anderson, M Bader, E Bard, E Boyle, G Doherty, S Garrod, S Isard, J Kowtko, J McAllister, J Miller, C Sotillo, H Thompson, and R Weinert. 1991. The HCRC Map Task corpus. *Language and Speech*, 34(4):351–366.

H H Clark and J E Fox Tree. 2002. Using uh and um in spontaneous speaking. *Cognition*, 84(1):73–111.

Deeplearning4j. 2017. Deeplearning4j: Open-source distributed deep learning for the JVM, Apache Software Foundation License 2.0.

Nina Dethlefs, Helen Hastie, Heriberto Cuayahuitl, Yanchao Yu, Verena Rieser, and Oliver Lemon. 2016. Information density and overlap in spoken dialogue. *Computer Speech and Language*, 37:82–97.

S Duncan and G Niederehe. 1974. On signalling that it's your turn to speak. *Journal of Experimental Social Psychology*, 10(3):234–247.

Jens Edlund and Mattias Heldner. 2005. Exploring prosody in interaction control. *Phonetica*, 62(2–4):215–226.

Florian Eyben, Felix Weninger, Stefano Squartini, Bjorn Schuller, and Björn Florian Eyben ; Felix Weninger ; Stefano Squartini ; Schuller. 2014. Real-life voice activity detection with LSTM Recurrent Neural Networks and an application to Hollywood movies. In *Proceedings of ICASSP*, volume 1, pages 3709–3713. IEEE, May.

L Ferrer, E Shriberg, and A Stolcke. 2002. Is the speaker done yet? Faster and more accurate end-of utterance detection using prosody. In *Proceedings of ICSLP*, pages 2061–2064.

Agustín. Gravano and Julia. Hirschberg. 2011. Turn-taking cues in task-oriented dialogue. *Computer Speech & Language*, 25(3):601–634.

Alex Graves, Abdel-rahman Mohamed, and Geoffrey Hinton. 2013. Speech recognition with deep recurrent neural networks. In *2013 IEEE International Conference on Acoustics, Speech and Signal Processing*, pages 6645–6649. IEEE, May.

Mattias Heldner and Jens Edlund. 2010. Pauses, gaps and overlaps in conversations. *Journal of Phonetics*, 38(4):555–568.

Anna Hjalmarsson. 2011. The additive effect of turn-taking cues in human and synthetic voice. *Speech Communication*, 53(1):23–35.

Sepp Hochreiter and Jürgen Schmidhuber. 1997. Long Short-Term Memory. *Neural Computation*, 9(8):1735–1780, November.

Martin Johansson, Tatsuro Hori, Gabriel Skantze, Anja Höthker, and Joakim Gustafson. 2016. Making turn-taking decisions for an active listening robot for memory training. In *Proceedings of the International Conference on Social Robotics*, volume 9979 LNAI, pages 940–949.

Martin Johansson and Gabriel Skantze. 2015. Opportunities and Obligations to Take Turns in Collaborative Multi-Party Human-Robot Interaction. In *Proceedings of SigDial*, number September, page 402.

Tatsuya Kawahara, Takuma Iwatate, and Katsuya Takanashi. 2012. Prediction of Turn-Taking by Combining Prosodic and Eye-Gaze Information in Poster Conversations. In *Proceedings of Interspeech*.

A Kendon. 1967. Some functions of gaze direction in social interaction. *Acta Psychologica*, 26:22–63.

Hanae Koiso, Yasuo Horiuchi, Syun Tutiya, Akira Ichikawa, and Yasuharu Den. 1998. An analysis of turn-taking and backchannels based on prosodic and syntactic features in Japanese map task dialogs. *Language and Speech*, 41 (Pt 3-4:295–321.

Bing Liu and Ian Lane. 2016. Joint Online Spoken Language Understanding and Language Modeling with Recurrent Neural Networks. In *Proceedings of Sigdial 2016*, number September, pages 22–30.

Raveesh Meena, Gabriel Skantze, and Joakim Gustafson. 2014. Data-driven models for timing feedback responses in a Map Task dialogue system. *Computer Speech and Language*, 28(4):903–922.

L P Morency, I de Kok, and J Gratch. 2008. Predicting listener backchannels: A probabilistic multimodal approach. In *Proceedings of IVA*, pages 176–190, Tokyo, Japan.

Daniel Neiberg and Joakim Gustafson. 2011. Predicting speaker changes and listener responses with and without eye-contact. In *Proceedings of Interspeech*, number August, pages 1565–1568.

Daniel Neiberg and Khiet P. Truong. 2011. Online detection of vocal Listener Responses with maximum latency constraints. In *Proceedings of ICASSP*, pages 5836–5839. IEEE, May.

Jan-Peter De Ruiter, Holger. Mitterer, and N. J. Enfield. 2006. Projecting the end of a speaker's turn: A cognitive cornerstone of conversation. *Language*, 82(3):515–535.

D Schlangen. 2006. From reaction to prediction: experiments with computational models of turn-taking. In *Proceedings of Interspeech 2006, Pittsburgh, PA, USA*, 2010-2013, September.

Ethan O Selfridge, Iker Arizmendi, Peter A Heeman, and Jason D Williams. 2013. Continuously Predicting and Processing Barge-in During a Live Spoken Dialogue Task. *SIGdial 2013*(August):384–393. NULL.

Kåre Sjölander and Jonas Beskow. 2000. WaveSurfer - an open source speech tool. In *Proceedings of ICSLP 2000*, volume 4, pages 464–467, Beijing.

Gabriel Skantze and David Schlangen. 2009. Incremental dialogue processing in a micro-domain. In *Proceedings of EACL*, number April, pages 745–753. Association for Computational Linguistics.

Marisa Tice and Tania Henetz. 2011. The eye gaze of 3rd party observers reflects turn-end boundary projection. In *Proceedings of SemDial*, pages 204–205, Los Angeles, CA, US, September.

Nigel G Ward, Olac Fuentes, and Alejandro Vega. 2010. Dialog Prediction for a General Model of Turn-Taking. In *Proceedings of Interspeech-2010*.

Victor H Yngve. 1970. On getting a word in edgewise. In *Papers from the sixth regional meeting of the Chicago Linguistic Society*, pages 567–578, Chicago, April.

Appendix – Examples of model predictions

These are some examples of the output of the model, when applied to unseen test data. The blue vertical bar shows the point of prediction (i.e., no predictions are shown before this point), and the curves show the predictions for the future 3 seconds window. One speaker is represented with black (the information giver) and the other with red (the information follower).

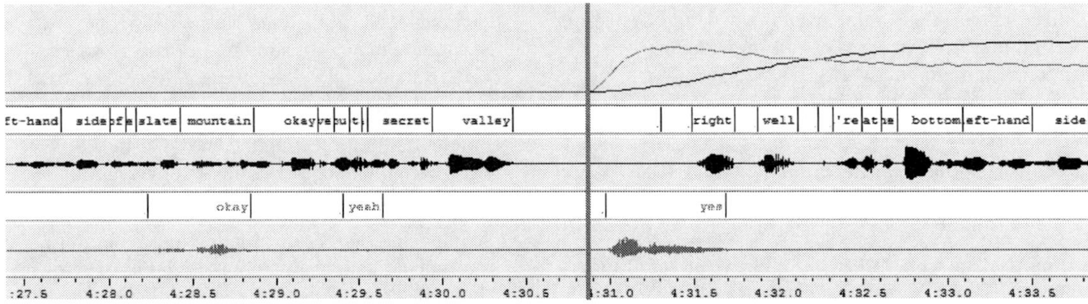

Example 1: Prediction in a pause. The model predicts that the red speaker will give a (short) response, but also that the black speaker will continue later on.

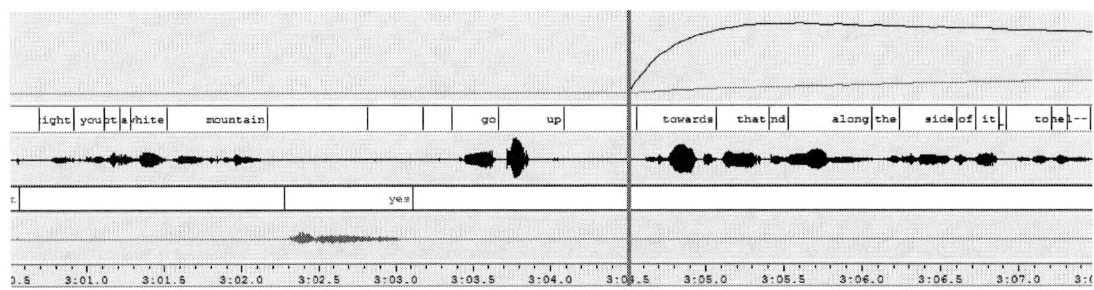

Example 2: Prediction in a pause. The model predicts that the black speaker will continue, and that the red speaker will not respond.

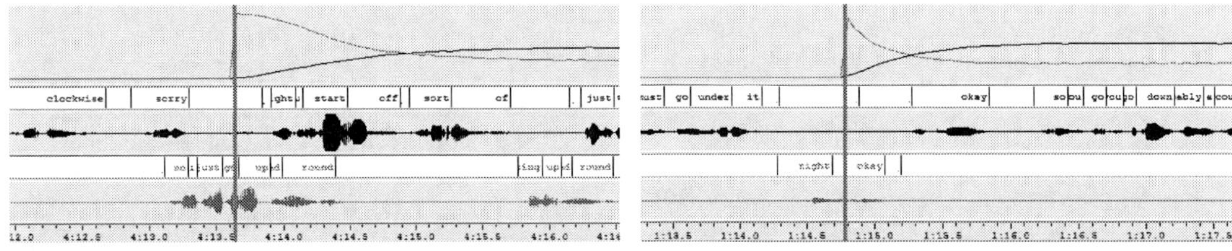

Example 3: Prediction at speech onset. On the left, the red speaker has just started a longer utterance (but is eventually interrupted by the black speaker). On the right, the speaker has only started a brief response (a backchannel). This is reflected by a stronger prediction for the red speaker in the left picture compared to the right picture.

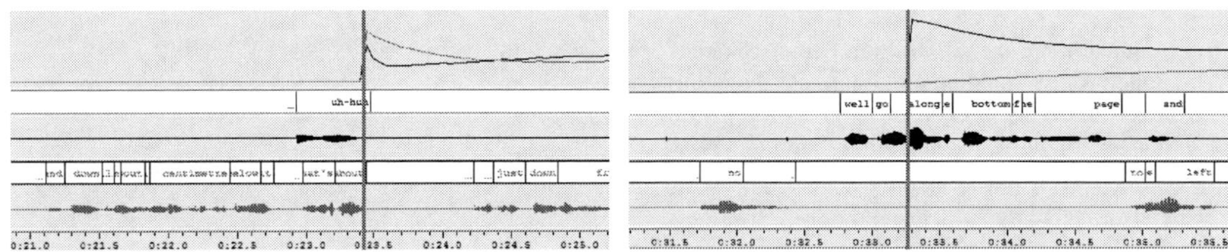

Example 4: Prediction at speech onset, similar to Example 3. However, notice that it is the information giver that gives the backchannel here, and that it is still correctly distinguished from the longer utterance on the right.

Neural-based Natural Language Generation in Dialogue using RNN Encoder-Decoder with Semantic Aggregation

Van-Khanh Tran[1,2], Le-Minh Nguyen[1,*] and Satoshi Tojo[1]

[1]Japan Advanced Institute of Science and Technology, JAIST
1-1 Asahidai, Nomi, Ishikawa, 923-1292, Japan
{tvkhanh, nguyenml, tojo}@jaist.ac.jp
[2]University of Information and Communication Technology, ICTU
Thai Nguyen University, Vietnam
tvkhanh@ictu.edu.vn

Abstract

Natural language generation (NLG) is an important component in spoken dialogue systems. This paper presents a model called Encoder-Aggregator-Decoder which is an extension of an Recurrent Neural Network based Encoder-Decoder architecture. The proposed Semantic Aggregator consists of two components: an Aligner and a Refiner. The Aligner is a conventional attention calculated over the encoded input information, while the Refiner is another attention or gating mechanism stacked over the attentive Aligner in order to further select and aggregate the semantic elements. The proposed model can be jointly trained both text planning and text realization to produce natural language utterances. The model was extensively assessed on four different NLG domains, in which the results showed that the proposed generator consistently outperforms the previous methods on all the NLG domains.

1 Introduction

Natural Language Generation (NLG) plays a critical role in a Spoken Dialogue System (SDS), and its task is to convert a meaning representation produced by the dialogue manager into natural language sentences. Conventional approaches to NLG follow a *pipeline* which typically breaks down the task into *sentence planning* and *surface realization*. *Sentence planning* decides the order and structure of a sentence, followed by a *surface realization* which converts the sentence structure into final utterance. Previous approaches to NLG still rely on extensive hand-tuning templates and rules that require expert knowledge of linguistic representation. There are some common and widely used approaches to solve NLG problems, including rule-based (Cheyer and Guzzoni, 2014), corpus-based n-gram generator (Oh and Rudnicky, 2000), and a trainable generator (Ratnaparkhi, 2000).

Recurrent Neural Network (RNN)-based approaches have recently shown promising results in NLG tasks. The RNN-based models have been used for NLG as a joint training model (Wen et al., 2015a,b) and an end-to-end training network (Wen et al., 2016c). A recurring problem in such systems requiring annotated corpora for specific dialogue acts* (DAs). More recently, the attention-based RNN Encoder-Decoder (AREncDec) approaches (Bahdanau et al., 2014) have been explored to tackle the NLG problems (Wen et al., 2016b; Mei et al., 2015; Dušek and Jurčíček, 2016b,a). The AREncDEc-based models have also shown improved results on various tasks, *e.g.*, image captioning (Xu et al., 2015; Yang et al., 2016), machine translation (Luong et al., 2015; Wu et al., 2016).

To ensure that the generated utterance represents the intended meaning of the given DA, the previous RNN-based models were conditioned on a 1-hot vector representation of the DA. Wen et al. (2015a) proposed a Long Short-Term Memory-based (HLSTM) model which introduced a heuristic gate to guarantee that the slot-value pairs were accurately captured during generation. Subsequently, Wen et al. (2015b) proposed an LSTM-based generator (SC-LSTM) which jointly learned the controlling signal and language model. Wen et al. (2016b) proposed an AREncDec based generator (ENCDEC) which applied attention mechanism on the slot-value pairs.

---

*A combination of an action type and a set of slot-value pairs). *E.g. inform(name='Piperade'; food='Basque').*

Proceedings of the SIGDIAL 2017 Conference, pages 231–240,
Saarbrücken, Germany, 15-17 August 2017. ©2017 Association for Computational Linguistics

---

*Corresponding author.

Table 1: Order issue in natural language generation, in which an incorrect generated sentence has wrong ordered slots.

Input DA	**Compare**(name=*Triton 52*; ecorating=*A+*; family=*L7*; name=*Hades 76*; ecorating=*C*; family=*L9*)
INCORRECT	The *Triton 52* has an *A+* eco rating and is in the *L9* product family, the *Hades 76* is in the *L7* product family and has a *C* eco rating.
CORRECT	The *Triton 52* is in the *L7* product family and has an *A+* eco rating, the *Hades 76* is in the *L9* product family and has a *C* eco rating.

Although these RNN-based generators have worked well, however, they still have some drawbacks, and none of these models significantly outperform the others in solving NLG tasks. While the HLSTM cannot handle cases such as the binary slots (*i.e., yes* and *no*) and slots that take *don't_care* value in which these slots cannot be directly delexicalized, the SCLSTM model is limited to generalize to the unseen domain, and the ENCDEC model has difficulty to prevent undesirable semantic repetitions during generation.

To address the above issues, we propose a new architecture, *Encoder-Aggregator-Decoder*, an extension of the AREncDec model, in which the proposed Aggregator has two main components: (i) an Aligner which computes the attention over the input sequence, and (ii) a Refiner which are another attention or gating mechanisms to further select and aggregate the semantic elements. The proposed model can learn from unaligned data by jointly training the sentence planning and surface realization to produce natural language sentences. We conduct comprehensive experiments on four NLG domains and find that the proposed method significantly outperforms the previous methods regarding BLEU (Papineni et al., 2002) and slot error rate ERR scores (Wen et al., 2015b). We also found that our generator can produce high-quality utterances with correctly ordered than those in the previous methods (see Table 1). To sum up, we make two key contributions in this paper:

- We present a semantic component called *Aggregator* which is easy integrated into existing (attentive) RNN encoder-decoder architecture, resulting in an end-to-end generator that empirically improved performance in comparison with the previous approaches.

- We present several different choices of attention and gating mechanisms which can be effectively applied to the proposed semantic Aggregator.

In Section 2, we review related works. The proposed model is presented in Section 3. Section 4 describes datasets, experimental setups and evaluation metrics. The results and analysis are presented in Section 5. We conclude with a brief of summary and future work in Section 6.

2 Related Work

Conventional approaches to NLG traditionally divide the task into a pipeline of sentence planning and surface realization. The conventional methods still rely on the handcrafted rule-based generators or rerankers. Oh and Rudnicky (2000) proposed a class-based n-gram language model (LM) generator which can learn to generate the sentences for a given dialogue act and then select the best sentences using a rule-based reranker. Ratnaparkhi (2000) later addressed some of the limitation of the class-based LMs by proposing a method based on a syntactic dependency tree. A phrase-based generator based on factored LMs was introduced by Mairesse and Young (2014), that can learn from a semantically aligned corpus.

Recently, RNNs-based approaches have shown promising results in the NLG domain. Vinyals et al. (2015); Karpathy and Fei-Fei (2015) applied RNNs in setting of multi-modal to generate caption for images. Zhang and Lapata (2014) also proposed a generator using RNNs to create Chinese poetry. For task-oriented dialogue systems, Wen et al. (2015a) combined two TNN-based models with a CNN reranker to generate required utterances. Wen et al. (2015b) proposed SC-LSTM generator which proposed an additional "reading" cell to the traditional LSTM cell to learn the gating mechanism and language model jointly. A recurring problem in such systems lacking of sufficient domain-specific annotated corpora. Wen et al. (2016a) proposed an out-of-domain model which is trained on counterfeited datasets by using semantic similar slots from the target-domain dataset instead of the slots belonging to the out-of-domain dataset. The empirical results indicated

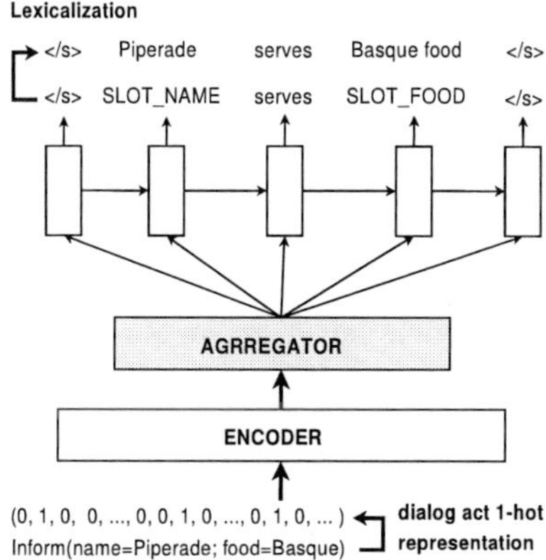

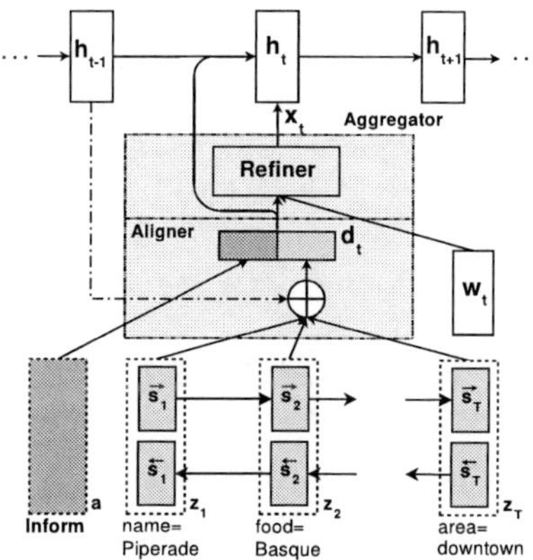

Figure 1: Unfold presentation of the RNN-based neural language generator. The encoder part is subject to various designs, while the decoder is an RNN network.

Figure 2: The RNN Encoder-Aggregator-Decoder for NLG proposed in this paper. The output side is an RNN network while the input side is a DA embedding with aggregation mechanism. The Aggregator consists of two parts: an Aligner and a Refiner. The lower part Aligner is an attention over the DA representation calculated by a Bidirectional RNN. Note that the action type embedding $\mathbf{a}$ is not included in the attention mechanism since its task is controlling the style of the sentence. The higher part Refiner computes the new input token $\mathbf{x}_t$ based on the original input token $\mathbf{w}_t$ and the dialogue act attention $\mathbf{d}_t$. There are several choices for Refiner, *i.e.*, gating mechanism or attention mechanism.

that the model can obtain a satisfactory results with a small amount of in-domain data by fine-tuning the target-domain on the out-of-domain trained model.

More recently, attentional RNN encoder-decoder based models (Bahdanau et al., 2014) have shown improved results in a variety of tasks. Yang et al. (2016) presented a review network in solving the image captioning task, which produces a compact thought vector via reviewing all the input information encoded by the encoder. Mei et al. (2015) proposed attentional RNN encoder-decoder based model by introducing two layers of attention to model content selection and surface realization. More close to our work, Wen et al. (2016b) proposed an attentive encoder-decoder based generator, which applied the attention mechanism over the slot-value pairs. The model indicated a domain scalability when a very limited proportion of training data is available.

3 Recurrent Neural Language Generator

The recurrent language generator proposed in this paper is based on a neural net language generator (Wen et al., 2016b) which consists of three components: an encoder to incorporate the target meaning representation as the model inputs, an aggregator to align and control the encoded information, and a decoder to generate output sentences. The generator architecture is shown in Figure 1. While the decoder typically uses an RNN model, there is a variety of ways to choose the encoder because it depends on the nature of the meaning

representation and the interaction between semantic elements. The encoder first encodes the input meaning representation, then the aggregator with a feature selecting or an attention-based mechanism is used to aggregate and select the input semantic elements. The input to the RNN decoder at each time step is a 1-hot encoding of a token[†] and the aggregated input vector. The output of RNN decoder represents the probability distribution of the next token given the previous token, the dialogue act representation, and the current hidden state. At generation time, we can sample from this conditional distribution to obtain the next token in a generated sentence, and feed it as the next input to the RNN decoder. This process finishes when a stop sign is generated (Karpathy and Fei-Fei, 2015), or some constraint is reached (Zhang and Lapata, 2014). The network can generate a sequence of tokens which can be lexicalized[‡] to form the required utterance.

[†] Input texts are delexicalized in which slot values are replaced by its corresponding slot tokens.

[‡] The process in which slot token is replaced by its value.

3.1 Gated Recurrent Unit

The encoder and decoder of the proposed model use a Gated Recurrent Unit (GRU) network proposed by Bahdanau et al. (2014), which maps an input sequence $\mathbf{W} = [\mathbf{w}_1, \mathbf{w}_2, .., \mathbf{w}_T]$ to a sequence of states $\mathbf{H} = [\mathbf{h}_1, \mathbf{h}_2, .., \mathbf{h}_T]$ as follows:

$$
\begin{aligned}
\mathbf{r}_i &= \sigma(\mathbf{W}_{rw}\mathbf{w}_i + \mathbf{W}_{rh}\mathbf{h}_{i-1}) \\
\mathbf{u}_i &= \sigma(\mathbf{W}_{uw}\mathbf{w}_i + \mathbf{W}_{uh}\mathbf{h}_{i-1}) \\
\tilde{\mathbf{h}}_i &= \tanh(\mathbf{W}_{hw}\mathbf{w}_i + \mathbf{r}_i \odot \mathbf{W}_{hh}\mathbf{h}_{i-1}) \\
\mathbf{h}_i &= \mathbf{u}_i \odot \mathbf{h}_{i-1} + (1 - \mathbf{u}_i) \odot \tilde{\mathbf{h}}_i
\end{aligned}
\tag{1}
$$

where: $\odot$ denotes the element-wise multiplication, $\mathbf{r}_i$ and $\mathbf{u}_i$ are called the reset and update gates respectively, and $\tilde{\mathbf{h}}_i$ is the candidate activation.

3.2 Encoder

The encoder uses a separate parameterization of the slots and values. It encodes the source information into a distributed vector representation $\mathbf{z}_i$ which is a concatenation of embedding vector representation of each slot-value pair, and is computed by:

$$
\mathbf{z}_i = \mathbf{o}_i \oplus \mathbf{v}_i
\tag{2}
$$

where: $\mathbf{o}_i$ and $\mathbf{v}_i$ are the i-th slot and value embedding, respectively. The i index runs over the given slot-value pairs. In this study, we use a Bidirectional GRU (Bi-GRU) to encode the sequence of slot-value pairs[§] embedding. The Bi-GRU consists of forward and backward GRUs. The forward GRU reads the sequence of slot-value pairs from left-to-right and calculates the forward hidden states $(\overrightarrow{s_1}, .., \overrightarrow{s_K})$. The backward GRU reads the slot-value pairs from right-to-left, resulting in a sequence of backward hidden states $(\overleftarrow{s_1}, .., \overleftarrow{s_K})$. We then obtain the sequence of hidden states $\mathbf{S} = [\mathbf{s}_1, \mathbf{s}_2, .., \mathbf{s}_K]$ where $\mathbf{s}_i$ is a sum of the forward hidden state $\overrightarrow{s_i}$ and the backward one $\overleftarrow{s_i}$ as follows:

$$
\mathbf{s}_i = \overrightarrow{s_i} + \overleftarrow{s_i}
\tag{3}
$$

3.3 Aggregator

The Aggregator consists of two components: an Aligner and a Refiner. The Aligner computes the dialogue act representation while the choices for Refiner can be varied.

[§]We treat the set of slot-value pairs as a sequence and use the order specified by slot's name (*e.g.*, slot *area* comes first, *price* follows *area*). We have tried treating slot-value pair sequence as natural order as appear in the DA, which even yielded worse results.

Firstly, the Aligner calculates dialogue act embedding $\mathbf{d}_t$ as follows:

$$
\mathbf{d}_t = \mathbf{a} \oplus \sum_i \alpha_{t,i}\mathbf{s}_i
\tag{4}
$$

where: $\mathbf{a}$ is vector embedding of the action type, $\oplus$ is vector concatenation, and $\alpha_{t,i}$ is the weight of i-th slot-value pair calculated by the attention mechanism:

$$
\begin{aligned}
\alpha_{t,i} &= \frac{\exp(e_{t,i})}{\sum_j \exp(e_{t,j})} \\
e_{t,i} &= a(\mathbf{s}_i, \mathbf{h}_{t-1}) \\
a(\mathbf{s}_i, \mathbf{h}_{t-1}) &= \mathbf{v}_a^\top \tanh(\mathbf{W}_a\mathbf{s}_i + \mathbf{U}_a\mathbf{h}_{t-1})
\end{aligned}
\tag{5}
$$

where: $a(.,.)$ is an alignment model, $\mathbf{v}_a, \mathbf{W}_a, \mathbf{U}_a$ are the weight matrices to learn.

Secondly, the Refiner calculates the new input $\mathbf{x}_t$ based on the original input token $\mathbf{w}_t$ and the DA representation. There are several choices to formulate the Refiner such as gating mechanism or attention mechanism. For each input token $\mathbf{w}_t$, the selected mechanism module computes the new input $\mathbf{x}_t$ based on the dialog act representation $\mathbf{d}_t$ and the input token embedding $\mathbf{w}_t$, and is formulated by:

$$
\mathbf{x}_t = f_R(\mathbf{d}_t, \mathbf{w}_t)
\tag{6}
$$

where: f_R is a refinement function, in which each input token is refined (or filtered) by the dialogue act attention information before putting into the RNN decoder. By this way, we can represent the whole sentence based on this refined input using RNN model.

Attention Mechanism: Inspired by work of Cui et al. (2016), in which an attention-over-attention was introduced in solving reading comprehension tasks, we place another attention applied for Refiner over the attentive Aligner, resulting in a model Attentional Refiner over Attention (ARoA).

- ARoA with Vector (*ARoA-V*): We use a simple attention where each input token representation is weighted according to dialogue act attention as follows:

$$
\begin{aligned}
\beta_t &= \sigma(\mathbf{V}_{ra}^\top \mathbf{d}_t) \\
f_R(\mathbf{d}_t, \mathbf{w}_t) &= \beta_t * \mathbf{w}_t
\end{aligned}
\tag{7}
$$

where: $\mathbf{V}_{ra}$ is a refinement attention vector which is used to determine the dialogue act attention strength, and σ is sigmoid function to normalize the weight β_t between 0 and 1.

- ARoA with Matrix (*ARoA-M*): ARoA-V uses only a vector $\mathbf{V}_{ra}$ to weight the DA attention. It may be better to use a matrix to control the attention information. The Equation 7 is modified as follows:

$$\mathbf{V}_{ra} = \mathbf{W}_{aw}\mathbf{w}_t$$
$$\beta_t = \sigma(\mathbf{V}_{ra}^\top \mathbf{d}_t) \qquad (8)$$
$$f_R(\mathbf{d}_t, \mathbf{w}_t) = \beta_t * \mathbf{w}_t$$

where: $\mathbf{W}_{aw}$ is a refinement attention matrix.

- ARoA with Context (*ARoA-C*): The attention in ARoA-V and ARoA-M may not capture the relationship between multiple tokens. In order to add context information into the attention process, we modify the attention weights in Equation 8 with additional history information $\mathbf{h}_{t-1}$:

$$\mathbf{V}_{ra} = \mathbf{W}_{aw}\mathbf{w}_t + \mathbf{W}_{ah}\mathbf{h}_{t-1}$$
$$\beta_t = \sigma(\mathbf{V}_{ra}^\top \mathbf{d}_t) \qquad (9)$$
$$f_R(\mathbf{d}_t, \mathbf{w}_t, \mathbf{h}_{t-1}) = \beta_t * \mathbf{w}_t$$

where: $\mathbf{W}_{aw}, \mathbf{W}_{ah}$ are parameters to learn, $\mathbf{V}_{ra}$ is the refinement attention vector same as above, which contains both DA attention and context information.

Gating Mechanism: We use simple element-wise operators (multiplication or addition) to gate the information between the two vectors $\mathbf{d}_t$ and $\mathbf{w}_t$ as follows:

- Multiplication (*GR-MUL*): The element-wise multiplication plays a part in word-level matching which learns not only the vector similarity, but also preserve information about the two vectors:

$$f_R(\mathbf{d}_t, \mathbf{w}_t) = \mathbf{W}_{gd}\mathbf{d}_t \odot \mathbf{w}_t \qquad (10)$$

- Addition (*GR-ADD*):

$$f_R(\mathbf{d}_t, \mathbf{w}_t) = \mathbf{W}_{gd}\mathbf{d}_t + \mathbf{w}_t \qquad (11)$$

3.4   Decoder

The decoder uses a simple GRU model as described in Section 3.1. In this work, we propose to apply the DA representation and the refined inputs deeper into the GRU cell. Firstly, the GRU reset and update gates can be further influenced on the DA attentive information $\mathbf{d}_t$. The reset and update gates are modified as follows:

$$\mathbf{r}_t = \sigma(\mathbf{W}_{rx}\mathbf{x}_t + \mathbf{W}_{rh}\mathbf{h}_{t-1} + \mathbf{W}_{rd}\mathbf{d}_t)$$
$$\mathbf{u}_t = \sigma(\mathbf{W}_{ux}\mathbf{x}_t + \mathbf{W}_{uh}\mathbf{h}_{t-1} + \mathbf{W}_{ud}\mathbf{d}_t) \qquad (12)$$

where: $\mathbf{W}_{rd}$ and $\mathbf{W}_{ud}$ act like background detectors that learn to control the style of the generating sentence. By this way, the reset and update gates learn not only the long-term dependency but also the attention information from the dialogue act and the previous hidden state. Secondly, the candidate activation $\tilde{\mathbf{h}}_t$ is also modified to depend on the DA representation as follows:

$$\tilde{\mathbf{h}}_t = \tanh(\mathbf{W}_{hx}\mathbf{x}_t + \mathbf{r}_t \odot \mathbf{W}_{hh}\mathbf{h}_{t-1} \\ + \mathbf{W}_{hd}\mathbf{d}_t) + \tanh(\mathbf{W}_{dc}\mathbf{d}_t) \qquad (13)$$

The hidden state is then computed by:

$$\mathbf{h}_t = \mathbf{u}_t \odot \mathbf{h}_{t-1} + (1 - \mathbf{u}_t) \odot \tilde{\mathbf{h}}_t \qquad (14)$$

Finally, the output distribution is computed by applying a softmax function g, and the distribution is sampled to obtain the next token,

$$P(w_{t+1} \mid w_t, w_{t-1}, ...w_0, \mathbf{z}) = g(\mathbf{W}_{ho}\mathbf{h}_t)$$
$$w_{t+1} \sim P(w_{t+1} \mid w_t, w_{t-1}, ...w_0, \mathbf{z}) \qquad (15)$$

3.5   Training

The objective function was the negative log-likelihood and simply computed by:

$$F(\theta) = -\sum_{t=1}^{T} \mathbf{y}_t^\top \log \mathbf{p}_t \qquad (16)$$

where: $\mathbf{y}_t$ is the ground truth word distribution, $\mathbf{p}_t$ is the predicted word distribution, T is length of the input sequence. The proposed generators were trained by treating each sentence as a mini-batch with l_2 regularization added to the objective function for every 10 training examples. The pre-trained word vectors (Pennington et al., 2014) were used to initialize the model. The generators were optimized by using stochastic gradient descent and back propagation through time (Werbos, 1990). To prevent over-fitting, we implemented early stopping using a validation set as suggested by Mikolov (2010).

3.6   Decoding

The decoding consists of two phases: (i) over-generation, and (ii) reranking.   In the over-generation, the generator conditioned on the given

Table 2: Comparison performance on four datasets in terms of the BLEU and the error rate ERR(%) scores; **bold** denotes the best and *italic* shows the second best model. The results were produced by training each network on 5 random initialization and selected model with the highest validation BLEU score. ♯ denotes the Attention-based Encoder-Decoder model.

Model	Restaurant		Hotel		Laptop		TV	
	BLEU	ERR	BLEU	ERR	BLEU	ERR	BLEU	ERR
HLSTM	0.7466	0.74%	0.8504	2.67%	0.5134	1.10%	0.5250	2.50%
SCLSTM	0.7525	0.38%	0.8482	3.07%	0.5116	0.79%	0.5265	2.31%
ENCDEC♯	0.7398	2.78%	0.8549	4.69%	0.5108	4.04%	0.5182	3.18%
GR-ADD♯	0.7742	0.59%	0.8848	1.54%	*0.5221*	*0.54%*	0.5348	0.77%
GR-MUL♯	0.7697	0.47%	0.8854	1.47%	0.5200	1.15%	0.5349	0.65%
ARoA-V♯	0.7667	*0.32%*	0.8814	**0.97%**	0.5195	0.56%	*0.5369*	0.81%
ARoA-M♯	**0.7755**	**0.30%**	**0.8920**	*1.13%*	**0.5223**	**0.50%**	**0.5394**	**0.60%**
ARoA-C♯	*0.7745*	0.45%	*0.8878*	1.31%	0.5201	0.88%	0.5351	*0.63%*

Table 3: Comparison performance of variety of the proposed models on four dataset in terms of the BLEU and the error rate ERR(%) scores; **bold** denotes the best and *italic* shows the second best model. The first two models applied gating mechanism to Refiner component while the last three models used attention over attention mechanism. The results were averaged over 5 randomly initialized networks.

Model	Restaurant		Hotel		Laptop		TV	
	BLEU	ERR	BLEU	ERR	BLEU	ERR	BLEU	ERR
GR-ADD	0.7685	0.63%	*0.8838*	1.67%	*0.5194*	*0.66%*	*0.5344*	0.75%
GR-MUL	0.7669	*0.61%*	0.8836	1.40%	0.5184	1.01%	0.5328	0.73%
ARoA-V	0.7673	0.62%	0.8817	*1.27%*	0.5185	0.73%	0.5336	0.68%
ARoA-M	**0.7712**	**0.50%**	**0.8851**	**1.14%**	**0.5201**	**0.62%**	**0.5350**	**0.62%**
ARoA-C	*0.7690*	0.70%	0.8835	1.44%	0.5181	0.78%	0.5307	*0.64%*

DA uses a beam search to generate a set of candidate responses. In the reranking, the cost of the generator is computed to form the reranking score R as follows:

$$R = -\sum_{t=1}^{T} \mathbf{y}_t^\top \log \mathbf{p}_t + \lambda ERR \qquad (17)$$

where λ is a trade off constant and is set to a large value in order to severely penalize nonsensical outputs. The slot error rate ERR, which is the number of slots generated that is either redundant or missing, and is computed by:

$$ERR = \frac{p + q}{N} \qquad (18)$$

where: N is the total number of slots in DA, and p, q is the number of missing and redundant slots, respectively. Note that the ERR reranking criteria cannot handle arbitrary slot-value pairs such as *binary* slots or slots that take the *dont_care* value because these slots cannot be delexicalized and matched.

4 Experiments

We conducted an extensive set of experiments to assess the effectiveness of our model using several metrics, datasets, and model architectures, in order to compare to prior methods.

4.1 Datasets

We assessed the proposed models using four different NLG domains: finding a restaurant, finding a hotel, buying a laptop, and buying a television. The Restaurant and Hotel were collected in (Wen et al., 2015b) which contain around 5K utterances and 200 distinct DAs. The Laptop and TV datasets have been released by Wen et al. (2016a). These datasets contain about 13K distinct DAs in the Laptop domain and 7K distinct DAs in the TV. Both Laptop and TV datasets have a much larger input space but only one training example for each DA so that the system must learn partial realization of concepts and be able to recombine and apply them to unseen DAs. As a result, the NLG tasks for the Laptop and TV datasets become much harder.

4.2 Experimental Setups

The generators were implemented using the TensorFlow library (Abadi et al., 2016) and trained by partitioning each of the datasets into training, validation and testing set in the ratio 3:1:1. The hidden layer size was set to be 80 for all cases, and the generators were trained with a 70% of dropout rate. We perform 5 runs with different random initialization of the network and the training is terminated by using early stopping as described in Section 3.5. We select a model that yields the highest BLEU score on the validation set as shown in Table 2. Since the trained models can differ depending on the initialization, we also report the results which were averaged over 5 randomly initialized networks. Note that, except the results reported in Table 2, all the results shown were averaged over 5 randomly initialized networks. The decoder procedure used beam search with a beam width of 10. We set λ to 1000 to severely discourage the reranker from selecting utterances which contain either redundant or missing slots. For each DA, we over-generated 20 candidate utterances and selected the top 5 realizations after reranking. Moreover, in order to better understand the effectiveness of our proposed methods, we (1) trained the models on the Laptop domain with a varied proportion of training data, starting from 10% to 100% (Figure 3), and (2) trained general models by merging all the data from four domains together and tested them in each individual domain (Figure 4) .

4.3 Evaluation Metrics and Baselines

The generator performance was assessed by using two objective evaluation metrics: the BLEU score and the slot error rate ERR. Both metrics were computed by adopting code from an open source benchmark NLG toolkit[¶]. We compared our proposed models against three strong baselines from the open source benchmark toolkit. The results have been recently published as an NLG benchmarks by the Cambridge Dialogue Systems Group[¶], including *HLSTM*, *SCLSTM*, and *ENCDEC* models.

5 Results and Analysis

5.1 Results

We conducted extensive experiments on the proposed models with varied setups of Refiner and

compared against the previous methods. Overall, the proposed models consistently achieve the better performances regarding both evaluation metrics across all domains.

Table 2 shows a comparison between the *AREncDec* based models (the models with $^\sharp$ symbol) in which the proposed models significantly reduce the slot error rate across all datasets by a large margin about 2% to 4% that are also improved performances on the BLEU score when comparing the proposed models against the previous approaches. Table 3 further shows the stable strength of our models since the results' pattern stays unchanged compared to those in Table 2. The *ARoA-M* model shows the best performance over all the four domains, while it is an interesting observation that the *GR-ADD* model with simple addition operator for Refiner obtains the second best performance. All these prove the importance of the proposed component Refiner in aggregating and selecting the attentive information.

Figure 3 illustrates a comparison of four models (*ENCDEC*, *SCLSTM*, *ARoA-M*, and *GR-ADD*) which were trained from scratch on the laptop dataset in a variety of proportion of training data, from 10% to 100%. It clearly shows that the BLEU increases while the slot error rate decreases as more training data was provided. Figure 4 presents a comparison performance of general models as described in Section 4.2. Not surprisingly, the two proposed models still obtain higher the BLEU score, while the *ENCDEC* has difficulties in reducing the ERR score in all cases. Both the proposed models show their ability to generalize in the unseen domains (TV and Laptop datasets) since they consistently outperform the previous methods no matter how much training data was fed or how training method was used. These indicate the relevant contribution of the proposed component Refiner to the original AREncDec architecture, in which the Refiner with gating or attention mechanism can effectively aggregate the information before putting them into the RNN decoder.

Figure 5 shows a different attention behavior of the proposed models in a sentence. While all the three models could attend the slot tokens and their surrounding words, the *ARoA-C* model with context shows its ability in attending the consecutive words. Table 4 shows comparison of responses generated for some DAs between different models.

[¶]https://github.com/shawnwun/RNNLG

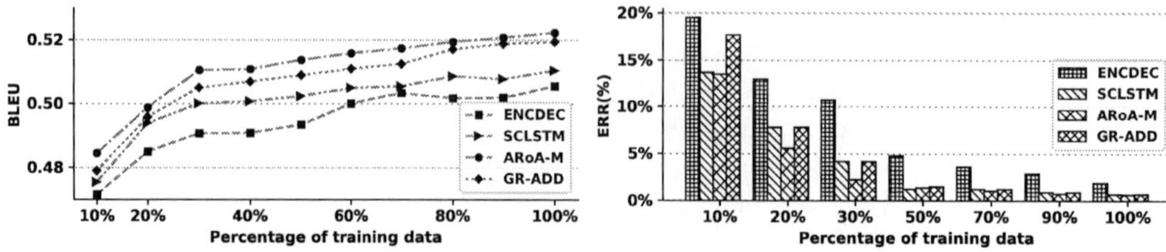

Figure 3: Performance comparison of the four models trained on Laptop (unseen) domain.

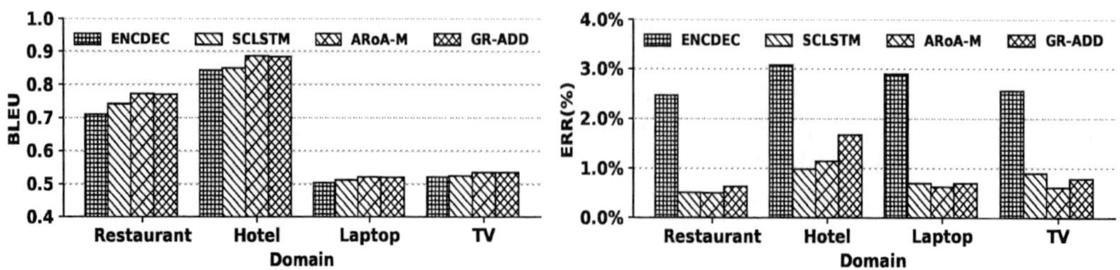

Figure 4: Performance comparison of the general models on four different domains.

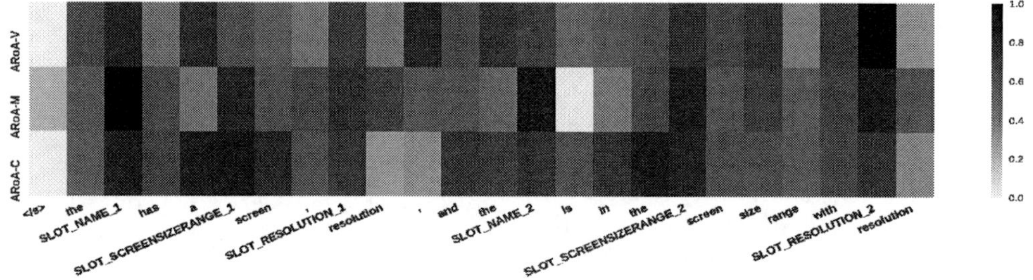

Figure 5: A comparison on attention behavior of three models in a sentence on given *DA* with sequence of slots [*Name_1, ScreenSizeRange_1, Resolution_1, Name_2, ScreenSizeRange_2, Resolution_2*].

The previous approaches (*ENCDEC*, *HLSTM*) still have missing and misplaced information, whereas the proposed models can generate complete and correct-order sentences.

6 Conclusion and Future Work

We present an extension of an Attentional RNN Encoder-Decoder model named Encoder-Aggregator-Decoder, in which a Refiner component is introduced to select and aggregate the semantic elements produced by the encoder. We also present several different choices of gating and attention mechanisms which can be effectively applied to the Refiner. The extension, which is easily integrated into an RNN Encoder-Decoder, shows its ability to refine the inputs and control the flow information before putting them into the RNN decoder. We evaluated the proposed model on four domains and compared to the previous generators. The proposed models empirically show consistent improvement over the previous methods in both BLEU and ERR evaluation metrics. In the future, it would be interesting to further investigate hybrid models which integrate gating and attention mechanisms in order to leverage the advantages of both mechanisms.

Acknowledgements

This work was supported by JSPS Kakenhi Grant Number JP15K16048 and the grant for the research cooperation between JAIST and TIS. The first author would like to thank the Vietnamese Government Scholarship (911 project).

Table 4: Comparison of top responses generated for some input dialogue acts between different models. Errors are marked in color (missing, misplaced slot-value pair). † and ♮ denotes the baselines and the proposed models, respectively.

Model	Generated Responses in Laptop domain
Input DA	*compare(name='aristaeus 59'; screensizerange='large'; resolution='1080p'; name='charon 61'; screensizerange='medium'; resolution='720p')*
Reference	*Compared to aristaeus 59 which is in the large screen size range and has 1080p resolution, charon 61 is in the medium screen size range and has 720p resolution. Which one do you prefer?*
ENCDEC†	the aristaeus 59 has a large screen , the charon 61 has a medium screen and 1080p resolution [1080p, 720p]
HLSTM†	the aristaeus 59 has a large screen size range and has a 1080p resolution and 720p resolution [720p, charon 61, medium]
SCLSTM†	the aristaeus 59 has a large screen and 1080p resolution , the charon 61 has a medium screen and 720p resolution
GR-ADD♮	the aristaeus 59 has a large screen size and 1080p resolution , the charon 61 has a medium screen size and 720p resolution
GR-MUL♮	the aristaeus 59 has a large screen size and 1080p resolution , the charon 61 has a medium screen size and 720p resolution .
ARoA-V♮	the aristaeus 59 has a large screen size and 1080p resolution , the charon 61 has a medium screen size , and has a 720p resolution
ARoA-M♮	the aristaeus 59 has a large screen and 1080p resolution , the charon 61 has a medium screen and 720p resolution
ARoA-C♮	the aristaeus 59 has a large screen size and 1080p resolution , the charon 61 has a medium screen size range and 720p resolution

References

Martın Abadi, Ashish Agarwal, Paul Barham, Eugene Brevdo, Zhifeng Chen, Craig Citro, Greg S Corrado, Andy Davis, Jeffrey Dean, Matthieu Devin, et al. 2016. Tensorflow: Large-scale machine learning on heterogeneous distributed systems. *arXiv preprint arXiv:1603.04467* .

Dzmitry Bahdanau, Kyunghyun Cho, and Yoshua Bengio. 2014. Neural machine translation by jointly learning to align and translate. *arXiv preprint arXiv:1409.0473* .

A. Cheyer and D. Guzzoni. 2014. Method and apparatus for building an intelligent automated assistant. US Patent 8,677,377. https://www.google.com/patents/US8677377.

Yiming Cui, Zhipeng Chen, Si Wei, Shijin Wang, Ting Liu, and Guoping Hu. 2016. Attention-over-attention neural networks for reading comprehension. *arXiv preprint arXiv:1607.04423* .

Ondřej Dušek and Filip Jurčíček. 2016a. A context-aware natural language generator for dialogue systems. *arXiv preprint arXiv:1608.07076* .

Ondřej Dušek and Filip Jurčíček. 2016b. Sequence-to-sequence generation for spoken dialogue via deep syntax trees and strings. *arXiv preprint arXiv:1606.05491* .

Andrej Karpathy and Li Fei-Fei. 2015. Deep visual-semantic alignments for generating image descriptions. In *Proceedings of the IEEE Conference CVPR*. pages 3128–3137.

Minh-Thang Luong, Hieu Pham, and Christopher D Manning. 2015. Effective approaches to attention-based neural machine translation. *arXiv preprint arXiv:1508.04025* .

François Mairesse and Steve Young. 2014. Stochastic language generation in dialogue using factored language models. *Computational Linguistics* .

Hongyuan Mei, Mohit Bansal, and Matthew R Walter. 2015. What to talk about and how? selective generation using lstms with coarse-to-fine alignment. *arXiv preprint arXiv:1509.00838* .

Tomas Mikolov. 2010. Recurrent neural network based language model.

Alice H Oh and Alexander I Rudnicky. 2000. Stochastic language generation for spoken dialogue systems. In *Proceedings of the 2000 ANLP/NAACL Workshop on Conversational systems-Volume 3*. Association for Computational Linguistics, pages 27–32.

Kishore Papineni, Salim Roukos, Todd Ward, and Wei-Jing Zhu. 2002. Bleu: a method for automatic evaluation of machine translation. In *Proceedings of the 40th ACL*. Association for Computational Linguistics, pages 311–318.

Jeffrey Pennington, Richard Socher, and Christopher D Manning. 2014. Glove: Global vectors for word representation. In *EMNLP*. volume 14, pages 1532–43.

Adwait Ratnaparkhi. 2000. Trainable methods for surface natural language generation. In *Proceedings of the 1st North American Chapter of the Association for Computational Linguistics Conference*. Association for Computational Linguistics, Stroudsburg, PA, USA, NAACL 2000, pages 194–201. http://dl.acm.org/citation.cfm?id=974305.974331.

Oriol Vinyals, Alexander Toshev, Samy Bengio, and Dumitru Erhan. 2015. Show and tell: A neural image caption generator. In *Proceedings of the IEEE Conference on Computer Vision and Pattern Recognition*. pages 3156–3164.

Tsung-Hsien Wen, Milica Gašić, Dongho Kim, Nikola Mrkšić, Pei-Hao Su, David Vandyke, and Steve Young. 2015a. Stochastic Language Generation in Dialogue using Recurrent Neural Networks with Convolutional Sentence Reranking. In *Proceedings SIGDIAL*. Association for Computational Linguistics.

Tsung-Hsien Wen, Milica Gasic, Nikola Mrksic, Lina M Rojas-Barahona, Pei-Hao Su, David Vandyke, and Steve Young. 2016a. Multi-domain neural network language generation for spoken dialogue systems. *arXiv preprint arXiv:1603.01232* .

Tsung-Hsien Wen, Milica Gašic, Nikola Mrkšic, Lina M Rojas-Barahona, Pei-Hao Su, David Vandyke, and Steve Young. 2016b. Toward multi-domain language generation using recurrent neural networks .

Tsung-Hsien Wen, Milica Gašić, Nikola Mrkšić, Pei-Hao Su, David Vandyke, and Steve Young. 2015b. Semantically conditioned lstm-based natural language generation for spoken dialogue systems. In *Proceedings of EMNLP*. Association for Computational Linguistics.

Tsung-Hsien Wen, David Vandyke, Nikola Mrksic, Milica Gasic, Lina M Rojas-Barahona, Pei-Hao Su, Stefan Ultes, and Steve Young. 2016c. A network-based end-to-end trainable task-oriented dialogue system. *arXiv preprint arXiv:1604.04562* .

Paul J Werbos. 1990. Backpropagation through time: what it does and how to do it. *Proceedings of the IEEE* 78(10):1550–1560.

Yonghui Wu, Mike Schuster, Zhifeng Chen, Quoc V Le, Mohammad Norouzi, Wolfgang Macherey, Maxim Krikun, Yuan Cao, Qin Gao, Klaus Macherey, et al. 2016. Google's neural machine translation system: Bridging the gap between human and machine translation. *arXiv preprint arXiv:1609.08144* .

Kelvin Xu, Jimmy Ba, Ryan Kiros, Kyunghyun Cho, Aaron C Courville, Ruslan Salakhutdinov, Richard S Zemel, and Yoshua Bengio. 2015. Show, attend and tell: Neural image caption generation with visual attention. In *ICML*. volume 14, pages 77–81.

Zhilin Yang, Ye Yuan, Yuexin Wu, William W Cohen, and Ruslan R Salakhutdinov. 2016. Review networks for caption generation. In *Advances in Neural Information Processing Systems*. pages 2361–2369.

Xingxing Zhang and Mirella Lapata. 2014. Chinese poetry generation with recurrent neural networks. In *EMNLP*. pages 670–680.

Beyond On-Hold Messages:
Conversational Time-Buying in Task-Oriented Dialogue

M Soledad López Gambino
CITEC, Bielefeld University
Universitätsstraße 25, 33615
Bielefeld, Germany

Sina Zarrieß
CITEC, Bielefeld University
Universitätsstraße 25, 33615
Bielefeld, Germany

David Schlangen
CITEC, Bielefeld University
Universitätsstraße 25, 33615
Bielefeld, Germany

`m.lopez_gambino, sina.zarriess, david.schlangen@uni-bielefeld.de`

Abstract

A common convention in graphical user interfaces is to indicate a "wait state", for example while a program is preparing a response, through a changed cursor state or a progress bar. What should the analogue be in a spoken conversational system? To address this question, we set up an experiment in which a human information provider (IP) was given their information only in a delayed and incremental manner, which systematically created situations where the IP had the turn but could not provide task-related information. Our data analysis shows that 1) IPs bridge the gap until they can provide information by "re-purposing" a whole variety of task- and grounding-related communicative actions (e.g. echoing the user's request, signaling understanding, asserting partially relevant information), rather than being silent or explicitly asking for time (e.g. *please wait*), and that 2) IPs combined these actions productively to ensure an ongoing conversation. These results, we argue, indicate that natural conversational interfaces should also be able to manage their time flexibly using a variety of conversational resources.

1 Introduction

How to best present information in a dialogue system is a central, and hence well-studied problem (Stent et al., 2004; Demberg and Moore, 2006; Rieser et al., 2010; Dethlefs et al., 2012b; Wen et al., 2015). What has received less attention is the question of what a system should do *until* it can present information, in the case that retrieval of this information takes time.

A simple option would be to remain silent. However, as observed in human conversation analysis, longer periods of silence appear to be marked in normal conversation and are typically avoided (Clark, 2002). As part of an effort to study online, incremental information presentation, we set up an experiment where an information provider (IP) was given their information in a delayed and piecemeal fashion, and hence was faced with the problem of having the turn before having the information to relay (Section 2). We devised a coding scheme for different types of dialogue moves used in this "time-buying phase" before task-related information is available (Section 3). Analyzing the distribution and sequencing of these moves (Section 4), we find that a variety of strategies is used, with direct requests for more time ("please wait", "one moment please") being relatively rare.

2 Data Collection

As task domain, we chose flight travel information.[1] Interactions were set up between a CALLER (C; a confederate), who had the information need, and a TRAVEL AGENT (A), who was to provide the information. The participants were assigned the role of travel agent, and assumed that they were talking to another participant. C and A were connected via audio only, through high-quality headsets. Each agent handled 10 calls (from the same caller, but treating each as separate), after two training calls. We had 10 participants (balanced for gender), all native German speakers.

To provide some control over the interaction, the task was set up so that after a greeting provided by a recording, C formulated their request in one turn (ostensibly, addressing a dialogue system that processed it) which A could hear, but not intervene

---

[1] A domain in which it is, to this date, realistic that a request needs significant time to be processed, as anyone who has recently used flight search engines can attest.

Proceedings of the SIGDIAL 2017 Conference, pages 241–246,
Saarbrücken, Germany, 15-17 August 2017. ©2017 Association for Computational Linguistics

RING +GREETING	CALLER'S REQUEST	BEEP	TR. AGENT WAITS FOR INFO DISPLAY/ SEARCHES FOR FLIGHT (TIME-BUYING STRETCH)	TR. AGENT'S ANSWER (+ NEGOTIATION)	CALLER'S DECISION

Figure 1: Phases of the call.

Hm, I'd like a flight from...	BEEP	A flight from Köln Bonn	to Lisbon	departure end of November	uh	one moment, please	the search for flights is in progress	There is an available flight...
CALLER'S REQUEST		ECHO: origin	ECHO: destination	ECHO: date	FILL.	WAIT REQUEST	SYSTEM STATE	ANSWER (flight offer)

Figure 2: Example interaction (gray: caller, white: travel agent)

in. C was given, as part of the experimental protocol, a schematic representation of their goal (e.g., "flight from Hannover to New York, early August, weekday, Lufthansa"), but no exact formulation. After the request was completed, the system (or so A was told) processed it and showed it in writing on a computer display placed in front of A. An audible signal was played, after which the line was assumed to be open and it was A's task to respond to the request, using information also displayed on their computer screen. This information, however, could be presented either immediately or after a certain delay (consisting of five seconds plus a random interval between 500 and 2500 ms). The information presentation itself was also varied. In 8 of the 10 calls handled by the same agent, 16 flights were presented; in the other 2, only 4. The 16 flight responses were presented either all in one go, with the 16 flights appearing individually with delays between them, or in two blocks. In some cases, flights were taken off the result list (greyed out) again after a delay. The intended effect of this presentation mode was to keep A uncertain of whether they already had the full flight list or not. Figure 1 shows a schematic illustration of the general call structure, and Figure 2 shows an example call (abbreviated, and translated from the German) with category labels explained next. Due to technical problems, some recorded calls were not useable, which left us with a total of 92 calls (1h:41min audio).

3 Annotation

Time-Buying Stretch   In this paper, we focus on what we call the "time-buying stretch", that is, the time from after the beep (when A gets the turn) until the moment at which A offers information about a specific flight, or declares definitely that no flight matches the request. One of the authors identified these stretches in the calls. There is one such stretch in each call, the length of which depends on the information delay mode (see previ-

ous section) and the individual selection speed of A. These stretches vary in duration from 4 seconds to 50 seconds, with the majority being shorter than 20 seconds.

Time Buyer Categories   To enable a fine-grained analysis of the strategies for bridging the time until information presentation, we annotated dialogue moves that do not directly move the task at hand forward (as per the definition of time-buying stretch). We started out from the general DAMSL scheme (Core and Allen, 1997) but, somewhat contrary to our expectations, found that the dialogue moves in our data correspond to various backward and forward-looking actions coded in different parts of the DAMSL hierarchy. Thus, we opted for a flat scheme, allowing us to label conversational actions specific to our domain. The categories are shown together with examples in Table 1. It is important to note here that we allow for multi-functionality of the dialogue moves. Moves in the "echo" category, for example, clearly also have a conversational grounding function (Clark, 1996; Bunt, 2011); however, our focus is on their function to avoid giving task information or being silent[2].

The TB stretches were segmented and annotated by one of the authors. An independent second annotator also labelled a randomly selected set of 20% of the time buyers, using the information from Table 1 as a guideline. For these segments, we calculated Cohen's $\kappa = 0.93$, indicating that the categories are well-recognisable.

4 Analysis

The first observation to make is that there is a similar amount of speech (629 seconds) and of silence (771 seconds) in the time-buying stretches. It seems clear, hence, that our agents do something else than just wait until they have task-related in-

---

[2]Interestingly, given our task setup, confirmation of the search parameters was not really necessary for A, as these were displayed on A's screen.)

Category	Description	DAMSL	Examples
acknowledgment	signaling understanding of the request/ acceptance of task	Signal Understanding → Acknowledge	C: I want to fly to Bristol. A: *Okay*
echoing	repeating the request or part of it	Signal Understanding → Repeat / Statement → Reassert	C: I'm looking for a flight to Izmir at the beginning of August. A: *A flight to Izmir . beginning of August*
conf./exp./rep. request	A asks C to clarify, repeat or expand on request	Influencing addressee future action → Directive → Info-Request	*Did you say Lufthansa?*
filler	conventional hesitation sound	?	*Uh, uhm, mm, etc.*
wait request	A asks C to wait	Influencing addressee future action → Directive → Action-Directive / Information Level → Task Management	*One moment, please*
agent/system state	providing information about factors which prevent A from offering information	Information Level → Task Management	*The search for flights is still in progress. I'm not sure if Emirates flies this route.*
commitment	expressing that A is (still) engaged in performing the task	Committing Speaker Future Action → Commit	*Let's have a look...*
availability	announcing information without presenting it	Statement → Assert / Committing Speaker Future Action → Commit	*I could offer you a number of flights...* Hmm, you said Quito, is that correct?
partial match	presenting information which only matches the request partially	Statement → Assert / Signal-Understanding → Repeat	*There's a flight to Sidney on 2.8 at 07:15*, but you would prefer to fly after lunchtime, so let's keep looking...
temporary non-availability	announcing lack of information at the current moment	Statement → Assert	*Until now I haven't found any flights for your request*, let's keep looking...
incomplete	partial utterance	Communicative Status → Abandoned	*Maybe I can find...*

Table 1: Time buyer categories (C: Customer, A: Agent)

Category	%
echoing	21
filler	19
agent/system state	10.4
acknowledgment	9.4
commitment	8.8
incomplete	6.7
wait request	6.3
conf./exp./rep. request	5.9
availability	5.1
other	3.5
partial match	2.2
temporary non-availability	1.6

Table 2: Distribution of time buyer categories

formation to provide. Table 2 shows the overall distribution of time buyer categories. As can be seen, echoing occurs frequently, as does production of fillers. Direct requests to wait are comparatively rare. As Figure 3 shows, there is considerable variation between speakers in their distribution of time buyer categories, in particular for echoing and filler, which can occur very frequently or rarely depending on the speaker. Finally, Figure 4 illustrates the temporal sequencing of the TB categories. The plot shows percentages of TB type for the first seven time-buyers uttered in each episode (where available). As this indicates, there seems to be a certain structure to the sequencing of these acts: First, taking over the floor (and accepting the task) is acknowledged, then some time is filled with echoing parts of the request; when information becomes available, the parameters are made present again through clarification / expansion requests, or announcements of partial or full availability. Task- and grounding-independent acts such as fillers, announcements of system state, or direct wait requests, are available at any time, but are most relevant after the initial grounding has been done and before partial information is available for presentation.

5   Related Work

To the best of our knowledge, delayed information presentation has so far not been systematically studied. Various systems, however, addressed the problem in an ad-hoc manner. The

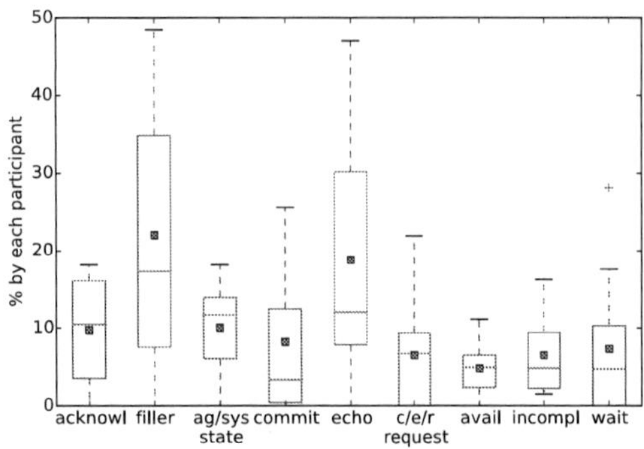

Figure 3: Distribution of TB categories per speaker (only categories with an overall frequency higher than 5%)

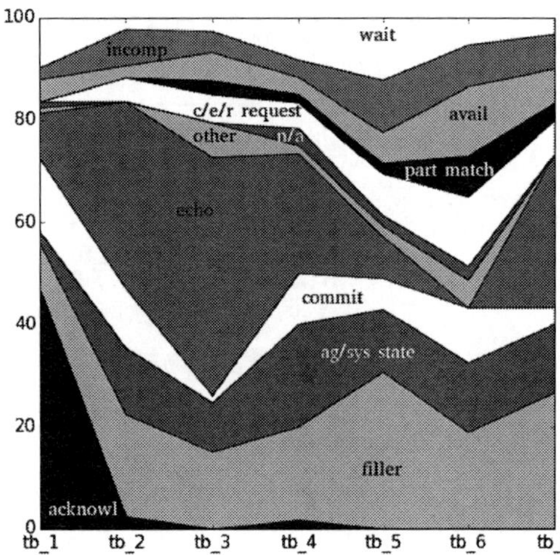

Figure 4: Distribution of time buyer categories for the first seven time-buyers in each episode (where available)

TRIPS system (Stent, 1999), for example, deals with pauses during language generation by inserting "turn-keeping" utterances, such as *um* and *wait a minute*. Funakoshi et al. (2008) conducted a Wizard-of-Oz experiment with a robot which blinked a light on its chest during long pauses, and participants successfully understood this signal as meaning that the robot was processing the incoming utterance. Wigdor et al. (2016) carried out an experiment in which a robot using "pensive fillers" (utterances such as *good question* and *let me think*) was viewed as more alive by participants than one which only postponed information by producing pauses. Although the motivation behind this experiment is not related to a real need to buy time, its results suggest that explicitly addressing collateral aspects of the task before conveying primary task information is not only not detrimental to the interaction, but might in fact be beneficial.

From a broader perspective, we see this study on time buying as contributing to research on incremental generation and information presentation for dialogue systems, cf. (Skantze and Hjalmarsson, 2010), and incremental processing in general (Schlangen and Skantze, 2009). In this line of research, it is typically acknowledged that dialogue systems should be set up in a way such that they are able to start speaking before a complete plan of what to say has been built. Skantze and Hjalmarsson (2010) present a model for incremental generation that includes the ability to insert small speech segments for hesitations and fillers, in case the system has not fully planned the current utterance. It is unclear how such a system would be able to deal with scenarios similar to the ones we have investigated in this work. Similarly, other work has looked at appropriate timings of feedback and barge-in in spoken dialogue systems (Dethlefs et al., 2012a; Meena et al., 2013), dealing with situations where the system does not need to buy time pro-actively.

6 Conclusions and Further Work

It is often difficult to systematically elicit conversational phenomena in human-human dialogue (Gustafson and Merkes, 2009), at least to an extent that would support robust data-driven systems for conversational dialogue. We have presented an experiment designed to investigate conversational strategies used to bridge time until a task can be fulfilled, or to say something before fully knowing what to say. We found that such phenomena can be successfully and systematically triggered by manipulating and delaying the information that an agent has to communicate in a typical travel information setup. Our analysis focused on the time-buying stretch, i.e. the phase of the interaction where the information provider cannot offer factual information. Even in this stretch, task- or interaction-management related acts are clearly preferable over explicit requests for more time.

In future work, we plan to analyze the remaining phases of the recorded interactions where agents actually provided information. This will allow us to compare conversational strategies in this initial time-buying stretch to grounding-related strategies used in the information presentation phase. It would also be interesting to analyze information postponing in actual telephone interactions from customer/passenger service lines, and see whether time-buying in the real world exhibits similar characteristics to those in our recordings. Clearly, this is subject to the possibility of obtaining access to such data.

On the other hand, it is necessary to devote more efforts to understanding the variation between the use of time-buyers by different individuals (Figure 3), as well as along time (Figure 4). In addition, while we think that the setup we devised is representative for the travel information domain specifically, it remains to be seen how information-postponing occurs in other conversational contexts. A similar remark could be made in connection to other languages: Since tolerance to silence has been shown to differ significantly across cultures (Lundholm Fors, 2015), observation of the phenomenon in non-German interactions might also prove revealing.

Finally, we still need to establish how to incorporate these insights in a human-agent interaction scenario. While our taxonomy was useful for annotation and analysis, it could be necessary to adjust it in order to implement time-buying in an actual system.

Acknowledgments

This research/work was supported by the Cluster of Excellence Cognitive Interaction Technology 'CITEC' (EXC 277) at Bielefeld University, which is funded by the German Research Foundation (DFG). Special thanks to our student assistants for their help with transcription and annotation, and to Julian Hough and Ting Han for enlightening discussions on the topic of time-buying.

References

Harry Bunt. 2011. The semantics of dialogue acts. In *Proceedings of the Ninth International Conference on Computational Semantics*. Association for Computational Linguistics, Stroudsburg, PA, USA, IWCS '11, pages 1–13.

Herbert H. Clark. 1996. *Using Language*. Cambridge University Press, Cambridge.

Herbert H. Clark. 2002. Speaking in time. In *Speech Communication*, Elsevier Science, volume 36, pages 5–13.

Mark G Core and James Allen. 1997. Coding dialogs with the damsl annotation scheme. In *AAAI fall symposium on communicative action in humans and machines*. Boston, MA, volume 56.

Vera Demberg and Johanna Moore. 2006. Information presentation in spoken dialogue systems. In *Proceedings of EACL*.

Nina Dethlefs, Helen Hastie, Verena Rieser, and Oliver Lemon. 2012a. Optimising incremental dialogue decisions using information density for interactive systems. In *Proceedings of the 2012 Joint Conference on Empirical Methods in Natural Language Processing and Computational Natural Language Learning*. Association for Computational Linguistics, pages 82–93.

Nina Dethlefs, Helen Hastie, Verena Rieser, and Oliver Lemon. 2012b. Optimising incremental generation for spoken dialogue systems: Reducing the need for fillers. In *Proceedings of the Seventh International Natural Language Generation Conference*. Association for Computational Linguistics, pages 49–58.

Kotaro Funakoshi, Kazuki Kobayashi, Mikio Nakano, Seiji Yamada, Yasuhiko Kitamura, and Hiroshi Tsujino. 2008. Smoothing human-robot speech interactions by using a blinking-light as subtle expression. In *Proceedings of the 10th International Conference on Multimodal Interfaces*. ACM, New York, NY, USA, ICMI '08, pages 293–296. https://doi.org/10.1145/1452392.1452452.

Joakim Gustafson and Miray Merkes. 2009. Eliciting interactional phenomena in human-human dialogues. In *Proceedings of the SIGDIAL 2009 Conference: The 10th Annual Meeting of the Special Interest Group on Discourse and Dialogue*. Association for Computational Linguistics, pages 298–301.

Kristina Lundholm Fors. 2015. *Production and Perception of Pauses in Speech*. Ph.D. thesis, University of Gothenburg.

Raveesh Meena, Gabriel Skantze, and Joakim Gustafson. 2013. A data-driven model for timing feedback in a map task dialogue system. In *14th Annual Meeting of the Special Interest Group on Discourse and Dialogue-SIGdial*. pages 375–383.

Verena Rieser, Oliver Lemon, and Xingkun Liu. 2010. Optimising information presentation for spoken dialogue systems. In *Proceedings of the 48th Annual Meeting of the Association for Computational Linguistics*. Association for Computational Linguistics, pages 1009–1018.

David Schlangen and Gabriel Skantze. 2009. A general, abstract model of incremental dialogue processing. In *Proceedings of the 12th Conference of the European Chapter of the Association for Computational Linguistics (EACL 2009)*. Athens, Greece, pages 710–718.

Gabriel Skantze and Anna Hjalmarsson. 2010. Towards incremental speech generation in dialogue systems. In *Proceedings of the 11th Annual Meeting of the Special Interest Group on Discourse and Dialogue*. Association for Computational Linguistics, Stroudsburg, PA, USA, SIGDIAL '10, pages 1–8.

Amanda Stent, Rashmi Prasad, and Marilyn Walker. 2004. Trainable sentence planning for complex information presentation in spoken dialog systems. In *Proceedings of the 42nd annual meeting on association for computational linguistics*. Association for Computational Linguistics, page 79.

Amanda J. Stent. 1999. Content planning and generation in continuous-speech spoken dialog systems. In *Proceedings of the KI'99 workshop "May I Speak Freely?"*.

Tsung-Hsien Wen, Milica Gašić, Dongho Kim, Nikola Mrkšić, Pei-Hao Su, David Vandyke, and Steve Young. 2015. Stochastic Language Generation in Dialogue using Recurrent Neural Networks with Convolutional Sentence Reranking. In *Proceedings of the 16th Annual Meeting of the Special Interest Group on Discourse and Dialogue (SIGDIAL)*. Association for Computational Linguistics.

Noel Wigdor, Joachim de Greeff, Rosemarijn Looije, and Mark A. Neerincx. 2016. How to improve human-robot interaction with conversational fillers. In *Proceedings of the 25th IEEE International Symposium on Robot and Human Interactive Communication (RO-MAN)*. IEEE, pages 219–224.

Neural-based Context Representation Learning
for Dialog Act Classification

Daniel Ortega   **Ngoc Thang Vu**

Institute for Natural Language Processing (IMS)
University of Stuttgart
Pfaffenwaldring 5b, 70569 Stuttgart, Germany
`{daniel.ortega, thang.vu}@ims.uni-stuttgart.de`

Abstract

We explore context representation learning methods in neural-based models for dialog act classification. We propose and compare extensively different methods which combine recurrent neural network architectures and attention mechanisms (AMs) at different context levels. Our experimental results on two benchmark datasets show consistent improvements compared to the models without contextual information and reveal that the most suitable AM in the architecture depends on the nature of the dataset.

1 Introduction

The study of spoken dialogs between two or more speakers can be approached by analyzing the dialog acts (DAs), which is the intention of the speaker at every utterance during a conversation. Table 1 shows a fragment of a conversation from the Switchboard (SwDA) dataset with DA annotation. Automatic DA classification is an important pre-processing step in natural language understanding tasks and spoken dialog systems. This classification task has been approached using traditional statistical methods such as hidden Markov models (HMMs) (Stolcke et al., 2000), conditional random fields (CRF) (Zimmermann, 2009) and support vector machines (SVMs) (Henderson et al., 2012). However, recent works with deep learning (DL) techniques have brought state-of-the-art models in DA classification, such as convolutional neural networks (CNNs) (Kalchbrenner and Blunsom, 2013; Lee and Dernoncourt, 2016), recurrent neural networks (RNNs) (Lee and Dernoncourt, 2016; Ji et al., 2016) and long short-term memory (LSTM) models (Shen and Lee, 2016).

Utterance	Dialog act
A: *Are you a musician yourself?*	Yes-no-question
B: *Uh, well, I sing.*	Affirmative non-yes answer
A: *Uh-huh.*	Acknowledge (Backchannel)
B: *I don't play an instrument.*	Statement-non-opinion

Table 1: Examples from the SwDA dataset.

Given an utterance in a dialog without any previous context, it is not always obvious even for human beings to find the corresponding dialog act. In many cases, the utterances are too short so that is hard to classify them, for example the utterance *'Right'* can be either an *Agreement* or a *Backchannel* indicating the interlocutor to go on talking, in this case the context plays a key role at disambiguating. Therefore, using context information from the previous utterances in a dialog flow is a crucial step for improving DA classification. Few papers in the literature have suggested to utilize context as a potential knowledge source for DA classification (Lee and Dernoncourt, 2016; Shen and Lee, 2016). Recently, Ribeiro et al. (2015) presented an extensive analysis of the influence of context on DA recognition concluding that contextual information from preceding utterances helps to improve the classification performance. Nonetheless, such information should be differentiable from the current utterance information, otherwise, the contextual information could have a negative impact.

Attention mechanisms (AMs) introduced by Bahdanau et al. (2014) have contributed to significant improvements in many natural language processing tasks, for instance machine translation (Bahdanau et al., 2014), sentence classification (Shen and Lee, 2016) and summarization (Rush et al., 2015), uncertainty detection (Adel and Schütze, 2017), speech recognition (Chorowski et al., 2015), sentence pair modeling (Yin et al., 2015), question-answering (Golub and He, 2016),

Proceedings of the SIGDIAL 2017 Conference, pages 247–252,
Saarbrücken, Germany, 15-17 August 2017. ©2017 Association for Computational Linguistics

document classification (Yang et al., 2016) and entailment (Rocktäschel et al., 2015) . AMs let the model decide what parts of the input to pay attention to according to the relevance for the task.

In this paper, we explore the use of AMs to learn the context representation, as a manner to differentiate the current utterance from its context as well as a mechanism to highlight the most relevant information, while ignoring unimportant parts for DA classification. We propose and compare extensively different neural-based methods for context representation learning by leveraging a recurrent neural network architecture with LSTM (Hochreiter and Schmidhuber, 1997) or gated recurrent units (GRUs) (Cho et al., 2014; Chung et al., 2014) in combination with AMs.

2 Model

The model architecture, shown on the left side of Figure 1, contains two main parts: the CNN-based utterance representation and the attention mechanism for context representation learning. Finally, the context representation is fed into a softmax layer which outputs the posterior of each predefined DA given the current dialog utterance.

2.1 CNN-based Dialog Utterance Representation

We used CNNs for the representation of each utterance. CNNs perform a discrete convolution on an input matrix with a set of different filters. For the DA classification task, the input matrix represents a dialog utterance and its context, this is n previous utterances: each column of the matrix stores the word embedding of the corresponding word. We use 2D filters f (with width $|f|$) spanning all embedding dimensions d. This is described by the following equation:

$$(w * f)(x, y) = \sum_{i=1}^{d} \sum_{j=-|f|/2}^{|f|/2} w(i, j) \cdot f(x-i, y-j)$$

$$(1)$$

After convolution, a max pooling operation is applied that stores only the highest activation of each filter. Furthermore, we apply filters with different window sizes 3-5 (multi-windows), i.e. spanning a different number of input words. Then, all feature maps are concatenated to one vector which represents the current utterance and its context.

2.2 Internal Attention Mechanism

Attention mechanisms can be applied in different sequences of input vectors, e.g. representations of consecutive dialog utterances. For each of the input vectors $u(t - i)$ at time step $t - i$ in a dialog and t is the current time step, the attention weights α_i are computed as follows

$$\alpha_i = \frac{exp(f(u(t - i)))}{\sum_{0<j<m} exp(f(u(t - j)))} \quad (2)$$

where f is the scoring function. In this work, f is the linear function of the input $u(t - i)$

$$f(u(t - i)) = W^T u(t - i) \quad (3)$$

where W is a trainable parameter. The output $attentive\_u$ after the attention layer is the weighted sum of the input sequence.

$$attentive\_u = \sum_i \alpha_i u(t - i) \quad (4)$$

Another option (*order-preserved attention* as proposed in Adel and Schütze (2017)) is to store the weighted inputs into a vector sequence $attentive\_v$ which preserves the order information.

$$attentive\_v = [\alpha_0 u(t), \alpha_1 u(t - 1), ...] \quad (5)$$

2.3 Neural-based Context Modeling

In this subsection, we present different methods, depicted on the right side of Figure 1, to learn the context representation.

(a) **Max** We apply max-pooling on top of the dialog utterance representations which spans all the contexts and the vector dimension.

(b) **Attention** We apply directly attention mechanism on the dialog utterance representations. The weighted sum of all the dialog utterances represents the context information.

(c) **RNN** We introduce a recurrent architecture with LSTM or GRU cells on top of the dialog utterance representations to model the relation between the context and the current utterance over time. The output of the hidden layer of the last state is the context representation.

(d) **RNN-Output-Attention** Based on the previous option, we apply the attention mechanisms on the output sequence of the RNN. The context representation is the weighted sum of all the output vectors.

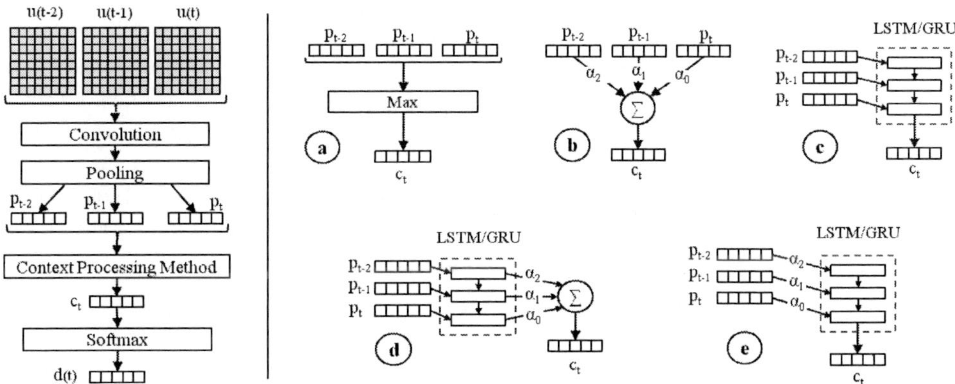

Figure 1: Model architecture for DA classification. On the left side is the overview of the model. The right site contains six neural-based methods for context representation learning.

(e) **RNN-Input-Attention** We first apply the order-preserved attention mechanism on the dialog utterance representations to obtain a sequence of weighted inputs. Afterwards, an RNN with LSTM or GRU cells is introduced to model the relation of the weighted context.

3 Experimental Setup

3.1 Data

We test our model on two DA datasets:

- **MRDA**: ICSI Meeting Recorder Dialog Act Corpus (Janin et al., 2003; Shriberg et al., 2004; Dhillon et al., 2004), a dialog corpus of *multiparty meetings*. The 5-tag-set used in this work was introduced by Ang et al. (2005).

- **SwDA**: Switchboard Dialog Act Corpus (Godfrey et al., 1992; Jurafsky et al., 1997), a dialog corpus of *2-speaker conversations*.

Train, validation and test splits on both datasets were taken as defined in Lee and Dernoncourt (2016)[1], summary statistics are shown in Table 2. In both datasets the classes are highly unbalanced, the majority class is 59.1% on MRDA and 33.7 % on SwDA.

3.2 Hyperparameters and Training

The hyperparameters for both datasets are summarized in Table 3, they were selected by vary-

---

[1]Concerning SwDA, the data setup in Lee and Dernoncourt (2016) was preferred over Stolcke et al. (2000)'s, because it was not clearly found in the latter which conversations belong to each split.

Dataset	C	|V|	Train	Validation	Test
MRDA	5	12k	78k	16k	15k
SwDA	43	20k	193k	23k	5k

Table 2: Data statistics: **C** is the number of classes, **|V|** is the vocabulary size and **Train/Validation/Test** are the no. of utterances.

ing one hyperparameter at a time while keeping the others fixed. The filter widths and feature maps were taken from the CNN architecture for sentence classification in Kim (2014). Dropout rate of 0.5 was found to be the most effective in the range of [0-0.9]. The rectified linear unit (ReLU) was used as non-linear activation function, 1-max as pooling operation at utterance level as suggested in Zhang and Wallace (2015). The only dataset specific hyperparameter is the mini-batch size: 150 and 50 for SwDA and MRDA, respectively. Word2vec (Mikolov et al., 2013) was used for word vector representation. Training was done for 30 epochs with averaged stochastic gradient descent (Polyak and Juditsky, 1992) over minibatches. The learning rate was initialized at 0.1 and reduced 10% every 2000 parameter updates. We kept the word vector unchanged during training. The context length was optimized on the development set, ranging from 1-5. Our best results were obtained with three context utterances for MRDA and two for SwDA.

4 Experimental Results

4.1 Baseline Models

We define two models as baseline, both are a one-layer CNN for sentence classification based on

Hyperparameter	Value
Filter width	3, 4, 5
Feature maps per filter	100
Dropout rate	0.5
Activation function	ReLU
Pooling	1-max pooling per utterance
Mini-batch size	50 (MRDA) – 150 (SwDA)
Word embeddings	word2vec (dim. 300)

Table 3: Hyperparameters.

Kim (2014) but with an input variation: a) Baseline I: The input is a single utterance a time without any contextual information and b) Baseline II: The input is the concatenation of the current utterance and previous utterances.

4.2 Results

Table 4 summarizes the results of all the models. Results on the Baseline I and the Baseline II on both datasets show that a simple context concatenation is not enough to model the context information for this task. While on SwDA the accuracy improves by 1.3%, it slightly drops on MRDA. Other simple methods such as *Max* and *Attention* do not improve the results over the baseline either.

Our results are consistently improved on both datasets after introducing RNN architecture to model the relation between the contexts. It indicates that hierarchical structure is crucial to learn the context representation. Attention mechanisms contribute to the overall improvements. On MRDA, the AM was more useful when it was applied to the inputs of the RNN, whereas on SwDA when it was applied to the outputs. Our intuition is that in multiparty dialogs the dependency between the utterances should be weighted before being processed by the RNN.

Model	MRDA	SwDA
Baseline I	83.6	71.3
Baseline II	83.5	72.6
Max	58.5	48.0
Attention	83.5	72.4
RNN (LSTM)	83.8	73.1
RNN (GRU)	83.8	72.8
RNN-Output-Attention (LSTM)	84.1	**73.8**
RNN-Output-Attention (GRU)	84.0	73.1
RNN-Input-Attention (LSTM)	**84.3**	73.3
RNN-Input-Attention (GRU)	83.6	73.1

Table 4: Accuracy (%) of baselines and models with different context processing methods.

4.3 Impact of Context Length

Our experiments revealed that context length plays an important role for DA classification and the best length is corpus dependent. By experimenting in the context range of 0-5 utterances, we found that the best context length for MRDA is three utterances and two for SwDA. Table 5 shows the results at different context lengths.

n-context	MRDA	SwDA
1	83.8	73.1
2	83.9	**73.8**
3	**84.3**	73.5
4	84.0	73.1
5	84.0	72.9

Table 5: Comparison of accuracy (%) on different context lengths (n-context, where n is the number of sentences as context).

5 Comparison with Other Works

Table 6 compares our results with other works. To the best of our knowledge, Lee and Dernoncourt (2016) is the newest research in DA classification, which published train/validation splits and claimed to be the state-of-the-art on that setup. Therefore, an accurate comparison of our results can be only done with this work. Our model yields comparable results to the state-of-the-art on both datasets, 84.3% against 84.6% on MRDA and 73.8% against 73.1% on SwDA. Ji et al. (2016) and Kalchbrenner and Blunsom (2013) obtained higher accuracy on SwDA but with different setup.

Model	MRDA	SwDA
Our best model	84.3	73.8
CNN-FF	84.6	73.1
LSTM-FF	84.3	69.6
HBM	81.3	—
LV-RNN	—	77.0
HCNN	—	73.9
CA-LSTM	—	72.6
HMM	—	71.0
Majority class	59.1	33.7

Table 6: Comparison of accuracy (%). *CNN-FF* and *LSTM-FF*: proposed in Lee and Dernoncourt (2016), *HBM*: hidden backoff model (Ji and Bilmes, 2006). *LV-RNN*: latent variable RNN with conditional training (Ji et al., 2016). *HCNN*: hierarchical CNN (Kalchbrenner and Blunsom, 2013). *CA-LSTM*: contextual attentive LSTM (Shen and Lee, 2016). *HMM* Stolcke et al. (2000).

6 Conclusions

We explored different neural-based context representation learning methods for dialog act classification which combine RNN architectures with attention mechanisms at different context levels. Our results on two benchmark datasets reveal that using RNN architecture is important to learn the context representation. Moreover, attention mechanisms contribute to the overall improvements, however, the place where AM should be applied depends on the nature of the dataset.

References

Heike Adel and Hinrich Schütze. 2017. Exploring different dimensions of attention for uncertainty detection. In *Proceedings of the 15th Conference of the European Chapter of the Association for Computational Linguistics: Volume 1, Long Papers*. Association for Computational Linguistics, Valencia, Spain, pages 22–34. http://www.aclweb.org/anthology/E17-1003.

Jeremy Ang, Yang Liu, and Elizabeth Shriberg. 2005. Automatic dialog act segmentation and classification in multiparty meetings. In *in Proc. IEEE Int. Conf. on Acoustics, Speech and Signal Processing (ICASSP*. pages 1061–1064.

Dzmitry Bahdanau, Kyunghyun Cho, and Yoshua Bengio. 2014. Neural machine translation by jointly learning to align and translate. *CoRR* abs/1409.0473. http://arxiv.org/abs/1409.0473.

KyungHyun Cho, Bart van Merrienboer, Dzmitry Bahdanau, and Yoshua Bengio. 2014. On the properties of neural machine translation: Encoder-decoder approaches. *CoRR* abs/1409.1259. http://arxiv.org/abs/1409.1259.

Jan Chorowski, Dzmitry Bahdanau, Dmitriy Serdyuk, KyungHyun Cho, and Yoshua Bengio. 2015. Attention-based models for speech recognition. *CoRR* abs/1506.07503. http://arxiv.org/abs/1506.07503.

Junyoung Chung, Çaglar Gülçehre, KyungHyun Cho, and Yoshua Bengio. 2014. Empirical evaluation of gated recurrent neural networks on sequence modeling. *CoRR* abs/1412.3555. http://arxiv.org/abs/1412.3555.

Rajdip Dhillon, Sonali Bhagat, Hannah Carvey, and Elizabeth Shriberg. 2004. Meeting Recorder Project: Dialog Act Labeling Guide. Technical report, ICSI Tech. Report. https://goo.gl/TtLJlE.

John J. Godfrey, Edward C. Holliman, and Jane McDaniel. 1992. Switchboard: Telephone speech corpus for research and development. In *Proceedings of the 1992 IEEE International Conference on Acoustics, Speech and Signal Processing - Volume 1*. IEEE Computer Society, Washington, DC, USA, ICASSP'92, pages 517–520. http://dl.acm.org/citation.cfm?id=1895550.1895693.

David Golub and Xiaodong He. 2016. Character-level question answering with attention. *CoRR* abs/1604.00727. http://arxiv.org/abs/1604.00727.

M. Henderson, M. Gai, B. Thomson, P. Tsiakoulis, K. Yu, and S. Young. 2012. Discriminative spoken language understanding using word confusion networks. In *2012 IEEE Spoken Language Technology Workshop (SLT)*. pages 176–181. https://doi.org/10.1109/SLT.2012.6424218.

Sepp Hochreiter and Jürgen Schmidhuber. 1997. Long short-term memory. *Neural Comput.* 9(8):1735–1780. https://doi.org/10.1162/neco.1997.9.8.1735.

Adam Janin, Don Baron, Jane Edwards, Dan Ellis, David Gelbart, Nelson Morgan, Barbara Peskin, Thilo Pfau, Elizabeth Shriberg, Andreas Stolcke, and Chuck Wooters. 2003. The icsi meeting corpus. pages 364–367.

Gang Ji and Jeff Bilmes. 2006. Backoff model training using partially observed data: Application to dialog act tagging. In *Proceedings of the Main Conference on Human Language Technology Conference of the North American Chapter of the Association of Computational Linguistics*. Association for Computational Linguistics, Stroudsburg, PA, USA, HLT-NAACL '06, pages 280–287. https://doi.org/10.3115/1220835.1220871.

Yangfeng Ji, Gholamreza Haffari, and Jacob Eisenstein. 2016. A latent variable recurrent neural network for discourse relation language models. *CoRR* abs/1603.01913. http://arxiv.org/abs/1603.01913.

D. Jurafsky, E. Shriberg, and D. Biasca. 1997. Switchboard SWBD-DAMSL shallow-discourse-function annotation coders manual. Technical Report Draft 13, University of Colorado, Institute of Cognitive Science.

Nal Kalchbrenner and Phil Blunsom. 2013. Recurrent convolutional neural networks for discourse compositionality. *CoRR* abs/1306.3584. http://arxiv.org/abs/1306.3584.

Yoon Kim. 2014. Convolutional neural networks for sentence classification. *CoRR* abs/1408.5882. http://arxiv.org/abs/1408.5882.

Ji Young Lee and Franck Dernoncourt. 2016. Sequential short-text classification with recurrent and convolutional neural networks. *CoRR* abs/1603.03827. http://arxiv.org/abs/1603.03827.

Tomas Mikolov, Ilya Sutskever, Kai Chen, Greg Corrado, and Jeffrey Dean. 2013. Distributed representations of words and phrases and their compositionality. *CoRR* abs/1310.4546. http://arxiv.org/abs/1310.4546.

B. T. Polyak and A. B. Juditsky. 1992. Acceleration of stochastic approximation by averaging. *SIAM J. Control Optim.* 30(4):838–855. https://doi.org/10.1137/0330046.

Eugénio Ribeiro, Ricardo Ribeiro, and David Martins de Matos. 2015. The influence of context on dialogue act recognition. *CoRR* abs/1506.00839. http://arxiv.org/abs/1506.00839.

Tim Rocktäschel, Edward Grefenstette, Karl Moritz Hermann, Tomás Kociský, and Phil Blunsom. 2015. Reasoning about entailment with neural attention. *CoRR* abs/1509.06664. http://arxiv.org/abs/1509.06664.

Alexander M. Rush, Sumit Chopra, and Jason Weston. 2015. A neural attention model for abstractive sentence summarization. In Lluís Màrquez, Chris Callison-Burch, Jian Su, Daniele Pighin, and Yuval Marton, editors, *Proceedings of the 2015 Conference on Empirical Methods in Natural Language Processing, EMNLP 2015, Lisbon, Portugal, September 17-21, 2015*. The Association for Computational Linguistics, pages 379–389. http://aclweb.org/anthology/D/D15/D15-1044.pdf.

Sheng-syun Shen and Hung-yi Lee. 2016. Neural attention models for sequence classification: Analysis and application to key term extraction and dialogue act detection. *CoRR* abs/1604.00077. http://arxiv.org/abs/1604.00077.

Elizabeth Shriberg, Raj Dhillon, Sonali Bhagat, Jeremy Ang, and Hannah Carvey. 2004. The icsi meeting recorder dialog act (mrda) corpus. In Michael Strube and Candy Sidner, editors, *Proceedings of the 5th SIGdial Workshop on Discourse and Dialogue*. Association for Computational Linguistics, Cambridge, Massachusetts, USA, pages 97–100. http://www.aclweb.org/anthology/W04-2319.

Andreas Stolcke, Noah Coccaro, Rebecca Bates, Paul Taylor, Carol Van Ess-Dykema, Klaus Ries, Elizabeth Shriberg, Daniel Jurafsky, Rachel Martin, and Marie Meteer. 2000. Dialogue act modeling for automatic tagging and recognition of conversational speech. *Comput. Linguist.* 26(3):339–373. https://doi.org/10.1162/089120100561737.

Zichao Yang, Diyi Yang, Chris Dyer, Xiaodong He, Alexander J. Smola, and Eduard H. Hovy. 2016. Hierarchical attention networks for document classification. In *HLT-NAACL*.

Wenpeng Yin, Hinrich Schütze, Bing Xiang, and Bowen Zhou. 2015. ABCNN: attention-based convolutional neural network for modeling sentence pairs. *CoRR* abs/1512.05193. http://arxiv.org/abs/1512.05193.

Ye Zhang and Byron C. Wallace. 2015. A sensitivity analysis of (and practitioners' guide to) convolutional neural networks for sentence classification. *CoRR* abs/1510.03820. http://arxiv.org/abs/1510.03820.

Matthias Zimmermann. 2009. Joint segmentation and classification of dialog acts using conditional random fields. In *INTERSPEECH*. pages 864–867.

Predicting Success in Goal-Driven Human-Human Dialogues

Michael Noseworthy, Jackie Chi Kit Cheung, Joelle Pineau
School of Computer Science
McGill University
michael.noseworthy@mail.mcgill.ca
{jcheung, jpineau}@cs.mcgill.ca

Abstract

In goal-driven dialogue systems, success is often defined based on a structured definition of the goal. This requires that the dialogue system be constrained to handle a specific class of goals and that there be a mechanism to measure success with respect to that goal. However, in many human-human dialogues the diversity of goals makes it infeasible to define success in such a way. To address this scenario, we consider the task of automatically predicting success in goal-driven human-human dialogues using only the information communicated between participants in the form of text. We build a dataset from *stackoverflow.com* which consists of exchanges between two users in the technical domain where ground-truth success labels are available. We then propose a turn-based hierarchical neural network model that can be used to predict success without requiring a structured goal definition. We show this model outperforms rule-based heuristics and other baselines as it is able to detect patterns over the course of a dialogue and capture notions such as gratitude.

1 Introduction

In this paper, we investigate goal-driven dialogues in large open-ended domains where one participant engages in a conversation with another participant in order to gain information or complete some task. Such dialogues are common in online communication channels where users help each other complete tasks with various requirements. For instance, many corporations have online chat systems where users can talk to a representative, and there are countless online forums (both technical and non-technical) where people go for help.

Current dialogue agents learn to assist users to complete tasks in relatively constrained domains such as restaurant reservation booking (see Table 1 of Serban et al., 2015 for a list of these domains). In such domains, agents can measure success by referring to a structured goal definition or ontology and learn to maximize this score (Young et al., 2013). However, in less-constrained domains, success can be difficult to define as it is often dependent on the specific dialogue and participants.

One difficulty arises when participants enter a conversation with intrinsically different goals which we cannot anticipate in advance. For example, on *stackoverflow*, a popular forum for programming-related help, users can ask for help fixing a bug (in which case success occurs when the bug is resolved), or ask for a recommendation (in which case success occurs when the user is satisfied with a recommendation). On top of this, different users may have differing definitions of success (e.g., a novice may require more information than an expert).

The aforementioned difficulties suggest that the definition of success is highly specific to the user who initiates the dialogue. Even in constrained domains it has been observed that a user's perception of success is more indicative of user satisfaction than an objective measure (Walker et al., 2000; Williams and Young, 2004). Thus, we aim to let the original participant be the judge of success and build models that can predict success based on information communicated rather than enforcing a rigorous definition in our models.

An impediment in building models that predict success (or interactive agents) in these domains is the lack of success labels in current datasets (Kim et al., 2010; Lowe et al., 2015). These labels can be difficult to collect as forums often do not pro-

Proceedings of the SIGDIAL 2017 Conference, pages 253–262,
Saarbrücken, Germany, 15-17 August 2017. ©2017 Association for Computational Linguistics

vide any structured process of indicating whether a problem was solved or not. Our model is trained to predict success in these interactions using only the dialogue text, which can then be used as automatic feedback to improve the quality of the dialogues and enable automatic dialogue agents to learn from large, previously unlabeled corpora.

We address the challenge of predicting success in goal-driven human-human dialogues with three contributions. First, we present a new dataset of human-human goal-driven dialogues in the technical domain.[1] The use of human-human dialogues allows our dataset to reach a size needed to work in and be representative of large domains. We focus on dialogues from *stackoverflow.com*, where we have success labels available. These dialogues consist of one participant asking a programming-related question and other participants interacting with them to come up with a solution. This dataset will allow the community to work in an open-ended domain with success labels.

Our second contribution consists of an investigation of new models to predict success using only the raw text of the dialogue history. Our most successful model is a turn-based hierarchical recurrent neural network (H-RNN). This model is inspired by the observation that dialogues consist of multi-level sequences. At the higher-level, we have a sequence of turns, which is commonly abstracted as a dialogue act, or intent (Traum and Hinkelman, 2011). For each turn, we also have a lower-level sequence of words which are a natural language realization of the dialogue act. We show that the H-RNN outperforms alternative models, and in particular can capture the semantics of a user expressing their gratitude.

Our final contribution is an analysis of the salient features for success prediction. We show that our models' performances significantly increase when they explicitly model the entire dialogue history (and learn more complicated indicators of success along with gratitude). Although our models only use each turn in their raw text form (as opposed to the dialogue act type such as *Confirmation* or *Rejection*), they implicitly benefit from this natural structure that arises in dialogue.

---

2 Related Work

There has been much work on automatically evaluating dialogue success. This work has largely focused on small domains where one can manually define every task the system or participants can perform and what it means to complete the task.

Success, as defined by task completion, is easier to evaluate in traditional dialogue systems which have been highly scripted. These systems are designed for restricted domains in which the relevant ontology and language generation prompts or templates have been specified. Such systems include the *Let's Go* Pittsburgh Bus System (Raux et al., 2003), the Cambridge Restaurant System (Thomson and Young, 2010), and the *ELVIS* email assistant (Walker et al., 1998). Scaling these systems to larger domains, such as those found in online forums, is difficult because expanding their ontologies becomes infeasible.

The PARADISE framework (Walker et al., 1997) was proposed to automatically evaluate dialogues where the quality of a dialogue can be seen to consist of task success and costs such as the dialogue length. Here, task success has a rigid definition, where for each dialogue system using this framework, the designer must specify what attributes need to be communicated by the system to achieve a goal. This definition makes it clear what success looks like; however, it is not clear how to apply PARADISE to open-ended human-human dialogues, where each dialogue could have a different goal that we cannot anticipate before the conversation, or to large domains, where it is not feasible to design such a reward.

Instead of requiring the designer of a dialogue system to specify what information needs to be communicated between users, work has been done that tries to learn this. Su et al. (2015) propose neural network models that operate on dialogue acts to learn what success means in a constrained domain with knowledge of the true goal. A limitation to this work is that it requires a domain specific feature vector. We consider domains where it is infeasible to acquire such features and instead work directly from text input. Vandyke et al. (2015) extend this model to work in unseen domains but still require we parse our input into slots.

Recently, *Amazon Mechanical Turk* (AMT) has been used to crowd-source the success of a dialogue (Yang et al., 2010; Jurcıcek et al., 2011). The first method presents the transcript of a dialogue to a worker and asks them to fill out a questionnaire rating success. The latter has users interact with a dialogue system by giving them a goal and asking them to evaluate the dialogue after its completion. It is unclear how to extend these methods to an open-ended domain as AMT workers are unlikely to have enough expertise to evaluate success or start a conversation on each possible dialogue topic (Lowe et al., 2016). Furthermore, although AMT is both faster and cheaper than running in-person experiments, we search for an automatic evaluation method with near zero costs.

Work has been done that aims to make data from online forums more accessible to both other users and computer models. The Ubuntu dataset (Lowe et al., 2015) was proposed for dialogue modeling from the *Ubuntu Internet Relay Chat* channel and the CNET (Kim et al., 2010) dataset was proposed to learn dialogue structure from these often unstructured forums. We build on this work by offering a way to provide success labels with this type of data.

Complementary work has been done that shares a common goal of extending dialogue systems to open-ended domains. One area of research focuses on extending intent detection to open-ended domains, where an intent is defined as an action a user wants to perform in the dialogue (e.g. request information or make a reservation). These methods look for semantic similarity with existing intents (Chen et al., 2016) or exploit the structure of knowledge graphs (El-Kahky et al., 2014). Another line of research is on extending natural language generation to multiple or open-ended domains. Domain adaptation techniques have proved useful to generate responses for unseen dialogues (Wen et al., 2016).

The *Community Question Answering* (CQA) literature has investigated predicting the success of answers posed on online forums but typically in a different scenario. Whereas we are interested with predicting the success of a single question and answer, CQA often looks to predict user satisfaction based on several answers (Liu et al., 2008). Furthermore, we restrict our models to only consider the text of the questions, answers, and comments (we do not include any information about users or votes). Kim and Oh (2009) observe that comments often contain useful information for predicting success. Our work investigates this hypothesis.

Question
User A (Lee): I accidentally closed the Stack Trace window in the Visual Studio 2008 debugger. How do I redisplay this window?
Answer
User B (Brian): While debugging: Debug\ Windows\Call stack
Comment
User A (Lee): Thanks, I don't know how I overlooked it.

Figure 1: Example dialogue from our *stackoverflow* dataset. Post taken from *http://stackoverflow.com/questions/612123/redisplay-stacktrace-window*.

3   Dataset

Our first contribution is a dataset from *stackoverflow.com* curated to allow training a success prediction function. *Stackoverflow* is a community-based website where users post programming-related questions and other users can respond with answers. Multiple users can provide answers to the same question and users can comment on any potential answer. This format allows us to extract dialogues from the website that consist of the aforementioned exchange. To limit the complexity, we restrict our dataset to dialogues between two users. These dialogues are goal-driven as each is an attempt to solve the question initially posted. Figure 1 is an example of a question, answer, and comment found on *stackoverflow*.

In addition, the user who posed a question can mark an answer as accepted if that answer successfully solved their problem. Only the original user can mark an answer as accepted and they can only mark a single answer. Any user can vote ($+1$ or -1) on answers based on how helpful they are.

Our goal when creating the dataset is to collect a label for dialogue success that is representative of the original user's goal. Note that their true goal may differ slightly from what they express in their question (for example, due to a poor explanation). Votes have a high variance that depend on how popular a question is and the difficulty of the question. Furthermore, users who vote for an answer may not be experiencing the exact same problem as the original user. For this reason, we do not use the vote count alone to judge dialogue success (only to ensure a high quality dataset as described below).

3.1 Collection

In our work, we are concerned with dialogues that consist of only two participants and are complete dialogues in the sense that either the initial user's question was accepted or rejected. We define an accepted dialogue to be one in which the original user's question was successfully answered. Similarly, a rejected dialogue is one in which the dialogue did not solve the original question. Because of the open-ended nature of *stackoverflow*, many posts do not conform to these requirements and we must perform filtering to collect a high quality dataset.

We use the *stackoverflow* posts from the *Stack Exchange Data Dump*.[2] A candidate dialogue consists of a question, answer, and series of comments. In order to be considered, this series of exchanges must take place only between two unique users. We do not consider dialogues where the comments consist of other users.[3] We require at least one comment so that the dialogue extends beyond just question answering. For this reason, all dialogues are at least three turns long where a single turn is one or more utterances by a single user.

On *stackoverflow*, it is possible for a user to edit their posts after seeing answers or comments. We exclude any dialogue where the question or answer was edited to ensure a linear structure.

To ensure a question was either accepted or rejected by the original user, we use information from *stackoverflow* outside of the text. As mentioned above, there are two methods to express satisfaction with an answer. For a post to be accepted, we require both of the following to hold:

1. The answer be marked as accepted by the user who posed the question.

2. There be a strictly positive score from the votes attributed to the answer.

On the contrary, for an answer to be rejected, we require:

3. No answer associated with the question be marked as accepted.

4. There be a non-positive score from the votes assigned to the answer.

---

[2]http://archive.org/details/
stackexchange
[3]Note that for questions with multiple answers, we treat each answer as a new dialogue.

# Accepted Dialogues	667,777
# Rejected Dialogues	297,145
Avg. # of Turns	4
Avg. Question Length	110 words
Avg. Answer Length	60 words
Avg. Comment Length	31 words

Table 1: Statistics of the *stackoverflow.com* dataset. *Accepted* and *Rejected* are the two class labels.

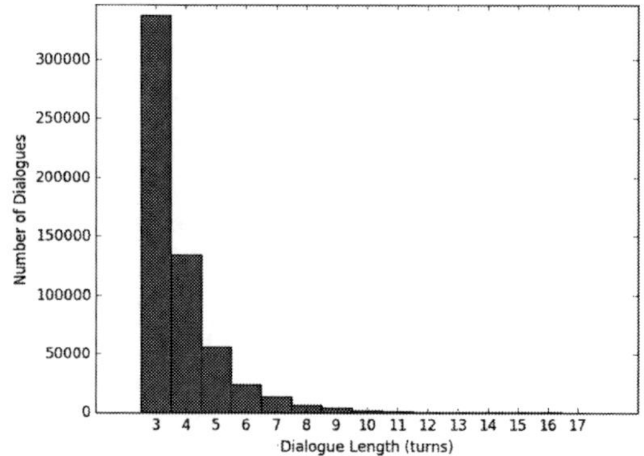

Figure 2: Turn distribution for the *stackoverflow.com* dataset.

Point (3) requires that no other answer be marked as accepted, in order to prevent less popular but nevertheless correct answers from being labelled as rejected. This situation often occurs because *stackoverflow* only allows one answer to be accepted by the user.

Note that (2) and (4) act as a form of validation as it requires the user and crowd be in agreement about the success of an answer. We performed label validation by blindly labelling randomly sampled dialogues from our dataset.

3.2 Statistics

After filtering through the *Data Dump* as described in the previous section, we have a dataset with 964,922 dialogues (reduced from 7,990,787 unfiltered posts). More statistics can be found in Table 1.

It is worth noting that the first and second turns will often be longer in these dialogues due to their question-answer nature. These types of dialogues are of particular interest in the tech-support (Kim et al., 2010; Lowe et al., 2015) and e-mail (Ulrich et al., 2008) domains where the bulk of the information is communicated in the first few turns (e.g. to explain a problem). As we will see, most of our models take advantage of features that appear in the comments which are more characteristic of traditional dialogues.

Figure 2 shows the distribution of number of turns in a dialogue. A single turn consists or a group of sentences by one user. For example, a question will be a single turn, as will an answer. Consecutive comments by the same user are considered as a single turn.

3.3 Preprocessing

Before continuing with any experiments, we preprocess each question, answer, and comment by removing HTML tags, and replacing numbers and code with generic tags.

4 Recurrent Neural Network Models for Dialogue Success Prediction

Presented with a dialogue that consists of a series of turns (question, answer, and comments), we would like to classify whether that dialogue was successful or not. We will denote the true labels as y and the model predictions as $success$. We refer to successful dialogues as $accepted$ ($y = 1$) and unsuccessful dialogues as $rejected$ ($y = 0$) as previously defined.

Formally, our input is the sequence of turns, $d = t_1, \ldots, t_n$, and the sequence of words within each turn, $t_i = w_{i,1}, \ldots, w_{i,n}$. The first turn will be a question, q, the second turn an answer, a, and the remaining turns a series of comments, $c_1, \ldots, c_n$.

We consider two recurrent neural network (RNN) models: a flat one that operates over the concatenated sequence of words from each turn, and a hierarchical one that explicitly models multi-level sequences.

No further information from *stackoverflow* is included in the models such as a user's reputation, tags, or the number of views. We want our models to be usable in other scenarios where this data may not be available. Thus, the only features the models have to work with are text from the dialogues.

A motivating example behind using RNNs is their ability to predict complex non-linear discourse features. For example, consider the following comments:

Rejected: *Thanks for the advice. I tried this change, but I am still encountering the same error.*

Accepted: *Hmm, I thought I already tried that but there probably were more errors in the regex at that time. It did the trick, thanks!*

Both these examples require reasoning across the complete utterance. A model that could capture longer dependencies within a discourse would be useful for differentiating these two examples.

4.1 Flat Recurrent Neural Network

The Flat RNN works by first converting each word of a dialogue into its word embedding. After seeing each word embedding, the RNN updates its hidden state. We insert a special token, $\langle t \rangle$ (with its own embedding), to denote the separation between turns of the dialogue. At the end of the dialogue, the RNN makes a prediction using a logistic regression unit on the final hidden state of the network. This allows us to learn discourse features beyond bag-of-words (BOW) as we maintain word ordering. See Figure 3(a) for the architecture.

In our implementation, we use *Long Short Term Memory* (LSTM) units (Hochreiter and Schmidhuber, 1997) to account for long-term dependencies. We use *Theano* (Bastien et al., 2012) and pretrained *GloVe* word embeddings (Pennington et al., 2014). Optimization is done using the *ADAM* optimizer (Kingma and Ba, 2014) to minimize cross-entropy between the model predictions, $success$, and the actual success labels, y.

4.2 Turn-Based Hierarchical Recurrent Neural Network

In this model, we extend the Flat RNN to model the natural hierarchy that occurs in dialogues. This allows our model to separate the flow of content throughout the dialogue from the natural language realization of each turn. Our model is similar to the encoder models used in previous work (Sordoni et al., 2015; Li et al., 2015).

Similar to the Flat RNN, each word is projected into its vectorized word embedding. Then for each turn t_i, we feed its word embeddings through the same RNN (the turn-level RNN) which outputs an encoded version of that turn, $t_{en,i}$. We feed all these encoded turn vectors into a higher-level RNN (the dialogue-level RNN) which takes into account the context of the dialogue.

We also use *LSTM* units (Hochreiter and Schmidhuber, 1997) with *GloVe* embeddings (Pennington et al., 2014). Refer to Figure 3 (b) for the model architecture.

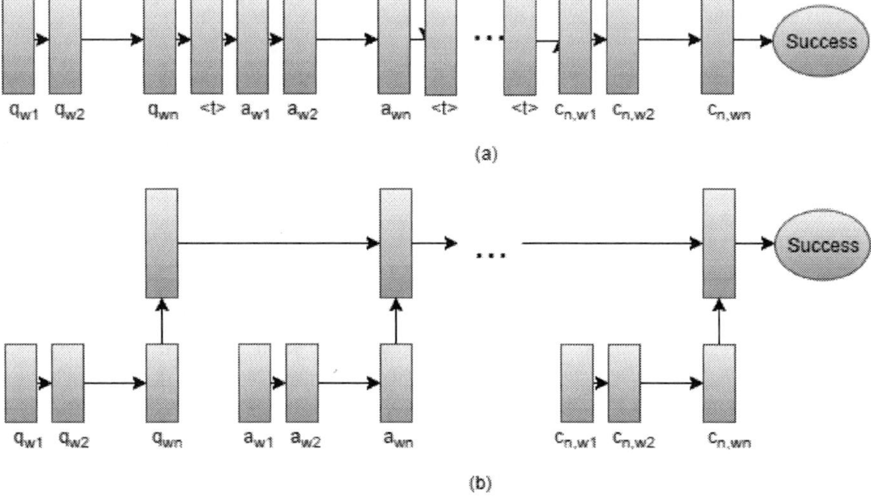

Figure 3: Flat (a) and Turn-Based Hierarchical (b) RNN models including features for a full dialogue.

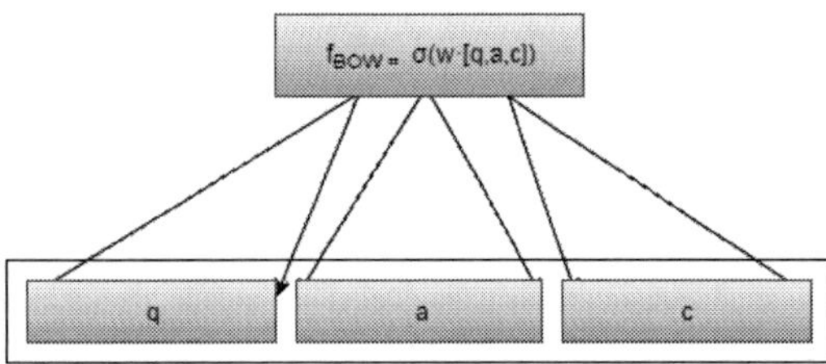

Figure 4: Logistic Regression BOW model including question, answer, and comment features.

5   Experiments

5.1   Baselines

We compare our two neural network models to several baselines ranging in complexity.

5.1.1   Majority Class

As our dataset suffers from class imbalance, we consider a majority class model which always predicts accepted.

5.1.2   Thanks Heuristic

The "Thanks" baseline operates on the intuition that users who ask a question will express gratitude for accepted answers in terms of thanking the user in a comment.

This method simply looks at the last comment, c_{-1}, by the user who posed the question and looks for the appearance of the word "thanks" or common variations of that word (we denote these words by the set $\mathrm{TH} =$ $\{thx, thanks, ty, thankyou, tx\}$). Our classification rule is:

$$f_{baseline}(c_{-1}) = \mathbb{1}_{\mathrm{TH}}(c_{-1}) \qquad (1)$$

5.1.3   Logistic Regression Classifier

We extend the "Thanks" baseline by considering the bag-of-word (BOW) vectors for each turn, and learning their respective weights when classifying a dialogue. In this model, we represent the dialogue as three concatenated BOW-vectors for the question, q, answer, a, and the sum of the comments, c. Together, these make up an input vector that is fed to a logistic regression classifier:

$$f_{BOW} = \sigma(w \cdot [q, a, c]) \qquad (2)$$

We learn the parameters by minimizing cross-entropy. See Figure 4 for a depiction of this model.

5.2   Evaluation

We performed multiple experiments to gain intuition about what our models are learning and their performance at predicting dialogue success. We divided our dataset into training, validation, and testing sets using a 60%/20%/20% split (there is equal class imbalance across sets). We present precision, recall, and F1 metrics for each class.

For the RNN models, we used the cross-validation set to optimize the model parameters. For the Flat-RNN this resulted in word embeddings of dimension 50 and hidden states of dimension 256. For the hierarchical model, we used

	Accepted			Rejected		
Model	Precision	Recall	F1	Precision	Recall	F1
Majority	69.20 ± 0.20	100 ± 0.0	81.66 ± 0.14	0.0 ± 0.0	0.0 ± 0.0	0.0 ± 0.0
Thanks	82.45 ± 0.20	73.51 ± 0.22	77.72 ± 0.17	52.13 ± 0.34	64.83 ± 0.36	57.79 ± 0.30
LR	81.95 ± 0.19	89.57 ± 0.17	85.59 ± 0.14	70.38 ± 0.43	55.68 ± 0.39	62.17 ± 0.35
Flat RNN	$\mathbf{87.08 \pm 0.18}$	87.39 ± 0.18	87.23 ± 0.14	71.42 ± 0.36	$\mathbf{70.85 \pm 0.37}$	71.13 ± 0.28
H-RNN	$\mathbf{87.28 \pm 0.17}$	$\mathbf{90.06 \pm 0.17}$	$\mathbf{88.65 \pm 0.13}$	$\mathbf{75.95 \pm 0.35}$	70.51 ± 0.37	$\mathbf{73.13 \pm 0.31}$

Table 2: 95% confidence intervals for Precision, Recall, and F1 for both classes for models trained using the entire dialogue. The highest metrics are bolded.

word embeddings of dimension 50, turn-level hidden states of dimension 100, and dialogue-level hidden states of dimension 200.

We can see the performance of various models and feature sets in Table 2. Confidence intervals were calculated using the bootstrap method (Efron and Tibshirani, 1994).

5.3 Results

We start with a comparison of the various models. From Table 2, we see that our RNN models, which can capture more complex dependencies, have the best F1-scores for each class. Their performances exceed that of the Logistic Regression model, the strongest baseline.

It is also interesting to note that the Turn-Based Hierarchical RNN has significantly higher F1-scores than the Flat RNN. This suggests that this model can better represent both a turn, and an entire dialogue. By explicitly building in the structure to represent a turn, we allow the model to learn the important information in a single turn in regards to predicting success. The lower-level RNN can learn the semantics of a single turn which leaves the higher-level RNN to focus solely on the aspects of each turn relevant to predicting success. We go on to examine this model further in the next section.

6 Discussion

6.1 Turn-Embedding Analysis

The Turn-Based Hierarchical RNN model allows us to inspect the turn embeddings through the turn-level RNN. We extract the final hidden layer embedding from this lower-level RNN which represents the last fully-encoded turn of a dialogue. These turn-vectors represent the part of the turn that is relevant to predicting dialogue success (as the model was optimized for this). We then use t-SNE (Maaten and Hinton, 2008) to visualize these embeddings for the last comment by the initial

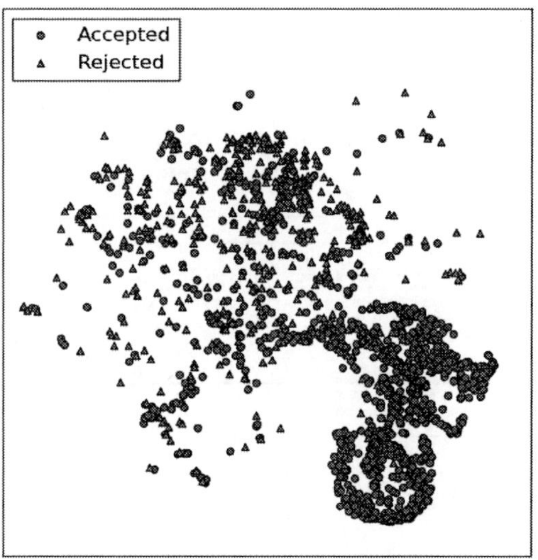

Figure 5: t-SNE visualization of the embedding of the last comment from the initial user from the H-RNN model.

user in two dimensions (see Figure 5). Here the circles denote a successful dialogue whereas the triangles denote a rejected one.

We see a cluster in the lower right of the visualization. In Table 3, we show examples sampled at random from the cluster, and from elsewhere in the visualization. We can see the cluster represents ways for the user to show their gratitude. This supports the hypothesis that the H-RNN model is picking up on various ways for a user to express their satisfaction with a proposed answer.

By incorporating a hierarchical structure the model was able to learn a useful embedding of a given turn before incorporating information from previous turns. We can see the turn-level RNN as a way of extracting the information relevant to the success prediction task from its natural language representation.

Lower Right Cluster	Elsewhere
thank you! this is perfect and youre my bestfriend.	for bordering the cells of a table as <code> do try the following. add a css class for the <code>. let say the class name be <code>. then add the style as below
ah alright thanks for the quick reply	selenium webdriver code to reply a mail in gmail. i tried writing code for replying a mail in gmail but was trapped in between i want to perform below task <ol> <li>open ...
really great helpful!! thanks a lot	make an absolutely positioned div stretch to <num> of the document height with no javascript. is there any neat cssonly way to make an absolutely positioned div element stretch ...
actually it worked. i missed the whereraw at first read. thanks!	the viewpager is for going between detail views. i want a custom action particularly to hide the list view.

Table 3: Example comments from the lower right cluster and everywhere else in the t-SNE plot. Comments are sampled at random from their respective clusters.

	Accepted			Rejected		
Model	Precision	Recall	F1	Precision	Recall	F1
LR (c_{-1})	79.86 ± 0.19	89.71 ± 0.17	84.50 ± 0.14	68.00 ± 0.46	49.13 ± 0.39	57.05 ± 0.36
LR (d_{-1})	73.07 ± 0.21	92.39 ± 0.14	81.60 ± 0.15	57.85 ± 0.64	23.49 ± 0.34	33.41 ± 0.40
LR (d)	81.95 ± 0.19	89.57 ± 0.17	85.59 ± 0.14	70.38 ± 0.43	55.68 ± 0.39	62.17 ± 0.35
RNN (c_{-1})	85.48 ± 0.18	87.43 ± 0.19	86.45 ± 0.13	70.23 ± 0.39	66.62 ± 0.39	68.38 ± 0.31
RNN (d_{-1})	69.23 ± 0.20	100.0 ± 0.0	81.81 ± 0.14	0.0 ± 0.0	0.0 ± 0.0	0.0 ± 0.0
RNN (d)	87.08 ± 0.18	87.39 ± 0.18	87.23 ± 0.14	71.42 ± 0.36	70.85 ± 0.37	71.13 ± 0.28
H-RNN (c_{-1})	85.48 ± 0.18	87.43 ± 0.19	86.45 ± 0.13	70.23 ± 0.39	66.62 ± 0.39	68.38 ± 0.31
H-RNN (d_{-1})	74.11 ± 0.22	93.75 ± 0.12	82.79 ± 0.16	65.30 ± 0.60	26.43 ± 0.34	37.63 ± 0.41
H-RNN (d)	87.28 ± 0.17	90.06 ± 0.17	88.65 ± 0.13	75.95 ± 0.35	70.51 ± 0.37	73.13 ± 0.31

Table 4: 95 % confidence intervals for Precision, Recall, and F1 for models trained using subsets of the dialogue that include or exclude the last turn by the initial user.

6.2 Feature Ablation

We now show that our models exploit features throughout the entire dialogue history to make their predictions. We define feature sets based on whether or not the dialogue contains the last comment by the initial user. We are interested in this comment in particular as it is often the comment where a user will express their satisfaction with the proposed answer. In human-human dialogues, people are generally polite, even if an answer wasn't helpful. It is important for our models to learn the difference between a true expression of gratitude, and that of just being polite - which the baseline methods fail to do.

We can define a dialogue as $d = q, a, c_1, \ldots, c_n$ and let c_{-1} be the last comment by the user who asked the question. Then we will let d_{-1} be the dialogue with c_{-1} removed.

For each model, we re-calculate the above metrics using just c_{-1} or d_{-1} as features. The Hierarchical RNN reduces to the Flat RNN when using c_{-1} features. The results can be seen in Table 4 (we include results from Table 2 for comparison).

We see that the models that utilize the entire dialogue outperform the respective models that use just the last comment in F1-score. This suggests that these models can pick up on more complicated indicators of success than just gratitude such as whether an answer was irrelevant or a question was ill-posed.

It is worth noting that the models that use just the last comment still significantly outperform the baselines (Table 2). We can see the importance of the last comment by observing that the Thanks Heuristic has a higher F1 score for the Rejected class than models that do not include the last turn by the initial user (d_{-1}).

When removing the last comment (going from d to d_{-1}), the models see a drop in precision for the *accepted* class but a rise in recall. This is likely a result of removing discriminative features (c_{-1}) which causes the model to predict the majority class more often (we see that the performance for the *rejected* class greatly drops). The Flat RNN predicts all answers as accepted when the last comment is removed.

Removing the last comment makes the problem more difficult as we no longer use the user's expression of gratitude. In this case, the hierarchical model improves upon the Logistic Regression and Flat RNN models. This can potentially be because it tries to model different dialogue acts such as clarification, or requests for information.

7 Conclusion

In this paper, we collected a *stackoverflow* dataset that consists of dialogues labeled with whether that dialogue was accepted or not. This dataset will allow the community to work in open-ended domains with a clear notion of success. We used this dataset to build models that accurately predict success in open-ended human-human dialogues.

Our Turn-Based Hierarchical RNN model takes advantage of the natural structure that occurs in dialogues by recognizing both expressions of gratitude and more complex indicators of success found throughout the entire dialogue history.

An extension of this work will apply similar methods to human-computer dialogues. Our methods will become more relevant as human-computer interactions become more naturalistic. To minimize the dependence on users expressing their gratitude, we can focus on improving our models that remove the last comment by the initial user from the dataset.

Our methods can also be used to label similar human-human corpora which can then be used to train a dialogue system. Success offers a notion of reward and can be used as such in dialogue systems trained with reinforcement learning.

Acknowledgements

The authors gratefully acknowledge financial support for this work by the Samsung Advanced Institute of Technology (SAIT) and the Natural Sciences and Engineering Research Council of Canada (NSERC).

References

Frédéric Bastien, Pascal Lamblin, Razvan Pascanu, James Bergstra, Ian J. Goodfellow, Arnaud Bergeron, Nicolas Bouchard, and Yoshua Bengio. 2012. Theano: new features and speed improvements. In *Deep Learning and Unsupervised Feature Learning NIPS 2012 Workshop*.

Yun-Nung Chen, Dilek Hakkani-Tur, and Xiaodong He. 2016. Zero-shot learning of intent embeddings for expansion by convolutional deep structured semantic models. In *Proceedings of the 2016 International Conference on Acoustics, Speech and Signal Processing*. IEEE, pages 6045–6049.

Bradley Efron and Robert J Tibshirani. 1994. *An introduction to the bootstrap*. CRC press.

Ali El-Kahky, Xiaohu Liu, Ruhi Sarikaya, Gokhan Tur, Dilek Hakkani-Tur, and Larry Heck. 2014. Extending domain coverage of language understanding systems via intent transfer between domains using knowledge graphs and search query click logs. In *Proceedings of the 2014 International Conference on Acoustics, Speech and Signal Processing*. IEEE, pages 4067–4071.

Sepp Hochreiter and Jurgen Schmidhuber. 1997. Long short-term memory. *Neural computation* 9(8):1735–1780.

F. Jurcıcek, S. Keizer, M. Gašic, F. Mairesse, B. Thomson, K. Yu, and S. Young. 2011. Real user evaluation of spoken dialogue systems using amazon mechanical turk. In *Proceedings of the 12th Annual Conference of the International Speech Communication Association*. pages 3061–3064.

Soojung Kim and Sanghee Oh. 2009. Users' relevance criteria for evaluating answers in a social Q&A site. *Journal of the American society for information science and technology* 60(4):716–727.

Su Nam Kim, Li Wang, and Timothy Baldwin. 2010. Tagging and linking web forum posts. In *Proceedings of the 14th Conference on Computational Natural Language Learning*. Association for Computational Linguistics, pages 192–202.

Diederik. Kingma and Jimmy Ba. 2014. Adam: A method for stochastic optimization. In *Proceedings of the 3rd International Conference for Learning Representations*.

Jiwei Li, Thang Luong, and Dan Jurafsky. 2015. A hierarchical neural autoencoder for paragraphs and documents. In *Proceedings of the 53rd Annual Meeting of the Association for Computational Linguistics and the 7th International Joint Conference on Natural Language Processing*. Association for Computational Linguistics, pages 1106–1115.

Yangdon Liu, Jiang Bian, and Eugene Agichtein. 2008. Predicting information seeker satisfaction in community question answering. In *Proceedings of the 31st annual international ACM SIGIR conference on Research and development in information retrieval*. ACM, pages 483–490.

Ryan Lowe, Nissan Pow, Iulian Serban, and Joelle Pineau. 2015. The ubuntu dialogue corpus: A large dataset for research in unstructured multi-turn dialogue systems. In *Proceedings of the 16th Annual Meeting of the Special Interest Group on Discourse and Dialogue*. Association for Computational Linguistics, pages 285–294.

Ryan Lowe, Iulian Vlad Serban, Michael Noseworthy, Laurent Charlin, and Joelle Pineau. 2016. On the evaluation of dialogue systems with next utterance classification. In *Proceedings of the 17th Annual Meeting of the Special Interest Group on Discourse and Dialogue*. Association for Computational Linguistics, pages 264–269.

Laurens van der Maaten and Geoffrey Hinton. 2008. Visualizing data using t-SNE. *Journal of Machine Learning Research* 9:2579–2605.

Jeffrey Pennington, Richard Socher, and Christopher Manning. 2014. Glove: Global vectors for word representation. In *Proceedings of the 2014 Conference on Empirical Methods in Natural Language Processing*. Association for Computational Linguistics, pages 1532–1543.

Antoine Raux, Brian Langner, Alan W. Black, and Maxine Eskenazi. 2003. LET'S GO: Improving spoken dialog systems for the elderly and non-natives. In *Proceedings of the 8th European Conference on Speech Communication and Technology*. pages 753–756.

Iulian V. Serban, Ryan Lowe, Laurent Charlin, and Joelle Pineau. 2015. A survey of available corpora for building data-driven dialogue systems. *arXiv preprint arXiv:1512.05742* .

Alessandro Sordoni, Yoshua Bengio, Hossein Vahabi, Christina Lioma, Jakob G. Simonsen, and Jian-Yun Nie. 2015. A hierarchical recurrent encoder-decoder for generative context-aware query suggestion. In *Proceedings of the 24th ACM International on Conference on Information and Knowledge Management*. ACM, pages 553–562.

Pei-Hao Su, David Vandyke, Mrksic Gasic, Dongho Kim, Nikola Mrksic, Tsung-Hsien Wen, and Steve Young. 2015. Learning from real users: Rating dialogue success with neural networks for reinforcement learning in spoken dialogue systems. In *Proceedings of the 16th Annual Conference of the International Speech Communication Association*. pages 2007–2011.

Blaise Thomson and Steve Young. 2010. Bayesian update of dialogue state: A POMDP framework for spoken dialogue systems. *Computer Speech & Language* 24(4):562–588.

David R. Traum and Elizabeth A. Hinkelman. 2011. Conversation acts in task-oriented spoken dialogue. Technical Report 425, Computer Science Department, University of Rochester.

Jan Ulrich, Gabriel Murray, and Giuseppe Carenini. 2008. A publicly available annotated corpus for supervised email summarization. In *Proceedings of the 2008 AAAI Enhanced Messaging Workshop*. AAAI, pages 77–82.

David Vandyke, Pei-Hao Su, Milica Gasic, Nikola Mrksic, Tsung-Hsien Wen, and Steve Young. 2015. Multi-domain dialogue success classifiers for policy training. In *In Proceedings of the 2015 IEEE Workshop on Automatic Speech Recognition and Understanding*. IEEE, pages 763–770.

Marilyn Walker, Candace Kamm, and Diane Litman. 2000. Towards developing general models of usability with paradise. *Natural Language Engineering* 6(3-4):363–377.

Marilyn A. Walker, Jeanne C. Fromer, and Shrikanth Narayanan. 1998. Learning optimal dialogue strategies: A case study of a spoken dialogue agent for email. In *Proceedings of the 36th Annual Meeting of the Association for Computational Linguistics and 17th International Conference on Computational Linguistics, Volume 2*. Association for Computational Linguistics, pages 1345–1351.

Marilyn A. Walker, Diane J. Littman, Candace A. Kamm, and Alicia Abella. 1997. PARADISE: A framework for evaluating spoken dialogue agents. In *Proceedings of the 35th Annual Meeting of the Association for Computational Linguistics*. Association for Computational Linguistics, pages 271–280.

Tsung-Hsien Wen, Milica Gašić, Nikola Mrkšić, Lina M. Rojas-Barahona, Pei-Hao Su, David Vandyke, and Steve Young. 2016. Multi-domain neural network language generation for spoken dialogue systems. In *Proceedings of the 2016 Conference of the North American Chapter of the Association for Computational Linguistics: Human Language Technologies*. Association for Computational Linguistics, pages 120–129.

Jason D. Williams and Steve Young. 2004. Characterizing task-oriented dialog using a simulated asr chanel. In *Proceedings of the 2004 International Conference on Spoken Language Processing*. pages 185–188.

Zhaojun Yang, Baichuan Li, Yi Zhu, Irwin King, Gina Levow, and Helen Meng. 2010. Collection of user judgments on spoken dialog system with crowdsourcing. In *Proceedings of the 2010 Spoken Language Technology Workshop*. IEEE, pages 277–282.

Steve Young, Milica Gasic, Blaise Thomson, and Jason D. Williams. 2013. POMDP-based statistical spoken dialog systems: A review. *IEEE* 101(5):1160–1179.

Generating and Evaluating Summaries for Partial Email Threads: Conversational Bayesian Surprise and Silver Standards

Jordon Johnson, Vaden Masrani, Giuseppe Carenini, and Raymond Ng
Department of Computer Science
University of British Columbia
Vancouver, British Columbia, Canada
{jordon, vadmas, carenini, rng}@cs.ubc.ca

Abstract

We define and motivate the problem of summarizing partial email threads. This problem introduces the challenge of generating reference summaries for partial threads when human annotation is only available for the threads as a whole, particularly when the human-selected sentences are not uniformly distributed within the threads. We propose an oracular algorithm for generating these reference summaries with arbitrary length, and we are making the resulting dataset publicly available[1]. In addition, we apply a recent unsupervised method based on Bayesian Surprise that incorporates background knowledge into partial thread summarization, extend it with conversational features, and modify the mechanism by which it handles redundancy. Experiments with our method indicate improved performance over the baseline for shorter partial threads; and our results suggest that the potential benefits of background knowledge to partial thread summarization should be further investigated with larger datasets.

1 Introduction

Despite the relatively early advent of emails compared to other forms of electronic communication, the continued proliferation of emails make them an ongoing focus of NLP research. With users experiencing an increasing flow of emails and decreasing screen sizes, there has been a growing interest in the *email summarization task*: given an email thread with multiple participants, provide a summary of the contents of the thread. Such

---

[1]http://www.cs.ubc.ca/cs-research/lci/research-groups/natural-language-processing/Software.html

summaries should contain the key information in a thread and free a user from having to comb through its entire contents. Also, given that email threads can span days, weeks, or months, and users often participate in multiple threads at once, such summaries can serve as memory aids to users returning to or joining a thread in progress (Ulrich et al., 2008).

Email threads are dynamic document collections, however, and the content of a summary may need to change over time as emails come in. Therefore, while the *full thread summarization problem* (extensively studied in the past as discussed in section 2) provides a single summary of a complete, archived email thread, we are interested in the *partial thread summarization problem* where we generate a succession of summaries, each summarizing the thread at different moments in time. More formally, for each email E_i in a given email thread $\{E_1...E_i...E_n\}$ we wish to generate a summary for the corresponding *partial thread* (PT) $\{E_1...E_i\}$. Given the novelty of the summarization task, in this paper we focus on investigating simple unsupervised extractive approaches, where the summary is a subset of the sentences in the source partial thread, and leave supervised and abstractive approaches for future work.

A *partial thread summary* will provide a summary of the thread so far, including the new email; it is intended to benefit users that may have forgotten the content of the preceding emails in the thread (or may be new to the thread) and need a quick refresh, possibly on the relatively small screen of a mobile device. Additionally, a user may want to "extend" a partial thread summary in order to get more information; and so we also investigate the ability to generate summaries of arbitrary length. The PT summarization problem is thus different from the *update summariza-*

Proceedings of the SIGDIAL 2017 Conference, pages 263–272,
Saarbrücken, Germany, 15-17 August 2017. ©2017 Association for Computational Linguistics

tion problem previously studied for news in the Text Analysis Conferences (Dang and Owczarzak, 2008). The update summarization problem, applied to email threads, would provide a summary of *only* the incoming email with the assumption that the user knows and remembers the content of the preceding emails.

The new NLP task of summarizing email PT is challenging, not only because new algorithms may need to be developed, but also with respect to evaluating the generated summaries. While there are publicly available datasets - including BC3 (Ulrich et al., 2008) and an Enron-derived dataset (Loza et al., 2014) - that provide gold standard summaries for completed email threads, none to our knowledge provides such summaries for PTs; such annotation by humans would be prohibitive, as it would require a summary for each partial thread (i.e., each email) in the corpus. So, a challenge we face in the evaluation of PT summaries is due to the dearth of human annotations. More specifically, given gold standard human annotations of a thread as a whole, how do we generate reference summaries of each PT against which to compare automatically generated extractive summaries?

Most current summarization techniques for full thread summarization rely on the analysis of only the content of the input thread to decide what sentences should be included in the summary. However, since PT can be rather short we hypothesize that the identification of the most informative sentences would benefit from examining the larger informational context in which the PT was generated (eg. all the email generated in an organization). We test this hypothesis by applying and extending a recent summarization method based on Bayesian Surprise that leverages such background information for PT summarization.

The main contributions of this paper are as follows:

- We propose an algorithm for exploiting existing extractive gold standard (EGS) summaries of full threads to automatically generate oracular "silver standard" PT summaries of arbitrary length, as discussed in section 3. Further, we are releasing these silver standard summaries for the dataset used in this work.

- For PT summary generation, we propose an unsupervised method extending previous work on full-thread summarization that considers not only the input thread, but also background knowledge synthesized from a large number of other email threads. In particular, we developed a summarization method based on Bayesian Surprise (Louis, 2014) which takes into account conversational features of the partial thread, as discussed in section 4. We then evaluate the system-generated summaries using our silver standards with ROUGE.

- Using our silver standard with ROUGE, we carry out experiments to compare the summaries generated by Bayesian-based methods with summarization techniques that do not take into account background information.

2 Related Work

To generate PT summaries we propose an unsupervised extractive approach. Although to the best of our knowledge no one has studied PT summarization directly, there has been extensive work done in extractive summarization in general, as well as work done on email summarization specifically. Supervised methods have been proposed which turn the extractive summarization task into a binary classification problem where sentences are labeled in/out using standard machine learning classifiers (Rambow et al., 2004; Murray and Carenini, 2008). Variations of this approach include adding sentence compression and using integer linear programming to evaluate candidate summaries and select the best ones (Berg-Kirkpatrick et al., 2011). Sentence classification assumes sentences are independent from one another; and so to capture dependencies between sentences, the extractive summarization problem has also been recast as a sequence labeling problem using hidden Markov models and conditional random fields (Fung et al., 2003; Jin et al., 2012; Oya and Carenini, 2014).

The weakness of supervised approaches is the reliance on human-annotated labeled data, which is often expensive and difficult to acquire due to privacy concerns. Our extractive approach, therefore, will focus on unsupervised extractive techniques which do not require labeled data. Another benefit of unsupervised methods is that they can serve as features for supervised methods, meaning improvements in unsupervised techniques can directly benefit supervised systems.

Many unsupervised extractive summarization methods have been proposed for generic documents, as well as for conversations. Some make use of textual features such as lexical chains, cue words ("In conclusion", "To summarize", etc.) or conversation structure to select the most informative sentences (Barzilay and Elhadad, 1999; Hatori et al., 2011; Carenini et al., 2008). Others make use of more advanced methods including topic modeling, latent semantic analysis or rhetorical parsing (Nagwani, 2015; Kireyev, 2008; Hirao et al., 2013). Our algorithm for generating silver standard summaries of partial threads incorporates a topic modeling framework that, in turn, makes use of lexical chains and conversational structure.

There is also a large class of methods which build graphs with textual units (words, sentences, paragraphs, etc) as vertices and use similarity measures between the text units to form the edge weights. Once a full graph is created, an extractive summary is generated by using a centrality measure to select central nodes from a cluster and concatenating them to form a summary. Two popular systems are LexRank and TextRank, which both use a variant of the PageRank algorithm (Erkan and Radev, 2004; Mihalcea and Tarau, 2004; Mihalcea and Radev, 2011). Graph methods are popular because of their simplicity and ease of implementation, and their performance has been shown to be competitive with other methods. Our silver standard algorithm and baseline summarizer both incorporate graph-based sentence scoring.

No matter how the information content (or the query relevance) of a sentence is computed, sentences should be included in the final summary not only if they are informative but also if they convey new information with respect to sentences already in the summary. One popular method known as *Maximum Marginal Relevance* (MMR) builds a summary with a scoring function that trades off between the "relevance" and "information-novelty" of a sentence, and builds a summary by selecting sentences which maximize relevance and minimize redundancy with previously selected sentences (Carbonell and Goldstein, 1998). While our silver standard generation system uses vanilla MMR, the Bayesian Surprise-based summarizers described in section 4 have a built-in means of handling information redundancy.

There has also been work on the task of unsupervised email summarization specifically. Carenini et al. (2008) proposed the use of "fragment quotation graphs" (FQGs) to summarize asynchronous conversations. FQGs use the fact that a given email often contains quoted material from previous emails. These quotations, or "fragments", can then be used to create fine-grained representations of the underlying structure of a given email thread, allowing a set of particularly informative *clue words* to be identified. In this paper, we also exploit FQGs in our silver standard generation system, and we use a summarizer based on clue words as a baseline in our evaluations.

Furthermore, a key limitation of (Carenini et al., 2008), common to other approaches to full-thread summarization, is to consider only the input thread in the summarization process; in contrast, a user's email history (or that of the user's organization) can provide valuable background knowledge. The summarizer we propose in this paper addresses this limitation by taking into account background knowledge synthesized from a large number of other email threads, which we argue is especially beneficial to PT summarization as the PT can be rather short and consequently unable to provide much ground for sentence selection.

3 Generating Silver Standard Summaries for Partial Email Threads

In order to automatically evaluate PT summaries (e.g., with ROUGE), human-generated EGS summaries are needed for comparison. However, because producing such EGS summaries is a time-consuming and often difficult task, all publicly available email corpora we are aware of only provide human-annotated EGS summaries for each email thread as a whole (Loza et al., 2014; Ulrich et al., 2008). Given a partial thread PT and a gold standard summary EGS of the corresponding full thread, an intuitive solution might be to simply use $EGS \cap PT$ as the silver standard. In this section we discuss potential problems with that approach as well as our solution.

3.1 Distribution of Summary Sentences

The distribution of EGS sentences across emails in a thread cannot be assumed to be uniform in all (or even most) cases; indeed, this is not the case in the dataset used in this work (a collection of 62 email threads, described further in section 5). As shown in Figure 1, while many threads in the dataset have highly ranked EGS sentences in the first part of the conversation, others have important EGS sentences in the middle or even at the end of the con-

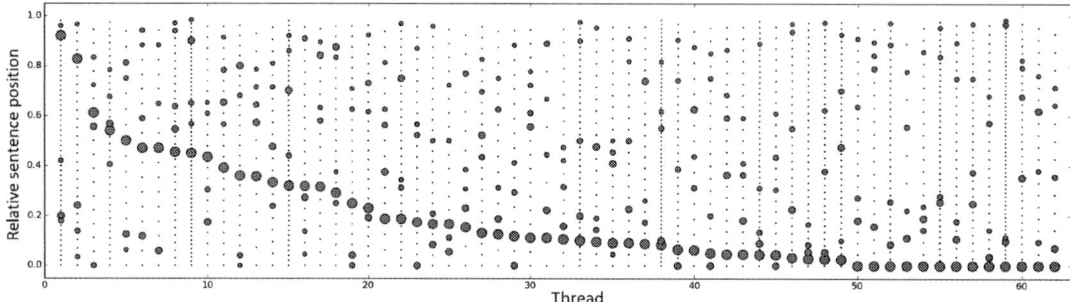

Figure 1: Distribution of EGS sentences in full threads. Each vertical column of dots represents a thread, with each dot representing a sentence at its relative position within the thread (beginning at 0, ending at 1). Non-EGS sentences are black dots, while EGS sentences are red circles; and larger circles indicate that a human annotator considered those sentences more important. The threads are sorted in descending order of the relative position of the highest-ranked sentences.

versation. Variations in EGS sentence distribution become a concern when generating silver standard PT summaries. In some cases, there may not be enough EGS sentences in a given PT to form a silver standard summary; in extreme cases, the PT may have no EGS sentences at all. In other cases, there may be too many EGS sentences in a PT to fit into the silver standard; and not all datasets rank EGS sentences by importance as part of the annotation. In other words, unless exactly the desired number of EGS sentences are present in each PT, some sentence selection is necessary; and this issue is exacerbated when generating silver standard summaries of arbitrary length. Our silver standard generation algorithm handles all these possibilities as described in the next section.

3.2 The Silver Standard Algorithm

We propose an oracular algorithm for generating silver standard extractive reference summaries of arbitrary length for partial threads; in other words, it references the existing gold standard for the full thread to generate silver standard summaries for the partial threads. Our silver standard system incorporates graph-based sentence scoring, which has been used extensively for summarization as discussed in section 2. Both the graph-based aspect of the algorithm and its redundancy minimization mechanism rely on word embeddings trained using a large email corpus.

Our silver standard system also makes use of topic modeling. We expect the discussions in email threads to be topically coherent (though, for both individual emails and threads, multiple topics may be covered). The topical coherence of a sen-

tence with both the PT and the gold standard are thus related to that sentence's importance in the discussion in the context of the PT as well as the thread as a whole. The topic modeling system we used exploits conversational structure.

The pseudocode for silver standard generation is given in Algorithm 1. The first step (lines 6-14) is to seed the silver standard with EGS sentences in the PT. If there are more EGS sentences than the desired silver standard length, then a sentence selection method (using human-annotated rankings if available) is applied. This first step is oracular because it directly references the gold standard. If there are fewer EGS sentences in the PT than desired for the silver standard, then the algorithm proceeds to the second step (lines 15-18), where the sentence selection method is applied to the rest of the PT sentences.

For this work, we have chosen an intuitive sentence selection method that can be used in both steps as needed. To maximize sentence importance while minimizing redundancy, the selection method uses maximal marginal relevance (MMR) (Carbonell and Goldstein, 1998). For a given candidate sentence s for inclusion in a summary S, its MMR score is

$$MMR(s) = \lambda I(s) - (1 - \lambda)Sim(s, S) \quad (1)$$

where $I(s)$ is an *importance function*, and *Sim(s,S)* is a similarity function comparing s to the sentences of S. For this work we set λ to 0.5.

The importance function used here incorporates graph centrality and topic segmentation. We first define $PR_{PT}(s)$ as the PageRank score of s in the fully-connected graph whose vertices are the sentences of the partial thread. We choose PageRank over LexRank in order to incorporate topic modeling designed for conversational data. For each sentence in PT, a vector representation is obtained by averaging 100-dimensional Word2Vec embeddings of its words (Goldberg and Levy, 2014). The edge weights are then set to the cosine similarity of the vector representations of the relevant sentences. The Word2Vec model was trained on the entire Enron email corpus of $\sim$500K emails.

We then define $T(s)$ as the topic of sentence s; in this work, we apply a topic segmentation method that uses fragment quotation graphs to represent conversational structure and that has been shown to work well on asynchronous conversations (Joty et al., 2013). We then define $Prom_{PT}(T(s))$, or the *prominence* of $T(s)$ within the partial thread, as the fraction of PT sentences that have that topic; so if a PT containing five sentences has a total of three whose topic is $T(s)$, then $Prom_{PT}(T(s))$ is 0.6. Similarly, $Prom_{EGS}(T(s))$ is the prominence of $T(s)$ within the gold standard summary. Together, the two prominence scores form the overall topic prominence score of s:

$$Prom(T(s)) = \frac{1}{2}\Big(Prom_{PT}(T(s))+ \\ Prom_{EGS}(T(s))\Big) \quad (2)$$

Note that $Prom_{EGS}(T(s))$ is a second oracular component of the silver standard algorithm, since it references the importance of a topic in the context of the entire thread as represented by the EGS. By increasing the likelihood of choosing sentences from the same topics as the EGS, this ensures the silver standard is oracular even in cases where there are no EGS sentences in the PT of interest.

Putting graph centrality and topic prominence together, we have:

$$I(s) = \frac{1}{2}\Big(PR_{PT}(s) + Prom(T(s))\Big) \quad (3)$$

It is worth noting that the PageRank score takes values in [0,1], as do both of the prominence scores. The weights in equations 2 and 3 are set to match the simplifying assumption that the centrality of a sentence in its PT is as important as the overall prominence of its topic, and that the prominence of a topic within a PT is as important as its prominence within the larger context of the

---

Algorithm 1: Silver Summary Generation

Result: SLV_m

1   - Let $EGS = \{egs_1...egs_j...egs_k\}$ be set of gold standard sentences;

2   - Let $PT_m = \{pt_1...pt_i...pt_n\}$ be set of sentences in the partial thread up to email m;

3   - Let $EGS_m^{PT} = \{egs_1^{PT}...egs_i^{PT}...egs_n^{PT}\} = (EGS \cap PT_m)$;

4   - Let $SLV_m = \emptyset$ be silver summary of PT_m;

5   - Let len be desired length of silver summary;

6   **while** $|SLV_m| <\min(len, |EGS|)$ **do**

7   **if** EGS has annotated sentence ranking **then**

8   - score each egs_i^{PT} using ranking

9   **end**

10   **else**

11   - score each egs_i^{PT} using $scoring\_function(egs_i^{PT})$;

12   **end**

13   - add highest scoring $egs_i^{PT} \notin SLV_m$ to SLV_m

14 **end**

15 **while** $|SLV_m|<len$ **do**

16   - score each pt_i using $scoring\_function(pt_i)$;

17   - Add highest scoring $pt_i \notin SLV_m$ to SLV_m

18 **end**

19 **return** SLV_m

---

full thread. Taken together, the importance function takes values in [0,1], which is appropriate for MMR.

The similarity function $Sim(s, S)$ in equation 1 is the maximum cosine similarity of the candidate sentence s and the sentences of the in-progress summary S, using the aggregated Word2Vec representations described for the PageRank score.

4 Generating Partial Thread Summaries

While previous work on unsupervised full-thread summarization essentially takes as input only the thread to be summarized, Louis (2014) has shown that background knowledge can be effectively taken into account in the summarization process by applying the idea of Bayesian Surprise.

The Bayesian Surprise method is based on the intuition that, given a collection of background knowledge (such as the email history of a user or organization), the most "surprising" new information is the most significant for inclusion in a summary.

Presumably, while background knowledge should be useful for summarization in general as an additional source of information from which to infer salience, it should be especially useful for PT summarization, since the partial threads can be rather short, and thus there is relatively little information available to a given summarizer. For this reason, our PT summarization method is based on Bayesian Surprise, but it extends the existing technique to consider conversational features and incorporates a less harsh redundancy management mechanism.

4.1 Bayesian Surprise

Let H be some hypothesis about a background corpus that is represented by a multinomial distribution over word unigrams. The prior probability of H is a Dirichlet distribution:

$$P(H) = Dir(\alpha_1, ... \alpha_V) \qquad (4)$$

where α_i is the count of word i in the background corpus, and V is the size of the background corpus vocabulary.

Suppose word w_i appears c_i times in the PT being summarized. We can then obtain the posterior

$$P(H|w_i) = Dir(\alpha_1, ..., \alpha_i + c_i, ... \alpha_V) \qquad (5)$$

The Bayesian Surprise score for w_i due to the PT is then the KL divergence between $P(H|w_i)$ and $P(H)$. Then, to obtain the Bayesian Surprise score of a sentence, one simply aggregates the scores of its words; and the sentence with the highest score is added to the summary. In order to minimize redundancy during summarization in the original proposal (Louis, 2014), once a sentence is added to a summary, the Bayesian Surprise scores of its words are set to zero. The process is repeated until the desired summary length has been reached.

4.2 Conversational Features

As discussed in section 2, conversational features have proved useful in summarizing asynchronous conversations such as email threads. We have extended the Bayesian Surprise method to include a number of these conversational features as additional concentration parameters in the Dirichlet distributions. In order to maintain consistency with the original Bayesian Surprise method, we limit our extensions to features that can be expressed as counts of word w_i; specifically, we use the number of times w_i was used:

- by the creator of the thread (whether in the initial email or afterwards)

- by the dominant participant in the thread (who may or may not be the thread creator)

- in emails where it also appears in the email subject line

- as a clue word

The prior for the extended Bayesian Surprise method then becomes

$$P(H) = Dir(\alpha_{1..V}, \beta_{1..V}, \gamma_{1..V}, \delta_{1..V}, \epsilon_{1..V})$$
$$(6)$$

where $\alpha_{1..V}$ are the original concentration parameters, and $\beta, \gamma, \delta, \epsilon$ are the corresponding feature counts.

4.3 Surprise Decay

As discussed in section 4.1, once a sentence containing a word is added to the summary, the Bayesian Surprise score of that word is set to zero in order to minimize redundancy. While this accomplishes that goal, it may impact the measured importance of words in the larger context of the PT too harshly. In order to mitigate this effect, we propose an alternative we call *surprise decay*, where each time a sentence is added to the summary, the Bayesian Surprise scores of its words are multiplied by some *decay factor* < 1. Intuitively, this corresponds to making these words "less surprising," rather than removing the surprise entirely; this allows salient words to continue to contribute to the overall surprise of sentences in a limited way as the summary is generated. The simplest decay factor would be a constant $df \in [0, 1)$, resulting in exponential decay of a given word's Bayesian Surprise score.

5 Dataset

We used the "corporate thread" subset of the publicly available annotated email dataset produced by Loza et. al., which was derived from the Enron email dataset (Loza et al., 2014). The data consists of 62 email threads (from which 282 PTs can be extracted) containing a total of 354 emails and 1654 sentences. Each thread is manually annotated with abstractive and extractive summaries, as well as five ranked keyphrases. This work focuses on extractive summarization, so only those annotations were used. The keyphrases were not used here, because it is not expected that most gold standard annotations will include keyphrases.

Each thread was annotated by two annotators, so for each thread we have two sets of extractive sentences. The annotators were asked to select up to five sentences *"that contained the most important information in the email, and also rank the sentences in reverse order of their importance"*.

To serve as a background corpus that could be used for both Bayesian Surprise methods, we used a publicly available collection of threads extracted from the Enron corpus (Jamison and Gurevych, 2013), of which threads ~43k had the metadata required (sender, recipient(s) and subject line in all emails) in order to extract the desired conversational features.

6 Experimental Setup and Results

We generated a number of summaries for each full thread as well as for its corresponding PTs. First, we generated summaries using both the original and our extended Bayesian Surprise methods (**BS** and **BSE**) discussed in sections 4.1 and 4.2. We then generated additional summaries for each method using the exponential surprise decay (**-d**) discussed in section 4.3 with $df = 0.5$.

In addition, we generated summaries using a method (**CWS**) that scores sentences based on the number of clue words they contain (Carenini et al., 2008). This method was shown to perform well in email summarization, and we use it here as a baseline.

6.1 Evaluation over Full Threads

Initially, we evaluated the system summaries over the full threads against the human-annotated EGS. The evaluation was carried out using ROUGE-1 F-scores. In the ROUGE evaluation, stemming was performed, but stopwords were not removed, consistent with previous evaluations of summarization based on Bayesian Surprise (Louis, 2014). The system summaries were truncated to the length (in words) of the corresponding EGS. As a baseline we used a PageRank-based summarizer (**PR-MMR**) that scores sentences using the same sentence graphs as the silver standard algorithm and employs MMR to minimize redundancy. The results for this evaluation over full threads are given in Table 1.

Method	Full threads
BS	0.573
BS-d	0.582
BSE	0.566
BSE-d	0.573
CWS	**0.598**
PR-MMR	0.509

Table 1: ROUGE-1 mean F-scores for full threads as compared to gold standard summaries.

The results of this experiment over full threads suggest that the Bayesian Surprise-based methods perform comparably to the clue words-based summarizer, and that they all significantly outperform the PR-MMR baseline ($p < 0.005$)[2]. In addition, there appears to be some benefit to the more gradual redundancy handling provided by surprise decay, though the differences in these cases do not appear to be significant.

6.2 Evaluation over Partial Threads

To evaluate the summarizers over partial threads, we generated two silver standard summaries (one for each annotator) per PT using the algorithm in section 3. The silver standard and system summaries for each PT were truncated to a fraction of

---

[2]Significance for all reported results was verified using ANOVA followed by paired t-tests (with Bonferroni corrections as needed).

the PT length (in words). Since the silver standard algorithm generates summaries of arbitrary length, we evaluated the summarizers at both 20% and 30% of the PT length.

The hypothesis behind our use of Bayesian Surprise-based methods is that they should work particularly well for PT summarization, because PTs can be rather short, and the identification of the most informative sentences would benefit from examining a larger informational context. To test this hypothesis we sorted the 282 PTs being summarized by length and binned them into quartiles (see Table 2). Since BSE-d is the Bayesian Surprise-based method incorporating all of our extensions, we focus our statistical analysis on comparing it to CWS. The results of this evaluation are given in Table 3.

	min	25%	median	75%	max
Length	22	104	197	329	1236

Table 2: Length (in words) of the partial threads in the dataset used to define the quartile bins.

We observe a number of trends in Table 3 from the experiments over PTs; however, only some cases exhibit at least marginal significance. This may be due in part to limited sample size; and so we argue that further work in applying background knowledge to PT summarization over larger datasets is warranted.

Over the shorter PTs (i.e. first and second quantiles) and at both summary lengths, we observe a trend favoring our hypothesis, namely that Bayesian Surprise-based methods seem to perform better than CWS; for example, the performance improvement of BSE-d over CWS is at least marginally significant ($p<0.1$) for the second quartile at both summary lengths. Conversely, for the longest PTs (i.e., the fourth quantile), we see that the effectiveness of clue words is more fully realized, allowing CWS to outperform the Bayesian Surprise-based summarizers. While this difference is significant ($p<0.05$) for summaries of 30% PT length, it is not significant at 20% PT length; this suggests that Bayesian Surprise-based summarizers may be more robust against changes in PT summary length than CWS.

Surprisingly, the conversational features used to extend the Bayesian Surprise method have not improved summarizer performance. It may be that treating these features as equivalent to word counts

is inappropriate for this task, in which case some other means of extracting these features as background knowledge should be devised. Alternatively, the inclusion of additional features, such as the number of times a word is used in the first sentence of each email in the thread, may improve the performance of the extended Bayesian Surprise summarizer.

As with the full threads, the inclusion of surprise decay seems to provide some benefit, though it appears to hamper the summarizers for the shortest PTs; this trend can be seen at 30% PT length, where BS-d outperforms BS in all quartiles except the first. This suggests that applying surprise decay factors derived from PT length and desired summary length may improve overall performance; we leave this endeavor for future work.

7 Conclusions and Future Work

In this work, we have defined and motivated the partial thread summarization problem. We have proposed an algorithm that uses gold standard summaries of complete threads in order to build oracular silver standard extractive summaries of arbitrary length for partial email threads. We have also applied an intuitive unsupervised summarization method to PT summarization, extended it with conversational features, and modified the mechanism by which it handles redundancy. Although in our experiments we did not find consistently significant improvements using Bayesian Surprise-based methods on partial threads, we argue that in light of the observed trends, the potential benefit of background knowledge to PT summarization (and email summarization in general) should be further investigated with larger datasets.

There are multiple directions of future work. While an obvious direction is the continued development of extractive PT summarization algorithms (eg. by applying recent summarization techniques such as ILP (Murray et al., 2010) or neural network-based summarizers (Cao et al., 2015)), another is the abstractive summarization of partial threads. Yet another is the application of the silver standard algorithm to other asynchronous conversations, such as discussion forums, as well as other domains where some human annotation is available but reference summaries for different portions of the source document(s) are desired.

Future work may also include finding additional

30% PT length	BS	BS-d	BSE	BSE-d	CWS	p
Q1	**0.666**	0.643	0.632	0.622	0.582	*0.310*
Q2	0.558	**0.576**	0.560	0.571	0.503	*0.041*
Q3	0.552	0.565	0.540	0.535	**0.568**	*0.088*
Q4	0.504	0.516	0.510	0.510	**0.548**	*0.011*
all PTs	0.570	**0.575**	0.560	0.559	0.550	*0.519*
20% PT length	BS	BS-d	BSE	BSE-d	CWS	p
Q1	**0.600**	0.577	0.558	0.557	0.512	*0.402*
Q2	0.504	**0.513**	0.495	0.494	0.424	*0.078*
Q3	**0.476**	0.470	0.469	0.469	0.467	*0.933*
Q4	0.435	0.441	0.439	0.448	**0.452**	*0.808*
all PTs	**0.504**	0.500	0.490	0.493	0.464	*0.114*

Table 3: ROUGE-1 mean F-scores over partial threads (binned into quartiles by length in words) as compared to silver standard summaries. Values are given for both summary lengths (20% and 30% of PT length). Bolded ROUGE scores are the highest for their quartile and summary length category. P-values are given for the comparisons between BSE-d and CWS; underlined p-values indicate at least marginal significance (p<0.1).

ways to incorporate background knowledge into email summarization. For example, Bayesian Surprise scores may be used in tandem with other features to develop summarizers that are more robust against changes in document length.

An advantage to the study of PT summarization is that it may reveal whether current summarization techniques perform differently on in-progress threads than on complete, archived ones. For example, if a summarizer uses features that may depend on the entire email thread (eg. the relative positions of sentences in the thread, completed dialog acts, etc.), then those features may have a different significance when applied to PTs than they do for complete threads. Similarly, PT summaries may give insights into the development of email threads over time. For example, the summaries generated for an earlier PT may have features that are useful in summarizing a later PT or in predicting aspects of a thread's future development. To further the study of PT summarization, another direction of future work is a thorough categorization of the differences between full and partial threads, as well as differences between PTs at different stages of development. Such differences may be found, for example, in lexical and topic diversity, as well as dialog act initiation and/or completion.

Acknowledgments

This research was funded in part under a grant from the Yahoo Faculty Research and Engagement Program (FREP).

References

Regina Barzilay and Michael Elhadad. 1999. Using lexical chains for text summarization. Advances in automatic text summarization pages 111–121.

Taylor Berg-Kirkpatrick, Dan Gillick, and Dan Klein. 2011. Jointly learning to extract and compress. In Proceedings of the 49th Annual Meeting of the Association for Computational Linguistics: Human Language Technologies-Volume 1. Association for Computational Linguistics, pages 481–490.

Ziqiang Cao, Furu Wei, Li Dong, Sujian Li, and Ming Zhou. 2015. Ranking with recursive neural networks and its application to multi-document summarization. In AAAI. pages 2153–2159.

Jaime Carbonell and Jade Goldstein. 1998. The use of mmr, diversity-based reranking for reordering documents and producing summaries. In Proceedings of the 21st annual international ACM SIGIR conference on Research and development in information retrieval. ACM, pages 335–336.

Giuseppe Carenini, Raymond T Ng, and Xiaodong Zhou. 2008. Summarizing emails with conversational cohesion and subjectivity. In ACL. volume 8, pages 353–361.

Hoa Trang Dang and Karolina Owczarzak. 2008. Overview of the tac 2008 update summarization task. In Proceedings of text analysis conference. pages 1–16.

Günes Erkan and Dragomir R Radev. 2004. Lexrank: Graph-based lexical centrality as salience in text summarization. Journal of Artificial Intelligence Research 22:457–479.

Pascale Fung, Grace Ngai, and Chi-Shun Cheung. 2003. Combining optimal clustering and hidden markov models for extractive summarization. In Proceedings of the ACL 2003 workshop on Multilingual summarization and question answering-Volume 12. Association for Computational Linguistics, pages 21–28.

Yoav Goldberg and Omer Levy. 2014. word2vec explained: deriving mikolov et al.'s negative-sampling word-embedding method. arXiv preprint arXiv:1402.3722 .

Jun Hatori, Akiko Murakami, and Junichi Tsujii. 2011. Multi-topical discussion summarization using structured lexical chains and cue words. In International Conference on Intelligent Text Processing and Computational Linguistics. Springer, pages 313–327.

Tsutomu Hirao, Yasuhisa Yoshida, Masaaki Nishino, Norihito Yasuda, and Masaaki Nagata. 2013. Single-document summarization as a tree knapsack problem. In EMNLP. volume 13, pages 1515–1520.

Emily Jamison and Iryna Gurevych. 2013. Headerless, quoteless, but not hopeless? using pairwise email classification to disentangle email threads. In RANLP. pages 327–335.

Wei Jin, Shafiq Joty, Giuseppe Carenini, and Raymond Ng. 2012. Detecting informative blog comments using tree structured conditional random fields. NW-NLP, Microsoft Research, Redmond.

Shafiq Joty, Giuseppe Carenini, and Raymond T Ng. 2013. Topic segmentation and labeling in asynchronous conversations. Journal of Artificial Intelligence Research 47:521–573.

Kirill Kireyev. 2008. Using latent semantic analysis for extractive summarization. In Proceedings of text analysis conference. volume 2008.

Annie P Louis. 2014. A bayesian method to incorporate background knowledge during automatic text summarization. Association for Computational Linguistics.

Vanessa Loza, Shibamouli Lahiri, Rada Mihalcea, and Po-Hsiang Lai. 2014. Building a dataset for summarization and keyword extraction from emails. In LREC. pages 2441–2446.

Rada Mihalcea and Dragomir Radev. 2011. Graph-based natural language processing and information retrieval. Cambridge University Press.

Rada Mihalcea and Paul Tarau. 2004. Textrank: Bringing order into texts. Association for Computational Linguistics.

Gabriel Murray and Giuseppe Carenini. 2008. Summarizing spoken and written conversations. In Proceedings of the Conference on Empirical Methods in Natural Language Processing. Association for Computational Linguistics, pages 773–782.

Gabriel Murray, Giuseppe Carenini, and Raymond Ng. 2010. Generating and validating abstracts of meeting conversations: a user study. In Proceedings of the 6th International Natural Language Generation Conference. Association for Computational Linguistics, pages 105–113.

NK Nagwani. 2015. Summarizing large text collection using topic modeling and clustering based on mapreduce framework. Journal of Big Data 2(1):1.

Tatsuro Oya and Giuseppe Carenini. 2014. Extractive summarization and dialogue act modeling on email threads: An integrated probabilistic approach. In 15th Annual Meeting of the Special Interest Group on Discourse and Dialogue. page 133.

Owen Rambow, Lokesh Shrestha, John Chen, and Chirsty Lauridsen. 2004. Summarizing email threads. In Proceedings of HLT-NAACL 2004: Short Papers. Association for Computational Linguistics, pages 105–108.

Jan Ulrich, Gabriel Murray, and Giuseppe Carenini. 2008. A publicly available annotated corpus for supervised email summarization. In Proc. of aaai email-2008 workshop, chicago, usa.

Enabling robust and fluid spoken dialogue with cognitively impaired users

Ramin Yaghoubzadeh
CITEC, Bielefeld University
P. O. Box 10 01 31
33501 Bielefeld, Germany
ryaghoubzadeh@uni-bielefeld.de

Stefan Kopp
CITEC, Bielefeld University
P. O. Box 10 01 31
33501 Bielefeld, Germany
skopp@techfak.uni-bielefeld.de

Abstract

We present the `flexdiam` dialogue management architecture, which was developed in a series of projects dedicated to tailoring spoken interaction to the needs of users with cognitive impairments in an everyday assistive domain, using a multimodal front-end. This hybrid DM architecture affords incremental processing of uncertain input, a flexible, mixed-initiative information grounding process that can be adapted to users' cognitive capacities and interactive idiosyncrasies, and generic mechanisms that foster transitions in the joint discourse state that are understandable and controllable by those users, in order to effect a robust interaction for users with varying capacities.

1   Introduction

In recent years, politics and society have placed emphasis on ways to enable an autonomous and self-determined life for those who were previously automatic recipients of stationary care. This is most overtly the case for older adults whose capacities start to degrade but are still sufficient to organize their life given some help; but also for people with general cognitive impairments, who until twenty or thirty years ago were often regarded as unable of being afforded a lifestyle with a workplace and an independent living space, tailored to their individual strenghths and capacities.

In order to support these individuals in those areas where deficits might manifest, use of mobile personal help for organization and management is regularly employed. There has been heightened interest in offsetting some of the burden of common routine tasks to technological implementations. Most unexperienced users report spoken interaction to be their preferred modality, which they are also used to in those domains, due to interactions with personnel. Human-computer interactions have to be designed in a way that suits their experience and preferences, their prior and their attainable special knowledge, and their other capacities. There is regular comorbidity with impaired articulation which can complicate interactions (Young and Mihailidis, 2010) – although for mild cases automated speech recognition software has caught up in recent years to ensure suitable operation. Additionally, their capacity of adhering to a recommended interaction style, or their general capacity for learning, might be reduced. Information density in interaction is another issue: tightly-packed information might be overwhelming and lead to incomplete appreciation and inadequate reflection of the contents (Yaghoubzadeh et al., 2013). At the same time, and especially if comorbidity with impulse control disorders is present (Swaffer and Hollin, 2000), the frustration tolerance in adverse situations might be lowered, although their stakes – of obtaining assistance – can provide extrinsic motivation.

Altogether, we have to address several areas which assistive systems for these user groups have to be aware of and cope with: less reliable input, idiosyncratic interaction style such as verbosity, limitations to cognitive processing and adaptation on the user side, and less reliable adherence to implicit system expectations and overt instruction.

In this paper, we will first look at systems that aim to provide assistance or company for these people in their everyday life, and address existing approaches to dialogue management with respect to the above properties. Then, we will describe our approach to dialogue management that is tailored to meet these requirements. Finally, we present initial results from an evaluation with older adults and people with cognitive impairments.

Proceedings of the SIGDIAL 2017 Conference, pages 273–283,
Saarbrücken, Germany, 15-17 August 2017. ©2017 Association for Computational Linguistics

2   Related work

2.1   Assistive and accompanying systems

Technical assistance can be provided to the aforementioned user groups in several domains, striving to improve their quality of life: in enabling their control of their environment, in enabling them to communicate more readily, in aiding self-organization, in supporting and tracking therapeutic efforts, in ameliorating the effects of ennui and social isolation, among others. In the following overview, we omit those technologies that rely on physical support or that use non-interactive spoken control (keyword commands for smart homes etc.). However, there has been relevant work in domains that transcend these limited scenarios, and evaluations relating to all mentioned aspects.

If speech is chosen as a modality for an assistive system, the role of personification, involuntary attribution, and the social effect of help rendered must not be underestimated, Meis (2013) commented that older subjects, having interacted with a spoken-dialogue scheduling helper for an extended time, first and foremost wished for it to be given a name and to react contingently to social affordances such as expressions of gratitude.

Bickmore et al. (2013) analyzed month-long phases of interactions of older adults with a personified exercise coaching system – it used spoken language, but user input was selected from sets of touchscreen buttons. Sidner et al. (2013) addressed the social support aspect, attempting to identify preferred domains of conversation or joint activity based on the same system design.

An autonomous spoken dialogue prototype with a humanoid assistive agent for older adults and people with cognitive impairments has been analyzed by Yaghoubzadeh et al. (2015); they found that users with terse interaction styles from both groups were able to successfully ground information with their system, their earlier studies showing that explicit confirmation patterns and a preference for packing all pieces of information in separate utterances helped the latter user group in particular in detecting and repairing system errors.

More recently, Wargnier et al. (2016) have evaluated a low-level attention monitoring and management module with a small sample of older adults with mild cognitive impairment; their system performed as well as with the control group.

The two latter teams also mentioned that interactions were unsuccessful for only their respective participant with the most overtly noticeable impairments. However, spoken interaction with users with cognitive impairments seems, in general, to be feasible and accepted by the user group.

2.2   Relation to other DM approaches

As a preliminary, we want to establish what we consider the bounds of the safe action space for a robust, noise-resistant communication system – particularly, the case of potential categorial confusion of positive and negative evidence in key issues of ensuring mutual understanding. Clark and Schaefer (1989) stated that positive evidence for understanding generally arrives in five categories of increasing strength: 'continued attention' (i.e. without any repair initiation), 'initiation of the relevant next contribution', explicit 'acknowledgment' (possibly via back channels or multimodal signals), as well as 'demonstration' and 'display', referring to (partial) paraphrase or cooperative completion and verbatim repetition, respectively. However, for the assessment of the strength of evidence, a system has to take into account the risk of confusion with conflicting categories. In particular, we posit that in the case of verbatim display – nominally providing the strongest evidence – there is significant structural overlap with possible 'bare revisions' (i.e. unmarked other-repairs containing only the corrected information – which are abundant and should be handled by an SDS, cf. Larsson (2015)) or even incredulous return questions. These ambiguities only disappear if the confidence values (or suitable correlates) of the ASR process are on the level of near-certainty – and can be trusted – and, in the case of unmarked questions, prosody is also considered. In terms of negative evidence of successful grounding, spontaneous repairs and repeated requests are examples of explicit evidence, while multimodal modulations that indicate confusion or surprise (furrowed brows, 'double-checking' gaze patterns) are more subtle signals.

For a comparison of the present work to existing approaches and implementations of dialogue systems, we will consider the following taxonomical properties: globally accessible versus locally encapsulated state; rule-based versus statistically grounded decision making; human-authored vs. learned policies; approaches with or without strictly disjoint modeling of task and discourse models, with or without incremental processing, and with or without modeling of probabilistic aspects or uncertainty in either their input, inner state, and/or output. Centrally, implementations differ in their presentation and modeling of revisions and repairs from the system or the user side.

With the information-state-update (ISU) approach, Traum and Larsson (2003) proposed a generic mechanism for the concurrent matching of a set of update rules to the current state of a globally accessible information blackboard – in contrast to plan-based or finite state machine-based approaches. `flexdiam` employs a hybrid approach, independent entry points can operate solely on the global state or in relation to their ancestors and children in the hierarchy. The designer and the domain define an emphasis on reliance on the global context for one globally active set of rules (flexible, but harder to scrutinize) or classical graph-based traversals (predictable, but rather rigid) – or a hybrid of both. The global context does not contain an additional logic-based representation of internal – or attributed – plans.

Larsson (2002) modeled the grounding process on earlier work by Ginzburg, implementing the 'questions under discussion' in the form of 'issues', with an explicit propositional model of the common ground between the parties and the system's short-term agenda and longer-term plan, and explicit signals on three levels (contact, semantic, and pragmatic understanding).

Skantze (2007) considered the effects of uncertainty on the grounding process, particularly in 'real-world' ASR scenarios. The approach included disjoint modules of (abstract) NLU and (contextualized) discourse model that performed contextual integration, and generic clarification request and display actions based on word and concept level estimations of confidence, driven by a rule-based decision policy. `flexdiam` features a similar dichotomy of NLU and discourse models for incremental processing, opting for hierarchical situative interpretation – enabling partial interpretation in the most specific context and additional interpretation (and forward-looking expansion) in the more general ones. Since we found our ASR to yield word confidence scores with domain dependent baselines, we decided to start with a pessimistic strategy to minimize the false-positive rate for assuming "certain" interpretation – thus, ambiguous slots from the lattice of hypotheses were weighted equally, producing the

primary source of inherent low-level uncertainty. The basic grounding criterion for our first evaluations was likewise a rule-based one, operating on concept entropy values.

Bohus and Rudnicky (2009), with RavenClaw, proposed an logic-based approach that separated the task domain model, provided in a domain specific language to yield a hierarchical description of tasks and dependent subtasks, and a generic dialogue engine, configured with the task model and capable of employing two strategies for resolving detected ambiguity ('misunderstandings') and several more for non-understanding, including declaration of non-understanding, requests, reprompts, and help messages. `flexdiam` does also provide hierarchical task modeling, repairs and grounding strategy selection are however encapsulated in a library of reusable, specialized patterns that are configured[1] for specific situations.

Baumann and Schlangen (2012), with InproTK, provide a fully incremental dialogue management toolkit that builds a fine-grained graphical representation of sequences of incremental information in the system, including revoked and revised paths – that can thus also encode a full implicit discourse history. Notably, input and output sides can operate in an incremental fashion. In `flexdiam`, input and processing modules operate incrementally, but there is currently no provision for incremental adaptation in the NLG (although other output modalities do operate in an incremental fashion).

Skantze and Moubayed (2012), with IrisTK, presented another hybrid approach that combined a generic 'attention manager' with a hierarchical task and dialogue model (IrisFlow) based on a generalized, extended version of Harel statecharts, which can be conveniently authored. Their extension does take into account, and attempts to integrate, the asynchronous character of the relation of intention and actual spoken interaction. It has been employed in the autonomous robotic head FurHat. In `flexdiam`, authoring cannot be undertaken using an abstract modeling description that automatically transfers to code, as in IrisTK or RavenClaw. However, since it is written in Python, there is arguably little difference between the two anyway; graphical authoring might be attractive, though, especially since the existing live and off-line visualizations could serve as a basis.

---

[1] The system is tailored to incremental, multimodal referential behavior, hence the dynamics of promoting and retracting references is quite dependent on the domain.

Lison and Kennington (2015), with Open-Dial, proposed another hybrid approach, combining logical and statistical methods. Probabilistic logical dialogue rules are parametrized with respect to probabilities of their outcomes and their estimated utility, and selected under consideration of uncertainty in their respective preconditions. The strength of the approach is the particular suitability for combining (or gradually replacing/adapting) hand-crafted parameters with learned ones. `flexdiam` presently foregoes any general representation of post-condition success estimations (although local planners are free to factor this in their plans opaquely). There is however a clearly defined way for monitoring the state of asynchronous output – and the user's closing of contingency pairs (or failure to) can be handled in the hierarchical situation model. Uncertainty in input and derived data is also represented.

As did most of the previous work, we also assert that our present system is a relatively loose framework that enables more than one philosophy to thrive within, though maybe not simultaneously.

3 Architecture and processing

`flexdiam` is an interaction framework that aims to unify the features of incrementality (to quickly update and relay discussed information), provisions for representation and resolution of uncertainty (resulting from input and unclear grounding) with explicit representation of topics, structured hierarchically in units intuitive to laymen.

The system is built on top of the `IPAACA` middleware, a distributed, platform-independent implementation Schlangen et al. (2010) of the 'general, abstract model for incremental dialogue processing' proposed by Schlangen and Skantze (2011). This provides the back-end for the connection of the core DM components to input (including ASR, tagger and parser, eye tracker, keyboard/mouse/touch etc.) and output modules (NLG, synthesis, graphical components / GUI changes, control of animated characters etc.).

An overview of the DM architecture is provided in Fig. 1. Temporal information, and the representation of `Events` is maintained in a functionally tiered structure called `TimeBoard`. Event-driven observers are used to derive events from interval relations between existing ones, and trigger higher-level functions, most centrally the dialogue manager proper, but also the contribution

manager, which schedules queued communicative intentions when the floor situation allows.

Propositional information is, in the general case, resident in the global `VariableContext` (subsequently 'Context'), containing a rewindable representation of certain and uncertain (distribution) variables with generic metrics – like entropy – that serve as the basis for local decision heuristics. Other types of variables include watchdogs that update their state based on other values; one such use case is the recalculation of possible referents in a certain domain whenever information restricts or extends its determining variables.

In `flexdiam`, there is generally a single joint task and discourse model for both interactants (i.e. no explicit full Theory of Mind-like simulation of the other party); its presence in the actual common ground is on the other hand promoted by the update heuristics, below. The basic structure of the joint task and discourse model is a forest of independent but hierarchically interdependent agents termed `Issues`[2], as well as generic update rules to transform this forest after DM invocations. An Issue $I := I(Pattern)$ with $Pattern :=$ $(Cls, name, config)$ is defined by a functional class Cls that implements its input handling and planning dynamics, an abstract $name$ (used e.g. for mapping to specific verbalizations in the NLG module), and a $configuration$ that defines its initial internal state. If $Pattern$ is identical for any Issues I_1, I_2, they are defined to *match functionally*. When an Issue is *instantiated*, it is at the same time made a *child* of the Issue that effected its creation. Issues can have zero or one parent (root / non-root) and any number of children.

Any path from a leaf Issue to the root of its tree corresponds to a specific (sub-)topic of discussion. Any number of topics can be active at any one time and will be considered valid points of reference in parallel, if applicable according to their grounding state. Any Issue can be in one of five canonical states that correspond to its status with respect to the common ground and its continued relevance: NEW (it is on the system's agenda, but has never been raised by successful communication by the system or relevant contribution of the user), ENTERED (an initial communication attempt has been completed to introduce it to the common ground; it is presently considered a

---

[2]Terminology adapted from Ginzburg, via Larsson (albeit in a slightly less rigorous sense) – since the basal Issues do in fact correspond to grounding and acceptance questions.

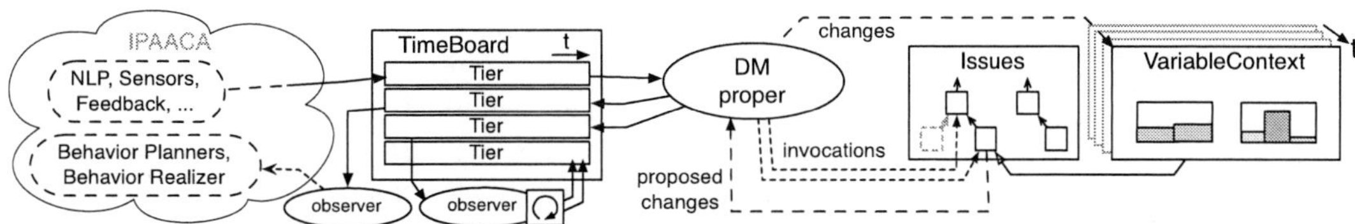

Figure 1: Overview of the architecture

valid target for DM invocations), FULFILLED or FAILED (terminal states decided locally by the Issue) or OBSOLETE (a terminal state which means that a replanning process in an ancestor has invalidated this instance explicitly, or implicitly through an intermediate ancestor).

3.1 Processing proper and plans

An invocation of the dialogue manager proper, triggered by the event structure on the TimeBoard, relays input records to all valid *entry points*. These refer to active topics (non-terminated leaves, see above), stored together with access time information to produce an implicit priority queue, similar to the 'partially ordered set' in Ginzburg (2012); however, rank is defined solely at invocation time since locally estimated utility is factored in.

Invocations that trigger processing in Issues come in two flavors: input handling and structure update handling. Under the umbrella of input handling, any abstract category of information can trigger a DM invocation (and Issues will decide along their local path in the hierarchy, and based on the current global Context, whether they can provide a plan to handle it). Two basic input categories for a general `flexdiam`-based SDS are `prompt_request` and `nluparse`, referring to calls for action at suitable points for contributions by the system, and partial incremental parses of user ASR, respectively. Under the umbrella of structure update handling, parent Issues are informed, and given the opportunity to contribute (or re-plan), when a plan is generated that involves either a child transitioning to a terminal state, or a child marking that it has made progress that might merit re-evaluation of the parent. Child Issues are informed, and given the opportunity for a final contribution, when they are invalidated (marked OBSOLETE) by an ancestor; the final contributions are usually limited to cleanup – especially retractions of situated referential behaviors.

For any invocation on an entry point E_x, starting at Issue I_x at time t, an individual clone over-lay ('clover') C_{I_y} is generated for any contributing Issue I_y (Copy-on-Write access) (cf. Fig. 2); the global Context $\mathscr{C}(t)$ is also accessed via a CoW overlay $\mathscr{C} + \Delta\mathscr{C}_{I_x}$. This enables the generation of competing plans involving a common subset of Issues. Any modifications to the internal state of Issues is made to the clovers instead and later merged in after the DM commits to a plan. Prior to any overlay production and processing (*handle_*), Issues may make a shallow assessment of the capability of handling the input in the given situation (*can_handle_*), for reasons of economy. For any invocation with input i that an Issue I_y can handle, it produces a partial plan $\mathscr{P}_{I_y} = \{C_{I_y}, O_{I_y}\}$ – with C the new 'clover' of the Issue, and O its *output record*. The latter may contain the following: a local *utility estimate*; a flag that signals *significant progress* to the ancestors; a preference for *propagation* of the input; a list of proposed *new child issues*; a list of *obsolete children* that are to be invalidated if the plan is selected; and, centrally, the current *communicative intentions*. The partial plans $\mathscr{P}_{I_{...}}$ contribute to the full plan for this input and entry point, $\mathscr{P}(E_x, i) = \{(C_{I_z}, O_{I_z}) \text{ for all contributing } I_z\}$. Additionally, Issues may annotate (or even transform) the input record (primarily marking input keys as used and 'accounted for', thus also marking interpretation coverage). The modified record i' is reused for all contributions by other issues to the same plan. The Context overlay $\mathscr{C} + \Delta\mathscr{C}_{I_x}$ is also reused, progressively accumulating changes from all contributions to the same plan.

If an Issue cannot handle an input handling invocation locally, a preference is marked to let its parent handle it instead. Partial localized processing does not preclude propagation, if flagged in the output record. A DM can enforce certain requirements beyond the marked propagation preferences in order to guarantee post-conditions (e.g. maximize opportunities that any prompt is generated).

Progressive propagation from the leaves

277

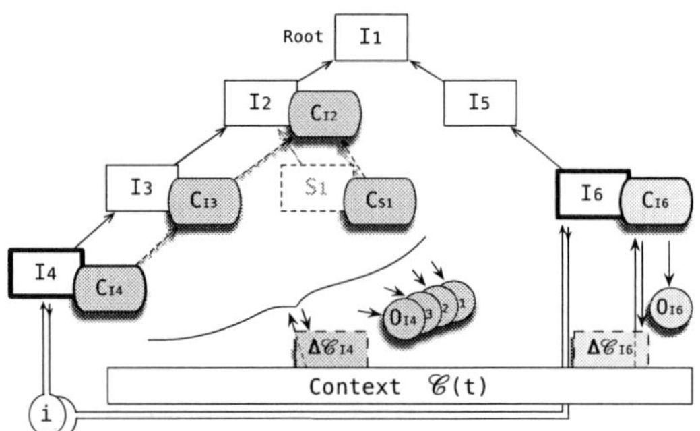

Figure 2: Invocation of the DM proper with input i leading to alternative plans starting at entry points I_4 and I_6, each yielding $i', \Delta\mathscr{C}, \{(C_{I_x}, O_{I_x})\}$. This example corresponds to two open topics (possible jump), the plan for I_4 includes deduced forward-looking agenda C_{S1}, contributed by shadow S_1.

through the ancestors thus allows for situated partial interpretation and processing; this is most specific and situation-dependent in the leaves, and most generic and general in the roots of the forest.

3.2 User-initiated agenda changes

Any Issue I_x can elect to define a set of anticipated Issue patterns that are not immediately on its local agenda (i.e. not actual children), but well-defined with respect to their arising at any time during the active life of I_x. This might include possible future child Issues, but also, crucially, anticipations about user behavior that stands outside the typical traversal though the local planning of I_x. In the former case, this is equivalent to defining precisely the opportunities of mixed-initiative approaches to subplan initiation. In the latter case, it simply affords offloading resources (and from the developers' perspective, code duplication and implementation time) to reusable patterns that are jointly servicing any number of issues with overlapping expectations. The anticipated patterns, implemented internally as specially-flagged Issues, are called *shadows*. Subtrees spanned by shadows must be cycle-free, and functionally matching shadows present in children and parents alike will always match only at the most specific location (the child). All shadows, leaf and non-leaf, are also defined to be valid entry points.

If a user contribution does not fit well into any active Issue, save for an existing shadow, a discourse transition based on user initiative can be as-

sumed to have taken place. Depending on the situation, this could be construed as either a forward-looking contribution (if anticipated by the currently invoked entrance point or a direct ancestor) or a real topic jump (when the shadow matches at another side branch of the current tree, opens a whole deep side branch, or belongs to an entirely different tree in the forest). From the point of time of plan selection using the DM policy, all employed shadows are copied into real instances and transplanted into their parents as proper children. The new branch is marked ENTERED and moved to the top of the entry point priority queue.

3.3 Decision making

The set of (non-empty) plans $\{\mathscr{P}(E_x, i)\}$ for all entry points E_x, with $\mathscr{P}(E_x, i) = \{(C_{I_z}, O_{I_z})$ for all contributing $I_z\}$, are ranked by a central policy using weighted criteria:

- local utility estimations placed in O_{I_z} by I_z,

- the coverage of the annotated input i', proportionally to the original,

- the recency of the topic, i.e. the latest invocation timestamp on the path from E_x to its root (freshly instantiated Issues are not considered),

- special rules (e.g. acting on estimated topic jumps can be deferred during an incremental interpretation phase).

The plan with the highest rank is selected for execution, which entails:

- merging the context overlay $\Delta\mathscr{C}_{I_x}$ into $\mathscr{C}$, producing the new global context (recalling that prior states remain accessible by obtaining a rewound view),

- merging the whole internal state of all clovers C_{I_z} into their respective Issue I_z – this also updates its canonical / grounding state,

- scheduling all *communicative intentions* from all O_{I_z} for the contribution manager to pick up, instantiate and post for asynchronous micro-planning and execution,

- updating the winning entry point with the most recent invocation time, and

- instantiating any newly proposed children, and adding new entry points for them.

4   Summary of approach

In terms of the basic approach, and in relation to existing work, discourse modeling in `flexdiam` most closely resembles Ginzburg's approach and its incarnations, in a formally less rigorous fashion. Some features of the info-state approach are present in the system (and it can in principle be employed as such), but the structural confinement afforded by the forest of hierarchical Issue agents helps to alleviate problems of inscrutability when the domain size increases, while still remaining very flexible. The present system is most suited to quick, interactive approaches to spoken interaction (and notably not designed for rigorous logical representation or explicit simulation of the interlocutor's mind), and to modeling real-world applications with limited domains. Manual extension is quite straightforward and seems to scale if 'best practices' are honored[3]. Incremental processing and the handling of uncertain input and information derived from it has received special focus, the 'output' side employs a similar notion of indeterminate state until evidence for communicative success provides a precondition for grounding being attested. Communicative plans are capable of employing several modalities and the (small) implemented suite of basic Issues for grounding problems can be fine-tuned to cover a wide space of varying explicitness, verbosity, and conversational styles, which will be used in upcoming long-term experiments to seed user models that best suit the estimated capabilities and preferences of participants. This extends to information density (configurable via different options for packaging and different approaches to confirmation requests), but also discourse structure: explicit ratification for topic jumps beyond a distance threshold (and implicit acceptance by means of contingent continuation by the user) is currently in development. The system is modular; the central decision policy is exchangeable and could in the future be parametrized using machine learning.

5   Initial evaluation

We have recently performed an initial evaluation of the described architecture in a setup for diverse user groups. For this experiment, we recruited 44 participants: 19 older adults (SEN), aged about 75+, with age-typical perception and cognition; 15

Figure 3: Scene from the first evaluation study with the present system; subject anonymized, and scene enhanced for clarity.

cognitively impaired adults (CIM) of working age; and 10 university controls (CTL).

Participants were asked to enter at least five items into a fictional weekly schedule at their leisure, in spoken interaction with a virtual assistant agent who also offered external activity suggestions. The agent was presented alongside a graphical calendar; the DM was able to generate dynamic references in the calendar and referential behavior for the agent (Fig. 3).

We selected the activity / scheduling domain because it was on the one hand the support domain most requested by our corporate partner, *von Bodelschwinghsche Stiftungen Bethel*, a large health care provider, but also by merit of its interesting properties: it can be reasonably well constrained in certain dimensions (days, times, intervals), while being potentially boundless in another (the activity being discussed) - though possibly constrained implicitly by priming and suggestions. This provides a relatively safe starting point for shallow, heuristic understanding of the only unconstrained dimension, because attribution to the other domains is fairly exclusive. (On the down side, out-of-domain discrimination would then amount to deep pragmatic understanding, so prior instruction about the restrictedness of the system capacities were necessary). A full dictation language model was used for ASR (provided via Dragon Client SDK 12.5)[4] to realize the free-form entering of the appointment. NLU performed heuristic extraction of best guesses for this slot from ASR hypotheses. Specifically, the parser identified sentences that might contain an appointment declaration, both in elliptic form (such as "<day> <time> <comment>") and various explicit

---

[3]Proper provisions for authoring are on the wish list for a future open release of the framework.

[4]Our health care partner required that a client-only, offline solution be employed in the project to guarantee privacy.

forms (such as "I was planning to <comment> on Monday"). The rule-based heuristics attempted to reduce the comment to a coherent sequence of V-N or N-N, optionally with declared participants ("with <proper-name>").

Aside from the scaffolding of social interaction and calendar entry commitment, we designed the grounding problem for the schedule items in three Issues: `VariableSetGrounding`, for accepting in free form, and integrating in a frame-like manner, the variables of day of the week (*dow*), the *start* and *end* times, and the activity (*what*) alongside many types of revisions, marked and unmarked; `VariableSetSequentialRephrase`, representing a situation where the system rephrased the previously uttered understood partial information; and `VariableValueConfirmation`, for explicit need for ratification and disambiguation when information was too uncertain to proceed silently. For the agent-initiated suggestions, the same approach was used, but pre-seeded with one variable (the agent's suggestion), and with the additional possibility of handling outright rejection of the suggestion. A final ratification with full multimodal presentation was also required before any activity was actually committed to the schedule.

The autonomous dialogue system was overseen by an experimenter, who had three options to aid the system in strategy selection: initiate the raising of an auto-generated partial suggestion ("Would you like to do something on *Saturday*?"); proceed to two fully-formed possible activities if the user had stated, or was assumed, to be done with their entries; or initiate the final valediction sequence.

All subjects managed to enter at least the required number of appointments into the calendar. The number of negotiated entries ranged between 5 and 18; the number of final entries averaged 10.4, 8.5, and 8.9 for CTL, SEN and CIM, respectively (including up to two agent-recommended items). The older adults spent 15% longer on average on a topic compared to controls, while the group with impairments spent 23% longer; some participants from the CIM group made long hesitations in isolated instances (up to tens of seconds). The number of required utterances was initially high especially for the older adults, but started to converge; most subjects from the CIM group relied slightly more on reacting to dynam-

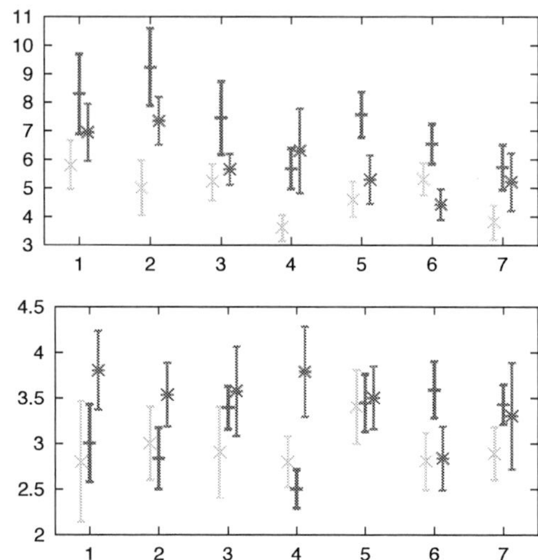

Figure 4: Top: user utterances per topic (for the first seven entered items, due to sample size); bottom: number of system variable prompts. User groups, ordered: CTL, pale; SEN, dark; CIM, red.

ically generated prompts, their performance compared to CTL indicates that the afforded structure was suitable for them (Fig. 4). As expected by us, most time per entry was spent on correcting the topic (*what*) of an activity, due to the heuristic extraction of possible topics from a multitude of alternative ASR hypotheses, which caused the majority of challenging situations. For the future, we aim to add deeper NLU capabilities to the system to better constrain the set of relevant candidates – currently, we are exploring the use of word embeddings to this effect.

The experiment was conducted to gain qualitative insight into the repair, revision and metacommunicative patterns exhibited by the user groups; as such, there was no clearly delineated 'right' and 'wrong' with respect to final entries (hence there was no baseline reference to match). Detailed conversational analysis has only recently started (see appendix for two example situations with a view of DM internals)[5]; a statistical description of the language used - and of word error rates - can only be sensibly made based on a comprehensive transcription of the corpus, which is still pending at the time of writing. For upcoming experiments, we are currently scaling up the possible activities to include revisions and removal of older entries,

---

[5]Additional material will be made available here: `https://purl.org/net/ramin/sigdial2017/`

queries about specific topics or time ranges, and installing and managing reminders.

6 Discussion and conclusion

We have presented the principal approach and current state of our dialogue management framework `flexdiam`, which is being used to evaluate spoken interaction with people with cognitive impairments, informed by prior work in this domain. It is designed to handle uncertainty, interruptions, and many kinds of revisions in a robust manner in order to provide a stable interaction in task-oriented domains. The approach makes for flexible interaction dynamics that are also straightforward to analyze and scrutinize in detail by humans. With respect to the requirements for the specific user groups, confusion due to e.g. problems in articulation is resolved in place using generic recipes, information density can be configured for specific users, and the system can cope both with increased and reduced pace. Regarding idiosyncrasies in floor behavior, we observed long hesitations in specific users, which from the point of view of the system primarily entails non-standard assumptions in assessing engagement and disengagement; in previous work (Yaghoubzadeh and Kopp (2016)), we conversely explored multimodal preemptive floor management to reduce user verbosity in a socially acceptable manner; this module has been integrated into the architecture but not employed in the present study.

We regard our architectural requirements to be fulfilled and will integrate the results from the emerging qualitative analysis to refine the recipes in the system.

We strove to highlight the mechanics of `flexdiam`, and its novel combination of features for the target user groups, in comparison to existing approaches, and we have performed an initial evaluation with the target user groups in which subjects were generally able to solve the set task, and the system was able to reach successful grounding of the desired contents in most cases. Implementation of the domain and communicative behavior was straightforward, and has already been scaled up to include competing alternative actions. We would also like to employ learning approaches to seed and adapt utility estimations and policy weights in the system.

Acknowledgments

This research was partially supported by the German Federal Ministry of Education and Research (BMBF) in the project 'KOMPASS' (FKZ 16SV7271K) and by the Deutsche Forschungsgemeinschaft (DFG) in the Cluster of Excellence 'Cognitive Interaction Technology' (CITEC).

References

Timo Baumann and David Schlangen. 2012. The InproTK 2012 release. In *NAACL-HLT Workshop on Future Directions and Needs in the Spoken Dialog Community: Tools and Data*. Association for Computational Linguistics, Stroudsburg, PA, USA, SDCTD '12, pages 29–32. http://dl.acm.org/citation.cfm?id=2390444.2390464.

Timothy W. Bickmore, Rebecca A. Silliman, Kerrie Nelson, Debbie M. Cheng, Michael Winter, Lori Henault, and Michael K. Paasche-Orlow. 2013. A randomized controlled trial of an automated exercise coach for older adults. *Journal of the American Geriatrics Society* 61(10):1676–1683. http://dx.doi.org/10.1111/jgs.12449.

Dan Bohus and Alexander I. Rudnicky. 2009. The RavenClaw dialog management framework: Architecture and systems. *Computer Speech and Language* 23.

Herbert H. Clark and Edward F. Schaefer. 1989. Contributing to discourse. *Cognitive Science* 13(2):259–294.

Jonathan Ginzburg. 2012. *The Interactive Stance*. Oxford University Press, Oxford, UK.

Staffan Larsson. 2002. *Issue-Based Dialogue Management*. Ph.D. thesis, University of Gothenburg, Gothenburg, SE.

Staffan Larsson. 2015. The state of the art in dealing with user answers. In *Proceedings of SemDial 2015*. pages 190–191.

Pierre Lison and Casey Kennington. 2015. Developing spoken dialogue systems with the OpenDial toolkit. In *Proceedings of SemDial 2015*. pages 194–195.

Markus Meis. 2013. Nutzerzentrierte Entwicklung eines Erinnerungsassistenten. Abschlusssymposium Niedersächsischer Forschungsverbund Gestaltung altersgerechter Lebenswelten.

David Schlangen, Timo Baumann, Hendrik Buschmeier, Okko Buß, Stefan Kopp, Gabriel Skantze, and Ramin Yaghoubzadeh. 2010. Middleware for incremental processing in conversational agents. In *Proceedings of the SIGDIAL 2010 Conference, The 11th Annual Meeting of the Special Interest Group on Discourse and Dialogue, 24-15 September 2010, Tokyo, Japan*. pages 51–54. http://www.aclweb.org/anthology/W10-4308.

David Schlangen and Gabriel Skantze. 2011. A general, abstract model of incremental dialogue processing. *Dialogue and Discourse* 2(1):83–111.

Candace Sidner, Timothy Bickmore, Charles Rich, Barbara Barry, Lazlo Ring, Morteza Behrooz, and Mohammad Shayganfar. 2013. An always-on companion for isolated older adults. In *14th Annual SIGdial meeting on discourse and dialogue*.

Gabriel Skantze. 2007. *Error Handling in Spoken Dialogue Systems*. Ph.D. thesis, KTH.

Gabriel Skantze and Samer Al Moubayed. 2012. IrisTK: a statechart-based toolkit for multi-party face-to-face interaction. In *Proceedings of ICMI '12*.

Tracey Swaffer and Clive R. Hollin. 2000. Anger and impulse control. In Rob Newell and Kevin Gournay, editors, *Mental health nursing*, Churchill Livingstone, chapter 15, pages 265–289.

David R. Traum and Staffan Larsson. 2003. The information state approach to dialogue management. *Current and new directions in discourse and dialogue* pages 325–353.

P. Wargnier, G. Carletti, Y. Laurent-Corniquet, S. Benveniste, P. Jouvelot, and A. S. Rigaud. 2016. Field evaluation with cognitively-impaired older adults of attention management in the embodied conversational agent Louise. In *2016 IEEE International Conference on Serious Games and Applications for Health (SeGAH)*. pages 1–8.

Ramin Yaghoubzadeh and Stefan Kopp. 2016. Towards graceful turn management in human-agent interaction for people with cognitive impairments. In *Proceedings of the 7th Workshop on Speech and Language Processing for Assistive Technologies (SLPAT 2016)*.

Ramin Yaghoubzadeh, Marcel Kramer, Karola Pitsch, and Stefan Kopp. 2013. Virtual agents as daily assistants for elderly or cognitively impaired people - studies on acceptance and interaction feasibility. In *Intelligent Virtual Agents - 13th International Conference, IVA 2013, Edinburgh, UK, August 29-31, 2013. Proceedings*. Edinburg, UK, pages 79–91.

Ramin Yaghoubzadeh, Karola Pitsch, and Stefan Kopp. 2015. Adaptive grounding and dialogue management for autonomous conversational assistants for elderly users. In *Proceedings of the 15th International Conference on Intelligent Virtual Agents*. Delft, The Netherlands.

Victoria Young and Alex Mihailidis. 2010. Difficulties in automatic speech recognition of dysarthric speakers and implications for speech-based applications used by the elderly: A literature review. *Assistive Technology* 22(2):99–112.

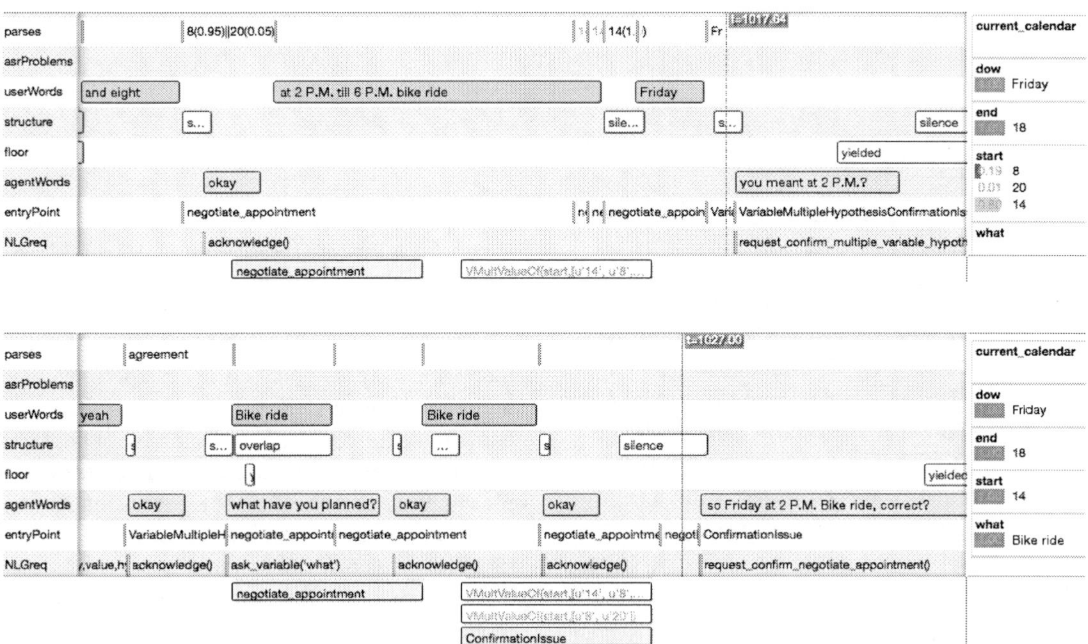

Figure 5: Example situation (via HTML transcript generated by `flexdiam`, and translated to English): top: user initiated new appointment, note that two possible start times were generated from the first fragment, and overridden by the second; bottom: final ratification phase after last information provided.

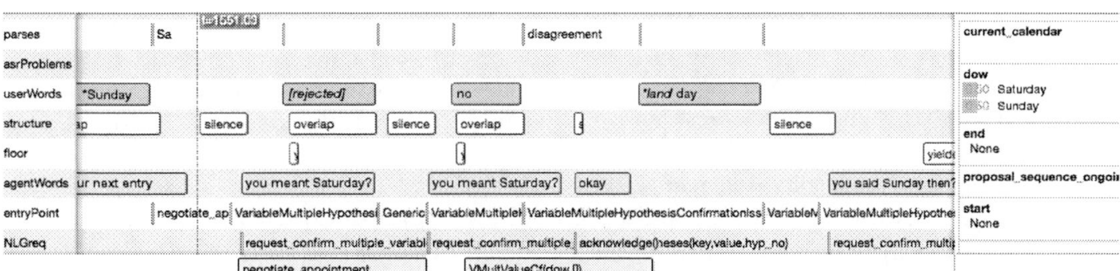

Figure 6: User with impaired articulation: cooperative repair. Prior to the blue cursor position (left), two equally valid hypotheses were generated for *dow* from the user's preceding utterance. The user provides negative evidence by rejection for the first grounding attempt, but their subsequent correction is not recognized – the system continues with the next hypothesis.

Adversarial Evaluation for Open-Domain Dialogue Generation

Elia Bruni and **Raquel Fernández**
Institute for Logic, Language and Computation
University of Amsterdam
`elia.bruni@gmail.com` `raquel.fernandez@uva.nl`

Abstract

We investigate the potential of adversarial evaluation methods for open-domain dialogue generation systems, comparing the performance of a discriminative agent to that of humans on the same task. Our results show that the task is hard, both for automated models and humans, but that a discriminative agent can learn patterns that lead to above-chance performance.

1 Introduction

End-to-end dialogue response generation systems trained to produce a plausible utterance given some limited dialogue context are receiving increased attention (Vinyals and Le, 2015; Sordoni et al., 2015; Serban et al., 2016; Li et al., 2016). However, for systems dealing with chatbot-style open-dialogue, where task completion is not applicable, evaluating the quality of their responses remains a challenge. Most current models are evaluated with measures such as perplexity and overlap-based metrics like BLEU, that compare the generated response to the ground-truth response in an actual dialogue. This kind of measures, however, correlate very weakly or not at all with human judgements on response quality (Liu et al., 2016).

In this paper, we explore a different approach to evaluating open-domain dialogue response generation systems, inspired by the classic Turing Test (Turing, 1950): measuring the quality of the generated responses on their indistinguishability from human output. This approach has been preliminary explored in recent work under the heading of *adversarial evaluation* (Kannan and Vinyals, 2016; Li et al., 2017), drawing a parallel with generative adversarial learning (Goodfellow et al., 2014). Here we concentrate on exploring the potential and the limits of such an adversarial eval-

uation approach by conducting an in-depth analysis. We implement a discriminative model and train it on the task of distinguishing between actual and "fake" dialogue excerpts and evaluate its performance, as well as the feasibility of the task more generally, by conducting an experiment with human judgements. Results show that the task is hard not only for the discriminative model, but also for human judges. We then implement a simple chatbot agent for dialogue generation and test the discriminator on this data, again comparing its performance to that of humans on this task. We show that both humans and the discriminative model can be fooled by the generator in a significant amount of cases.

2 The Discriminative Agent

Our discriminative agent is a binary classifier which takes as input a sequence of dialogue utterances and predicts whether the dialogue is real or fake. The agent treats as positive examples of coherent dialogue actual dialogue passages and as negative examples passages where the last utterance has been randomly replaced. Random replacement has been used in the past to study discourse coherence (Li and Hovy, 2014).

2.1 Model

The classifier is modelled as an attention-based bidirectional LSTM. LSTMs are indeed very effective to model word sequences, and are especially suited for learning on data with long distance dependencies (Hochreiter and Schmidhuber, 1997) such as multi-turn dialogues. The bidirectional LSTM includes both a forward function ($\overrightarrow{\text{LSTM}}$, which reads the sentence s_i from w_{i1} to w_{iT}) and a backward function ($\overleftarrow{\text{LSTM}}$, which reads the sentence s_i from w_{iT} to w_{i1}):

$$x_{it} = W_e w_{it}, t \in [1, T] \tag{1}$$

Proceedings of the SIGDIAL 2017 Conference, pages 284–288,
Saarbrücken, Germany, 15-17 August 2017. ©2017 Association for Computational Linguistics

$$\overrightarrow{h}_{it} = \overrightarrow{\mathrm{LSTM}}(x_{it}), t \in [1, T] \qquad [2]$$

$$\overleftarrow{h}_{it} = \overleftarrow{\mathrm{LSTM}}(x_{it}), t \in [T, 1] \qquad [3]$$

The words of a dialogue turn do not always contribute equally to determine coherence. We thus use an attention mechanism to extract words that are important to detect plausibility or coherence of a dialogue passage and parametrize their aggregation accordingly. Having an aggregated vector representation which is adaptive to the content of each time step allows the classifier to assign large weights to the most "discriminative" words. Contemporarily, the attention should also have an advantage in modelling long sequences by considering different word locations in the dialogue in a relatively even manner:

$$u_{it} = \tanh(W_w h_{it} + b_w) \qquad [4]$$

$$\alpha_{it} = \frac{\exp(u_{it}^T u_w)}{\sum_t \exp(u_{it}^T u_w)}, \quad \sum_i \alpha_i h_i \qquad [5]$$

We first compute the hidden representation of h_{it} through a one-layer MLP u_{it}; we then weight the importance of u_{it} by computing its similarity to a word-level context vector, normalized via a softmax function. The context vector is learned end-to-end by the classifier and is meant to represent a general query about the level of "discriminability" of a word (see, e.g., Sukhbaatar et al. 2015 or Yang et al. 2016). The output of the attention is then fed to a sigmoid function, which returns the probability of the input being real or fake:

$$p = \mathrm{sigmoid}(W_c^v + b_c) \qquad [6]$$

As loss function we then use the negative log likelihood of the correct labels:

$$L = - \sum_d \log p_{dj} \qquad [7]$$

2.2 Training Details

We trained the discriminator with a combination of three different datasets: *MovieTriples*, *SubTle* and *Switchboard*. MovieTriples (Serban et al., 2016) has been created from the Movie-Dic corpus of film transcripts (Banchs, 2012) and contains 3-utterance passages between two interlocutors who alternate in the conversation. SubTle

(Ameixa et al., 2014) is made of 2-utterance passages extracted from movie subtitles. To discourage the pairing of utterances coming from different movie scenes, we selected only those pairs with a maximum difference of 1 second between the first and the second turn. Switchboard (Godfrey et al., 1992) is a corpus of transcribed telephone conversations. We ignored utterances that consist only of non-verbal acts such as laughter, and selected sequences of three consecutive utterances. In all cases, we consider the last utterance of a passage the target response, and the previous utterances, the context. For the three datasets, we restrict ourselves to dialogue passages where the context and the response have a length of 3 to 25 tokens each. We concatenated the three datasets, obtaining a total of 3,289,835 dialogue passages (46,499 from MovieTriples, 3,211,899 from Sub-Tle, and 77,936 from Switchboard).

For training, we limit the vocabulary size to the top 25K most frequent words.[1] We used mini-batch stochastic gradient descent, shuffling the batches each epoch. We use a bidirectional layer, with 500 cells, and 500-dimensional embeddings (we tried with more layers and higher number of cells without significant improvements). All model parameters are uniformly initialized in $[-0.1, 0.1]$ and as optimizer we used Adam with an initial learning rate of 0.001. Dropout with probability 0.3 was applied to the LSTMs.

3 Human Evaluation

To assess the performance of our discriminative model, we conduct an experiment with human annotators. To our knowledge, this is the first study of its kind ever conducted. Previous human evaluation experiments of dialogue generation systems have mostly consisted in asking participants to choose the better response between two options generated by different models or to rate a generated dialogue along several dimensions (Vinyals and Le, 2015; Lowe et al., 2017; Li et al., 2017). In contrast, here we present humans with the same task faced by the discriminator: We show them a dialogue passage and ask them to decide whether, given the first one or two utterances of context, the shown continuation is the actual follow-up utterance in the original dialogue or a random response.

The data for this experiment consists of 900 pas-

---

[1] All remaining words are converted into the universal token <unk>.

data	discriminator							humans							agreement	
		real			random				real			random			Fleiss' π	
	Acc	P	R	F1	P	R	F1	Acc	P	R	F1	P	R	F1	hum	disc
SWB	.583	.549	.933	.691	.778	.233	.359	.670	.650	.714	.690	.695	.604	.647	.299	.068
MOV	.677	.645	.787	.709	.726	.567	.637	.677	.664	.713	.688	.690	.640	.664	.303	.258
SUB	.737	.763	.687	.723	.715	.787	.749	.640	.635	.660	.647	.646	.620	.633	.304	.301

Table 1: Accuracy, Precision, Recall, and F-score of discriminator and humans against ground-truth. Inter-annotator agreement among humans and between the discriminator and the human majority class.

sages: 300 randomly selected per dataset, with 50% real and 50% fake dialogues. We use the CrowdFlower platform to recruit annotators, restricting the pool to English native speakers.[2] Each item is classified as real or random by three different annotators. A total of 137 annotators participated in the experiment, with each of them annotating between 10 and 150 items.

We test the discriminator on the same data and compare its performance to the human judgements. Chance level accuracy for both humans and the discriminator is 50%, namely when real and fake passages are indistinguishable from each other. The results are summarised in Table 1. Let us first consider the performance of humans on the task. We compute inter-annotator agreement using Fleiss π (Fleiss, 1971), suitable for assessing multi-coder annotation tasks. Agreement is low: $\pi = 0.30$ across the 3 corpora, indicating that the task is challenging for humans (there is limited consensus on whether the shown dialogue passages are plausible or not). Looking into the human performance with respect to the ground truth, we see similar accuracy scores for Switchboard and MovieTriples, while accuracy is lower for SubTle, where the context consists of one utterance only. Across the three datasets, we observe slightly higher F-score for positive instances (real) than negative instances (random). For the positive instances, recall is higher than precision, while the opposite is true for negative instances. Arguably, this indicates that humans tend to accommodate responses that in fact are random as possible coherent continuations of a dialogue, and will only flag them as fake if they are utterly surprising.

We compute the agreement of the discriminator's predictions and the human majority class over 3 annotators. For Switchboard, agreement is at chance level ($\pi = .07$), while for the other two

datasets it is on a par with agreement among humans. As for the discriminator's performance with respect to the ground truth, not surprisingly we obtain low accuracy on Switchboard, but slightly higher accuracy than humans in the other datasets, in particular SubTle, possibly due to the larger amount of training data from this corpus. In what follows, we investigate what information the discriminator may be exploiting to make its predictions.

4 Analysis

To inspect the discriminator's internal representation of the dialogue turns, at testing time we run two extra forward passes, inputting context and target separately, and compute the cosine similarity between the respective LSTM hidden states. We find some clear patterns: The context and response of the dialogue passages classified as coherent by the discriminator (true and false positives) have significantly higher cosine similarity than the passages classified as fake (true and false negatives). This holds across the 3 datasets ($p < .001$ on a two-sample Wilcoxon rank sum test) and indicates that the discriminator is exploiting this information to make its predictions. We also observe that, while there is a tendency to higher cosine similarity in the ground-truth positive instances than in the negative ones in Switchboard ($p = .05$) and MovieTriples ($p = .03$), the effect is highly significant in SubTle ($p < .001$), which is in line with the higher performance of the discriminator on this corpus. Since accuracy is higher than humans in this case, presumably the discriminator is sensitive to patterns that may not be apparent to humans. Whether this capacity is useful for developing generative models that interact with humans, however, is an open question.

We find another interesting pattern within the attention mass distribution between context and target: For true and false positives, higher attention is concentrated on the response ($\approx 90\%$),

[2]We use strict quality controls, only accepting annotators considered "highly trusted" by CrowdFlower (www. crowdflower.com) and requiring 90% accuracy on socalled "test questions". Annotators are paid $4 cents per item.

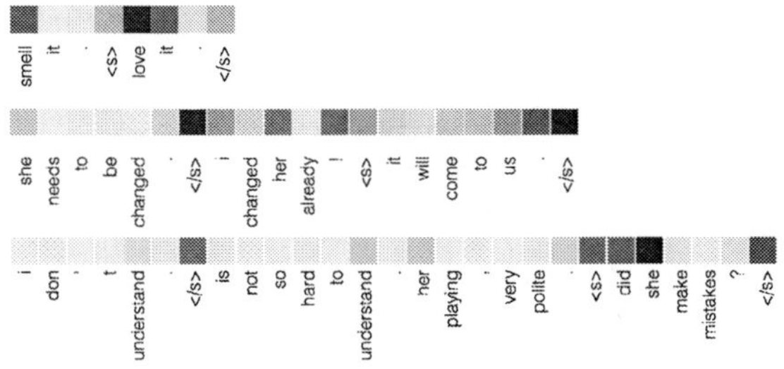

Figure 1: Attention visualization.

while for true and false negatives the attention is more balanced between the two ($\approx 50\%$). Figure 1 shows three sample dialogue passages with word-level attention weights displayed in different color intensities. The token <s> separates the context from the target response. The sample at the top is a passage from SubTle that humans judged to be incoherent, but that was rightly classified by the discriminator as a positive instance (the passage is real). The sample in the middle (a passage from MovieTriples where the target is random) illustrates how attention weights are more balanced in negative instances. Finally, the sample at the bottom shows a passage from MovieTriples rightly classified as coherent by human annotators and by the discriminative agent. As can be seen, attention is more prominent on the target response, with particular focus on the pronoun 'she' whose antecedent 'her' in the context also receives some attention mass. In all cases the token </s> receives high attention, suggesting that the discriminative agent is keeping track of turn alternations.

5 Discriminating Generated Responses

We implement a baseline generative agent to test the extent to which the discriminator's ability to distinguish between generated and actual responses is comparable to humans.

5.1 The Generator Agent

The generator directly models the conditional probability $p(y|x)$ of outputting the subsequent dialogue turn $y_1, ..., y_m$ given some previous context $x_1, ..., x_n$. The model consists of a SEQ2SEQ model, divided into two components: an *encoder* which computes a representation for the dialogue context and a *decoder* which generates the subsequent dialogue turn one word at a time. A natural choice for implementing both the *encoder* and the *decoder* is to use an LSTM (see Section 2). The *decoder* is also equipped with an attention system.

We train the generator to predict the next dialogue turn given the preceding dialogue history on the OpenSubtitles dataset (Tiedemann, 2009). We considered each line in the dataset as a target to be predicted by the model and the concatenation of the two foregoing lines as the source context. We opt for OpenSubtitles rather than for the cleaner datasets used for training the discriminative agent, because the SEQ2SEQ model requires a very large amount of data to converge, and with more than 80 million triples, OpenSubtitles is one of the largest dialogue dataset available.

During training, we filtered out passages with context or target longer than 25 words. We used mini-batch stochastic gradient descent, shuffling the batches each epoch. We use stacking LSTM with 2 bidirectional layers, each with 2048 cells, and 500-dimensional embeddings. All model parameters are uniformly initialized in $[-0.1, 0.1]$; we train using SGD, with a start learning rate of 1, and after 5 epochs we start halving the learning rate at each epoch; the mini-batch size is set to 64 and we rescale the normalized gradients whenever the norm exceeds 5. We also apply dropout with probability 0.3 on the LSTMs.

5.2 Results

We test our discriminative agent on the task of distinguishing passages with real responses versus generated responses and, as before, compare its performance to human performance. For this evaluation, we selected a random sample of 30 generated instances per corpus, avoiding repeated generated responses and responses with <unk> tokens since these would make the human judgements trivial. A summary of results is shown in Table 2. We can see that human accuracy is at chance level, while the discriminator's is above chance, again suggesting that the discriminator may pick up on patterns that are not discernible to humans. The higher performance on SubTle may again be explained by the larger amount of training data from this dataset. We also observe very low inter-annotator agreement, with even negative π for the discriminator with respect to humans in the case of Switchboard.

6 Conclusions

In this paper, we investigated the use of an adversarial setting for open domain dialogue eval-

data	discriminator							humans							agreement	
		real			generated				real			generated			Fleiss' π	
	Acc	P	R	F1	P	R	F1	Acc	P	R	F1	P	R	F1	hum	disc
SWB	.567	.538	.933	.683	.750	.200	.316	.517	.511	.755	.610	.532	.277	.365	.194	−.130
MOV	.633	.618	.700	.656	.654	.567	.607	.467	.478	.733	.579	.428	.200	.273	.177	.062
SUB	.700	.773	.567	.654	.658	.833	.736	.511	.508	.678	.581	.517	.344	.413	.258	.129

Table 2: Performance of discriminator and humans against ground-truth for generator experiment. Inter-annotator agreement among humans and between the discriminator and the human majority class.

uation, providing novel results on human performance that are informative of the difficulty of the task and the strategies employed to tackle it. We found that there is limited consensus among human annotators on what counts as a coherent dialogue passages when only 1 or 2 utterances of context are provided, but that nevertheless a discriminative model is able to learn patterns that lead to above-chance performance.

References

David Ameixa, Luisa Coheur, Pedro Fialho, and Paulo Quaresma. 2014. *Luke, I am your father*: Dealing with out-of-domain requests by using movies subtitles. In *International Conference on Intelligent Virtual Agents*. Springer, pages 13–21.

Rafael E Banchs. 2012. Movie-DiC: a movie dialogue corpus for research and development. In *Proceedings ACL-2012: Short Papers-Volume 2*. pages 203–207.

Joseph L. Fleiss. 1971. Measuring nominal scale agreement among many raters. *Psychological Bulletin* 76(5):378–382.

John J Godfrey, Edward C Holliman, and Jane McDaniel. 1992. Switchboard: Telephone speech corpus for research and development. In *Proceedings of the IEEE International Conference on Acoustics, Speech, and Signal Processing (ICASSP-92)*. volume 1, pages 517–520.

Ian Goodfellow, Jean Pouget-Abadie, Mehdi Mirza, Bing Xu, David Warde-Farley, Sherjil Ozair, Aaron Courville, and Yoshua Bengio. 2014. Generative adversarial nets. In *Advances in neural information processing systems*. pages 2672–2680.

Sepp Hochreiter and Jürgen Schmidhuber. 1997. Long short-term memory. *Neural computation* 9(8):1735–1780.

Anjuli Kannan and Oriol Vinyals. 2016. Adversarial evaluation of dialogue models. In *NIPS Workshop on Adversarial Training*.

Jiwei Li and Eduard H. Hovy. 2014. A model of coherence based on distributed sentence representation. In *Proceedings of EMNLP*.

Jiwei Li, Will Monroe, Alan Ritter, Michel Galley, Jianfeng Gao, and Dan Jurafsky. 2016. Deep reinforcement learning for dialogue generation. In *Proceedings of EMNLP*.

Jiwei Li, Will Monroe, Tianlin Shi, Alan Ritter, and Dan Jurafsky. 2017. Adversarial learning for neural dialogue generation. *Preprint arXiv:1701.06547* .

Chia-Wei Liu, Ryan Lowe, Iulian Serban, Mike Noseworthy, Laurent Charlin, and Joelle Pineau. 2016. How NOT To Evaluate Your Dialogue System: An Empirical Study of Unsupervised Evaluation Metrics for Dialogue Response Generation. In *Proceedings of the 2016 Conference on EMNLP*.

Ryan Lowe, Michael Noseworthy, Iulian Serban, Nicolas Angelard-Gontier, Yoshua Bengio, and Joelle Pineau. 2017. Towards an automatic Turing test: Learning to evaluate dialogue responses. In *Proceedings of ACL*.

Iulian V Serban, Alessandro Sordoni, Yoshua Bengio, Aaron Courville, and Joelle Pineau. 2016. Building end-to-end dialogue systems using generative hierarchical neural network models. In *Proceedings of the Thirtieth AAAI Conference on Artificial Intelligence*.

Alessandro Sordoni, Michel Galley, Michael Auli, Chris Brockett, Yangfeng Ji, Margaret Mitchell, Jian-Yun Nie, Jianfeng Gao, and Bill Dolan. 2015. A neural network approach to context-sensitive generation of conversational responses. In *Proceedings of NAACL-HLT*. pages 196–205.

Sainbayar Sukhbaatar, Jason Weston, Rob Fergus, et al. 2015. End-to-end memory networks. In *Advances in neural information processing systems*.

Jörg Tiedemann. 2009. News from opus-a collection of multilingual parallel corpora with tools and interfaces. In *Recent advances in natural language processing*. volume 5, pages 237–248.

Alan M Turing. 1950. Computing machinery and intelligence. *Mind* 59(236):433–460.

Oriol Vinyals and Quoc V. Le. 2015. A neural conversational model. In *ICML Deep Learning Workshop*.

Zichao Yang, Diyi Yang, Chris Dyer, Xiaodong He, Alex Smola, and Eduard Hovy. 2016. Hierarchical attention networks for document classification. In *Proceedings of NAACL-HLT*. pages 1480–1489.

Exploring Joint Neural Model for Sentence Level Discourse Parsing and Sentiment Analysis

Bita Nejat   **Giuseppe Carenini**   **Raymond Ng**

Department of Computer Science, University of British Columbia
Vancouver, BC, V6T 1Z4, Canada
{nejatb, carenini, rng}@cs.ubc.ca

Abstract

Discourse Parsing and Sentiment Analysis are two fundamental tasks in Natural Language Processing that have been shown to be mutually beneficial. In this work, we design and compare two Neural models for jointly learning both tasks. In the proposed approach, we first create a vector representation for all the text segments in the input sentence. Next, we apply three different Recursive Neural Net models: one for discourse structure prediction, one for discourse relation prediction and one for sentiment analysis. Finally, we combine these Neural Nets in two different joint models: Multi-tasking and Pre-training. Our results on two standard corpora indicate that both methods result in improvements in each task but Multi-tasking has a bigger impact than Pre-training. Specifically for Discourse Parsing, we see improvements in the prediction on the set of contrastive relations.

1   Introduction

This paper focuses on studying two fundamental NLP tasks, Discourse Parsing and Sentiment Analysis. The importance of these tasks and their wide applications (e.g., (Gerani et al., 2014), (Rosenthal et al., 2014)) has initiated much interest in studying both, but no method yet exists that can come close to human performance in solving them.

Discourse parsing is the task of parsing a piece of text into a tree (called a Discourse Tree), the leaves of which are typically clauses (called Elementary Discourse Units or EDUs in short) and nodes (Discourse Units) represent text spans that are concatenations of their corresponding sub-

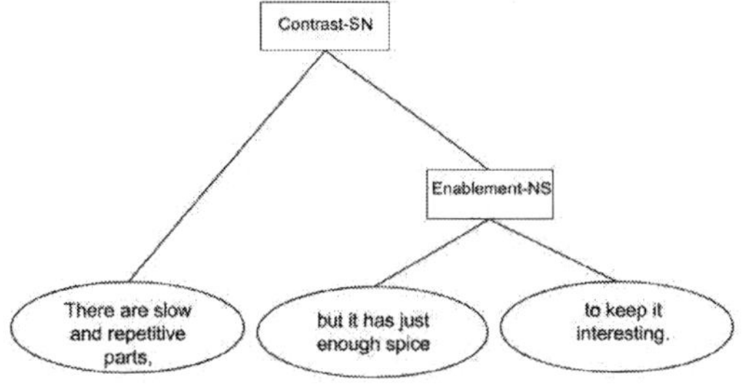

Figure 1: The Discourse Tree of a sentence from Sentiment Treebank dataset

trees' text spans [1]. Nodes also have labels identifying discourse relationships (*"contrast"*, *"evidence"*, etc.) between their corresponding subtrees. The relation also specifies nucliearity of the children. Nuclei are the core parts of the relation and Satellites are the supportive ones.

A Relation can take one of the following forms: (1) Satellite-Nucleus: First Discourse Unit is Satellite and second Discourse Unit is Nucleus. (2) Nucleus-Satellite: First Discourse Unit is Nucleus and second Discourse Unit is Satellite. (3) Nucleus-Nucleus: Both Discourse Units are Nuclei. In this approach relation identification and nuclearity assignment is done simultaneously. Figure 1 shows the Discourse Tree of a sample sentence. In this sentence, the Discourse Unit "There are slow and repetitive parts," holds a *"Contrast"* relationship with "but it has just enough spice to keep it interesting.". Furthermore, we can see that the former Discourse Unit is the satellite of the relation and the later part is the Nucleus.

Discourse Parsing is such a critical task in NLP because previous work has shown that information

---

[1] A text span is a piece of text consisting of one or more clauses (or EDUs).

Proceedings of the SIGDIAL 2017 Conference, pages 289–298,
Saarbrücken, Germany, 15-17 August 2017. ©2017 Association for Computational Linguistics

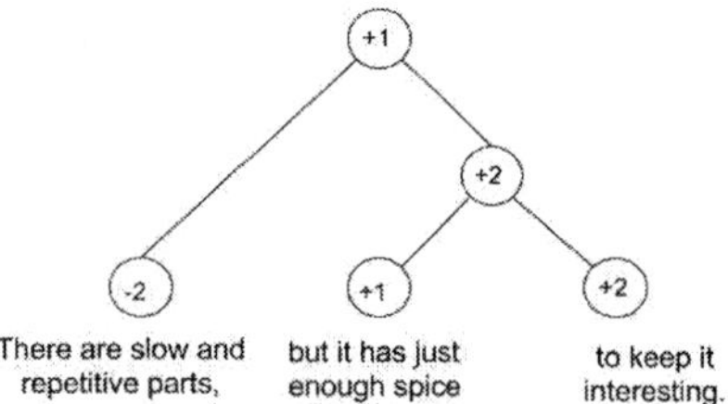

Figure 2: The Sentiment annotation (over Discourse Tree structure) of a sentence from Sentiment Treebank dataset

contained in the resulting Discourse Tree can benefit many other NLP tasks including but not restricted to automatic summarization (e.g., (Gerani et al., 2014), (Marcu and Knight, 2001), (Louis et al., 2010)), machine translation (e.g., (Meyer and Popescu-Belis, 2012),(Guzmán et al., 2014)) and question answering (e.g., (Verberne et al., 2007)). In contrast to traditional syntactic and semantic parsing, Discourse Parsing can generate structures that cover not only a single sentence but also multi-sentential text. However, the focus of this paper is on sentence level Discourse Parsing, leaving the study of extensions to multi-sentential text as future work.

The second fundamental task we consider in this work is assigning a contextual polarity label to text (sentiment analysis). Analyzing the overall polarity of a sentence is a challenging task due to the ambiguities that can be introduced by combinations of words and phrases. For example in the movie review excerpt shown in Figure 2, the phrase "There are slow and repetitive parts" has a negative sentiment. However when it is combined with the positive phrase "but it has just enough spice to keep it interesting", it results in an overall positive sentence.

It has been suggested that the information extracted from Discourse Trees can help with Sentiment Analysis (Bhatia et al., 2015) and likewise, knowing the sentiment of two pieces of text might help with the identification of discourse relationships between them (Lazaridou et al., 2013). For instance, taking the sentence in Figure 1 as an example, knowing that the two text spans "There are slow and repetitive parts" and "but it has just enough spice to keep it interesting" are in a *Contrast* relationship to each other, also signals that the sentiment of the two text spans is less likely

to be of the same type[2]. Likewise, knowing that the sentiment of the former text span is "very negative", while the sentiment of the later text span is "very positive", helps to narrow down the choice of discourse relation between these two text spans to the *Contrastive* group which contains relations *Contrast, Comparison, Antithesis, Antithesis-e, Consequence-s, Concession* and *Problem-Solution*.

To the best of our knowledge there is no previous work that learns both of these tasks in a joint model, using deep learning architectures. The main contribution of this paper is to address this gap by investigating how the two tasks can benefit from each other at the sentence level within a deep learning joint model. More specific contributions include:

(i) The development of three independent recursive neural nets: two for the key sub-tasks of discourse parsing, namely structure prediction and relation prediction; the third net for sentiment prediction.

(ii) The design and experimental comparison of two alternative neural joint models, Multi-tasking and Pre-training, that have been shown to be effective in previous work for combining other tasks in NLP (e.g., (Collobert and Weston, 2008),(Erhan et al., 2010),(Liu et al., 2016a)).

Our results indicate that a joint model performs better than individual models in either of the tasks with Multi-tasking outperforming Pre-training. Upon closer inspection, we also find that the improvement of Multi-tasking system in Relation prediction is mainly for the Contrastive set of relations, which confirms our hypothesis that knowing the sentiment of two text spans can help narrow down the choice of discourse relations that holds between them.

2 Previous Work

Traditionally, **Discourse Parsing and Sentiment Analysis** have been approached by applying machine learning methods with predetermined, engineered features that were carefully chosen by studying the properties of the text.

---

[2]Contrast can also hold between factual clauses as in [But from early on, Tigers workers unionized,] and [while Federals never have.] (wsj_1394 from RST-DT).

Examples of effective sentence level and document level Discourse Parsers include CODRA (Joty et al., 2015) and the parser of (Feng and Hirst, 2014) . These parsers use organizational, structural, contextual, lexical and N-gram features to represent Discourse Units and apply graphical models for learning and inference (i.e. Conditional Random Fields). The performance of these parsers critically depends on a careful selection of informative and relevant features, something that is instead performed automatically in the neural models we propose in this paper.

(Nakagawa et al., 2010), (Pang et al., 2008) and (Rentoumi et al., 2010), approach Sentiment Analysis using carefully engineered features as well as polarity rules. The choice of features also plays a key role in the high performance of these models.

Yet, with the rapid advancements of Neural Nets, there has been increased interest in applying them to different NLP tasks. (Socher et al., 2013) approached the problem of Sentiment Analysis by recursively assigning sentiment labels to the nodes of a binarized syntactic parse tree over a sentence. At each non-leaf node, the Sentiment Neural Net first creates a distributed embedding for the node using the embedding of its two children and then assigns a sentiment label to that node. Their approach achieves state of the art results. In our work, we borrow from the same idea of Recursive Neural Nets to learn the Sentiment labels. However, the structure over which we learn the Sentiment labels is the Discourse Tree of the sentence as opposed to the syntactic parse tree, with the goal of testing if Sentiment Analysis can benefit directly from discourse information within a neural joint model.

Motivated by Socher's success on Sentiment Analysis, (Li et al., 2014) approached the problem of Discourse Parsing by recursively building the Discourse Tree using two Neural Nets. A Structure Neural Net decides whether two nodes should be connected in the Discourse Tree or not. If two nodes are determined to be connected by the Structure Neural Net, a Relation Neural Net then decides what rhetorical relation should hold between the two nodes. Their approach also yields promising results. In terms of representation, the recursive structure of a Discourse Tree is used to learn the embedding of each non-leaf node from its children. For leaf nodes (EDUs), the representation is learned recursively using the syntac-tic parse tree of the node. One problem with their work is that it is unclear how they combine the labeled Discourse Structure Tree with the unlabeled syntactic parse trees to learn the vector representations for the text spans.

(Bhatia et al., 2015) trained a Recursive Neural Network for Sentiment Analysis over a Discourse Tree and showed that the information extracted from the Discourse Tree can be helpful for determining the Sentiment at document level. In their work however, they did not attempt to learn a distributed representation for the sub-document units. To represent EDUs, they used the bag-of-words features. For our work, we not only apply a Recurrent Neural Net approach to learn embeddings for the EDUs, but we also jointly learn models for the two tasks, instead of simply feeding a pre-computed discourse structure in a neural model for sentiment.

Learning text embeddings is a fundamental step in using Neural Nets for NLP tasks. An embedding is a fixed dimensional representation of the data (text) without the use of handpicked features. As words are the building blocks of text, previous studies have created fixed dimensional vector representations for words (Mikolov et al., 2013) that capture syntactic and semantic properties of the words. However, creating meaningful fixed dimensional vector representations for text spans is an ongoing challenge.

Both (Socher et al., 2013) and (Li et al., 2014) learn the embedding of a text span in a recursive manner, given a binary tree over the text span with leaves being the words. The embedding of a parent is computed from the embedding of its two children using a non-linear projection. The embedding is then used for training the task under study (Sentiment Analysis and Discourse Parsing respectively) and updated according to how useful it was for the task.

Recently Recurrent Neural Nets (RNNs) have become a more popular alternative for learning the embedding of a sentence (Kiros et al., 2015). In this setting, an encoder RNN encodes a sentence into a fixed vector representation that is then used by a decoder RNN to predict the following and preceding sentences and based on how good the predictions were, updates both the decoder and encoder RNNs. Once training is done, the encoder RNN can be used to create an embedding for any text span. In this paper, we have used the encoder

RNN to represent our EDUs, but we further compress the resulting embeddings with a neural based compressor to limit the number of parameters.

When training a neural model, the weights are usually initialized with random numbers taken from a uniform distribution. However, in their work, (Erhan et al., 2010) argue that **Pre-training** a neural model results in better generalization and can enhance the performance of the model. More recently, this general idea has been successfully applied in several scenarios (e.g., (Chung et al., 2015), (Seyyedsalehi and Seyyedsalehi, 2015)). In our work, we use the trained weights of one neural model (e.g. sentiment) as an initialization form for another task (e.g. discourse structure) to see if the features learned for one can be helpful for the other.

Neural **Multi-tasking** was originally proposed by (Collobert and Weston, 2008), who experimented with the technique using deep convolutional neural networks. In essence, the basic idea is that a network is alternatively trained with instances for different tasks, so that the network is learning to perform all these tasks jointly. In (Collobert and Weston, 2008) a model is trained to perform a variety of predictions on a given sentence, including part-of-speech tags, chunks, named entity tags, semantic roles, semantically similar words and the likelihood that the sentence makes sense using a language model. They showed that multitasking using a neural net structure can improve the generalization of the shared tasks and result in better performance. Following up on this initial success, many researchers have applied the neural multi-tasking strategy to several tasks, including very recent work in vision (Kaneko et al., 2016) and NLP (e.g., text classification (Liu et al., 2016a) and the classification of implicit discourse relations (Liu et al., 2016b)).

3 Corpora

For the task of Discourse Parsing, we use RST-DT ((Carlson and Marcu, 2001), (Carlson et al., 2002)). This dataset contains 385 documents along with their fully labeled Discourse Trees. The annotation is based on the Rhetorical Structure Theory (RST), a popular theory of discourse originally proposed in (Mann and Thompson, 1988). All the documents in RST-DT were chosen from Wall Street Journal news articles taken from the Penn Treebank corpus (Marcus et al.,

1993). Since we are focusing only on sentence-level discourse parsing, the documents as well as their Discourse Trees were first preprocessed to extract the sentences and sentence-level Discourse Trees. The sentence-level Discourse Trees were extracted from the document-level Discourse Tree by finding the sub-tree that exactly spans over the sentence. This resulted in a dataset of 6846 sentences with well-formed Discourse Trees, out of which 2239 sentences had only one EDU. Since sentences with only one EDU have trivial Discourse Trees, these sentences were excluded from our dataset, leaving a total of 4607 sentences.

For the task of Sentiment Analysis, we use the Sentiment Treebank (Socher et al., 2013). This dataset consists of 11855 sentences along with their syntactic parse trees annotated with sentiment labels at each node. For this work, since our models label sentiment over a Discourse Tree, we had to preprocess the Sentiment Treebank in the following way. For each sentence in the dataset, a Discourse Tree was created using (Joty et al., 2015). Next, for each node of the discourse tree, a sentiment label was extracted from the corresponding labeled syntactic tree by finding a sub-tree that exactly (or almost exactly [3]) matches the text span represented by the node in the discourse tree.

4 Proposed Joint Model

Our framework consists of three main sub parts. Given a segmented sentence, the first step is to create meaningful vector representations for all the EDUs. Next, we devise three different Recursive Neural Net models, each designed for one of discourse structure prediction, discourse relation prediction and sentiment analysis. Finally, we join these Neural Nets in two different ways: Multi-tasking and Pre-training. Below, we discuss each of these steps in more detail.

4.1 Learning Text Embeddings

One of the most challenging aspects of designing effective Neural Nets is to have meaningful representations for the inputs. Our inputs to the Neural Nets are text spans consisting of multiple words. Initially, we considered directly applying the Skip-

---

[3]Exact match was not possible when the syntactic and the discourse structures were not fully aligned, which happened in 31.9% of the instances. In this case, an approximation of the sentiment was computed by considering the sentiment of the two closest subsuming and subsumed syntactic sub-trees.

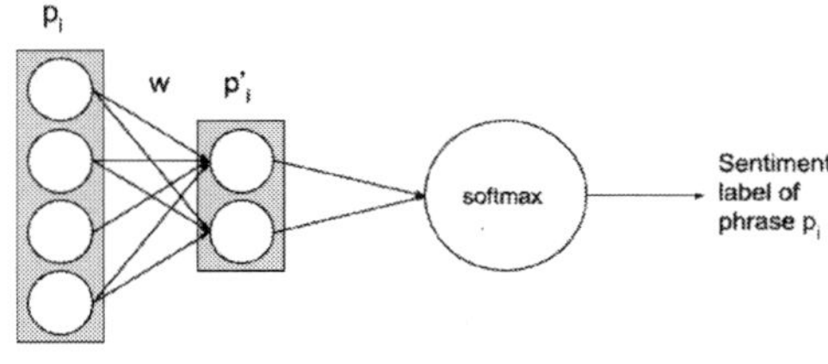

Figure 3: The Sentiment Neural Compressor

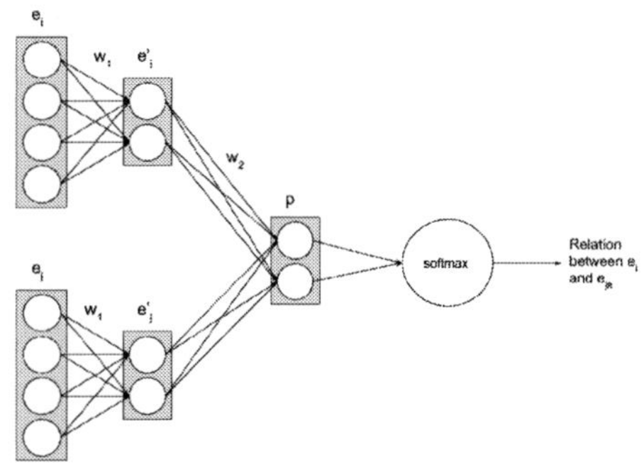

Figure 4: The Discourse Neural Compressor

thought framework (Kiros et al., 2015) to each text span to get a generic vector representations for them, since the original Skip-thought vectors were shown in (Kiros et al., 2015) to be useful for many NLP tasks. However, given the size of our datasets (only in the thousands of instances), it was clear that using 4800-dimensional Skip-thought would have created an over-parametrized network prone to over-fitting. Based on this observation, in order to simultaneously reduce the dimensionality and to produce vectors that are meaningful for our tasks, we devised a compression mechanism that takes in the Skip-thought produced vectors and compresses them using a Neural Net. Figures 4 and 3 show the structure of these compressors for our two different tasks. Each compressor is learned on the training set used for that task.

The sentiment neural compressor (Figure 3) takes as input, the skip-thought produced vector representations for all phrases in the Sentiment Treebank. For example, consider a phrase i with skip-thought produced vector $P_i \in R^{4800}$. The Sentiment Neural Compressor learns compressed vector $P_i' \in R^d$ through

$$P_i' = f(W.P_i) \qquad (1)$$

where f is a non-linear activation function such as $relu$ and $W \in R^{d \times 4800}$ is the matrix of weights. This Neural Net uses the sentiment of phrase i for supervised learning of the weights.

Similarly, the Discourse Parsing neural compressor (Figure 4) takes the skip-thought produced vector representations for two EDUs e_i, e_j and learns the compressed vectors e_i' and e_j', each with d dimensions where

$$\begin{aligned} e_i' &= f(W_1.e_i) \\ e_j' &= f(W1.e_j) \end{aligned} \qquad (2)$$

where f is again a non-linear activation function such as $relu$ and $W_1 \in R^{d \times 4800}$ is the matrix of weights. Note that the same set of weights are used for both EDUs because we are looking for a unique set of weights to compress an EDU.

4.2 Neural Net Models

Following (Socher et al., 2013)'s idea of Sentiment Analysis using recursive Neural Nets, we designed three Recursive Neural Nets for each task of Discourse Structure prediction, Discourse Relation prediction and Sentiment Analysis. All these three Neural Nets are classifiers.

The Structure Neural Net takes in the compressed vector representation ($\in R^d$) for two Discourse Units and learns whether they will be connected in the Discourse Tree (Figure 5). In this process, it also learns the vector representation for the parent of these two children. So for a parent p with children c_l and c_r, the vector representation for the parent is obtained by:

$$p = f(W_{str}[c_l, c_r] + b_{str}) \qquad (3)$$

where $[c_l, c_r]$ denotes the concatenating vector for the children; f is a non-linearity function; $W_{str} \in R^{d \times 2d}$ and $b_{str} \in R^d$ is the bias vector.

The Relation Neural Net takes as input the compressed vector representation for two Discourse Units that are determined to be connected in the Discourse Tree and learns the relation label for the parent node. The Relation Neural Net is the same in structure as the Structure Neural Net in Figure 5.

The Sentiment Neural Net takes as input the compressed vector representation for two Dis-

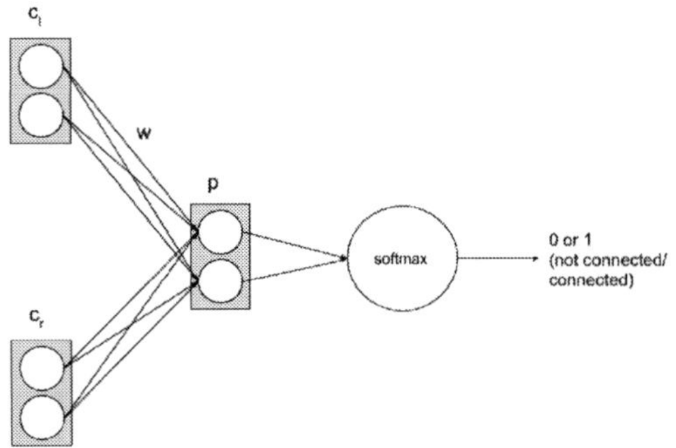

Figure 5: The Discourse Structure Neural Net

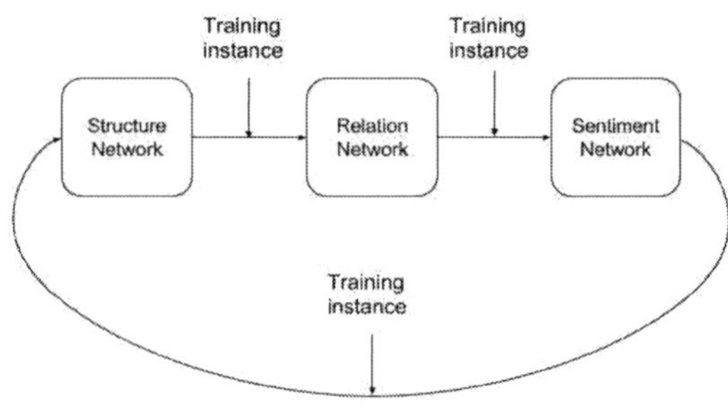

Figure 6: Multi-tasking

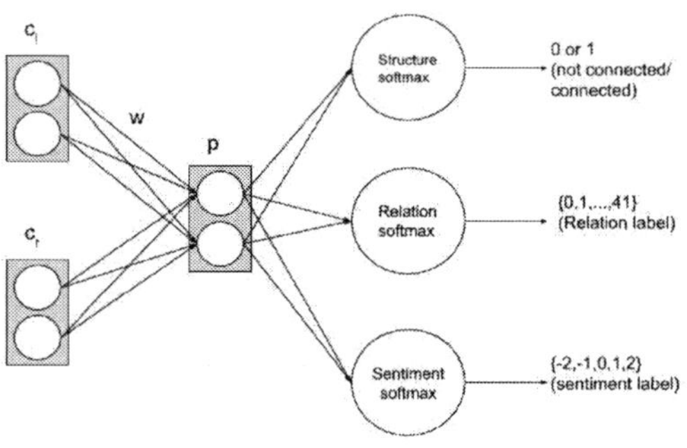

Figure 7: Multi-tasking Network

course Unit that are determined to be connected in the Discourse Tree and learns the sentiment label for the parent node. This Neural net also shares the same structure as the one in Figure 5.

4.3 Joining Neural Nets

Our hypothesis in creating a joint model is that the accuracy of prediction obtained in a joint design would be higher than the accuracy of prediction coming from independent Neural Nets applied to each task. We explore two ways of creating a joint model. For both approaches, we train three neural nets (Discourse Structure, Discourse Relation and Sentiment Neural Nets) that interact with one another for improved training. The input to the Structure net are all possible pairs of text spans that can be connected in a Discourse Tree. The input to the Relation and Sentiment nets are the pairs of text spans that are determined to be connected by the Structure net.

Inspired by **Multitasking** (Collobert and Weston, 2008), our goal is to find a representation for the input that will benefit all the tasks that need to be solved. Since the first layer in a Neural Net learns relevant features from the input embedding, in this approach, the first layer is shared between the three Neural Nets and training is achieved in a stochastic manner by looping over the three tasks. As shown in Figure 6, at each time step, one of the tasks is selected along with a random training example for that task. Afterwards, the neural net corresponding to this task is updated by taking a gradient step with respect to the chosen example. The end product of this design is a joint input representation that could benefit both Sentiment Analysis and Discourse Parsing.

Inspired by **Pre-training Neural Nets** (Erhan et al., 2010), in this approach we study how the parameters of one Neural Net after training can be used as a form of initialization for the network applied to the other task. As shown in Figure 8, in this setting, we first fully train the Discourse Structure Neural Net, then the weights from this trained net are used to initialize the Discourse Relation Neural Net and once this net is fully trained, its weights are used to initialize the weights of the Discourse Structure Neural Net again. After another round of training the Discourse Structure Neural Net, its weights are used to initialize the Sentiment Neural Net. After training the Sentiment Neural Net, its weights are again used to initialize the Structure Neural Net. [4]

5 Training and Evaluating the Models

All the neural models presented in this paper were implemented using the TensorFlow python pack-

---

[4]We experimented with 2,3 and 10 iterations using 10-fold cross validation on the datasets and achieved best results with 3 iterations, which appears to be a good compromise between accuracy and training time.

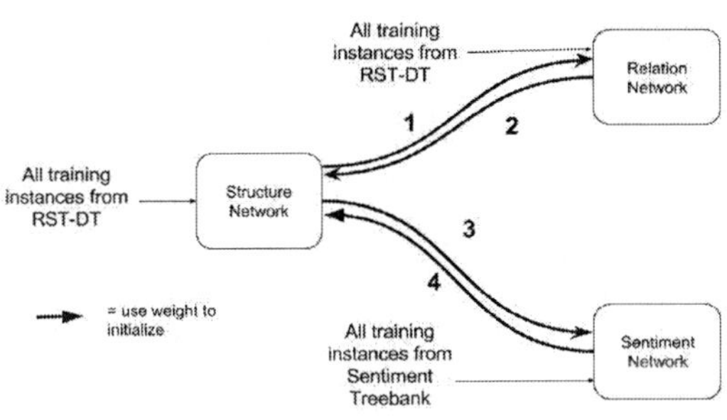

Figure 8: Using the weights of one network as a form of pre-training for another network

Approach	Span	Nuclearity	Relation
Discourse Parser (Before Joining)	93.37	73.38	57.05
Joined Model Pre-training	**94.35**	74.92	58.82
Joined Model Multi-tasking	94.31	**75.91***	**60.91***

Table 1: Discourse Parsing results based on manual discourse segmentation

Relation \ Setting	Individual	Pre-training	Multi-tasking
Comparison	18.97	20.87	27.08
Contrast	15.19	17.74	20.83
Cause	7.6	8.11	8.61
Average	13.92	15.57	18.84

Table 2: Contrastive Relation Prediction results under different training settings

age (Abadi et al., 2015). We minimize the cross-entropy error using the Adam optimizer and L2-regularization on the set of weights. For the individual models (before joining), we use 200 training epochs and a batch size of 100.

We evaluate our models using 10-fold cross validation on the sentiment treebank and on RST-DT. In Table 1 and Table 3, a star indicates that there is statistical significance with a p-value less than 0.05. The significance is with respect to the joint model vs the model before joining. The results for Discourse Parsing are shown in Table 1. To build the most probable tree, a CKY-like bottom-up parsing algorithm that uses dynamic programming to compute the most likely parses is applied (Joty et al., 2015) and we have used the 41 relations outlined in (Mann and Thompson, 1988) for training and evaluation of the Relation prediction. From the results, we see some improvement on Discourse Structure prediction when we are using a joint model but the improvement is statistically significant only for the Nuclearity and Relation predictions. The improvements on the Relation predictions were mainly on the Contrastive set (Bhatia et al., 2015), specifically the class of *Contrast*, *Comparison* and *Cause* relations as defined in (Mann and Thompson, 1988). The result for each of these relations under different training settings are shown in Table 2. Notice that the accuracies may seem low, but because we train over 41 classes of relations, a random prediction would result in 2.43% accuracy. Among the contrastive relations, the *Problem-Solution* did not improve due to the fact that this relation is hardly seen at the sentence level. This confirms our hypothesis that knowing the sentiment of the two Discourse

Units that are connected in a discourse tree can help with the identification of the discourse relation that holds between them.

For the task of Sentiment Analysis, the results are shown in Table 3. To train the model, we use the five classes of sentiment used in (Socher et al., 2013)[5]. We measure the accuracy of prediction in two different settings. In the fine grained setting we compute the accuracy of exact match across five classes. In the Positive/Negative setting, if the prediction and the target had the same sign, they were considered equal. Notice that this is different from training a classifier for binary classification, which is a much easier task (see (Bhatia et al., 2015)). The difference in accuracy between these two settings signals that distinguishing between *very positive* and *positive* and distinguishing between *very negative* and *negative* is rather hard. The results of sentiment shown in Table 3 are also consistent with our hypothesis. When jointly trained with Discourse Parsing, we can get a better performance on labeling nodes of the Discourse Tree with sentiment labels compared to an individual sentiment analyzer applied to a Discourse Tree.

Interestingly, if we compare the two joint models across both tasks it appears that Multi-tasking does better that Pre-training in all cases except for discourse structure. A possible explanation is that by transferring weights from one network to another (as done in Pre-training), the neural net starts learning with a possibly better initialization of the weights. However Multi-tasking performs a joint

---

[5] {*very negative, negative, neutral, positive, very positive*}

Approach	Fine grained		Positive Negative	
	All	Root	All	Root
Sentiment Analyzer (Before Joining)	43.37	40.6	52.86	51.27
Joined Model Pre-training	42.46	40.36	53.82	53.15
Joined Model Multi-tasking	**45.49***	**44.82***	**55.52***	**54.72***

Table 3: Sentiment Analysis over Discourse Tree

learning at the finer granularity of single training instances and so an improvement in learning one task immediately affects the next.

All results in Table 1 and 3 were obtained by setting the dimension d of the compressed vectors to 100. Experimentally, we found that the performance of the model was rather stable for $d \in \{1200, 600, 300, 100\}$ and was substantially lower for $d \in \{50, 25\}$.

In terms of actual runtime, Pre-training and the individual models are an order of magnitude faster than the Multi-tasking model. This is because even though they require a larger number of epochs to converge (200 for individual, vs 6 for Multi-tasking), they can be trained in parallel. Notice that training and testing of the networks is done on Sentiment Treebank for sentiment analysis and on RST-DT for discourse parsing. (Joty et al., 2015)'s Discourse parser was run on Sentiment Treebank to get the sentiment annotation at the granularity required for the joint model with discourse. However, having a gold dataset of sentiment labels corresponding to discourse units could further improve the results.

6 Comparison With Previous Work

Several differences between this work and previous approaches make direct comparisons challenging and possibly not very informative.

(Socher et al., 2013) use syntactic trees, as opposed to discourse trees, as recursive structures for training. Thus we cannot compare with his "All"-level results. For "Root"-level, (Socher et al., 2013) reports 45.7% fine-grained sentiment accuracy compared to 44.82% of our Multi-tasking. This difference is unlikely to be significant and the sentiment annotation of syntactic structure is definitely more costly than one at the EDU level.

(Bhatia et al., 2015) focuses on document level sentiment analysis, using bag-of-word features for EDUs; and only training a binary model while assuming the discourse tree as given, which is very different from our approach.

Since our work focuses on sentence-level discourse parsing, we cannot compare with (Li et al., 2014) because they only report overall results without differentiating sentence vs document level.

Finally, (Joty et al., 2015) achieves better performance on sentence level. First, we believe that with more training data, as it has been shown with other NLP tasks, we would eventually outperform CODRA. Second, the goal of our work is not to beat the state of the art on each single task, but to show how the two tasks can be jointly performed in a neural model.

7 Conclusion

Discourse Parsing and Sentiment Analysis are two fundamental NLP tasks that have been shown to be mutually beneficial. Evidence from previous work indicates that information extracted from Discourse Trees can help with Sentiment Analysis and likewise, knowing the sentiment of two pieces of text can help with identification of discourse relationships between them. In this paper, we show how synergies between these two tasks can be exploited in a joint neural model. The first challenge entailed learning meaningful vector representations for text spans that are the inputs for the two tasks. Since the dimension of vanilla skip-thought vectors is too high compared to the size of our corpora, in order to simultaneously reduce the dimensionality and to produce vectors that are meaningful for our tasks, we devised task specific neural compressors, that take in Skip-thought vectors and produce much lower dimensional vectors.

Next, we designed three independent Recursive Neural Nets classifiers; one for Discourse Structure prediction, one for Discourse Relation prediction and one for Sentiment Analysis. After that, we explored two ways of creating joint models from these three networks: Pre-training and Multitasking. Our experimental results show that such models do capture synergies among the three tasks with the Multi-tasking approach being the most successful, confirming that latent Discourse features can help boost the performance of a neural sentiment analyzer and that latent Sentiment features can help with identifying contrastive relations between text spans.

In the short term, we plan to verify how syntactic information could be explicitly leveraged in the three task-specific networks as well as in the joint models. Then, our investigation will move from making predictions about a single sentence to the much more challenging task of dealing with multisentential text, which will likely require not only more complex models, but also models with scalable time performance in both learning and inference. Next, we intend to study how pre-training and multitasking could be both exploited simultaneously in the same model, something that to the best of our knowledge has not been tried before. Finally, as another venue for future research, we plan to explore how sentiment analysis and discourse parsing could be modeled jointly with text summarization, since these three tasks can arguably inform each other and therefore benefit from joint neural models similar to the ones described in this paper.

References

Martín Abadi, Ashish Agarwal, Paul Barham, Eugene Brevdo, Zhifeng Chen, Craig Citro, Greg S. Corrado, Andy Davis, Jeffrey Dean, Matthieu Devin, Sanjay Ghemawat, Ian Goodfellow, Andrew Harp, Geoffrey Irving, Michael Isard, Yangqing Jia, Rafal Jozefowicz, Lukasz Kaiser, Manjunath Kudlur, Josh Levenberg, Dan Mané, Rajat Monga, Sherry Moore, Derek Murray, Chris Olah, Mike Schuster, Jonathon Shlens, Benoit Steiner, Ilya Sutskever, Kunal Talwar, Paul Tucker, Vincent Vanhoucke, Vijay Vasudevan, Fernanda Viégas, Oriol Vinyals, Pete Warden, Martin Wattenberg, Martin Wicke, Yuan Yu, and Xiaoqiang Zheng. 2015. TensorFlow: Large-scale machine learning on heterogeneous systems. Software available from tensorflow.org. http://tensorflow.org/.

Parminder Bhatia, Yangfeng Ji, and Jacob Eisenstein. 2015. Better document-level sentiment analysis from rst discourse parsing. In *Proceedings of Empirical Methods for Natural Language Processing (EMNLP)*. http://www.aclweb.org/anthology/D/D15/D15-1263.pdf.

Lynn Carlson and Daniel Marcu. 2001. Discourse tagging reference manual. *ISI Technical Report ISI-TR-545* 54:56.

Lynn Carlson, Mary Ellen Okurowski, and Daniel Marcu. 2002. *RST discourse treebank*. Linguistic Data Consortium, University of Pennsylvania.

Yu-An Chung, Hsuan-Tien Lin, and Shao-Wen Yang. 2015. Cost-aware pre-training for multiclass cost-sensitive deep learning. *arXiv preprint arXiv:1511.09337* .

Ronan Collobert and Jason Weston. 2008. A unified architecture for natural language processing: Deep neural networks with multitask learning. In *Proceedings of the 25th international conference on Machine learning*. ACM, pages 160–167.

Dumitru Erhan, Yoshua Bengio, Aaron Courville, Pierre-Antoine Manzagol, Pascal Vincent, and Samy Bengio. 2010. Why does unsupervised pre-training help deep learning? *Journal of Machine Learning Research* 11(Feb):625–660.

Vanessa Wei Feng and Graeme Hirst. 2014. A linear-time bottom-up discourse parser with constraints and post-editing. In *Proceedings of the 52nd Annual Meeting of the Association for Computational Linguistics (Volume 1: Long Papers)*. Association for Computational Linguistics, Baltimore, Maryland, pages 511–521. http://www.aclweb.org/anthology/P14-1048.

Shima Gerani, Yashar Mehdad, Giuseppe Carenini, Raymond T Ng, and Bita Nejat. 2014. Abstractive summarization of product reviews using discourse structure. In *EMNLP*. pages 1602–1613.

Francisco Guzmán, Shafiq R Joty, Lluís Màrquez, and Preslav Nakov. 2014. Using discourse structure improves machine translation evaluation. In *ACL (1)*. pages 687–698.

Shafiq Joty, Giuseppe Carenini, and Raymond T Ng. 2015. Codra: A novel discriminative framework for rhetorical analysis. *Computational Linguistics* .

Takuhiro Kaneko, Kaoru Hiramatsu, and Kunio Kashino. 2016. Adaptive visual feedback generation for facial expression improvement with multitask deep neural networks. In *Proceedings of the 2016 ACM on Multimedia Conference*. ACM, pages 327–331.

Ryan Kiros, Yukun Zhu, Ruslan R Salakhutdinov, Richard Zemel, Raquel Urtasun, Antonio Torralba, and Sanja Fidler. 2015. Skip-thought vectors. In *Advances in neural information processing systems*. pages 3294–3302.

Angeliki Lazaridou, Ivan Titov, and Caroline Sporleder. 2013. A bayesian model for joint unsupervised induction of sentiment, aspect and discourse representations. In *ACL (1)*. pages 1630–1639.

Jiwei Li, Rumeng Li, and Eduard H Hovy. 2014. Recursive deep models for discourse parsing. In *EMNLP*. pages 2061–2069.

Pengfei Liu, Xipeng Qiu, and Xuanjing Huang. 2016a. Recurrent neural network for text classification with multi-task learning. *arXiv preprint arXiv:1605.05101* .

Yang Liu, Sujian Li, Xiaodong Zhang, and Zhifang Sui. 2016b. Implicit discourse relation classification via multi-task neural networks. *arXiv preprint arXiv:1603.02776* .

Annie Louis, Aravind Joshi, and Ani Nenkova. 2010. Discourse indicators for content selection in summarization. In *Proceedings of the 11th Annual Meeting of the Special Interest Group on Discourse and Dialogue*. Association for Computational Linguistics, pages 147–156.

William C Mann and Sandra A Thompson. 1988. Rhetorical structure theory: Toward a functional theory of text organization. *Text-Interdisciplinary Journal for the Study of Discourse* 8(3):243–281.

Daniel Marcu and Kevin Knight. 2001. Discourse parsing and summarization. US Patent App. 09/854,301.

Mitchell P Marcus, Mary Ann Marcinkiewicz, and Beatrice Santorini. 1993. Building a large annotated corpus of english: The penn treebank. *Computational linguistics* 19(2):313–330.

Thomas Meyer and Andrei Popescu-Belis. 2012. Using sense-labeled discourse connectives for statistical machine translation. In *Proceedings of the Joint Workshop on Exploiting Synergies between Information Retrieval and Machine Translation (ESIRMT) and Hybrid Approaches to Machine Translation (HyTra)*. Association for Computational Linguistics, pages 129–138.

Tomas Mikolov, Ilya Sutskever, Kai Chen, Greg S Corrado, and Jeff Dean. 2013. Distributed representations of words and phrases and their compositionality. In *Advances in neural information processing systems*. pages 3111–3119.

Tetsuji Nakagawa, Kentaro Inui, and Sadao Kurohashi. 2010. Dependency tree-based sentiment classification using crfs with hidden variables. In *Human Language Technologies: The 2010 Annual Conference of the North American Chapter of the Association for Computational Linguistics*. Association for Computational Linguistics, pages 786–794.

Bo Pang, Lillian Lee, et al. 2008. Opinion mining and sentiment analysis. *Foundations and Trends® in Information Retrieval* 2(1–2):1–135.

Vassiliki Rentoumi, Stefanos Petrakis, Manfred Klenner, George A Vouros, and Vangelis Karkaletsis. 2010. United we stand: Improving sentiment analysis by joining machine learning and rule based methods. In *LREC*.

Sara Rosenthal, Alan Ritter, Preslav Nakov, and Veselin Stoyanov. 2014. Semeval-2014 task 9: Sentiment analysis in twitter. In *Proceedings of the 8th international workshop on semantic evaluation (SemEval 2014)*. Dublin, Ireland, pages 73–80.

Seyyede Zohreh Seyyedsalehi and Seyyed Ali Seyyedsalehi. 2015. A fast and efficient pre-training method based on layer-by-layer maximum discrimination for deep neural networks. *Neurocomputing* 168:669–680.

Richard Socher, Alex Perelygin, Jean Y Wu, Jason Chuang, Christopher D Manning, Andrew Y Ng, Christopher Potts, et al. 2013. Recursive deep models for semantic compositionality over a sentiment treebank. *Proceedings of the conference on empirical methods in natural language processing (EMNLP)* 1631:1642.

Suzan Verberne, Lou Boves, Nelleke Oostdijk, and Peter-Arno Coppen. 2007. Evaluating discourse-based answer extraction for why-question answering. In *Proceedings of the 30th annual international ACM SIGIR conference on Research and development in information retrieval*. ACM, pages 735–736.

Predicting Causes of Reformulation in Intelligent Assistants

Shumpei Sano, Nobuhiro Kaji, and Manabu Sassano
Yahoo Japan Corporation
1-3 Kioicho, Chiyoda-ku, Tokyo 102-8282, Japan
{shsano, nkaji, msassano}@yahoo-corp.jp

Abstract

Intelligent assistants (IAs) such as Siri and Cortana conversationally interact with users and execute a wide range of actions (e.g., searching the Web, setting alarms, and chatting). IAs can support these actions through the combination of various components such as automatic speech recognition, natural language understanding, and language generation. However, the complexity of these components hinders developers from determining which component causes an error. To remove this hindrance, we focus on reformulation, which is a useful signal of user dissatisfaction, and propose a method to predict the reformulation causes. We evaluate the method using the user logs of a commercial IA. The experimental results have demonstrated that features designed to detect the error of a specific component improve the performance of reformulation cause detection.

1 Introduction

Intelligent assistants (IAs) such as Apple's Siri and Cortana have gained considerable attention as mobile devices have become prevalent in our daily lives. They are hybrids of search and dialogue systems that conversationally interact with users and execute a wide range of actions (e.g., searching the Web, setting alarms, making phone calls and chatting). IAs can support these actions through the combination of various components such as automatic speech recognition (ASR), natural language understanding (NLU), and language generation (LG). One major concern in the development of commercial IAs is how to speed up the cycle of the system performance enhancement. The

enhancement process is often performed by manually investigating user logs, finding erroneous data, detecting the component responsible for that error, and updating the component. As IAs are composed of various components, the error cause detection becomes an obstacle in the manual process. In this paper, we attempt to automate the error cause detection to overcome this obstacle.

One approach to do this is to utilize user feedback. In this work, we focus on reformulation, i.e., when a user modifies the previous input. In web search and dialogue systems, reformulation is known as an implicit feedback signal that the user could not receive a desired response to the previous input due to one or more system components failing. In IAs, ASR error is a major cause of reformulation and has been extensively studied (Hassan et al., 2015; Schmitt and Ultes, 2015).

Besides correcting ASR errors, users of IAs reformulate their previous utterances when they encounter NLU errors, LG errors, and so on. For example, when a user utters "alarm", the NLU component may mistakenly conclude that s/he wants to perform a Web search, and consequently the system shows the search results for "alarm." Sarikaya (2017) reported that only 12% of the errors in an IA system are related to ASR components, which is the smallest percentage across six components. They also reported that the NLU component is the biggest source of errors (24%). Therefore, the errors related to the other components should not be ignored to improve system performance. However, previous work mainly focused on reformulation caused by ASR error, and reformulation caused by the other components has received little attention.

In this work, we propose a method to predict reformulation causes, i.e., detect the component responsible for causing the reformulation in IAs. Features are divided into several categories mainly

Proceedings of the SIGDIAL 2017 Conference, pages 299–309,
Saarbrücken, Germany, 15-17 August 2017. ©2017 Association for Computational Linguistics

on the basis of their relations with the components in an IA. The experiments demonstrate that these features can improve the error detection performances of corresponding components. The proposed method which combines all features sets, outperforms the baseline, which uses component-independent features such as session information and reformulation related information.

Our work makes the following contributions. First, we investigate the reformulation causes among the components in IAs from real data of a commercial IA. Second, we create dataset of human annotated data obtained from a commercial IA. Finally, we develop the method to predict reformulation causes in IAs.

2　Related Work

Three research areas are related to our work, and the most closely related is reformulation (also called correction). As reformulation is frequently caused by system errors, the second related area is error analysis and error detection in search or dialogue systems. The third area is system evaluation in search or dialogue systems. Reformulation is a useful feature for system evaluation.

2.1　Reformulation and Correction

Users of search or dialogue systems often reformulate their previous inputs when trying to obtain better results (Hassan et al., 2013) or correct errors (e.g., ASR errors) (Jiang et al., 2013; Hassan et al., 2015). Our research focuses on the latter category of reformulation, which relates to correction. Studies on correction have mainly focused on automatic detection of correction (Levow, 1998; Hirschberg et al., 2001; Litman et al., 2006). Some studies have also tried to improve system performance beyond correction detection. Shokouhi et al. (2016) constructed a large-scale dataset of correction pairs from search logs and showed that the database enables ASR performance to be improved.

The research most related to ours is that of Hassan et al. (2015). In addition to reformulation detection, they proposed a method to detect whether a reformulation is caused by ASR error or not. We extend their study to determine which component (e.g., ASR, NLU, and LG) is responsible for the error.

2.2　Error Analysis and Error Detection

Besides reformulation, researchers have studied system errors in search or dialogue systems. For example, Meena et al. (2015) and Hirst et al. (1994) focused on miscommunication in spoken dialogue systems and Feild et al. (2010) focused on user frustrations in search systems. In this paper, we focus on predicting the cause of errors among the different components in IAs. In spoken dialogue systems, Georgiladakis et al. (2016) reported that ASR error is the most frequent cause of errors among seven components (65.9% in Let's Go datasets (Raux et al., 2005). On the other hand, Sarikaya (2017) reported that ASR error is the least frequent cause of errors among six components (12% in an IA). These results indicate that errors in IA have various causes and that the causes other than ASR error also should not be ignored. In this paper, we focus on reformulation and propose a method to automatically detect the reformulation causes in IAs.

2.3　System Evaluation

Users of the search or conversational systems often reformulate their inputs when they are dissatisfied with the system responses to their previous inputs. Therefore, reformulation is a useful signal of user dissatisfaction and information related to reformulation has been widely used as a feature to automatically evaluate system performance in web search (Hassan et al., 2013), dialogue (Schmitt and Ultes, 2015), and IA systems (Jiang et al., 2015; Kiseleva et al., 2016; Sano et al., 2016). However, these studies paid little attention to detecting causes of user dissatisfaction. Information of these causes is beneficial to the developers for both improving system design and engineering feature of automatic evaluation methods. Thus, we propose a method to automatically detect the reformulation causes in IAs.

3　Reformulation Cause Prediction

In this section, we describe the task of reformulation cause prediction in IAs.

3.1　Definition

First, we define notations used in this paper.

U_1 : The user utterance

R : The corresponding system response to U_1

Label	U1	R	U2
No error	What's the weather?	It will be sunny today.	What's the weather tomorrow?
ASR error	What's the.	Sorry?	What's the weather?
NLU error	Alarm.	Here are the search results for "Alarm".	Open alarm.
LG error	What's your name?	I'm twenty years old.	Tell me your name.
Unsupported action	Play videos of cats.	Sorry, I can't support that action.	Search for videos of cats.
Endpoint error	Search Obama's age.	No results found in for "Obama's age".	Search Obama.
Uninterpretable input	Aaaa.	Sorry?	Aaa.

Table 1: List of annotation labels. U1, R, and U2 are example conversations.

Label	Rate	Error Rate
No error	38.7%	N.A.
ASR error	31.7%	57.2%
NLU error	17.3%	31.2%
LG error	5.1%	9.2%
Unsupported action	0.8%	1.4%
Endpoint error	0.5%	0.9%
Uninterpretable input	5.9%	N.A.

Table 2: Percentage of annotation labels in our dataset. Error rate is calculated using labels related to reformulation causes.

U_2 : The next utterance to U_1

Reformulation : A pair of (U_1, U_2) is a *reformulation* if U_2 is uttered to modify U_1 in order to satisfy the same intent as in U_1

To define the *reformulation*, we referred to the definition in the work of Hassan et al. (2015) that is used for voice search systems.

3.2 Corpus

We constructed a dataset of user logs of a commercial IA[1] for analyzing and predicting reformulation causes. We randomly sampled 1,000 utterance pairs of (U_1, U_2) and corresponding information with the following conditions.

- U_1 and U_2 are text or voice inputs

- Interval time between U_1 and U_2 is equal to or less than 30 minutes (the same as in previous research (Jiang et al., 2015; Sano et al., 2016).)

- Samples where normalized Levenshtein edit-distance (Li and Liu, 2007) between U_1 and U_2 is equal to 0 (i.e., U_1 and U_2 are identical utterances) or more than 0.5 are excluded

- U_1 and U_2 were both uttered in June, 2016

With the first three conditions, we can exclude utterances that are not reformulations and can focus on reformulation. We calculated character-based, rather than word-based, edit-distance (white spaces are ignored), because we found word-based edit-distances sometimes fail to identify reformulation pairs such as "what's up" and "whatsapp."

All samples in the dataset are manually annotated with the label of the reformulation causes between different components in IAs. Table 1 lists the annotation labels. Here, we explain them. In this paper, we assume an IA system that has the components shown in Figure 1. *ASR error* means that the ASR component misrecognizes U_1. *NLU error* means that ASR is correct but the NLU component misunderstands the intent of U_1 or fails to fill one or more slots correctly. *LG error* means that ASR and NLU are correct but the LG component fails to generate appropriate response. This error mainly caused by response generation failure in chat intent. Note that the NLU component only determines whether or not an utterance is chat intent and the LG component generates appropriate response of the utterance in our system. Therefore, we consider that the case shown in Table 1 is LG error rather than NLU error. *Endpoint error* means that endpoint API (application program interface) fails to respond with correct information. *Unsupported action* means that the system cannot support the action that the user expects and so cannot generate a correct response. *No error* means that a sample contains no error. Submitting similar utterances to obtain better results in search intents (e.g., U_1 is "Search for image of strawberry wallpaper" and U_2 is "Search for image of strawberry") and using similar functions (e.g., U_1 is "Turn on Wi-Fi" and U_2 is "Turn off Wi-Fi") are typical utterances in this label. Finally, *Uninterpretable input* means that U_1 is uninterpretable.

As expert knowledge about the components of

---

[1]Because the IA supports only Japanese, all utterances are made in Japanese. In this paper, we present English translations rather than the original Japanese to facilitate non-Japanese readers' understanding.

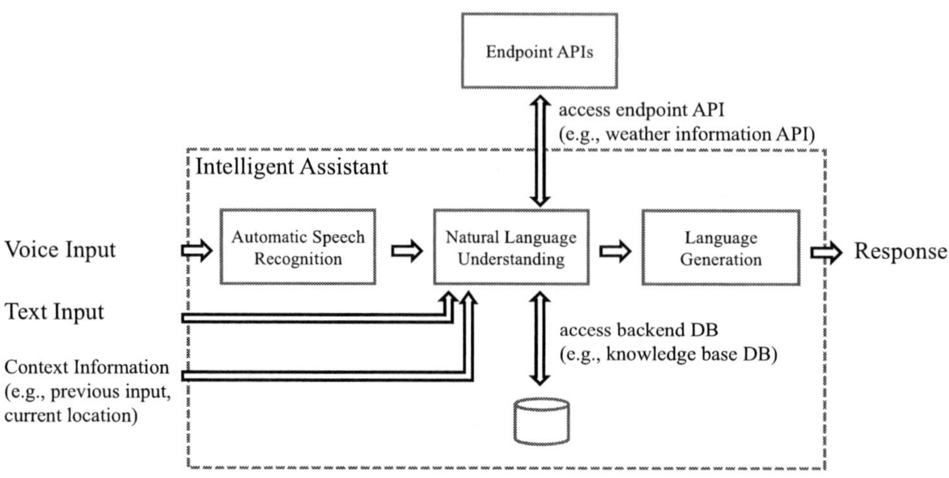

Figure 1: Components and processes of typical IA system.

IAs is required for the annotation, annotation is performed by an expert developer of the commercial IA. Figure 2 shows the annotation flowchart. First, we listen to the voice of U_1 and read the texts of U_1, R, and U_2. Text information is used to support guessing the user intent of U_1. *Uninterpretable input* such as one-word utterances and misrecognized input of background noises is distinguished in this phase. Next, *ASR error* samples are distinguished using transcription of U_1. Afterwards, *No error* samples are distinguished if R of the samples correctly satisfies the intent of U_1. Finally, one of the other four error causes is annotated to the remaining samples. The annotation results are shown in Table 2. We ignored the cases where the latter components could recover from the errors generated by the former components because these cases were rarely observed. For example, a percentage that the NLU component could recover from ASR errors is 1.2% in our dataset.

3.3 Discussion on Annotated Labels

Here, we discuss the annotation results and which labels should be included or excluded in reformulation cause prediction. To come to the point, we do not use *Uninterpretable input*, *Unsupported action*, or *Endpoint error* for reformulation cause prediction. We will explain why these labels are excluded.

As shown in Table 2, the most frequent cause is *ASR error*. This result differs from that of Sarikaya (2017) in which ASR error is the least frequent cause. The reason for the difference is that Sarikaya (2017) used whole samples, whereas we use only reformulation samples. These results indicate that the reformulation tendency when a user encounters an error differs depending on the cause of errors. For example, the percentage of unsupported actions is 1.4%, which is much smaller than that reported by Sarikaya (2017), 14%. This finding indicate that when users encounter a response that notifies them that the action they expected was unsupported, they would rather give up than reformulate their previous utterances. The same is true for endpoint error.

Next, we discuss which labels should be included or excluded in the task. First, *Uninterpretable input* should be excluded because these utterances have no appropriate responses and become noise for the task. We also exclude *Unsupported action* and *Endpoint error*. An IA do not require user feedback for these errors because no components in the IA is responsible for the errors and the IA is aware the error causes in these labels. In addition, the benefits of detecting these errors are limited because these errors are rarely observed in reformulation as shown in Table 2. In conclusion, we use *No error*, *ASR error*, *NLU error*, and *LG error* for the task.

302

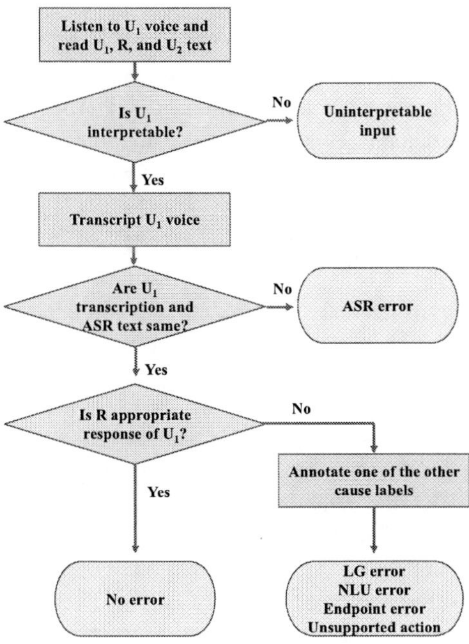

Figure 2: Annotation flowchart.

3.4 Task Definition

Here, we describe the task of reformulation cause prediction. Our goal is to predict the reformulation cause of U_1 between different components using the information from U_1 and U_2. Specifically, we predict one of the four labels in Table 1, *No error*, *ASR error*, *NLU error*, and *LG error*. For example, we want to predict as *NLU error* from the conversation logs of (U_1:"Alarm.", R:"Here are the search results for Alarm.", U_2:"Open alarm."). These labels are useful for IA developers to improve system performance.

4 Analysis

We analyze the statistical differences between reformulation causes prior to the experiments and exploit the findings for engineering features.

4.1 Analysis of Correction Types

Here, we analyze the correction types when an IA user is trying to correct a previous utterance. We simplify the definition of (Swerts et al., 2000) and define four correction types: ADD, $OMIT$, PAR, and $OTHER$. Their definitions are as follows.

ADD A sequence of words is added to U_1.

Type	Example
ADD	What's the weather in Nara today?
OMIT	What's the weather?
PAR	How about the weather today?
OTHER	How about the humidity today?

Table 3: Example corrections of "What's the weather today?" in each correction type.

	ADD	OMIT	PAR	OTHER
No error	27.1	7.2	58.1	7.4
ASR error	7.5	6.0	74.2	12.3
NLU error	27.9	19.8	41.9	10.5
LG error	23.5	19.6	47.1	9.8

Table 4: Distribution of correction types (%).

OMIT A sequence of words in U_1 is omitted in U_2.

PAR A sequence of words in U_1 changes into another sequence of words in U_2.

OTHER Match none of preceding correction types.

Note that U_1 and U_2 have at least one word in common in ADD, $OMIT$, and PAR. Table 3 shows examples of each correction type.

Table 4 presents the distribution of correction types. As shown in Table 4, the percentage of PAR in *ASR error* is higher than those of other correction types. In *No error*, the percentages of ADD and PAR are large. We can also see that *NLU error* and *LG error* have similar distributions and that $OMIT$ is more frequent than the other correction types. This is because when users encounter *NLU error* or *LG error*, they use different types of corrections depending on the situation: adding words to clarify their intent, omitting words that seem to be the noise for the system, and so on. We expect correction types to be useful for detecting reformulation causes as the distribution of correction types differs for different error types.

4.2 Analysis of Input Types

Here, we analyze the correlation between error causes and input types. Input types sometimes differ between U_1 and U_2. For example, Jiang et al. (2013) have reported that users switch from voice inputs to text inputs when they encounter ASR errors. Table 5 presents the distribution of input

	V2V	T2T	V2T	T2V
No error	75.2	23.5	1.3	0.0
ASR error	94.6	0.0	5.4	0.0
NLU error	70.5	23.8	1.7	4.6
LG error	76.5	23.5	0.0	0.0

Table 5: Distribution of input type switches (%). For example, V2T means input type of U_1 is voice input and that of U_2 is text input.

type switches. As shown in Table 5, distribution of input type switches differs slightly among the error causes. As Jiang et al. (2013) have shown, voice-to-text switches are more frequent for *ASR error* than in other causes. We can also see that both text-to-voice and voice-to-text switches are observed for *NLU error*. Compared with these causes, input type switches are rarely observed for *No error*. Interestingly, text-to-voice switches are not observed for *No error* either. On the other hand, small number of voice-to-text switches are observed for *No error*. We guess that some users switch input from voice to text when they submit similar query by copy and paste the part of ASR result of their previous utterances. These findings suggest that users tend to keep using the same input type while their intents are correctly recognized. Unlike the other causes, no input type switches are observed for *LG error*. We expect this is due to insufficient data.

5 Features

We divide the features into five categories by their functions. Session features and reformulation features, which are useful for reformulation prediction (Hassan et al., 2015) and system evaluation (Jiang et al., 2015), are designed to distinguish between errors or non-errors. Though these features are also useful for reformulation cause detection, these are not specialized for detecting reformulation causes. ASR, NLU, and LG features are designed to detect reformulation causes related to their corresponding components from causes related to the other components. Table 6 lists the features.

5.1 Session Features

Features related to session information belong to this category. In *InputType*, 1 if an utterance is text input and 0 if an utterance is voice input (Hassan et al., 2015). In a web search system, the interval time between inputs is a useful indicator of search success (Huang and Efthimiadis, 2009). Therefore, *Interval* is useful for distinguishing *No error* from the other labels. If *CharLen* or *WordLen* of the utterance is long or short, the utterance possibly contains noise information or lacks information for the system.

5.2 Reformulation Features

Features related to reformulation belong to this category. Features in this category are widely used in previous methods such as query reformulation detection (Hassan et al., 2015), error detection (Litman et al., 2006), and system performance evaluation (Jiang et al., 2015). The correction type t of *Correction(t)* is one of ADD, OMIT, PAR, or OTHER described in Section 4.1. As shown in Section 4.1, the distribution of correction types differs among annotation labels. Therefore, *Correction(t)* is useful information for predicting reformulation causes. *Voice2Text* and *Text2Voice* are designed to distinguish *ASR error* and *NLU error* from other errors on the basis of analysis in Section 4.2.

5.3 ASR Features

Features related to the ASR component belong to this category. Low *ASRConf* indicates speech recognition errors (Hassan et al., 2015). The probability of misrecognition increases as the recognized voice length increases (Hassan et al., 2015). Therefore, long *VoiceLen* may be one signal related to ASR error. Note that these features are calculated only when the input type of the utterance is voice input.

5.4 NLU Features

Features related to the NLU component belong to this category. When a user's intent in U_1 is misunderstood and that in U_2 is correctly understood, recognized intents or filled slots between the utterances are different. On the other hand, when a user's intent in U_1 is correctly understood by the system, the user sometimes uses similar functions subsequently (e.g., requesting weather information for Osaka after requesting it for Tokyo.). Therefore, *DifferentIntent* and *DifferentSlot* are useful to distinguish *NLU error* from the other errors, and *SameIntent* is useful to distinguish *No error* from the other errors. Note that the intents used in these features are the intents recognized by

Category	Name	Definition
Session	**CharLen***	Number of characters in utterance.
	WordLen*	Number of words in utterance.
	InputType*	1 if utterance is text input else 0
	Interval	Time between U_1 and U_2
Reformulation	**EditDistance**	Normalized Levenshtein edit distance between U_1 and U_2
	Correction(t)	1 if U_2 is correction type t of U_1
	CommonWords	Number of words appearing in both U_1 and U_2
	Voice2Text	1 if U_1 is voice input and U_2 is text input
	Text2Voice	1 if U_1 is text input and U_2 is voice input
ASR	**ASRConf***	Speech recognition confidence
	VoiceLen*	Speech recognition time
NLU	**SameIntent**	1 if recognized intents between U_1 and U_2 are same
	DifferentIntent	1 if recognized intents between U_1 and U_2 are different
	DifferentSlot	1 if some slots in U_2 are different from those in U_1
	IntentType(t)*	1 if recognized intent of utterance is t
LG	**DialogAct**(t)*	1 if utterance contains phrases in dialogue act t

Table 6: List of features. Features marked with "*" were computed for both U_1 and U_2.

Type	Examples
Praise	Wow!; Great.
Thanking	Thanks.; Thank you.
Backchannel	I see.; Yeah.
Accept	Yes.; Exactly.
Abuse	Shit.; Shut up.
Reject	No.; Not like that.
IDU	What do you mean?

Table 7: List of dialog acts.

the IA system such as weather information, web search, application launch, and chat.

5.5 LG Features

Features related to the LG component belong to this category. If users expect the system to chat, their utterances may contain phrases commonly used in chatting. *DialogAct(t)* is designed to detect these phrases in the utterance. User utterances of chat intent in IAs have unique characterictics (e.g., some users curse at the intelligent assistants (Akasaki and Kaji, 2017)). We defined seven types of dialogue acts that are common in chats between users and IAs, as listed in Table 7. Frequently occurring phrases in the user log of the commercial IA are used for the phrases of each dialogue act.

6 Experiments

6.1 Experimental Settings

The experimental settings of reformulation cause prediction are as follows.

- The dataset described in Section 3.2 is used for evaluation. It contains 928 samples.

- We evaluate the performance of the model with 10-fold cross validation.

- We train the model using a linear SVM classifier with the features described in section 5.

- We optimize hyper parameters of the classifier with an additional 5-fold cross validation using only training sets (9-folds used for a training set is combined and split into 5 new folds in each validation).

- The baseline model is trained in the same conditions except that the model uses only Session and Reformulation features. Comparison between the proposed and the baseline methods enables us to evaluate the effect of the features related to the components of IA.

We choose linear SVM because it has scalability and has outperformed RBF-kernel SVM.

	Precision	Recall	F_1
Baseline (B.)	0.51	0.53	0.51
Proposed	**0.67**	**0.66**	**0.67**$^+$
B. + ASR	0.56	0.59	0.57$^+$
B. + NLU	0.63	0.60	0.61*
B. + LG	0.50	0.50	0.49

Table 8: The results of the reformulation cause prediction.

Gold \ Predict	No	ASR	NLU	LG
No error	**216**	132	29	10
ASR error	67	**219**	21	10
NLU error	61	54	**52**	6
LG error	19	17	14	**1**

(a) Baseline

Gold \ Predict	No	ASR	NLU	LG
No error	**284**	55	27	21
ASR error	38	**230**	37	12
NLU error	44	29	**81**	19
LG error	8	12	11	**20**

(b) Proposed

Table 9: Confusion matrix of reformulation cause prediction of (a) baseline and (b) proposed methods.

	No	ASR	NLU	LG
Baseline (B.)	0.58	0.59	0.36	0.03
Proposed	**0.75**$^+$	**0.72**$^+$	**0.49***	**0.33**$^+$
B. + ASR	0.66$^+$	0.67$^+$	0.35	0.16
B. + NLU	0.71$^+$	0.65	0.43	0.25*
B. + LG	0.55	0.57	0.32	0.08

Table 10: F_1-measure in reformulation cause prediction for each label.

other methods. Focusing on individual labels, F_1-measures of the proposed method are better for *No error* and *ASR error* than for *NLU error* and *LG error*. In other words, F_1-measures for *NLU error* and *LG error* are not high. As the performances of individual labels are in the order of the number of samples belonging to the label, we expect that these low performances are mainly due to insufficient data and will improve given sufficient data. Focusing on individual feature sets, ASR and NLU features are useful for distinguishing *No error* from other labels. Note that statistical significant differences from the baseline detected by the paired t-test are denoted by $+$ ($p < 0.01$) and $\star$ ($p < 0.05$).

6.2 Results

Table 8 presents the results for the reformulation cause prediction. The first row compares the proposed method with the baseline. The proposed method obtains a 0.67-point F_1-measure and outperforms the baseline. This result shows the effectiveness of the features related to the components of IA. The second row illustrates the performance when one feature set is added to the baseline. We can see that ASR and NLU features improve the performance of the baseline. In F_1-measure, statistical significant differences from the baseline detected by the paired t-test are denoted by $+$ ($p < 0.01$) and $\star$ ($p < 0.05$).

Table 9 presents the confusion matrix of the proposed and baseline methods. The results going diagonally show agreement between the gold labels and the predicted labels. As shown in Table 9, the proposed method outperforms the baseline regardless of the gold labels. Again, these results indicate the effectiveness of the features related to the components of IA.

Table 10 presents F_1-measures of each gold label. Again, the proposed method outperforms the other methods.

6.3 Results by Input Types

Here we analyze the result of Table 8 by input types. Table 11 presents the results of reformulation cause prediction by input types. As shown in Table 11, Both the F_1-measures of the proposed method in voice inputs and text inputs are 0.66. These results suggest that the proposed method is robust for both input types. On the other hand, the F_1-measure of the baseline method in voice inputs is lower than that in text inputs. Particularly, the F_1 measure of *No error* in voice inputs is lower than that in text inputs. Table 12 presents the distribution of predicted labels with the following two conditions. First, U_1 and U_2 are voice inputs. Second, gold labels of all samples are *No error*. As shown in Table 12, misclassification rate of the proposed method in *No error* as *ASR error* is less than that of the baseline method. In other words, the proposed method distinguishes between *No error* and *ASR error* more accurately compared to the baseline method. These results suggest that ASR features contribute to the performance improvement of the proposed method.

	No	ASR	NLU	LG	total
Baseline	0.49	0.58	0.33	0.03	0.47
Proposed	**0.73**	**0.71**	**0.49**	**0.30**	**0.66**
# samples	291	300	122	39	752

(a) U_1 and U_2 are voice inputs.

	No	ASR	NLU	LG	total
Baseline	0.80	N.A.	0.32	0.00	0.60
Proposed	**0.81**	N.A.	**0.42**	**0.39**	**0.66**
# samples	91	N.A.	40	12	143

(b) U_1 and U_2 are text inputs.

Table 11: F_1-measure in reformulation cause prediction of each label between input types.

Predicted label	No	ASR	NLU	LG
Baseline	129	129	25	8
Proposed	205	53	16	17

Table 12: The number of predicted samples in reformulation cause prediction in following two conditions. First, U_1 and U_2 are voice inputs. Second, gold labels of all samples are *No error*.

6.4 Investigation of Feature Weights

We investigate weights of the features learned by the linear-kernel SVM to clarify what features contribute to the reformulation cause prediction.

Table 13 presents top and bottom feature weights in each label. The median value of the 10 models which are obtained with cross validation are used for weights in Table 13. Features calculated from U_1 appear in Table 13 but that calculated from U_2 do not appear. This result is not surprising because information related to U_1 has more relationship to reformulation causes compared to that related to U_2. Next, we focus on the features in individual labels. Features related to their corresponding components appear in Table 13 such as *ASRConf* in *ASR error*, *SameIntent* in *NLU error*, and *DialogAct* in *LG error*. These results indicate that features designed to detect reformulation causes related to their corresponding components work as designed. Finally, we focus on the individual features. We observe that features of input type switches are useful for predicting reformulation causes. In particular, *Voice2Text* is useful for detecting *ASR error* and *Text2Voice* is useful for detecting *NLU error*. These results are consistent with findings in section 4.2.

Label	Feature	Weight
No error	ASRConf*	1.07
	IntentType(SingSong)*	1.05
	Voice2Text	-1.01
	IntentType(DeviceControl)*	-1.10
ASR error	Voice2Text	1.27
	IntentType(Search)*	0.90
	ASRConf*	-1.51
	InputType*	-1.77
NLU error	Text2Voice	1.43
	InputType*	0.94
	SameIntent	-0.61
	IntentType(Dictionary)*	-0.77
LG error	IntentType(DeviceControl)*	1.08
	DialogAct(IDU)*	0.81
	DialogAct(Praise)*	-0.95
	Voice2Text	-1.04

Table 13: Top and Bottom two feature weights of the proposed method. Features marked with "*" were computed for U_1.

7 Future Work

While the proposed method has outperformed the baseline, there is room for improvement on the performance. As mentioned in section 6.2, the performances of individual labels are in the order of the number of samples belonging to the labels. Therefore, we expect that the performance improves as the dataset size increases. The performance will also improve if some features used in previous studies are added to our features. For example, linguistic features such as word n-gram and language model score are used in previous studies (Hassan et al., 2015; Meena et al., 2015) but not used in ours.

8 Conclusion

This paper attempted to predict reformulation causes in intelligent assistants (IAs). Prior to the prediction, we first analyzed the cause of reformulation in IAs using user logs obtained from a commercial IA. Based on the analysis, we defined reformulation cause prediction as four-class classification problem of classifying user utterances into *No error*, *ASR error*, *NLU error*, or *LG error*. Features are divided into five categories mainly on the basis of the relations with the components in the IA. The experiments demonstrated that the proposed method, which combines all feature sets, outperforms the baseline which uses component-independent features such as session information and reformulation related information.

References

Satoshi Akasaki and Nobuhiro Kaji. 2017. Chat detection in an intelligent assistant: Combining task-oriented and non-task-oriented spoken dialogue systems. In *Proceedings of the 55th Annual Meeting of the Association for Computational Linguistics (Volume 1: Long Papers)*. Association for Computational Linguistics (to appear).

Henry A. Feild, James Allan, and Rosie Jones. 2010. Predicting searcher frustration. In *Proceedings of the 33rd International ACM SIGIR Conference on Research and Development in Information Retrieval*. ACM, SIGIR '10, pages 34–41. https://doi.org/10.1145/1835449.1835458.

Spiros Georgiladakis, Georgia Athanasopoulou, Raveesh Meena, Jos Lopes, Arodami Chorianopoulou, Elisavet Palogiannidi, Elias Iosif, Gabriel Skantze, and Alexandros Potamianos. 2016. Root cause analysis of miscommunication hotspots in spoken dialogue systems. In *Proceedings of Interspeech 2016*. ISCA, pages 1156–1160. https://doi.org/10.21437/Interspeech.2016-1273.

Ahmed Hassan, Ranjitha Gurunath Kulkarni, Umut Ozertem, and Rosie Jones. 2015. Characterizing and predicting voice query reformulation. In *Proceedings of the 24th ACM International on Conference on Information and Knowledge Management*. ACM, pages 543–552. https://doi.org/10.1145/2806416.2806491.

Ahmed Hassan, Xiaolin Shi, Nick Craswell, and Bill Ramsey. 2013. Beyond clicks: Query reformulation as a predictor of search satisfaction. In *Proceedings of the 22nd ACM International Conference on Information and Knowledge Management*. ACM, pages 2019–2028. https://doi.org/10.1145/2505515.2505682.

Julia Hirschberg, Diane Litman, and Marc Swerts. 2001. Identifying user corrections automatically in spoken dialogue systems. In *Proceedings of the Second Meeting of the North American Chapter of the Association for Computational Linguistics on Language Technologies*. Association for Computational Linguistics, NAACL '01, pages 1–8. https://doi.org/10.3115/1073336.1073363.

Graeme Hirst, Susan McRoy, Peter Heeman, Philip Edmonds, and Diane Horton. 1994. Repairing conversational misunderstandings and non-understandings. *Speech Communication* 15(3-4):213–229. https://doi.org/10.1016/0167-6393(94)90073-6.

Jeff Huang and Efthimis N. Efthimiadis. 2009. Analyzing and evaluating query reformulation strategies in web search logs. In *Proceedings of the 18th ACM Conference on Information and Knowledge Management*. ACM, pages 77–86. https://doi.org/10.1145/1645953.1645966.

Jiepu Jiang, Ahmed Hassan Awadallah, Rosie Jones, Umut Ozertem, Imed Zitouni, Ranjitha Gurunath Kulkarni, and Omar Zia Khan. 2015. Automatic online evaluation of intelligent assistants. In *Proceedings of the 24th International Conference on World Wide Web*. International World Wide Web Conferences Steering Committee, pages 506–516. https://doi.org/10.1145/2736277.2741669.

Jiepu Jiang, Wei Jeng, and Daqing He. 2013. How do users respond to voice input errors?: Lexical and phonetic query reformulation in voice search. In *Proceedings of the 36th International ACM SIGIR Conference on Research and Development in Information Retrieval*. ACM, pages 143–152. https://doi.org/10.1145/2484028.2484092.

Julia Kiseleva, Kyle Williams, Jiepu Jiang, Ahmed Hassan Awadallah, Aidan C. Crook, Imed Zitouni, and Tasos Anastasakos. 2016. Understanding user satisfaction with intelligent assistants. In *Proceedings of the 2016 ACM on Conference on Human Information Interaction and Retrieval*. ACM, pages 121–130. https://doi.org/10.1145/2854946.2854961.

Gina-Anne Levow. 1998. Characterizing and recognizing spoken corrections in human-computer dialogue. In *Proceedings of the 36th Annual Meeting of the Association for Computational Linguistics and 17th International Conference on Computational Linguistics - Volume 1*. Association for Computational Linguistics, ACL '98, pages 736–742. https://doi.org/10.3115/980845.980969.

Yujian Li and Bo Liu. 2007. A normalized Levenshtein distance metric. *Pattern Analysis and Machine Intelligence, IEEE Transactions on* 29(6):1091–1095. https://doi.org/10.1109/TPAMI.2007.1078.

Diane Litman, Julia Hirschberg, and Marc Swerts. 2006. Characterizing and predicting corrections in spoken dialogue systems. *Computational Linguistics* 32(3):417–438. https://doi.org/10.1162/coli.2006.32.3.417.

Raveesh Meena, Jose Lopes, Gabriel Skantze, and Joakim Gustafson. 2015. Automatic detection of miscommunication in spoken dialogue systems. In *Proceedings of the 16th Annual Meeting of the Special Interest Group on Discourse and Dialogue*. Association for Computational Linguistics, pages 354–363. https://doi.org/10.18653/v1/W15-4647.

Antoine Raux, Brian Langner, Dan Bohus, Alan W Black, and Maxine Eskenazi. 2005. Let's go public! taking a spoken dialog system to the real world. In *Proceedings of Interspeech 2005*. ISCA, pages 885–888.

Shumpei Sano, Nobuhiro Kaji, and Manabu Sassano. 2016. Prediction of prospective user engagement with intelligent assistants. In *Proceedings of the*

54th Annual Meeting of the Association for Computational Linguistics (Volume 1: Long Papers). Association for Computational Linguistics, pages 1203–1212. https://doi.org/10.18653/v1/P16-1114.

Ruhi Sarikaya. 2017. The technology behind personal digital assistants: An overview of the system architecture and key components. *IEEE Signal Processing Magazine* 34(1):67–81. https://doi.org/10.1109/MSP.2016.2617341.

Alexander Schmitt and Stefan Ultes. 2015. Interaction quality: Assessing the quality of ongoing spoken dialog interaction by experts—and how it relates to user satisfaction. *Speech Commun.* 74(C):12–36. https://doi.org/10.1016/j.specom.2015.06.003.

Milad Shokouhi, Umut Ozertem, and Nick Craswell. 2016. Did you say u2 or youtube?: Inferring implicit transcripts from voice search logs. In *Proceedings of the 25th International Conference on World Wide Web*. International World Wide Web Conferences Steering Committee, WWW '16, pages 1215–1224. https://doi.org/10.1145/2872427.2882994.

Marc Swerts, Diane J Litman, and Julia Hirschberg. 2000. Corrections in spoken dialogue systems. In *Proceedings of ICSLP-2000*. ISCA, pages 615–618.

Are you serious?: Rhetorical Questions and Sarcasm in Social Media Dialog

Shereen Oraby[1], Vrindavan Harrison[1], Amita Misra[1], Ellen Riloff [2] and Marilyn Walker[1]

[1] University of California, Santa Cruz

[2] University of Utah

{soraby,vharriso,amisra2,mawalker}@ucsc.edu

riloff@cs.utah.edu

Abstract

Effective models of social dialog must understand a broad range of rhetorical and figurative devices. Rhetorical questions (**RQs**) are a type of figurative language whose aim is to achieve a pragmatic goal, such as structuring an argument, being persuasive, emphasizing a point, or being ironic. While there are computational models for other forms of figurative language, rhetorical questions have received little attention to date. We expand a small dataset from previous work, presenting a corpus of 10,270 RQs from debate forums and Twitter that represent different discourse functions. We show that we can clearly distinguish between RQs and sincere questions (0.76 F1). We then show that RQs can be used both sarcastically and non-sarcastically, observing that non-sarcastic (other) uses of RQs are frequently argumentative in forums, and persuasive in tweets. We present experiments to distinguish between these uses of RQs using SVM and LSTM models that represent linguistic features and post-level context, achieving results as high as 0.76 F1 for SARCASTIC and 0.77 F1 for OTHER in forums, and 0.83 F1 for both SARCASTIC and OTHER in tweets. We supplement our quantitative experiments with an in-depth characterization of the linguistic variation in RQs.

1 Introduction

Theoretical frameworks for figurative language posit eight standard forms: *indirect questions, idiom, irony and sarcasm, metaphor, simile, hyperbole, understatement,* and *rhetorical questions*

1	**Then why do you call a politician who ran such measures liberal** *OH yes, it's because you're a republican and you're not conservative at all.*
2	**Can you read?** *You're the type that just waits to say your next piece and never attempts to listen to others.*
3	**Pray tell, where would I find the atheist church?** *Ridiculous.*
4	**You lost this debate Skeptic, why drag it back up again?** *There are plenty of other subjects that we could debate instead.*

(a) RQs in Forums Dialog

5	**Are you completely revolting?** *Then you should slide into my DMs, because apparently thats the place to be. #Sarcasm*
6	**Do you have problems falling asleep?** *Reduce anxiety, calm the mind, sleep better naturally [link]*
7	**The officials messed something up?** *I'm shocked I tell you.SHOCKED.*
8	**Does ANY review get better than this?** *From a journalist in New York.*

(b) RQs in Twitter Dialog

Table 1: RQs and Following Statements in Forums and Twitter Dialog

(Roberts and Kreuz, 1994). While computational models have been developed for many of these forms, rhetorical questions (**RQs**) have received little attention to date. Table 1 shows examples of RQs from social media in debate forums and Twitter, where their use is prevalent.

RQs are defined as utterances that have the structure of a question, but which are *not intended* to seek information or elicit an answer (Rohde, 2006; Frank, 1990; Ilie, 1994; Sadock, 1971). RQs are often used in arguments and expressions of opinion, advertisements and other persuasive domains (Petty et al., 1981), and are frequent in social media and other types of informal language.

Corpus creation and computational models for

Proceedings of the SIGDIAL 2017 Conference, pages 310–319,
Saarbrücken, Germany, 15-17 August 2017. ©2017 Association for Computational Linguistics

some forms of figurative language have been facilitated by the use of hashtags in Twitter, e.g. the `#sarcasm` hashtag (Bamman and Smith, 2015; Riloff et al., 2013; Liebrecht et al., 2013). Other figurative forms, such as similes, can be identified via lexico-syntactic patterns (Qadir et al., 2016, 2015; Veale and Hao, 2007). RQs are not marked by a hashtag, and their syntactic form is indistinguishable from standard questions (Han, 2002; Sadock, 1971).

Previous theoretical work examines the discourse functions of RQs and compares the overlap in discourse functions across all forms of figurative language (Roberts and Kreuz, 1994). For RQs, 72% of subjects assign *to clarify* as a function, 39% assign *discourse management*, 28% mention *to emphasize*, 56% percent of subjects assign negative emotion, and another 28% mention positive emotion.[1] The discourse functions of clarification, discourse management and emphasis are clearly related to argumentation. One of the other largest overlaps in discourse function between RQs and other figurative forms is between RQs and irony/sarcasm (62% overlap), and there are many studies describing how RQs are used sarcastically (Gibbs, 2000; Ilie, 1994).

To better understand the relationship between RQs and irony/sarcasm, we expand on a small existing dataset of RQs in debate forums from our previous work (Oraby et al., 2016), ending up with a corpus of 2,496 RQs and the self-answers or statements that follow them. We use the heuristic described in that work to collect a completely novel corpus of 7,774 RQs from Twitter. Examples from our final dataset of 10,270 RQs and their following self-answers/statements are shown in Table 1. We observe great diversity in the use of RQs, ranging from sarcastic and mocking (such as the forum post in Row 2), to offering advice based on some anticipated answer (such as the tweet in Row 6).

In this study, we first show that RQs can clearly be distinguished from sincere, information-seeking questions (0.76 F1). Because we are interested in how RQs are used sarcastically, we define our task as distinguishing sarcastic uses from other uses RQs, observing that non-sarcastic RQs are often used argumentatively in forums (as opposed to the more mocking sarcastic uses), and persua-

sively in Twitter (as frequent advertisements and calls-to-action). To distinguish between sarcastic and other uses, we perform classification experiments using SVM and LSTM models, exploring different levels of context, and showing that adding linguistic features improves classification results in both domains.

This paper provides the first in-depth investigation of the use of RQs in different forms of social media dialog. We present a novel task, dataset[2], and results aimed at understanding how RQs can be recognized, and how sarcastic and other uses of RQs can be distinguished.

2 Related Work

Much of the previous work on RQs has focused on RQs as a form of figurative language, and on describing their discourse functions (Schaffer, 2005; Gibbs, 2000; Roberts and Kreuz, 1994; Frank, 1990; Petty et al., 1981). Related work in linguistics has primarily focused on the differences between RQs and standard questions (Han, 2002; Ilie, 1994; Han, 1997). For example Sadock (1971) shows that RQs can be followed by a *yet* clause, and that the discourse cue *after all* at the beginning of the question leads to its interpretation as an RQ. Phrases such as *by any chance* are primarily used on information seeking questions, while negative polarity items such as *lift a finger* or *budge an inch* can only be used with RQs, e.g. *Did John help with the party?* vs. *Did John lift a finger to help with the party?*

RQs were introduced into the DAMSL coding scheme when it was applied to the Switchboard corpus (Jurafsky et al., 1997). To our knowledge, the only computational work utilizing that data is by Battasali et al. (2015), who used n-gram language models with pre- and post-context to distinguish RQs from regular questions in SWBD-DAMSL. Using context improved their results to 0.83 F1 on a balanced dataset of 958 instances, demonstrating that context information could be very useful for this task.

Although it has been observed in the literature that RQs are often used sarcastically (Gibbs, 2000; Ilie, 1994), previous work on sarcasm classification has not focused on RQs (Bamman and Smith, 2015; Riloff et al., 2013; Liebrecht et al., 2013; Filatova, 2012; González-Ibáñez et al., 2011; Davi-

---

[1] Subjects could provide multiple discourse functions for RQs, thus the frequencies do not add to 1.

[2] The Sarcasm RQ corpus will be available at: `https://nlds.soe.ucsc.edu/sarcasm-rq`.

dov et al., 2010; Tsur et al., 2010). Riloff et al. (2013) investigated the utility of sequential features in tweets, emphasizing a subtype of sarcasm that consists of an expression of positive emotion contrasted with a negative situation, and showed that sequential features performed much better than features that did not capture sequential information. More recent work on sarcasm has focused specifically on sarcasm identification on Twitter using neural network approaches (Poria et al, 2016; Ghosh and Veale, 2016; Zhang et al., 2016; Amir et al., 2016).

Other work emphasizes features of semantic incongruity in recognizing sarcasm (Joshi et al., 2015; Reyes et al., 2012). Sarcastic RQs clearly feature semantic incongruity, in some cases by expressing the certainty of particular facts in the frame of a question, and in other cases by asking questions like *"Can you read?"* (Row 2 in Table 1), a competence which a speaker must have, prima facie, to participate in online discussion.

To our knowledge, our previous work is the first to consider the task of distinguishing sarcastic vs. not-sarcastic RQs, where we construct a corpus of sarcasm in three types: generic, RQ, and hyperbole, and provide simple baseline experiments using ngrams (0.70 F1 for SARC and 0.71 F1 for NOT-SARC) (Oraby et al., 2016). Here, we adopt the same heuristic for gathering RQs and expand the corpus in debate forums, also collecting a novel Twitter corpus. We show that we can distinguish between SARCASTIC and OTHER uses of RQs that we observe, such as argumentation and persuasion in forums and Twitter, respectively. We show that linguistic features aid in the classification task, and explore the effects of context, using traditional and neural models.

3 Corpus Creation

Sarcasm is a prevalent discourse function of RQs. In previous work, we observe both sarcastic and not-sarcastic uses of RQs in forums, and collect a set of sarcastic and not-sarcastic RQs in debate by using a heuristic stating that an RQ is a question that occurs in the middle of a turn, and which is answered immediately by the speaker themselves (Oraby et al., 2016). RQs are thus defined *intentionally*: the speaker indicates that their intention is not to elicit an answer by not ceding the turn.[3]

---

[3]We acknowledge that this method may miss RQs that do not follow this heuristic, but opt to use this conservative pat-

SARCASTIC

1	**Do you even read what anyone posts?** *Try it, you might learn something.......maybe not.......*
2	**If they haven't been discovered yet, HOW THE BLOODY HELL DO YOU KNOW?** *Ten percent more brains and you'd be pondlife.*

OTHER

3	**How is that related to deterrence?** *Once again, deterrence is preventing through the fear of consequences.*
4	**Well, you didn't have my experiences, now did you?** *Each woman who has an abortion could have innumerous circumstances and experiences.*

(a) SARC vs. OTHER RQs in Forums

SARCASTIC

5	**When something goes wrong, what's the easiest thing to do?** *Blame the victim! Obviously they had it coming #sarcasm #itsajoke #dontlynchme*
6	**You know what's the best?** *Unreliable friends. They're so much un. #sarcasm #whatever.*

OTHER

7	**And what, Socrates, is the food of the soul?** *Surely, I said, knowledge is the food of the soul. Plato*
8	**Craft ladies, salon owners, party planners?** *You need to state your #business [link]*

(b) SARC vs. OTHER RQs in Twitter

Table 2: Sarcastic vs. Other Uses of RQs

In this work, we are interested in doing a closer analysis of RQs in social media. We use the same RQ-collection heuristic from previous work to expand our corpus of SARCASTIC vs. OTHER uses RQs in debate forums, and create another completely novel corpus of RQs in Twitter. We observe that the other uses of RQs in forums are often argumentative, aimed at structuring an argument more emphatically, clearly, or concisely, whereas in Twitter they are frequently persuasive in nature, aimed at advertising or grabbing attention. Table 2 shows examples of sarcastic and other uses of RQs in our corpus, and we describe our data collection methods for both domains below.

Debate Forums: The Internet Argument Corpus (IAC 2.0) (Abbott et al., 2016) contains a large number of discussions about politics and social issues, making it a good source of RQs. Following our previous work (2016), we first extract RQs in

---

tern for expanding the data to avoid introducing extra noise.

posts whose length varies from 10-150 words, and collect five annotations for each of the RQs paired with the context of their following statements.

We ask Turkers to specify whether or not the RQ-response pair is sarcastic, as a binary question. We count a post as "sarcastic" if the majority of annotators (at least 3 of the 5) labeled the post as sarcastic. Including the 851 posts per class from previous work (Oraby et al., 2016), this resulted in 1,248 sarcastic posts out of 4,840 (25.8%), a significantly larger percentage than the estimated 12% sarcasm ratio in debate forums (Swanson et al., 2014). We then balance the 1,248 sarcastic RQs with an equal number of RQs that 0 or 1 annotators voted as sarcastic, giving us a total of 2,496 RQ pairs. For our experiments, all annotators had above 80% agreement with the majority vote.

Twitter: We also extract RQs defined as above from a set of 80,000 tweets with a `#sarcasm`, `#sarcastic`, or `#sarcastictweet` hashtag. We use the hashtags as "labels", as in other work (Riloff et al., 2013; Reyes et al., 2012). This yields 3,887 sarcastic RQ tweets, again balanced with 3,887 RQ pairs from a set of random tweets (not containing any sarcasm-related hashtags). We remove all sarcasm-related hashtags and username mentions (prefixed with an "@") from the posts, for a total of 7,774 total RQ tweets.

4 Experimental Results

In this section, we present experiments classifying rhetorical vs. information-seeking questions, then sarcastic vs. other uses of RQs.

4.1 RQs vs. Information-Seeking Qs

By definition, fact-seeking questions are not RQs. We take advantage of the annotations provided for subsets of the IAC, in particular the subcorpus that distinguishes FACTUAL posts from EMOTIONAL posts (Abbott et al., 2016; Oraby et al., 2015).[4] Table 3 shows examples of FACTUAL/INFO-SEEKING questions.

To test whether RQ and FACTUAL/INFO-SEEKING questions are easily distinguishable, we randomly select a sample of 1,020 questions from our forums RQ corpus, and balance them with the same number of questions from FACT corpus. We divide the question data into 80% train and

---

[4]`https://nlds.soe.ucsc.edu/factfeel`

FACTUAL/INFO-SEEKING QUESTIONS

1	How do you justify claims about covering only a fraction more ?
2	If someone is an attorney or in law enforcement, would you please give an interpretation?

Table 3: Examples of Information-Seeking Questions

20% test, and use an SVM classifier (Pedregosa et al., 2011), with GoogleNews Word2Vec (W2V) (Mikolov et al., 2013) features. We perform a grid-search on our training set using 3-fold cross-validation for parameter tuning, and report results on our test set. Table 4 shows the precision (P), recall (R) and F1 scores we achieve, showing good classification performance for distinguishing both classes, at 0.76 F1 for the RQ class, and 0.74 F1 for the FACTUAL/INFO-SEEKING class.

#	Class	P	R	F1
1	RQ	0.74	0.79	0.76
2	FACT	0.77	0.72	0.74

Table 4: Supervised Learning Results for RQs vs. Fact/Info-Seeking Questions in Debate Forums

4.2 Sarcastic vs. Other Uses of RQs

Next, we focus on distinguishing SARCASTIC from OTHER uses of RQs in forums and Twitter. We divide the full RQ data from each domain (2,496 forums and 7,774 tweets, balanced between the two classes) into 80% train and 20% test data. We experiment with two models, an SVM classifier from Scikit Learn (Pedregosa et al., 2011), and a bidirectional LSTM model (Chollet, 2015) with a TensorFlow backend (Abadi et al., 2016). We perform a grid-search using cross-validation on our training set for parameter tuning, and report results on our test set.

For each of the models, we establish a baseline with W2V features (Google News-trained Word2Vec size 300 (Mikolov et al., 2013) for the debate forums, and Twitter-trained Word2Vec size 400 (Godin et al., 2015), for the tweets). We experiment with different embedding representations, finding that we achieve best results by averaging the word embeddings for each input when using SVM, and creating an embedding matrix (number of words by embedding size for each in-

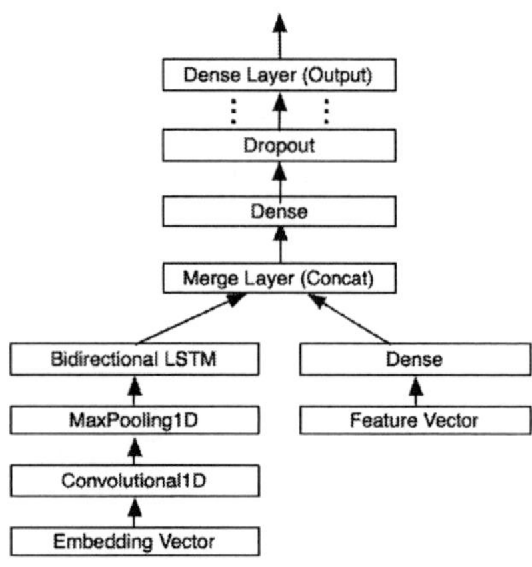

Figure 1: LSTM Network Architecture

Debate Forums	Tweets
2nd PERSON	2nd PERSON
3rd PERSON PLURAL	3rd PERSON PLURAL
3rd PERSON SINGULAR	ARTICLES
ADVERBS	AUXILIARY VERBS
AFFILIATION	CERTAINTY
ASSENT	COLON
AUXILIARY VERBS	COMMA
COMPARE	CONJUNCTION
EXCLAMATION MARKS	FRIENDS
FOCUS FUTURE	MALE
FRIENDS	NEGATIONS
FUNCTION	NEGATIVE EMOTION
HEALTH	PARENTHESIS
INFORMAL	QUOTE MARKS
INTERROGATIVES	RISK
NETSPEAK	SADNESS
NUMERALS	SEMICOLON
QUANTIFIERS	SWEAR WORDS
REWARDS	WORD COUNT
SADNESS	WORDS PER SENTENCE

Table 5: LIWC Features by Domain

put) as input to an embedding layer when using LSTM.[5]

For our LSTM model, we experiment with various different layer architectures from previous work (Poria et al, 2016; Ghosh and Veale, 2016; Zhang et al., 2016; Amir et al., 2016). For our final model (shown in Figure 1), we use a sequential embedding layer, 1D convolutional layer, maxpooling, a bidirectional LSTM, dropout layer, and a sequence of dense and dropout layers with a final sigmoid activation layer for the output.

For additional features, we experiment with using post-level scores (frequency of each category in the input, normalized by word count) from the Linguistic Inquiry and Word Count (LIWC) tool (Pennebaker et al., 2001). We experiment with which LIWC categories to include as features on our training data, and end up with a set of 20 categories for each domain[6], as shown in Table 5. When adding features to the LSTM model, we include a dense and merge layer to concatenate features, followed by the dense and dropout layers and sigmoid output.

We experiment with different levels of textual context in training for both the forums and Twitter data (keeping our test set constant, always testing on only the RQ and self-answer portion of the text). We are motivated by the intuition that training on larger context will help us identify more informative segments of RQs in test. Specifically,

we test four different levels of context representation:

- RQ: only the RQ and its self-answer
- $Pre + RQ$: the preceding context and the RQ
- $RQ + Post$: the RQ and following context
- $FullText$: the full text or tweet (all context)

Table 6 presents our results on the classification task by model for each domain, showing P, R, and F1 scores for each class (forums in Table 6a and Twitter in Table 6b). For each domain, we present the same experiments for both models (SVM and LSTM), first showing a W2V baseline (Rows 1 and 6 in both tables), then adding in LIWC (Rows 2 and 7), and finally presenting results for W2V and LIWC features on different context levels (Rows 2-5 for SVM and Rows 7-10 for LSTM).

Debate Forums: From Table 6a, for both models, we observe that the addition of LIWC features gives us a large improvement over the baseline of just W2V features, particularly for the SARC class (from 0.72 F1 to 0.76 F1 SARC and 0.73 F1 to 0.77 F1 OTHER for SVM in Rows 1-2, and from 0.68 F1 to 0.72 F1 SARC and 0.74 F1 to 0.75 F1 OTHER for LSTM in Rows 6-7). Our best results come from the SVM model, with best scores of 0.76 F1 for SARC and 0.77 OTHER in Row 2 from using

---

[5]In future work, we plan to further explore the effects of different embedding representations on model performance.

[6]We discuss some of the highly-informative LIWC categories by domain in Sec. 5.

#	Domain	Model	Features	Training		SARCASTIC				OTHER	
						P	R	F1		P	R	F1
1	**Forums**	SVM	$W2V_{Google}$	RQ		0.74	0.70	0.72		0.71	0.75	0.73
2			$W2V_{Google}+LIWC$	RQ		0.78	0.74	**0.76**		0.75	0.79	**0.77**
3				$Pre+RQ$		0.76	0.72	0.74		0.73	0.78	0.76
4				$RQ+Post$		0.75	0.76	0.75		0.76	0.74	0.75
5				$Full\ Text$		0.75	0.77	**0.76**		0.76	0.74	0.75
6		LSTM	$W2V_{Google}$	RQ		0.76	0.62	0.68		0.68	0.80	0.74
7			$W2V_{Google}+LIWC$	RQ		0.76	0.68	0.72		0.71	0.79	0.75
8				$Pre+RQ$		0.81	0.60	0.69		0.68	0.86	0.76
9				$RQ+Post$		0.74	0.76	0.75		0.76	0.74	0.75
10				$Full\ Text$		0.76	0.67	0.71		0.70	0.78	0.74

(a) Supervised Learning Results on Debate Forums

#	Domain	Model	Features	Training		SARCASTIC				OTHER	
						P	R	F1		P	R	F1
1	**Twitter**	SVM	$W2V_{Tweet}$	RQ		0.77	0.85	0.80		0.83	0.74	0.78
2			$W2V_{Tweet}+LIWC$	RQ		0.80	0.86	**0.83**		0.85	0.79	0.82
3				$Pre+RQ$		0.80	0.87	**0.83**		0.86	0.78	0.82
4				$RQ+Post$		0.79	0.87	**0.83**		0.86	0.77	0.81
5				$Full\ Text$		0.80	0.86	**0.83**		0.85	0.79	0.82
6		LSTM	$W2V_{Tweet}$	RQ		0.76	0.70	0.73		0.72	0.78	0.75
7			$W2V_{Tweet}+LIWC$	RQ		0.80	0.82	0.81		0.82	0.79	0.80
8				$Pre+RQ$		0.78	0.84	0.81		0.83	0.76	0.80
9				$RQ+Post$		0.83	0.81	0.82		0.82	0.84	**0.83**
10				$Full\ Tweet$		0.80	0.83	0.82		0.83	0.79	0.81

(b) Supervised Learning Results on Twitter

Table 6: Supervised Learning Results for RQs in Debate Forums and Twitter

only the RQ and self-response in training (with the same F1 for SARC when training on the full text).

We observe that while the SVM results with LIWC features do not change significantly depending on the training context (Rows 3-5), the LSTM model is highly sensitive to context changes for the SARC class (Rows 8-10). Some interesting findings emerge when training on different context granularities for LSTM: our best LSTM results for the SARC class come from training on the $RQ+Post$ context (0.75 F1 in Row 9), and for the $Pre+RQ$ context for the OTHER class (0.76 F1 in Row 8). We note that this increase in the SARC class from plain word embeddings to word embeddings combined with LIWC and context is larger than the increase in the OTHER class, indicating that post-level context for SARC captures more diverse instances in training. We also note that these results beat our previous baselines using only ngram features on the smaller original dataset of 851 posts per class (0.70 F1 for SARC, 0.71 F1 for NOT-SARC) (Oraby et al., 2016).

We investigate why certain context features benefit each class differently for LSTM. Table 7 shows examples of single posts, divided into Pre, RQ, and $Post$. Looking at Row 1, it is clear that while the RQ and self-answer portion may not appear to be sarcastic, the $Post$ context makes the sarcasm much more pronounced. This is frequent in the case of sarcastic debate posts, where the speaker often ends with a sharp remark or an interjection (like *"gasp!!!"*), or emoticons (like winking *;)* or roll-eyes *8-)*). In the case of the OTHER forums posts, the RQ is often nestled within sequences of questions, or other RQ and self-answer pairs (Row 2).

		SARCASTIC
1	*Pre*	[...] the argument I hear most often from so-called 'pro-choicers' is that you cannot legislate morality.
	RQ	**Well then what can you legislate?** *Every law in existence is legislation of morality!*
	Post	By that way of thinking, then we should have no laws. If someone kidnaps and murders your 3-year-old child, then let's hope the murderer goes free because we cannot legislate morality!

		OTHER
2	*Pre*	what that man did isn't illegal in the us? you couldn't claim self defence if someone running away like that.
	RQ	**you think that the fact that man had a gun stopped people getting shot?** *what would have happened if he hadn't would be that the robbers got away with some money.*
	Post	nothing to do with taking lives. [...]

(a) SARC vs. OTHER RQs in Context on Forums

		SARCASTIC
3	*Pre*	Gasp!
	RQ	**Two football players got into it with each other?!** *How uncivilized!*
	Post	Lets make a big deal about it! #NFLlogic #cowboys

		OTHER
4	*Pre*	
	RQ	**Are you willing to succeed?** *The answer isn't as simple as you may think.*
	Post	Read my blog post and you'll see why.... [link]

(b) SARC vs. OTHER RQs in Context on Twitter

Table 7: Sarcastic vs. Other Uses RQs in Context

Twitter: From Table 6b, we observe that the best result of 0.83 F1 for the SARC class come from the SVM model (for all context levels), while the best result of 0.83 F1 for the OTHER class comes from the LSTM model. We observe a strong performance increase from adding in LIWC features for both models, even more pronounced than for forums (0.80 F1 to 0.83 F1 SARC and 0.78 F1 to 0.82 F1 OTHER for SVM in Rows 1-2, and 0.73 F1 to 0.81 F1 SARC and 0.75 F1 to 0.80 F1 OTHER for LSTM in Rows 6-7).

Again, while the SVM results do not vary based on changes in context, there is a large improvement in the OTHER class for LSTM when using $RQ + Post$ level context, giving us our best

OTHER class results. From Table 9 Row 4, we see an example of a "call-to-action" that are frequent and distinctive in non-sarcastic Twitter RQs, asking users to visit a link at the end of a tweet (*Post* RQ). In the case of the SARC tweet in Row 3, the extra tweet-level context (such as initial exclamations/interjections) aids in highlighting the sarcasm, but is limited in length compared to the forums posts, explaining the smaller gain from context in the Twitter domain for SARC.

Comparing both domains, we observe that the results for tweets in Table 6b are much higher than the results for forums in Table 6a, noting that this could be a result of less lexical diversity and a larger amount of data, making them more distinguishable than the more varied forums posts. We plan to explore these differences more extensively in future work.

5 Linguistic Characteristics of RQs by Class and Domain

In this section, we discuss linguistic characteristics we observe in our SARCASTIC vs OTHER uses of RQs using the most informative LIWC features.

Previous work has observed that FACTUAL utterances are often very heavy on technical jargon (Oraby et al., 2015): this is also true of factual questions. When analyzing differences in LIWC categories in our factual vs. RQ data, we find that our factual questions are slightly longer on average than the RQs (14 words on average compared to 12). We also find significant differences in "function" word categories ($p < 0.05$, unpaired t-test) in LIWC, marking use of personal references, and "affective processes" ($p < 0.005$). Both categories are more prevalent in the RQs than in the FACT questions, indicating more emotional language that is targeted towards the second party.

A qualitative analysis of our SARCASTIC vs. OTHER data shows that sarcastic RQs in forums are often followed by short statements that serve to point attention or mock, whereas the other RQ-self-response pairs often serve as a technique to concisely structure an argument. RQs in Twitter are frequently advertisements (persuasive communication) (Petty et al., 1981), making them more distinguishable from the more diverse sarcastic instances. Tables 8 and 9 show examples of LIWC features that are most characteristic of each domain and class based on our experiments. For ranking, we show the learned feature weight (FW)

Table 8: Forums LIWC Categories

SARCASTIC

#	FW	Feature	Example
1	15.19	2nd Person	**Do you ever read headers?** *You got a mouth on you as big as grand canyon.*
2	12.09	Informal	**The hate you're spewing is palpable, yet you can't even see that can you?** *Hypocrites, ya gotta luv em.*
3	8.92	Exclamation	**Force the children to learn science?** *How obscene!!*
4	4.66	Netspeak	**To make fun of my title?** *lol, how that stings...*

OTHER

#	FW	Feature	Example
5	8.98	Interrog.	**How do you know it's the truth?** *If it were definitive [...]*
6	8.54	3rd Person Plural	**what's the difference?** *both are imposing their ideologies*
7	3.93	Quantifiers	**[...] we have minimum wage, why can't we have a maximum wage?** *some of [...]*
8	3.88	Health	**When will the people press congress to take up abortion?** *It's the job of congress [...]*

Table 9: Tweet LIWC Categories

SARCASTIC

#	FW	Feature	Example
1	15.71	Comma	**Wait, wait, I can't...it's impossible...NO WAY?!** *- a stiffer track pad?!*
2	6.86	Word Count	**Shouldn't you be in power?** *You know best after all.*
3	5.89	Negations	**Can't we do that already without brain imaging?** *I think it's called empathy*
4	3.91	3rd Person Plural	**How intelligent, they make the laws and then violate [them]?** *That is absurd!*

OTHER

#	FW	Feature	Example
5	4.51	Swear Words	**Idk why I'm fighting my sleep?!** *Ain't shit else to do*
6	3.60	Risk	**Have their been launch pad explosions?** *That would be a risk.*
7	3.01	2nd Person	**Do you want a great deal on [...]?** *Check out the latest*
8	2.83	Friends	**Can I get 12.7k followers today?** *:) xo Thanks to everyone who is following me.*

for each class, found by performing 10-fold cross-validation on each training set using an SVM model with only LIWC features.

In Table 8, Row 1, we observe that 2nd person mentions are frequent in the sarcastic debate forums posts (referring to the other person in the debate), while in the Twitter domain, they come up as significant features in the *non-sarcastic* tweets, where they are used as methods to persuade readers to interact: click a link, like, comment, share (Table 9, Row 6). Likewise, "informal" words and more "verbal speech style" non-fluencies, including exclamations and social media slang ("netspeak"), also appear in sarcastic debate (Table 8, Rows 2 and 4). Features of sarcastic forums include exclamations (Table 8, Rows 3), often used in a hyperbolic or figurative manner (McCarthy and Carter, 2004; Roberts and Kreuz, 1994). We find that sarcastic tweets frequently include sets of exclamations/interjections strung together with commas (Table 9, Row 1), and are often shorter than the tweets in the non-sarcastic class (Table 9, Row 3).

Table 8 shows that "interrogatives" are a strong feature of argumentative forums (Row 7), as well as the use of technical jargon (including quantifiers health words with some domain-specific topics, such as abortion) (Row 8). Table 9 indicates that OTHER tweets frequently contain forms of advertisement and calls-to-action involving 2nd person references (Row 7). Similarly, RQ tweets are sometimes used to express frustration ("swear words" in Row 5), or increase engagement with references to "friends" and followers (Row 8).

6 Conclusions

In this study, we expand on a small corpus from previous work to create a large corpus of RQs in two domains where RQs are prevalent: debate forums and Twitter. To our knowledge, this is the first in-depth study dedicated to sarcasm and other uses of RQs in social media. We present supervised learning experiments using traditional and neural models to classify sarcasm in each domain, providing analysis of unique features across domains and classes, and exploring the effects of training of different levels of context.

We first show that we can distinguish between information-seeking and rhetorical questions (0.76 F1). We then focus on classifying sarcasm in only the RQs, showing that there are distinct linguistic differences between the methods of expression used in RQs across forums and Twitter. For forums, we show that we are able to distinguish be-

317

tween the sarcastic and other uses (noting they are often argumentative) in forums with 0.76 F1 for SARC and 0.77 F1 for NOT-SARC, improving on our baselines from previous work on a smaller dataset (Oraby et al., 2016).

We also explore sarcastic and other uses of RQs on Twitter, noting that other non-sarcastic uses of RQs are often advertisements, a form of persuasive communication not represented in debate dialog. We show that we can distinguish between sarcastic and other uses of RQ in Twitter with scores of 0.83 F1 for both the SARC and OTHER classes. We observe that tweets are generally more easily distinguished than the more diverse forums, and that the addition of linguistic categories from LIWC greatly improves classification performance. We also note that the LSTM model is more sensitive to context changes than the SVM model, and plan to explore the differences between the models in greater detail in future work.

Other future work also includes expanding our dataset to capture more instances of what may characterize RQs across these domains to improve performance, and also to analyze other interesting domains, such as Reddit. We believe that it will be possible to improve our results by using more robust models, and also by developing features to represent the *sequential* properties of RQs by further utilizing the larger context of the surrounding dialog in our analysis.

Acknowledgments

This work was funded by NSF CISE RI 1302668, under the Robust Intelligence Program.

References

Martin Abadi, Paul Barham, Jianmin Chen, Zhifeng Chen, Andy Davis, Jeffrey Dean, Matthieu Devin, Sanjay Ghemawat, Geoffrey Irving, Michael Isard, Manjunath Kudlur, Josh Levenberg, Rajat Monga, Sherry Moore, Derek G. Murray, Benoit Steiner, Paul Tucker, Vijay Vasudevan, Pete Warden, Martin Wicke, Yuan Yu, and Xiaoqiang Zheng. 2016. Tensorflow: A system for large-scale machine learning. In *Proceedings of the 12th USENIX Conference on Operating Systems Design and Implementation.*

Robert Abbott, Brian Ecker, Pranav Anand, and Marilyn Walker. 2016. Internet argument corpus 2.0: An sql schema for dialogic social media and the corpora to go with it. In *Language Resources and Evaluation Conference, LREC2016.*

Silvio Amir, Byron Wallace, Hao Lyu, Paula Carvalho, and Mario Silva. 2016. Modelling Context with User Embeddings for Sarcasm Detection in Social Media *The SIGNLL Conference on Computational Natural Language Learning (CoNLL2016).*

David Bamman and Noah A Smith. 2015. Contextualized sarcasm detection on twitter. In *Ninth International AAAI Conference on Web and Social Media.*

Shohini Bhattasali, Jeremy Cytryn, Elana Feldman, and Joonsuk Park. 2015. Automatic identification of rhetorical questions. In *Proc. of the 53rd Annual Meeting of the Association for Computational Linguistics and the 7th International Joint Conference on Natural Language Processing (Short Papers).*

Francois Chollet. 2015. Keras. https://github.com/fchollet/keras

Dmitry Davidov, Oren Tsur, and Ari Rappoport. 2010. Semi-supervised recognition of sarcastic sentences in twitter and amazon. In *Proceedings of the Fourteenth Conference on Computational Natural Language Learning.* pages 107–116.

Elena Filatova. 2012. Irony and sarcasm: Corpus generation and analysis using crowdsourcing. In *Language Resources and Evaluation Conference, LREC2012.*

Jane Frank. 1990. You call that a rhetorical question?: Forms and functions of rhetorical questions in conversation. *Journal of Pragmatics* 14(5):723–738.

Aniruddha Ghosh and Tony Veale. 2016. Fracking Sarcasm using Neural Network In *Proc. of the 7th Workshop on Computational Approaches to Subjectivity, Sentiment and Social Media Analysis.* WASSA 2016.

Raymond Gibbs. 2000. Irony in talk among friends. *Metaphor and Symbol* 15(1):5–27.

Fréderic Godin, Baptist Vandersmissen, Wesley De Neve, and Rik Van de Walle. 2015. Multimedia lab@ acl w-nut ner shared task: named entity recognition for twitter microposts using distributed word representations. *ACL-IJCNLP* 2015:146–153.

Roberto González-Ibáñez, Smaranda Muresan, and Nina Wacholder. 2011. Identifying sarcasm in twitter: a closer look. In *Proceedings of the 49th Annual Meeting of the Association for Computational Linguistics: Human Language Technologies: short papers.* Citeseer, volume 2, pages 581–586.

Chung-hye Han. 1997. Deriving the interpretation of rhetorical questions. In *The Proc. of the Sixteenth West Coast Conference on Formal Linguistics, WCCFL16.*

Chung-hye Han. 2002. Interpreting interrogatives as rhetorical questions. *Lingua* 112(3):201–229.

Cornelia Ilie. 1994. *What else can I tell you?: a pragmatic study of English rhetorical questions as discursive and argumentative acts.* Acta Universitatis Stockholmiensis: Stockholm studies in English. Almqvist & Wiksell International. https://books.google.com/books?id=T2wiAQAAIAAJ.

Aditya Joshi, Vinita Sharma, and Pushpak Bhattacharyya. 2015. Harnessing context incongruity for sarcasm detection. In *Proceedings of the 53rd Annual Meeting of the Association for Computational Linguistics and the 7th International Joint Conference on Natural Language Processing.* volume 2, pages 757–762.

Dan Jurafsky, Liz Shriberg, and Debra Biasca. 1997. Swbd-damsl labeling project coder's manual. Technical report, University of Colorado. Available as http://stripe.colorado.edu/ jurafsky/manual.august1.html.

Christine Liebrecht, Florian Kunneman, and Antal van den Bosch. 2013. The perfect solution for detecting sarcasm in tweets #not. In *Proc. of the 4th Workshop on Computational Approaches to Subjectivity, Sentiment and Social Media Analysis.* WASSA 2013.

Michael McCarthy and Ronald Carter. 2004. 'There's millions of them': hyperbole in everyday conversation *Journal of Pragmatics* 36:149–184.

Tomas Mikolov, Ilya Sutskever, Kai Chen, Greg S Corrado, and Jeff Dean. 2013. Distributed representations of words and phrases and their compositionality. In *Advances in Neural Information Processing Systems.* pages 3111–3119.

Shereen Oraby, Vrindavan Harrison, Ernesto Hernandez, Lena Reed, Ellen Riloff, and Marilyn Walker. 2016. Creating and characterizing a diverse corpus of sarcasm in dialogue. In *Proc. of the SIGDIAL 2015 Conference: The 17th Annual Meeting of the Special Interest Group on Discourse and Dialogue.*

Shereen Oraby, Lena Reed, Ryan Compton, Ellen Riloff, Marilyn Walker, and Steve Whittaker. 2015. And thats a fact: Distinguishing factual and emotional argumentation in online dialogue. *NAACL HLT 2015* page 116.

Fabian Pedregosa, Gael Varoquaux, Alexandre Gramfort, Vincet Michel, Bertrand Thirion, Oliver Grisel, Mathieu Blondel, Peter Prettenhofer, Ron Weiss, Vincent Dubourg, Jake Vanderplas, Alexandre Passos, David Cournapeau, Matthieu Brucher, Matthieu Perrot, and Edouard Duchesnay. 2011. Scikit-learn: Machine learning in Python. *Journal of Machine Learning Research* 12:2825–2830.

James Pennebaker, Martha Francis, and Rojer Booth. 2001. *LIWC: Linguistic Inquiry and Word Count.*

Richard Petty, John Cacioppo, and Martin Heesacker. 1981. Effects of rhetorical questions on persuasion: A cognitive response analysis. *Journal of personality and social psychology* 40(3):432.

Soujanya Poria, Erik Cambria, Devamanyu Hazarika, and Prateek Vij. 2016. A Deeper Look into Sarcastic Tweets Using Deep Convolutional Neural Networks. In *26th International Conference on Computational Linguistics (COLING2016)*

Ashequl Qadir, Ellen Riloff, and Marilyn A. Walker. 2015. Learning to recognize affective polarity in similes. In *Conferenece on Empirical Methods in NLP, EMNLP-2015.*

Ashequl Qadir, Ellen Riloff, and Marilyn A Walker. 2016. Automatically inferring implicit properties in similes. In *Proceedings of NAACL-HLT.* pages 1223–1232.

Antonio Reyes, Paolo Rosso, and Davide Buscaldi. 2012. From humor recognition to irony detection: The figurative language of social media. *Data & Knowledge Engineering* .

Ellen Riloff, Ashequl Qadir, Prafulla Surve, Lalindra De Silva, Nathan Gilbert, and Ruihong Huang. 2013. Sarcasm as contrast between a positive sentiment and negative situation. In *Proceedings of the 2013 Conference on Empirical Methods in Natural Language Processing.*

Richard M Roberts and Roger J Kreuz. 1994. Why do people use figurative language? *Psychological Science* 5(3):159–163.

Hannah Rohde. 2006. Rhetorical questions as redundant interrogatives. *Department of Linguistics, UCSD* .

Jerrold M Sadock. 1971. Queclaratives. In *Seventh Regional Meeting of the Chicago Linguistic Society.* volume 7, pages 223–232.

Deborah Schaffer. 2005. Can rhetorical questions function as retorts? : Is the pope catholic? *Journal of Pragmatics* 37:433–600.

Reid Swanson, Stephanie Lukin, Luke Eisenberg, Thomas Chase Corcoran, and Marilyn A Walker. 2014. Getting reliable annotations for sarcasm in online dialogues. In *Language Resources and Evaluation Conference, LREC 2014.*

Oren Tsur, Dmitry Davidov, and Ari Rappoport. 2010. Icwsm–a great catchy name: Semi-supervised recognition of sarcastic sentences in online product reviews. In *Proceedings of the fourth international AAAI conference on weblogs and social media.* pages 162–169.

Tony Veale and Yanfen Hao. 2007. Learning to understand figurative language: from similes to metaphors to irony. In *Proceedings of the Cognitive Science Society.* volume 29.

Meishan Zhang, Yue Zhang, and Guohong Fu. 2016. Tweet Sarcasm Detection Using Deep Neural Network. In *26th International Conference on Computational Linguistics (COLING2016)*

Finding Structure in Figurative Language: Metaphor Detection with Topic-based Frames

Hyeju Jang, Keith Maki, Eduard Hovy, Carolyn Penstein Rosé
Language Technologies Institute
Carnegie Mellon University
Pittsburgh, PA 15213, USA
{hyejuj, kmaki, hovy, cprose}@cs.cmu.edu

Abstract

In this paper, we present a novel and highly effective method for induction and application of metaphor frame templates as a step toward detecting metaphor in extended discourse. We infer implicit facets of a given metaphor frame using a semi-supervised bootstrapping approach on an unlabeled corpus. Our model applies this frame facet information to metaphor detection, and achieves the state-of-the-art performance on a social media dataset when building upon other proven features in a nonlinear machine learning model. In addition, we illustrate the mechanism through which the frame and topic information enable the more accurate metaphor detection.

1 Introduction

Computational work on metaphor has largely focused on metaphor detection within individual sentences, for the purpose of identification of literal meaning, with an eye towards improvement of downstream applications like Machine Translation. This limited conceptualization of metaphor within these restricted contexts has allowed prior work to leverage local indicators to identify metaphorical language, such as the violation of selectional preferences (Martin, 1996; Shutova et al., 2010; Huang, 2014) or the use of abstract vs concrete descriptors (Turney et al., 2011; Brysbaert et al., 2014; Tsvetkov et al., 2013). When detecting metaphor in an extended discourse, and especially for the purpose of modeling the use of metaphor in interaction, however, a broader conceptualization of metaphor is needed in order to accommodate the many places where these simplifying assumptions break down (Jang

et al., 2015, 2016). Detection of metaphors in naturalistic discourse remains an open problem.

To begin to address this gap, this paper suggests adopting a concept of *framing* in discourse (Tannen, 1993; Tannen and Wallat, 1987; Gee, 2014; Minsky, 1975; Schank and Abelson, 1975; Fillmore, 1976; Fauconnier and Turner, 1998). *Framing* is a well-known approach for conceptualizing discourse processes, with variants that have arisen in linguistics, cognitive psychology, and artificial intelligence. This approach stands in contrast to conceptualizations of metaphor as a violation of narrowly defined linguistic rules such as selectional restrictions, instead adopting a softer, Gricean notion that an expectation of coherence broadly construed has been flouted. Specifically, a metaphor occurs when a speaker brings one frame into a context governed by another frame, and explicitly relates parts of each, so that the original frame's expectations are extended or enhanced according to the new frame.

We propose a novel and highly effective method for induction and application of metaphor frame templates as a step toward detecting metaphor in an extended discourse. Our contributions are three-fold. (1) We computationally induce frames, which can be either metaphorically or literally used, from unannotated text. Our approach infers the facets of a given frame through template induction using a semi-supervised bootstrapping approach. Then, (2) we evaluate the obtained template in an established metaphor detection task which distinguishes whether a target word from the given frame is used metaphorically or literally in text. We demonstrate that this frame information is effective in metaphor detection in combination with features from Jang et al. (2016) in a nonlinear machine learning model, which significantly outperforms Jang et al. (2016), the state-of-the-art baseline on a social media dataset. Ad-

320

Proceedings of the SIGDIAL 2017 Conference, pages 320–330,
Saarbrücken, Germany, 15-17 August 2017. ©2017 Association for Computational Linguistics

ditionally, (3) through error analysis, we illustrate the mechanism through which the frame and topic information that are germane to our approach enable the more accurate metaphor detection it achieves. Frame switching can occur not only for metaphor but also for other reasons e.g., topic switches. Our model provides more fine-grained information about what pieces of the frame make the frame metaphorical or literal. Specifically, in our model, semantically-related words from the same frame that co-exist around a target word aid metaphor detection whereas they confuse metaphor detection in other prior approaches.

The remainder of the paper is organized as follows. Section 2 relates our work to prior work. Section 3 shows how adopting the concept of a *frame* may be useful for studying metaphor in discourse from a social perspective. Section 4 explains our semi-supervised approach of template induction to model a metaphor frame in detail. Section 5 presents the effectiveness of the frame information through metaphor detection experiments. Section 6 analyzes the results and identifies when the frame information is beneficial. Section 7 concludes the paper.

2 Relation to Prior Work

In this section, we discuss previous computational work on metaphor that is most relevant to our study. (For more thorough review, refer to (Shutova, 2015).) Next, Section 2.1 introduces approaches to metaphor detection by modeling metaphorical mapping patterns instead of relying on the idea of violation of linguistic expectations. Section 2.2 reviews work that specifically aims to address problems of metaphor detection in discourse. As a direction related to metaphor detection, Section 2.3 introduces computational work that extracts properties of similes, which provides inspiration for our template induction approach used to induce properties (facets) of a metaphor frame.

2.1 Modeling Metaphorical Mapping

There are many different types of metaphor including metaphors that do not violate any local linguistic expectations (Jang et al., 2015, 2016). In order to find other patterns not predicated on the assumption of constraint violation, one might investigate which domains are frequently mapped metaphorically, or what target and source domains are frequently used together in metaphors.

Within these approaches that model frequent target and source domain mappings, Shutova et al. (2010) identified new metaphors by expanding seed metaphors. The idea in this approach is that target concepts that are frequently used with the same source concept occur in similar lexico-syntactic settings. They cluster nouns (target domain) and verbs (source domain), and search the corpus for metaphors that use the verbs in the source domain lexicon to represent the target domain concepts. Extending Shutova et al. (2010), (Shutova and Sun, 2013) find metaphorical mappings by building and traversing a graph of concepts. Then, they generate lists of salient features for the metaphorically connected clusters, and search the corpus for metaphors that use the verbs in the salient features to represent the target domain concepts.

Another approach, Hovy et al. (2013) detected metaphors using certain semantic patterns appearing in metaphor manifestations. For example, "sweet" with *food* is literal, but is metaphorical with *people*. By finding these patterns on different levels, they extended the application of this mapping information from a narrow focus on verb relations to other syntactic relations.

Along the same lines, Mohler et al. (2013) presented a domain-aware semantic signature to capture source and target domains for a text. A semantic signature represents the placement of a text on a semantic space by using a set of related Word-Net senses, and it includes source concept dimensions and target concept dimensions. The primary idea is that the signature of a known metaphor is used to detect the same conceptual metaphor.

These approaches are effective for capturing frequent domain specific metaphorical mappings, and in appropriate contexts are helpful for metaphor detection. They also provided valuable insight to our approach. Nevertheless, they may overgeneralize in cases where frequent mappings are metaphorical when applied to an extended discourse.

2.2 Metaphor Detection in Discourse

Other approaches, which share more conceptually with our approach, use context information above the clause level to more directly address problems related to metaphor detection in discourse.

In these contexts, using only local indicators has less predictive power since metaphor is not always confined to a single clause in discourse.

In detection of metaphor in running discourse, coherence in context is an important ingredient. For example, Jang et al. (2015) detected metaphor in discourse focusing on modeling the context of a target word that may or may not have been used metaphorically. They modeled context as global and local, using lexical categories and topic distributions to detect whether cohesion in context was disrupted. In addition, within a sentence, they used the idea that interplay between the target words category and that of other words is indicative of the non-literalness of the target word. Jang et al. (2016), building on the work of Jang et al. (2015), more aggressively tackle the problem that distinguishes metaphorical/literal usage when there has been a recent topic transition. They do so by modeling topic transitions in conjunction with situational context. These approaches begin to grapple with the challenges of leveraging context, but encounter problems when related metaphors co-exist around a target word i.e., extended metaphor. In contrast, in our approach, nearby related words are strategically used to assist rather than obfuscate metaphor detection.

Detecting extended metaphor is important for modeling the use of metaphor in communication. Beigman Klebanov and Beigman (2010) offers an example of studying extended metaphor, showing that extended metaphors can reveal motivations behind metaphor use and the effect of metaphor use on social dynamics in political communication. However, this study was conducted using manually-annotated extended metaphors on a small dataset, and to our knowledge there has been no computational work on detecting extended metaphor. In this paper, we demonstrate promising improvement over prior approaches by leveraging frame facet information on an established metaphor detection task. There is no existing corpus for extended metaphor detection; however, our error analysis suggests that the broad conceptualization of metaphor we employ will be applicable to extended metaphor.

2.3 Extraction of Properties

So far very little computational work has focused on facets, or properties, of metaphor specifically. However, the Qadir et al. (2016) approach auto-matically infers implicit properties evoked by similes. They generate candidate properties from different sources using a vehicle and an event. Then, properties are evaluated based on the influence of multiple simile components: using PMI or similarity between a candidate property and the second component of a simile, and aggregate ranking of the properties from different sources. This work is similar to our work in that it extracts properties related to the source domain. However, this work only focuses on similes, which have more formulaic structural patterns compared to metaphors, e.g. *He's as cold as ice*. In addition, the grammatical patterns used in their work are fixed manually by human intuition whereas we automatically infer the patterns in our work.

3 Metaphor Frames

A metaphor occurs when a speaker brings one frame into a context/situation governed by another. In this section, we offer a qualitative analysis of the data from this standpoint, and the technical approach described in Section 4 will build on this understanding.

The same or related metaphors from the frame may be used repeatedly. For example, EX(1) compares people to a gun and bullets, and EX(2) compares the world and people to a stage and players. Related metaphors can be used not only within a sentence, but also beyond a sentence. For instance, EX(3) compares the author's imagination to a circus and imagination-related things to circus-related things throughout the paragraph.

EX(1) "He is the pointing gun, we are the bullets of his desire."

EX(2) "All the world's a stage and men and women merely players." (Shakespeare, Twelfth Night)

EX(3) "Bobby Holloway says my imagination is a three-hundred-ring circus. Currently I was in ring two hundred and ninety-nine, with elephants dancing and clowns cart wheeling and tigers leaping through rings of fire. The time had come to step back, leave the main tent, go buy some popcorn and a Coke, bliss out, cool down." (Dean Koontz, Seize the Night. Bantam, 1999)

In the breast cancer discussion forum we use in our work, community participants frequently bring in *journey* and *battle* frames when talking about their cancer experience. Depending on what aspects of the cancer experience they choose to focus on, they invoke different frames accordingly even within the same text. For example, in EX(4), the *journey* and *road* metaphors are used to say that the speaker is having a similar experience with the hearer. Further on, *weapons* from the *battle* frame are used to emphasize the power of faith and prayer in cancer treatment. In this way, metaphor introduces specific facets for specific communicative purposes.

> EX(4) "I know, the age thing struck me too when I read about **your bc journey — we have been going down the same road at the same time, only in another part of the country!** It does help to know you are not alone! How amazing with the size of your tumor, that you did not have positive nodes. That is a miracle in itself. I do believe faith and prayer are our most powerful **weapons against this disease.** It is what gets me thru each day."

While metaphor provides resources for the speaker to use in communication, it also creates corresponding resources for the hearer. For example, EX(5)–EX(8) from the same thread in the breast cancer discussion forum shows how conversational participants repeat and expand one another's metaphors. The speaker in EX(5) starts using the *falling off the wagon* metaphorical idiom to convey her opinion that failing to stay on a controlled diet is okay. EX(6) relays the *falling off* part, and connects it to *journey*. EX(7) and EX(8) carry the *wagon* part of the initial post, and use *on the wagon* to describe her status (EX(7)) and her wish to the other person with the extension of *get back on after you fall*. Although *falling off the wagon* and *on the wagon* are metaphorical idioms, *get back on after you fall* is a novel metaphor created by the following speaker. This novel metaphor is drawn from the *wagon* frame that has been brought into this conversation. In this way, a metaphor that is taken up by multiple speakers may increase empathetic understanding as well as add creative opportunities (e.g., for "fun") to the conversation.

> EX(5) "**falling off the wagon** is no big thing in my opinion, the psychological good feelings of enjoyment weigh in big for feeling good."
>
> EX(6) "Tina **falling off is part of this journey**, it is stupid to deny yourself everything."
>
> EX(7) "I am **on the wagon** so far today ... ongoing battle."
>
> EX(8) "Tina — hope you **stay on the wagon**, or at least **get back on after you fall!**"

As shown in the above examples, metaphor performs social functions through the switching of frames. In other words, observing frame switches offers insight into the ways in which people use metaphor to achieve social goals. The goal of our work is to lay a computational foundation for detection of such switches so that social strategies regarding metaphor use in interaction can be accomplished as follow-up work. Thus, in this paper, we empirically construct a metaphor frame, and model the linguistic signals of frame switches.

4 Our Approach

To investigate how a metaphor frame appears in discourse, we computationally model frames that can be either metaphorically or literally used. A frame characterizes a conceptual domain, a "world" that is defined by a number of co-occurring facets. For example, the *journey* domain in *"life is a journey"* or *"he took a journey to Sweden"* could have facets such as *origin*, *destination*, *path*, *vehicle*, *companion*, and *guide*. Using a *journey*-related metaphor activates this domain and its facets, which become available as conversational resources in communication. In our work, we identify facet "slots" of a frame such as the *origin* and *destination* of the *journey* frame, and discover linguistic manifestations of the facets that fill the slots. We later use this frame information for metaphor detection, and observe how the same frame is used metaphorically or literally depending on its facets. We will call the facet slots *facets*, *facet categories*, or *facet slots*, and the linguistic manifestations *facet instances*.

In order to obtain both facets (template slots) and facet instances (slot instances), we propose a simple bootstrapping algorithm (Figure 1) which expands on the number of the facet instances, inspired by earlier bootstrapping approaches such

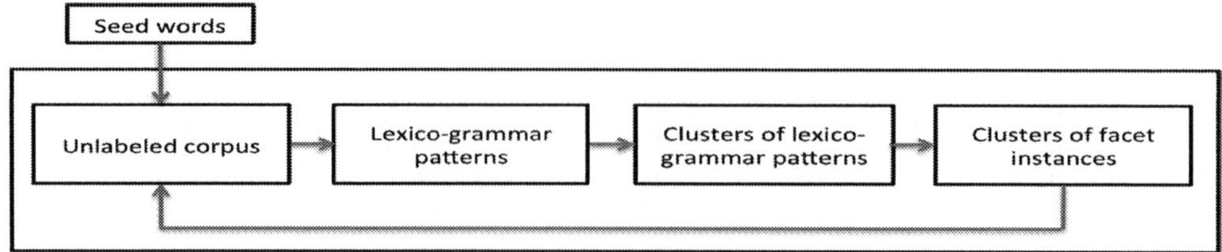

Figure 1: System flow diagram.

as (Riloff et al., 1999, 2003; Qadir and Riloff, 2013). In our model, we assume that a sentence tends to contain more than one important facet of a metaphor frame. In other words, if a sentence contains one facet of a metaphor frame, the sentence is likely to contain additional facets. Additionally, we assume that facets and dependency relations have some relationship. There are certain grammatical patterns that represent semantic relations that connect facets in context. Note that we disregard frame facet instances that do not co-occur with a keyword (e.g., *journey*) within the same sentence. This can be considered as a limitation of this approach.

Our bootstrapping process begins with several seed words (Section 4.1) that specify the domain and provide seed facet instances. Using the seed words, we collect lexico-grammatical patterns (Section 4.2) in unannotated texts and cluster them to find facets (template slots) (Section 4.3). Next, the induced patterns are used for identifying facet instances which comprise a facet cluster (Section 4.4). Then, the most representative facet instances for each cluster are identified and added to the seed word set. Repeating this process expands the seed facet instances and lexico-grammatical patterns into larger sets. The overall sequence is illustrated in Table 1.

4.1 Seed Words

The mutual bootstrapping process begins with pre-defined seed words and a text corpus. The seed words are the frame related words including the domain (e.g. *journey*) and a few examples of representative facet instances (e.g. *train, long*) for one or more unspecified facets. The corpus is then filtered for sentences that contain the frame (e.g. *journey*) and at least one example seed facet instance. Note that the sentences in the corpus are not annotated metaphorical or literal. Since we are building a frame that can be used either metaphorically or literally, we do not require sen-

1.	Harvest sentences containing the seed words from the unannotated texts.
2.	Parse the harvested sentences, and obtain lexico-grammatical patterns of the sentences.
3.	Cluster the lexico-grammatical patterns.
4.	Extract candidate facet instances from the lexico-grammatical patterns in each cluster.
5.	Compute the score of each candidate facet instance.
6.	Top ranked candidate facet instances of each cluster are added to the original seed words.
7.	Repeat starting with step 1.

Table 1: The bootstrapping process.

tences where the seed words are used in a desired sense. For this reason, any general corpus that contains sufficient amount of sentences that include frame-related words can be used.

4.2 Collect Lexico-Grammar Patterns

We collect lexico-grammatical patterns using the seed words to represent relations between the domain and its facets. Representing relations in this way is a common approach in event extraction where relations often appear in text within a verb relation. For example, in a Bombing event, *perpetrator* can be represented as a *person/org* who detonates, blows up, plants, hurls, stages, launches, or is detained, suspected, or blamed for the bombing (Chambers and Jurafsky, 2009). However, representing a relation for a domain and its facets for our purpose is not as straightforward as it is in event extraction because facets appear in more diverse ways than merely as verb relations. In particular, facets appear in a diversity of syntactic contexts.

As a solution, we propose using lexico-grammatical patterns generated from dependency paths between a domain word and facet words via the *ROOT*. The lexico-grammatical patterns are defined as the shortest path that passes through the *ROOT* in dependencies between the domain name and seed facet instances. For example, StanfordCoreNLP (Manning et al., 2014) outputs the dependencies in Table 2 for the sentence *She resumed her journey through the city*. The lexico-grammatical pattern that connects *journey* with other candidate property words such as *she* and *city* is defined as the reverse path from *journey* to *ROOT* combined with the path from *ROOT* to *journey*. The paths for the example are shown in Table 3. Words are lemmatized to reduce sparsity.

This lexico-grammatical pattern representation has advantages. First, it allows representing patterns connecting pairs of words in a position invariant manner. For example, in our baseline bootstrapping model, it is difficult to represent the pattern *reach __ of my journey* because *reach* is not located between the slot for a property instance and *journey*. However, using the lexico-grammatical pattern enables formalization of this pattern. Second, the lexico-grammar pattern is not affected by modifiers in the path. For example, the patterns representing the relationships between *journey* and *she*, and between *journey* and *city* do not change even for the sentence "She resumed her long journey through the city", in which *long* has been added.

4.3 Cluster Lexico-Grammar Patterns

Using the idea that lexico-grammar patterns can approximate semantic relations, we first cluster collected lexico-grammar patterns so that each cluster may represent a different relation (facet slot).

The feature representation of each pattern is based on all arguments (e.g., *origin* and *destination* in Table 3) the pattern has in the corpus. For example, the pattern "dobj_r(*origin*, resume), root_r(resume, root), root(root, resume), nmod:through(resume, *destination*)" in Table 3 may have other *origins* and *destinations* in the corpus in addition to many occurrences of "city". We use all arguments appearing with the pattern as features for the pattern, with the feature space size of the whole vocabulary. This is based on the idea that patterns with similar arguments would have

similar roles that can be facet slots, which is similar to the distributional hypothesis (Harris, 1954).

For the clustering algorithm, we use Nonnegative Matrix Factorization (NMF) (Lin, 2007). We adopt this algorithm because our feature space is greatly sparse and NMF is effective for sparse data. We use the scikit-learn (Pedregosa et al., 2011) implementation of NMF.

4.4 Identify Representative Facet Instances

After obtaining pattern clusters, we extract tokens that match patterns in each pattern cluster. Tokens extracted for each pattern cluster are facet instance candidates.

Although we have clusters of similar facet instance candidates, there are many noisy instances in each cluster. To determine which instances are most reliable, we score each instance based on how far its generating patterns are from the center of the cluster. Specifically, an instance is scored high if it is found in more patterns in the cluster, and in patterns with higher within-cluster scores. We also take into account how semantically close each instance is to the other words in the same cluster. We use the GloVe vector representations (Pennington et al., 2014) to compute cosine similarity between two words. The scoring formula is shown below, where N_i is the number of different patterns that extracted $word_i$, Sim is the average cosine similarity with all other words in the same cluster, $score\_pattern_k$ is within-cluster score computed by NMF.

$$score(word_i) = Sim * \sum_{k=1}^{N_i} 1 + (.01 * score\_pattern_k)$$

$$(1)$$

Once the best facet instances are identified in this ranking step, the new instances are added to the original seed words, and the process repeats. The lexico-grammar patterns and property instances are clustered again and rescored after each iteration. The process stops after a specified number of iterations. For our experiments, we found five iterations to be sufficient. We leave an exploration of more heuristic stopping criteria to future work.

5 Evaluation

We evaluate our learned facet clusters, which define a particular metaphor frame template, with

Sentence	She resumed her journey through the city.
Dependencies	nsubj(resumed-2, She-1) root(ROOT-0, resumed-2) nmod:poss(journey-4, her-3)
	dobj(resumed-2, journey-4) case(city-7, through-5) det(city-7, the-6)
	nmod:through(resumed-2, city-7)

Table 2: Dependencies from parsed result

origin	destination	pattern
journey	she	dobj_r(*origin*, resume), root_r(resume, root), root(root, resume),
		nsubj(resume, *destination*)
journey	city	dobj_r(*origin*, resume), root_r(resume, root), root(root, resume),
		nmod:through(resume, *destination*)

Table 3: Examples of lexico-grammar patterns. _r represents a reverse dependency.

Model	κ	F1	P-L	R-L	P-M	R-M	A
Frame	.204	.602	.381	.369	.826	.833	.732
Unigram	.446	.720	.707	.434	.858	.950	.837
Unigram + Frame	.485	.742	.665	.520	.874	.927	.838
Jang et al. (2016)	.618	.808	.789	.615	.899	.954	.880
Jang et al. (2016) + Frame***	.655	.827	.814	.648	.907	.959	.891

Table 4: Performance on metaphor detection. (**Metrics**) κ: Cohen's kappa, F1: average F1 score on M/L, P-L: precision on literals, R-L: recall on literals, P-M: precision on metaphors, R-M: recall on metaphors, A: accuracy, ***: highly statistically significant ($p < 0.01$) improvement over Jang et al. (2016) by Student's t-test.

respect to how well they perform for an application, metaphor detection. In so doing, we assess the performance of the represented frame information and compare to state-of-the-art models for the same task. The evaluation results are presented in Table 4. The results show that our model performs significantly better than the state-of-the-art model, which indicates that modeling metaphor in terms of frames is promising for distinguishing metaphorical and literal usage of words.

Section 5.1 explains our evaluation task, and which datasets we have used for the evaluation. Section 5.2 describes baseline systems we compare our model with. Section 5.3 illustrates how we model the frame information as features for classification, and explains the classification settings used in our experiments. Finally, Section 5.4 provides the experiment results.

5.1 Evaluation Task

For our experiments, we use the metaphor detection task as in Jang et al. (2016). The task is to decide whether a given target word is metaphorically or literally used. Because there is a set of pre-determined target words, this task is beneficial

to see whether the applied model has disambiguating power.

We conducted our metaphor detection experiments on a subset of the breast cancer metaphor dataset annotated by Jang et al. (2015). We chose to work on this dataset because this dataset contains conversational texts so that we can observe how people use metaphor in discourse. In addition, more importantly, this dataset has multiple target metaphors from a single frame, *journey*. From the cross-validation and development datasets used in (Jang et al., 2016), we select the journey-related words *road*, *train*, and *ride* to evaluate the journey frame template we built. We exclude other target words, *spice*, *boat*, *light*, and *candle* for our experiments because they do not belong to the journey frame. After filtering out these target words that are not relevant to the journey frame, the development dataset contains 488 instances, and the cross-validation dataset contains 1,119 instances.

To learn templates for the *journey* frame, we use unannotated data from the BookCorpus (Zhu et al., 2015). The corpus contains 11,038 books in 16 different genres. Particularly for our experiments, we use 74,004,228 sentences from the books, which are provided together with the original book files in the corpus. We use this data instead of more conversational data in order to minimize errors from detecting sentence boundaries and parsing, and to ensure broad topical coverage.

5.2 Baselines

First, we compare our model with a baseline Context Unigram Model that uses all the words in a post as features. Additionally, we compare our model with (Jang et al., 2016), a state-of-the-art model on this dataset. Their model uses sentence-level topic transition features and emotion and cognition related features. We use their best configuration of features, which includes unigram, lexical contrast between a target word and its global and local context (Jang et al., 2015), and topic transition surrounding the target word and emotion and cognition features (Jang et al., 2016). For comparison to approaches using only local indicators, see (Jang et al., 2015).

5.3 Features and Classification Settings

We extract a vector of binary features for each target word to indicate which of the learned facets of the journey frame appear in its immediate context. The presence of each cluster in the same sentence, preceding sentence, and following sentence relative to the target word; as well as the presence of each cluster in any of those three contexts, is indicated respectively by features in a vector of length four times the number of clusters.

We used the support vector machine (SVM) classifier provided in the `LightSIDE` toolkit (Mayfield and Rosé, 2010) with sequential minimal optimization (SMO) and a polynomial kernel of exponent 2. This enables the model to make use of contingencies between features. We expect that in order for a frame to be meaningfully identified, an appropriate topic shift coupled with identification of associated slot fillers in the nearby context is needed. The nonlinearity in this model enables this. For each experiment, we performed 10-fold cross-validation. We also trained the baselines with the same SVM settings.

5.4 Results

The results of our classification experiment are shown in Table 4. We tested our frame features alone (Frame), with context unigram features (Un-

igram + Frame), and with features from the previous state of the art ((Jang et al., 2016) + Frame).

Adding our frame features to the baselines improved performance in predicting metaphor detection. We see that our features combined with the unigram features slightly improved over the Unigram baseline. However, when our features are combined with the features from Jang et al. (2016), we see large gains in performance, which suggests that there is an synergistic interaction between our frame features and the features from Jang et al. (2016).

6 Discussion

Our experiments show that frame facets that appear in surrounding sentences can be strong indicators of metaphor detection. This is promising, and suggests that observing frame facets can be crucial key to understanding how metaphor is used in discourse. However, the frame facets themselves are not as informative as when used with other features from the baseline. The improved performance when the frame facets are used with baseline features in the nonlinear model suggests that there are interactions among the features. In this section, we discuss the benefits of our model by examining prediction errors of our model and the (Jang et al., 2016) baseline.

The majority of the instances where the baseline model and our model do not agree is where our model improves on classifying literal instances as literal. In these cases, a topic shift is sufficient evidence of a metaphor, but the model without our template slots is not able to determine that. EX(9) and EX(10) show some specific examples where the baseline failed by incorrectly predicting metaphor. In both of these examples, a target word *road* is used literally, but the baseline classified it as metaphorical. Although their own topic transition features correctly captured that there is no topic transition in both cases, in combination with Jang et al. (2015) features, the baseline model did not make a correct prediction.

> EX(9) ... Planning on having my right removed then reconstruction on both sides . I am an avid runner , road biker and downhill skier . Was looking at the tram flap. ...

> EX(10) ... I did go to my son 's for Christmas , 500 miles away . My husband drove and we spent one night

at our daughters to break up the time on the *road* .

When our frame features are added, however, the model correctly predicted that they are literal. This is probably because our frame features that picked up frame facet words surrounding the target word in combination with topic transition features strongly signaled literal usage of the target word. In EX(10), for example, our model picked up the distance word, *miles*, in the sentence prior to the sentence where the target word *road* resides.

From this, we can see that adding the frame facet information allows having more complete frame information for distinguishing metaphorical and literal usage of the topic frame. Our model seems to provide more fine-grained information about what pieces of the frame make it metaphorical or literal.

Conducting an error analysis on the instances where both baseline and our model failed reveals the limitations of using a topic frame based approach in general. EX(11) shows that *train* is used literally in the post. However, because there are different topical words around the target word and there is no other journey frame words, both (Jang et al., 2016) model and our model classify the target word as metaphorical by picking up the topic transition.

> EX(11) ... I woke at 2 a.m. because it was so quiet . I could n't hear the frogs or crickets and then I heard a *train* getting louder and louder and then it threw us around . When we got out the giant trees looked like x-mas trees from all the clutter in the tops of them . ...

7 Conclusion

In this paper, we argued that a frame-based approach is useful for metaphor detection and may be useful in subsequent work for studying metaphor from a social perspective. In particular, we described a semi-supervised computational approach for constructing a metaphor frame from unlabeled text. We demonstrated the effectiveness of this frame information in metaphor detection when used together with other proven features in a nonlinear machine learning model, which suggests interactions among the features. We discussed the ways in which the frame and topic information

anchor the classifier to allow for more accurate metaphor detection.

Although our approach showed promising results which suggest that how the frame facet information is used in text helps determine the frame's metaphorical usage, applying frame information to metaphor detection in this way has a limitation in scalability – we need to know which frame target words belong to in advance. Our contributions here demonstrated the potential of modeling metaphor through the lens of frame theory; we hope to address scalable ways to leveraging frame information in future work, for example, by automatically detecting primary frames that exist in text.

In addition, we hope to exploit this frame information for detecting extended metaphor, a series of related metaphors under the same frame. Obtaining a metaphor corpus that contains a sufficient amount of extended metaphors is a big challenge. However, once such a dataset becomes available, we believe that the findings from this paper will be applicable in that context.

Acknowledgments

We thank the reviewers for their helpful and insightful comments. This research was supported in part by NSF grant IIS 1546393.

References

Beata Beigman Klebanov and Eyal Beigman. 2010. A game-theoretic model of metaphorical bargaining. In *Proceedings of the 48th annual meeting of the association for computational linguistics*. Association for Computational Linguistics, pages 698–709.

Marc Brysbaert, Amy Beth Warriner, and Victor Kuperman. 2014. Concreteness ratings for 40 thousand generally known english word lemmas. *Behavior research methods* 46(3):904–911.

Nathanael Chambers and Dan Jurafsky. 2009. Unsupervised learning of narrative schemas and their participants. In *Proceedings of the Joint Conference of the 47th Annual Meeting of the ACL and the 4th International Joint Conference on Natural Language Processing of the AFNLP: Volume 2-Volume 2*. Association for Computational Linguistics, pages 602–610.

Gilles Fauconnier and Mark Turner. 1998. Conceptual integration networks. *Cognitive science* 22(2):133–187.

Charles J Fillmore. 1976. Frame semantics and the nature of language. In *Annals of the New York*

Academy of Sciences: Conference on the origin and development of language and speech. volume 280, pages 20–32.

James Paul Gee. 2014. *An introduction to discourse analysis: Theory and method*. Routledge, fourth edition.

Zellig S Harris. 1954. Distributional structure. *Word* 10(2-3):146–162.

Dirk Hovy, Shashank Srivastava, Sujay Kumar Jauhar, Mrinmaya Sachan, Kartik Goyal, Huiying Li, Whitney Sanders, and Eduard Hovy. 2013. Identifying metaphorical word use with tree kernels. *Meta4NLP 2013* page 52.

Ting-Hao Kenneth Huang. 2014. Social metaphor detection via topical analysis. In *Sixth International Joint Conference on Natural Language Processing*. page 14.

Hyeju Jang, Yohan Jo, Qinlan Shen, Michael Miller, Seungwhan Moon, and Carolyn Rose. 2016. Metaphor detection with topic transition, emotion and cognition in context. In *Proceedings of the 54th Annual Meeting of the Association for Computational Linguistics (Volume 1: Long Papers)*. Association for Computational Linguistics, pages 216–225. https://doi.org/10.18653/v1/P16-1021.

Hyeju Jang, Seunghwan Moon, Yohan Jo, and Carolyn Penstein Rosé. 2015. Metaphor detection in discourse. In *16th Annual Meeting of the Special Interest Group on Discourse and Dialogue*. page 384.

Chih-Jen Lin. 2007. Projected gradient methods for nonnegative matrix factorization. *Neural computation* 19(10):2756–2779.

Christopher D. Manning, Mihai Surdeanu, John Bauer, Jenny Finkel, Steven J. Bethard, and David McClosky. 2014. The Stanford CoreNLP natural language processing toolkit. In *Proceedings of 52nd Annual Meeting of the Association for Computational Linguistics: System Demonstrations*. pages 55–60. http://www.aclweb.org/anthology/P/P14/P14-5010.

James H Martin. 1996. Computational approaches to figurative language. *Metaphor and Symbol* 11(1):85–100.

Elijah Mayfield and Carolyn Rosé. 2010. An interactive tool for supporting error analysis for text mining. In *Proceedings of the NAACL HLT 2010 Demonstration Session*. Association for Computational Linguistics, pages 25–28.

Marvin Minsky. 1975. A framework for representing knowledge .

Michael Mohler, David Bracewell, David Hinote, and Marc Tomlinson. 2013. Semantic signatures for example-based linguistic metaphor detection. In *Proceedings of the First Workshop on Metaphor in NLP*. pages 27–35.

F. Pedregosa, G. Varoquaux, A. Gramfort, V. Michel, B. Thirion, O. Grisel, M. Blondel, P. Prettenhofer, R. Weiss, V. Dubourg, J. Vanderplas, A. Passos, D. Cournapeau, M. Brucher, M. Perrot, and E. Duchesnay. 2011. Scikit-learn: Machine learning in Python. *Journal of Machine Learning Research* 12:2825–2830.

Jeffrey Pennington, Richard Socher, and Christopher D. Manning. 2014. Glove: Global vectors for word representation. In *Empirical Methods in Natural Language Processing (EMNLP)*. pages 1532–1543. http://www.aclweb.org/anthology/D14-1162.

Ashequl Qadir and Ellen Riloff. 2013. Bootstrapped learning of emotion hashtags# hashtags4you. In *Proceedings of the 4th workshop on computational approaches to subjectivity, sentiment and social media analysis*. pages 2–11.

Ashequl Qadir, Ellen Riloff, and Marilyn A Walker. 2016. Automatically inferring implicit properties in similes. In *Proceedings of NAACL-HLT*. pages 1223–1232.

Ellen Riloff, Rosie Jones, et al. 1999. Learning dictionaries for information extraction by multi-level bootstrapping. In *AAAI/IAAI*. pages 474–479.

Ellen Riloff, Janyce Wiebe, and Theresa Wilson. 2003. Learning subjective nouns using extraction pattern bootstrapping. In *Proceedings of the seventh conference on Natural language learning at HLT-NAACL 2003-Volume 4*. Association for Computational Linguistics, pages 25–32.

Roger C Schank and Robert P Abelson. 1975. *Scripts, plans, and knowledge*. Yale University.

Ekaterina Shutova. 2015. Design and evaluation of metaphor processing systems. *Computational Linguistics* 41(4):579–623.

Ekaterina Shutova and Lin Sun. 2013. Unsupervised metaphor identification using hierarchical graph factorization clustering. In *HLT-NAACL*. pages 978–988.

Ekaterina Shutova, Lin Sun, and Anna Korhonen. 2010. Metaphor identification using verb and noun clustering. In *Proceedings of the 23rd International Conference on Computational Linguistics*. Association for Computational Linguistics, pages 1002–1010.

Deborah Tannen. 1993. *Framing in discourse*. Oxford University Press.

Deborah Tannen and Cynthia Wallat. 1987. Interactive frames and knowledge schemas in interaction: Examples from a medical examination/interview. *Social Psychology Quarterly* pages 205–216.

Yulia Tsvetkov, Elena Mukomel, and Anatole Gershman. 2013. Cross-lingual metaphor detection using common semantic features .

Peter D Turney, Yair Neuman, Dan Assaf, and Yohai Cohen. 2011. Literal and metaphorical sense identification through concrete and abstract context. In *Proceedings of the 2011 Conference on the Empirical Methods in Natural Language Processing*. pages 680–690.

Yukun Zhu, Ryan Kiros, Richard Zemel, Ruslan Salakhutdinov, Raquel Urtasun, Antonio Torralba, and Sanja Fidler. 2015. Aligning books and movies: Towards story-like visual explanations by watching movies and reading books. In *arXiv preprint arXiv:1506.06724*.

Using Reinforcement Learning to Model Incrementality
in a Fast-Paced Dialogue Game

Ramesh Manuvinakurike[1,2]**, David DeVault**[2]**, Kallirroi Georgila**[1,2]
[1]Institute for Creative Technologies, University of Southern California
[2]Computer Science Department, University of Southern California
`manuvina|devault@usc.edu, kgeorgila@ict.usc.edu`

Abstract

We apply Reinforcement Learning (RL) to
the problem of incremental dialogue policy learning in the context of a fast-paced
dialogue game. We compare the policy
learned by RL with a high performance
baseline policy which has been shown to
perform very efficiently (nearly as well as
humans) in this dialogue game. The RL
policy outperforms the baseline policy in
offline simulations (based on real user data).
We provide a detailed comparison of the
RL policy and the baseline policy, including information about how much effort and
time it took to develop each one of them.
We also highlight the cases where the RL
policy performs better, and show that understanding the RL policy can provide valuable insights which can inform the creation
of an even better rule-based policy.

1 Introduction

Building incremental spoken dialogue systems
(SDSs) has recently attracted much attention. One
reason for this is that incremental dialogue processing allows for increased responsiveness, which
in turn improves task efficiency and user satisfaction. Incrementality in dialogue has been studied in
the context of turn-taking, predicting the next user
utterances/actions, and generating fast system responses (Skantze and Schlangen, 2009; Schlangen
et al., 2009; Selfridge and Heeman, 2010; DeVault
et al., 2011; Dethlefs et al., 2012a,b; Selfridge
et al., 2012, 2013; Hastie et al., 2013; Baumann and
Schlangen, 2013; Paetzel et al., 2015). Over the
years researchers have tried a variety of approaches
to incremental dialogue processing. One such approach is using rules whose parameters may be
optimized using real user data (Buß et al., 2010;

Ghigi et al., 2014; Paetzel et al., 2015). Reinforcement Learning (RL) is another method that has
been used to learn policies regarding when the system should interrupt the user (barge-in), stay silent,
or generate backchannels in order to improve the
responsiveness of the SDS or increase task success
(Kim et al., 2014; Khouzaimi et al., 2015; Dethlefs
et al., 2016).

We apply RL to the problem of incremental dialogue policy learning in the context of a fast-paced
dialogue game. We use a corpus of real user data
for both training and testing. We compare the policies learned by RL with a high performance baseline policy which uses parameterized rules (whose
parameters have been optimized using real user
data) and has a carefully designed rule (CDR) structure. From now on, we will refer to this baseline as
the CDR baseline.

Our contributions are as follows: We provide
an RL method for incremental dialogue processing
based on simplistic features which performs better
in offline simulations (based on real user data) than
the high performance CDR baseline. Note that this
is a very strong baseline which has been shown
to perform very efficiently (nearly as well as humans) in this dialogue game (Paetzel et al., 2015).
In many studies that use RL for dialogue policy
learning, the focus is on the RL algorithms, the
state-action space representation, and the reward
function. As a result, the rule-based baselines used
for comparing the RL policies against are not as
carefully engineered as they could be, i.e., they are
not the result of iterative improvement and optimization using insights learned from data or user
testing. This is understandable since building a very
strong baseline would be a big project by itself and
would detract attention from the RL problem. In
our case, there was a pre-existing strong CDR baseline policy which inspired us to investigate whether
it could be outperformed by an RL policy. One of

Proceedings of the SIGDIAL 2017 Conference, pages 331–341,
Saarbrücken, Germany, 15-17 August 2017. ©2017 Association for Computational Linguistics

our main contributions is that we provide a detailed comparison of the RL policy and the CDR baseline policy, including information about how much effort and time it took to develop each one of them. We also highlight the cases where the RL policy performs better, and show that understanding the RL policy can provide valuable insights which can inform the creation of an even better rule-based policy.

2 RDG-Image Game

For this study we used the RDG-Image (Rapid Dialogue Game) (Paetzel et al., 2014) dataset and the high performance baseline Eve system (Section 2.2). RDG-Image is a collaborative, two player, time-constrained, incentivized rapid conversational game, and has two player roles, the Director and the Matcher. The players are given 8 images as shown in Figure 1 in a randomized order. One of the images is highlighted with a red border on the Director's screen (called target image - TI). The Matcher sees the same 8 images in a different order but does not know the TI. The Director has to describe the TI in such a way that the Matcher will be able to identify it from the distractors as quickly as possible. The Director and Matcher can talk back-and-forth freely to accomplish the task. Once the Matcher believes that he has made the right selection, he clicks on the image and communicates this to the Director. If the guess is correct then the team earns 1 point, otherwise 0 points. Now the Director can press a button so that the game can continue with a new TI. The game consists of 4 rounds called Sets (from 1 - 4) with varying levels of complexity. Each round has a predefined time limit. The goal is to complete as many images as possible, and thus as a team to earn as many points as possible.

2.1 Human-Human Data

The RDG-Image data comes in two flavors, human-human (HH) and human-agent (HA) spoken conversations. The HH data was collected by pairing 2 human players in real time and having their conversation recorded. The HA conversations were recorded by pairing a human Director with the agent Matcher (Section 2.2). In this section, we describe the HH part of the corpus. The HH data was collected in two separate experiments, in-lab (Paetzel et al., 2014) and over the web (Manuvinakurike and DeVault, 2015). Figure 1 shows an excerpt from the HH corpus.

The HH corpus contains the user speech transcribed, and labeled dialogue acts (DAs) along with carefully annotated time stamps as shown in Figure 1. This timing information is important for modeling incrementality. We can observe that the game conversation involves rapid exchanges with frequent overlaps. Each episode (dialogue exchange for each TI) typically begins with the Director describing the TI and ends with the Matcher acknowledging the TI selection with the Assert-Identified (As-I) DA (e.g., "got it") or As-S (skipping action) DA (e.g., "let's move on to the next image"). The Director then requests the next TI and the game continues until time runs out. Sometimes the Matcher may interrupt the Director with questions or other illocutionary acts. A complete list of DAs can be found in (Manuvinakurike et al., 2016).

In this paper, we are interested in modeling incrementality for DAs related to TI selection by the Matcher. As-I is the most common DA used by the human Matchers. As-S was not frequently used by the human Matchers but is used by the baseline matcher agent to give up on the current TI and proceed to the next TI to try to increase the total points scored. Further distinctions between As-I and As-S are made in Section 2.2. The most common DA generated by the Director was D-T (Describe-Target).

2.2 Eve

The baseline agent called Eve (Paetzel et al., 2015) was developed to play the role of the Matcher using the HH data. The agent Eve relies on several kinds of incremental processing. It obtains the 1-best automatic speech recognition (ASR) hypothesis every 100ms and forwards it to the natural language understanding (NLU) module. The NLU module is a Naive Bayes classifier trained on bag-of-words features which are generated using a frequency threshold (frequency >5) on unigrams and bigrams (d_t). The NLU assigns confidence values to the 8 images (called the image set). Let the image set at time t be $\mathcal{I}_t = \{i_1, ..., i_8\}$, with the correct target image $T \in \mathcal{I}_t$ unknown to the agent. The maximum probability assigned to any image at time t is $P_t^* = \max_j P(T = i_j | d_t)$. We call these probability values $(P(T = i_j | d_t))$ as confidence. The image with the highest confidence is chosen as the best selection TI by the agent. Let t_c be the

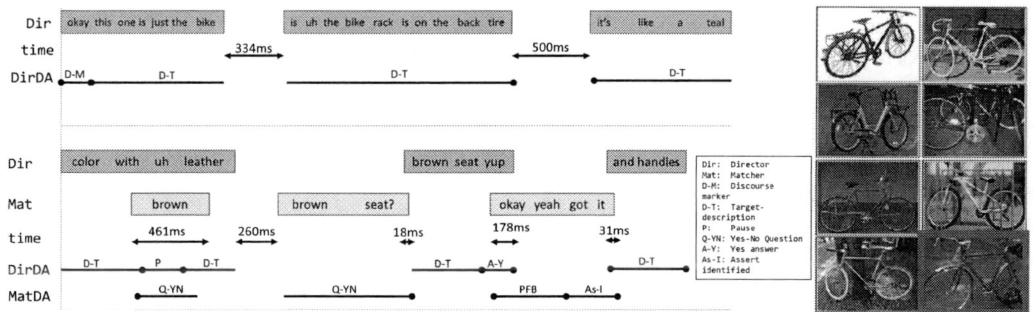

Figure 1: Example interaction for a set of images in the human-human corpus.

time consumed on the current TI.

Eve's policy decides between waiting and interrupting the user with As-I or As-S to maximize the score in the game. She can do it by taking three actions: i) WAIT: Listen more in the hope that the user provides more information; ii) As-I: Make the selection and request the next TI; iii) As-S: Make the selection and request the next TI as it might not be fruitful to wait more.[1] Eve's policy depicted in Algorithm 1, uses two threshold values namely identification threshold (IT) and give-up threshold (GT) to select these actions. The IT learned is the least confidence value (P_t^*) above which the agent uses the As-I action. GT is the maximum time the agent should WAIT before giving up on the current image set and requesting the human Director to move on to the next TI. The IT and GT values are learned using an offline policy optimization method called the Eavesdropper simulation, which performs an exhaustive grid search to find the optimal values of IT and GT for each image set (Paetzel et al., 2015). In this simulation, the agent is trained offline on the HH conversations and learns the best values of IT and GT, i.e., the values that result in scoring the maximum points in the game. For example, the optimal values learned for the image set shown in Figure 1 were IT=0.8 and GT=18sec.

The Eve agent is very efficient and carefully engineered to perform well in this task, and serves as a very strong baseline. In the real user study reported in Paetzel et al. (2015), Eve in the HA gameplay scored nearly as well as human users in HH gameplay. Thus this study provides an opportunity to compare an RL policy with a strong baseline

---

Algorithm 1 Eve's dialogue policy

if $P_t^* >$ IT & $|\text{filtered}(d_t)| \geq 1$ **then**
　　Assert-Identified (As-I)
else if $\text{elapsed}(t) <$ GT **then**
　　WAIT (continue listening)
else
　　Request-Skip (As-S)
end if

---

policy that uses a hand-crafted carefully designed rule structure (CDR baseline). In the Appendix, Figure 6 shows an example from the HA corpus. The data used in the current work comes from both the HH and HA datasets (see Table 1).

Branch	# users	# sub-dialogues
Human-Human lab	64	1485
Human-Human web	196	5642
Human-Agent web	175	7393

Table 1: Number of users and number of TI sub-dialogues used for our study.

2.3 Improving NLU with Agent Conversation Data

Obviously, the success of the agent heavily depends on the accuracy of the NLU module. In the earlier work by Paetzel et al. (2015), the NLU module was trained on HH conversations. We investigated whether using HA data would improve the NLU accuracy or not. Using data from all of the users director's speech for all the TIs in the HH branch only the NLU accuracy was found to be 59.72%. Using data from the HA branch only resulted in a lower NLU accuracy of 48.70%. Combining the HH and HA training data resulted in a higher accuracy of 61.89%. The improvement associated with training on HH and HA data is significant

---

[1] For As-S Eve's utterance is 'I don't think I can get that one. Let's move on. I clicked randomly' and for As-I it is 'Got it'.

across all sets of images[2]. Thus in this work we use the best performing NLU with the data trained from both the HH and HA subsets of the corpus. The overall reported NLU accuracy was averaged across all the image sets. The NLU module was trained with the same method as in Paetzel et al. (2015). Note that for all our experiments, 10% of the HH data and 10% of the HA data was used for testing, and the rest was used for training.

2.4 Room for Improvement

Though the baseline agent is impressive in its performance there are a few shortcomings. We investigated the errors being made by the baseline policy and identified four primary limitations in its decision-making. Examples of these limitations are shown in Figure 2, depicting the NLU assigned confidence (y-axis) for the human TI descriptions plotted against the time steps (x-axis).

First, the baseline commits to As-I as soon as the confidence reaches a high enough value (IT threshold), or As-S when the time consumed exceeds the GT threshold. In Case 1 the agent decides to skip (As-S) because the time consumed has exceeded the GT threshold, instead of waiting more which would allow for a more distinguishing description to come from the human Director.

Second, its performance can be negatively affected by instability in the partial ASR results. Examples of partial ASR results are shown in Figure 8 in the Appendix. In Case 2, the agent could learn to wait for higher time intervals as the ASR partial outputs become more stable.

Third, the baseline only commits at high confidence values. Case 3 shows an instance where the agent can save time by committing to a selection at a much lesser confidence value.

Fourth, as we can see from Algorithm 1, the baseline policy does not use "combinations" (or joint values) of time and confidence to make detailed decisions.

Perhaps using RL can not only help the agent learn a more complex strategy but could also provide insights into developing a better engineered policy which would not have been intuitive for a dialogue designer to come up with. That is, RL could potentially help in building better rules that would be much easier to incorporate into the agent and thus improve its performance. For example, is there

a combination of time and confidence which is not currently used by the baseline i.e., not committing at some initial time slices for high confidence values and committing at lower confidence values as the user consumes more time?

3 Design of the RL Policy

The incremental policy decision making is modeled as an MDP (Markov decision process), i.e., a tuple (S, A, TP, R, γ). S is a set of states that the agent can be in. In this task S is represented by (P_t^*, t_c) features where P_t^* is the highest confidence score assigned by the NLU for any image in the image set ($P_t^* \longmapsto \mathbb{R}; 0.0 \leq P_t^* \leq 1.0$) and t_c is the time consumed for the current TI ($t_c \longmapsto \mathbb{R}; 0.0 \leq t_c \leq 45.0$)[3]. The RL learns a policy π mapping the state (S) to the action (A), $\pi : S \to A$, where $A = \{$As-I, As-S, WAIT$\}$ are the actions to be performed by the agent to maximize the overall reward in the game. The As-I and As-S actions map to their corresponding utterances. R is the reward function and γ a discount factor weighting long-term rewards. TP is the set of transition probabilities after taking an action.

When the agent is in the state $S_t = (P_t^*, t_c)$, executing the WAIT action results in moving to the state S_{t+1} which corresponds to a new d_{t+1} which corresponds to the new utterance (See Section 2.2) and thus yielding new P_t^* and t_c for the given episode. The As-I and As-S actions result in goal states for the agent. Separate policies are trained per image set similar to the baseline. The difference between the As-I and As-S action is in the rewards assigned. The reward function R is as follows. After the agent performs the As-I action, it receives a high positive reward for the correct image selection and a high negative penalty for the wrong selection. This is to encourage the agent to learn to guess at the right point of time. There is a small positive reward of δ for "WAIT" actions, to encourage the agent to wait before committing to As-I selections. No reward is provided for the As-S actions. This is to discourage the agent from choosing to skip and scoring the points by chance, and at the same time not penalize the agent for wanting to skip when it is really necessary. The reward function for As-S prevents the agent from getting heavy negative penalties in case the wrong images are selected by the NLU. In those cases the confidence would probably be low and thus the

---

[2]All the significance tests are performed using student's t test.

[3]Each round lasts a maximum of 45 seconds.

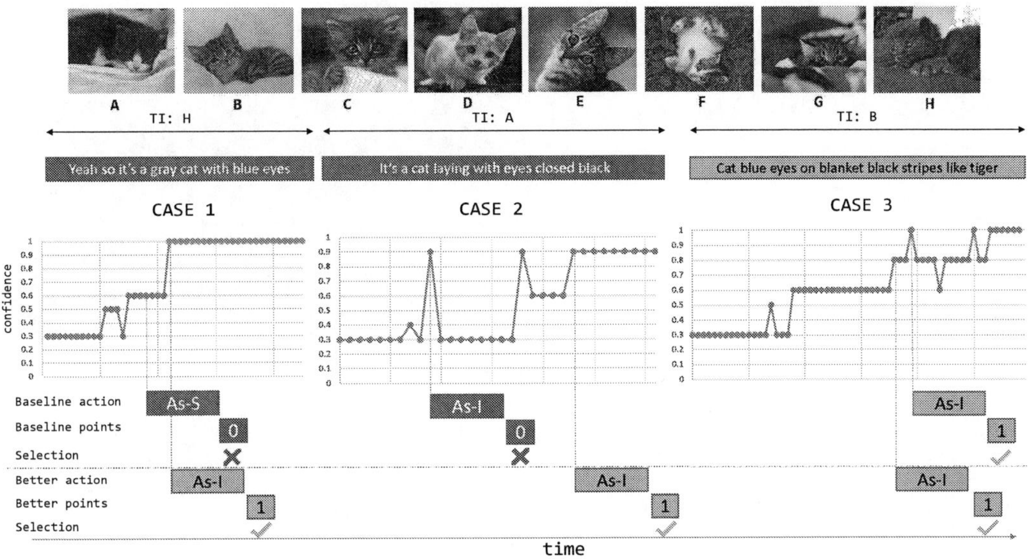

Figure 2: Examples where the agent can do better. The red boxes show the wrong selection by the agent.

agent would not commit to As-I but choose the action As-S instead.

$$R = \begin{cases} +\delta & \text{if action is WAIT} \\ +100 & \text{if As-I is right} \\ -100 & \text{if As-I is wrong} \\ 0 & \text{if action is As-S} \end{cases}$$

In this work we use the least squares policy iteration (LSPI) (Lagoudakis and Parr, 2003) RL algorithm implemented in the BURLAP[4] java code library to learn the optimal policy. LSPI is a sample efficient model-free off-policy method that combines policy iteration with linear value function approximation. LSPI in our work uses State-Action-Reward-State (SARS) transitions sampled from the human interactions data (HH and HA). We use Gaussian radial basis value function (RBF) representation for the confidence (P_t^*) and time consumed (t_c) features. We treat the state features as continuous values. The confidence values and time consumed values are continuous in nature within the bounds defined i.e., $0.0 \leq P_t^* \leq 1.0$ and $0.0 \leq t_c \leq 45.0$. We define 10 basis functions distributed uniformly for the confidence features (P_t^*) and 45 basis functions for the time consumed (t_c) features. The basis function returns a value between 0 and 1 with a value of 1 when the query state has a distance of zero from the function's "center" state. As the state gets further away, the

basis function's returned value degrades to a value of zero.

Initial experimentation with the Vanilla Q-learning algorithm (Sutton and Barto, 1998) did not yield good results, due to the very large state space and consequently data sparsity. Binning the features, in order to transform their continuous values into discrete values and thus reduce the size of the state space, did not help either. That is, having a large number of bins did not deal with the data sparsity problem, and having a small number of bins made it much harder to learn fine-grained distinctions between the states. Note that LSPI is generally considered as a more sample efficient algorithm than Q-learning.

We run LSPI with a discount factor of 0.99 until convergence occurs or a maximum of 50 iterations is reached, whichever happens first. We use 250k available SARS transitions from the HH and HA interactions to train the policy. The LSPI returns a Greedy-Q policy which we use on the test data.

Figure 3 shows the modus operandi of the policy in this domain. For every time step the ASR provides a 1-best partial hypothesis for the speech uttered by the test user. This partial speech recognition hypothesis is input to the NLU module which returns the confidence value (P_t^*). The time consumed (t_c) for the current TI is tracked by the game logic.

---

[4]http://burlap.cs.brown.edu/

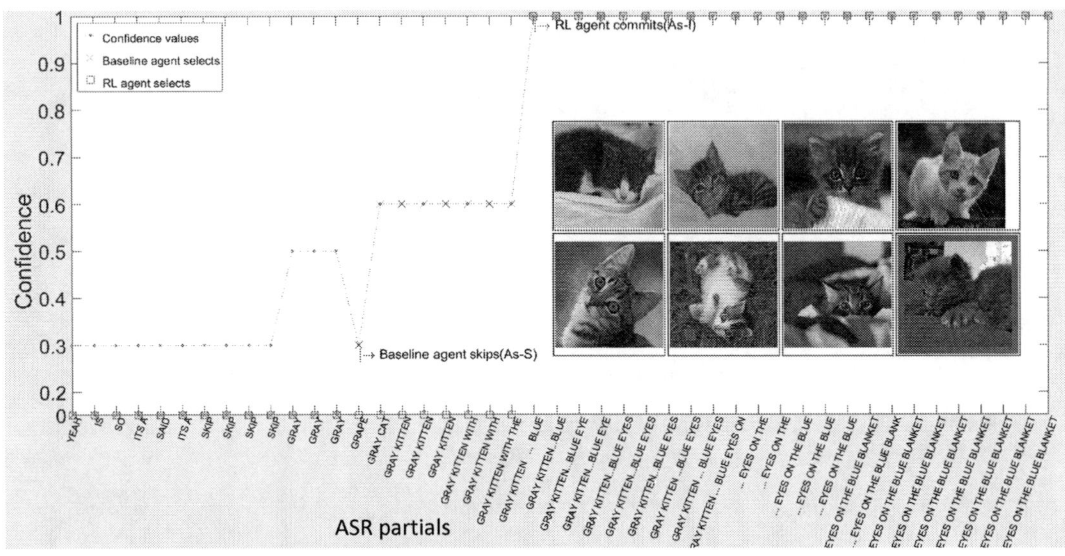

Figure 3: Actions taken by the baseline and the RL agent.

	pets		zoo		kitten		cocktail		bikes		yoga		necklace	
	PPS	P	PPS	P	PPS	P	PPS	P	PPS	P	PPS	P	PPS	P
Baseline	0.22	37	0.28	27	0.14	14	0.18	23	0.09	13	0.20	3	0.20	4
RL agent	0.23	39	0.31	32	0.13	16	0.19	25	0.14	22	0.11	18	0.12	20

Table 2: Comparison of points per second (PPS) and points (P) earned by the baseline and the RL agent on the test set.

4 Experimental Setup

For testing, we use the real user held out conversation data from the HH and HA datasets. The IT and GT thresholds for the baseline Eve were also retrained (Paetzel et al., 2015) using the same data and NLU as used to train the RL policy. Figure 3 shows the setup for testing and comparing the actions of the RL policy and the baseline. Every ASR partial corresponds to a state. For every ASR partial we obtain the highest assigned confidence score from the NLU, use the time consumed feature from the game, and obtain the action from the policy. If the action chosen by the policy is "WAIT" then we sample the next state. For each pair of confidence and time consumed values we obtain the actions from the baseline and the RL policy separately and compare them with the ground truth to evaluate which policy performs better. Once the policy decides to take either the As-I or As-S action then we advance the simulated game time by an additional interval of 750ms or 1500ms respectively. This is to simulate the conditions in the real user game where we found that the users on average take 500ms to click the button to load the next set of TIs, and the agent takes 250ms to say the As-I utterance and 1000ms to say the As-S utterance. The next TI is loaded at this point and then the process is repeated until the game time runs out for each user round.

5 Results

The policy learned using RL (LSPI with RBF functions) performs significantly better ($p<0.01$) in scoring points compared to the baseline agent in offline simulations. Also, the RL policy takes relatively more time to commit (As-I or As-S) compared to the baseline.[5] The idea of setting the IT and GT threshold values in the baseline (Section 2.2) originally aimed at scoring points rapidly in the game, i.e., the baseline agent was optimized at scoring the highest number of points per second (PPS). The PPS parameter is a measure of how effective the agent is at scoring points overall, and is calculated as the ratio of the total points scored by the

---

[5] $p=0.06$; we cannot claim that the time taken is significantly higher but there is a trend.

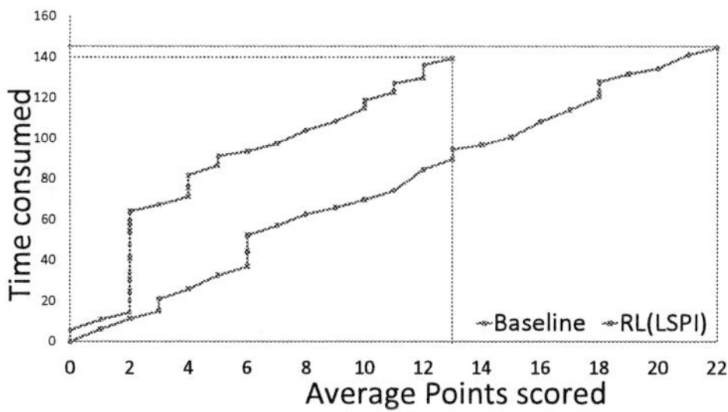

Figure 4: The RL policy scores significantly more points than the baseline by investing slightly more time (graph generated for one of the image sets).

agent divided by the total time consumed. Table 2 shows the points per second and the total points scored in some of the image sets by the baseline and the RL. We can observe that the RL consistently scores more points than the baseline, however this comes at the cost of additional time. By scoring more points overall than the baseline, the RL also scores higher in the PPS metric ($p<0.05$). Table 3 shows the total points scored and the total time spent across all the users by the baseline and the agent. Each set here refers to one round in a game.

	Baseline		RL	
Set	P	t (s)	P	t (s)
1	96	510.8	107	528.1
2	75	525.0	85	537.9
3	42	298.9	74	595.2
4	49	531.9	76	592.3

Table 3: The points scored (P) and the time consumed (t) in seconds for different image sets (Set).

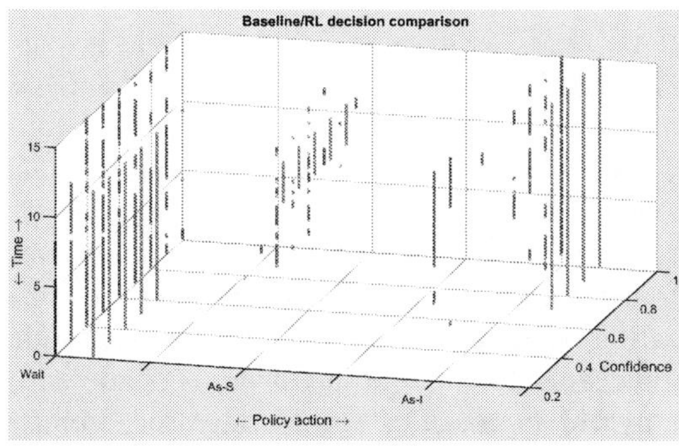

Figure 5: Decisions of the RL policy (in blue) vs. the baseline policy (in red).

Figure 4 depicts this result for an image set of bikes (images shown in Figure 1). We plot the total time spent by the agent and the total points

scored. Clearly, the RL policy manages to score more points than the baseline in a given amount of time. In order to understand the differences in the actions taken by the RL policy and the baseline policy, we plot on a 3 dimensional scatter plot, the action taken by the policy for confidence values between 0 and 1 (spaced at 0.1 intervals) and the time consumed between 0s to 15s (spaced at 100ms intervals) for one of the image sets (bikes). Figure 5 shows the decisions made by the RL (in blue) compared to the decisions made by the baseline (in red). As we can see there is not much variety in the decisions of the baseline policy; it basically uses thresholds (see Algorithm 1) optimized using real user data. Below we summarize our observations regarding the actions taken by the RL policy.

i) Regardless of whether the confidence value is high or low, the RL policy learns to wait for low values of the time consumed. This may be helping the RL policy to avoid the problem illustrated in Case 2 in Figure 2, where instability in the early ASR results for a description can lead an incorrect guess to be momentarily associated with high confidence. The RL policy is more keen on waiting and decides to commit early only when the confidence value is really high (almost 1.0). ii) Requiring a lower degree of confidence when the time consumed is high was also found to be an effective strategy to score more points in the game. Thus the RL policy learns to guess (As-I) even at lower confidence values when the time consumed reaches high values. This combination of time and confidence values helps the RL agent perform better w.r.t. points and consequently PPS in the task.

It is also important to note that the agent does not wait eternally to make its selection. The human TI descriptions are collected from real user gameplay that lasts for a limited number of time steps. That is, the maximum number of points that the RL policy can score in simulation is limited by the number of images described in the real user gameplay. In the case of the "WAIT" action beyond this point the agent fails to gather high rewards as the As-I action was never selected. By the virtue of this design feature, the RL agent has implicitly learned the notion of playing the game at a high pace.

Note also that the RL agent has not learned to always commit at a later time than the baseline. Table 4 shows the percentage of times (in the test games) where the RL policy chooses a different strategy than the baseline. We can see that the RL

% times Same commit times	48.06
% times Baseline has faster commit	44.77
% times RL has faster commit	7.17

Table 4: Comparison of commit strategies between baseline and RL (%).

policy commits at the same time instances as the baseline about 48% of the time. 44.77% of the time the baseline commits to the TI faster and about 7% of the time the RL decides to commit earlier to the TI compared to the baseline.

6 Discussion & Future Work

The cases shown in Figure 2 provide examples of how the RL policy can outperform the baseline. i) As the RL agent has learned to not commit to a decision early it can wait enough time to observe more user words and thus reach higher confidence (Case 1). ii) The RL agent is not keen on committing when it sees an early high confidence value (like IT for the baseline) but rather waits which may enable the ASR partials to become more stable (Case 2). iii) The RL agent also learns to commit at low confidence values as the time consumed increases and sometimes even committing earlier than the baseline (Case 3).

6.1 Contrasting Baseline and RL Policy Building Efforts

Building an SDS with carefullly crafted rules has often been criticized as a laborious and time consuming exercise. This is in contrast to the alternative data oriented approaches, which are often argued to require less time to engineer a solution and be more scalable. Development of the baseline system's policy component took an NLP researcher approximately two months, including experimentation with alternative rule structures and development of the parameter optimization framework. Note that this effort does not include data collection. The same amount of effort was put into developing the RL policy by a researcher with similar skills. Building the RL policy involved experimenting with various reward functions to suit the task. Though the reward function is simplistic in our case, a high negative reward for wrong As-I actions was required for RL to learn useful policies. It also takes effort and experimentation to select the right algorithm (LSPI with value function approximation vs. Vanilla Q-learning). It is thus hard to claim which approach is more time-efficient (in terms of development effort). Figure 7 in the Appendix shows a comparison of the baseline policy and the RL policy learned with the Vanilla Q-learning algorithm which did not perform well. It performed worse than the baseline. We also need to keep in mind that: i) We cannot claim that the rules learned by the RL policy could not be implemented in the hand-crafted system. Bounds on the time and confidence (for example: do not commit as soon as the confidence exceeds a threshold but rather wait for a few additional time steps, it is okay to commit at lower confidence values for higher time values to perform better, etc.) can be included in the Algorithm 1 and the system can be deployed with ease. ii) It usually takes time and effort to build a common infrastructure to experiment between the two strategies. In this case, experimenting with the incremental RL policy was simpler as the infrastructure and the methodology existed from the previous work by Manuvinakurike et al. (2015) and Paetzel et al. (2015). Despite the fact that both approaches required similar development effort, in the end, RL did learn a better strategy automatically, at least in our offline simulations (based on real user data). RL provides advantages compared to the baseline method. Adding new constraints into the baseline can be hard. This is because the baseline method uses exhaustive grid search to set its parameter values, and it might be exponentially costly to do this with more constraints. On the other hand, RL is more scalable as adding features is relatively easy with RL.

6.2 Future Work

In this work we have showed that RL has potential for learning policies to make incremental decisions that yield better results than a high performance CDR baseline. Our experiments were performed in simulation (albeit using real user data) and the next step is to investigate whether these improvements transfer to real time experiments (real time interaction of the agent with human users). Another interesting avenue for future work is to implement a hybrid approach of engineering a hand-crafted policy using the intuitions learned from using RL. There are still regions of the state space that were not fully explored by RL. On the other hand, as we saw, RL can potentially learn interesting policies which would not have been intuitive for a dialogue designer to come up with. Therefore, we plan to explore incorporating intuitions from the RL into the high performance CDR baseline and see which avenue would be more fruitful and if we can get the best of both worlds. Finally, another idea for future work is to experiment with Inverse Reinforcement Learning (Abbeel and Ng, 2004; Nouri et al., 2012; Kim et al., 2014) in order to potentially learn a better reward function directly from the data.

Acknowledgments

This work was supported by the National Science Foundation under Grant No. IIS-1219253 and by the U.S. Army Research Laboratory (ARL) under contract number W911NF-14-D-0005. Any opinions, findings, and conclusions or recommendations expressed in this material are those of the author(s) and do not necessarily reflect the views, position, or policy of the National Science Foundation or the United States Government, and no official endorsement should be inferred. We would like to thank Maike Paetzel. Thanks to Hugger Industries, Eric Sorenson and fixedgear for images published under CC BY-NC-SA 2.0. Thanks to Eric Parker and cosmo flash for images published under CC BY-NC 2.0, and to Richard Masonder / Cyclelicious and Florian for images published under CC BY-SA 2.0. Thanks to wikimedia for images published under CC BY-SA 2.0.

References

Pieter Abbeel and Andrew Y. Ng. 2004. Apprenticeship learning via inverse reinforcement learning. In *Proceedings of the International Conference on Machine Learning (ICML)*. Banff, Alberta, Canada.

Timo Baumann and David Schlangen. 2013. Open-ended, extensible system utterances are preferred, even if they require filled pauses. In *Proceedings of the Annual Meeting of the Special Interest Group on Discourse and Dialogue (SIGDIAL)*. Metz, France, pages 280–283.

Okko Buß, Timo Baumann, and David Schlangen. 2010. Collaborating on utterances with a spoken dialogue system using an ISU-based approach to incremental dialogue management. In *Proceedings of the Annual Meeting of the Special Interest Group on Discourse and Dialogue (SIGDIAL)*. pages 233–236.

Nina Dethlefs, Helen Hastie, Heriberto Cuayáhuitl, Yanchao Yu, Verena Rieser, and Oliver Lemon. 2016. Information density and overlap in spoken dialogue. *Computer Speech & Language* 37:82–97.

Nina Dethlefs, Helen Hastie, Verena Rieser, and Oliver Lemon. 2012a. Optimising incremental dialogue decisions using information density for interactive systems. In *Proceedings of the Joint Conference on Empirical Methods in Natural Language Processing and Computational Natural Language Learning (EMNLP-CoNLL)*. Jeju Island, South Korea, pages 82–93.

Nina Dethlefs, Helen Hastie, Verena Rieser, and Oliver Lemon. 2012b. Optimising incremental generation for spoken dialogue systems: Reducing the need for fillers. In *Proceedings of the International Natural Language Generation Conference (INLG)*. Utica, IL, USA, pages 49–58.

David DeVault, Kenji Sagae, and David Traum. 2011. Incremental interpretation and prediction of utterance meaning for interactive dialogue. *Dialogue & Discourse* 2(1).

Fabrizio Ghigi, Maxine Eskenazi, M. Ines Torres, and Sungjin Lee. 2014. Incremental dialog processing in a task-oriented dialog. In *Proceedings of INTERSPEECH*. Singapore, pages 308–312.

Helen Hastie, Marie-Aude Aufaure, Panos Alexopoulos, Heriberto Cuayáhuitl, Nina Dethlefs, Milica Gašić, James Henderson, Oliver Lemon, Xingkun Liu, Peter Mika, Nesrine Ben Mustapha, Verena Rieser, Blaise Thomson, Pirros Tsiakoulis, Yves Vanrompay, Boris Villazon-Terrazas, and Steve Young. 2013. Demonstration of the Parlance system: a data-driven, incremental, spoken dialogue system for interactive search. In *Proceedings of the Annual Meeting of the Special Interest Group on Discourse and Dialogue (SIGDIAL)*. Metz, France, pages 154–156.

Hatim Khouzaimi, Romain Laroche, and Fabrice Lefèvre. 2015. Optimising turn-taking strategies with reinforcement learning. In *Proceedings of the Annual Meeting of the Special Interest Group on Discourse and Dialogue (SIGDIAL)*. Prague, Czech Republic, pages 315–324.

Dongho Kim, Catherine Breslin, Pirros Tsiakoulis, Milica Gašić, Matthew Henderson, and Steve Young. 2014. Inverse reinforcement learning for micro-turn management. In *Proceedings of INTERSPEECH*. Singapore, pages 328–332.

Michail G. Lagoudakis and Ronald Parr. 2003. Least-squares policy iteration. *Journal of Machine Learning Research* 4:1107–1149.

Ramesh Manuvinakurike and David DeVault. 2015. *Natural Language Dialog Systems and Intelligent Assistants*, chapter Pair Me Up: A web framework for crowd-sourced spoken dialogue collection, pages 189–201.

Ramesh Manuvinakurike, Maike Paetzel, and David DeVault. 2015. Reducing the cost of dialogue system training and evaluation with online, crowd-sourced dialogue data collection. In *Proceedings of the Workshop on the Semantics and Pragmatics of Dialogue (SemDial)*. Gothenburg, Sweden.

Ramesh Manuvinakurike, Maike Paetzel, Cheng Qu, David Schlangen, and David DeVault. 2016. Toward incremental dialogue act segmentation in fast-paced interactive dialogue systems. In *Proceedings of the Annual Meeting of the Special Interest Group on Discourse and Dialogue (SIGDIAL)*. Los Angeles, CA, USA, pages 252–262.

Elnaz Nouri, Kallirroi Georgila, and David Traum. 2012. A cultural decision-making model for negotiation based on inverse reinforcement learning. In *Proceedings of the Annual Meeting of the Cognitive Science Society (CogSci)*. Sapporo, Japan, pages 2097–2102.

Maike Paetzel, Ramesh Manuvinakurike, and David DeVault. 2015. "So, which one is it?" The effect of alternative incremental architectures in a high-performance game-playing agent. In *Proceedings of the Annual Meeting of the Special Interest Group on Discourse and Dialogue (SIGDIAL)*. Prague, Czech Republic, pages 77–86.

Maike Paetzel, David Nicolas Racca, and David DeVault. 2014. A multimodal corpus of rapid dialogue games. In *Proceedings of the Language Resources and Evaluation Conference (LREC)*. Reykjavik, Iceland, pages 4189–4195.

David Schlangen, Timo Baumann, and Michaela Atterer. 2009. Incremental reference resolution: The task, metrics for evaluation, and a Bayesian filtering model that is sensitive to disfluencies. In *Proceedings of the Annual Meeting of the Special Interest Group on Discourse and Dialogue (SIGDIAL)*. London, UK, pages 30–37.

Ethan Selfridge, Iker Arizmendi, Peter Heeman, and Jason Williams. 2013. Continuously predicting and processing barge-in during a live spoken dialogue task. In *Proceedings of the Annual Meeting of the Special Interest Group on Discourse and Dialogue (SIGDIAL)*. Metz, France, pages 384–393.

Ethan Selfridge and Peter Heeman. 2010. Importance-driven turn-bidding for spoken dialogue systems. In *Proceedings of the 48th Annual Meeting of the Association for Computational Linguistics (ACL)*. Uppsala, Sweden, pages 177–185.

Ethan O. Selfridge, Iker Arizmendi, Peter A. Heeman, and Jason D. Williams. 2012. Integrating incremental speech recognition and POMDP-based dialogue systems. In *Proceedings of the Annual Meeting of the Special Interest Group on Discourse and Dialogue (SIGDIAL)*. Seoul, South Korea, pages 275–279.

Gabriel Skantze and David Schlangen. 2009. Incremental dialogue processing in a micro-domain. In *Proceedings of the 12th Conference of the European Association for Computational Linguistics (EACL)*. Athens, Greece, pages 745–753.

Richard S. Sutton and Andrew G. Barto. 1998. *Reinforcement learning: An introduction*. MIT Press Cambridge.

Appendix

Example dialogue

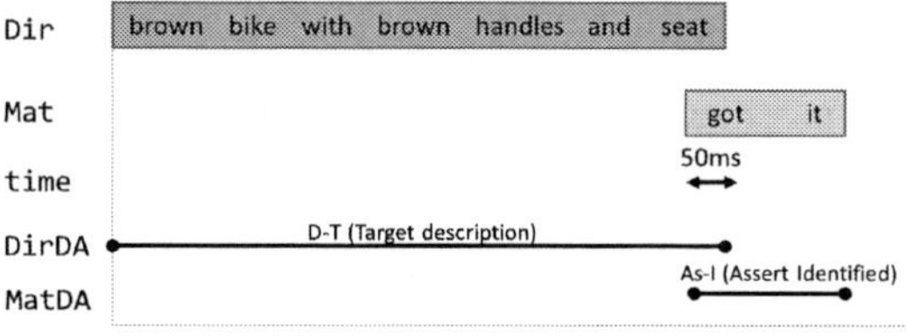

Figure 6: Example dialogue for an episode in the human-agent corpus for the same TI as in Figure 1.

Policy differences

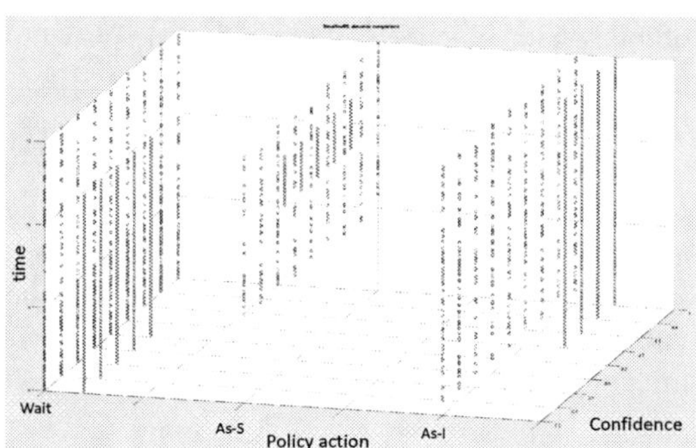

Figure 7: Policy learned by the Vanilla Q-learning algorithm (blue) compared to the baseline (red).

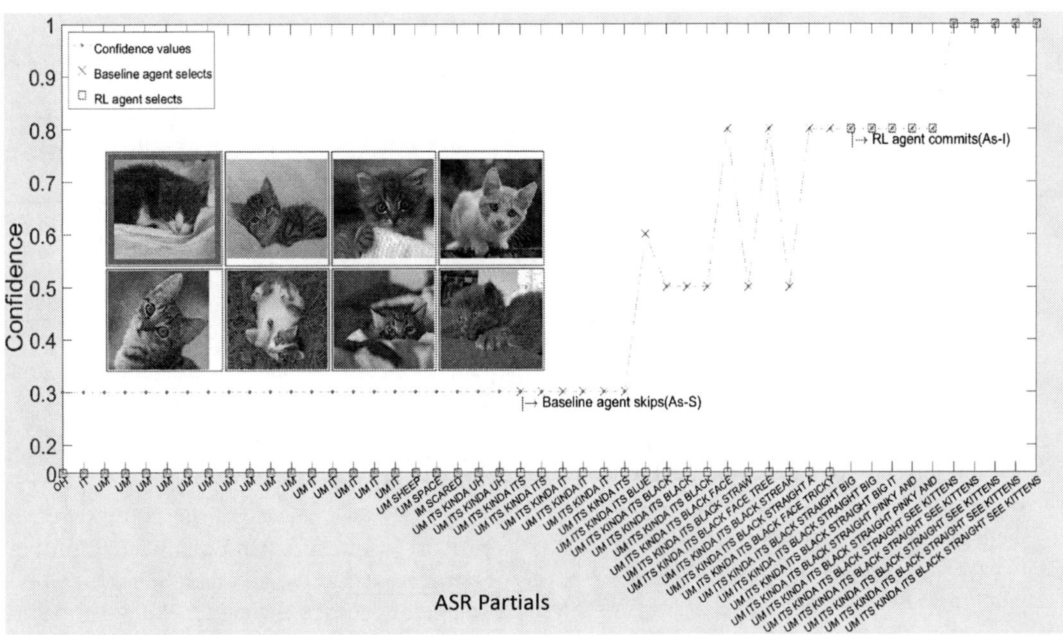

Figure 8: Actions taken by the baseline and the RL agent for the 1-best ASR increments. The image set is also shown.

Inferring Narrative Causality between Event Pairs in Films

Zhichao Hu and Marilyn A. Walker
Natural Language and Dialogue Systems Lab
Department of Computer Science, University of California Santa Cruz
Santa Cruz, CA 95064, USA
`zhu@soe.ucsc.edu, mawalker@ucsc.edu`

Abstract

To understand narrative, humans draw inferences about the underlying relations between narrative events. Cognitive theories of narrative understanding define these inferences as four different types of causality, that include pairs of events A, B where A physically causes B (X drop, X break), to pairs of events where A causes emotional state B (Y saw X, Y felt fear). Previous work on learning narrative relations from text has either focused on "strict" physical causality, or has been vague about what relation is being learned. This paper learns pairs of causal events from a corpus of film scene descriptions which are action rich and tend to be told in chronological order. We show that event pairs induced using our methods are of high quality and are judged to have a stronger causal relation than event pairs from Rel-grams.

1 Introduction

Telling and understanding stories is a central part of human experience, and many types of human communication involve narrative structures. Theories of narrative posit that NARRATIVE CAUSALITY underlies human understanding of a narrative (Warren et al., 1979; Trabasso et al., 1989; Van den Broek, 1990). However previous computational work on narrative schemas, scripts or event schemas learn "collections of events that tend to co-occur" (Chambers and Jurafsky, 2008; Balasubramanian et al., 2013; Pichotta and Mooney, 2014), rather than causal relations between events (Rahimtoroghi et al., 2016). Another limitation of previous work is that it has mostly been applied to newswire, limiting what is learned to relations between newsworthy events, rather than everyday

events (Rahimtoroghi et al., 2016; Hu et al., 2013; Beamer and Girju, 2009; Manshadi et al., 2008).

Our focus here is on NARRATIVE CAUSALITY (Trabasso et al., 1989; Van den Broek, 1990), the four different relations posited by narrative theories to underly narrative coherence:

- PHYSICAL: Event A physically causes event B to happen

- MOTIVATIONAL: Event A happens with B as a motivation

- PSYCHOLOGICAL: Event A brings about emotions (expressed in event B)

- ENABLING: Event A creates a state or condition for B to happen. A enables B.

Previous work on learning causal relations has primarily focused on physical causality (Riaz and Girju, 2010; Beamer and Girju, 2009), while our aim is to learn event pairs manifesting all types of narrative causality, and test their generality as a source of causal knowledge. We posit that film scene descriptions are a good resource for learning narrative causality because they are: (1) action rich; (2) about everyday events; and (3) told in temporal order, providing a primary cue to causality (Beamer and Girju, 2009; Hu et al., 2013).

Film scenes contain many descriptions encoding PHYSICAL CAUSALITY, e.g. in Fig. 1, Scene 1, Frodo grabs Pippin's sleeve, causing Pippin to spill his beer (*grab - spill*). Pippin then pushes Frodo away, causing Frodo to stumble backwards and fall to the floor (*push - stumble, stumble - fall*, and *push - fall*). But they also contain all other types of narrative causality: in Scene 2, Gandalf has to stoop, because he wants to avoid hitting his head on the low ceiling (*stoop - avoid*: MOTIVATIONAL). He then looks around, and enjoys the result of looking: the familiarity of Bag End (*look - enjoy*: PSYCHOLOGICAL). He turns, which causes

Proceedings of the SIGDIAL 2017 Conference, pages 342–351,
Saarbrücken, Germany, 15-17 August 2017. ©2017 Association for Computational Linguistics

#	Scene
1	Pippin, sitting at the bar, chatting with Locals. Frodo leaps to his feet and pushes his way towards the bar. Frodo **grabs** Pippin's sleeve, **spilling** his beer. Pippin **pushes** Frodo away... he **stumbles** backwards, and **falls** to the floor.
2	Bilbo leads Gandalf into Bag End... Cozy and cluttered with souvenirs of Bilbo's travels. Gandalf has to **stoop** to **avoid** hitting his head on the low ceiling. Bilbo hangs up Gandalf's hat on a peg and trots off down the hall. Bilbo disappears into the kitchen as Gandalf **looks** around.. **enjoying** the familiarity of Bag End... He **turns**, **knocking** his head on the light and then walking into the wooden beam. He groans.
3	Bilbo **pulls out** the ring... he **stares at** it in his palm. With all his will power, Bilbo **allows** the ring to slowly **slide off** his palm and drop to the floor. The tiny ring lands with a heavy thud on the wooden floor.
4	GANDALF... lying unconscious on a cold obsidian floor. He **wakes** to the sound of ripping and tearing ... **rising** onto his knees... lifting his head... Gandalf stands as the camera pulls back to reveal him stranded on the summit of Orthanc.

Figure 1: Film Scenes from Lord of the Rings

him to knock his head on the light (*turn - knock*: the weak causality of ENABLING).[1]

This paper learns causal pairs from a corpus of 955 films. Because previous work shows that more specific, detailed causal relations can be learned from topic-sorted corpora (Riaz and Girju, 2010; Rahimtoroghi et al., 2016), we explore differences in learning between genres of film, positing e.g. that horror films may feature very different types of events than comedies. We also test the quality of what is learned when we train on genre specific texts vs. the whole collection. Our results show that:

- human judges can distinguish between strong and weakly causal event pairs induced using our method (Section 3.1);

- our strongly causal event pairs are rated as more likely to be causal than those provided by the Rel-gram corpus (Balasubramanian et al., 2013) (Section 3.2);

- human judges can recognize different types of narrative causality (Section 3.3);

- using both whole-corpus and genre-specific methods yields similar results for quality, despite the smaller size of the genre-specific sub-corpora. Moreover, the genre-specific method learns some event pairs that are different than whole corpus event-pairs, while still being high-quality. (Section 3.4);

We explain our method in Section 2, and then present experimental results in Section 3. We leave a more detailed discussion of related work until Section 4 when we can compare it more directly with our own.

2 Experimental Method

We estimate the likelihood of a narrative causality relation between events in film scenes.

2.1 Film Scenes & Pre-Processing.

We chose 11 genres with more than 100 films from a corpus of film scene descriptions (Walker et al., 2012; Hu et al., 2013),[2] resulting in 955 unique films. Film scripts were scraped from the IMSDb website, film dialogs and scene descriptions were then automatically separated. Films per genre range from 107 to 579. Films can belong to multiple genres, e.g. the scenes from *The Fellowship of the Ring* shown in Figure 1 would become part of the genres of Action, Adventure, and Fantasy. Each film's scene descriptions ranges from 2000 to 35000 words. Table 1 enumerates the sizes of each genre, illustrating the potential tradeoff between getting good probability estimates for event co-occurrence when the same events are repeated **within** a genre, vs. across the whole corpus. We use Stanford CoreNLP 3.5.2 to tokenize, lemmatize, POS tag, dependency parse and label named entities (Manning et al., 2014).

2.2 Compute Event Representations.

An event is defined as a verb lemma, as in previous work (Chambers and Jurafsky, 2008; Do et al., 2011; Riaz and Girju, 2010; Manshadi et al., 2008).

---

[1]Gandalf did not *turn* in order to *knock*, which would have been MOTIVATIONAL. Nor was it entailed that *turning* would cause *knocking*, which would have been PHYSICAL, because he clearly could have missed hitting his head if he had been more careful.

[2]From https://nlds.soe.ucsc.edu/fc2

Genre	# Films	Word Count	Example
Action	290	3,758,387	The Avengers
Adventure	166	2,115,247	Indiana Jones and the Temple of Doom
Comedy	347	3,434,612	All About Steve
Crime	201	2,342,324	The Italian Job
Drama	579	6,680,749	American Beauty
Fantasy	113	1,186,587	Lord of the Rings: Fellowship of the Ring
Horror	149	1,789,667	Scream
Mystery	107	1,346,496	Black Swan
Romance	192	2,022,305	Last Tango in Paris
Sci-Fi	155	1,964,856	I, Robot
Thriller	373	4,548,043	Ghost Rider

Table 1: Distribution of Films By Genre.

We extract events by keeping all tokens whose POS tags begin with VB: VB, VBD, VBG, VBN, VBP, and VBZ. This results in extracting deverbal nouns that implicitly evoke events, such as the events of *ripping* and *tearing* in Scene 4 of Figure 1. This definition also allows us to pick up *resultative clauses* along with the action that caused the result (Hovav and Levin, 2001; Goldberg and Jackendoff, 2004), e.g. in *He slammed the door shut*, both *slammed* and *shut* are picked up as verbs. We exclude light verbs e.g. *be, let, do, begin, have, start, try*, because they often only represent a meaningful event when combined with their complements.

We extract the subject (*nsubj, agent*), direct object (*dobj, nsubjpass*), indirect object (*iobj*) and particle of the verb (*compound:prt*), if any. In order to abstract and merge different arguments, we generalize the arguments to two types: *person* and *something*. We generalize an argument to *person* when: (1) its named entity type is PERSON; or (2) it is a pronoun (except "it"); or (3) it is a noun in WordNet with more than half of its Synsets having lexical filename `noun.person`, e.g. *doctor, soldier, waiter, man, woman*. Our narrative causal semantics would be more specific if we could generalize over other types of named entities as well, such as *location*. However Stanford NER identifiable named entities rarely occur in film data.

For every event, we record the combinations of its arguments and particle for every instance. For example, the instance of event "pick" in sentence: *He picked it up... a pearl*, has combination *subj: person, dobj: something, iobj: none, particle: up*. We pick the combination with the highest frequency to represent the arguments and particle for each event.

2.3 Calculating Narrative Causality.

We use the Causal Potential (CP) measure in (1), shown to work well in previous work (Beamer and Girju, 2009; Hu et al., 2013):

$$CP(e_1, e_2) = PMI(e_1, e_2) + \log \frac{P(e_1 \rightarrow e_2)}{P(e_2 \rightarrow e_1)} \tag{1}$$

$$\text{where } PMI(e_1, e_2) = \log \frac{P(e_1, e_2)}{P(e_1)P(e_2)}$$

where the arrow notation means ordered event pairs, i.e. event e_1 occurs before event e_2. CP consists of two terms: the first is pair-wise mutual information (PMI) and the second is relative ordering of bigrams. PMI measures how often events occur as a pair (without considering their order); whereas relative ordering accounts for the order of the event pairs because temporal order is one of the strongest cues to causality (Beamer and Girju, 2009; Riaz and Girju, 2010).

We obtain the frequency of every event and event pair for each genre. Unseen event pairs are smoothed with frequency equal to 1. In this paper, the notion of window size indicates how many events after the current event are paired with the current event. We use window sizes 1, 2 and 3, and calculate narrative causality for each window size. In film scenes, events are very densely distributed, (see Figure 1), thus related event pairs are often adjacent to one another, but the discourse structure of film scenes, not surprisingly, also contain related events separated by other events (Grosz and Sidner, 1986; Mann and Thompson, 1987). For example, in Scene 3 of Figure 1, Bilbo pulling out the ring enables him to slide it off his palm later (*pull out - slide off*). Moreover, while related events are less

In this task, we will present you with two pairs of events (upper case verbs) that were automatically extracted from film scripts, and ask you to tell us which event pair is more likely to have a narrative causality relation. According to the theories of narrative, in a pair of events [A -> B], the narrative causality relation consists of 4 possible types of event relations, given below with defining examples. Note that the order of event A and B matters.

(1) Physical Causality: event A physically causes event B to happen. Thus the assumption is that when A is put into the context of the story, B will inevitably follow.
[person PUSH person -> person FALL]: Pippin pushes Frodo away...he stumbles backwards, and falls to the floor.
(2) Motivational Causality: event A happens with B as a motivation.
[person SWERVE -> AVOID something]: He swerves to avoid an ugly pickup truck crawling like a snail ahead.
(3) Psychological Causality: event A brings about emotions (expressed in event B).
[person LOOK -> ENJOY]: Bilbo disappears into the kitchen as Gandalf looks around.. enjoying the familiarity of Bag End.
(4) Enabling Causality: event A creates a state or condition for B to happen. A enables B.
[person GRAB something -> YANK something]: Thor grabs the barrel, yanks it out of DeLancey's hands and thrusts the hilt back...

Given any common story context that you can imagine, which event pair is more likely to have a narrative causality relation?
(1) All the events are in their verb base forms. But they can be in any tense in order to satisfy the narrative causality relation.
(2) Please use the arguments (subject, object etc) as reference only and focus on the events. Arguments are extracted automatically and could be incorrect. "person" and "something" are merely indicators of types of arguments (human or thing). In an event pair, "person" does not necessarily refer to the same person, and "something" does not necessarily refer to the same thing either.

1. ◯ person UNCORK something -> person POUR something
    ◯ person SPEAK -> person CHECK something

......

20. ◯ person BEND -> person PICK up something
    ◯ person LIFT something -> person CROSS

Figure 2: Instructions for the MT HIT.

frequently separated (window size 3), we assume that unrelated events will be filtered out by their low probabilities. We thus define a *CPC* measure, shown in (2) that combines the frequencies across window size:

$$CPC(e_1, e_2) = \sum_{i=1}^{w_{max}} \frac{CP_i(e_1, e_2)}{i} \qquad (2)$$

where w_{max} is the max window size. $CP_i(e_1, e_2)$ is the CP score for event pair e_1, e_2 calculated using window size i. The *CPC* measure combines frequencies across window sizes, but punishes event pairs from larger window sizes, thus assuming that nearby events are more likely to be causal.

3 Evaluation and Results

We posit that human judgments are the best way to evaluate the quality of the induced event pairs, as opposed to automatic measures such as Narrative Cloze, which assume that the event pairs in a particular instance of text can be used as held-out test data (Chambers and Jurafsky, 2008). Our first experiment tests whether event pairs with high *CPC* scores are more likely to have a narrative causality relation. Our second experiment compares pairs with high *CPC* scores with their corresponding top Rel-gram pairs. Our third experiment tests whether annotators can distinguish narrative causality types. Our final experiment compares the quality and type of causal pairs learned on a per genre basis, vs. those learned on the whole film corpus.

3.1 High vs. Low CPC Event Pairs

After processing all the data, we have a list of event pairs scored by *CPC*, and rank-ordered within each genre. Some of the genre specific event pairs seem to intuitively reflect their genre, however there are many learned pairs that are in overlap across genres. We select the top 3000 event pairs with high scores from all the genres ("high pairs"). The number of event pairs from a genre is proportional to the number of films in that genre. We also select the bottom 6000 event pairs with low scores from all the genres using similar method ("low pairs"). Since many pairs are duplicated across genre, the high pairs and low pairs are then de-duplicated (two event pairs are defined as equal if they have the same verbs in the same order). We keep the arguments with the highest frequencies. This result in 960 high pairs. If an event has no subject, "person" is added as

#	High CPC Pair	Low CPC Pair
1	[person] *clink* [smth] - [person] *drink* [smth]	[person] *strike* - [person] *give* [person] [smth]
2	[person] *beckon* - [person] *come*	[smth] *become* - [person] *hide*
3	[person] *bend* - [person] *pick* up [smth]	[person] *lift* [smth] - [person] *cross*
4	[person] *cough* - [person] *splutter*	[person] *force* - [smth] *show* [smth]
5	[person] *crane* - [person] *see* [smth]	[person] *fade* - [person] *allow* [person]

Table 2: Narratively Causal Pairs where all 5 annotators selected the High CPC pair.

subject, since most events have human agents.

For every event pair in the 960 high pairs, we randomly select a low pair in order to collect human judgments on Mechanical Turk. The task first introduces event and event pair definitions, then defines the four types of narrative causality with corresponding examples. Turkers are asked to select the event pair that is more likely to manifest a narrative causality relation. Each HIT consists of 20 judgements, and we collect 5 judgements per HIT. Because this task requires some care, Turkers had to be prequalified. The qualification test aims to test Turkers' understanding of narrative causality. It is similar to the task itself, but with more obvious choices, such as high CPC pair *open - reveal* vs low CPC pair *pay - fade*. Figure 2 shows a simplified version of the HIT instructions.[3]

Genre	# High Pairs	% Causality
Action	320	86.3
Adventure	171	86.6
Comedy	384	84.9
Crime	23	84.9
Drama	**665**	**82.6**
Fantasy	**127**	**90.7**
Horror	156	87.2
Mystery	122	87.7
Romance	215	86.0
Sci-Fi	158	88.0
Thriller	405	87.7

Table 3: Percentages of high pairs that receive majority vote results by genre.

The results show that humans judge the high pairs as more likely to have a narrative causality relation in 82.8% of items. Among those, all the items receive 3 or more votes for the high pairs. Overall, all five Turkers select the high CPC pairs in 51% of the items. The average pairwise Krippendorff's Alpha score is respectable at 0.56.

Table 2 shows items where all 5 Turkers selected the high pair. For example, *clink - drink* in Row 1 could have either a MOTIVATIONAL or ENABLING narrative causality depending on the context, but the causal relation in either case is much clearer than with the low CPC pair *strike - give*. Row 2 and Row 5 *beckon - come* and *crane -see* both have ENABLING causality which is a weakly causal relation, but again more meaningful than their low CPC counterparts. In Row 3, it is clear that a person often *bends* with the motivation to *pick up* something. In row 4 a person *coughs*, PHYSICALLY causes him to *splutter* everywhere.

Table 3 shows majority vote results for percentages of high pairs that are considered to exhibit more narrative causality, sorted by genre. The results for all genres are good, ranging from ~82% to ~91%. Interestingly, Drama has the highest number of films with the lowest percentage of judged narrative causality, while Fantasy has the lowest number of films with the highest judged narrative causality. This may be because the Drama category is a catch-all (over half of the films are categorized this way suggesting that it has low coherence as a genre). The poor performance on Drama would then be consistent with previous work that shows that topical coherence (genre in this case) improves causal relation learning (Rahimtoroghi et al., 2016; Riaz and Girju, 2010). We will return to this point in Section 3.4.

3.2 CPC vs. Rel-gram Event Pairs

We then compare the narrative causality event pairs (high pairs) with event pairs from the Rel-grams corpus (Balasubramanian et al., 2012, 2013). Rel-grams (Relational n-grams) are pairs of open-domain relational tuples (T,T'). They are analogous to lexical n-grams, but is computed over relations rather than over words. For example, "A person who gets arrested is typically charged with some activity." yield the tuple: T = ([police] *arrest* [person]) and T' = ([person] *be charge with* [activity]).

---

[3]The full instructions provide more examples and background information.

#	Narrative Causality (CPC) Pairs	Rel-gram Pairs	CPC Vote #
1	[person] *clear* [smth] - [person] *reveal* [smth]	[person] *clear* [smth] - [person] *hit* [smth]	5
2	[person] *embrace* - [person] *kiss*	[person] *embrace* [person] - [person] *meet* [person]	5
3	[person] *empty* [something] -[person] *reload*	[person] *empty* [smth] - [person] *shoot* [person]	5
4	[person] *marry* [person] - [person] *think*	[person] *marry* [person] - [person] *die* [something]	5
5	[person] *stumble* - [smth] *fall*	[person] *stumble* upon [person] - [person] *take* [person]	5
6	[person] *gaze* - [smth] *drift*	[person] *gaze* at [person]- [person] *see* [person]	0
7	[person] *reveal* [smth] - [person] *sit*	[person] *reveal* [person] - [person] *see* [person]	0
8	[person] *watch* - [person] *appal*	[person] *watch* [person] - [person] *see* [person]	0

Table 4: Items where either CPC event pairs or Rel-gram event pairs were strongly preferred.

Over 1.8M news wire documents are used to build a database of Rel-grams co-occurence statistics.

Using a similar HIT template, we randomly sample 100 high CPC event pairs from the 960 high CPC pairs, where we ensure that each of the first events of the pairs are distinct. We use the publicly available search interface for Rel-grams[4] to find Rel-gram statement pairs that have the same first event. Modeling our own experimental setup we set the co-occurrence window to 5[5], and select the Rel-gram pair with the highest #50(FS) (frequency of first statement occurring before second statement within a window of 50).

To make Rel-gram event pairs similar to ours, we generalize their arguments to "person" and "something" manually. We keep the verb particle if any. For example, the Rel-gram pair "[person] *remain* in [location] - [person] *become* [leader]" is generalized to "[person] *remain* in [something] - [person] *become* [something]". It is possible that this disadvantages Rel-grams in some way, but our main focus is on the causality relation between verbs, which should not be affected. Moreover the two sets of event pairs cannot be compared without this generalization. The same 5 annotators participate in this 5 HITs (100 items).

The results show that humans judge the CPC pairs to be more likely to manifest a narrative causality relation 81% of the time. The average pairwise Krippendorff's Alpha score of all Turkers is 0.482. Table 4 shows items where all Turkers judge the CPC pairs as more likely to be causally related. For example, in Row 1 to *clear* seems more likely to enable something being *revealed*, instead of causing a person to *hit* something. In Row 2, even though *embrace* and *kiss* might only have an ENABLING narrative causality relation, the

reversed causality between *embrace* and *meet* in the Rel-gram pair is based on symmetric conditional probability (SCP) rather than explicit causal modeling. SCP combines Bigram probability in both directions as follows:

$$SCP(e_1, e_2) = P(e_2|e_1) \times P(e_1|e_2) \quad (3)$$

In Row 4, *marrying* someone might just possibly enable one to think about something, but could hardly enable/cause someone to die. In Row 5 *stumble* physically causes one to *fall*, while it is more difficult to see the causal relation between *stumbling on* someone and then a person *taking* another person (somewhere).

Narrative Causality Type	Count	Example Pair
Physical	13	*fire - blast*
Motivational	29	*bend - retrieve*
Psychological	9	*look - astonish*
Enabling	28	*lean - whisper*

Table 5: Distribution of narrative causality types .

3.3 Narrative Causality Types

Although theories of narrative posit four different types of narrative causality, previous work has not conducted reliability studies with non-experts such as Turkers. Here we explore whether humans can distinguish narrative causality types, by asking Turkers to decide which relation holds between an event pair. The instructions contain descriptions of narrative causality types and the strength of these relations (from strong to weak: PHYSICAL, MOTIVATIONAL, PSYCHOLOGICAL and ENABLING (Trabasso et al., 1989)). Because the stronger types of narrative causality could also be considered ENABLING, Turkers are instructed to choose the strongest narrative causality that could be applied to the event pair.

---

[4]http://relgrams.cs.stonybrook.edu/

[5]The search interface does not support a window size of 3, thus we chose 5 as it's the closest window size larger than 1.

Fantasy	CPC	Action	CPC
[person] *slam* [smth] - *shut*	4.95	[person] *huff* - [person] *puff*	5.57
send [smth] - [smth] *fly*	4.89	*bind* - *gag*	5.50
[person] *watch* - [smth] *disappear*	4.87	[smth] *swerve* - *avoid* [smth]	5.21
[person] *turn* - *face* [person]	4.83	[person] *bend* - [person] *pick* up [smth]	5.01
[person] *pull* [smth] - *reveal* [smth]	4.70	*send* [smth] - [smth] *tumble*	4.85
[person] *pick* up [smth] - *carry* [smth]	4.54	*send* [smth] - *sprawl*	4.83
[person] *reach* - [person] *pull* [smth]	4.42	[person] *slam* [smth] - *shut*	4.79
Sci-Fi	**CPC**	**Thriller**	**CPC**
[person] *bend* - [person] *pick* up [smth]	4.88	*bind* - *gag*	5.66
follow - [person] *gaze*	4.83	[smth] *swerve* - *avoid* [smth]	5.37
[person] *grab* [smth] - [person] *yank* [smth]	4.83	[person] *rummage* - [person] *find* [smth]	5.05
send [smth] - [smth] *fly*	4.81	[person] *inhale* - peroson *exhale*	5.04
[person] *slam* [smth] - *shut*	4.78	[person] *slam* [smth] - *shut*	5.00
[person] *grab* [smth] - [person] *drag* [person]	4.77	*send* [smth] - [smth] *fly*	4.97
[person] *reach* - *touch* [smth]	4.67	[person] *reach* - [person] *produce* [smth]	4.81

Table 6: Event pairs with Highest CPC scores from Fantasy, Action, Sci-Fi and Thriller genres.

We select 100 pairs randomly from the high CPC pairs of the 479 questions that had the highest Turker agreement. Among all 100 questions, 79% of the items receive a majority vote result (3 or more Turkers selecting the same answer). The distribution of narrative causality types of the 79 items is shown in Table 5. Interestingly, films are full of motivational causality, which often reflect action sequences where protagonist pursue particular narratively relevant goals (Rapp and Gerrig, 2006, 2002).

3.4 Genre Specific Causality

Previous work suggests that topical coherence and similarity of events within the corpus used for learning causal/contingent event relations might be as important as the size of the corpus (Riaz and Girju, 2010; Rahimtoroghi et al., 2016). In other words, smaller corpora filtered by topic or genre might be more useful than large undifferentiated sets (Riloff, 1996), although obviously very large corpora that are topic or genre sorted could be even more useful. We therefore test whether separating films by genre yields higher quality event pairs than a method that combines all films, irrespective of genre. We assume that the very notion of a film genre defines a set of films with similar types of events.

We first compute a list of *CPC* scores using films from all genres and take 960 event pairs with highest scores. Comparing the 960 event pairs from all films with the 960 pairs from merging genres described in Section 3.1, we find that 728 pairs overlap between the two sets. Thus with the smaller genre-specific corpora we learn more than 70% of the same causal pairs. The results shown in Table 3 suggest furthermore that the genre-specific pairs are high quality.

However, it is still possible that the 232 pairs from each set that are not in overlap vary in quality from the 728 pairs that are in overlap. We therefore pick 100 random pairs from each set, match the pairs randomly to form items, and repeat the event pairs comparison HIT with these pairs. The results suggest that there are no differences between the two methods as far as quality: in 48 of the 100 questions, pairs from genre-separated method have Turkers' majority vote, vs. in 52 of the 100 questions pairs from combined genres have the majority vote.

Moreover we obtain **more** high-quality, reliable narrative causality relations using both methods, and we learn some genre-specific causal relations that we do not learn on the whole corpus. Table 8 shows the the overlap in learned pairs amongst the top 30 CPC pairs in five of the most distinct genres (genres with highest percentages in Table 3: Fantasy, Sci-Fi, Horror, Mystery and Thriller) vs. all films (All). Mystery has the smallest overlap with All, followed by Fantasy and Sci-Fi.

To illustrate some of the differences, Table 6 shows event pairs with the highest *CPC* scores in Fantasy, Action, Sci-Fi and Thriller genres. Table 7 shows event pairs unique to each genre within its top 30 CPC pairs.

We also compare our 960 pairs from merging genres described in Section 3.1 with 200 event pairs extracted from camping and storm personal blog stories in Rahimtoroghi et al. (2016). The only pairs that overlap are: *sit - eat, play - sing*, illustrating again that causal relations learned are not as dependent on the size of the corpus, as they are on its topical and event-based coherence. Since most previous work on narrative schemas, scripts,

Genre	Event pairs
Fantasy	*struggle - get, reveal - stand, see - stand, get - marry, sit - sip, nod - head, make - break, spin - face, take - bite, watch - disappear, pick - carry*
Sci-Fi	*hear - echo, see - come, look - alarm, widen - see, head - stop, clear - reveal, sit - study, look - puzzle, peek - see*
Horror	*listen - hear, stare - fascinate, hear - muffle, slow - stop, peel - reveal, reach - yank, reach - handle, grab - handle*
Mystery	*slip - fall, dig - pull, walk - reach, look - confuse, sit - eat, knock - open, look - horrify, stop - look, sit - look, seem - lose*
Thriller	*look - wonder, raise - fire, poise - strike, sit - hunch, rape - murder*
All	*sit - leg, whoop - holler, huff - puff, disappear - reappear, cease - exist, dive - swim, spur - gallop, offer - decline, contain - omit, hoot - holler, pay - heed*

Table 7: Event pairs unique to Fantasy, Sci-Fi, Horror, Mystery, Thriller genres and all films.

Genre	All	Thr	Mys	Hor	Sci
Fan	8	9	13	15	14
Sci	8	12	14	18	
Hor	10	14	14		
Mys	7	12			
Thr	18				

Table 8: Overlap in learned pairs among the most distinct genres (Fantasy, Sci-Fi, Horror, Mystery and Thriller) vs. all films (All).

event schemas or rel-grams has only been applied to one large corpus of newswire (Gigaword corpus), these methods have only learned relations about newsworthy topics, and even then, perhaps only the most frequent, highly common news events. In contrast, both our approach and that of Rahimtoroghi et al. (2016) learn fine-grained causal relations that underly narratives, which we believe are more in the spirit of Schank's original motivation for scripts (Lehnert, 1981; Schank et al., 1977; Wilensky, 1982; de Jong, 1979).

4 Related Work

Hu et al. (2013) tested four methods for inducing pairs of adjacent events with contingency/causality relations from film scenes, including Causal Potential, Pointwise Mutual Information, Bigram Model and Protagonist-based Model. Rahimtoroghi et al. (2016) also used a modified version of the the CP measure, adjusted to account for the discourse structure of personal narratives in blogs. Here we use a much larger set of films and apply different techniques and a detailed evaluation. Our learned causal pairs and supporting film data are available for download [6].

Do et al. (2011) used a minimally supervised approach, based on focused distributional similarity methods and discourse connectives, to identify causality relations between events in PDTB in context (both verbs and nouns) (Prasad et al., 2008). They present a detailed formula for calculating contingency/causality that takes into account several different kinds of argument overlap between adjacent events. However they do not provide any evidence that all the components of this formula actually contribute to their results.

Gordon et al. (2011) used event ngrams and discourse cues to learn causal relations from first person stories posted on weblogs and evaluated them with respect to the COPA SEM-EVAL task. Other related work learns likely sequences of temporally ordered events but does not explicitly model CAUSALITY (Chambers and Jurafsky, 2009; Balasubramanian et al., 2013; Manshadi et al., 2008).

Work on VerbOcean (Chklovski and Pantel, 2004) use lexical patterns to learn semantic verb relations of similarity, strength, antonymy, enablement and happens-before relations. Balasubramanian et al. (2013) use symmetric probability to learn semantically typed relational triples (actor, relation, actor), which they call Rel-grams (relational n-grams), and show that their schemas outperform previous work (Chambers and Jurafsky, 2009). We thus compared our event pairs with Rel-grams, showing that humans are more likely to perceive narrative causality in our event pairs.

5 Discussion and Future Work

We present an unsupervised model based on Causal Potential (Beamer and Girju, 2009) to induce event pairs with narrative causality relations from film scenes in 11 genres. Results from four human evaluations show that narrative causality event pairs induced using our method are of high quality, and are perceived as more causally related than corresponding Rel-grams. We show that humans can identify different types of narrative causality, but we leave automatic identification of these to future work. We also show that inducing narrative causality event

---

[6] https://nlds.soe.ucsc.edu/narrativecausality

pairs using both whole-corpus and genre-specific methods yields similar results for quality, despite the smaller size of the genre-specific subcorpora. Moreover, the genre-specific method learns high quality event pairs that are different than whole corpus event-pairs.

We are looking into applying and evaluating our CPC method to other genre and topic sorted datasets such as books and personal blogs. We want to expand our set of event pairs with narrative causality relations, which could potentially aid text understanding, information extraction, question answering, and content summarization. We also aim to explore features for narrative causality type classification. Information such as event A physically causes event B, or event C enables event D could further help aforementioned applications.

Acknowledgements

This research was supported by Nuance Foundation Grant SC-14-74, NSF #IIS-1302668-002, NSF CISE CreativeIT #IIS-1002921 and NSF CISE RI EAGER #IIS-1044693.

References

Niranjan Balasubramanian, Stephen Soderland, Oren Etzioni, et al. 2012. Rel-grams: a probabilistic model of relations in text. In *Proceedings of the Joint Workshop on Automatic Knowledge Base Construction and Web-scale Knowledge Extraction*. Association for Computational Linguistics, pages 101–105.

Niranjan Balasubramanian, Stephen Soderland, Oren Etzioni Mausam, and Oren Etzioni. 2013b. Generating coherent event schemas at scale. In *EMNLP*. pages 1721–1731.

Brandon Beamer and Roxana Girju. 2009. Using a bigram event model to predict causal potential. In *Computational Linguistics and Intelligent Text Processing*, Springer, pages 430–441.

Nathanael Chambers and Dan Jurafsky. 2008. Unsupervised learning of narrative event chains. *Proceedings of ACL-08: HLT* pages 789–797.

Nathanael Chambers and Dan Jurafsky. 2009. Unsupervised learning of narrative schemas and their participants. In *Proceedings of the 47th Annual Meeting of the ACL*. pages 602–610.

Timothy Chklovski and Patrick Pantel. 2004. Verbocean: Mining the web for fine-grained semantic verb relations. In *EMNLP*. volume 4, pages 33–40.

G. F. de Jong. 1979. *Skimming Stories in Real Time: An Experiment in Integrated Understanding*. Ph.D. thesis, Computer Science Department, Yale University.

Quang Xuan Do, Yee Seng Chan, and Dan Roth. 2011. Minimally supervised event causality identification. In *Proceedings of the Conference on Empirical Methods in Natural Language Processing*. Association for Computational Linguistics, pages 294–303.

Adele E Goldberg and Ray Jackendoff. 2004. The english resultative as a family of constructions. *Language* pages 532–568.

Andrew Gordon, Cosmin Bejan, and Kenji Sagae. 2011. Commonsense causal reasoning using millions of personal stories. In *Twenty-Fifth Conference on Artificial Intelligence (AAAI-11)*.

Barbara J. Grosz and Candace L. Sidner. 1986. Attention, intentions and the structure of discourse. *Computational Linguistics* 12:175–204.

Malka Rappaport Hovav and Beth Levin. 2001. An event structure account of english resultatives. *Language* pages 766–797.

Zhichao Hu, Elahe Rahimtoroghi, Larissa Munishkina, Reid Swanson, and Marilyn A Walker. 2013. Unsupervised induction of contingent event pairs from film scenes. In *Proceedings of Conference on Empirical Methods in Natural Language Processing*. pages 370–379.

Wendy G Lehnert. 1981. Plot units and narrative summarization. *Cognitive Science* 5(4):293–331.

W.C. Mann and S.A. Thompson. 1987. Rhetorical structure theory: A framework for the analysis of texts. Technical Report RS-87-190, USC/Information Sciences Institute.

Christopher D Manning, Mihai Surdeanu, John Bauer, Jenny Rose Finkel, Steven Bethard, and David McClosky. 2014. The Stanford CoreNLP natural language processing toolkit. In *ACL (System Demonstrations)*. pages 55–60.

Mehdi Manshadi, Reid Swanson, and Andrew S Gordon. 2008. Learning a probabilistic model of event sequences from internet weblog stories. In *Proceedings of the 21st FLAIRS Conference*.

Karl Pichotta and Raymond J Mooney. 2014. Statistical script learning with multi-argument events. *EACL 2014* page 220.

R. Prasad, N. Dinesh, A. Lee, E. Miltsakaki, L. Robaldo, A. Joshi, and B. Webber. 2008. The penn discourse treebank 2.0. In *Proceedings of the 6th International Conference on Language Resources and Evaluation (LREC 2008)*. pages 2961–2968.

Elahe Rahimtoroghi, Ernesto Hernandez, and Marilyn A. Walker. 2016a. Learning fine-grained knowledge about contingent relations between everyday events. In *Proceedings of SIGDIAL 2016*. pages 350–359.

D.N. Rapp and R.J. Gerrig. 2002. Readers' reality-driven and plot-driven analyses in narrative comprehension. *Memory & Cognition* 30(5):779.

D.N. Rapp and R.J. Gerrig. 2006. Predilections for narrative outcomes: The impact of story contexts and reader preferences. *Journal of Memory and Language* 54(1):54–67.

Mehwish Riaz and Roxana Girju. 2010. Another look at causality: Discovering scenario-specific contingency relationships with no supervision. In *Semantic Computing (ICSC), 2010 IEEE Fourth International Conference on*. IEEE, pages 361–368.

Ellen Riloff. 1996. Automatically generating extraction patterns from untagged text. In *Proceedings of the national conference on artificial intelligence*. pages 1044–1049.

R Schank, Robert Abelson, and Roger C Schank. 1977. *Scripts Plans Goals*. Lea.

Tom Trabasso, Paul Van den Broek, and So Young Suh. 1989. Logical necessity and transitivity of causal relations in stories. *Discourse processes* 12(1):1–25.

Paul Van den Broek. 1990. The causal inference maker: Towards a process model of inference generation in text comprehension. *Comprehension processes in reading* pages 423–445.

Marilyn Walker, Grace Lin, and Jennifer Sawyer. 2012. An annotated corpus of film dialogue for learning and characterizing character style. In *Language Resources and Evaluation Conference, LREC2012*.

William H Warren, David W Nicholas, and Tom Trabasso. 1979. Event chains and inferences in understanding narratives. *New directions in discourse processing* 2:23–52.

Robert Wilensky. 1982. Points: A theory of the structure of stories in memory. In Wendy G. Lehnert and Martin H. Ringle, editors, *Strategies for Natural Language Processing*.

Lessons in Dialogue System Deployment

Anton Leuski and **Ron Artstein**
USC Institute for Creative Technologies
12015 E Waterfront Dr
Los Angeles, CA 90094, USA
{leuski|artstein}@ict.usc.edu

Abstract

We analyze deployment of an interactive dialogue system in an environment where deep technical expertise might not be readily available. The initial version was created using a collection of research tools. We summarize a number of challenges with its deployment at two museums and describe a new system that simplifies the installation and user interface; reduces reliance on 3rd-party software; and provides a robust data collection mechanism.

1 Introduction

New Dimensions in Testimonies (NDT) is a dialogue system that allows for two-way communication with a person who is not available for conversation in real time: a large set of statements is prepared in advance, and users access these statements through natural conversation that mimics face-to-face interaction (Artstein et al., 2014). Users interact with a recording of Holocaust survivor Pinchas Gutter. The system listens to their questions, selects and plays back Mr. Gutter's responses from a collection of video clips. We deployed the system at the Illinois Holocaust Museum and Education Center in Skokie since March 2015 (Traum et al., 2015a), where a museum docent relays questions from a large group audience to the system. The system was also installed for a few months at the U.S. Holocaust Memorial Museum in Washington, DC, and was demonstrated at other locations by our collaborators from the USC Shoah Foundation (SFI).

The installation proved to be a successful teaching aid: student gains were reported in interest in historical topics, critical thinking, and knowledge of issues going on in the world. The NDT system provided an engaging and emotional experi-

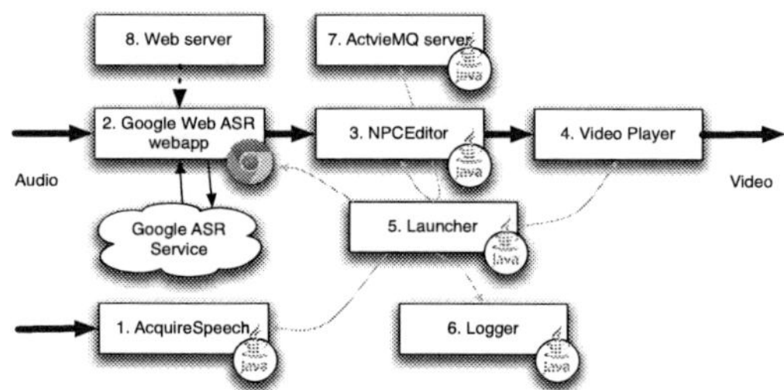

Figure 1: The initial NDT system architecture.

ence (Traum et al., 2015b). However, we discovered a number of issues with the system maintenance and support: system installation was a delicate process, there were issues maintaining the 3rd party system dependencies, the system user interface tended to overwhelm and confuse the operators, and reliable data collection proved to be a challenge.

The lessons we learned from the deployment of the NDT system led us back to the drawing board. We created a new version of the NDT system that we call Alfred. Our goal was to make the system easier to install and maintain. We looked to simplify and streamline the user interface; create a better data collection and archiving mechanism; develop support for multiple survivor databases; and optimize the system for better performance. This paper describes the initial NDT system architecture and compares Alfred's design to it. We enumerate the challenges with encountered in the initial deployment and discuss how we addressed each challenge in Alfred.

2 Deployment Challenges

The initial NDT system was created from components of the Virtual Human Toolkit (Hartholt et al., 2013). It consists of 9 applications running on a single computer (Figure 1).

Proceedings of the SIGDIAL 2017 Conference, pages 352–355,
Saarbrücken, Germany, 15-17 August 2017. ©2017 Association for Computational Linguistics

The NDT system listens to the user's audio streaming from a microphone. Two components handle the audio stream: AcquireSpeech (1) records the user's audio to a file for later analysis, and the Google Web ASR webapp (2) sends the audio to Google speech recognition services, receives the speech transcription, and forwards the text to the language understanding module. The webapp is loaded from a web server (8) running in the background. We chose the Google speech service because it has been shown to be highly effective and robust (Morbini et al., 2013). At the time of the system development, the only way to access the Google ASR was to use the Web Speech API in the Chrome web browser[1]; we thus had to include Chrome as an additional component of the NDT system (the ninth component, not explicitly shown on Figure 1).

The language understanding and dialogue management are handled by NPCEditor (3) (Leuski and Traum, 2011). It uses a statistical classifier to analyze the speech transcript and selects the appropriate response from a collection of Mr. Gutter's video clips. It passes the clip identifier to a custom Video Player (4), which handles on-the-fly video composition such as the crossfade effect between clips and custom backgrounds for the video.

The interprocess communication between individual components is handled by messages that flow through the ActiveMQ message server (7). Logger (6) records and stores all the messages for further analysis. Finally, Launcher (5) starts and terminates the individual components. The video clips and the language data are packaged with the system components inside the Launcher application. A typical NDT installation is run on a 15-inch MacBook Pro, connected via HDMI to an external monitor or television.

Architecture The multi-component design stems from the origins of the VH Toolkit as a research and development enviromnent, where individual components can be swapped as needed. If a component crashes, the rest of the system continues to work. This design created several issues for museum deployment: the system was slow to start as each component had to be loaded and initialized separately, and if a component crashed, the system appeared to be running but stopped responding. This confused system operators, many of whom were museum volunteers

---

[1]http://tinyurl.com/mxdocae

with little technical training.

To simplify operation while preserving the multi-component design, Alfred appears as a single application, but internally it integrates a number of dynamically loaded plugins corresponding to individual parts of the architecture (Figure 2). The plugins deal with audio acquisition, speech recognition, response selection, video playback, logging, and external communication. The plugins use an internal messaging protocol to exchange information while isolating internal plugin details from each other. The Alfred application framework also maintains an internal database (a whiteboard) where the plugins can share data about the current state of the execution.

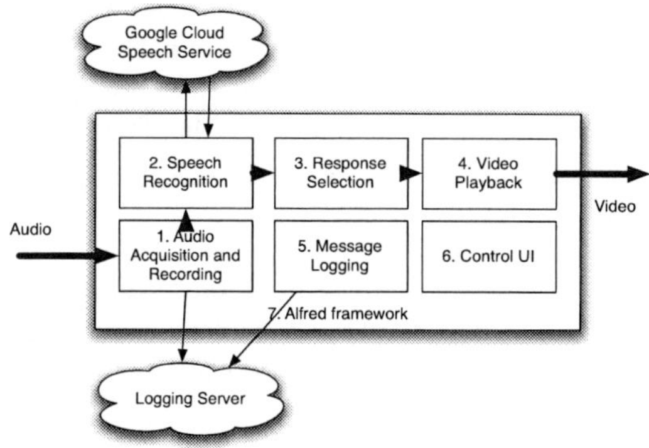

Figure 2: The Alfred NDT system architecture. Each box represents a dynamically loaded plugin that shares code in the Alfred framework.

Installation The original system installation and maintenance process is complicated by the need to install and maintain system-level 3rd party dependencies: Java SDK for Components 1, 3, 5, 6, and 7, and Google Chrome browser and Apache web server for Component 2. Configuring both web and ActiveMQ servers requires modifying the OS configuration. Google Chrome's update mechanism runs in background without user's control and can break the system without warning. This issue came to light when the NDT system stopped working one morning after the web browser updated itself overnight.

While many of the original toolkit components are cross-platform, the installation packaging for the NDT system was specific to MacOS, as both the museum staff and SFI personnel showed that they are more familiar with that environment. We therefore created Alfred as a native MacOS application. It has all the traditional UI features that a native application has. It is installed by downloading an archive file, unpacking and dragging the application icon into place. It does not require administrative level OS privileges for installation. It can be removed by dragging the application icon into the trash. Alfred has no external dependencies that we do not control – no Java runtime or Google Chrome to maintain. Alfred integrates an auto-update mechanism that checks our server at regular intervals and prompts the user to update the application if a new version is available.

User Interface Each original VH Toolkit component was created as a research tool, with its own user interface (UI). As the components were developed independently, the UIs are not consistent across them. During the system startup each component presents its own window interface. Additionally, as all the components in the system are built to be cross-platform using Java or C libraries, the UI elements in the components often do not match what a user is expecting from a native application. The number of windows and the amount of information presented in the windows overwhelm unexperienced system operators.

To simplify the UI design, we separated the user interface into regular and expert configurations. In the regular configuration, Alfred presents a single window with the survivor's video. This mode is all that is required to interact with the system. The expert mode provides an additional window with detailed information from individual plugins. The window contains tabs; each tab corresponds to a UI plugin that displays concise information summary in the tab itself, with space for more detailed information in the pane associated with the tab. For example, a UI plugin corresponding to the audio acquisition module displays the current audio power level in its tab, while providing user controls for selecting the audio source and toggling the audio recording in its pane. A number of UI plugins are provided, including one that supports a Wizard-of-Oz interface (Artstein et al., 2015).

The expert mode is disabled by default, but can be displayed on request. The expert interface is implemented as a web app that runs in a browser window, to allow observation and control from another computer. The connection is done via the standard http protocol so it is capable of crossing most firewalls without issues.

Performance The overall NDT system performance was acceptable while running on a top-of-the-line laptop. However, we encountered several challenges. Firstly, the system operators reported that the system would stop responding to the user's input for short amounts of time. We traced the issue to a Java garbage collection process effectively pausing the system at random times. Secondly, the Video Player would occasionally stutter during clip transitions. That issue was attributed to the open source, cross-platform OpenCV[2] library used for video decoding, which was not efficient enough for video playback of high resolution clips. Finally, Google Web Speech API is nonstandard and poorly documented. For example, while we could request transcription in US English, that feature never worked reliably; when installing and demonstrating the system in Canada or United Kingdom, Google Chrome would detect the computer location, and the speech recognition result would default to Canadian or British spellings, throwing off the language understanding component.

As a native application, Alfred does not suffer from garbage collection issues. Some native components show higher efficiency than Java-based counterparts. For example, we re-implemented the NPCEditor text classification and dialogue management algorithms as a C++ library, and the implementation is noticeably more efficient. We continue to author the language classifiers in NPCEditor, and convert the final files into the Alfred format before deployment.

We replaced the video decoding OpenCV library with AVFoundation – the native macOS media framework. We were able to optimize the playback, decrease the computational requirements by a factor of three, and eliminate playback stutter.

Alfred uses the platform-native Google Cloud Speech API library.[3] The speech recognition plugin streams the audio from the acquisition plugin directly to the Google Cloud server. The native Google Cloud API is efficient, robust, and allows us to control the spelling variety reliably.

Scaling The initial NDT system stores both the software and the data together into a single application. Our assumption was that it would provide a single package that encapsulated the relevant pieces in one place. However, after the suc-

---

[2] `http://opencv.org`
[3] `https://cloud.google.com/speech/`

cess of the initial installation, the decision was made to extend the project by recording 11 additional Holocaust survivors, allowing the museum docents to switch between them. In Alfred, each survivor database is a document bundle – a folder masquerading as a single file. The document contains the video clips, the language database, and the dialogue manager scripts. Alfred opens the survivor document and loads the required information initializing the individual plugins. The document interface is a window that presents the survivor video on the screen. Closing the window closes the document and unloads its resources from memory. Switching between survivors is as easy as closing a document and opening another.

Data Collection The NDT system records both the user's audio and the inter-component messages as log files which are stored locally on the computer. The logs are used to monitor the system, evaluate its performance, and adapt the response selection algorithm. Our intention was to download the logs from the machine at the museum at regular intervals. However, access to these logs proved to be a challenge as the computer was located behind a firewall. Alfred archives both the user utterance audio and the inter-plugin messages and uploads them to our server automatically. The files are uploaded as soon as they are created. If the upload fails or the network is unavailable, Alfred attempts to upload the files again at a later time. Alfred uses a lossless codec to archive the audio, which results in files that approximately four times smaller than the files produced by the initial NDT system.

3 Conclusion

In this paper we described our analysis of an interactive dialogue system deployment in an environment where deep technical expertise might not be readily available. The initial version was created using a collection of research components and deployed at two museums. As the result of observations from the deployment, we designed a new system architecture to simplify and streamline the system installation and user interface; create a better data collection and archiving mechanism; develop support for multiple dialogue databases; and optimize the system for better performance.

We have deployed a beta version of the Alfred system both at SFI and Illinois earlier this year. The response was overwhelmingly positive: our users love the improved performance, simplified interface, and support for multiple survivor databases. We had no reports of system performance issues and the data is being collected on our servers automatically.

Acknowledgments

New Dimensions in Testimony is a collaboration between the USC Institute for Creative Technologies, the USC Shoah Foundation, and Conscience Display, and was made possible by generous donations from private foundations and individuals. We are extremely grateful to the Illinois Holocaust Museum and Education Center for hosting the exhibit and providing invaluable feedback.

References

Ron Artstein, Anton Leuski, Heather Maio, Tomer Mor-Barak, Carla Gordon, and David Traum. 2015. How many utterances are needed to support time-offset interaction? In *Proceedings of FLAIRS 28*.

Ron Artstein, David Traum, Oleg Alexander, Anton Leuski, Andrew Jones, Kallirroi Georgila, Paul Debevec, William Swartout, Heather Maio, and Stephen Smith. 2014. Time-offset interaction with a Holocaust survivor. In *Proceedings of IUI'14*. pages 163–168.

Arno Hartholt, David Traum, Stacy C. Marsella, Ari Shapiro, Giota Stratou, Anton Leuski, Louis-Philippe Morency, and Jonathan Gratch. 2013. All together now: Introducing the Virtual Human toolkit. In *Proceedings of IVA'13*. Edinburgh, UK.

Anton Leuski and David Traum. 2011. NPCEditor: Creating virtual human dialogue using information retrieval techniques. *AI Magazine* 32(2):42–56.

Fabrizio Morbini, Kartik Audhkhasi, Kenji Sagae, Ron Artstein, Doğan Can, Panayiotis Georgiou, Shri Narayanan, Anton Leuski, and David Traum. 2013. Which ASR should I choose for my dialogue system? In *Proceedings of the SIGDIAL'13*. Metz, France, pages 394–403.

David Traum, Kallirroi Georgila, Ron Artstein, and Anton Leuski. 2015a. Evaluating spoken dialogue processing for time-offset interaction. In *Proceedings of SIGDIAL'15*. Prague, Czech Republic.

David Traum, Andrew Jones, Kia Hays, Heather Maio, Oleg Alexander, Ron Artstein, Paul Debevec, Alesia Gainer, Kallirroi Georgila, Kathleen Haase, Karen Jungblut, Anton Leuski, Stephen Smith, and William Swartout. 2015b. New dimensions in testimony: Digitally preserving a holocaust survivor's interactive storytelling. In *Proceedings of ICIDS'15*. Copenhagen, Denmark, pages 269–281.

Information Navigation System with Discovering User Interests

Koichiro Yoshino, Yu Suzuki and Satoshi Nakamura

Graduate School of Information Science

Nara Institute of Science and Technology

8916-5, Takayama-cho, Ikoma, Nara, 6300192, Japan

{koichiro,ysuzuki,s-nakamura}@is.naist.jp

Abstract

We demonstrate an information navigation system for sightseeing domains that has a dialogue interface for discovering user interests for tourist activities. The system discovers interests of a user with focus detection on user utterances, and proactively presents related information to the discovered user interest. A partially observable Markov decision process (POMDP)-based dialogue manager, which is extended with user focus states, controls the behavior of the system to provide information with several dialogue acts for providing information. We transferred the belief-update function and the policy of the manager from other system trained on a different domain to show the generality of defined dialogue acts for our information navigation system.

1 Introduction

A large number of dialogue systems to assist daily life of users have been deployed in the real world, however, most are handled on goal-oriented architecture (Young et al., 2010), on which clear goals of users are assumed. In contrast, an information navigation system (Yoshino and Kawahara, 2015) to clarify ambiguous user goals through a dialogue was proposed. The system provides information about current talking topics with several dialogue acts of providing information according to the ky strength of the user's interest to the current topic. If the user's intention is ambiguous and the user does not have any strong interest or focus, the system provides general information about the current discussion topic to help the user decide. However, if the user has specified interests or focus for some contents, the system answers the user's question and presents additional information proactively according to the detected user's interests, even if the user can not find the exact words to express his or her interests.

The partially observable Markov decision process (POMDP)-based management architecture of information navigation was proposed (Yoshino and Kawahara, 2014) with several dialogue acts of providing information, however, this study ran the system only on one limited domain. In this demonstration, we used the belief-update function and the policy function trained on the different domain (news navigation for baseball news) for the proposed system (information navigation for tourist) to investigate the robustness of the defined system architecture. We also introduce a new mechanism to select more related topics when the system selects a topic to be presented in the next sub-dialogue by introducing semantic similarity of dialogue topics (content).

The proposed system has speech interfaces with open-source speech recognition system Julius (Lee and Kawahara, 2009)[1] and text to speech system OpenJtalk[2]. This system runs on a standalone machine without connecting other servers, however, any modules can be replaced by other modules on other severs because modules connect each other on TCP/IP protocol.

2 System Architecture

Information providing is a sub-function of the general purpose function defined in ISO-24617-2 standard dialogue act set (Bunt et al., 2012), which includes dialogue acts of providing new or requested information from the dialogue partner. We defined seven dialogue modules to fulfill the information demand of a user though interactions

---

[1] https://github.com/julius-speech/julius
[2] http://open-jtalk.sourceforge.net/

356

Proceedings of the SIGDIAL 2017 Conference, pages 356–359,
Saarbrücken, Germany, 15-17 August 2017. ©2017 Association for Computational Linguistics

Table 1: Relations between defined dialogue modules in our system and dialogue acts defined in ISO-24617-2 (Bunt et al., 2012)

Category in ISO-24617-2			DAs in the proposed system
General purpose function	Information Providing	Inform	Topic presentation (TP)
			Storytelling (ST)
			Proactive presentation (PP)
		Answer	Question Answering (QA)
	Information seeking	Propositional question	Confirmation (CO)
Dimension specific function	Social Obligation	*	Greeting (GR)
	Turn Management	Turn release	Keep Silent (KS)

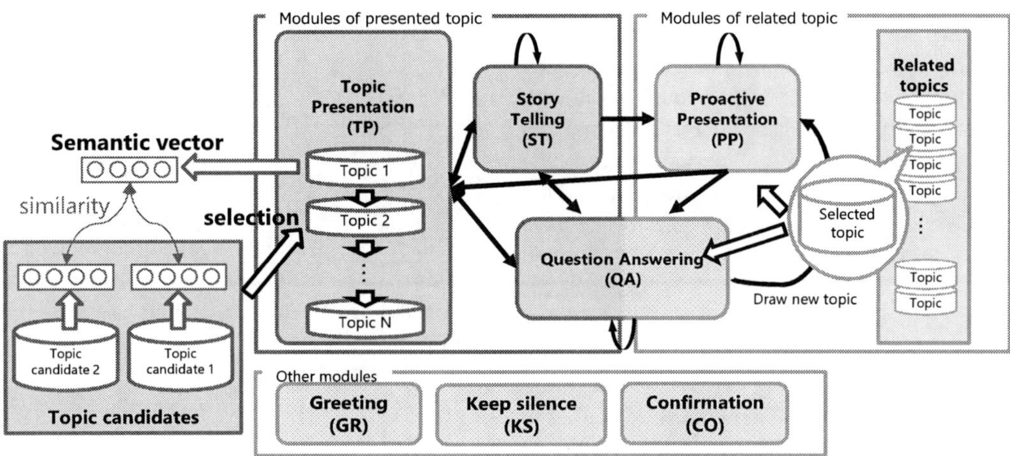

Figure 1: Overall architecture of proposed system.

by following this standard. The relations of defined modules and ISO-24617-2 dialogue acts are summarized in Table 1. We defined three sub-categories of dialogue act of "Inform" in the information providing function i.e., topic presentation (TP), storytelling (ST), and proactive presentation (PP), to enable smart information provision. The dialogue act "Answer" is also implemented as the question answering (QA) module in the same function. Our information navigation system basically provides information, but only one case in which the system uses the information-seeking function is confirmation (CO) to clarify the previous user intent. Dimension-specific functions support the general-purpose function; thus, minimum social obligation and turn-management functions are implemented as Greeting (GR) and Keep silent (KS).

Dialogue modules for these functions are defined for the task of news navigation (Yoshino and Kawahara, 2015), and the call of these modules at each turn is managed by the POMDP-based man-ager. The call of system action is managed by the policy of POMDP, which takes into account the interests of the user (=user focus). The belief update is defined as,

$$b'_{s',f'} = P(s', f'|o'_{s'}, o'_{f'}) \sum_s P(s', f'|s, f, a) b_{s,f}, \quad (1)$$

where s denote the dialogue act of the user, f is the focus of the user on the current topic, and a is the selected dialogue module (dash means the next turn). The policy is trained in Q-learning as

$$\pi(b_{s,f}) = a \quad (2)$$

by using defined rewards and a user simulator constructed from dialogue data with users. The details are described in a previous study (Yoshino and Kawahara, 2015). The dialogue data of a different domain (news navigation for baseball news) is used to train the belief-update function and policy function for the current domain (sightseeing domain).

The order of topics (=documents of the information source) to be presented at each sub-dialogue is pre-defined in the current system. However, topics to be introduced by the system should be selected according to user interests in the dialogue history, which can be captured in the past dialogue. Thus, we introduce a mechanism to introduce new topics that will be more attractive for the user by using past topics that the user and system already discussed. We defined a semantic similarity measure to define the similarities of each pair of topics (=news). The system determines the next topic of the dialogue by using the similarity from topics that the user is interested in, to topic candidates to be presented as the next topic. A binary flag of user interest (=focus) can be predicted for each presented topic by using the existence of user focus in user utterances. Only vectors of flagged documents are used to select the next presenting document. If TP module is called by the dialogue manager, the TP module selects the next dialogue topic according to the similarity. The system calculates a vector of a document with word2vec (Mikolov et al., 2013) and the long-short term memory neural network (LSTM)-based encoder-decoder model (Cho et al., 2014) to define the similarity. Each word of new text is embedded into a fixed-length distributed representation with word2vec, and inputted into the LSTM-based encoder model. The LSTM-based encoder-decoder model is trained to restore the original sentences of news texts. The final vector of the encoding phase in this architecture is used as the vector of the document. News texts collected from a Kyoto prefecture sightseeing Web site[3] was used as the training data of word2vec, LSTM-based encoder-decoder model, and content of the dialogue system. We used cosine similarity between the vectors of documents to calculate the similarities of each topic (news texts). The overall architecture is illustrated in Figure 1.

3 Dialogue example (translation from Japanese)

In the following example, the system starts a dialogue from the presentation of the system about some interesting places in Kyoto. In **User 2**, the user requires an overall description of the presented topic, however, the user does not have any specified focus word that indicates his inter-

---

[3]http://www.kyototourism.org/en/

est. Thus, the system drastically changes the topic when the system is requested to change the topic (**System 3**). In **System 4**, the user shows an interest with a focus on the word "matcha" and the focus detection module of the system detects that the user is interested in this current topic. The vector of the second topic (document) is used to select the third topic in **System 5**, and the selected topic is similar to the second topic (about "matcha").

— Dialogue example ——————

System 0 (GR): Hello, I would like to introduce you to some interesting places in Kyoto. Let me know if you are interested.

System 1 (TP): There is a cherry blossom illumination event at the Kamo-gawa river.

User 2 (ST): Could you give me the details?

System 2 (ST): We have an illumination event at the banks of the Kamo-gawa river from Oike to Gojo, which is called the "flower corridor".

User 3 (TP): Thanks, do you have any other topics?

System 3 (TP): There is a tea ceremony in Kyoto.

User 4 (QA): Does it involve matcha (traditional style green tea)?

System 4 (QA): Shoka-do added a new green-tea course in a quality tea room.

User 5 (TP): Interesting. Any other news?

System 5 (TP): There is a long line to wait for a new matcha parfait.

...

Acknowledgement

Part of this work is supported by Japan Science and Technology Agency PRESTO (JP-MJPR165B). Part of this work have been achieved by "Research and Development on Fundamental and Utilization Technologies for Social Big Data" ,the Commissioned Research of National Institute of Information and Communications Technology (NICT) , JAPAN.

References

Harry Bunt, Jan Alexandersson, Jae-Woong Choe, Alex Chengyu Fang, Koiti Hasida, Volha Petukhova, Andrei Popescu-Belis, and David R Traum. 2012. Iso 24617-2: A semantically-based standard for dialogue annotation. In *In Proc. 8th edition of the Lan-*

guage Resources and Evaluation Conference. Citeseer, pages 430–437.

Kyunghyun Cho, Bart Van Merriënboer, Caglar Gulcehre, Dzmitry Bahdanau, Fethi Bougares, Holger Schwenk, and Yoshua Bengio. 2014. Learning phrase representations using rnn encoder-decoder for statistical machine translation. In *In Proc. The 2014 Conference on Empirical Methods on Natural Language Processing*. pages 1724–1734.

Akinobu Lee and Tatsuya Kawahara. 2009. Recent development of open-source speech recognition engine julius. In *Proceedings: APSIPA ASC 2009: Asia-Pacific Signal and Information Processing Association, 2009 Annual Summit and Conference*. Asia-Pacific Signal and Information Processing Association, 2009 Annual Summit and Conference, International Organizing Committee, pages 131–137.

Tomas Mikolov, Ilya Sutskever, Kai Chen, Greg S Corrado, and Jeff Dean. 2013. Distributed representations of words and phrases and their compositionality. In *Advances in neural information processing systems*. pages 3111–3119.

Koichiro Yoshino and Tatsuya Kawahara. 2014. Information navigation system based on pomdp that tracks user focus. In *In Proc. Annual SIGdial Meeting on Discourse and Dialogue*. pages 32–40.

Koichiro Yoshino and Tatsuya Kawahara. 2015. Conversational system for information navigation based on POMDP with user focus tracking. *Computer Speech & Language* 34(1):275 – 291.

Steve Young, Milica Gašić, Simon Keizer, François Mairesse, Jost Schatzmann, Blaise Thomson, and Kai Yu. 2010. The hidden information state model: A practical framework for pomdp-based spoken dialogue management. *Computer Speech & Language* 24(2):150–174.

Modelling Protagonist Goals and Desires in First-Person Narrative

Elahe Rahimtoroghi, Jiaqi Wu, Ruimin Wang,
Pranav Anand and **Marilyn A Walker**
University of California Santa Cruz
Santa Cruz, CA, US
{erahimto,jwu64,ruiwang,panand,mawalker}@ucsc.edu

Abstract

Many genres of natural language text are narratively structured, a testament to our predilection for organizing our experiences as narratives. There is broad consensus that understanding a narrative requires identifying and tracking the goals and desires of the characters and their narrative outcomes. However, to date, there has been limited work on computational models for this problem. We introduce a new dataset, **DesireDB**, which includes gold-standard labels for identifying statements of desire, textual evidence for desire fulfillment, and annotations for whether the stated desire is fulfilled given the evidence in the narrative context. We report experiments on tracking desire fulfillment using different methods, and show that LSTM Skip-Thought model achieves F-measure of 0.7 on our corpus.

1 Introduction

Humans appear to organize and remember everyday experiences by imposing a narrative structure on them (Nelson, 1989; Thorne and Nam, 2009; Bruner, 1991; McAdams et al., 2006), and many genres of natural language text are therefore narratively structured, e.g. dinner table conversations, news articles, user reviews and blog posts (Polanyi, 1989; Jurafsky et al., 2014; Bell, 2005; Gordon et al., 2011). Moreover, there is broad consensus that understanding a narrative involves activating a representation, early in the narrative, of the protagonist and her goals and desires, and then maintaining that representation as the narrative evolves, as a vehicle for explaining the protagonist's actions and tracking narrative outcomes (Elson, 2012; Rapp and Gerrig, 2006; Trabasso

People did seem pleased to see me but all I **[wanted to]** do was talk to a particular friend.
I'm off this weekend and had really **[hoped to]** get out and dance.
We **[decided to]** just go for a walk and look at all the sunflowers in the neighborhood.
I **[couldn't wait to]** get out of our cheap and somewhat charming hotel and show James a little bit of Paris.
We drove for just over an hour and **[aimed to]** get to Trinity beach to set up for the night.
She called the pastor, and he had time, too, so, we **[arranged to]** meet Saturday at 9am.
Even though my deadline wasn't until 4 p.m., I **[needed to]** write the story as quickly as possible.

Figure 1: Desire expressions in personal narratives

and van den Broek, 1985; Lehnert, 1981).

To date, there has been limited work on computational models for recognizing the expression of the protagonist's goals and desires in narrative texts, and tracking their corresponding narrative outcomes. We introduce a new corpus **DesireDB** of ~3,500 first-person informal narratives with annotations for desires and their fulfillment status, available online.[1] Because first-person narratives often revolve around the narrator's private states and goals (Labov, 1972), this corpus is highly suitable as a testbed for identifying human desires and their outcomes. Moreover, first-person narratives allow the narrative protagonist (first-person) to be easily identified and tracked. Figure 1 illustrates examples of desire and goal expressions in our corpus.

DesireDB is open domain. It contains a broad range of expressions of desires and goal statements in personal narratives. It also includes the narrative context for each desire statement as shown in Figure 2. We include both prior and

---

[1]https://nlds.soe.ucsc.edu/DesireDB

Proceedings of the SIGDIAL 2017 Conference, pages 360–369,
Saarbrücken, Germany, 15-17 August 2017. ©2017 Association for Computational Linguistics

post context of the desire expressions, since theories of narrative structure suggest that the evaluation points of a narrative can precede the expression of the events, goals and desires of the narrator (Labov, 1972; Swanson et al., 2014).

Our approach builds on seminal work on a computational model of Lehnert's plot units, that applied modern NLP tools to tracking narrative affect states in Aesop's Fables (Goyal et al., 2010; Lehnert, 1981; Goyal and Riloff, 2013). Our framing of the problem is also inspired by recent work that identifies three forms of desire expressions in short narratives from MCTest and SimpleWiki and develops models to predict whether desires are fulfilled or unfulfilled (Chaturvedi et al., 2016). However DesireDB's narrative and sentence structure is more complex than either MCTest or SimpleWiki (Richardson et al., 2013; Coster and Kauchak, 2011).

We propose new features (Sec 4.1), as well as testing features used in previous work, and apply different classifiers to model desire fulfillment in our corpus. We also directly compare to results on MCTest and SimpleWiki (Sec 4.4). We apply LSTM models that distinguish between prior and post context and capture the flow of the narrative. Our best system, a Skip-Thought RNN model, achieves an F-measure of 0.70, while a logistic regression system achieves 0.66. Our models and features outperform Chaturvedi et al. (2016) on MCTest and SimpleWiki, while providing new results for a new corpus for tracking desires in first-person narratives. Moreover, analysis of our results shows that features representing the discourse structure (such as overt discourse relation markers) are the best predictors of fulfillment status of a desire or goal. We also show that both prior and post context are important for this task.

We discuss related work in Sec. 2 and describe our corpus and annotations in Sec. 3. Section 4 presents our features and methods for modeling desire fulfillment in narratives along with the experiments and results including comparison to previous work. Finally, we present conclusions and future directions in Sec. 5.

2   Related Work

There has recently been an upsurge in interest in computational models of narrative structure (Lehnert, 1981; Wilensky, 1982) and story understanding (Rahimtoroghi et al., 2016; Swanson

---

Prior-Context: (1) I ran the Nike+ human Race 10K new York in under 57 minutes! (2) Then at the all-American rejects concert, I somehow ended up right next to this really cute guy and he seemed interested in me. (3) Was I imagining things? He was really nice; (4) I dropped something and it was dark, he bent with his cell phone light to help me look for it. (5) We spoke a little, but it was loud and not suited for conversation there.
Desire-Expression-Sentence: I [**had hoped to**] ask him to join me for a drink or something after the show (if my courage would allow such a thing) but he left before the end and I didn't see him after that.
Post-Context: (1) Maybe I'll try missed connections lol. (2) I didn't want to tell him I think he's cute or make any gay references during the show because if I was wrong that would make standing there the whole rest of the concert too awkward... (3) Afterward, I wandered through the city making stops at several bars and clubs, met some new people, some old people (4) As in people I knew - I actually didn't met any old people, unless you count the tourist family whose dad asked me about my t-shirt. (5) And when I thought the night was over (and the doorman of the club did insist it was over) I met this great guy going into the subway.

Figure 2: A desire expression with its surrounding context extracted from a personal narrative

et al., 2014; Ouyang and McKeown, 2015, 2014). However there has been limited work on computational models for recognizing the expression of the protagonist's goals and desires in narrative genres.

Our approach builds on work by Goyal and Riloff (2013) that applied modern NLP tools to track narrative affect states in Aesop's Fables (Goyal et al., 2010). They present a system called AESOP that uses a number of existing resources to identify affect states of the characters as part of deriving plot units. The motivation of modeling plot units is the idea that emotional reactions are central to the notion of a narrative and the main plot of a story can be modeled by tracking the transition between the affect states (Lehnert, 1981). The AESOP system identifies affect states and creates links between them to model plot units and is evaluated on a small set of two-character fables. They performed a manual annotation to examine different types of affect expressions in the narratives. Their study shows that many affect states arise from events where a character is acted upon in positive or negative ways, not explicit expression of emotions. They also show that most of the affect states emerge by the expression of goals and plans and goal completion. Some of our features are motivated by the idea that implicit sentiment polarity can represent success or failure of goals and can be used to better model desire and goal

361

fulfillment in a narrative (Reed et al., 2017), although we cannot directly compare our findings to theirs because their annotations are not publicly available.

Chaturvedi et al. (2016) exploit two deliberately simplified datasets in order to model desire and its fulfillment: **MCTest** which contains 660 stories limited to content understandable by 7-year old children, and, **SimpleWiki** created from a dump of the Simple English Wikipedia discarding all the lists, tables and titles. They use desire statements matching a list of three verb phrases, *wanted to, hoped to,* and *wished to.* Their context representation consists of five or fewer sentences following the desire expression. They use BOW (Bag of Words) as baseline and apply unstructured and structured models for desire fulfillment modeling with different features motivated by narrative structure. Their best result is achieved with a structured prediction model called Latent Structured Narrative Model (LSNM) which models the evolution of the narrative by associating a latent variable with each fragment of the context in the data. Their best unstructured model is a Logistic Regression classifier that uses all of their features.

Recent work on computational models of semantics provides an evaluation test for story understanding (Mostafazadeh et al., 2017). The task includes four-sentence stories, each with two possible endings where only one is correct. The goal is for each system to select the correct ending of the story by modeling different levels of semantics in narratives, such as lexical, sentential and discourse-level. The highest performing model with 75% accuracy used a linear regression classifier with several features such as neural language models and stylistic features to model the story coherence (Schwartz et al., 2017). The results from other systems showed that sentiment is an important factor and using only sentiment features could achieve about 65% accuracy on the test.

3   DesireDB Corpus

DesireDB aims to provide a testbed for modeling desire and goals in personal narrative and predicting their fulfillment status. We develop a systematic method to identify desire and goal statements, and then collect annotations to create gold-standard labels of fulfillment status as well as spans of text marked as evidence.

3.1   Identifying Desires and Goals

Our corpus is a subset of the Spinn3r corpus (Burton et al., 2011, 2009), consisting of first-person narratives from six personal blog domains: *livejournal.com, wordpress.com, blogspot.com, spaces.live.com, typepad.com, travelpod.com.* To create our dataset, we select only desire expressions involving some version of the first-person. In first-person narratives, the narrator and protagonist naturally align which makes it much easier to identify and track the protagonist than in fiction or historical genre. Thus, selecting narrative passages with expressions of desire relating to the first-person are very likely to discuss subsequent behaviors to achieve that desire and the end result. Put simply, zooming in on first-person desires means that desire and its aftermath are more likely to be highly topical for the narrative. This corpus, then, is highly suitable as a testbed for modeling human desires and their fulfillment.

Human desires and goals can be expressed linguistically in many different ways, including both explicit verbal and nominal markers of desire or necessity (e.g., *want, hope*) and more general markers of urges (e.g., *craving, hunger, thirst*). To systematically discover predicates that specify desires, we browsed FrameNet 1.7 (Baker et al., 1998) selecting frames that seemed likely to contain lexical units specifying desires: *Being-necessary, Desiring, Have-as-a-demand, Needing, Offer, Purpose, Request, Required-event, Scheduling, Seeking, Seeking-to-achieve, Stimulus-focus, Stimulate-emotion,* and *Worry.* We then selected 100 representative instances of that frame in English Gigaword (Parker et al., 2011) by first selecting the 10 most frequent lexical units in that frame, and then selecting 10 random instances per lexical unit. One of the authors examined each set of 100 instances, estimating for each sentence whether the predicate specifies a goal that the surrounding text picks up on. Because we were looking for predicates that reliably specify desires that motivate a protagonist's actions, we eliminated frames where less than 80% of the sentences showed this characteristic.

This resulted in a downsample to the following four frames: *Desiring, Needing, Purpose,* and *Request.* We selected only the verbal lexical units because we found that verbs were more likely to introduce goals than nouns or adjectives. We examined 100 instances for each verbal lex-

Figure 3: Example of data in DesireDB

Pattern	Count	Ful	Unf	Unk	None
wanted to	2,510	49%	35%	14%	2%
needed to	202	65%	16%	16%	3%
ordered	201	71%	21%	6%	2%
arranged to	199	68%	13%	16%	3%
decided to	68	87%	9%	4%	0%
hoped to	68	19%	68%	12%	1%
couldn't wait	68	79%	3%	15%	3%
wished to	66	27%	35%	30%	8%
scheduled	60	43%	25%	27%	5%
asked for	60	53%	27%	15%	5%
required	58	69%	16%	15%	0%
requested	30	60%	20%	20%	0%
demanded	30	60%	23%	17%	0%
ached to	20	50%	40%	10%	0%
aimed to	20	55%	30%	15%	0%
desired to	20	50%	25%	25%	0%
Total	3,680	53%	31%	14%	2%

Table 1: Distribution of desire verbal patterns and fulfillment labels in DesireDB

ical unit, discarding as before. This resulted in 37 verbs. For each verb, we systematically constructed and coded all past forms of the verb (e.g., *was [verb]ing, had [verb]ed, had been [verb]ing, [verb]ed, didn't [verb]*, etc.) because we posited that morphological form itself may convey likelihood of fulfillment (e.g., a past perfect *I had wanted to ...* signals that something changed, either the desire or fulfillment). We initially experimented with both past and (historical) present, but past tense verb patterns resulted in much higher precision. We counted the instances of these patterns in our dataset, and retained only those lemmas with at least 1000 instances across the corpus.

We extract stories containing the verbal patterns of desire, with five sentences before and after the desire expression sentence as context (See Fig. 2). Our annotation results provide support that the evidence of desire fulfillment can be expressed before the desire statement. We also study the effect of prior and post context in understanding desire fulfillment in our experiments (Section 4) and show that using the narrative context preceding the desire statement improves the results.

3.2 Data Annotation

We extracted ∼600K desire expressions with their context, and then sample 3,680 instances for annotation. This subset consists of 16 verbal patterns (when collapsing all morphological forms to their head word). A group of pre-qualified Mechanical Turkers then labelled each instance. The annotators labelled the fulfillment status of the desire expression sentence based on the prior and post context, by choosing from three labels: *Fulfilled, Unfulfilled,* and *Unknown from the context*. They were also asked to mark the evidence for the label they had chosen by specifying a span of text in the narrative. For each data instance, we asked the Turkers to mark the subject of the desire expression and determine if the expressed desire is hypothetical (e.g., a conditional sentence) or not.

The annotators were selected from a list of prequalified workers who had successfully passed a test on a textual entailment task with 100% correct answers. They were provided with detailed instructions and examples as to how to label the desires and mark the evidence. We also specified the desire expression verbal pattern using square brackets (as shown in Fig. 1 and 2) for more clarity. Three annotators were assigned to work on each data instance. To generate the gold-standard labels we used majority vote and the cases with no agreement were labeled as *'None'*.

Table 1 reports the distribution of data and goldstandard labels (Ful:Fulfilled, Unf:Unfulfilled, Unk:Unknown from the context). About half of the desire expressions (53%) were labeled *Fulfilled* and about one third (31%) were labeled *Unfulfilled*. The annotators didn't agree on about 2% of the instances, that were labeled *None*. As Tabel 1 shows, the distribution of labels is not uniform across different verbal patterns. For instance, *decided to* and *couldn't wait* are highly skewed towards Fulfilled as opposed to *hoped to* which includes 68% Unfulfilled instances. Some patterns seem to be harder to annotate, like *wished to*, which has the highest rate of Unknown (30%) and None (8%) among all.

Other than fulfillment status, for each data instance in our corpus we include the agreement-score which is the number of annotators that agreed on the assigned label. In addition, we provide the *evidence* as a part of the DesireDB data, by merging the text spans marked by the annotators as evidence. We compared the evidence spans pairwise to measure the overlap-score, indicating the number of pairs of annotators with overlapping responses. An example is shown in Figure 3. The first part is the extracted data including the desire expression with prior and post context, and the second part is the gold-standard annotations.

To assess inter-annotator agreement for Fulfillment, we calculated Krippendorff-alpha Kappa (Krippendorff, 1970, 2004) for pairwise inter-annotator reliability, and, the average of Kappa between each annotator and the majority vote. These two metrics are 0.63 and 0.88 respectively. Overall, 66% of the data was labeled with total agreement (where all three annotators agreed on the same label) and about 32% of data was labeled by two agreements and one disagreement. We also examined the agreements across each label separately. For *Fulfilled* class, total agreement rate is 75%, which for *Unfulfilled* is 67%, and on *Unknown from the context* is 41%. We believe this indicates that annotating unfulfilled desires was harder than fulfilled cases. For evidence marking, in 79% of the data all three annotators marked overlapping spans.

4 Modeling Desire Fulfillment

We conducted a range of experiments on predicting fulfillment status of desires and goals, using different features and models, including LSTM architectures that can encode the sequential structure of the narratives. We first describe our features and models. Then, we present our feature analysis study to examine their importance in modeling fulfillment. Finally we provide results of direct comparison to previous work on the existing corpora.

Sentiment: Negative Prior-Context(4): "I had been working for hours on boring paperwork and financial stuff, and I was really crabby."
Sentiment: Negative Prior-Context(5): I decided it was time to take a break and thought, should I read a magazine or watch best Week Ever?
Sentiment: Negative Desire-Epxression-Sentence: But I realized that what I really **[wanted to]** do was go for a run!
Sentiment: Positive Post-Context(1): That was pretty amazing, to transition mentally from 'having to' to 'wanting to' run.
Sentiment: Positive Post-Context(2): So I did a quick, fun 2.75 miles.

Figure 4: Example of sentiment features, where prior context is negative while the post context is positive, implying fulfillment of the desire

4.1 Features Description

In our original informal examination of the DesireDB development data, we noticed several ways that a writer can signal (lack of) fulfillment of a desire like "I hoped to pick up a dictionary". First, they may mention an outcome that entails ("The book I bought was...") or strongly implies fulfillment ("I went back home happily."). However, we noticed that in many cases of fulfillment, the 'marker' was simply the absence of any mention that things went wrong. For lack of fulfillment, while we found cases where writers explicitly state that their desire wasn't met, we noted many instances where evidence came from mentioning that an enabling condition for fulfillment wasn't met ("The bookstore was closed.").

True machine understanding of these kinds of narrative structures requires robust models of the complex interplay of semantics (including negation) as well as world knowledge about the scripts for tasks like buying books, including what count as enabling conditions and entailers for fulfillment. While we hope to explore more articulated models in the future, for our experiments we considered reasonable proxies for the conditions mentioned above using existing resources (note that we also tested LSTM models described below, which may implicitly learn such relationships with sufficient data). One set (**Desire Features**) indexes properties of the desire expression (e.g., the desire verb) as well as overlap between the desired object/event and the surrounding context. The remaining features attempt to find general markers for success or failure. One set (**Discourse Features**) looks for overt discourse relation markers that signal violation of expectation (e.g., 'but', 'however') or its opposite (e.g., 'so'). Another uses the Connotation Lexicon (Feng et al., 2013) to model whether the context provides a positive or negative event. All of these features are inspired by Chaturvedi et al. (2016). Finally, motivated by the AESOP modeling of affect states for identifying plot units (Goyal and Riloff, 2013), one set of features (**Sentiment-Flow-Features**) indexes whether there has been a change in sentiment in the surrounding context (which might be the mention of a thwarted effort or a hard won victory). Figure 4 provides an example of this.

In addition to a BOW (Bag of Words) baseline, we extracted the four types of features mentioned above. For features that examine the context around the desire expression, our experiments used the pre-context, the post-context, or both, as discussed below; context features are computed per sentence i of the context. We also tested various ablations of these features described below as well. We now describe the full set of features in more detail.

Desire-Features. From a desire expression of the form 'X Ved S', we extract the lexical feature *Desire-Verb*, the lemma for V. We also extract a list of *focal words*, the content words in embedded sentence S. In Figure 4, these are 'do', 'go', and 'run'. The features *Focal-{Word,Synonym,Antonym}-Mention-i* counts how many times each word, its synonyms, or its antonyms in WordNet (Fellbaum, 1998) are in the context, respectively. Similarly, *Desire-Subject-Mention-i* marks if subject X is mentioned in the context. Finally, boolean *First-Person-Subject* indicates if X is first person ('I', 'we').

Discourse-Features. This class of features count how many of two classes of discourse relation markers (*Violated-Expectation–i* vs. *Meeting-Expectation–i*) occur in the context. For the classes, we manually coded all overt discourse relation markers in the Penn Discourse Treebank three ways(violation, meeting, or neutral), leading to 15 meeting markers ('accordingly', 'so', 'ultimately', 'finally') and 31 violating ('although', 'rather', 'yet', 'but'). In addition, we also tracked the presence of the most frequent of these ('so' and 'but', respectively) in the desire sentence itself by the booleans *So-Present* and *But-Present*.

Fulfilled	Unfulfilled	Unknown	None	Total
1,366	953	380	70	2,780

Table 2: Simple-DesireDB dataset

Connotation-Features. Beyond the use of WordNet expansion for *Focal-Word-Mention-i*, we also used the Connotation Lexicon (Feng et al., 2013), a lexical resource marking very general connotation polarities (positive or negative) of words (as opposed to more specific sentiment lexicons). *Connotation-Agree-i* counts for each word w in *focal words* the number of words in the context that have the same connotation polarity as w. *Connotation-Disgree-i* is defined similarly.

Sentiment-Flow-Features. To model affect states, we compute a sentiment score for the desire expression sentence as well as each sentence in the context. Then for each sentence of the context, the booleans *Sentiment-Agree-i* and *Sentiment-Disagree-i* mark whether that sentence and the desire expression sentence have the same sentiment polarity (see Figure 4). While there is evidence suggesting that models of implicit sentiment (e.g., (Goyal et al., 2010; Reed et al., 2017)) could do much better at tracking affect states, here we use the Stanford Sentiment system (Socher et al., 2013).

4.2 LSTM Models

Our features are motivated by narrative characteristics but do not directly capture the sequential structure of the narratives. We thus apply neural network models suitable for sequence learning, in order to directly encode the order of the sentences in the story and distinguish between prior and post context. We use two different architectures of LSTM (Long Short-Term Memory) (Hochreiter and Schmidhuber, 1997) models to generate sentence embeddings and then apply a three-layer RNN (Recurrent Neural Network) for classification. We used Keras (Chollet, 2015) as a deep learning toolkit for implementing our experiments.

Skip-Thoughts. This is a sequential model that uses pre-trained skip-thoughts model (Kiros et al., 2015) as the embedding of sentences. It first concatenates features, if any, with embeddings, and then uses LSTM to generate a single representation for the context sequence, which is the output of the last unit. That single representation is then

Method	Features	Ful-P	Ful-R	Ful-F1	Unf-P	Unf-R	Unf-F1	Precision	Recall	F1
Skip-Thought	BOW	0.75	0.70	0.72	0.54	0.61	0.57	0.65	0.65	0.65
	ALL	**0.80**	**0.71**	**0.75**	**0.59**	**0.70**	**0.64**	**0.70**	**0.70**	**0.70**
CNN-RNN	BOW	0.75	0.73	0.74	0.57	0.60	0.58	0.66	0.66	0.66
	ALL	0.75	0.79	0.77	0.61	0.56	0.59	0.68	0.68	0.68

Table 3: Results of LSTM models on Simple-DesireDB

Data	Ful-P	Ful-R	Ful-F1	Unf-P	Unf-R	Unf-F1	Precision	Recall	F1
Desire	0.74	0.75	0.75	0.57	0.56	0.57	0.66	0.66	0.66
Desire+Prior	0.78	0.73	0.75	0.58	0.65	0.61	0.68	0.69	0.68
Desire+Post	0.76	0.70	0.73	0.55	0.62	0.59	0.66	0.66	0.66
Desire+Context	**0.80**	**0.71**	**0.75**	**0.59**	**0.70**	**0.64**	**0.70**	**0.70**	**0.70**

Table 4: Results of Skip-Thought using different parts of data, with ALL features on Simple-DesireDB

concatenated with embedding-feature concatenation of desire sentence and is fed into a multi-layer network to yield a single binary output.

CNN-RNN. The only difference between the CNN-RNN model and Skip-Thought is that it uses the 1-dimensional convolution with max-over-time pooling introduced in (Kim, 2014) to generate the sentence embedding from word embedding, instead of using skip-thoughts. We use Google News Vectors (Mikolov et al., 2013) for the word embedding with different sizes from 1 to 7 for the kernel.

For our experiments, we first constructed a subset of DesireDB that we will call **Simple-DesireDB**, in order to be able to compare more directly to the models and data used in previous work. Chaturvedi et al. (2016) used three verb phrases to identify desire expressions (*wanted to*, *hoped to*, and *wished to*), so we selected a portion of our corpus including these patterns along with two other expressions (*couldn't wait to* and *decided to*) to have sufficient data for experiments. Table 2 shows the distribution of labels in this subset. For classification experiments we use data labeled as *Fulfilled* and *Unfulfilled*, thus the majority class accuracy is 59%. We split the data into Train (1,656), Dev (327), and Test (336) sets for the experiments.

Results of our two LSTM models for Fulfilled (Ful) and Unfulfilled (Unf) classes and the overall classification task (P:precision, R:recall) on Simple-DesireDB are presented in Table 3. ALL feature set includes all the features described in Sec. 4.1 (without BOW). The results indicate that our features can considerably improve the model, compared to the BOW baseline (F1 improved from

0.65 to 0.70 for Skip-Thought). We also conducted 4 sets of experiments to study the importance of prior, post and the whole context in predicting fulfillment status, using our best model. The results of Skip-Thought using different contextual representations are in Table 4 with ALL features. The results indicate that adding features from prior context **alone** improves the results. The best results are obtained by including the whole context and desire sentence.

We then experimented with our best model on all of DesireDB. We also trained Naive Bayes, SVM and Logistic Regression (LR) classifiers as baselines, with the best results on the Dev set achieved by Logistic Regression. Table 5 shows the results of Skip-Thought and LR on DesireDB for different features on the test set. Our feature ablation study on the Dev set, discussed in Sec. 4.3, indicates that Discourse features are better predictors of fulfillment status, so we present results using only Discourse features in addition to BOW and ALL.

All of the results indicate that similar features and methods achieve better results for the *Fulfilled* class as compared to *Unfulfilled*. We believe the reason is that identifying unfulfillment of a desire or goal is a more difficult task, as discussed in the annotation description in Section 3.2. To further our analysis on the annotation disagreements, we examined the cases where only two annotators agreed on the assigned label. From the expressions labeled **Fulfilled** by two annotators, 64% were labeled *Unknown from the context* by the disagreeing annotator, and only 36% were labeled *Unfulfilled*. However, these numbers for the **Unfulfilled** class are respectively 49% and 51%, indicating a

Method	Features	Ful-P	Ful-R	Ful-F1	Unf-P	Unf-R	Unf-F1	Precision	Recall	F1
Skip-Thought	BOW	0.78	0.78	0.78	0.57	0.56	0.57	0.67	0.67	0.67
	All	0.78	0.79	0.79	0.58	0.56	0.57	0.68	0.68	0.68
	Discourse	**0.80**	**0.79**	**0.80**	**0.60**	**0.60**	**0.60**	**0.70**	**0.70**	**0.70**
Logistic Regression	BOW	0.69	0.65	0.67	0.53	0.57	0.55	0.61	0.61	0.61
	All	0.79	0.70	0.74	0.52	0.64	0.58	0.66	0.67	0.66
	Discourse	0.75	0.84	0.80	0.60	0.45	0.52	0.67	0.65	0.66

Table 5: Results of best LSTM model with different feature sets, compared to LR on DesireDB

Features	Precision	Recall	F1
ALL	0.64	0.64	0.64
Discourse	0.66	0.64	0.65
But-Present	**0.72**	**0.64**	**0.68**
ALL w/o But-Present	0.58	0.58	0.58

Table 6: Results of Logistic Regression classifier with different feature sets on Simple-DesireDB

Dataset	Method	Precision	Recall	F1
MCTest	BOW	0.41	0.50	0.45
	Unstruct-LR	0.71	0.63	0.67
	LSNM	0.70	0.84	0.74
	Discourse-LR	**0.63**	**0.83**	**0.71**
	SkipTh-BOW	**0.72**	**0.68**	**0.70**
	SkipTh-ALL	**0.70**	**0.84**	**0.76**
Simple Wiki	BOW	0.28	0.20	0.23
	Unstruct-LR	0.50	0.09	0.15
	LSNM	0.38	0.21	0.27
	Discourse-LR	**0.32**	**0.82**	**0.46**
	SkipTh-BOW	**0.71**	**0.26**	**0.38**
	SkipTh-ALL	**0.33**	**0.16**	**0.22**

Table 7: Previous work and **our results** for the Fulfilled class, on MCTest and SimpleWiki.

stronger disagreement between annotators when labeling Unfulfilled expressions.

4.3 Feature Selection Experiments

We used the InfoGain measure to rank features based on their importance in modeling desire fulfillment. The top 5 features are: But-Present, Post-Context-Connotation-Disagree, Post-Context-Violated-Expectation, Desire-Verb, Is-First-Person. We also tested different feature sets separately. We describe our experiment results below.

The results of the feature ablation experiments using LR model are shown in Table 6. The ALL feature set includes all the features described in Sec. 4.1 (without BOW). We obtained high precision and F-measure using the Discourse features. We also experimented with our top feature from the InfoGain analysis, *But-Present*, which surprisingly achieves a high F-measure, compared to using ALL and Discourse feature sets. The last row of Table 6 shows the results of using ALL features excluding *But-Present*. This indicates that features motivated by narrative structure are primarily driving improvement. In previous work Chaturvedi et al. (2016) show that a model representing narrative structure could beat the BOW baseline, but they performed no systematic feature ablation. Our results suggest that ultimately, the presence of *"but"* is likely a central driver for their improvements as well.

4.4 Comparison to Previous Work

We directly compare our methods and features to the most relevant previous work (Chaturvedi et al., 2016). They applied their models on two datasets and reported the results for the Fulfilled class. We present the same metrics in Table 7, using our best model **Skip-Thought** (SkipTh). We also present results of our LR model with our Discourse features, **Discourse-LR**, trained and tested on their corpora to compare to their features. The first three rows show the results from Chaturvedi et al. (2016) for comparison. As described in Sec. 2, they used BOW as baseline, LSNM is their best model, and Unstruct-LR is their unstructured model that uses all of their features with LR.

On both corpora, **Discourse-LR** outperforms Unstruct-LR, showing that the Discourse features are stronger indicators of the desire fulfillment status when used with LR classifier. In addition, on SimpleWiki, LR-Discourse outperforms their structured model, LSNM (0.46 vs. 0.27 on F-1).

5 Conclusion and Future Work

We created a novel dataset, DesireDB, for studying the expression of desires and their fulfillment in narrative discourse. We show that contextual features help with classification, and that both prior and post context are useful. Finally, we show that exploiting narrative structure is helpful, both directly in terms of the utility of discourse relation features and indirectly via the superior performance of a Skip-Thought LSTM model.

In future work, we plan to explore richer features and models for semantic and discourse-based features, as well as the utility of more narratively-aware features. For instance, the sentiment flow features roughly track the notion that the arc of a narrative may implicitly reveal resolution of a goal via changes in affect states. We hope to examine whether there are other similar rough-grained measures of change over the entire narrative that can improve the results.

DesireDB contains annotator-labeled spans for evidence for the annotator's conclusions. While we have not used this labeling, we plan to use it in future work. Finally, we hope to turn to automatically detecting instances of desire expressions that give rise to the kind of goal-oriented narratives DesireDB contains. Here we have used high-precision search patterns but our annotations show that such patterns still admitted 134 hypothetical desires (e.g., 'If I had wanted to buy a book'). It would appear that distinguishing hypothetical vs. real desires itself could be an interesting problem.

Acknowledgments

This research was supported by Nuance Foundation Grant SC-14-74, NSF Grant IIS-1302668-002 and IIS-1321102.

References

C.F. Baker, C.J. Fillmore, and J.B. Lowe. 1998. The berkeley framenet project. In *Proceedings of the 36th Annual Meeting of the Association for Computational Linguistics and 17th International Conference on Computational Linguistics-Volume 1*. Association for Computational Linguistics, pages 86–90.

Allan Bell. 2005. News stories as narratives. *The Language of Time: A Reader* page 397.

Jerome Bruner. 1991. The narrative construction of reality. *Critical Inquiry* 18:1–21.

Kevin Burton, Akshay Java, and Ian Soboroff. 2009. The ICWSM 2009 Spinn3r dataset. In *Proceedings of the Third Annual Conference on Weblogs and Social Media (ICWSM 2009)*.

Kevin Burton, Niels Kasch, and Ian Soboroff. 2011. The icwsm 2011 spinn3r dataset. In *Proceedings of the Annual Conference on Weblogs and Social Media (ICWSM)*.

Snigdha Chaturvedi, Dan Goldwasser, and Hal Daume III. 2016. Ask, and shall you receive? understanding desire fulfillment in natural language text. In *Proceedings of the National Conference on Artificial Intelligence*.

Francois Chollet. 2015. Keras.

William Coster and David Kauchak. 2011. Simple english wikipedia: a new text simplification task. In *Proceedings of the 49th Annual Meeting of the Association for Computational Linguistics: Human Language Technologies: short papers-Volume 2*. Association for Computational Linguistics, pages 665–669.

David K. Elson. 2012. *Modeling Narrative Discourse*. Ph.D. thesis, Columbia University, New York City.

Christiane Fellbaum. 1998. *WordNet: An Electronic Lexical Database*. MIT Press.

Song Feng, Jun Seok Kang, Polina Kuznetsova, and Yejin Choi. 2013. Connotation lexicon: A dash of sentiment beneath the surface meaning. In *Association for Computational Linguistics (ACL)*.

Andrew Gordon, Cosmin Bejan, and Kenji Sagae. 2011. Commonsense causal reasoning using millions of personal stories. In *Twenty-Fifth Conference on Artificial Intelligence (AAAI-11)*.

Amit Goyal and Ellen Riloff. 2013. A computational model for plot units. *Computational Intelligence* 29(3):466–488.

Amit Goyal, Ellen Riloff, and Hal Daumé III. 2010. Automatically producing plot unit representations for narrative text. In *Proceedings of the 2010 Conference on Empirical Methods in Natural Language Processing*. pages 77–86.

Sepp Hochreiter and Jürgen Schmidhuber. 1997. Long short-term memory. *Neural computation* 9(8):1735–1780.

Dan Jurafsky, Victor Chahuneau, Bryan R Routledge, and Noah A Smith. 2014. Narrative framing of consumer sentiment in online restaurant reviews. *First Monday* 19(4).

Yoon Kim. 2014. Convolutional neural networks for sentence classification. *arXiv preprint arXiv:1408.5882* .

Ryan Kiros, Yukun Zhu, Ruslan R Salakhutdinov, Richard Zemel, Raquel Urtasun, Antonio Torralba, and Sanja Fidler. 2015. Skip-thought vectors. In *Advances in neural information processing systems*. pages 3294–3302.

Klaus Krippendorff. 1970. Bivariate agreement coefficients for reliability of data. *Sociological methodology* 2:139–150.

Klaus Krippendorff. 2004. *Content analysis: An introduction to its methodology*. Sage.

William Labov. 1972. The transformation of experience in narrative syntax. In *Language in the Inner City*, University of Pennsylvania Press, Philadelphia, pages 354–396.

Wendy G Lehnert. 1981. Plot units and narrative summarization. *Cognitive Science* 5(4):293–331.

Dan P McAdams, Ruthellen Ed Josselson, and Amia Ed Lieblich. 2006. *Identity and story: Creating self in narrative.*. American Psychological Association.

Tomas Mikolov, Ilya Sutskever, Kai Chen, Greg S Corrado, and Jeff Dean. 2013. Distributed representations of words and phrases and their compositionality. In *Advances in neural information processing systems*. pages 3111–3119.

Nasrin Mostafazadeh, Michael Roth, Annie Louis, Nathanael Chambers, and James F Allen. 2017. Lsdsem 2017 shared task: The story cloze test. *LSDSem 2017* page 46.

Katherine Nelson. 1989. *Narratives from the Crib.* University Press, Cambridge, MA.

Jessica Ouyang and Kathleen McKeown. 2015. Modeling reportable events as turning points in narrative. In *EMNLP*. pages 2149–2158.

Jessica Ouyang and Kathy McKeown. 2014. Towards automatic detection of narrative structure. In *LREC*. Citeseer, pages 4624–4631.

Robert Parker, David Graff, Junbo Kong, Ke Chen, and Kazuaki Maeda. 2011. English gigaword. *Linguistic Data Consortium* .

Livia Polanyi. 1989. *Telling the American Story: A Structural and Cultural Analysis of Conversational Storytelling*. MIT Press.

Elahe Rahimtoroghi, Ernesto Hernandez, and Marilyn A. Walker. 2016. Learning fine-grained knowledge about contingent relations between everyday events. In *Proceedings of SIGDIAL 2016*. pages 350–359.

D.N. Rapp and R.J. Gerrig. 2006. Predilections for narrative outcomes: The impact of story contexts and reader preferences. *Journal of Memory and Language* 54(1):54–67.

Lena Reed, Jiaqi Wu, Shereen Oraby, Pranav Anand, and Marilyn Walker. 2017. Learning lexico-functional patterns for first-person affect. In *Proceedings of the 55th annual meeting of the Association for Computational Linguistics (ACL-17)*. ACL.

Matthew Richardson, Christopher JC Burges, and Erin Renshaw. 2013. Mctest: A challenge dataset for the open-domain machine comprehension of text. In *EMNLP*. volume 3, page 4.

Roy Schwartz, Maarten Sap, Ioannis Konstas, Leila Zilles, Yejin Choi, and Noah A Smith. 2017. Story cloze task: Uw nlp system. *LSDSem 2017* page 52.

Richard Socher, Alex Perelygin, Jean Wu, Jason Chuang, Christopher D. Manning, Andrew Ng, and Christopher Potts. 2013. Recursive deep models for semantic compositionality over a sentiment treebank. In *Proceedings of the 2013 Conference on Empirical Methods in Natural Language Processing*. pages 1631–1642.

Reid Swanson, Elahe Rahimtoroghi, Thomas Corcoran, and Marilyn A Walker. 2014. Identifying narrative clause types in personal stories. In *15th Annual Meeting of the Special Interest Group on Discourse and Dialogue*.

Avril Thorne and V. Nam. 2009. The storied construction of personality. In Kitayama S. and Cohen D., editors, *Handbook of Cultural Psychology*, pages 491–505.

Tom Trabasso and Paul van den Broek. 1985. Causal thinking and the representation of narrative events. *Journal of Memory and Language* 24:612–630.

Robert Wilensky. 1982. Points: A theory of the structure of stories in memory. In Wendy G. Lehnert and Martin H. Ringle, editors, *Strategies for Natural Language Processing*.

SHIHbot: A Facebook chatbot for Sexual Health Information on HIV/AIDS

Jacqueline Brixey, Rens Hoegen, Wei Lan, Joshua Rusow, Karan Singla, Xusen Yin,
Ron Artstein, Anton Leuski
University of Southern California
brixey, rhoegen, artstein, leuski at ict.usc.edu
weilan, rusow, singlak, xusenyin at usc.edu

Abstract

We present the implementation of an autonomous chatbot, SHIHbot, deployed on Facebook, which answers a wide variety of sexual health questions on HIV/AIDS. The chatbot's response database is compiled from professional medical and public health resources in order to provide reliable information to users. The system's backend is NPCEditor, a response selection platform trained on linked questions and answers; to our knowledge this is the first retrieval-based chatbot deployed on a large public social network.

1 Introduction

HIV (human immunodeficiency virus) is an incurable virus that leads to chronic illness and is the precursor for the potentially fatal disease, AIDS (acquired immunodeficiency syndrome). Approximately 73% of those infected are aware of their HIV-status[1]. Without diagnosis information, HIV-infected people are unable to access medication that improves their health, and reduces their risk of passing HIV on to their partners. However, stigma and discrimination, particularly in the form of homophobia, may prevent people from accessing providers for support.

Of the approximately 20 million per year sexually transmitted infections diagnosed, half occur among individuals between the ages of 15 and 24[2], thus sexual education for youths is vital. Yet youths indicate that sexual education does not meet their needs, as many report discomfort discussing sensitive topics in front of peers and with teachers who they feel might inform their parents about inquiries (DiCenso et al, 2001). However,

access to medically accurate information or confidential, individual counseling decreases negative consequences by increasing condom and contraception use (Kirby et al.,1994).

In the United States, overall technology usage (including Internet and mobile phone use) for those age 12 to 29 years was over 90% in 2014, and social media use was also high: 12-17 year olds: 81%; and 18-29 year olds: 89%[3]. Technology, particularly mobile technologies and social media, thus offers a powerful method to not only reach, but also engage and retain youth and young adults in HIV prevention and care. To inform our target group of youths, we implemented a chatbot, named SHIHbot, to dispense relevant, professionally vetted, and easy to access HIV/AIDS information on Facebook. Continuation of current work will strengthen the system before full public deployment. SHIHbot will undergo several rounds of testing and evaluation by cohorts of participants in the target demographic. Evaluation will include metrics for satisfying social work goals as well as dialogue system goals.

2 Motivation

Recent research has investigated the acceptability of sharing sexual health information via technology due to high technology use among youths, particularly vulnerable minorities in this demographic. One online survey distributed to over 5000 youth age 13 to 18 found that 19% of heterosexual youth versus 78% of gay/lesbian/queer youth used the Internet to search for sexual health information. The sizable difference in usage was attributed to sexual minority youth reporting lack of credible offline information sources (Mitchell et al., 2014).

---

[1] https://www.cdc.gov/hiv/group/msm/index.html
[2] http://www.cdc.gov/std/stats/

[3] http://www.pewinternet.org/three-technology-revolutions/

Type	Purpose	Example dialogue
Don't know	No relevant response in domain above threshold	User: What is the weather in LA? SHIHbot: I am not confident on an answer for that question.
Personal	Questions about the chatbot	User: are you a robot? SHIHbot: I am a computer, but I have lots of human colleagues who helped make me so smart.
Greeting	Greetings and pleasantries	User: hello SHIHbot: Hi there! Do you have any questions about HIV/AIDS?
Alternative	Suggests a new conversation topic after 3 off topic inputs from user	User: will it rain today? SHIHBot: I'm not sure on that. I would be happy to answer any questions you have about HIV/AIDS though.
Say more	Gives a random response with the same topic as the previous response	User: Should I get tested even if I do not have symptoms? SHIHBOT: If you think that you may have been exposed to HIV: you should get tested as soon as possible. You may have HIV and have no symptoms for many years. User: tell me more about this topic. SHIHBot: The CDC recommends that everyone between the ages of 13 and 64 get tested for HIV at least once as part of routine health care. About 1 in 8 people in the United States who have HIV don't know they have it.
Repeat	Repeats previous response	
QR	In-domain responses annotated with topics	

Table 1: dialogue-type description for all responses in SHIHbot domain.

We are aware of two chat services have been developed and evaluated to deliver health information to youths via social media. One, named MiChat, is a live chat intervention for 18 to 29 year olds delivered on Facebook and consists of eight one-hour motivational interviewing and cognitive behavioral skills-based online sessions designed to reduce condomless anal sex and substance use. In a pre-posttest design among 41 participants with no control group, investigators found that participation in at least one session of the intervention (n= 31) was associated with reductions in instances of condomless anal sex (Lelutiu-Weinberger et al., 2015). Another chatbot developed in 2011 was deployed on Windows Live Messenger and exclusively answered questions dealing with sex, drugs, and alcohol. The chatbot was rated highly by adolescent participants and demonstrated the potential to reach youths via chatbots (Crutzen et al., 2011). As of time of writing the chatbot is no longer accessible.

Facebook has over 1.23 billion daily active users[4], providing a platform to reach a large audience. Facebook also currently hosts over 30,000 unique automated chatbots, nonetheless users have reported disappointing experiences[5]. Our system, hence, aims to give a satisfying and informative experience to users by providing reliable information through a service that is always available on a ubiquitous social network.

3 Question-Answer Corpus

To build a system that answers a variety of personal and relevant questions about HIV/AIDS concerns, we created a corpus containing linked questions and answers (QA). Although a lot of information can be obtained from the web, the information might contain errors. To counteract this, our chatbot only provides information from reliable sources.

We extracted questions and their respective answers from the Center for Disease Control (CDC), New York State Department of Health HIV guide (NY), and i-Base, a treatment advocacy group that provides information vetted by medical professionals on an online forum.

The QA corpus forms the domain knowledge for SHIHbot and also provides the training data for the response classifier. The three sources pro-

---

[4] https://newsroom.fb.com/company-info/.

[5] https://techcrunch.com/2016/09/12/messenger-bot-payments/

provided over 3000 questions; some were curated by medical professionals but most submitted directly by users seeking information. The questions cover more than forty categories, encompassing questions dealing with transmission of HIV, potential drug interactions, and the history of the disease, among others. The inclusion of questions from i-Base provided real-world questions from users, rounding out the "frequently-asked questions" nature of the questions from the CDC and NY.

We also pulled all responses linked with their original questions from the three sources. All responses are either provided by medical professionals directly (CDC and NY) or approved by medical professionals (i-Base). Due to the larger variety in domain for questions from the forum on i-Base, the responses from this source also demonstrate a large variety. We reduced the total number of responses as more questions were provided from i-Base than answers. This was due to a new question being referred to the answer for a similar question previously responded to. In these cases, both questions were matched with the same answer in the corpus. In addition, when answers repeated the same information, only one answer was repeated where appropriate. For example, synonymous questions about a cure for HIV were all provided with the same response. An expert in social work manually annotated answers with topic tags in order to provide topic information to the dialogue manager.

4 Architecture

The architecture of SHIHbot comprises NPCEditor, a dialogue manager, and plugins to Facebook.

4.1 Dialogue Management

To drive our chatbot responses we used NPCEditor, a response classifier and dialogue management system (Leuski and Traum, 2011). NPCEditor employs a statistical classifier that is trained on linked questions and responses; for each new user utterance, the classifier ranks all the available responses. We train the classifier on our QA corpus, which is augmented by questions and responses about the chatbot itself and utterances that maintain dialogue flow such as greetings and closings (Table 1).

The dialogue manager functionality within NPCEditor chooses which response to return back to the user. Typically it will choose the response that was ranked highest by the classifier, but it may choose a lower ranked response in order to avoid repetition. If the score of the top ranked response is below a predefined threshold (determined during training), the dialogue manager will instead select an off-topic response that indicates non-understanding (such as "please repeat that" or "I don't understand"). The classifier also has special tokens to recognize when a user asks the chatbot to repeat an answer or elaborate on a pervious answer, and when such a token is identified, the dialogue manager will repeat or elaborate, based on the topic annotation of the responses. A counter keeps track of the number of consecutive times the chatbot has failed to provide a direct answer, and on the 3rd instance, an "alternative" response is given to suggest returning to the HIV/AIDS domain. The counter restarts after giving an "alternative" response.

Previous applications of NPCEditor have been used to drive interactive characters in various domains such as interactive museum guides (Swartout et al., 2010), entertainment experiences (Hartholt et al., 2009), and interviews with Holocaust survivors (Artstein et al., 2016). NPCEditor was applied to the HIV/AIDS domain in the development of a virtual reality application designed for HIV positive young men who have sex with men (YMSM) to practice disclosing their status to intimate partners in an immersive, nonjudgmental environment (Knudtson et al., 2016). While NPCEditor has been used for custom chat applications, this is the first deployment of NPCEditor with Facebook Messenger.

4.2 Facebook API

Facebook launched the Messenger platform supporting chatbots, as well as sending and receiving APIs in 2016.[6] SHIHbot is the first deployment of a Facebook bot using NPCEditor, and to our knowledge, is the first Facebook bot to use information retrieval based response selection.

To create a chatbot on Messenger, the free Facebook API was used. This API was then connected with NPCEditor plugins, bridging NPCEditor and Facebook. When a message event occurs, it notifies our web-hook and calls a predefined function. Once all the actions of NPCEditor are completed and a response has been selected, the response is then sent to Facebook to deliver to the

---

[6] http://newsroom.fb.com/news/2016/04/messenger-platform-at-f8

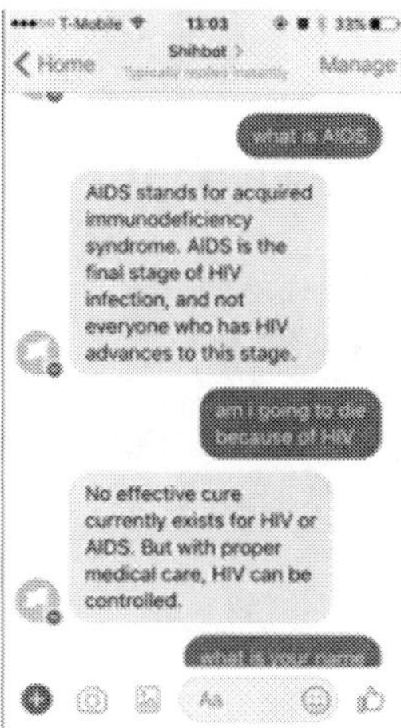

Figure 1: Interaction with mobile user on Facebook messenger.

user. A screenshot of an interaction with a mobile user is shown in Figure 1.

5 Demonstration outline

Participants will engage with SHIHbot via an open portal on Facebook Messenger available on a laptop at the demonstration. Participants will be invited to type input to the chatbot or welcome to provide suggestions for input. The live conversations will exhibit SHIHbot's ability to understand new questions, the chatbot's ability to cope with being asked questions outside of the domain knowledge, and the overall flow of dialogue. Participants will also be invited to view the real-time visualizations (Swartout et al., 2010) of how responses are selected based on user input.

Acknowledgments

Many thanks to Professors Milind Tambe and Eric Rice for helping to develop this work and for promoting artificial intelligence for social good. The first, seventh and eighth authors were supported in part by the U.S. Army; statements and opinions expressed do not necessarily reflect the position or the policy of the United States Government, and no official endorsement should be inferred.

References

Ron Artstein, Alesia Gainer, Kallirroi Georgila, Anton Leuski, Ari Shapiro, and David Traum. 2016. New dimensions in testimony demonstration. In *Proceedings of the 2016 Conference of the North American Chapter of the ACL: Demonstrations*, pages 32–36.

Rik Crutzen, Gjalt-Jorn Y. Peters, Sarah Dias Portugal, Erwin M. Fisser, and Jorne J. Grolleman. 2011. An artificially intelligent chat agent that answers adolescents' questions related to sex, drugs, and alcohol: an exploratory study. *Journal of Adolescent Health*, 48(5):514-519.

Alba DiCenso, Vicki W. Borthwick, and Catia Creatura. 2011. Completing the picture: adolescents talk about what's missing in sexual health services. *Canadian Journal of Public Health.* 92(1):35.

rno Hartholt, Jonathan Gratch, and Lori Weiss. 2009. At the virtual frontier: Introducing Gunslinger, a multi-character, mixed-reality, story-driven experience. In *International Workshop on Intelligent Virtual Agents*. Springer Berlin Heidelberg, pages 500-501.

Kirby, D., et al.,1994. *School-based programs to reduce sexual risk behaviors: a review of effectiveness.* Public health reports, 109(3): p. 339.

Kelly Knudtson, Karina Soni, Kate Muessig, Margo Adams-Larsen, Ron Artstein, Anton Leuski, David Traum, Willa Dong, Donaldson Conserve, Lisa Hightow-Weidman. 2016. Tough Talks: Developing a virtual reality application to support HIV status disclosure among young MSM. In *21st International AIDS Conference (AIDS 2016) Abstract Book*, page 717.

Corina Lelutiu-Weinberger, John E. Pachankis, Kristi E. Gamarel, Anthony Surace, Sarit A. Golub, and Jeffrey T. Parsons. 2015. Feasibility, acceptability, and preliminary efficacy of a live-chat social media intervention to reduce HIV risk among young men who have sex with men. *AIDS and Behavior* ,19(7):1214-1227.

Anton Leuski and David Traum. 2011. NPCEditor: Creating virtual human dialogue using information retrieval techniques." *AI Magazine,* 32(2): 42-56.

Kimberly J. Mitchell, Michele L. Ybarra, Josephine D. Korchmaros, and Joseph G. Kosciw. 2014. Accessing sexual health information online: use, motivations and consequences for youth with different sexual orientations. *Health Education Research*, 29(1):147–57.

William Swartout, David Traum, Ron Artstein, Dan Noren, Paul Debevec, Kerry Bronnekant, Josh Williams, Anton Leuski, Shrikanth Narayanan, Diane Piepol, Chad Lane, Jacquelyn Morie, Priti Aggrawal, Matt Liewer, Jen-Yuan Chiang, Jillian Gerten, Selina Chu, and Kyle White. 2010. Ada and Grace: Toward realistic and engaging virtual museum guides. In *International Conference on Intelligent Virtual Agents*. Springer Berlin Heidelberg, pages 286-300.

How Would You Say It?
Eliciting Lexically Diverse Data for Supervised Semantic Parsing

Abhilasha Ravichander[1]*, Thomas Manzini[1]*, Matthias Grabmair[1]
Graham Neubig[1], Jonathan Francis[12], Eric Nyberg[1]
[1]Language Technologies Institute, Carnegie Mellon University
[2]Robert Bosch LLC, Corporate Sector Research and Advanced Engineering
`{aravicha, tmanzini, mgrabmai, gneubig, ehn}@cs.cmu.edu`
`jon.francis@us.bosch.com`

Abstract

Building dialogue interfaces for real-world scenarios often entails training semantic parsers starting from zero examples. How can we build datasets that better capture the variety of ways users might phrase their queries, and what queries are actually realistic? Wang et al. (2015) proposed a method to build semantic parsing datasets by generating canonical utterances using a grammar and having crowdworkers paraphrase them into natural wording. A limitation of this approach is that it induces bias towards using similar language as the canonical utterances. In this work, we present a methodology that elicits meaningful and lexically diverse queries from users for semantic parsing tasks. Starting from a seed lexicon and a generative grammar, we pair logical forms with mixed text-image representations and ask crowdworkers to paraphrase and confirm the plausibility of the queries that they generated. We use this method to build a semantic parsing dataset from scratch for a dialog agent in a smart-home simulation. We find evidence that this dataset, which we have named SMARTHOME, is demonstrably more lexically diverse and difficult to parse than existing domain-specific semantic parsing datasets.

1 Introduction

Semantic parsing is the task of mapping natural language utterances to their underlying meaning representations. This is an essential component for many tasks that require understanding natural language dialogue (Woods, 1977; Zelle and

*The indicated authors contributed equally to this work.

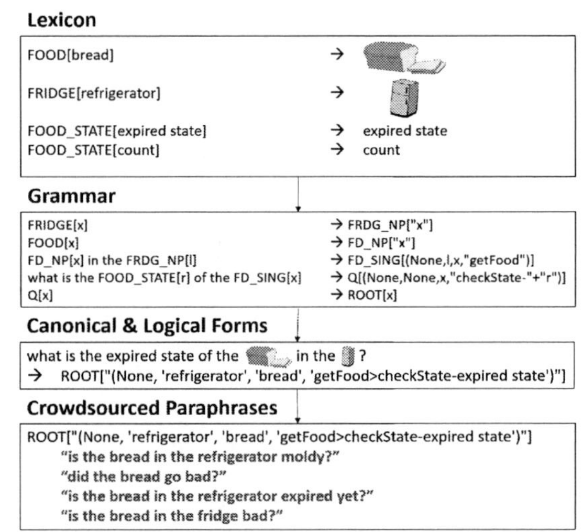

Figure 1: Crowdsourcing pipeline for building semantic parsers for new domains

Mooney, 1996; Berant et al., 2013; Branavan et al., 2009; Azaria et al., 2016; Gulwani and Marron, 2014; Krishnamurthy and Kollar, 2013). Orienting a dialogue-capable intelligent system is accomplished by training its semantic parser with utterances that capture the nuances of the domain. An inherent challenge lies in building datasets that have enough lexical diversity for granting the system robustness against natural language variation in query-based dialogue. With the advent of data-driven methods for semantic parsing (Dong and Lapata, 2016; Jia and Liang, 2016), constructing such realistic and sufficient-sized dialog datasets for specific domains becomes especially important, and is often the bottleneck for applying semantic parsers to new tasks.

Wang et al. (2015) propose a methodology for efficient creation of semantic parsing data that starts with the set of target logical forms, and

Proceedings of the SIGDIAL 2017 Conference, pages 374–383,
Saarbrücken, Germany, 15-17 August 2017. ©2017 Association for Computational Linguistics

generates example natural language utterances for these logical forms. Specifically, the authors of the parser specify a seed lexicon with canonical phrase/predicate pairs for a particular domain, and subsequently a generic grammar constructs canonical utterances paired with logical forms. Because the canonical utterances may be ungrammatical or stilted, they are then paraphrased by crowd workers to be more natural queries in the target language. We argue that this approach has three limitations when constructing semantic parsers for new domains: (1) the seed utterances may induce bias towards the language of the canonical utterance, specifically with regards to lexical choice, (2) the generic grammar suggested cannot be used to generate all the queries we may want to support in a new domain, and (3) there is no check on the correctness or naturalness of the canonical utterances themselves, which may not be logically plausible. This is problematic as even unlikely canonical utterances can be paraphrased fluently.

In this paper, we propose and evaluate a new approach for creating lexically diverse and plausible utterances for semantic parsing (Figure 1.). Firstly, inspired by the use of images in the creation of datasets for paraphrasing (Lin et al., 2014) or for natural language generation (Novikova et al., 2016), we seek to reduce this linguistic bias by using a lexicon consisting of images. Secondly, a generative grammar, which is tailored to the domain, combines these images to form mixed text-image representations. Using these two approaches, we retain many of the advantages of existing approaches such as *ease of supervision* and *completeness* of the dataset, with the added bonus of promoting *lexical diversity* in the natural language utterances, and supporting queries relevant to our domain. Finally, we add a simple step within the crowdsourcing experiment where crowd-workers evaluate the plausibility of the generated canonical utterances. At training time, we conjecture that optionally adding a term to upweight plausible queries might be useful to deploy a semantic parser in real world settings. Encouraging the parser to focus on queries that make sense reduces emphasis on things that a user is unlikely to ask.

We evaluate our method by building a semantic parser from scratch for a dialogue agent in a smart home simulation. The dialogue agent will be capable of answering questions about various sen-

sor activations, and higher-level concepts which map to these activations. Such a task requires understanding the natural language queries of the user, which could be varied and even indirect. For example, in SMARTHOME, *'where can I go to cool off?'* corresponds to the canonical utterance 'which room contains the AC that is in the house?'. Similarly, *'is the temp in the chillspace broke?'* corresponds to 'are the thermometers in the living room malfunctioning?'.

As a result of our analysis, we find that the proposed method of eliciting utterances using image-based representations results in considerably more diverse utterances than in the previous text-based approach. We also find evidence that the SMARTHOME dataset, constructed using this approach, is more diverse than other domain-specific datasets for semantic parsing, such as GEOQUERY or ATIS. We release this dataset to the community[1] as a new benchmark.

2 Example Domain: Smart Home

While our proposed data collection methodology could conceivably be used in a number of domains, for illustrative purposes we choose the domain of a smart home simulation for all our examples. We define a smart home as a home populated with sensors and appliances that are streaming data which can be read. A fully connected dialog agent could reason about and discuss these data streams. Our work attempts to develop a question answering system to support dialogue in this environment.

In the smart home domain, queries could range from complex, such as a user trying to determine the optimal time to start cooking dinner given a party schedule, to simple, asking for a temperature reading. While we believe that many queries could be handled with the methodology that we describe, we have limited the types of queries that can be asked to a reasonable subset, primarily single-turn queries about entity states (for example, *'did I leave the lights in the bedroom on?'* or *'is the dog safe?'*).

3 Approach Overview

Our approach to building a dialog interface for a new domain D, first requires analysis of the domain and identification of the entities involved. This builds on the methodology of Wang et al.

---

[1]https://github.com/oaqa/resources

(2015), but with three significant additions to elicit diversity and capture domain-relevant queries:

1. An additional step of specifying images for the entities in the domain, and

2. A domain-specific grammar that captures queries relevant to the particular domain.

3. A crowdsourcing methodology that includes crowdworkers annotating canonical utterances for plausibility

After analyzing the domain and the queries we want to support, we construct a seed lexicon and a generative grammar. The generative grammar generates matched pairs of canonical utterances and logical forms. As our seed lexicon contains images, the canonical forms generated are mixed text-image representations. These representations are then shown to workers from Amazon Mechanical Turk[2] to paraphrase in natural language.

3.1 Seed Lexicon

Essential to the goal of reducing lexical bias, is the use of images to describe the entities in the domain. It is beneficial here to choose images which are representative and will be well-understood. The images we used for entities within the SMARTHOME domain are shown in Figure. 3. It is not necessary that all entities be assigned images, in fact it is possible for entities to be named or abstract, and not have any associated images. In these cases, we simply use the natural language description of the image.

We specify a seed lexicon L, consisting of entities e in our domain and associated images (when available) i. Our lexicon consists of a set of rules $\langle e, (i) \rightarrow t[e] \rangle$, where t is a domain type. For our smart home domain, we define possible domain types to be appliances, rooms, food, weather and entities, and their associated subtypes and states (Figure 2.).

3.2 Generative Grammar

Next, we utilize a generative grammar G to produce canonical utterance and logical form pairs (c, z), similar to Wang et al. (2015). Our grammar differs from theirs, in that in our work, the grammar G is not a generic grammar, but is written to generate the kinds of queries we would actually like to support in our domain D. The rules are of

the form $\alpha_! \beta_1 \gamma_1 ... \rightarrow t[z]$, where $\alpha\beta\gamma$ are token sequences and t is the domain type. A complete description of our grammar is included in the supplementary material.

3.3 Canonical Utterances and Logical Forms

We generate canonical form - logical form pairs (c, z) exhaustively using the seed lexicon L and grammar G for domain D. This resulted in exactly 948 canonical and logical form pairs in our domain.

The logical formalism we utilize closely corresponds to Python syntax. It consists of functional programs where all questions in our smart-home domain are formulated with the help of a context tree. Each questions is defined as spans over this tree as shown in Figure. 4. The root node of the tree is the environment that we are operating in, and at the surface-level are sensors. These spans are then used to construct a single-line Python statement that is executed against our smart home simulation to retrieve an answer. From this construct, we are able to execute logical forms against the simulation seamlessly after having retrieved them.

3.4 Data Collection Methodology

The next step after forming canonical utterance and logical form pairs, is generating paraphrases for each pair. We use Amazon Mechanical Turk to distribute our data collection task. Over a span of three days, we collected data from nearly 200 Turkers, some of whom participated in the data collection task multiple times.

During the first stage of the task, the Turkers were instructed to paraphrase canonical utterances as naturally as possible, as well as mark the utterances themselves as likely to be asked or not asked. They were also shown a small number of examples, and possible paraphrases. These examples were created using images not present in the lexicon, so as to avoid biasing the Turkers.

In the next stage, the Turkers were asked to enter their paraphrases. Each worker was asked to enter a total of 60 paraphrases over the course of the task. These paraphrases were presented to the worker over 3 pages, with 2 paraphrases per canonical utterance. Turkers were also asked to state if they believed that the question that they were paraphrasing was likely or not. This annotation could subsequently be used for curation, or to bias semantic parsing models towards answers

---

[2]https://www.mturk.com/mturk/welcome

Lexicon

television | AC | light | humidifier | clock | radio | phone	→ APPLIANCE[television | …]
refrigerator | stove | dishwasher | toaster | microwave | blender | grill	→ KITCHEN_APPLIANCE[refrigerator | …]
on| off | malfunctioning | not malfunctioning	→ S_STATE[on | …]
bedroom | kitchen | livingroom | diningroom| hallway | bathroom | gym | home office	→ ROOM[bedroom | …]
Bob | Alice | dog | cat	→ ENTITY [Bob | …]
eggs | bread | milk	→ FOOD[eggs| …]
expired_state | count	→ FOOD_STATE[expired_state | …]
rain | sun | wind | snow	→ WEATHER_TYPE[rain | …]
intensity | duration	→ WEATHER_STATE[intensity | …]
news | cartoon | comedy	→ TV_PROG_TYPE[news | …]]
airtime | duration | channel number	→ TV_PROG_STATE[airtime | …]
safe | hungry | tired	→ ENTITY_STATE[safe | …]

Figure 2: The lexicon used to generate canonical and logical forms.

Figure 3: Images for terms in the seed lexicon

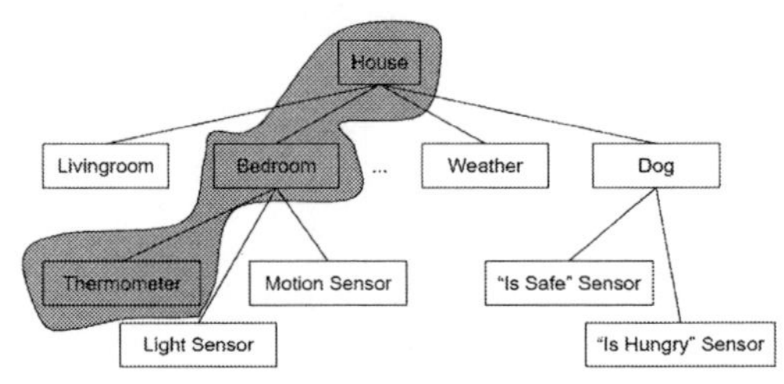

Figure 4: An example of a concept tree that could be used to define the logical form structure.

that users labeled as likely. Most canonical forms had a single image inserted into the text (875 or 92.3%), some had no images inserted into the text (58 or 6.1%), and even fewer had two images inserted into the text (15 or 1.6%). Each logical form was shown to five Turkers for paraphrasing, resulting in approximately ten paraphrases for each logical form.

Finally, we took several post-processing steps to remove improper paraphrases from our dataset. Firstly, a large portion of Turker mistakes arose because of them making real-world assumptions and neglecting to mention locations in their utterances. We automatically shortlisted all paraphrases missing location information. We then manually inspected each of these paraphrases and discarded the ones identified as invalid. In all, this post processing step took less than one day and could have easily been delegated to crowd workers, had it been necessary. Secondly, we automatically pruned all paraphrases in our dataset which were associated with more than one logical form. This left us with 8294 paraphrases.

4 Data Statistics and Analysis

In this section, we describe some statistics of our data set, perform a comparative analysis with the data collection paradigm of existing work, and contrast the statistics of our dataset with other semantic parsing datasets.

4.1 Data Statistics

In its uncurated form, our dataset consists of 10522 paraphrases spread across 948 distinct canonical and logical form pairs. Each pair has a minimum of 10 paraphrases and a maximum of 28 paraphrases. These paraphrases were collected over 195 Turker sessions using the methodology described in the previous section. Following the removal of duplicate paraphrases, and paraphrases missing location information, we are left with 8294 paraphrases over the same 948 logical forms.

4.2 Effect of Data Collection Methodology

We ran an experiment on purely text-based representations as suggested in (Wang et al., 2015) to compare and contrast with our mixed text-image representations. In an effort to subdue domain variance, we utilize our domain-specific grammar to generate text-based canonical representations. We randomly subsample 100 logical form and canonical utterance pairs from this dataset, and recreate the crowdsourcing experiment suggested by Wang et al. (2015), wherein each canonical utterance is shown to ten Turkers to paraphrase and each Turker receives four canonical utterances to paraphrase. The workers are asked to reformulate the canonical utterance in natural language or state that it is incomprehensible. In this way, we collect 1000 paraphrases associated with the 100 logical forms. For each of these logical forms, we randomly subsample paraphrases from the set gathered using the proposed mixed text-image methodology. We then compare the two and observe the results shown in Table 3. We evaluate the results on three metrics:

Lexical Diversity   We estimate the lexical diversity elicited from the two methodologies by comparing the total vocabulary size as well as the type-to-token ratio as shown in Table 1. We find that both the total vocabulary size, as well as the type-to-token ratio of the paraphrases collected using the proposed crowdsourcing methodology is considerably higher than that of an equivalent number of paraphrases collected using the methodology suggested in (Wang et al., 2015).

Lexical Bias   We estimate bias by computing the average lexical overlap between the paraphrase generated by the Turker and the canonical utterance they were shown. For the text-image experiment, we consider the equivalent text representation of the canonical utterance, by substituting the images by terms from the lexicon. We find that the proposed crowd sourcing methodology elicits considerably less lexical bias as shown in Table 1.

Relevance   We estimate relevance by randomly sampling one paraphrase each for one hundred logical forms using the two methodologies. We then manually annotate them for relevance. Here, relevance is defined as a paraphrase exactly expressing the meaning of the original canonical form.

We performed this analysis on both our final dataset and the the data that was collected in the same manner as described in (Wang et al., 2015). We find that our data set had an estimated relevance of 60% when compared directly with the same random logical forms sampled from the data collected in the manner of (Wang et al., 2015),

Representation	Vocab Size	TTR	Lexical Overlap
Text (Wang et al., 2015)	291	.044	5.50
Text-Image (ours)	**438**	**.066**	**4.79**

Table 1: Comparison of data creation methodology of (Wang et al., 2015) and this work. 'Vocab size' is the total vocabulary size across an equal number of paraphrase collected for the same logical forms using the two methodologies. TTR represents the word-type:token ratio. Lexical overlap measures the average number of words that are common between the canonical utterances and the paraphrases in the two methodologies.

which had an estimated relevance of 69%.

Randomly sampling from our entire curated dataset, we find that we have an estimated relevance of 66%.

4.3   Comparison with Other Data Sets

In order to examine the lexical diversity in the original dataset, we examine the ratio of the total number of word types seen in the natural language representations to the total number of token types in the meaning representation. We compare against four publicly accessible datasets:

OVERNIGHT The Overnight dataset (Wang et al., 2015) consists of 26k examples distributed across eight different domains. These examples are obtained by asking crowdworkers to paraphrase slightly ungrammatical natural language realizations of a logical form.

GEO880 Geoquery is a benchmark dataset for semantic parsing (Zettlemoyer and Collins, 2005) which contains 880 queries to a U.S geography database. The dataset is divided into canonical test-train splits with the first 680 examples being used for training and the last 200 examples being used for testing.

ATIS This dataset is another benchmark semantic parsing dataset that contains queries for a flights database, each with an associated meaning representation in lambda calculus. The dataset consists of 5,410 queries and is traditionally divided into 4,480 training instances, 480 development instances and 450 test instances.

Dataset	Example
GEO	how many states border the state with the largest population? answer(A,count(B,(state(B),next_to(B,C),largest(D,(state(C), population(C,D)))),A))
JOBS	what jobs desire a degree but don't use c++? answer(A, (job(A), des_deg(A),+((language(A,C),const(C,'c++')))))
ATIS	what flights from tacoma to orlando on saturday (_lambda $0e(_and(_flight0)$) (_from $0tacoma :_c i)(_to0$ orlando:_ci) (_day \$0 saturday:_da)))
OVERNIGHT	what players made less than three assists over a season (call SW.listValue (call SW.getProperty ((lambda s (call SW.filter (var s) (call SW.ensureNumericProperty (string num_assists)) (string <) (call SW.ensureNumericEntity (number 3 assist)))) (call SW.domain (string player))) (string player)))
SMARTHOME	has the milk gone bad? ROOT["(None, 'refrigerator', 'milk', 'getFood>checkState-expired state')"]

Table 2: Example from datasets GEO, JOBS, ATIS, OVERNIGHT and SMARTHOME

Dataset	NL Types	MR Types	NL/ MR Ratio
GEO	283	148	1.91
ATIS	934	489	1.91
JOBS	387	226	1.71
OVERNIGHT	1422	199	7.14
SMARTHOME (Ours)	1356	83	**16.33**

Table 3: Number of word types in the language compared to number of word types in the logical form. Larger ratio indicates more lexical diversity for the same complexity of the logical form

JOBS The JOBS dataset (Zettlemoyer and Collins, 2005) consists of 640 queries to a job listing database where each query is associated with Prolog-style semantics. This dataset is traditionally divided into 500 examples for training and 140 examples for testing.

An example of the kind of query that can be found in each of these datasets is given in Table 2.

In the analysis, we find that on average SMARTHOME exhibits nearly twice the word type to meaning representation token ratio, as compared to most existing semantic parsing datasets as shown in Table 3.

4.4 Logical Form Plausibility

For each canonical utterance, Turkers were asked to state if the canonical form was 'likely' or 'not likely'. By examining the most polar of these ratings, we see interesting patterns. For example, the canonical form *'what are the readings of the thermometers in the hallway¿* is rated as a highly likely form according to Turkers and does indeed seem like a question that could be asked in the real world. On the other hand, one of the less likely forms according to the Turkers, *'are the televisions in the bathroom on?'*, is indeed not likely, as bathrooms are arguably one of the least likely rooms that one would encounter multiple televisions in. Overall, 752 out of 948 logical forms were identified as very plausible by at least 60% of the Turkers who paraphrased them, indicating they were reasonable questions to ask.

5 Semantic Parsing Experiments

Finally, it is of interest how the data collection methodology influences the realism and difficulty of the semantic parsing task. In this section, we run several baseline models to measure this effect.

5.1 Models

We present three different baselines on our dataset, including a state-of-the-art neural model with an attention-copying mechanism (Jia and Liang, 2016).

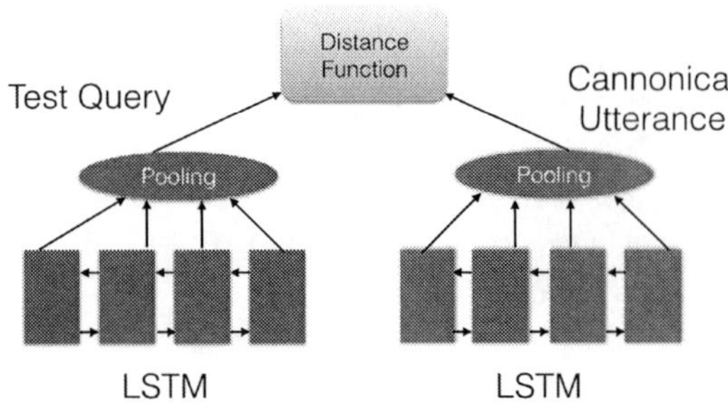

Figure 5: Neural Reranking Model

Jaccard   First, we experiment with a simple baseline using Jaccard Similarity which is given by $J(A, B) = \frac{|A \cap B|}{|A \cup B|}$. For each query in the test set, we find the paraphrase in the training set which has the highest Jaccard similarity score with the test query and return its associated logical form.

Neural Reranking Model   We next experiment with a neural reranking model for semantic parsing which learns a distribution over the logical forms by means of learning a distribution over their associated paraphrases as a proxy. This model has the added advantage of being independent of the choice of the formal language, and has been used for tasks such as answer selection (Wang and Nyberg, 2015; Tan et al., 2015), but not for semantic parsing. The basic model is shown in Figure. 5. We generate a representation of both the test query and the paraphrasing using a bidirectional-LSTM and use a hinge loss function as specified:

$$L = max(0, M - d(p*, p+) + d(p*, p-))$$

where M is the margin, d is a distance function, p* is the test query, p+ is a paraphrase that has the same meaning representation as p* and p- is a paraphrase that does not. For our experiments, we choose d to be the product of the Euclidean distance and the sigmoid of the cosine distance between the two representations, and M to be 0.05.

We group all the paraphrases by logical form, and create training examples by picking all possible combinations within one grouping as positive samples, and randomly sampling from the remaining top-25 matching paraphrases for negative examples. At test time, we first identify twenty five most likely candidates utilizing a Jaccard-based search engine over the paraphrases in the training

data. We then identify the most likely paraphrase from amongst these using the Neural Reranking model.

Neural Semantic Parsing Model   We also implement the neural semantic parsing model with an attention-based copying mechanism from (Jia and Liang, 2016). We use the same setting of hyperparameters that gave the best results on GEO, OVERNIGHT and ATIS. Specifically, we run the experiments with 200 hidden units, 100 dimensional word vectors and all the parameters of the network are initialized from the interval [-0.1, 0.1]. We also train the model for 30 epochs starting with a learning rate of 0.1 and halving the learning rate at every 5 epochs from the 15th epoch onwards. We refer the readers to (Jia and Liang, 2016) for further details about the model.

5.2   Results and Discussion

We evaluate these models on independent data in the form of the OVERNIGHT and GEO datasets. We use the standard train-test splits suggested by (Zettlemoyer and Collins, 2005) and (Wang et al., 2015). The full results are presented in Table 4. We observe that the neural semantic parsing model performs relatively poorly on the SMARTHOME dataset compared to OVERNIGHT or GEO. Careful error analysis suggests that most of the errors stem due to the following types of queries in our dataset, which are not present in OVERNIGHT or GEO

- The model not differentiating between the singular and plural forms (For example, *which room in the house can you find the stereo?* maps to the logical form for plural radios instead of the singular)

- The model not recognizing terms which have not been seen in the training data i.e unseen vocabulary (for example, *does bob not have any energy?* does not map to the logical form for checking if Bob is tired, because the model has never seen that to not have energy means being tired for living entities),

- The model not being able to respond to indirect queries in the test set (for example, *how long will the heat have to run?* does not map to the logical form for how long the weather will be cold, or *do i need to change the lights*

System	SMARTHOME(ours)	OVERNIGHT	GEO
Jaccard	18.0%	24.82%	40.7%
Neural Reranker	30.3%	41.91%	60.2%
Seq2Seq (Jia and Liang, 2016)	**42.1%**	75.8%	85.0%

Table 4: Test accuracy results of different systems on the SMARTHOME dataset as compared to OVERNIGHT and GEO

in the living room? does not map to the logical form for the living room lights not working correctly)

- Errors with and between complementary valued variables such as on/off and malfunctioning/not malfunctioning. (For example, *does the tv in the bathroom work?* maps to the logical form for the TV malfunctioning, when it should map to the logical form for the TV not malfunctioning)

We are aware that by accounting for plural nouns, we added a dimension of difficulty for all canonical forms that have a plural/singular sibling which is not present in the datasets which we compare to . We found that 29.7% of the Seq2Seq model's mistakes contained a wrong quantity. Similarly, the smart-home domain includes complementary terms that sometimes form the only difference between two canonical forms (e.g. functioning vs malfunctioning, on vs off). We measure that 43.2% of the Seq2Seq model's errors contain an incorrect complementary term. 9.8% percent contain both a wrong quantity and a wrong complementary term. We conclude that handling plurals and complementary forms makes the task more difficult, particularly as they are often not differentiated well in conversational language. The remaining 36.9% of errors made by the model can largely be attributed to lexical diversity, indirect queries or confusion between entity states.

This work represents a first step in considering lexical diversity as an important criteria while creating semantic parsing datasets. Due to the ambiguity introduced by images (though it is hard to make claims on whether it is ambiguity based only on the interpretation of these images by crowdworkers, or overall difficulty of trying to paraphrase a mixed text-image representation), this could come at the cost of generating slightly less relevant queries. We hope this starts the conversation and inspires further research in finding better ways of introducing lexical diversity.

6 Related Work

Semantic parsing has been used in dialog systems with significant success.(Zhu et al., 2014; Padmakumar et al., 2017; Engel, 2006). Supervised semantic parsing is of special practical interest as while trying to build dialogue systems for new domains, it is important to be able to adapt to domain-specific language. Domains exhibit varied linguistic phenomena and every domain has it's own vocabulary (Kushman and Barzilay, 2013; Matuszek et al., 2012; Tellex et al., 2011; Krishnamurthy and Kollar, 2013; Wang et al., 2015; Quirk et al., 2015). Training a semantic parser for these domains involves understanding the kinds of language used in a domain, however, the cost of supervision of associating natural language with equivalent logical forms is prohibitive.

In an attempt to overcome this overhead of supervision, several approaches have been suggested including learning from denotation-match (Clarke et al., 2010; Liang et al., 2011). As the authors of (Wang et al., 2015) point out, paraphrasing overcomes this overhead by being a considerably lightweight form of supervision. However, methods such as theirs which utilize text induce lexical bias.

Novikova et al. (2016) show that using images reduces this lexical bias for natural language generation tasks. In this work, we unite these strands of research by presenting a methodology where we construct a seed lexicon from images, and use a generative grammar to combine these images into questions, each paired with an associated logical form. These can then be paraphrased by workers from Amazon Mechanical Turk. Our experiment provides evidence that partially replacing canonical form text with images leads to measurably higher lexical diversity in crowd-sourced paraphrases. By contrast to (Wang et al., 2015), we operate only inside a single domain and observe the linguistic patterns specific to the smarthome setting (see Sec 5.2). It remains to be examined whether the observed large increase in diversity can be reproduced in a different domain with different language patterns and colloquialisms. Another immediate research direction, inspired by (Novikova et al., 2016) is replacing more of the canonical form representation with images to further reduce lexical bias and increase variety. This would require the development of a symbol set that is sufficiently expressive while not being overly ambiguous. We anticipate this converging to a tradeoff between the diversity and relevance measures (see Sec 4.2).

7 Conclusion

The primary goal of this paper is to highlight steps to be taken in order to apply semantic parsing in the real world, where systems need robustness against variation in natural language. In this work, we propose a novel crowdsourcing methodology for semantic parsing that elicits lexical diversity in the training data, with the aim of promoting future research in constructing less brittle semantic parsing systems. We utilize combined text-image representations which we believe reduces lexical bias towards language from the lexicon, at the cost of additional ambiguity introduced by the use of images. We find that this crowdsourcing methodology elicits demonstrably more lexical diversity compared to previous crowdsourcing methodologies suggested for creating semantic parsing datasets. The dataset created utilizing this methodology offers unique challenges that result in lower performance of semantic parsing models as compared to standard semantic parsing benchmark datasets. The dataset contains both direct and indirect conversational queries, and we believe that learning to recognize the semantics of such varied queries will open up new directions of research for the community.

Acknowledgments

This research has been supported by funds provided by Robert Bosch LLC to Eric Nyberg's research group as part of a joint project with CMU on the development of a context-aware, dialog-capable personal assistant. The authors are grateful to Bosch Pittsburgh researcher Alessandro Oltramari for valuable insights and productive collaboration. We would also like to thank Alan Black and Carolyn Rose for helpful discussions and Shruti Rijhwani, Rajat Kulshreshtha and Pengcheng Yin for their suggestions on the writing of this paper. We are grateful to all the students from the Language Technologies Institute who helped us test our methodology before releasing it to Turkers including especially Maria Ryskina, Soumya Wadhwa and Evangelia Spiliopoulou. We also thank the anonymous reviewers for helpful and constructive feedback.

References

Amos Azaria, Jayant Krishnamurthy, and Tom M. Mitchell. 2016. Instructable intelligent personal agent. In Dale Schuurmans and Michael P. Wellman, editors, *Proceedings of the Thirtieth AAAI Conference on Artificial Intelligence, February 12-17, 2016, Phoenix, Arizona, USA.*. AAAI Press, pages 2681–2689.

Jonathan Berant, Andrew Chou, Roy Frostig, and Percy Liang. 2013. Semantic parsing on freebase from question-answer pairs. In *EMNLP*. Association for Computational Linguistics, pages 1533–1544.

S. R. K. Branavan, Harr Chen, Luke S. Zettlemoyer, and Regina Barzilay. 2009. Reinforcement learning for mapping instructions to actions. In *Proceedings of the Joint Conference of the 47th Annual Meeting of the ACL and the 4th International Joint Conference on Natural Language Processing of the AFNLP: Volume 1 - Volume 1*. Association for Computational Linguistics, Stroudsburg, PA, USA, pages 82–90.

James Clarke, Dan Goldwasser, Ming-Wei Chang, and Dan Roth. 2010. Driving semantic parsing from the world's response. In *Proceedings of the fourteenth conference on computational natural language learning*. Association for Computational Linguistics, pages 18–27.

Li Dong and Mirella Lapata. 2016. Language to logical form with neural attention. *CoRR* abs/1601.01280. http://arxiv.org/abs/1601.01280.

Ralf Engel. 2006. Spin: A semantic parser for spoken dialog systems. In *Proceedings of the Fifth Slovenian And First International Language Technology Conference (IS-LTC 2006).*.

Sumit Gulwani and Mark Marron. 2014. Nlyze: Interactive programming by natural language for spreadsheet data analysis and manipulation. In *Proceedings of the 2014 ACM SIGMOD International Conference on Management of Data*. ACM, New York, NY, USA, SIGMOD '14, pages 803–814.

Robin Jia and Percy Liang. 2016. Data recombination for neural semantic parsing. volume abs/1606.03622. http://arxiv.org/abs/1606.03622.

Jayant Krishnamurthy and Thomas Kollar. 2013. Jointly learning to parse and perceive: Connecting natural language to the physical world. *Transactions of the Association for Computational Linguistics* 1:193–206.

Nate Kushman and Regina Barzilay. 2013. Using semantic unification to generate regular expressions from natural language. North American Chapter of the Association for Computational Linguistics (NAACL).

Percy Liang, Michael I Jordan, and Dan Klein. 2011. Learning dependency-based compositional semantics. In *Proceedings of the 49th Annual Meeting of the Association for Computational Linguistics: Human Language Technologies-Volume 1*. Association for Computational Linguistics, pages 590–599.

Tsung-Yi Lin, Michael Maire, Serge Belongie, James Hays, Pietro Perona, Deva Ramanan, Piotr Dollár, and C Lawrence Zitnick. 2014. Microsoft coco: Common objects in context. In *European Conference on Computer Vision*. Springer, pages 740–755.

Cynthia Matuszek, Nicholas FitzGerald, Luke Zettlemoyer, Liefeng Bo, and Dieter Fox. 2012. A joint model of language and perception for grounded attribute learning. *arXiv preprint arXiv:1206.6423* .

Jekaterina Novikova, Oliver Lemon, and Verena Rieser. 2016. Crowd-sourcing nlg data: Pictures elicit better data. In *Proceedings of the 9th International Natural Language Generation conference*. Association for Computational Linguistics, pages 265–273.

Aishwarya Padmakumar, Jesse Thomason, and Raymond J Mooney. 2017. Integrated learning of dialog strategies and semantic parsing. In *Proceedings of the 15th Conference of the European Chapter of the Association for Computational Linguistics (EACL)*.

Chris Quirk, Raymond J Mooney, and Michel Galley. 2015. Language to code: Learning semantic parsers for if-this-then-that recipes. Association for Computational Linguistics.

Ming Tan, Cicero dos Santos, Bing Xiang, and Bowen Zhou. 2015. Lstm-based deep learning models for non-factoid answer selection. *arXiv preprint arXiv:1511.04108* .

Stefanie Tellex, Thomas Kollar, Steven Dickerson, Matthew Walter, Ashis Banerjee, Seth Teller, and Nicholas Roy. 2011. Understanding natural language commands for robotic navigation and mobile manipulation. In *AAAI Conference on Artificial Intelligence*.

Di Wang and Eric Nyberg. 2015. Cmu oaqa at trec 2015 liveqa: Discovering the right answer with clues. Technical report, Carnegie Mellon University Pittsburgh United States.

Yushi Wang, Jonathan Berant, and Percy Liang. 2015. Building a semantic parser overnight. In *Association for Computational Linguistics*.

William A. Woods. 1977. Lunar rocks in natural English: Explorations in natural language question answering. In *Linguistic Structures Processing*. North Holland, pages 521–569.

John M. Zelle and Raymond J. Mooney. 1996. Learning to parse database queries using inductive logic programming. In *Proceedings of the Thirteenth National Conference on Artificial Intelligence - Volume 2*. AAAI Press, AAAI'96, pages 1050–1055.

Luke S. Zettlemoyer and Michael Collins. 2005. Learning to map sentences to logical form: Structured classification with probabilistic categorial grammars. In *In Proceedings of the 21st Conference on Uncertainty in AI*. pages 658–666.

Su Zhu, Lu Chen, Kai Sun, Da Zheng, and Kai Yu. 2014. Semantic parser enhancement for dialogue domain extension with little data. In *Spoken Language Technology Workshop (SLT), 2014 IEEE*. IEEE, pages 336–341.

Not All Dialogues are Created Equal:
Instance Weighting for Neural Conversational Models

Pierre Lison
Norwegian Computing Center
Oslo, Norway
`plison@nr.no`

Serge Bibauw[*]
KU Leuven, imec
Université catholique de Louvain
`serge.bibauw@kuleuven.be`

Abstract

Neural conversational models require substantial amounts of dialogue data to estimate their parameters and are therefore usually learned on large corpora such as chat forums, Twitter discussions or movie subtitles. These corpora are, however, often challenging to work with, notably due to their frequent lack of turn segmentation and the presence of multiple references external to the dialogue itself. This paper shows that these challenges can be mitigated by adding a *weighting model* into the neural architecture. The weighting model, which is itself estimated from dialogue data, associates each training example to a numerical weight that reflects its intrinsic quality for dialogue modelling. At training time, these sample weights are included into the empirical loss to be minimised. Evaluation results on retrieval-based models trained on movie and TV subtitles demonstrate that the inclusion of such a weighting model improves the model performance on unsupervised metrics.

1 Introduction

The development of conversational agents (such as mobile assistants, chatbots or interactive robots) is increasingly based on data-driven methods aiming to infer conversational patterns from dialogue data. One major trend in the last recent years is the emergence of neural conversation models (Vinyals and Le, 2015; Sordoni et al., 2015; Shang et al., 2015; Serban et al., 2016; Lowe et al., 2017; Li et al., 2017). These neural models can be directly estimated from raw (non-annotated) dialogue corpora, allowing them to be deployed with a limited amount of domain-specific knowledge and feature engineering.

Due to their large parameter space, the estimation of neural conversation models requires considerable amounts of dialogue data. They are therefore often trained on conversations collected from various online resources, such as Twitter discussions (Ritter et al., 2010) online chat logs (Lowe et al., 2017), movie scripts (Danescu-Niculescu-Mizil and Lee, 2011) and movie and TV subtitles (Lison and Tiedemann, 2016).

Although these corpora are undeniably useful, they also face some limitations from a dialogue modelling perspective. First of all, several dialogue corpora, most notably those extracted from subtitles, do not include any explicit turn segmentation or speaker identification (Serban and Pineau, 2015; Lison and Meena, 2016). In other words, we do not know whether two consecutive sentences are part of the same dialogue turn or were uttered by different speakers. The neural conversation model may therefore inadvertently learn responses that remain within the same dialogue turn instead of starting a new turn.

Furthermore, these dialogues contain multiple references to named entities (in particular, person names such as fictional characters) that are specific to the dialogue in question. These named entities should ideally not be part of the conversation model, since they often draw on an external context that is absent from the inputs provided to the conversation model. For instance, the mention of character names in a movie is associated with a visual context (for instance, the characters appearing in a given scene) that is not captured in the training data. Finally, a substantial portion of the utterances observed in these corpora is made of neutral, commonplace responses (*"Perhaps"*, *"I*

---

[*] Also affiliated with Universidad Central del Ecuador (Quito, Ecuador).

Proceedings of the SIGDIAL 2017 Conference, pages 384–394,
Saarbrücken, Germany, 15-17 August 2017. ©2017 Association for Computational Linguistics

don't know", "*Err*", ...) that can be used in most conversational situations but fall short of creating meaningful and engaging conversations with human users (Li et al., 2016a).

The present paper addresses these limitations by adding a *weighting model* to the neural architecture. The purpose of this model is to associate each ⟨*context, response*⟩ example pair to a numerical *weight* that reflects the intrinsic "quality" of each example. The instance weights are then included in the empirical loss to minimise when learning the parameters of the neural conversation model. The weights are themselves computed via a neural model learned from dialogue data. Experimental results demonstrate that the use of instance weights improves the performance of neural conversation models on unsupervised metrics. Human evaluation results are, however, inconclusive.

The rest of this paper is as follows. The next section presents a brief overview of existing work on neural conversation models. Section 3 provides a description of the instance weighting approach. Section 4 details the experimental validation of the proposed model, using both unsupervised metrics and a human evaluation of the selected responses. Finally, Section 5 discusses the advantages and limitations of the approach, and Section 6 concludes this paper.

2 Related Work

Neural conversation models are a family of neural architectures (generally based on deep convolutional or recurrent networks) used to represent mappings between dialogue contexts (or queries) and possible responses. Compared to previous statistical approaches to dialogue modelling based on Markov processes (Levin et al., 2000; Rieser and Lemon, 2011; Young et al., 2013), one benefit of these neural models is their ability to be estimated from raw dialogue corpora, without having to rely on additional annotation layers for intermediate representations such as state variables or dialogue acts. Rather, neural conversation models automatically *derive* latent representations of the dialogue state based on the observed utterances.

Neural conversation models can be divided into two main categories, *retrieval models* and *generative models*. Retrieval models are used to select the most relevant response for a given context amongst a (possibly large) set of predefined responses, such as the set of utterances extracted from a corpus (Lowe et al., 2015; Prakash et al., 2016). Generative models, on the other hand, rely on sequence-to-sequence models (Sordoni et al., 2015) to generate new, possibly unseen responses given the provided context. These models are built by linking together two recurrent architectures: one encoder which maps the sequence of input tokens in the context utterance(s) to a fixed-sized vector, and one decoder that generates the response token by token given the context vector (Vinyals and Le, 2015; Sordoni et al., 2015). Recent papers have shown that the performance of these generative models can be improved by incorporating attentional mechanisms (Yao et al., 2016) and accounting for the structure of conversations through hierarchical networks (Serban et al., 2016). Neural conversation models can also be learned using adversarial learning (Li et al., 2017). In this setting, two neural models are jointly learned: a generative model producing the response, and a discriminator optimised to distinguish between human-generated responses and machine-generated ones. The discriminator outputs are then used to bias the generative model towards producing more human-like responses.

The linguistic coherence and diversity of the models can be enhanced by including speaker-addressee information (Li et al., 2016b) and by expressing the objective function in terms of Maximum Mutual Information to enhance the diversity of the generated responses (Li et al., 2016a). As demonstrated by (Ghazvininejad et al., 2017), neural conversation models can also be combined with external knowledge sources in the form of factual information or entity-grounded opinions, which is an important requirement for developing task-oriented dialogue systems that must ground their action in an external context.

Dialogue is a sequential decision-making process where the conversational actions of each participant influence not only the current turn but the long-term evolution of the dialogue (Levin et al., 2000). To incorporate the prediction of future outcomes in the generation process, several papers have explored the use of reinforcement learning techniques, using deep neural networks to model the expected future reward (Li et al., 2016c; Cuayáhuitl, 2017). In particular, the Hybrid Code Networks model of (Williams et al., 2017) demonstrate how a mixture of supervised learning, reinforcement learning and domain-specific knowledge can be used to optimise dialogue strategies from limited amount of training data.

In contrast with the approaches outlined above, this paper does not present a new neural architecture for conversational models. Rather, it investigates how the performance of existing models can be improved "upstream", by adapting how these models can be trained on large, noisy corpora with varying levels of quality. It should be noted that, although the experiments presented in Section 4 focus on a limited range of neural models, the approach presented in this paper is designed to be model-independent and can be applied as a preprocessing step to any data-driven model of dialogue.

3   Approach

As mentioned in the introduction, the interactions extracted from large dialogue corpora do not all have the same intrinsic quality, due for instance to the frequent lack of turn segmentation or the presence of external, unresolvable references to person names. In other words, there is a discrepancy between the actual ⟨context, response⟩ pairs found in these corpora and the conversational patterns that should be accounted for in the neural model.

One way to address this discrepancy is by framing the problem as one of *domain adaptation*, the source domain being the original dialogue corpus and the target domain representing the dialogues we want our model to produce. The target domain is in this case not necessarily another dialogue domain, but simply reflects the fact that the distribution of responses in the raw corpus does not necessarily reflect the distribution of responses we ultimately wish to encode in the conversational model.

A popular strategy for domain adaptation in natural language processing, which has notably been used in POS-tagging, sentiment analysis, spam filtering and machine translation (Bickel et al., 2007; Jiang and Zhai, 2007; Foster et al., 2010; Xia et al., 2013), is to assign a higher weight to training instances whose properties are similar to the target domain. We present below such an instance weighting approach tailored for neural conversational models.

3.1   Weighting model

The quality of a particular ⟨context, response⟩ pair is difficult to determine using handcrafted rules – for instance, the probability of a turn bound-

ary may depend on multiple factors such as the presence of turn-yielding cues or the time gap between the utterances (Lison and Meena, 2016). To overcome these limitations, we adopt a data-driven approach and automatically learn a weighting model from examples of "high-quality" responses. What constitutes a high-quality response depends in practice on the specific criteria we wish to uphold in the conversation model – for instance, favouring responses that are likely to form a new dialogue turn (rather than a continuation of the current turn), avoiding the use of dull, commonplace responses, or disfavouring the selection of responses that contain unresolved references to person names.

The weighting model can be expressed as a neural model which associates each ⟨context, response⟩ example pair to a numerical weight. The architecture of this neural network is depicted in Figure 1. It is composed of two recurrent sub-networks with shared weights, one for the context and one for the response. Each sub-network takes a sequence of tokens as input and pass them through an embedding layer and a recurrent layer with LSTM or GRU cells. The fixed-size vectors for the context and response are then fed to a regular densely-connected layer, and finally to the final weight value through a sigmoid activation function. Additional features can also be included whenever available – for instance, timing information for movie and TV subtitles (such as the duration gap between the context and its response, in milliseconds), or document-level features such as the dialogue genre or the total duration of the dialogue.

To estimate its parameters, the neural model is provided with positive examples of "high-quality" responses along with negative examples sampled at random from the corpus. Based on this training data, the network learns to assign higher weights to the ⟨context, response⟩ pairs whose output vectors (combined with the additional inputs) are close from the high-quality examples, and a lower weight for those further away. In practice, the selection of high-quality example pairs from a given corpus can be performed through a combination of simple heuristics, as detailed in Section 4.1.

3.2   Instance weighting

Once the weighting model is estimated, the next step is to run it on the entire dia-

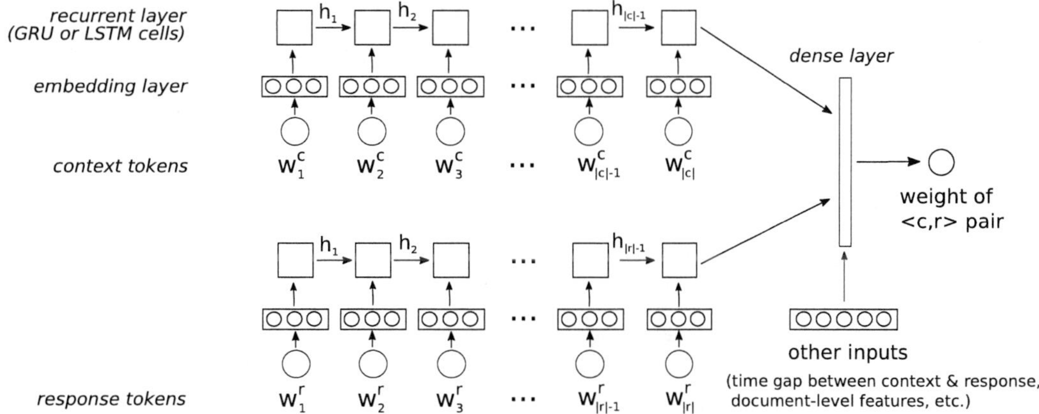

Figure 1: Neural weighting model, taking as input the ⟨context, response⟩ pairs, possibly along additional features (such as timing information for subtitles), and returning an associated weight value.

logue corpus to compute the expected weight of each ⟨context, response⟩ pair. These sample weights are then included in the empirical loss that is being minimised during training. Formally, assuming a set of context-response pairs $\{(c_1, r_1), (c_2, r_2), ...(c_n, r_n)\}$ with associated weights $\{w_1, ...w_n\}$, the estimation of the model parameters θ is expressed as a minimisation problem. For retrieval models, this minimisation is expressed as:

$$\theta^* = min_{\theta} \sum_{1}^{n} w_i \, L(y_i, f(c_i, r_i; \theta)) \quad (1)$$

where L is a loss function (for instance, the cross-entropy loss), and y_i is set to either 1 if r_i is the response to c_i, and 0 otherwise (when r_i is a negative example). For generative models, the minimisation is similarly expressed as:

$$\theta^* = min_{\theta} \sum_{1}^{n} w_i \, L(r_i, f(c_i; \theta)) \quad (2)$$

In both cases, the loss computed from each example pair is multiplied by the weight value determined by the weight model. Examples associated with a larger weight w_i will therefore have a larger influence on the gradient update steps.

4 Evaluation

The approach is evaluated on the basis of retrieval-based neural models trained on English-language subtitles from (Lison and Tiedemann, 2016). Three alternative models are evaluated:

1. A traditional TF-IDF model,

2. A Dual Encoder model trained directly on the corpus examples,

3. A Dual Encoder model combined with the weighting model from Section 3.1.

4.1 Models

TF-IDF model

The TF-IDF (Term Frequency - Inverse Document Frequency) model computes the similarity between the context and its response using methods from information retrieval (Ramos, 2003). TF-IDF measures the importance of a word in a "document" (in this case the context or response) relative to the whole corpus. The model transforms the context and response (represented as bag-of-words) into TF-IDF-weighted vectors. These vectors are sparse vectors of a size equivalent to the vocabulary size, where each row corresponds, if the given word is present in the context or response, to its TF-IDF weight, and is 0 otherwise. The matching score between the context and its response is then determined as the cosine similarity between the two vectors:

$$similarity = \frac{v^c \cdot v^r}{\|v^c\|_2 \, \|v^r\|_2} \quad (3)$$

where v^c and v^r respectively denote the TF-IDF-weighted vectors for the context and response.

Dual Encoder

The Dual Encoder model (Lowe et al., 2017) consists of two recurrent networks, one for the context and one for the response. The tokens are first

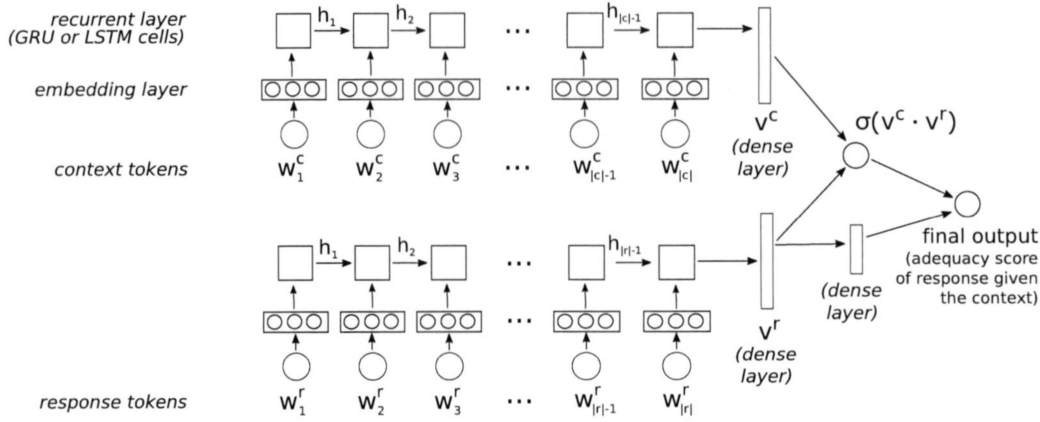

Figure 2: Dual encoder model, taking as input the ⟨context, response⟩ pairs and returning a score expressing the adequacy of the response given the context.

passed through an embedding layer and then to a recurrent layer with LSTM or GRU cells. In the original formalisation of this model (Lowe et al., 2015), the context vector is transformed through a dense layer of same dimension, representing the "predicted" response. The inner product of the predicted and actual responses is then calculated and normalised, yielding a similarity score. This model, however, only seeks to capture the semantic similarity between the two sequences, while the selection of the most adequate response in a given context may also need to account for other factors such as the grammaticality and coherence of the response. We therefore extend the Dual Encoder model in two ways. First, both the context and response vectors are transformed through a dense layer at the end of the recurrent layer (instead of just the context vector). Second, the final prediction is connected to both the inner product of the two vectors and to the response vector itself, as depicted in Figure 2.

Dual Encoder with instance weighting

Finally, the third model relies on the exact same Dual Encoder model as above, but applies the weighting model described in Section 3.1 prior to learning in order to assign weights to each training example. The weighting model is estimated on a subset of the movie and TV subtitles augmented with speaker information and filtered through heuristics to ensure a good cohesion between the context and its response. These heuristics are detailed in the next section.

Although the architecture of the Dual Encoder

is superficially similar to the weighting model of Figure 1, the two models serve a different purpose: the weighting model returns the expected *quality* of a training example, while the Dual Encoder returns a score expressing the *adequacy* between the context and the response.

4.2   Datasets

Training data for the conversation models

The dataset used for training the three retrieval models is the English-language portion of the OpenSubtitles corpus of movie and TV subtitles (Lison and Tiedemann, 2016). The full dataset is composed of 105 445 subtitles and 95.5 million utterances, each utterance being associated with a start and end time (in milliseconds).

Training data for the weighting model

For training the weighting model, we extracted a small subset of the full corpus of subtitles corresponding to ⟨context, response⟩ pairs satisfying specific quality criteria. The first step was to align at the sentence level the subtitles with an online collection of movie and TV scripts (1 069 movies and 6 398 TV episodes), following the approach described in (Lison and Meena, 2016).

This alignment enabled us to annotate the subtitles with speaker names and turn boundaries. Based on these subtitles, we then selected example pairs with two heuristics:

1. To ensure the response constitutes an actual reply from another speaker and not simply a continuation of the current turn, the

subtitles were segmented into sub-dialogues. $\langle$context, response$\rangle$ pairs including a change of speaker from the context to the response were then extracted from these sub-dialogues. Since multi-party dialogues make it harder to determine who replies to whom, only sub-dialogues with two participants were considered in the subset.

2. To ensure the response is intelligible given the context (without drawing on unresolved references to e.g. fictional person names), we also filtered out from the subset the dialogue turns including mentions of fictional character names and out-of-vocabulary words.

A total of 95 624 $\langle$context, response$\rangle$ pairs can be extracted using these two heuristics. This corresponds to about 0.1 % of the total number of examples for the OpenSubtitles corpus. These pairs are used as positive examples for the weighting model, along with negative pairs sampled at random from the corpus.

Test data

Two distinct corpora are used as test sets for the evaluation. The first corpus, whose genre is relatively close to the training set, is the Cornell Movie Dialog Corpus (Danescu-Niculescu-Mizil and Lee, 2011), which is a collection of fictional conversations extracted from movie scripts (unrelated to the ones used for training the weighting model). The transcripts from this corpus are segmented into conversations. Each conversation is represented as a sequence of dialogue turns. As this paper concentrates on the selection of relevant responses in a given context, we limited the test pairs to the ones where the context ends with a question, which yields a total of 67 305 $\langle$context, response$\rangle$ pairs.

The second test set comes from a slightly different conversational genre, namely theatre plays. The scripts of 62 English-language theatre plays were downloaded from public websites. We also limited the test pairs to the pairs where the context ends with a question, for a total of 3 427 pairs.

4.2.1 Experimental design

Preprocessing

The utterances from all datasets were tokenised, lemmatised and POS-tagged using the spaCy NLP library[1]. We also ran the named entity recogniser

---

[1] https://spacy.io/

from the same library to extract named entities. Since the person names mentioned in movies and theatre plays typically refer to fictional characters, we replaced their occurrences by tags, one distinct tag per entity. For instance, the pair:

Dana: Frank, do you think you could give me a hand with these bags?

Frank: I'm not a doorman, Miss Barrett. I'm a building superintendent.

is simplified as:

Dana: <person1>, do you think you could give me a hand with these bags?

Frank: I'm not a doorman, <person2>. I'm a building superintendent.

Named entities of locations and numbers are also replaced by similar tags. To account for the turn structure, turn boundaries were annotated with a <newturn> tag. The vocabulary is capped to 25 000 words determined from their frequency in the training corpus. Tokens not covered in this vocabulary are replaced by <unknown>.

Training details

The dialogue contexts were limited to the last 10 utterances preceding the response and a maximum of 60 tokens. The responses were defined as the next dialogue turn after the context, and limited to a maximum of 5 utterances and 30 tokens.

The embedding layers of the Dual Encoders were initialised with Skip-gram embeddings trained on the OpenSubtitles corpus. For the recurrent layers, we tested the use of both GRU and LSTM cells, along with their bidirectional equivalents (Chung et al., 2014), without noticeable differences in accuracy. As GRU cells are faster to train than LSTM cells, we opted for the use of GRU-based recurrent layers. The dimensionality of the output vectors from the recurrent layers was 400. The neural networks are trained with a batch size of 256, binary cross-entropy as cost function and RMSProp as optimisation algorithm. To avoid overfitting issues, a dropout of 0.2 was applied at all layers of the neural model.

Both the weighting model and the Dual Encoder models were training with a 1:1 ratio between positive examples (actual $\langle$ context, response $\rangle$ pairs) and negative examples with a response sampled at random from the training set.

Model name	Cornell Movie Dialogs			Theatre plays		
	$R_{10}@1$	$R_{10}@2$	$R_{10}@5$	$R_{10}@1$	$R_{10}@2$	$R_{10}@5$
TF-IDF	0.33	0.44	0.67	0.33	0.44	0.53
Dual Encoder	0.44	0.62	0.83	0.52	0.67	0.75
Dual Encoder + weighting	**0.47**	**0.63**	**0.85**	**0.56**	**0.70**	**0.80**

Table 1: Performance of the 3 retrieval models on the two test sets, namely the Cornell Movie Dialogs Dataset and the smaller dataset of theatre plays, using the $\text{Recall}_{10}@i$ metric.

4.3 Results

The three models (the TF-IDF model, the baseline Dual Encoder and the Dual Encoder combined with the weighting model) are evaluated using the $\text{Recall}_m@i$ metric, which is the most common metric for the evaluation of retrieval-based models. Let $\{\langle c_i, r_i \rangle, 1 \leq i \leq n\}$ be the list of m context-response pairs from the test set. For each context c_i, we create a set of m alternative responses, one response being the actual response r_i, and the $m{-}1$ other responses being sampled at random from the same corpus. The m alternative responses are then ranked based on the output from the conversational model, and the $\text{Recall}_m@i$ measures how often the correct response appears in the top i results of this ranked list. The $\text{Recall}_m@i$ metric is often used for the evaluation of retrieval models as several responses may be equally "correct" given a particular context.

The experimental results are shown in Table 1. As detailed in the table, the Dual Encoder model combined with the weighting model outperforms the Dual Encoder baseline on both test sets (the Cornell Movie Dialogs corpus and the smaller corpus of theatre plays). Our hypothesis is that the weighting model biases the responses selected by the conversation model towards more cohesive adjacency pairs between context and response[2].

Figure 3 illustrates the learning curve for the two Dual Encoder models, where the accuracy is measured on a validation set composed of the high-quality example pairs described in the previous section along with randomly sampled alternative responses (using a 1:1 ratio of positive vs. negative examples). We can observe that the Dual Encoder with instance weights outperforms the baseline model on this validation set – which is not *per se* a surprising result, since the purpose of the weighting model is precisely to bias the conversation model to give more importance to these types of example pairs.

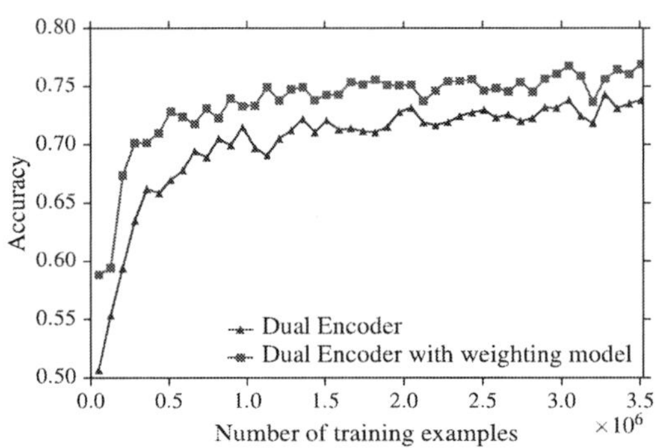

Figure 3: Learning curve for the two Dual Encoder models, showing the evolution of their accuracy on the validation set as a function of the number of observed training examples.

4.4 Human evaluation

To further investigate the potential of this weighting strategy for neural conversational models, we conducted a human evaluation of the responses generated by the two neural models included in the evaluation. We collected human judgements on $\langle \text{context}, \text{response} \rangle$ pairs using a crowdsourcing platform. We extracted 115 random contexts from the Cornell Movie Dialogs corpus and used four distinct strategies to generate dialogue responses: a random predictor (used to identify the lower bound), the two Dual Encoder models (both without and with instance weights), and expert responses (used to identify the upper bound). The expert responses were manually authored by two human annotators. The resulting 460 $\langle \text{context}, \text{response} \rangle$ pairs were evaluated by 8 distinct human judges each (920 ratings per model). The human judges were asked to rate the consistency between context and response on a 5-points scale, from *Inconsistent* to *Consistent*. In total,

---

[2]Contrary to the OpenSubtitles corpus which is made of subtitles with no turn segmentation, the Cornell Movie Dialogs corpus and the corpus of theatre plays are derived from scripts and are therefore segmented in dialogue turns.

118 individuals participated in the crowdsourced evaluation.

The results of this human evaluation are presented in Figure 4. There is unfortunately no statistically significant difference between the baseline Dual Encoder ($M = 2.97$, $SD = 1.27$) and the one combined with the weighting model ($M = 3.04$, $SD = 1.27$), as established by a Wilcoxon rank-sum test, $W(1838) = 410360$, $p = 0.23$. These inconclusive results are probably due to the very low agreement between the evaluation participants (Krippendorff's α for continuous variable $= 0.36$). The fact that the lower and upper bounds are only separated by 2 standard deviations confirms the difficulty for the raters to discriminate between responses. We hypothesise that the nature of the corpus, which is heavily dependent on an external context (the movie scenes), makes it particularly difficult to assess the consistency of the responses.

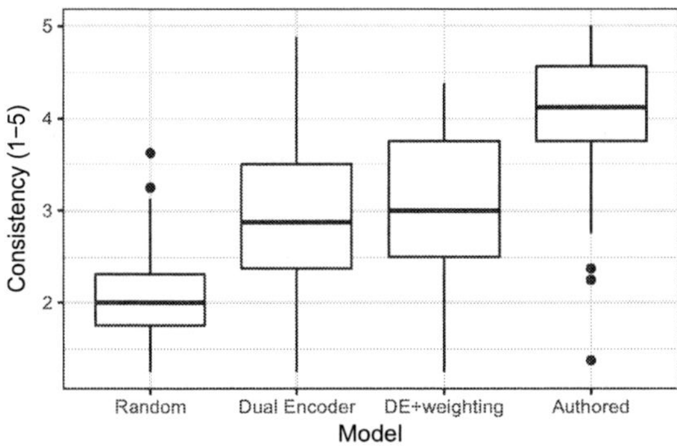

Figure 4: Distribution of human ratings of the responses generated by the four models tested.

Some examples of responses produced by the two Dual Encoder models illustrate the improvements brought by the weighting model. In (1), the baseline Dual Encoder selected a turn continuation rather than a reply, while the second model avoids this pitfall. Both (1) and (2) also show that the dual encoder with instance weighting tends to select utterances with fewer named entities.

(1) *Context of conversation:*
  – This is General Ripper speaking.
  – Yes, sir.
  – Do you recognize my voice?"
  ⇒ *Response of Dual Encoder:*
  – This is General Nikolas Pherides, Commander of the Third Army. I'm Oliver Davis.
  ⇒ *Response of Dual Encoder + weighting:*
  – Yes, sir. I'm Gideon.

(2) *Context of conversation:*
  – Let me finish dinner before you eat it... Chop the peppers...
  – Are you all right?
  ⇒ *Response of Dual Encoder:*
  – No thanks, not hungry. Harry Dunne.
  ⇒ *Response of Dual Encoder + weighting:*
  – Yes I'm fine. Everything is ok.

5 Discussion

The limitations of neural conversational models trained on large, noisy dialogue corpora such as movie and TV subtitles have been discussed in several papers. Some of the issues raised in previous papers are the absence of turn segmentation in subtitling corpus (Vinyals and Le, 2015; Serban and Pineau, 2015; Lison and Meena, 2016), the lack of long-term consistency and "personality" in the generated responses (Li et al., 2016b), and the ubiquity of dull, commonplace responses when training generative models (Li et al., 2016a). To the best of our knowledge, this paper is the first to propose an instance weighting approach to address some of these limitations. One related approach is described in (Zhang et al., 2017) which also relies on domain adaptation for neural response generation, using a combination of online and offline human judgement. Their focus is, however, on the construction of personalised conversation models and not on instance weighting.

The empirical results corroborate the hypothesis that assigning weights to the training examples of "noisy" dialogue corpora can boost the performance of neural conversation models. In essence, the proposed approach replaces a one-pass training regime with a two-pass procedure: the first pass to determine the quality of each example pair, and a second pass to update the model based on the observed pair and its associated weight. We also showed that these weights can be determined in a data-driven manner with a neural model trained on example pairs selected for their adherence to specific quality criteria.

Instead of this two-pass procedure, an alternative approach is to directly learn a conversation model on the subset of example pairs that are known to be of high-quality. However, one major shortcoming of this approach is that it considerably limits the size of the training set that can be exploited. For instance, the data used to estimate the weighting model in Section 4.2 corresponds to a mere 0.1 % of the total English-language part of the OpenSubtitles corpus (since the utterances had to be associated with speaker names derived from aligned scripts in order to apply the heuristics). In contract, the proposed two-pass procedure can scale to datasets of any size.

The results from Section 4 are limited to retrieval-based models. One important question for future work is to investigate whether the results carry over to generative, sequence-to-sequence models. As generative models are more computationally intensive to train than retrieval models, the presented approach may bring another important benefit, namely the ability to filter out part of the training data to concentrate the training time on "interesting" examples with a high cohesion between the context and its response.

6 Conclusion

Dialogue corpora such as chat logs or movie subtitles are very useful resources for developing open-domain conversation models. They do, however, also raise a number of challenges for conversation modelling. Two notable challenges are the lack of segmentation in dialogue turns (at least for the movie subtitles) and the presence of external context that is not captured in the dialogue transcripts themselves (leading to mentions of person names and unresolvable named entities).

This paper showed how to mitigate these challenges through the use of a *weighting model* applied on the training examples. This weighting model can be estimated in a data-driven manner, by providing example of "high-quality" training pairs along with random pairs extracted from the same corpus. The criteria that determine how these training pairs should be selected depend in practice on the type of conversational model one wishes to learn. This instance weighting approach can be viewed as a form of *domain adaptation*, where the data points from the source domain (in this case, the original corpus) are re-weighted to improve the model performance in a target domain (in this case, the interactions in which the conversation model will be deployed).

Evaluation results on retrieval-based neural models demonstrate the potential of this approach. The weighting model is essentially a preprocess-

ing step and can therefore be combined with any type of conversational model.

Future work will focus on two directions. The first is to extend the weighting model to account for other criteria, such as ensuring diversity of responses and coherence across turns. The second is to evaluate the approach on other types of neural conversational models, and more particularly on generative models.

References

Steffen Bickel, Michael Brückner, and Tobias Scheffer. 2007. Discriminative learning for differing training and test distributions. In *Proceedings of the 24th International Conference on Machine Learning*. ACM, New York, NY, USA, ICML '07, pages 81–88.

Junyoung Chung, Çaglar Gülçehre, KyungHyun Cho, and Yoshua Bengio. 2014. Empirical evaluation of gated recurrent neural networks on sequence modeling. *CoRR* abs/1412.3555.

Heriberto Cuayáhuitl. 2017. SimpleDS: A simple deep reinforcement learning dialogue system. In Kristiina Jokinen and Graham Wilcock, editors, *Dialogues with Social Robots: Enablements, Analyses, and Evaluation*, Springer, Singapore, Lecture Notes in Electrical Engineering, pages 109–118.

Cristian Danescu-Niculescu-Mizil and Lillian Lee. 2011. Chameleons in imagined conversations: A new approach to understanding coordination of linguistic style in dialogs. In *Proceedings of the Workshop on Cognitive Modeling and Computational Linguistics, ACL 2011*. Association for Computational Linguistics.

George Foster, Cyril Goutte, and Roland Kuhn. 2010. Discriminative instance weighting for domain adaptation in statistical machine translation. In *Proceedings of the 2010 Conference on Empirical Methods in Natural Language Processing*. Association for Computational Linguistics, Stroudsburg, PA, USA, EMNLP '10, pages 451–459.

Marjan Ghazvininejad, Chris Brockett, Ming-Wei Chang, Bill Dolan, Jianfeng Gao, Wen-tau Yih, and Michel Galley. 2017. A knowledge-grounded neural conversation model. *CoRR* abs/1702.01932.

Jing Jiang and Chengxiang Zhai. 2007. Instance weighting for domain adaptation in NLP. In *Proceedings of the 45th Annual Meeting of the Association of Computational Linguistics*. Association for Computational Linguistics, Prague, Czech Republic, pages 264–271.

E. Levin, R. Pieraccini, and W. Eckert. 2000. A stochastic model of human-machine interaction for learning dialog strategies. *IEEE Transactions on Speech and Audio Processing* 8(1):11–23.

Jiwei Li, Michel Galley, Chris Brockett, Jianfeng Gao, and Bill Dolan. 2016a. A diversity-promoting objective function for neural conversation models. In *Proceedings of the 2016 Conference of the North American Chapter of the Association for Computational Linguistics: Human Language Technologies*. Association for Computational Linguistics, San Diego, California, pages 110–119.

Jiwei Li, Michel Galley, Chris Brockett, Georgios Spithourakis, Jianfeng Gao, and Bill Dolan. 2016b. A persona-based neural conversation model. In *Proceedings of the 54th Annual Meeting of the Association for Computational Linguistics (Volume 1: Long Papers)*. Association for Computational Linguistics, Berlin, Germany, pages 994–1003.

Jiwei Li, Will Monroe, Alan Ritter, Michel Galley, Jianfeng Gao, and Dan Jurafsky. 2016c. Deep reinforcement learning for dialogue generation. *CoRR* abs/1606.01541.

Jiwei Li, Will Monroe, Tianlin Shi, Alan Ritter, and Dan Jurafsky. 2017. Adversarial learning for neural dialogue generation. *CoRR* abs/1701.06547.

Pierre Lison and Raveesh Meena. 2016. Automatic turn segmentation of movie & TV subtitles. In *Proceedings of the 2016 Spoken Language Technology Workshop*. IEEE, San Diego, CA, USA, pages 245–252.

Pierre Lison and Jörg Tiedemann. 2016. Opensubtitles2016: Extracting large parallel corpora from movie and TV subtitles. In *Proceedings of the 10th International Conference on Language Resources and Evaluation (LREC 2016)*.

Ryan Lowe, Nissan Pow, Iulian Serban, and Joelle Pineau. 2015. The Ubuntu Dialogue Corpus: A large dataset for research in unstructured multi-turn dialogue systems. In *Proceedings of the 16th Annual Meeting on Discourse and Dialogue (SIGDIAL 2015)*. pages 285–294.

Ryan Lowe, Nissan Pow, Iulian V. Serban, Laurent Charlin, Chia-Wei Liu, and Joelle Pineau. 2017. Training end-to-end dialogue systems with the Ubuntu Dialogue Corpus. *Dialogue & Discourse* 8(1):31–65.

Abhay Prakash, Chris Brockett, and Puneet Agrawal. 2016. Emulating human conversations using convolutional neural network-based IR. *CoRR* abs/1606.07056.

Juan Ramos. 2003. Using TF-IDF to Determine Word Relevance in Document Queries. In *Proceedings of the First Instructional Conference on Machine Learning*. Rutgers University, New Brunswick, NJ, USA.

V. Rieser and O. Lemon. 2011. *Reinforcement Learning for Adaptive Dialogue Systems*. Springer, Berlin, Heidelberg.

Alan Ritter, Colin Cherry, and Bill Dolan. 2010. Unsupervised modeling of twitter conversations. In *Human Language Technologies: The 2010 Annual Conference of the North American Chapter of the ACL*. Association for Computational Linguistics, Stroudsburg, PA, USA, HLT '10, pages 172–180.

Iulian V Serban and Joelle Pineau. 2015. Text-based speaker identification for multi-participant open-domain dialogue systems. In *NIPS Workshop on Machine Learning for Spoken Language Understanding*. Montreal, Canada.

Iulian V. Serban, Alessandro Sordoni, Yoshua Bengio, Aaron Courville, and Joelle Pineau. 2016. Building end-to-end dialogue systems using generative hierarchical neural network models. In *Proceedings of the Thirtieth AAAI Conference on Artificial Intelligence*. AAAI Press, AAAI'16, pages 3776–3783.

Lifeng Shang, Zhengdong Lu, and Hang Li. 2015. Neural responding machine for short-text conversation. In *Proceedings of the 53rd Annual Meeting of the Association for Computational Linguistics and the 7th International Joint Conference on Natural Language Processing (Volume 1: Long Papers)*. Association for Computational Linguistics, Beijing, China, pages 1577–1586.

Alessandro Sordoni, Michel Galley, Michael Auli, Chris Brockett, Yangfeng Ji, Margaret Mitchell, Jian-Yun Nie, Jianfeng Gao, and Bill Dolan. 2015. A neural network approach to context-sensitive generation of conversational responses. In *Proceedings of the 2015 Conference of the North American Chapter of the Association for Computational Linguistics: Human Language Technologies*. Denver, CO, USA, pages 196–205.

Oriol Vinyals and Quoc Le. 2015. A Neural Conversational Model. *CoRR* abs/1506.05869.

Jason D. Williams, Kavosh Asadi, and Geoffrey Zweig. 2017. Hybrid code networks: practical and efficient end-to-end dialog control with supervised and reinforcement learning. *CoRR* abs/1702.03274.

Rui Xia, Xuelei Hu, Jianfeng Lu, Jian Yang, and Chengqing Zong. 2013. Instance selection and instance weighting for cross-domain sentiment classification via pu learning. In *Proceedings of the Twenty-Third International Joint Conference on Artificial Intelligence*. AAAI Press, IJCAI '13, pages 2176–2182.

Kaisheng Yao, Baolin Peng, Geoffrey Zweig, and Kam-Fai Wong. 2016. An attentional neural conversation model with improved specificity. *CoRR* abs/1606.01292.

S. Young, M. Gai, B. Thomson, and J. D. Williams. 2013. POMDP-based statistical spoken dialog systems: A review. *Proceedings of the IEEE* 101(5):1160–1179.

Weinan Zhang, Ting Liu, Yifa Wang, and Qingfu Zhu.
2017. Neural personalized response generation as
domain adaptation. *CoRR* abs/1701.02073.

A data-driven model of explanations for a chatbot that helps to practice conversation in a foreign language

Sviatlana Höhn
AI Minds
Vianden, Luxembourg
`s.hoehn@aiminds.ai`

Abstract

This article describes a model of other-initiated self-repair for a chatbot that helps to practice conversation in a foreign language. The model was developed using a corpus of instant messaging conversations between German native and non-native speakers. Conversation Analysis helped to create computational models from a small number of examples. The model has been validated in an AIML-based chatbot. Unlike typical retrieval-based dialogue systems, the explanations are generated at run-time from a linguistic database.

1 Introduction

Conversational agents tailored for communication with language learners are studied in the area of Communicative Intelligent Computer-Assisted Language Learning (CommICALL). Starting with the idea of creating a machine that behaves like a language expert in an informal chat, specific interactional practices need to be described where linguistic identities of interaction participants become visible. Such practices include repair with linguistic trouble source where non-native speakers address troubles in comprehension or production (Danilava et al., 2013).

Repair is a building block of conversation that helps to deal with troubles in understanding and production of talk. Depending on who produced a trouble source and who initiates a repair we distinguish between self-initiated and other-initiated repair. A repair can be carried out by the same speaker who produced the trouble source or by the other speaker (self-repair and other-repair).

Because there is a preference for self-repair, other-initiated self-repair is the most frequent repair type. It may become even more frequent in conversations where one of the speakers is more knowledgeable in some matters than the other, for instance in mastering professional terminology or communication in a second language not yet fully mastered. Therefore it is crucial for conversational agents acting in such environments to recognize and to handle repair initiations properly.

Repair sequences where the machine is the trouble-speaker are in focus of this article. The learner initiates a repair in response to something not (fully) understood, and the machine explains. This type of repair corresponds to *other-initiated self-repair with a linguistic trouble source where the language learner is the recipient of the trouble talk* ($OISR_L$).

CommICALL research is mainly grounded in Second Language Acquisition (SLA) theory (Petersen, 2010; Wilske, 2014). The model of explanation sequences, so called *negotiations of meaning* introduced by (Varonis and Gass, 1985) received a lot of attention and was highly re-used in subsequent CALL research (Fredriksson, 2012; Satomi Kawaguchi, 2012). The model includes a trigger, an indicator, a response and a reaction to response. However, this model has been criticized for its view on repair as something "marring the flow" of a conversation and for being inapplicable to non-institutional settings (Markee, 2000). Although repair in native/non-native speaker talk has been intensively studied in Conversation Analysis (CA) (Markee, 2000; Gardner and Wagner, 2004; Hosoda, 2006), the results have not been operationalized for an implementation in a CommICALL system. Therefore, this article has two objectives:

1. Identify typical interactional resources employed for initiation and carry-out of repair using methods of Conversation Analysis.

2. Create a computation models of the repair

395

Proceedings of the SIGDIAL 2017 Conference, pages 395–405,
Saarbrücken, Germany, 15-17 August 2017. ©2017 Association for Computational Linguistics

of the type $OISR_L$ to be implemented in a CommICALL application.

We use a dataset of German native/non-native instant messaging conversations (Höhn, 2015) to analyze practices of repair in native/non-native speaker informal chat. All repair sequences have been annotated. Collections of similar cases have been built. Interactional resources used by language learners for repair initiations have been analyzed. Patterns of repair initiations have been obtained through generalization. In this way, rules for recognition of repair initiations have been created. An implementation case study was set up to validate the resulting computational models in an AIML-based chatbot.

2   Repair in Conversational Agents

Non-native speakers are usually not considered as the main user group of general-purpose dialogue systems. The assumption dominates that human users understand everything what an agent may say. This assumption is reflected in the two main problems addressed by research on repair for conversational agents: dealing with user's self-corrections which may make speech recognition difficult and managing system's lack of information in order to satisfy user's request.

These two research areas may be found under keywords *self-repairs*, sometimes *speech repairs* (Zwarts et al., 2010) or *disfluencies* (Shriberg, 1994; Martin and Jurafsky, 2009), and *clarification dialogues* or *clarification requests, CRs* in AI and NLP publications. What is referred to by the term *self-repair* in speech recognition domain corresponds to user's self-initiated self-repair in CA terminology.

Shriberg (1994) uses the term *reparandum* to refer to what is called *trouble source* in CA. The model considers pauses (moment of interruption) and lexicalised means to focus on the replacement (editing terms). These are interactional recourses used by speakers to signal trouble in production and to pre-announce a coming replacement.

The term *clarification dialogues* is mostly used to describe repairs dealing with insufficient information available for a system after speech recognition and language understanding (Kruijff et al., 2008; Jian et al., 2010; Buß and Schlangen, 2011). The term *miscommunication* was introduced to distinguish between *non-understandings* (the system could not match user's input to a representa-

tion) and *misunderstandings* (the system matched user's input to a wrong representation) (Dzikovska et al., 2009; Meena et al., 2015). These repair types correspond to other-initiated self-repair when the user is the trouble-speaker.

Clarification requests in AI and NLP publications should not be confused with clarification requests in SLA publications where this term is used to refer to only a particular form of corrective feedback (Lyster et al., 2013), or to a dialogue move in meaning negotiations (Varonis and Gass, 1985).

Emphasising the importance of correct recognition of user's clarification requests, Purver (2004) provides a study of various types of clarification requests, see also follow-up publications (Purver, 2006; Ginzburg et al., 2007; Ginzburg, 2012). Purver (2004) uses the HPSG framework to cover the main classes of the identified classification scheme. Because different functions might be expressed by a clarification request of the same form, Purver (2004) analyses the *clarification readings* to cover the correspondence between the form and the meaning of the repair initiations. However, several points for critiques arise. For instance, some utterances may be formatted as repair initiations but have a different interactional function, such as expressing surprise and topicalization (not listed as possible readings). In addition, repair initiations designed to deal with troubles in understanding are put together with strategies for dealing with troubles in production (e.g. *gap fillers*). From the CA perspective, Purver (2004)'s *gap fillers* correspond to self-initiated other-repair, thus are sequentially completely different. Therefore, modifications in the classification proposed by (Purver, 2004) are needed in order to better comply with studies in CA, and therefore better reflect the state-of-the-art in CA-informed dialogue research.

Example 2.1. Different types of causes for clarification used in (Schlangen, 2004, Ex. (12)).

a.	A	I ate a Pizza with chopsticks the other day
	B	A Pizza with chopsticks on it?
b.	A	Please give me a double torx.
	B	What's a torx?
c.	A	Please give me a double torx.
	B	Which one?
d.	A	Every wire has to be connected to a power source.
	B	Each to a different one, or can it be the same for every wire?

Schlangen (2004) analyses communication problems leading to clarification requests focusing on trouble source types (what caused the communication problem). Schlangen (2004) makes clear that a more fine-grained classification of causes for requesting clarification in dialogue may be needed, specifically, a model distinguishing between different cases in Example 2.1.

From the CA perspective, speakers' linguistic and professional identities and preferences play a role in speaker's selection of a specific format of a repair initiation. Speaker B in Example 2.1.b. positions herself as a novice in torx matters with her repair initiation, while speakers B in Examples 2.1.c. positions herself as knowledgeable in torx matters. In addition, utterances may be designed as repair initiations, but may in fact have a different function. For instance, the repair initiation produced by B in Example 2.1.a. may be analysed as a joke not requiring any explanation.

Other-initiated self-repair when the machine is the trouble-speaker is explored in (Gehle et al., 2014). Based on a corpus of video-recorded human-robot-interactions in a museum, the authors analyse interactional resources used by museum visitors to signal troubles in understanding robot's talk and dealing with misunderstandings. It was observed that people deal with different sorts of trouble similarly.

The potential user of a CommICALL system is a language learner who may have troubles in comprehension. While user-initiated repair has been subject of research of studies in human-robot interaction and general dialogue systems, not much attention has been paid to it in CommICALL. This article seeks to contribute to the research on repair in CommICALL by a microanalytic study of sequences of other-initiated self-repair when the native speaker is the trouble-speaker. Based on the results of the empirical study, the problem of computational modeling of system's reaction to the learner's repair initiation will be approached. The machine will need to recognize repair initiations, to extract the trouble source and to deliver an appropriate response. The the study contributes to language understanding for dialogue systems targeting language learners and has implications for user and expert models for CommICALL.

3   Practices of repair in chat

This section analyses interactional resources used by the non-native speakers in chat in order to other-initiate repair with a linguistic trouble source, that is to signal trouble and to reference the trouble source. Turn formats are specifically important for the future recognition of repair initiations by chatbots.

3.1   Repair initiations

Two abstract types of repair other-initiations were identified in the dataset: *statements of non-understanding* where a part of partner's utterance is marked as unclear, and *candidate understandings* where the own version of understanding of the problematic unit is provided. Non-understandings require an explanation of the trouble source in the repair while candidate understandings require a yes/no answer.

Repair other-initiations were found at two distinct types of position: *immediate* and *delayed*. The first type comes immediately after the trouble source turn. The second type comes later than the adjacent turn. Sequentially, both correspond to the next-turn repair initiation or second position repair described in CA literature as the first structurally specified place for other-initiated repair (Schegloff, 2000; Liddicoat, 2011). Delayed repair initiations occur because speakers in chat can produce turns simultaneously and follow distinct interleaved conversation threads. There is a dependency between the position of the repair initiation and the interactional recourses for repair initiation. Some resources are used exclusively in the immediate position.

Example 3.1. Open class repair initiation

```
615   L08   danke. good night)
              thank you. good night
617   N04   gn8 :-)
618   L08   ???
              ??? [repair initiation]
619   N04   gn8 ist ein zusammengeschrumpftes "gute
              Nacht" (lies: "g" = "gut" und "n8" = "N-Acht")
              gn8 is an abbreviation of "good night" (read:
              "g"="good" and "n8" = "n-ight")
620   N04   oder englisch, g=good, n-eight
              or English, g=good, n-eight
621   L08   aach sooo))
              I see
```

In Example 3.1, the learner initiates a repair by posting three question marks directly after the trouble source turn. The native speaker N04 is able to locate the trouble source, which is the abbreviation. In Example 3.1, the reference to the trouble source is realised by the immediate adjacent position, and signaling trouble with comprehension is realised by the questions marks.

Candidate understanding is another possibility

to mark a unit of an utterance as not (completely) clear. Example 3.2 shows a fragment of a chat where the native speaker N04 uses the word *über-fülltes* to describe an event in Munich (turn 222). The learner L08 checks her understanding of this term in turn 223 by copying the trouble source and providing her own understanding of the word. The trouble source is referenced through its repetition in the repair initiation. Signalling trouble is re-alised through the comparison token, the candidate understanding and the question mark.

Example 3.2. Many many people

221 L08 ja ich habe über Oktoberfest gehört, etwas lustiges und buntes))
yes I have heard about Oktoberfest, something funny and colourful
222 N04 ja, und teures und überfülltes ;-)
yes, and expensive and overfilled
223 L08))überfülltes bedeutet "viele viele Leute"?
overfilled means "many many people"?
224 N04 genau
exactly

The repair initiations produced by the learners in the dataset always try to resolve problems with the meaning, none of them was concerned with the form by itself.

3.2 Repair carry-out

Repair carry-out strategies depend on the type of the trouble source and the repair initiation for-mat and include confirmations / disconfirmations, definition work and paraphrasing of the trouble source. Direct definition work can be replaced or extended by a hyperlink to an example or a demon-stration of an instance of the trouble source.

If the trouble source is an abbreviation, the def-inition work contained a full spelling of the abbre-viated words and their explanation. For chat ab-breviations, a full reading of the abbreviation was normally provided and enough for explanation, as Example 3.1 demonstrates. Problematic abbrevia-tion were always repeated in the dataset, followed by the full spelling or reading.

If the trouble source is one semantic unit (one word or an idiomatic expression), a dictionary-like definition (synonyms + examples) is often selected to provide a repair. For longer messages or longer parts of longer messages, a strategy of splitting the message into smaller semantic units and a separate explanation of each unit can be chosen. Paraphras-ing is also one of the strategies used by the native speakers to explain longer messages.

Example 3.3 shows how a machine translation service can be used for definition work. Turn 376 contains an expression that the learner does not (fully) understand: "in sachen essen". This expres-sion is being formally made to a trouble source in the repair initiation in turns 377 and 378. Turn 377 locates the trouble source and marks the expres-sion as unclear. Turn 378 contains an instruction of what kind of explanation is desired.

Example 3.3. In Sachen Essen: repair is carried out with the help of machine translation.

376 N03 gibt es irgendwas moskau typisches in sachen essen?
is there something of food which is typical for moscow?
377 L07 in sachen essen???
in things food???
378 L07 übersetze bitte)))
translate please [smile]
379 N03 какая пища является типичным Москве?
which food is typical for Moscow?

4   Empirical findings

Regarding repair initiations, it was found that:

(1) Questioning is *the* practice to initiate repair in chat, confirming the results in the academic literature for oral interaction (Dingemanse et al., 2014). Other practices are declarations of lack of understanding such as *unklar* and *ich verstehe nicht*.

(2) Devices for signalling are question marks, dashes, explicit statements of non-understanding and presenting candidate understandings.

(3) References to trouble sources may be re-alised through the adjacent position, demonstra-tive expressions and full or partial repeats.

(4) Though all repair initiations were second-position initiations, they were not all immediate. Delayed repair initiation require more specific ref-erencing to trouble source, open-class repair initi-ations cannot be used in a delayed second position.

(5) Repetition-based repair initiations may con-tain repetitions of one specific unit from the previ-ous turn and contain a copy of the preceding turn regardless the unit boundaries. The latter may be placed between open class and restricted class re-pair initiations. Such types of repetitions have not been previously described in the academic litera-ture and may be typical for non-native speakers.

(6) The communication medium influences re-pair initiation types and formats. In particular, re-pair initiations eliciting a repetition of the trouble source are uncommon in chat. Misreadings are

possible, but they are made visible through mis-productions in repetition-based repair initiations.

(7) The non-native speakers' identity influences the format of candidate understandings which differ from those in native speaker talk.

(8) Repair initiation is one option to deal with trouble in comprehension. Other options include dictionary look-up and the "let-it-pass" strategy.

Regarding repair carry-outs, it was found that:

(1) Explanations of the meaning through synonyms or paraphrases, translations and demonstrations are common forms of repair carry-outs.

(2) Repair design is linked to expectation of what is known to the repair recipient. Consequently, repairs are designed for the language learners targeting difficulties in linguistic matters.

(3) Repair carry-outs may be immediate and delayed. Consequently, references to trouble source may be realised by the same resources as for repair initiations. However, there are dependencies between types of trouble source and participants' selection of resources for referencing the trouble source. For instance, abbreviations are usually repeated.

(4) *Split-repeat* is a type of a reference to the trouble source which did not appear in repair other-initiations but was found in the corresponding self-repair carry-outs. This way of referencing corresponds to self-repairs where native speakers only explained a few words from a longer turn or longer part of a turn marked as a trouble source. The trouble source was split in tokens, and only tokens that were supposed to cause the trouble were explained.

Repair carry-out is the preferred and the most frequent response to a repair initiation but other forms of responses are also possible, for instance a new repair initiation to deal with difficulties in identification of the trouble and responses which do not address the trouble. Finally, repair initiation and carry-out formats need to be "translated" into patterns and then into computational models of repair to make the findings applicable for computational purposes.

5   Computational model of $OISR_L$

In order to "serve computational interests" (Schegloff, 1996), the following needs to be taken into account for the purpose of modelling. Because repair initiations may occur *everywhere*, each user's utterance may be a repair initiation. Therefore, a repair initiation recognition routine needs to be activated after *every* user's turn. Two essential problems must be solved by a computer program in order to react to a repair initiation properly:
(1) Recognition of a repair initiation,
(2) Extraction of the trouble source.

A repair proper needs to be generated after that.

5.1   Recognition of repair initiations

Each class of repair initiations implies a specific form of referencing the trouble source. We consider the following types of referencing for modelling of the $OISR_L$-sequences:

1. Repeat-based initiations: *reuse* (a 1:1-copy of the trouble source), *recycle* the trouble source (rewriting it in a slightly different way),

2. Demonstratives-based initiations: using demonstrative determiners and pronouns.

3. Open-class initiations: referencing by a statement of non-understanding in the immediate position. The adjacent position of the repair initiation references the whole preceding turn as a trouble turn. Therefore we refer to this type of referencing as *reference by position*.

Each class of repair initiations references trouble of a particular size: either it is the whole preceding message (open-class and demonstratives-based repair initiations) or it is only a part of it (repeat-based and recycle-based initiations). Therefore, we consider three cases of trouble sources: single word (part of a longer message or a one-word message), part of a message (PoM) of two or more words and a whole message consisting of two or more words.

Signalling trouble involves symbolic and/or lexicalised means and a specific format designed either to mark something as unclear or to compare the trouble source with the own version of understanding. We call this *signalling format*.

The architecture of the repair initiation (RI) for $OISR_L$ can be formalised as follows. Depending on the time, different formats for the repair initiation may be used:

$$RI = TIME \times RIFormat$$

Time may be immediate or delayed: $TIME = \{immediate,\ delayed\}$. A repair initiation format is a combination of a reference to the trouble source and a selected signalling format:

$$RIFormat = REF \times SignalFormat$$

The referencing types are repeat-based $repeat(x)$, based on demonstratives Dem and reference by position AP. Signalling format may mark something in the trouble-turn as unclear $unclear(x)$ or present a candidate understanding $equals(x, y)$. The trouble source x and the candidate understanding y may be a single word, an idiomatic expression, part of a message or a complete turn (utterance).

$$REF = \{repeat(x),\ AP,\ Dem\}$$
$$SignalFormat = \{unclear(x),\ equals(x, y)\}$$
$$x, y \in \{word,\ idiom,\ PoM,\ utterance\}$$

This repair recognition procedure is also expected to differentiate between ordinary questions related to the subject of the ongoing talk and repair initiations. It works because ordinary questions are not formatted as $unclear(x)$ or $equals(x, y)$.

If a complete turn is recognised as a trouble source and this turn is a longer message, further filters may be applied to identify more precisely, which of the parts of the longer message may cause a problem with comprehension. This may be influenced by the learner model, but also by the system's capabilities to generate a repair proper. Section 5.3 will address this problem and provide examples of possible filters.

5.2 Generation of a repair carry-out

Repair carry-outs can contain a lexical reference to the trouble source, such as repeat-based and demonstratives-based references, or point to it just by the adjacent position to the repair initiation.

A confirmation or a disconfirmation is an appropriate type of self-repair carry-out after a repair other-initiation presenting candidate understandings $equals(x, y)$. All other self-repair carry-outs are expected to provide an explanation of the unit that is marked as problematic $explain(x)$. Because different options are available for referencing trouble source in immediate and delayed repair carry-outs, time needs to be taken into account in the abstract description:

$$RCO = TIME \times RCOFormat$$
$$TIME = \{immediate,\ delayed\}.$$

A self-repair carry-out is a product of a reference to the trouble source and the function $RCOF$, which it is expected to perform: confirming/disconfirming answer or an explanation.

$$RCOFormat = REF \times RCOF$$
$$REF = \{repeat(x),\ AP,\ Det, splitRepeat(x)\}$$
$$RCOF = \{explain(x),\ conf(equals(x, y))\}$$

Delayed self-repairs need to update the focus of the talk, and therefore, a repeat-based reference makes more sense than other types of referencing.

In practice, the function $explain(x)$ needs to be implemented differently for different types of trouble source. The quality of the response is highly dependent on the linguistic resources available for the generation of the explanations. We discuss various practical issues in the next section.

5.3 Model validation

The purpose of this section is to validate the practical applicability of the abstract model described in the preceding section. Because language understanding and generation capabilities of each dialogue system determines the possibilities for implementation of the $OISR_L$ model, we took the simplest form of such a system, namely an AIML-based chatbot (Bush, 2006). AIML (Artificial Intelligence Markup Language) covers the language understanding and generation task (Droßmann, 2005) in form of pattern-template pairs shown below. If the chatbot finds an input that matches to WIE GEHTS, the utterance stored in the template tag will be delivered to the user as a response.

```
<category>
    <pattern>WIE GEHTS</pattern>
    <template>Gut, und selbst?
    Alles paletti?</template>
</category>
```

Example 5.1 illustrates how a chatbot can benefit from patterns extracted from the dataset to come closer to the behaviour of a language expert.

Example 5.1. A sub-dialogue with the chatbot: other-initiated self-repair where the chatbot is the trouble-speaker.

1	User	wie gehts?
		how are you?
2	Bot	Gut, und selbst? Alles paletti?
		I'm fine, and you? Everything okay?
3	User	paletti?
4	Bot	umgangssprachlich alles gut, alles in Ordnung, alles okay.
		colloquial everything good, everything fine, everything okay.

The bot uses a colloquial expression in turn 2 which is not clear for the user. The user initiates the repair in turn 3. The bot recognises turn 3 as a repair initiation and extracts the trouble source: the repeated word *paletti* and the corresponding idiomatic expression *alles paletti*. Bot's response in turn 4 is a repair carry-out generated from a linguistic database.

The work of the repair manager is organised in two steps determined by the model. Every user's input that requires an explanation of a single entity (word, idiom) is redirected to the category that implements this function. The implementation of ProgramD includes so called `processors` to process specific AIML tags. A new AIML tag has been introduced for the purpose of this work: `<explanation>`. An additional processor named `explanation processor` has been implemented to generate a response.

The model for the recognition of repair initiations described in Section 5.1 is used for the implementation in form of the rules describing repair initiation formats. For instance, to recognise the repair initiation from Example 5.1, the chatbot matches the rule:

$$RI = immediate, repeat(x), unclear(x)$$

because the user repeats a part of bot's utterance placing a question mark after the repeated token and it happens immediately after the bot's turn.

In Example 5.1, the repair initiation contains only a part of an idiomatic expression and only the entire expression can be found in the linguistic database. Because all chatbot's utterances are known beforehand in AIML-based chatbots, it is possible to list all idioms to make their recognition easier. For this test implementation, a short list of idiomatic expressions and their parts was created. The explanation processor would first check, if the trouble source may be an idiom (comparing with the list and own preceding turns). If so, the entire expression will be set as the trouble source.

AIML provides a possibility to forward inputs with the same or similar meanings to a particular category handling responses to this meaning. Int this way, all recognised repair initiations with the meaning $unclear(x)$ are redirected to the category with the pattern:

```
<pattern>ICH VERSTEHE * NICHT</pattern>
```

where * is the matching token for the trouble source x.

The following template is responsible for the generation of repair carry-outs for all such trouble sources. The `<think>` tag allows processing of an input without without immediate output. The explanation processor searches for the trouble source in the linguistic database which contains only meanings, examples and notes about usage for German nouns, verbs, adjectives and adverbs. The database was automatically generated from Wiktionary. If the trouble source cannot be found in the linguistic database, the ex-

planation processor returns `<NOENTITY>` and the pre-stored *Response-1* is sent to the user. If the trouble source is found but its meaning is not stored in the database, the explanation processor returns `<ENTITY NOMEANING>`. A predefined *Response-2* is then sent to the user. Finally, if the explanation processor finds the trouble source in the database and at least one meaning of it is described, an explanation will be rendered. Five additional categories not shown here are responsible for rendering of the explanation and process meanings, examples and notes.

```
<template>
  <think>
   <set name="explanation-tmp">
    <explanation><star/></explanation>
   </set>
  </think>
  <condition name="explanation-tmp">
   <li value="NOENTITY">Response-1</li>
   <li value="ENTITY NOMEANING">
      Response-2</li>
   <li><srai>GETFIRSTMEANING
    <get name="explanation-tmp"/></srai>
   </li>
  </condition>
</template>
```

Every user's input that corresponds to an inquiry "does x mean y?" is redirected to the AIML category implementing meaning checks. An additional tag `<meaningcheck>` has been added to carry out the repair of this type. The handling of the meaning checks works in a similar way as the explanations described above. The program has been extended by a `meaning check processor` to process this tag in the following way. To generate a response to a candidate understanding, the chatbot needs to answer the question if x means the same as y? This is an instance of the textual entailment problem. If x is a single word, an idiom, a collocation or a proverb, the system can check the list of the synonyms of the corresponding entry in the linguistic database. If x and y are listed as synonyms, a confirming answer will be generated. Otherwise, the system will explain the meaning of x.

Only simple versions for each of paraphrasing and word-by-word explanation (split-reuse) were implemented. A word-by-word explanation only makes sense for words that could be difficult for the learner. We use a list of 100 and 1000 most frequently used German words[1] to filter those words that are supposed to be well known to everybody. The remaining words are explained separately.

---

[1] http://wortschatz.uni-leipzig.de/html/wliste.html

6 Results

The new model of other-initiated self-repair when the machine is the trouble-speaker allows recognising learner repair initiations and extracting the trouble source based on a description of language-specific and medium-specific resources for repair initiation. The model is created on a necessary level of abstraction to be applicable for text chat interaction in languages other than German. This assumption builds on (Dingemanse et al., 2014)'s finding that similar repair initiation formats exist across languages. Therefore, when provided a set of language-specific devices for repair initiation, it can be implemented for other languages. The extraction of the trouble source is based on abstract features like repetition of parts of the trouble-turn and adjacent position. These features are language independent.

The problem of the trouble source extraction is related to referring expression recognition or reference resolution described in NLP textbooks (Martin and Jurafsky, 2009, Ch. 21), which is addressed in a large number of scientific publications (Dahan et al., 2002; Iida et al., 2010). Usually only noun phrases or their pronominalised alternatives are considered for reference resolution in NLP. These are usually definite and indefinite noun phrases, pronouns, demonstratives and names. The analysis of repair initiations shows that verbs or parts of utterances may be used to refer to the trouble source. The presented model implicitly includes a local *discourse model* which "contains representations of entities which have been referred to in the discourse" (Martin and Jurafsky, 2009, p. 730). The local discourse model in repair sequences only conserns possible representations of the trouble source.

Compared to the model of clarification requests proposed in (Purver, 2004), the model introduced in this work has the following advantages. First, the inconsistencies form CA perspective found in (Purver, 2004)'s classification do not exist in the model presented in this work because of a close cross-disciplinary connection with CA. The model for repair initiations presented here strictly differentiates next-turn repair other-initiations from all other types of repair and describes only these repair initiations. Second, (Purver, 2004) introduced the model for clarification requests in a strong connection to the HPSG formalism. In contrast, the model presented in this work is already implementable with a simple language understanding technology. The separation between resources for signalling trouble and resources for referencing trouble source allows creating a rule-based grammar which can be implemented in dialogue systems with different levels of complexity.

With regard to the analysis of causes of troubles in understanding introduced in (Schlangen, 2004), mainly problems on the level of meaning and understanding were subject of learner's repair initiations. Consequently, the modelling was approached in this work with the assumption that the required kind of clarification is mainly determined by the user model targeting language learners. Similarly to the (Schlangen, 2004)'s approach to map the variance in form to a small number of readings, repair initiations in this work are mapped either to a content question *What does X mean?* or to a polar question *Does X mean Y?* where X is the trouble source and Y is the candidate understanding. In this way, the two approaches to modelling repair initiations are similar.

Models of repair covering repair initiations proposed in (Purver, 2004) and (Schlangen, 2004) and extended in follow-up work (Purver, 2006; Ginzburg et al., 2007; Ginzburg, 2012) were motivated by Conversation Analysis research. However, other approaches for modelling were preferred because of the insufficient operationalisation of CA findings for computational modelling. As an implication, the factors influencing the interaction that have been identified as important in CA studies and building a *system* did not become part of the baseline models in (Purver, 2004) and (Schlangen, 2004). Such factors include repair, turn taking, membership categorisation, adjacency pairs and preference organisation. In contrast to the previous models of repair (Purver, 2004; Schlangen, 2004) this work analyses repair initiations in a system of interconnected factors in conversation. More specifically, the proposed model of repair initiations takes turn taking and sequential organisation of interaction explicitly into account by distinguishing between immediate and delayed repair initiations and respective options for trouble source extraction. In addition, the new model takes virtual adjacency in chat into account. It explicitly differentiates repair initiated by the user from repair initiated by the system taking the sequential organisation into account. Finally, the preference organisation and recipient design were taken into account by the user model. Based on the empirical findings, the user model assumes that language learners will request a special kind of clarification.

While recognition of repair initiations and trouble source extraction can be implemented using the simplest type of language understanding, namely, pattern-based language understanding, most repair carry-outs require more sophisticated linguistic capabilities.

Definitions provide an explanation of the trouble source. Existing online dictionaries such as Wiktionary or Wikipedia may be used to create linguistic knowledge bases. Because one term may have multiple meanings, a linking to the correct meaning may be required. This problem is related to lexical ambiguity resolution also known as meaning resolution (Small et al., 1987) and is part of a larger area of computational lexical semantics (Martin and Jurafsky, 2009, Ch. 20).

Paraphrases provide a reformulation of the trouble source. A lot of efforts have been put in automatic paraphrase generation and recognition. Several recent publications are (Metzler et al., 2011; Regneri and Wang, 2012; Marton, 2013).

Synonyms provide usually a short reformulation of the trouble source. Existing language resources such as WordNet (Fellbaum, 2010) and GermaNet (Hamp et al., 1997) can be used for finding synonyms. Multiple meanings of a word may need to be resolved.

Translations may be generated by using existing machine translation systems (Avramidis et al., 2015; Burchardt et al., 2014). Open source statistical machine translation systems such as Moses[2] make experimental implementations feasible. Commercial machine translation API can be integrated into the dialogue manager, for instance Google Translate API[3].

Demonstrations include hyperlinks to websites containing relevant information examples of an object referenced by the trouble source. For semi-automatically created databases of linguistic knowledge, such information may be included into examples. Wikipedia articles sometimes also contain links to example websites and pictures, which may be used as examples of concepts described in the article.

Explicit handling of repairs targeted for lan-guage learners allows an implementation in a CommICALL system that helps to practice conversation. In this way, this research advances state-of-the-art in ICALL and strengthens multidisciplinary connections to related disciplines, such as Conversation Analysis and NLP. Other types of tutorial dialogues where a clarification of the terminology may be necessary would also benefit from the presented model.

7 Conclusions

This article describes typical interactional resources employed for repair in native/non-native speaker chat with the purpose of computation modelling of repair for a conversational agent in a CommICALL application. The study shows that CA methods provide a valuable set of tools for computational modelling of rare phenomena in talk from a small number of examples. To be successful, such approaches require datasets replicating the speech exchange systems that are envisioned in the communication with the agent. In particular, this research showed that native/nonnative speaker chat data can be used for computational models of dialogues in a CommICALL application.

Acknowledgements

This research has been carried out at the University of Luxembourg with the great help and support of my scientific advisors Stephan Busemann (DFKI GmbH), Christoph Schommer, Gudrun Ziegler (MultiLearn Institute), Leon van der Torre and Charles Max.

References

Eleftherios Avramidis, Maja Popovic, and Aljoscha Burchardt. 2015. DFKI's experimental hybrid MT system for WMT 2015. In *Proceedings of the 10th Workshop on Statistical Machine Translation*. ACL, pages 66–73.

Aljoscha Burchardt, Arle Richard Lommel, Georg Rehm, Felix Sasaki, Josef van Genabith, and Hans Uszkoreit. 2014. Language technology drives quality translation. *MultiLingual* 143:33–39.

Noel Bush. 2006. Program D. http://www.aitools.org/Program_D.

Okko Buß and David Schlangen. 2011. DIUM – An Incremental Dialogue Manager That Can Produce Self-Corrections. In *SEMDIAL*.

---

[2]http://www.statmt.org/moses/
[3]https://cloud.google.com/translate/docs

Delphine Dahan, Michael K Tanenhaus, and Craig G Chambers. 2002. Accent and reference resolution in spoken-language comprehension. *Journal of Memory and Language* 47(2):292–314.

Sviatlana Danilava, Stephan Busemann, Christoph Schommer, and Gudrun Ziegler. 2013. Towards Computational Models for a Long-term Interaction with an Artificial Conversational Companion. In *Proc. of ICAART'13*.

Mark Dingemanse, Joe Blythe, and Tyko Dirksmeyer. 2014. Formats for other-initiation of repair across languages: An exercise in pragmatic typology. *Studies in Languag* 3(81):5–43.

Christian Droßmann. 2005. German AIML set. http://www.drossmann.de/wordpress/alicebot/.

Myroslava O Dzikovska, Charles B Callaway, Elaine Farrow, Johanna D Moore, Natalie Steinhauser, and Gwendolyn Campbell. 2009. Dealing with interpretation errors in tutorial dialogue. In *Proceedings of the SIGDIAL 2009 Conference: The 10th annual meeting of the special interest group on discourse and dialogue*. Association for Computational Linguistics, pages 38–45.

Christiane Fellbaum. 2010. Princeton university: About WordNet. http://wordnet.princeton.edu. WordNet.

Christine Fredriksson. 2012. About collaboration, interaction, and the negotiation of meaning in synchronous written chats in l2-german. In Linda Bradley and Sylvie Thouësny, editors, *CALL: Using, Learning, Knowing, EUROCALL Conference, Gothenburg, Sweden, 22-25 August 2012, Proceedings*. Research-publishing.net, pages 88–92.

Rod Gardner and Johannes Wagner. 2004. *Second Language Conversations: Studies of Communication in Everyday Settings*. A&C Black - Verlag.

Raphaela Gehle, Karola Pitsch, and Sebastian Wrede. 2014. Signaling trouble in robot-to-group interaction. emerging visitor dynamics with a museum guide robot. In *Proceedings of the second international conference on Human-agent interaction*. ACM, pages 361–368.

Jonathan Ginzburg. 2012. *The interactive stance*. Oxford University Press.

Jonathan Ginzburg, Raquel Fernández, and David Schlangen. 2007. Unifying self-and other-repair. In *Proceeding of DECALOG, the 11th International Workshop on the Semantics and Pragmatics of Dialogue (SemDial07)*.

Birgit Hamp, Helmut Feldweg, et al. 1997. Germanet-a lexical-semantic net for german. In *Proceedings of ACL workshop Automatic Information Extraction and Building of Lexical Semantic Resources for NLP Applications*. Citeseer, pages 9–15.

Sviatlana Höhn. 2015. deL1L2IM: Corpus of long-term instant messaging NS-NNS conversations. ELRA http://islrn.org/resources/339-799-085-669-8/.

Yuri Hosoda. 2006. Repair and relevance of differential language expertise in second language conversations. *Applied Linguistics* 27(1):25–50.

Ryu Iida, Shumpei Kobayashi, and Takenobu Tokunaga. 2010. Incorporating extra-linguistic information into reference resolution in collaborative task dialogue. In *Proceedings of the 48th Annual Meeting of the Association for Computational Linguistics*. Association for Computational Linguistics, pages 1259–1267.

Cui Jian, Desislava Zhekova, Hui Shi, and John Bateman. 2010. Deep Reasoning in Clarification Dialogues with Mobile Robots. In *Proceedings of the 19th European Conference on Artificial Intelligence*. IOS Press, pages 177–182.

Geert-Jan M. Kruijff, Michael Brenner, and Nick Hawes. 2008. Continual planning for cross-modal situated clarification in human-robot interaction. In *The 17th IEEE International Symposium on Robot and Human Interactive Communication*. IEEE, pages 592–597.

Anthony J. Liddicoat. 2011. *An Introduction to Conversation Analysis*. Continuum.

Roy Lyster, Kazuya Saito, and Masatoshi Sato. 2013. Language teaching. *Oral corrective feedback in second language classrooms*. 46.

Numa Markee. 2000. *Conversation Analysis*. Mahwah, N.J.: Lawrence Erlbaum.

James H Martin and Daniel Jurafsky. 2009. *Speech and language processing: an introduction to natural language processing, computational linguistics and speech resognition*. Pearson International Edition, second edition edition.

Yuval Marton. 2013. Distributional phrasal paraphrase generation for statistical machine translation. *ACM Transactions on Intelligent Systems and Technology (TIST)* 4(3):39.

Raveesh Meena, José Lopes Gabriel Skantze, and Joakim Gustafson. 2015. Automatic detection of miscommunication in spoken dialogue systems. In *16th Annual Meeting of the Special Interest Group on Discourse and Dialogue*. pages 354 – 363.

Donald Metzler, Eduard Hovy, and Chunliang Zhang. 2011. An empirical evaluation of data-driven paraphrase generation techniques. In *Proceedings of the 49th Annual Meeting of the Association for Computational Linguistics: Human Language Technologies: short papers-Volume 2*. Association for Computational Linguistics, pages 546–551.

Kenneth A Petersen. 2010. *Implicit Corrective Feedback in Computer-Guided Interaction: Does Mode Matter?*. Ph.D. thesis, Georgetown University.

Matthew Purver. 2004. *The theory and use of clarification requests in dialogue*. Ph.D. thesis, King's College, University of London.

Matthew Purver. 2006. CLARIE: Handling clarification requests in a dialogue system. *Research on Language and Computation* 4(2-3):259–288.

Michaela Regneri and Rui Wang. 2012. Using discourse information for paraphrase extraction. In *Proceedings of the 2012 Joint Conference on Empirical Methods in Natural Language Processing and Computational Natural Language Learning*. Association for Computational Linguistics, pages 916–927.

Yuan Ma Satomi Kawaguchi. 2012. Corrective feedback, negotiation of meaning and grammar development: Learner-learner and learner-native speaker interaction in esl. *Open Journal of Modern Linguistics* 2:57–70.

Emanuel A Schegloff. 1996. Issues of relevance for discourse analysis: Contingency in action, interaction and co-participant context. In *Computational and conversational discourse: Burning Issues – An Interdisciplinary Account*, Springer-Verlag Berlin Heidelberg, pages 3–35.

Emmanuel A. Schegloff. 2000. When 'others' initiate repair. *Applied Linguistic* 21(2):205–243.

David Schlangen. 2004. Causes and Strategies for Requesting Clarification in Dialogue. In *5th Workshop of the ACL SIG on Discourse and Dialogue*.

Elizabeth Ellen Shriberg. 1994. *Preliminaries to a Theory of Speech Disfluencies*. Phd, University of California at Berkeley.

Steven Small, Garrison Cottrell, and Michael Tanenhaus. 1987. *Lexical ambiguity resolution*. Morgan Kaufman Publishers, Inc., Los Altos, CA.

Evangeline Marlos Varonis and Susan Gass. 1985. Non-native/non-native conversations: A model for negotiation of meaning. *Applied Linguistics* 6(1):71–90.

Sabrina Wilske. 2014. *Form and Meaning in Dialog-Based Computer-Assisted Language Learning*. Ph.D. thesis, University of Saarland.

Simon Zwarts, Mark Johnson, and Robert Dale. 2010. Detecting Speech Repairs Incrementally Using a Noisy Channel Approach. In *Proceedings of the 23rd International Conference on Computational Linguistics (Coling 2010)*. August, pages 1371–1378.

Association for Computational Linguistics
209 N. Eighth Street
Stroudsburg, Pennsylvania 18360

ISBN 978-1-5108-4860-3